A HISTORY OF
GREEK PHILOSOPHY

VOLUME V

A HISTORY OF
GREEK PHILOSOPHY

BY

W. K. C. GUTHRIE

VOLUME V

THE LATER PLATO
AND THE ACADEMY

CAMBRIDGE UNIVERSITY PRESS

CAMBRIDGE

LONDON · NEW YORK · MELBOURNE

Published by the Syndics of the Cambridge University Press
The Pitt Building, Trumpington Street, Cambridge CB2 1RP
Bentley House, 200 Euston Road, London NW1 2DB
32 East 57th Street, New York, NY 10022, USA
296 Beaconsfield Parade, Middle Park, Melbourne 3206, Australia

First published 1978

Printed in Great Britain at the
University Press, Cambridge

Library of Congress Cataloguing in Publication Data
Guthrie, William Keith Chambers, 1906–
A history of Greek philosophy.
Includes bibliographies
CONTENTS: v. 1. The earlier Presocratics and Pythagoreans.—v. 2. The Presocratic
tradition from Parmenides to Democritus.—v. 3. The fifth-century enlightenment [etc.]
1. Philosophy, Ancient – History. I. Title. B171.G83   182   62–52735

ISBN 0 521 20003 2

CONTENTS

Contents

Contents

Contents

Contents

Contents

Contents

The device on the front cover is the head of Plato from a herm in the Staatliche Museen, Berlin

PREFACE

There is no break in subject-matter between this volume and its immediate predecessor, and their division is purely a matter of physical convenience. Perhaps therefore they might better have been called 'Volume IV parts 1 and 2', but since they are in fact two separate and fairly bulky volumes that did not sound right either. It does mean however that what was said in the previous preface about the general approach adopted in this study of Plato, its aims and methods, applies equally to this second half and need not be repeated. No interpreter of Plato can feel fully satisfied with his work, if only because of the inevitable choice, whether to make the main part of the exposition an analysis and appreciation of separate dialogues or a synthetic or systematic treatment by subjects. I do not regret the decision for which I gave reasons in my last preface, but as I also admitted, there are drawbacks in either method. In the present volume (ch. VIII) I have tried to do justice to the modern school of interpreters who see Plato as from his early days a systematic thinker with a settled doctrine of first principles, orally, even secretly, expounded, which, though we can now only glimpse it through the veil of Aristotelian and later criticism and comment, must be assumed as the unwritten background to every stage of his written work. On these premises it is of course wrong to hold back the esoteric teaching until after the dialogues, but as will appear, I cannot regard the thesis as established beyond question, whereas on the other hand I do perceive, and hope I have brought out, a number of lines of genuinely philosophical development in the dialogues themselves. (It is this development which I hoped would save volume IV from appearing, as it did to one critic, more like a series of monographs than parts of a continuous history.) On the question of arrangement see also my 'Postscript' (ch. IX).

I should like to express my thanks to friends who have read some of my chapters on the dialogues and made valuable suggestions, many of which I have adopted to the great improvement of the chapters concerned. Vol. IV ch. VII (*Republic*) was read by Sir Desmond Lee, and in the present volume ch. III (*Philebus*) by Professor Sandbach and Dr G. E. R. Lloyd. Dr Lloyd also read ch. IV (*Timaeus*) and Dr T. J. Saunders ch. V (*Laws*). To Dr Saunders in particular I owe a number of useful references which had escaped me. For these as for all other chapters, however, I remain solely responsible, especially as I did not adopt every suggestion offered. To Miss R. M. Goroo I am indebted for three things: her impeccable typing, her classical education, and a friendship extending over many years.

Unattributed references to 'vol. I' etc. refer as before to the earlier volumes of this work.

I should like to correct a somewhat elusive misprint in the preface to the first impression of vol. IV. On p. xv, l. 10, for 'effect' read 'defect'. I also apologize for the blank space on p. 4, n. 1. The reference should be to pages 63 f.

CAMBRIDGE
DECEMBER 1976

W. K. C. G.

LIST OF ABBREVIATIONS

Most works cited in abbreviated form in the text will be easily recognizable under the author's or editor's name in the bibliography. It may be however helpful to list the following:

PERIODICALS

AGPh	*Archiv für Geschichte der Philosophie*
AJP	*American Journal of Philology*
APQ	*American Philosophical Quarterly*
BICS	*Bulletin of the Institute of Classical Studies* (London)
BJPS	*British Journal for the Philosophy of Science*
CJ	*Classical Journal*
CP	*Classical Philology*
CQ	*Classical Quarterly*
CR	*Classical Review*
G and R	*Greece and Rome*
GGA	*Göttingische Gelehrte Anzeigen*
HSCP	*Harvard Studies in Classical Philology*
IPQ	*International Philosophical Quarterly*
JHI	*Journal of the History of Ideas*
JHP	*Journal of the History of Philosophy*
JHS	*Journal of Hellenic Studies*
JP	*Journal of Philosophy*
PAS	*Proceedings of the Aristotelian Society*
PCPS	*Proceedings of the Cambridge Philological Society*
PR	*Philosophical Review*
Phron.	*Phronesis*
PQ	*Philosophical Quarterly*
RCSF	*Rivista Critica di Storia della Filosofia*
REG	*Revue des Études Grecques*
TAPA	*Transactions of the American Philological Association*

OTHER WORKS

(Full particulars are in the bibliography)

CGF	*Comicorum Graecorum Fragmenta*, ed. Meineke
DK	Diels–Kranz, *Die Fragmente der Vorsokratiker*
D.L.	Diogenes Laertius
KR	G. S. Kirk and J. E. Raven, *The Presocratic Philosophers*
LSJ	Liddell–Scott–Jones, *A Greek–English Lexicon*, 9th ed.
OCD	*Oxford Classical Dictionary*
OP	*Oxyrhynchus Papyri*
Posidonius, EK	The fragments of Posidonius, ed. Edelstein and Kidd.
PS	G. Vlastos, *Platonic Studies*
RE	*Realencyclopädie der classischen Altertumswissenschaft*, ed. Wissowa, Kroll *et al.*
SPM	*Studies in Plato's Metaphysics*, ed. R. E. Allen
SVF	*Stoicorum Veterum Fragmenta*, ed. von Arnim
TGF	*Tragicorum Graecorum Fragmenta*, ed. Nauck

Note: The dialogues known in England as *Republic* and *Politicus* are in some countries called *Politeia* and *Statesman* (in the language of the country) respectively. Non-English readers should be warned that the abbreviation *Pol.* indicates the latter work.

I

CRATYLUS[1]

If you are on your guard against taking names too seriously, you will be richer in wisdom as you grow old. Plato, *Pol.* 261 e

Date. The placing of this dialogue immediately after the *Republic* is not intended as a pronouncement on its date, which, like its purpose, has been a matter of lively debate. Earlier critics (e.g. all five in Ross's table, *PTI* 3) thought it an early dialogue, before *Phaedo, Symposium, Phaedrus* and *Republic,* and von Arnim's stylistic studies made him date it around 390, before Plato's first Sicilian visit, though others (see Ross, *ib.* 4–5) had seen affinities with later dialogues. Ross himself argued in 1955 for an early date, and Taylor thought it earlier than any of the 'great dramatic group', even the *Protagoras.* But since the fifties the argument from apparent affinities in content with the so-called 'critical group' (*Parmenides, Theaetetus, Sophist, Statesman*) has won much more favour, though still without unanimity. Runciman (1962) places it 'with reasonable confidence' before that group on grounds both of style and less sophisticated treatment and thinks *Phaedrus* is later, Luce (1965) takes it as preceding *Phaedo* and *Republic* and Brentlinger (1972) still puts it before *Symposium, Phaedo* and *Republic,* as in 1931 did Méridier. On the other hand Owen (1953) thinks the argument at 439 d 8–9 'alone would vindicate its place in the critical group', Kirk (1951) and Allan (1954) put it contemporary with *Theaetetus,* and Schadewaldt (1971) also argues for a fairly late date, as an immediate preliminary to the critical group. In 1953 Jowett's editors disputed his comparatively early dating of the *Cratylus* and emphasized its affinities with the later dialogues.[2]

[1] A descriptive bibliography of works on the *Cratylus* 1804–1972 will be found in Derbolav, *Sprachphil.* 1972, 234–308.

[2] Reff. not supplied in the text are: Ross, *R. Int. de Phil.* 1955; Taylor, *PMW* 75; Runciman, *PLE* 2 and 129; Luce, *Phron.* 1965, 21 and 36; Méridier in his Budé ed., 46; Owen, *SPM* 323 n. 3; Kirk, *AJP* 1951, 226; Allan, *AJP* 1954, 272; Schadewaldt, *Essays Merlan* 3–11; Brentlinger, *AGPh* 1972, 116 n. 1; Jowett, *Dial.*[4] III, 10 n. 1. For a conspectus of views before 1941 see Leisegang, *RE* 40. Halbb. 2428. He himself, like Méridier and Wilamowitz, found it impossible to

I

Lest it appear that the arguments for an early or late date depend on giving chief weight to style or content respectively, it should be added that an important argument for the earlier date concerns the stage which has been reached in the doctrine of Forms. Thus Méridier, Ross (*PTI* 18–20) and Luce (*Phron.* 1965, 36) have maintained that they are not yet fully transcendent or 'separated' (Aristotle's word) from particulars, a view which would of course put the *Cratylus* before the *Phaedo*.

The above selection of opinions will suffice to justify Crombie's assessment of the *Cratylus* as 'a dialogue whose date must be left uncertain' (*EPD* II, 323). More even than most, it is a unique and self-contained whole.

Dramatic date. It is usually thought (see e.g. Méridier 46) that the dialogue contains no indication of when the conversation was supposed to have taken place, but Allan has argued (*AJP* 1954, 272–4) that it was during the last year of Socrates's life.

Characters. Apart from this dialogue, we know of *Cratylus* only from Aristotle's statements that Plato was acquainted with him in his youth, and learned from him the doctrine that everything was in flux, which at some time he held in a more extreme form than that taught by Heraclitus himself. (See vol. III, 201.) Plato too speaks of him as a Heraclitean (437a1, 440d–e) and even attacks Heracliteanism in the extreme form in which Cratylus himself (according to Aristotle) held it: if all things are in flux, they cannot even be spoken of (439d). Scholars have found difficulty in reconciling this with all the beliefs ascribed to him in the dialogue, and some have sought to avoid it by assuming that Plato is only using his name to make a veiled attack on someone else. Antisthenes was a favourite guess in the past, but is less popular now.[1] Though in

separate *Crat.* from *Euthyd.* Nakhnikian has argued persuasively for the priority of *Crat.* to *Tht.* from their respective treatments of Protagorean and Heraclitean views (*R. of Metaph.* 1955–6, 308f.). Latest of all, Kahn (*Exegesis* 154) in 1973 agrees with Ross in placing it near the beginning of the middle group.

[1] 'In fact the Antisthenes-theory is almost dead' (Kirk, *AJP* 1951, 238). A useful list of reff. is given by Levinson in *R. of Metaph.* 1957–8, and a summary of those in favour by Méridier (44f.), whose sensible conclusions should be noted. Since Levinson mentions Derbolav as supporting it, it is fair to say that in his later book (*Sprachphil.* 1972, 30f.) he concludes that all attempts at identification rest on such scanty evidence that to decide between them is to act on faith rather than knowledge.

general highly suspicious of such conjectural identifications,[1] I have tried to show in vol. III (p. 215) that the central theory of Plato's *Cratylus*, that names have a natural affinity with their objects, was also upheld by Antisthenes, as, certainly, was the impossibility of false speaking. The importance which he attached to language is indicated by his pronouncement that the basis of education was the study of names.[2] Since the nature and use of words was a favourite topic of discussion among the Sophists (vol. III, 205 f.), there were probably more than one champion of each of the opposing views. Another suggestion is that the etymological theories of 'Cratylus' are directed against Plato's own gifted pupil Heraclides Ponticus. This was put forward by Warburg in 1929, but as Méridier says, it 'repose sur une base des plus fragiles'.[3] Protagoras has also had his turn,[4] and is mentioned in the dialogue itself as an expert on 'the correctness of names', whose central doctrine identifying appearance with reality is rejected by Hermogenes (391 c, 385 e–86 c). It was a leading theme of vol. III that the Sophists shared a common scepticism resting on a plausible interpretation of Heraclitus's flux-doctrine.[5] At the same time they were fascinated by the compulsion of Eleatic logic, as is plain from Gorgias's use of purely Eleatic arguments to maintain the equally paradoxical thesis that nothing exists (vol. III, 193 ff.); and their thesis of the impossibility of falsehood seems to have rested *both* on the Heraclitean assertion of the identity of opposites (vol. III, 166, 182 n. 2) *and* on the Parmenidean dictum that 'what is not' cannot be uttered. For their purposes Heraclitean and Eleatic doctrine were at one in 'abolishing the criterion' for any comparative assessment of judgements about the

[1] See vol. III, xiv, 310 f., 323, 347.

[2] Vol. III, 209–11, cf. *Crat.* 383 *et al.* (natural rightness of names), 429 d (impossibility of falsehood).

[3] Budé ed. 41, where reff. for the thesis and its critics will be found. It is an odd coincidence that the father of Heraclides should have been called Euthyphro (Heraclides fr. 3 Wehrli, where see W.'s note). See also Skemp, *TMPLD*, 2 f.

[4] First argued by Stallbaum. See Derbolav, *Sprachphil.* 30 and 297.

[5] Though H. himself would not have drawn the same epistemological conclusions, for πάντα ῥεῖ was not the whole of his teaching. Cf. frr. 1 and 2 (the common *logos* and the folly of acting 'as if each had his own private wisdom'), fr. 107 (the senses bad witnesses if not checked by the *psyche*), fr. 114 (the need for νόος; the one divine νόμος which feeds human νόμοι). See for these vol. I, 425, 415, and cf. vol. III, 185. Jackson (*Praelections* 17–19) has some judicious remarks on the question whether the theory of the natural rightness of names goes back to Heraclitus himself.

2-2

sensible world and human affairs.[1] It is a reasonable conclusion that Plato found Cratylus the Heraclitean a suitable character through which to criticize prevailing beliefs of the Sophists about the relationship between words and reality. How far the historical Cratylus shared their linguistic doctrines we cannot be sure, but at least it is unjustified to say with Warburg and Heinimann that because the Sophists were not pure Heracliteans, Heracliteanism and etymology were unconnected until Plato himself combined them in the person of Cratylus.

ADDITIONAL NOTE: CRATYLUS, HERACLITUS AND THE CORRECTNESS OF NAMES

For the view just mentioned see Heinimann, *N. u. Ph.* 54. In the exchange of views between Kirk and Allan in *AJP* 1951 and 1954, I do not find either entirely convincing. It is difficult to believe with K. (p. 244; cf. Allan 281 f.) that Aristotle's accounts of C.'s Heracliteanism (*Metaph.* 989a29 and 1078b9) are taken from Plato (though it was suggested in 1829; see Derbolav, *Sprachphil.* 283), and A.'s hypothesis of two stages in his development is precarious. K.'s view is influenced by his belief that Plato regularly misrepresented Heraclitus, on which see vol. 1, 488–92. His argument that in the dialogue C. only welcomes Heracliteanism because it supports his belief in the natural correctness of names, not vice versa, is weakened by the fact that C. was a historical person *known* to be a Heraclitean. In his book on Heraclitus (*HCF* 118f.) K. actually argues that H. himself did believe that names give some indication of the nature of their objects and bear an essential relation to it. The crucial passage is fr. 48 (βιός-βίος). (Others quoted by Heinimann and Kirk offer less compelling evidence.) Contrary to what Heinimann says (*o.c.* 55), this does not deny the view of names attributed to C., which was not that names commonly in use are correct, but that they are attached to things by convention (383a), being either the name of something else or mere noises. Heraclitus with his example of the bow may have meant the same, but more probably he used it to illustrate his doctrine of the identity of opposites: life and death are the same (fr. 88; vol. 1, 445 f.).

Hermogenes, son of Hipponicus and brother of Callias the wealthy patron of Sophists (vol. III, 31 and IV, 216), was a close associate of Socrates who according to Plato was one of those present during his last hours in prison. Xenophon says he had also been at the trial, and had previously tried to persuade Socrates to give some thought to his

[1] On 'abolition of the criterion' as a mark of the Sophists, see Gorg. fr. 3 DK (vol. III, 195 f.).

defence. He appears again as a participant in Xenophon's *Symposium*. Diogenes Laertius called him a follower of Parmenides, but this is doubtful, and perhaps an inference from his appearance here as the opponent of Cratylus.[1] Otherwise nothing is known of his views apart from what is here attributed to him by Plato, who represents him as a young man with no great aptitude for philosophical discussion. Both the respondents are depicted as younger than Socrates (429b, 440d), but Cratylus shows much more self-assurance and tenacity in maintaining his opinions.

The dialogue[2]

(*Direct dramatic form*)

Hermogenes and Cratylus have been arguing about the status of names[3] in terms of the current *nomos–physis* antithesis,[4] and agree to refer the dispute to Socrates. Hermogenes holds that they are merely conventional labels imposed by agreement or custom (*nomos*) and changeable at will, whereas Cratylus, he says, claims that everything has a naturally correct name, the same for Greeks and foreigners, irrespective of those in current use. Hermogenes cannot understand what he means, and he refuses to explain himself. Socrates as usual disclaims knowledge but is willing to go into the matter with them and starts his questions. The rest of the dialogue falls into two parts, carried on with Hermogenes and Cratylus respectively.

---

[1] *Phaedo* 59b, Xen. *Apol.* 2 and 3, *Mem.* 4.8.4, D.L. 3.6. That the last is an inference from *Crat.* was suggested by Natorp, *RE* VIII, 865.

[2] A brief indication of the contents has been given in vol. III, 206–10.

[3] I shall in general keep 'name' for the Greek ὄνομα, even though 'word' would sometimes be a more natural translation. As Robinson said (*Essays* 100), there is no exact English equivalent. Examples in *Crat.* include proper names, nouns, adjectives and even adverbs (427c), and in *Soph.* (262a) (though not always) they are distinguished from verbs. Thus P.'s use approximates more to Mill's than to present usage. (Mill, *Logic* bk 1 ch. 2.) M. Roth has a good discussion, in an unpublished Illinois dissertation on the *Crat.* (1969), 33–6.

[4] In vol. III, 206 n. 2, I followed Fehling in saying that the contrast is not between φύσει and θέσει. (So also Robinson, *Essays* 110ff.) This is literally true, but not really important. The contrast is between names which are formed φύσει (i.e. although man-made, they possess a natural rightness to which the makers conformed) and θέσει (only). I think therefore that anything known about φύσις *versus* θέσις on this matter is relevant, e.g. Simpl.'s statement (*in Catt.*, Schol. Bekk. 43b31) that the Pythagoreans said names were φύσει not θέσει.

Cratylus

(1) *Discussion with Hermogenes: there is a natural correctness of names* (385a–427d). Hermogenes repeats his belief that what even a single individual chooses to call something is as much its name as any other. If I call 'man' what everyone else calls 'horse', no one can challenge me, though its 'public' name is different. But he admits that speech may be true or false, and it follows, says Socrates, that the components of speech, including names, must be true or false.[1] If each object has as many names as anyone chooses to give to it, so long as he gives them, Protagoras must have been right in saying that things themselves are only what they appear to each one of us. They agree in rejecting Protagoras, but the only alternative is that every existing thing has a stable nature or essence (οὐσία) of its own, irrespective of our beliefs about it.

Actions too (Socrates proceeds) are realities, whose character is shown by the fact that we can only perform them as, and with the instruments which, their nature demands, not according to our own whim. You cannot cut with a box of matches or light a fire with a knife. Speech is an action, performed with words which are its proper instruments just as shuttles are for weaving. They have a dual function, (*a*) communication (lit. 'teaching one another'), and (*b*) the distinguishing or differentiation of one real thing from another.[2] Any tool, to perform its function properly, must be made by a skilled worker, and names are no exception. Since (as Hermogenes has said) they are the product of *nomos*, their maker must have been a lawgiver (*nomothete*), the rarest of all human craftsmen.[3]

Taking the analogy a step further, when a carpenter makes a shuttle, he has in view its function, and if one breaks under his hand he does not take the broken one as his model but 'the sort of thing which is fitted by nature to be a shuttle', which we may call the ideal shuttle ('what a shuttle is in itself', 389b). Within their generic function shuttles serve

---

[1] The truth or correctness of a name, as S. says later, depends on its revealing the nature of its object (οἷόν ἐστι τὸ πρᾶγμα, 428e).

[2] S. is continuing the analogy from weaving: as the shuttle separates (διακρίνει) the threads, so names separate the realities which they name.

[3] There have of course been plenty of lawgivers, but S. is speaking of the *expert*, whose names will correctly distinguish the essence of their objects, and as we know, for P. this is none other than the philosopher. S. is running rings round poor H., who will not of course see this point, and apart from that, he takes *nomos* to mean law, when H. obviously used it in its other sense of custom. Goldschmidt's defence (*Essai* 62f.), that the two concepts were indissoluble in the Greek mind, fails. *Nomos* as custom is not the work of a *nomothete*.

6

specific ends, for fine or coarse weaving, in wool, linen or other materials. Each must be given both the generic form and the character (*physis*) suited to its specific purpose. Similarly the master name-giver must put the name naturally formed for each purpose into sounds and syllables as well as keeping an eye on the ideal name. Different syllables may be used, as the same tools (say two hammers) are made out of different pieces of metal. Provided they are correct in form, they serve their purpose equally well, and so do names whether in Greek or another language.

The man who will know the proper form for an instrument, under whose instructions the maker must work, is the user—weaver, musician, or in the case of a rudder, a sailor; and the user from whom the name-maker must take his instructions is the dialectician, the skilled asker and answerer of questions. Naming is no light undertaking. Things, as Cratylus says, have names by nature, and their giver must look to the natural name of each thing and be able to put its form into letters and syllables.

Hermogenes would be happier about this if he knew what 'natural correctness of names' meant. He has forgotten that Socrates is just a fellow-enquirer, and 'correctness of names' is the province of Sophists. However, even Homer and the other poets can teach us something. Homer speaks of different names given by gods and men,[1] and presumably the gods know the right one. Without meddling in such high matters, even we can judge between the two names he gave Hector's son, Scamandrios and Astyanax.[2] Both are Greek, and since Hector means 'holder (or sustainer)' of the city and Astyanax 'lord of the city', obviously Astyanax is right, on the principle that son resembles father, as a lion's cub is called a lion. This does not always work. Even in nature there are freak births, and a pious man may have an impious son. In that case Theophilos ('God-friend') or Mnesitheos ('mindful-of-God') are incorrect names for him. The correct one would signify

[1] As examples S. quotes *Il.* 20.74, 24.291 and 2.813f.
[2] *Il.* 6.402f. S. says that because the Trojan men called him Astyanax, it must have been the women (the sillier sex) who called him Scamandrios! Unless there was an alternative version now lost, he was relying on H.'s imperfect memory of Homer to pull his leg, for in Homer Hector himself called the boy Scamandrios. The derivations of Hector and Astyanax are of course correct, and in fact most Greek proper names have a transparent meaning.

the opposite. Others are merely examples of wishful thinking, like Eutychides ('son of good fortune'). (This example comes to life when we read a funerary inscription in which a dead man called Eutychides complains that he was wrongly named. See Luce, *CQ* 1969, 225.) On an earlier point, we see how little the material constituents matter, for Hector and Astyanax have scarcely a letter in common. Similarly Iatrokles ('famous physician') and Akesimbrotos ('healer of men'), though so different in sound, are both correct names for doctors.[1]

Socrates now proceeds to show, by a torrent of etymologies,[2] how other names or words also reveal the nature of their objects. He, the ignorant, has been filled with a miraculous wisdom, doubtless caught from the inspired seer Euthyphro, to whom he has earlier been listening.[3] Tomorrow he will exorcize the spirit 'through some priest or Sophist', but today he will exploit it. Beginning with some basic words —god, man, soul,[4] body—he passes to the gods, of whom he avers that a claim to know their true names would be blasphemous: we can only say what was in the minds of men when they gave them their names. In spite of this, he proceeds as if the known names do reveal the gods' real natures, e.g. Demeter means 'the giving mother', Pluto means 'wealthy' and his other name Hades 'knowing'. There follows a purely Platonic digression on Pluto's philosophic nature: he consorts only with souls that are freed from the body and its insane desires, and keeps them spellbound by the riches of his wisdom. Hephaestus is 'obviously' Phaestus ('lord of light'), the first syllable being a mere extraneous addition. 'Probably—until you get another idea', says Hermogenes. 'Well, to prevent that, ask me about Ares.'

[1] For different languages (cf. 389d–90a) S. gives no examples, but 'Zimmermann' and 'Carpenter' might be said to reveal the identical nature of their nominates as workers in wood (the latter originally as a maker of chariots). As surnames, S. would say, they are only correct for families pursuing this trade.

[2] These obviously cannot be fully recounted in an English summary. A few will be included as illustrations, and for the whole collection I would refer (though without necessarily agreeing with his conclusions) to Boyancé in *REG* 1941, who goes through them in detail to prove his point that they are to be taken seriously, especially for their religious significance and as evidence of P.'s debt to the Pythagoreans. See also Dümmler, *Akad.* 131ff., Haag, *P.'s K.* ch. 4, Goldschmidt, *Essai* 185–99.

[3] P.'s real opinion of Euthyphro has appeared in the *Euthyphro*. See especially vol. IV, 107f.

[4] After very reasonably connecting ψυχή with ἀναψύχω, he abandons this for a wildly implausible etymology on the grounds that Euthyphro would be more likely to approve it.

The dialogue

But the gods are a dangerous subject. Let Hermogenes 'learn the mettle of Euthyphro's horses'[1] in another sphere. So they turn to the heavenly bodies, seasons and elements.[2] On 'fire' (πῦρ) the muse of Euthyphro deserts Socrates, and he falls back on the idea that it might be a loan-word from a non-Greek source, possibly Phrygian.[3] (This is invoked again for the intractable *kakon* ('bad') at 416a and *ōphelimon* ('beneficial') at 421c, but dismissed at 425e–26e, along with the hypothesis of corruption through age, as merely an ingenious device to escape the burden of explanation.)

After this section Hermogenes remarks that Socrates is making great progress, and he replies with satisfaction, 'Yes, I do seem to be far advanced in this skill, and you will soon have even better reason to say so.' They pass to the virtues which, like some of the gods, seem to have been named by Heracliteans, for they all have to do with movement and flow, e.g. *dikaion* ('just') is really *diiaion* ('penetrating') with a *k* for euphony. In this part, Hermogenes says, Socrates seems to be only repeating things he has heard, and Socrates replies that he will now try to fool him into believing that he is being original. His derivation of *technē*, which involves removing the *t* and inserting an *o* between *ch* and *n* and *n* and *e*, seems even to Hermogenes a bit far-fetched. Ah, but he doesn't understand. The original names have suffered not only from lapse of time but from unscrupulous titivating. People with no respect for truth have distorted them for euphony in all sorts of ways until no one knows what on earth they mean. If people can add or remove letters at will, any name can be fitted to any object, so Hermogenes as a wise overseer must check them in the cause of limit and probability.[4]

[1] An adaptation of *Il.* 5.221f. Perhaps here the steeds which bore E. up to his heavenly visions, like Parmenides (vol. II, 7).

[2] A point of interest for P.'s cosmology was noted by Boyancé (*REG* 1941, 147). At 410b–c S. mentions five elements, distinguishing air from *aither* as in *Epin.* (981c), whereas in *Tim.* (58d) *aither* is a form of air. No one has thought of using this to help in dating the *Crat.* Neither shall I. The distinction is in any case plain enough in *Phaedo* (109b). See vol. I, 270–2, and pp. 284f. below.

[3] S. says the Phrygian word for fire is very similar to πῦρ, and Méridier noted that in Armenian t is 'hur', and the Armenians were thought to be Phrygian colonists. Phrygian did contain words milar to, or identical with, Greek, including κακόν itself. See *Mon. As. Min. Ant.* 4, nos. 16, 17, 16, 239–43.

[4] This invitation to act in direct opposition to his own theory H. accepts with a meek 'I should like to' (414e).

But he mustn't be too pedantic or he will unnerve Socrates just as he is reaching his climax. More astonishing etymologies follow until Hermogenes is moved to remark that names become pretty complicated under Socrates's hands. That, says Socrates, is the fault of those who made them, and he proceeds unabashed. Derivations rain 'thicker and faster' as he nears the end, most of them offering remarkable confirmation of the Heraclitean view of the world as all flow and movement, for they contain these ideas in their roots:[1] in fact, he says, the ancient namegivers must have been like some contemporary philosophers who in their search for reality make so many turns and twists that they get giddy, and project the whirl and motion of their own minds on to the external world.[2] Finally Hermogenes asks about the 'really big and fine' names like 'truth' and 'falsehood', 'being' and 'name' itself. ('Being' —*on*—has simply lost an *i*. It should be *ion*, 'going', and Heraclitus is right again!) Socrates has 'knocked them to pieces manfully', says his admiring partner, but what of short, simple words like *ion* itself? Well, one could always claim foreign origin or irremediable distortion, but such excuses are cowardly. A new procedure is needed.

The problem is this. So far we have explained names by analysing them into their elements, but some names are simple and elemental themselves. How can we test the correctness of these? The secondary (compound) names revealed the nature of their nominates by means of the primary. How do the primary names do it?

If we had no voices, we should, like the dumb, try to indicate things by gestures, e.g. lightness or upward direction by raising the hand, heaviness or downward by lowering it, miming their nature, and similarly with a galloping horse and other animals. Perhaps then a name is a *vocal* imitation of something. This is not to say that to utter 'Baa' or 'Moo' is to *name* a sheep or a cow. So far as a thing has sound, shape or colour, its imitation is the province of music or painting. But besides sensible qualities, everything (including colour and sound themselves) has an *essence*. If one could imitate that through letters and

---

[1] For λυσιτελεῖν, 'to be profitable', S. rejects the vulgar, commercial (and incidentally correct) origin in favour of a wonderful theory that it conforms to the Heraclitean canons by meaning 'swiftest in motion' (417b–c).

[2] Goldschmidt aptly compares *Phaedo* 79c: the soul grows dizzy and confused when it relies on the bodily senses, which can only show it what is constantly changing.

syllables, then names could make plain what each thing is. The next question therefore is whether this is possible.

The method we must suppose to have been followed by the ancient name-givers is this. First the simplest units, letters, are classified into vowels, consonants and semi-vowels, and the vowels into their sub-divisions.[1] Then the objects to be named are similarly analysed to see if they too can be reduced to elements[2] which will show what they are and whether they can be referred to types like the letters. The next step is to apply the letters to the objects[3] according to their resemblance, either one to one or combining the letters in syllables. From syllables are built nouns and verbs,[4] and from them a great and splendid whole, the *Logos*, 'formed by the art of naming or rhetoric or whatever it may be, as a living figure is composed by the art of painting'.[5]

The present task is to split up language once more into its components to see whether primary as well as secondary names were rightly given. To complete it is beyond us, and the very idea that letters and syllables can reveal things through imitation will sound ridiculous, but unless it is true the whole theory of 'correctness of names' must be abandoned. To Socrates his own conjectures sound arrogant and absurd, but he gives them *faute de mieux*.

In principle, letters imitate basic notions by the movement or shape of mouth and tongue in pronouncing them. Thus the rapid vibration of the tongue in *r* suggests motion (so flow in 'river', also 'run', 'rush', 'tremble', and violent actions like 'strike', 'crush', 'break').[6] From

---

[1] Semi-vowels (neither φωνήεντα nor ἄφθογγα) include liquids and nasals (Haag, *P.'s K.* 12). Aristotle's examples are *s* and *r* (*Poet.* 1456b26). The subdivisions of vowels are presumably the Greek equivalents of *a e i o* and *u*, and are only mentioned *exempli gratia*, for there is no reason why the consonants should not be similarly specified. (At *Phil.* 18b–d, where the division of letters into vowels etc. is attributed to the Egyptian god Theuth, he is said to have subdivided all classes, not vowels only.)

[2] As words to syllables and they to letters. P. uses στοιχεῖα both for elements (422a) and letters of the alphabet.

[3] 424d5–6. Cf. e4–5 τὰ στοιχεῖα ἐπὶ τὰ πράγματα ἐποίσομεν.

[4] ῥῆμα in this context is a verb, as at *Soph.* 262d, though at 399a–b Διὶ φίλος is a ῥῆμα. (Cf. 421c1.) See vol. III, 220f., for this and the exaltation of the *Logos* (speech). Perhaps one should also remember the supremacy of the *Logos* in Heraclitus's philosophy.

[5] The above is a fairly close paraphrase of the important and difficult passage 424c–25a. (Those of Haag (*P.'s K.* 12) and Crombie (*EPD* II, 376) may be compared.) It may well repay further study.

[6] I have suggested English examples for amusement: sometimes a translation from the Greek will serve, sometimes not. (Not even S. can bring κίνησις itself into line, 426c.)

'breathy' letters (*f*, *s*, *ʒ*) come 'windy' words—'zephyr', 'puff', 'sizzle' and so on. *D* and *t* compress and hold up the tongue, hence words like 'stop', 'bind', 'stand'.[1] With *l* the tongue s*l*ides or s*l*ips, whence these and words of similar import ('level', 'sleek'), whereas *g* arrests its motion, so that the combination indicates stickiness ('glue'). *A* and *ē* are 'big' letters, hence 'large', 'length'; and of course *o* is for roundness as in 'orb', 'ovum' (Greek *ōön*, egg).

But what has Cratylus to say to all this?

(2) *Discussion with Cratylus: Truth is not to be got from names (428c–40e).* Cratylus is delighted with Socrates's 'oracles', by whomsoever inspired. Socrates however is suspicious of such a sudden access of wisdom, and to test it will go over the ground again. The premise stands that correctness of names lies in their power to reveal the nature of their objects. Their purpose then is instruction, which is an art, practised, as has been said, by lawgivers; and will not some of these be better at their profession than others? Cratylus will not admit this: no law is better than another,[2] and so it is with names. They are either correct or not names at all. So if someone calls him Hermogenes he is not even uttering a falsehood? No, for false speech is impossible. To speak falsely would be to say what is not, and to say what is not is not to say anything,[3] but only utter meaningless sounds.

Socrates starts again. Names, we agree, are imitations of their objects. Pictures too are imitations, and (*a*) they may be wrongly attributed: one may mistake a portrait of a man for one of a woman. Cratylus retorts that the cases are not parallel, but Socrates presses the agreed point that both pictures and names are representations. One can *say* 'man', pointing to a picture of a man or a woman, and this is what he

[1] S. made the point much earlier (393 d–e) that provided the operative letter is there, the name is correct even if others are added. Thus 'beta' is allowable as the name of the letter *b*.

[2] This sounds an astonishing statement, but (*a*) Grote (*Pl.* II, 534 n. *q*) drew attention to *Minos* 317 c, where the author makes S. himself claim that a bad law is no real law, but only seems so to the ignorant, and to Xen. *Mem.* 1.2.42–6. (*b*) It accords with Protagoras's opinion that whatever a city thinks right *is* right for it so long as it thinks so (*Tht.* 167 c, vol. III, 172). (*c*) Possibly C. is speaking as a Heraclitean. Cf. fr. 114: all human laws are nourished by the one divine law.

[3] The argument attributed to Protagoras and Antisthenes (vol. III, 182 n. 2 and 209–11). Its ultimate dependence on Parmenides has been adduced to show that our C. was not the Heraclitean, but Protagoras and Antisthenes were hardly followers of Parmenides. (Cf. pp. 3 f. above.) The problem of 'saying what is not' is deliberately shelved (429 d), and only solved in *Soph.*

means by false attribution. (*b*) By means of drawing and colour, a painter may produce a good or bad likeness. So too one who imitates the essence of things through letters and syllables may not get them all right, making a bad (inaccurate) name which yet is a name. Cratylus sticks to his guns. A name cannot be wrongly written. Either all the letters are right or it is not a name at all, for the alteration has made it something else.

That is true in some cases, replies Socrates—a number for instance. If one adds to or subtracts anything from ten, it becomes an entirely different number.[1] An image, on the contrary, *must* differ in some respect from its original. If some god could reproduce Cratylus in every detail—his flesh, life and mind—there would be, not Cratylus and an image or copy of him [such as a painter or sculptor might make], but two Cratyluses.

Names, then, as copies, cannot be perfect, or they would be indistinguishable from their objects, which is absurd. Inappropriate letters may be inserted in a name, and names in a sentence, and inappropriate sentences may be included in a composition. Yet the subject is still being named or spoken about so long as its general stamp (τύπος) is retained, as Hermogenes and Socrates were saying about letters.[2] Cratylus agrees that this is reasonable, but without wanting to quarrel about it, still stubbornly denies that a faulty name is a name at all.

Patiently Socrates starts again from the first premises. A name indicates its object, there are compound and simple names, and the latter indicate by resembling the object. The only alternative is the view of Hermogenes that the name-makers had prior knowledge of the objects[3] and assigned them names by an arbitrary convention which alone authenticates them. It would not matter if they had named 'small' what is called 'large'. Cratylus is emphatic that the resemblance-theory is the right one.

[1] This might be thought perverse, the point being not that instead of ten one might write nine or eleven, but that one might distort the name 'ten' (assuming it is correct) by saying or writing e.g. 'teen' or 'tine'. But although the word *deka* for ten occurs in full in the text, we have to remember that the Greeks represented numbers by single letters. Thus ι corresponds to our 10. Add one letter, α, and it becomes 11.

[2] P. 12 n. 1 above.

[3] Note how S. slips in something that H. never said. At 438a he will make C. say it and thereby get him into a corner.

Then the letters (elements) of names must also bear this resemblance, and we agreed that *r* represents motion and hardness, *l* smoothness and softness. Now take the Greek word for hardness (*sklērotēs*). In Eretrian dialect it ends in *r*, but we understand each other though *s* and *r* have different import. Also we understand it as 'hard' although it contains an *l*. 'Well, as you and Hermogenes said, letters got wrongly inserted in course of time, but we understand the intent through custom.' And what is custom but convention? At the least it means that letters can indicate to us an object to which they have no resemblance. No doubt in an ideal language names would always resemble their objects, but as things are, convention plays a part too.

Cratylus still insists that the resemblance between names and their objects is so close that names are the only source of information and 'he who knows the names knows the objects too'. This applies to the discovery of new knowledge as well as the communication of acquired. But surely, in original research, to take names as a guide to realities is dangerous. What if whoever bestowed them did so under an erroneous impression of what they stood for? But this on the Cratylean theory is impossible: he must have known the truth, or they would not be names at all. Besides, look at their consistency: Socrates himself has argued that they all express the same world-view. Against this, (*a*) consistency is no guarantee of rightness if the initial hypothesis is faulty; (*b*) it is doubtful whether the implied outlook is consistent. Words so far examined supported the principle of universal flow and motion, but others suggest the opposite.[1]

Besides, if names are the only source of knowledge, how could the first namer make his names with knowledge of the objects? Cratylus can only suppose that they were given by some infallible 'power greater than human', and therefore must be right. Any others (like those suggesting a static world) are not names at all. All very well, but if two sets conflict, what are we to do? Names can no longer help us, and we need other criteria by which to judge the truth about existing things and see which set of names is genuine. It must therefore be possible to

[1] Here S. takes a number of words, e.g. those for knowledge, enquiry, faith, memory, and conversely ignorance, licentiousness etc., and thinks up fanciful etymologies to show that the 'good' words are derived from 'standstill', 'rest', 'stopping the flow' and so on, and the bad from 'going with the god', or 'following realities'. Clearly their inventor was no Heraclitean!

learn of realities otherwise than through names, and if possible, surely also best. That is, we should understand them directly, through themselves, or each other where they have affinities. Things unrelated to them cannot signify them.[1] Names at the best (as all have agreed) are copies of realities, and it is more enlightening to learn from an original both about itself and the accuracy of the copy than to learn from a copy its own success as a likeness as well as the original it represents. *How* this is to be done—how to discover realities not through names but directly—is probably beyond our comprehension.

As a final question, if the name-makers did act on a belief in universal and continuous flux and motion, were they right? Not if what Socrates 'dreams' (and Cratylus says 'must be so') is correct, namely that there is an absolute beauty and absolute good, 'and so with all existing things'. It is these that demand our attention, not particular beautiful things and the question whether they are in flux, but beauty itself, which never changes. What is continually changing cannot be spoken of or known. We cannot say 'this' or 'such'; it is not anything, for if it stays the same for a moment, it is not changing. Nor can we know it, for even as the knower approaches it becomes something different. Knowledge itself cannot exist. Either it remains the same (which contradicts the flux doctrine) or if the very form of knowledge is always changing, it will no longer be knowledge. No, if there is always a knower and a known, if there is beauty, and goodness and every other existing thing, they bear no resemblance to flux or motion.[2]

Whichever view is right, no man of sense will trust to names and their makers as proof that everything runs like a leaky pot or a cold in the nose. It may be so, but the question calls for more hard thought. Cratylus promises not to shirk this, but all his study so far has confirmed him in the Heraclitean view, and he hopes S. will think it over too.

[1] Lit. 'What is other than and different from them would signify not them but what is other and different.' The meaning and reference of this are puzzling. Does P. no longer believe that all reality is akin (*Meno* 81c)? Or is it a hint that names do not after all resemble realities, as S. has all along said they do? But in the very next sentence he repeats this.

[2] See further on this passage pp. 81 f. below.

Comment[1]

This is real dialectic, with Plato at his most teasing in his effort to make us think. To examine the topical question of 'correctness of names' from all sides, he has taken full advantage of the dialogue form. It enables him to set out opposing theories, to show that neither is wholly right and conclude only that the matter needs more thought. Socrates is as wayward and wicked as he has ever been, taking first one side and then the other. No wonder scholars have differed widely over what Plato was trying to do, but in fact he leaves no doubt what was important to him. Throughout the discussions his own convictions (now familiar to us) flash in and out among those he thinks absurd, in the unique way which we know from his treatment of Sophists like Hippias, and are openly and plainly stated at the end. His choice of the status of names as subject had a double motive: first, it was a recent topic of debate among Sophists on which he could show up their errors with his favourite blend of seriousness and humour (especially the latter), and secondly it affected his cherished doctrine of Forms. (Proclus, *In Crat.*, p. 3 Pasqu., remarked that to understand the correctness of names was a necessary preliminary to dialectic.)

The idea that the correct concept of a thing must be inherent in its name was not confined to professionals but is attested by many passages in Greek literature, especially tragedy.[2] Since it is foreign to our thought, Wilamowitz did a service in pointing out what a natural, indeed inevitable assumption it was at the time (*Pl.* I, 287f.), and we need not be surprised at the Heraclitean Cratylus accepting it, even if we suspect that it is Socrates who puts into his head the welcome thought that any etymology can be made to support the flux-doctrine.

[1] I gladly acknowledge that in addition to published sources I have received help from a notebook of Cornford's containing notes on the *Crat*. References to Cornford in what follows are to these notes.

[2] Kirk (*HCF* 119) mentioned some examples from tragedy, which could easily be multiplied. A good one is Eur. *Tro.* 889f., connecting Aphrodite with ἄφρων, 'foolish', instead of the more usual ἀφρός, 'foam', which S. retains at 406d, though calling it her 'playful' name. There is evidence that Democritus, who certainly theorized on language (vol. III, 474–6), etymologized the names of gods (fr. 2). Kahn has pointed out that this too, and the emphasis on names and etymology in the fourth-cent. Orphic papyrus from Derveni, illustrate an extant fashion of explaining divine names allegorically which, if we knew more about it, might throw light on S.'s behaviour under the influence of Euthyphro. See esp. *Crat.* 401 ff. and Kahn in *Exegesis* 155 f.

Comment

Conversation with Hermogenes. In his discussion with Hermogenes, Socrates constructs a theory, such as Cratylus (who has so far refused explanation) might bring against him, of how names can have natural rightness. Hence he gives it a Heraclitean basis as agreeable to Cratylus, who in fact declares it all much to his mind (428c). As to Hermogenes's extreme view that even a single individual is entitled to call a man 'horse',[1] though all the world call him 'man', Socrates himself in the *Charmides* gave Critias licence to use any name he chose, provided he made clear what he meant by it. Grote accused Hermogenes of contradicting himself, because convention and agreement imply an intention to serve communication, which they would not do if everyone had his private vocabulary. But Hermogenes has not mentioned communication, and at 388b is unable to say what a name is for until Socrates prompts him. His present point is different, that the sounds in 'horse' can just as suitably indicate a man as a horse. If others acquiesced in the change, nothing would be lost, for there is no natural affinity, as Cratylus would claim, between a thing and its name.[2]

A fallacy of division? At 385b Socrates argues that just as statements can be true or false, so can the names of which they are composed. Robinson comments that the argument is bad, 'for names have no truthvalue, and the reason given for saying that they do is a fallacy of division'.[3] He thus offers two objections. (*a*) Socrates's words imply the universal proposition that if a whole has a certain characteristic, so will its parts. This is obviously a fallacy. (*b*) Socrates is wrong in this particular case because names have no 'truthvalue'. Here we should note the definition

[1] Apparently he could 'agree with himself' (435a); but in any case H. uses indifferently 'agreement' (συνθήκη, ὁμολογία) and 'wont' (ἦθος). He is usually thought to be confusing two theories of names, the 'Humpty Dumpty' one that the name of anything is what I choose to call it, and the more serious view of language as a social institution with word–thing correlations conventionally established by the tradition of a particular language (Kahn, *Exegesis* 158f.).

[2] Cf. B. Heath, *JPh* 17 (1888), 195.

[3] *Essays* 123. S.'s statement had already been called a sophism by Steinthal in 1890, and defended by Goldschmidt, *Essai* 51f. R. has been challenged by Lorenz and Mittelstrass in *Mind* 1967 and Luce in *CQ* 1969. (One must of course avoid the *petitio principii* of replying that it is validated by the theory of natural names, which is what S. is using it to prove.) Aristotle too distinguished between names and propositions by saying of a name: '"Man" signifies something, but not that it exists or does not exist' (or 'is or is not the case', ἔστιν ἢ οὐκ ἔστιν *De int.* 16b26–8). So P. says that one can point to a portrait and say 'man' or 'woman', thus conveying information or misinformation.

of 'true' at 385 b7 (remembering that *alēthes* means 'real' or 'genuine' as opposed to 'imitation', as well as 'true' in describing statements: see p. 69 below): 'a true *logos* is one which speaks of (or describes) things as they are'. In Greek eyes names themselves (including proper names, nouns and adjectives) fulfilled this condition,[1] and as we have noticed, most Greek names are transparently descriptive. Another example, quoted by Luce (*l.c.* 225), is Aesch. *P.V.* 85 f.: 'Falsely do the gods call you Prometheus'—Prometheus meaning 'foresight'. For nouns and adjectives the same is obvious when they are compound like *philosophos*, and it was easy to believe that when simple they had the same function, even if it was now difficult to detect. This is what Socrates is going to try to demonstrate. It is also true that a single name or word can serve as a statement, as 'Cratylus' answers the question 'Who is that?', 'Walking' answers 'What is he doing?' As a newspaper heading, 'Parliament' gives information, true if above a report of proceedings in Parliament, false if above the report of a murder. It would be unfair to object that a word so used is *virtually* a statement, or implies a statement, e.g. 'Cratylus is walking' or 'What follows is a parliamentary report'. Only one word is uttered, and that word gives the information. Plato is not speaking of words apart from any context, but as 'parts of discourse'.[2]

Hermogenes and Protagoras (386a). Hermogenes need not have worried about his reluctance to accept Protagorean relativism,[3] for his own theory of names by no means implies it. He holds that there exist objects with permanent and definable characteristics, e.g. (to take the

[1] A note of Cornford's is worth transcribing here: 'The use of ἀληθής is only intelligible by keeping its definition in mind, τὸ τὰ ὄντα λέγειν ᾗ ἔστιν. (*a*) If the ὄν in question is a relation between two things, the corresponding speech is a proposition affirming such a relation. (*b*) If the ὄν is a thing, the corresponding speech is a name. Just as the proposition is true if it rightly reflects the objectively existing relation, so the name is true if it rightly reflects the objectively existing thing, i.e. speaks of it ᾗ ἔστιν. This it can do if, and only if, the material (sounds) has a natural (φύσει) correspondence with the forms of things (οὐσίαι) as is shown to be the case at 434a–b.'

[2] Cf. Luce's 1969 article *passim*, esp. 224f.: 'A name, by being uttered in a context, i.e. as a label for a person or thing, acquires truth-value.' For another treatment of Robinson's criticism see now Kahn, *Exegesis* 159–61, and just as this book was finished there has appeared Mary Richardson, 'True and false names in the "*Cratylus*"', *Phron.* 1976.

[3] For Protagoras's relativism or subjectivism see vol. III, 183–8. His relation to Euthydemus (introduced here at 386d) is mentioned at 186 n. 1.

example from *Phdr.* 260b) 'tame animal with the longest ears', but that it makes no difference whether you call it donkey or horse, or for that matter 'blip' or 'cump', since any name is only an arbitrarily chosen label. Protagoras's theory was that though language is constant, and two men refer to the same sensation when they say 'cold' or 'warm', one may may feel cold in the same situation in which another feels warm. They cannot contradict each other, not because one man has a private language in which 'cold' is the name for the sensation which others call 'warm', but because they are having different sensations. Protagoras is dismissed very briefly here, for Plato is after other game. He gets his turn in the *Theaetetus*.

Essence and form. At 386d–e, Hermogenes agrees with Socrates that, if Protagoras was wrong, 'things must have a certain stable essence (or being, *ousia*) of their own, not in relation to us, dragged this way and that by our own imaginings, but as naturally constituted, in themselves and in relation to their own essence'. It will be convenient to take here some other passages in which the Platonic Socrates gives his own view on objective reality and its relation to names.

423e: 'Don't you think each thing has an *essence* just as it has a colour and the other qualities we mentioned just now? Isn't there an essence of colour and sound themselves, and everything else that is rightly said to "be"?'

393d: The precise syllables and letters do not matter 'so long as the essence of the object prevails and is revealed in the name'.

422d: 'The correctness of the names we have reviewed meant that they revealed each object as it was.' Similarly 428e: 'We agree that the correctness of a name means that it shall show the object as it is.'

438d: The discussion has now shown that names by their formation appear to give contradictory explanations of reality, so 'we must look for something else' to show us 'the true nature of existing things'.

There is also the statement of the twofold function of names at 388b: they are instruments used for (*a*) informing, (*b*) distinguishing things as they really are.

Finally there is the much discussed passage 386e ff., where Socrates introduces the well-worn analogy from the crafts which made him so unpopular in real life. A name is an instrument used for a purpose, just like an auger or a shuttle, and it is the purpose which the shuttle-maker has in mind as he shapes his wood. The proper definition of a shuttle is not 'a piece of wood of such-and-such shape and dimensions', but 'a tool ideally fitted to separate the threads'. This therefore may be called 'the shuttle itself' or the *eídos* 'shuttle' (which to Hermogenes, a Socratic but not a Platonist, could mean either form, appearance, or class, species), and this is, or should be, the object of a definition, 'what a shuttle essentially is' (389 b 5)—the old Socratic lesson as exemplified e.g. in *Hippias Major* and *Meno*. Moreover, since there are different shuttles for different materials and styles of weaving, the maker of an individual shuttle must give his wood both the general *eidos* of shuttle and the specific character (*physis*) required for its special work.[1]

In the context of the dialogue the application to names is this. Steel (to borrow an illustration from Cornford) is used to inscribe stone, a diamond to inscribe glass. For each purpose the *eidos* of cutting tool is put into a different kind of matter, and, owing to the different quality of the material to be treated, the diamond is shaped into a point for scratching, the steel into a blade (chisel) for chopping. The general *eidos* (390 a 5–6) or essence (389 d 6–7) of a name is to be an informative and diacritical instrument. The subordinate *eidos*, corresponding to sharp point or flat blade, appears in the difference between significant letters (*r* = motion etc.), each combination of which indicates a particular kind of things. The difference in matter (as between the steel of two chisels), which can be ignored, is the difference between (*a*) a Greek and a foreign combination of letters with the same meaning, or (*b*) two Greek combinations with the same meaning, like Hector and Astyanax, or *iatros* (physician) and *akestēr* (healer). At 390 e the true craftsman in names is he who 'looks solely to that which is the natural name for each thing and can implant its *form* in the letters and syllables',[2] but it has just been said that he can only do this by working under the

---

[1] This may be an indication of how Socrates thought that the relativity of the concept 'good' was compatible with the notion of a general *eidos*. See vol. III, 463 ff.

[2] Aristotle (*De int.* 17a1) said that what is κατὰ συνθήκην cannot be an ὄργανον. His point seems to be the one made acutely by Crombie (*EPD* II, 477), that 'whereas the function of a shuttle does determine its form, the function of a name does not'. Here P.'s whole argument, supported by the examples of 'imitative' letters, is that it does, but by the end of the talk with Cratylus he has shown that his own view coincides with Aristotle's and Crombie's.

Comment

instructions of the dialectician, that is, the philosopher. Plato is making the same point here as at *Rep.* 601 c ff., where the user has knowledge and the maker only 'right opinion'. It is quite in his dialectical manner to make a looser statement first (the carpenter looks to the Form) and then refine on it.[1]

Once again we see the teleological (that is, *practical*) basis of all Socraticism and Platonism.[2] We also see how easily the Socratic view developed in Plato's mind into the belief in independent Forms existing prior to their material instantiations, for obviously the function of a shuttle preceded any actual shuttles; that is to say, no shuttles would have been made until someone had felt the need of an implement of that kind to do the work he wanted done. The *Cratylus* provides a clear example of the Form being spoken of as not only an internal character or essence but an *ideal*. It is what the weaver and the carpenter 'look to' and embody in their material as far as they can. Plato adds that if a shuttle is damaged, the maker will not simply try to copy it but will consider 'that Form which he looked to when he made the broken one'. Strang[3] quotes a fascinating modern parallel. The 'standard yard' was made in 1760. In 1834 it was damaged, 'and the commission set up to replace it decided to reconstruct it as accurately as possible in terms of its certified copies'. But in this they contravened an act of 1824 'that the restoration should be in terms of the length of a pendulum which, swinging in a vacuum in the latitude of London, should have a periodic time of two solar seconds exactly'. That was the 'Form', to which both maker and replacer had to 'look'.

Plato might have been suspicious of even this formula, for a swinging pendulum suggests the world of sense, where accuracy is never more than approximate. (Cf. his treatment of astronomy, vol. IV, 524.)

[1] According to Ross (*PTI* 19), at 389c3–6 and 390b1–2 P. speaks of a skilful carpenter as succeeding [completely] in embodying the Form in particulars. In the first passage he is pressing the words too hard and ignoring the point, which is only that the function of a tool demands that it be given an objective form or character, irrespective of our whims, if we want it to perform that function. You may find a hammer a more pleasing object than an axe, but if you want to chop wood you must subdue your aesthetic leanings and fit an axe-blade to the haft and not a hammer-head. In the second passage P. is actually saying that *not* the artificer but the user of his product knows 'the *eidos* proper to a shuttle'.

[2] Socratic before it was Platonic. See vol. III, index s.v. *Socrates: teleology.*

[3] In *Plato* (ed. Vlastos) I, 188. He develops the theme as a fatal objection to P.'s 'paradigmatism'.

In the *Cratylus*, as in the *Phaedo*, a Form (*a*) is both logically and temporally prior to its instantiations, (*b*) represents a perfection to which they can only approximate by imitating, or as he says elsewhere, 'sharing in' them, (*c*) is an object of intelligence, not of sense.[1] (For the last point see 423 d–e, where sensible colours and sounds are contrasted with the essence of colour and sound.) At the same time, the vocabulary of this doctrine has so much in common with the Socratic (as exemplified in the *Euthyphro*, vol. IV, 114 ff.) that Hermogenes can follow and approve the argument without (one may assume) an inkling of its transcendent implications. Of course the notion of an essential shuttle existing eternally, independent of the invention of weaving, is absurd,[2] and as we shall see, the range of application of the doctrine of Forms became a serious stumbling-block, of which Plato does not yet seem aware. At present it serves as an illustration, whose philosophical pitfalls have not yet struck him. His interest is not in weaving, but in the ethico-aesthetic Forms in which Socrates dealt—the Good, the Beautiful and their similars (439 c). (Cf. vol. IV, 548–51.)

If the function of names is to inform by distinguishing the essence of things, they become in fact potted definitions, and a definition is of necessity universal, a statement of the *eidos*,[3] which means both

[1] The question whether P.'s doctrine of Forms had advanced so far in *Crat.* has led to much discussion. An early sceptic was Ritter (*N. Unters.* 262 ff., esp. 266). Ross (*PTI* 19) says P. 'has not yet reached the point of thinking that an Idea is never perfectly exemplified, but only imitated', and Luce that the *Crat.* 'constitutes . . . a stage distinctly prior to the position reached in the *Phaedo*' (*Phron.* 1965, 21: in a note he refers to other opinions). Contrast Hackforth (*Phaedo* 9): 'Surely Plato could hardly have used plainer language to indicate that he conceives the Form as existing apart from its particulars, and indeed before any of its particulars.' He adds a criticism of Ross. Cf. however the strikingly similar language at *Gorg.* 503 d, and Dodds *ad loc.*

[2] The point brings out well the difference between the Platonic and Aristotelian conceptions of form. For Aristotle too the form is both logically and chronologically prior to the product, because it must pre-exist *in the mind of the maker* (*Metaph.* 1032a32–b1).

[3] Or of the οὐσία (e.g. *Laws* 895 d). P.'s theory of definitions is in modern terms realist or essentialist, not, like most modern theories, nominal or linguistic (terms which mean that, in Mill's words (*Logic*, bk 1 ch. 8, 6), 'all definitions are of names, and of names only'). So Hospers, *Phil. Anal.* 54: 'In these cases [i.e. what are claimed as real definitions], what is defined is always a word or a phrase—a symbol. The language of "essence", however, may mislead us into thinking that we are defining things', and Russell and Whitehead, *Pr. Math.* 1, p. 11 (quoted by Abelson in his article 'Definition', *Ency. Phil.* 2,319): 'A definition is concerned wholly with the symbols, not with what they symbolize.' Moore on the other hand (*Pr. Eth.* 6–7) calls this kind of definition comparatively unimportant except in lexicography: the definitions he wants are 'those which describe the real nature of the object or notion denoted by a word', only possible when the object or notion is something complex. Both Antisthenes and Plato had anticipated him in the latter point (see vol. III, 211 f. and *Tht.* 201 d–202 b). It led him to conclude that 'good'

Comment

essential character (like *ousia*) and class. This is why Plato concentrates on common nouns rather than proper names. Even in the case of portraits he speaks (improbably) of mistaking a man's for a woman's, not (as would seem more natural) one of Hermogenes for one of Cratylus. In his etymologies he includes both, but once the proper name has been explained as descriptive of an essence, it immediately puts its holder in a class: there are many lords of cities besides Astyanax. It is the *typos*, general character or stamp, which the name must show (432e). The true power (*dynamis*) of names and their relation to realities, as Plato sees it, is made clear in the second part of the dialogue; but to say that they deal with essences is at least to this extent true, that only by using words can we exercise the uniquely human capacity to generalize (vol. IV, 427).

The etymologies.[1] These are a bewildering and sometimes ludicrous collection. They reminded Crombie of Lewis Carroll, and certainly some are in the same class as the Gryphon's association of 'lesson' with 'lessen'. Others are on sound lines and even correct, and the whole section is a regular encyclopaedia (as Goldschmidt called it) of Plato's knowledge of earlier and contemporary lore in physical science, cosmology, anthropology, and philosophical and religious ideas. The common element in the etymologies of 391c–427d is that all are made to support the Heraclitean and Cratylean theory of cosmological flux. (See especially 411c.) No one knows how seriously to take them. One can hardly accept the correct or reasonable derivations as evidence when they are treated as exactly on a par with the silly ones. Grote, it is true, argued that in Plato's eyes none were extravagant, and cited examples of derivations apparently meant seriously elsewhere.[2] Never-

was indefinable, and P. to say that whereas dialectical argument was an indispensable preliminary to the grasp of its essence, the full comprehension of it could only be the result of an intuitive leap or sudden illumination.

[1] 'Greek etymologies are not to be compared with our scientific etymologies because they are a different thing; they must in fact be regarded as an attempt to penetrate the mystery of things: their meaning is philosophical, not linguistic.' (Untersteiner, *Sophists* 224 n. 42 *ad fin.*)

[2] *Phdr.* 238c ἔρως from ῥώμη, 244b μαντική = μανική (very like *Crat.* in dismissing the τ as an 'insensitive' addition) and 244c οἰωνιστική from οἴησις, νοῦς and ἱστορία (though even Grote has doubts about this), *Tim.* 43c αἴσθησις from ἀίσσω, 62a θερμόν from κερματίζειν. But Taylor (*Comm.* 269, 432) calls both *Tim.* examples 'fancies' or 'sportive', and it is incredible that those from *Phdr.* had any serious philological intent. At *Tim.* 45b, P. offers for ἡμέρα the deriva-

theless—to cite one example only—I do not believe Plato thought the name of Kronos to be derived from the clean-swept purity of his mind (396b).

Others have maintained that although individual etymologies may be bad, they illustrate sound principles scarcely out of date even today.[1] Such are the effect of euphony (404d) and other changes in use, and the necessity to seek out the oldest form (418e), the beginnings of comparative philology (especially at 410a), 'sound-symbolism' and the clear way in which the theory of speech as vocal gesture is distinguished from the cruder onomatopoeia. Yet the principles themselves mix sense and nonsense. Women, for instance, are said to be, or to have been, particularly fond of the sound of *i* and *d*, and to be especially conservative in their speech (418b–c). We may note too that Socrates himself finally rejects the resort to foreign origin as 'escapist' (426a), and about sound-symbolism (more accurately imitation of essences through movements and positions of the organs of speech), which he admits seems ridiculous, he does not say that it is a true explanation but that it is the only rational way to defend the correctness of primary names (which in fact neither Hermogenes nor Plato himself believes in). Its uselessness is subtly shown in the very course of expounding it, e.g. by the true observation that even names with an obvious meaning may have been given for the wrong reasons (family connexions, wishful thinking) and have therefore no natural affinity with their nominates (394d–e, 397b), and that some names have been twisted to unintelligibility by 'people with no regard for the truth' until 'any name can be fitted to any object' (414c–d). Again, the professed purpose of the exercise is to show that words are connected with their objects by a theory of significant sounds, yet after refuting Cratylus on the basis of his assumption that they are so connected, Socrates upsets the whole thing by showing that etymologies could as easily be made to support a

tion from ἥμερον which at *Crat.* 418d he explicitly rejects. Other Platonic etymologies are given by Méridier on p. 18, n. 2. More impressive is the sober Aristotle: *HA* 493a22 ὀσφύς from ἰσοφυές, *EN* 1113a13 δίκαιον from δίχα, *Phys.* 198b22 αὐτόματον from αὐτὸ μάτην. Grote adds μεθύειν from μετὰ τὸ θύειν, but fr. 102 Rose suggests that this was not Aristotle's own idea. G. also quotes opinions from later antiquity to support the view that P. was serious. His 2nd vol., pp. 518–29 with their notes, should not be missed, if only as a brilliant display of scholarship.

[1] See e.g. Jowett, *Dials.* III, 2, Friedländer, *Pl.* II, 206 with n. 30, Pfeiffer, *Hist. Cl. Sch.* I, 63f., Méridier, *Crat.* 26.

theory of immobility as one of flux, even offering contrary explanations of the same word.[1]

Finally, whether or not either single examples or general principles are defensible, the idea that Plato meant them as a serious linguistic exercise is ruled out by the consistently humorous and ironic vein in which they are proposed. This I have tried to bring out in the summary. One of the things which has to be accepted about Plato and makes him so baffling a philosopher, and so delightful a writer, is the way that his Socrates plays with a naive or Sophistic respondent by tumbling together with an equally straight face absurdities and deeply held convictions. Perhaps agreement will never be reached, but for one reader at least the philological lessons are in the former class, a take-off of the current pseudo-science of etymology.

The right relation between names and reality. It may be that the terminology in 386e–88e closely resembles that at *Rep.* 596aff.,[2] which ostensibly posits a single form (*eidos*) for 'every set of things to which we apply the same name'. This would conflict with *Crat.* 387b–d, where Socrates points out to Hermogenes that 'if a man speaks as things are intended by nature to be spoken of, and with the appropriate instrument [*sc.* name], his action—that is, his speech—will accomplish something. Otherwise he will be in error, and his action nullified.' I hope I have shown, however, that the meaning of the *Republic* passage is not quite what it appears to be on the surface. (See vol. IV, 550.) The purpose of names is to classify according to essence (388b–c), but a wrong name may be given, and it will then be untrue that everything included under it will have the same *eidos*. If names are entirely conventional, there is no guarantee that a common name indicates a common idea.

The Socratic conception of *eidos* and method of definition left a series of problems for Plato, of which he only gradually became aware, when the instability of particulars forced him to conclude that this

---

[1] ἐπιστήμη. See 412a and 437a. Note also that on the theory of sound-symbolism names (in spite of 423e) can only imitate sensible attributes like speed, smoothness and shape, whereas essences or Forms are for Plato νοητά, grasped by the intellect not the senses. And νοητά are the only true objects of knowledge, therefore knowledge cannot be obtained from words.

[2] So Allan, *AJP* 1954, 281.

'Form' was not only the general character determining a class but also a separate, perfect exemplar to which the particulars could only partially aspire. The Socratic method of induction from cases where the same term is currently employed (justice, courage, self-control are all virtues, *therefore* they must share a common characteristic 'by which' they are virtues) could be taken to assume that use of the same name points to a resemblance between things, i.e. it infers from names to things. It looks as if the *Cratylus* is designed to correct this misconception. In its extreme form the assumption is that of Cratylus: 'It is quite simple: whoever knows the names knows the things too' (435 d). Against this 'Socrates' argues: (*a*) Whoever bestowed names doubtless formed them according to his notion of the things, but he could have been mistaken (436a–b);[1] (*b*) Knowledge of things cannot depend *solely* on knowledge of names, for there must have been a first name-maker, and how did *he* get his knowledge? Things then must be knowable, some-how, directly ('through themselves and each other') (438e),[2] and the correctness of names, as he said to Hermogenes, must be tested by their capacity to distinguish the essences, or indwelling nature, of things (422d).

Cornford put forward a tempting possibility, in terms of the earlier and later theory of Forms. On this view the assumption that a common name always indicates a common *eidos* would be both a Socratic and an early Platonic one, which the *Cratylus* is designed to examine. It shows that the assumption is unjustifiable and that consequently the basis of the early theory must be modified to render it independent of the caprices and imperfections of language. 'Is not', he continued, 'this modification the chief difference between the earlier and later theories, the later being based not on common names or on language at all, but on natural kinds distinguished by observed characteristics?' One thinks of *Pol.* 262b–e, with its warning not to think you are dividing 'according to form' because something is given a single name, or *Tim.* 83c which speaks of 'someone who can look at a variety of things and see within them a single genus justifying one name for all'.

---

[1] He might, says S., have been wrong in his initial assumption; and the errors would multiply as he forced the rest into agreement with it, as occurs in geometrical proofs. The importance of testing a hypothesis in every way possible is brought out in *Phaedo*. See vol. IV, 352f.

[2] Haag p. 5 compares *Tht.* 186a–b.

Comment

Nevertheless this would be difficult to maintain. As an illustration of the earlier theory Cornford cited *Rep.* 596a about positing a Form for everything with the same name. But in the same dialogue (454a) Socrates distinguishes eristics, or sharp debaters, from dialectical philosophers as people 'who cannot analyse their subject into its natural kinds (διαιρούμενοι κατ' εἴδη) but chase a contradiction in it through going by the mere name'.[1] The need to 'divide by (natural) kinds' has met us in the *Phaedrus* (vol. IV, 428) and recurs here, when at 424c–d Socrates gives Hermogenes a lesson in the method by showing how letters can be divided into natural kinds (διελέσθαι κατ' εἴδη) which can be fitted to the natural divisions between things. It goes back to Socrates, and perhaps further. A passage from the Hippocratic *De arte* 2 is worth quoting: 'I believe the *technai* took even their names from their natures (*eidē*), for it would be absurd and impossible to suppose that the forms originate from names. Names are conventions imposed on nature, but forms are not conventions but natural growths.' As for Socrates, according to Xenophon he suggested that dialectic was so called because its practitioners in their converse 'divided things according to their classes' (διαλέγοντας κατὰ γένη).[2] Evidently the method of definition by division, exemplified in the *Sophist* and *Statesman*, was not a new departure, but a technical elaboration of something with which Plato was familiar from the beginning. It and 'collection' were never, even in their earliest stages, dependent on inference from names to things. The assumption implied in the Socratic method was rather 'that the kinds or classes to which particulars belong, the "forms" which they possess, have a quasi-substantial nature and hence a stability which enables the essence of each to be grasped,

---

[1] The context is S.'s proposal that women and men should share the same occupations. To object that they are 'different' could be like saying that bald men and men with hair should not pursue the same trade. The question is, *in what respect* are they different? The mere name 'different' is no help in determining the natures of men and women.

[2] Xen. *Mem.* 4.5.12. (γένος and εἶδος are used indifferently in the passage on διαίρεσις at *Pol.* 262d–e.) See also vol. III, 440f. for S., and for the fifth cent. in general the ref. to Morrison on p. 204. Note in contrast to the Socratic κατ' εἴδη διαιρεῖν that Prodicus is more than once ironically lauded for his skill at ὀνόματα διαιρεῖν (*Charm.* 163d, *Laches* 197d). *De arte* is arguing against those who would deny reality to the τέχναι, especially medicine. I cannot believe that it is 'after' Plato, as some have suggested, rather than belonging to the fifth-cent. controversy over the status of names. (Heinimann, *N.u.Ph.* 160 dates it thus.) My translation of τὰ ὀνόματα λαβεῖν in vol. III, p. 204 probably needs correcting.

described, and clearly distinguished from all other essences'.[1] As the *Phaedo* says (102b), 'Things take their names from the Forms in which they participate.'

But modern comment on *Rep.* 596a shows how easily it could all be misunderstood as making correct classification and definition depend on the accidents of nomenclature. Such misapprehension would have horrified Plato, as undoing his master's work and striking at the very roots of the Socratic as well as his own belief in Forms, and the *Cratylus* may be seen, not as a correction of his own earlier teaching but a defence of it against unjustified criticism, and perhaps a lesson for his pupils.[2]

The upshot of the *Cratylus* is that names do give information by distinguishing between classes or essences of things ('It wasn't a burglar, only a cat'), *but only if the essences are known beforehand* (438a–b). We are left therefore with the problem of how we can know and distinguish between things in themselves. They must be known

---

[1] Vol. III, 440. There is an argument about this which goes well back into the last century, and in which prejudice has played a considerable part, as Stenzel rightly saw. Reacting against it, he declared (*PMD* 80) that *Rep.* 454a in its context has nothing to do with the technical procedure of the division of a genus in *Soph.* P., he says, used the word διαιρεῖν even in the earlier dialogues to mean 'division into parts' (what else could it mean?), but it must have been quite different considerations that led him to the consciously-held theory of *Soph.* and *Pol.* Cornford too (*PTK* 184f.) contrasts Socratic and Platonic methods in this respect, taking *Meno* as typical of the former, and Dodds (*Gorg.* 226) calls *diairesis* a Platonic invention, though seeing it already (as one must) in *Gorg. Soph.* and *Pol.* certainly represent a development in technique, but I believe it is going too far to say that this has nothing to do with Socratic method and arose from quite different considerations. (Cf. esp. vol. IV, 430.) Cornford (*PTK* 180) says that 'collection must not be confused with the Socratic muster of individual instances', because it is confined to Forms, but S. himself (if, as Cornford does, we take P.'s earlier dialogues to illustrate his method) normally operated with forms or species as units. It is the main thesis of Sayre's *PAM* that there is no sharp distinction between the method of hypothesis in *Phaedo* or *Rep.* and the collection and division of the later dialogues: they are a single method in two stages of development. Ten years after the German original of *PMD*, Stenzel himself wrote (*RE*, 2. Reihe, 5. Halbb. 862): 'P. saw in the general notion of "separating", sharpened perhaps by S., . . . an earlier form of his technical method of definition by *diairesis*.'

[2] Wilamowitz (*Pl.* I, 289) argued that P. himself had once been very attracted to the idea that the essence of things could be found in words, and the *Crat.* was written to rescue himself and his pupils from this illusion. He declares it wrong, but enjoys playing with it as only a man could who had ventured far on this path before discovering that it led nowhere. (One might think of S.'s reluctance to give up the 'imitation' theory of words at 535c. Cf. also the evidence presented with admirable impartiality by Goldschmidt, *Essai* 185–99.) This is possible, and would explain very satisfactorily the length and gusto of the etymological section, which some scholars have found disproportionate, though it is its own justification, far too ingenious and entertaining to merit such strictures as Méridier's (p. 33): 'P. croyait avoir ses raisons, mais il est certain que du point de vue artistique l'économie de l'œuvre en a souffert.'

directly, 'through themselves and each other' (438e), but how to do this is set aside as a problem 'too big for you and me'. It is reserved for the *Theaetetus* and *Sophist*. The obvious way would seem to be through sensation, whose claim to be called knowledge is fully discussed in the former. In the *Sophist* the hint that there is a definite relationship between the Forms ('through each other') is taken up and developed. From our knowledge of other dialogues, especially *Phaedrus* and *Phaedo*, we can see the answer which, so far at least, has appealed to Plato himself. Sensation must indeed be the starting-point (*Phdr.* 249b, *Phaedo* 74b). From sensations[1] all human beings have the power of forming general concepts, making possible the use of general terms. The philosopher however, by his skill in dialectic, carries further the process of recollecting the perfect Forms which his soul saw when free from the body, until, having recovered them, he can use them as standards for his classification of things on earth. The effective resemblance is not between things and their names, but between things and Forms, those steadfast, unchanging Forms which Socrates suddenly brings in at the end and which Cratylus cannot deny—not, surely, because he held any Platonic theory of their transcendence, but as Protagoras did, because it seems absurd to say that there is no such thing as beauty or goodness. (Cf. vol. IV, 223.)

What is meant by correctness of names? This does not settle one of the central questions raised by the *Cratylus*: how serious is Plato in saying that names reveal the nature of their objects by actually imitating them in sound? It is not decided by saying that the original legislator on names worked with a knowledge of the things named. Socrates's own purpose (which as we have often reminded ourselves was ultimately moral or social) did not require any resemblance between words and things but only *consistency*. Assuming as he did that 'justice itself' existed and was immutable, it did not matter whether within a society it was called *justice*, *dikaiosynē* or *Gerechtigkeit*, provided its users indicated its true nature when they used the same word, having through the work of the dialectician rid themselves of confusion such

[1] Perhaps better 'perceptions'. P. was not worried by any distinction between these and pure sense-data.

that one meant 'obedience to the laws' and another 'the right of the stronger'.[1]

Roth has pointed out[2] that not only are there two theories of naturally correct names in the *Cratylus*, but also, though not formally inconsistent themselves, they rest on inconsistent assumptions. The proper conclusion of the first is that a name is only correct if it makes clear the nature of the things it names; of the second, that a name is only correct if its letters and syllables imitate the nature of the thing named. In drawing the first conclusion Socrates insists that the letters and syllables chosen have no bearing on it whatever. At 390a the legislator on names does his work well provided he renders the form proper to each thing 'in whatever syllables, here or elsewhere'; and at 394b the expert in names in considering their *dynameis* will not be disturbed by a few changes or even if 'the force of a name is expressed in entirely different letters'. These are only the material, and the same form can be realized in different materials (389d–e). The validity of the second theory, on the other hand, obviously depends on the assumption that correctness of name is equivalent to correctness of vocal sound. At 433d–34a Socrates demands that Cratylus choose between the convention and resemblance theories as the only alternatives, and Cratylus naturally prefers the latter, which Socrates then (*a*) disputes by showing that even if some words indicate their objects by resembling them, others can do so by other means, and (*b*) makes fun of by showing that it could support a static theory of the universe as easily as Cratylus's own theory of flux. So we reach the seriously meant conclusion of the whole dialogue, that names offer no help in discovering the essential natures of things, though they serve to communicate those natures when known. With cats and burglars this is easy, but not so with the supremely important Forms of Good, Beautiful and Just, and others which are the Platonic philosopher's primary concern.[3]

[1] This point is made in the *Crat.* itself at 434e–35a.
[2] Diss. 1969, p. 88. (See p. 5 n. 3 above.)
[3] *Alc. I*, 111b–12a is relevant here.

Comment

Since Benfey's monograph in 1866, a question that has interested many is whether in the *Cratylus* Plato had in mind as an aim the creation of an ideal, artificial or technical language. This has been inferred from the analogy with the crafts, especially the comparison between carpenter and legislator and their relation to their respective overseers (390b-d). Thus Grote wrote with reference to this passage (*Pl.* II, 506): 'Plato aspires here to a philosophical language fit for those who conversed with forms or essences: something like ... a technical nomenclature.' And in modern times Weingartner (*Unity* 35): 'It seems that Plato was looking forward to a technical language which could reflect the classifications that result when dialectic becomes collection and division.' Runciman (*PLE* 21, n. 4 to p. 20) says that Grote was probably right in his view 'that Plato thought an absolute standard of naming to be theoretically desirable though not existing in fact', and supports this by reference to three other dialogues. I do not wish to continue the debate beyond what can be gathered from the above comments. The question is only peripheral to the main aims of the dialogue, and statements like those of 438c and 439a tell strongly against a positive answer: names are only confusing, so that we must find *something other than names* to reveal the truth; and even if we could learn from them, there is a better way. If one must answer for Plato, therefore, it will be in the negative, but in a dialogue in which, on everything but the main point, he so skilfully covers up his tracks, it would be rash to dogmatize.[1]

The Seventh Letter (343a) states that the names 'round' and 'straight' have no permanent validity, and could as well be reversed. They would be just as well established for those who changed them round. This is often quoted in connexion with the *Cratylus*, but it is dangerous to wrench it thus from its context, where it is only ancillary to a particular point, that nothing in the sensible world contains a pure quality unmixed with its opposite. No sensible circle, whether drawn or turned on a lathe, is perfectly circular. All contain elements of straightness as well.

---

[1] See also the judicious remarks of Goldschmidt, *Essai* 199–206. Since the above was written, Kahn has appeared on the same side (*Exegesis* 167). As evidence for 'a vision of an ideal language' Anagnostopoulos quotes 424c–25a. See his article on 'The significance of P.'s *Crat.*' in *R. of Metaph.* 1973–4, 327.

II

PARMENIDES, THEAETETUS, SOPHIST, POLITICUS

INTRODUCTION

With these dialogues Plato's thought takes a remarkable turn. So far the figure of Socrates has dominated the rest and his point of view has prevailed. His companions are either convinced or at least silenced, and the reader is plainly meant to follow his lead. Secondly, the assumption, or hypothesis, of the existence of unchanging Forms—the Good, the Beautiful and the rest—which though separate from particular actions or things are in some way responsible for their being what they are, has never been challenged. It is received as something well known and accepted, and used as the basic premise from which deductions can safely be made. (Cf. especially *Phaedo* 100 b–c, *Rep.* 476 a, *Crat.* 439 c.)

Suddenly in the *Parmenides* we meet a new Socrates, a very young man, unsure of himself and putting forward this same hypothesis, of separate Forms and particulars that 'share in' them, only to have it attacked by the old and famous Parmenides, who counters all his arguments in its defence and after leaving him helpless kindly offers to give him the lesson in method which he so obviously needs. For the first time, what we have come to regard as the corner-stone of Platonism, bound up with visions of an immortal soul and a place beyond the heavens, is itself made the subject of a searching examination. In the *Theaetetus* Socrates is again in the lead, but an attempt is made to define knowledge without recourse to the Forms, whose existence is scarcely hinted at in the main argument. As to *Sophist* and *Politicus*,[1] Socrates is reduced to a silent listener, and the discussion is conducted by a nameless character tailor-made for the occasion, and described precisely as a native of Elea and follower of Parmenides and Zeno, but nevertheless

---

[1] This latinized form of the Greek word for 'statesman' (abbr. *Pol.*) is usual in England, though in some countries *Pol.* is used for the *Republic* (*Politeia*).

no eristic or logic-chopper and not afraid of challenging his revered teacher himself. In the *Sophist* he severely criticizes some people referred to as 'friends of Forms' for their belief that reality is changeless. There and in the *Statesman* the technique of defining by 'collection and division', explained in the *Phaedrus* (vol. IV, 427–31), is refined and developed into the primary method of reaching a definition.

Plato makes clear that he meant the four dialogues to be read in conjunction, and in the order given above.[1] In both *Theaetetus* (183e) and *Sophist* (217c) Socrates mentions his long-past meeting with the aged Parmenides. In the *Sophist* the three speakers of the *Theaetetus* meet again 'according to yesterday's agreement' and introduce the visitor who is asked to explain the nature and mutual relations of three types: Sophist, Statesman and Philosopher; and the *Statesman* begins with explicit references to the *Sophist*, and includes others at 258b, 266d, 284b and 286b. Theaetetus talks to Socrates in the *Theaetetus*, to the visitor in the *Sophist*, and is present but 'let off' in the *Statesman*, where his place is taken by the younger Socrates, who has been silently present at the two earlier discussions.[2]

(1) PARMENIDES

The *Parmenides*, especially its second part, has had the strangest fate of any of Plato's dialogues. That he was a theist, deeply religious and with more than a touch of mysticism in him, no one would deny; nor would anyone be surprised at finding the *Phaedo*, *Phaedrus* or *Timaeus* cited in evidence of this. But that the dry antithetical arguments of the *Parmenides* about the One, sophistic in form at least and inseparable, one would have thought, from fifth–fourth-century controversy, should have been seen as an exposition of the sublimest truths of theology, is surely one of the oddest turns in the history of human

[1] This is probably also the order of composition, but since they were thought out as a group, it is of no great importance. For their relation to *Phdr.* see vol. IV, 396. Campbell, it is true (*Tht.* lv), gives his reasons for supposing that 'It does not appear that at the time of writing the *Theaetetus* Plato had distinctly planned the other three', and McDowell disputes the priority of *Parm.* to *Tht.* See his *Tht.* p. 113 and the other notes there referred to. Mrs Walker (*PR* 1938, 503) writes of 'the advance of the *Parmenides* beyond the *Philebus*', but this is a highly unusual view.

[2] For his presence in *Tht.* see 147d.

thought. Yet the Neoplatonists claimed to see in the One their own highest, ineffable and unknowable God, and as such it passed into medieval and later Christianity and into philosophy as far as Hegel. Even the analytic approach of the present century has its rivals, as in Wahl's talk (1926) of a union of 'transcendent mysticism and immanent pantheism', and Wundt's conclusion (1935) that 'the Neoplatonists were not so far from Plato's doctrine as is often believed today'. Today's disputes go a long way back, for Proclus himself divided earlier interpreters into a logical and a metaphysical school.[1]

Date. Of its position in the series of dialogues enough has already been said. It has been conjectured (Ritter, *Essence* 28) that it was written during Plato's second sojourn in Syracuse after Dion's exile, and if this is hardly susceptible of proof (cf. Taylor, introd. p. 2), the period 370–367 is generally agreed to be very probable. It has also been asserted that the two parts into which the dialogue naturally falls were written independently at a considerable interval of time, and later stitched together. This is an old theory, revived by Ryle, if turning it inside out can be called revival, for according to the older view the second part was the earlier, whereas Ryle puts it later than the first.[2] The strongest argument is the complete change of style at 137c from narrated dialogue, naming the speakers and with occasional mention of laughter and other descriptive touches, to direct speech and the abandonment of all pretence at narration. It is not however decisive, and the denial of an original and organic connexion between the two parts has not found general favour.

Dramatic date. Plato is at pains to place the main discussion in its temporal setting. Parmenides, grey-haired and distinguished-looking,

---

[1] Wahl, *Étude* 43 and 88, Wundt, *P.'s Parm.* 26. Wyller's work (1959 and later) has been described as 'a strange mixture of Proclus and Heidegger'. See Tigerstedt, *Interpreting P.* 143–7. Similar views are taken by Speiser (1937) and Huber (1951). For a brief historical summary of interpretations see Cornford, *P. and P.* v–ix, and for the Neoplatonists app. E to Taylor's trans. and Wundt, *o.c.* 7–26. A more recent Neoplatonic interpretation of the *Parm.* is Hager's in *Der Geist und das Eine* (1970).

[2] Ryle in *SPM* 145, *P.'s P.* 287–93, correcting his earlier statement in *SPM* (p. 100) that 'there is a clear connexion between the two parts'. His argument for separation is rebutted by Crombie, *PR* 1969, 372. For the earlier view of Apelt, Wilamowitz and Wundt see Wundt, *P.'s Parm.* 4–7.

is about sixty-five, Zeno approaching forty, and Socrates 'very young', so their meeting must have taken place about 450. But this is now a long time ago, nor do we get the story at first hand. As presented, the whole dialogue is narrated by one Cephalus of Clazomenae[1] (otherwise unknown), who tells how he brought some fellow-philosophers to Athens to hear an account of the meeting from Plato's half-brother Antiphon who had it from Zeno's friend Pythodorus who was present. If Cephalus had to get it in this roundabout way, one can only assume (with Taylor) that the Athenian participants—Socrates, Pythodorus and Aristoteles—were dead, and Antiphon's narration took place after 400. In the nearest comparable work, the *Symposium*, the narration takes place a mere sixteen years after the event, and the narrator has confirmed some points from Socrates himself.

Setting and characters. The involved introduction may indicate that Plato wanted to prepare a reader for the fictional nature of the main discussion, but it could equally well be intended to emphasize its importance, if a group of philosophers from the home of Anaxagoras thought it worth while to journey to Athens to hear it over fifty years after the event. In any case, as always, Plato enjoys the personal touches for which it gives an opportunity. Cephalus and his friends meet Glaucon and Adeimantus in the market-place, who confirm that their half-brother Antiphon heard the discussion in his youth and took great pains to learn it by heart, though now his main interest is in horses. Together they go to Antiphon's house, and when he has settled the important matter of a new bit with his harness-maker, and grumbled about the difficulty of recalling the story now, he agrees to tell it.

Zeno and Parmenides, on a visit to Athens, were staying with Pythodorus, at whose house in the Cerameicus the discussion took place. He is mentioned again in *Alc.I* as a paying pupil of Zeno,[2] and as an Athenian general his name occurs several times in Thucydides in connexion with events in Sicily during the Peloponnesian War and the signing of the Peace of Nicias in 421. Also present, besides Socrates,

---

[1] The home of Anaxagoras. On the significance of this see Schofield in *Mus. Helv.* 1973, 4.
[2] But on the payment see Vlastos in *JHS* 1975, 155–61.

was Aristoteles, the youngest of the company, the Greek form of whose name will serve to distinguish him from the philosopher Aristotle. The unlikelihood of the idea[1] that by the name Plato intended to link his famous pupil and critic with some objections to the doctrine of Forms is shown by more than one consideration: (*a*) Plato takes the trouble to point out at 127d that he was the Aristoteles who became one of the Thirty Tyrants (known also from Xenophon, *Hell.* 2.3.2, 13 and 46); (*b*) he was pretty certainly writing at about the time when Aristotle first came down from Macedonia, aged about 17, to join the Academy.

Of the historical Parmenides and Zeno nothing need be added here,[2] but it may be noted that the former is not a mere lay-figure. True, he does not always speak in the terms of his own Way of Truth. How could he? He is the first in a long line of philosophers who have propounded theories which they must ignore in practice. Could a solipsist act as such in communicating his ideas? But he suggests as subject for a dialectical exercise 'my own hypothesis about the One itself', and the main strength of his arguments in the first part lies in his historical denial of any possible connexion between the sensible and intelligible worlds, precisely the dilemma which Plato's doctrine of Forms was designed to solve.[3]

Part One (*126a–35d*)

Introductory conversation: Zeno's arguments countered by the doctrine of Forms (127d–30a). Zeno has been reading his treatise, the object of which, as he agrees with Socrates, was to defend Parmenides's thesis that 'All is One' (128a) indirectly by demonstrating that if there is a plurality things must have contrary characters, being e.g. both like and unlike, and this is absurd. Socrates counters with his familiar question: Are there not Forms of Similarity and Dissimilarity apart from particu-

---

[1] Revived by Wundt (*o.c.* 5 n. 2) and several other scholars, including recently Koutsouyanno-poulou in *Platon* 1966 and Newiger, *Gorgias über das Nichtseiende* (1973), 108. Against it see Taylor, trans. 129f. and Cornford, *P. and P.* 109 n. 1. Bury's suggestion (*J. Phil.* 1894, 176f.) that Aristotle could have already been pressing the objections because he had only taken them over from the Megarians is more ingenious than convincing.

[2] On Zeno and his relationship with Parmenides see Vlastos's article mentioned on previous page, n. 2.

[3] Schofield in *CQ* 1973, 44, sees P. as in the second part making Parmenides draw from his own hypothesis, and by Eleatic arguments, conclusions embarrassing to an Eleatic.

lar people and things, which are similar or dissimilar according as they partake in one or the other? There is no reason why a particular should not partake in contrary Forms, as Socrates for instance is one person but comprises many parts. It would be surprising if Forms themselves could exhibit contrary characteristics by combining with their opposites —Similarity with Dissimilarity, Unity with Plurality, Rest with Motion and so on[1]—but the difficulty raised by Zeno and Parmenides affects only sensibles, not the intelligible Forms which exist apart.

Zeno takes no further part in the discussion, which is conducted entirely by Parmenides. This is in keeping with Plato's opinion of the two men. Zeno is dismissed in the *Phaedrus* as a living demonstration that captious and contentious argument is not confined to lawyers and politicians. For Parmenides, who had changed the whole face of Greek philosophy, Plato had enormous respect tempered with fundamental disagreement.[2]

The theory of Forms, as stated here and elaborated in reply to Parmenides's questions, is exactly that of the *Phaedo*,[3] so before encountering Parmenides we may recall its chief features. Forms (1) exist apart from particulars, as changeless and eternal exemplars, accessible to the mind in thought, but not to the senses. At the same time (2) they are the causes of particulars being what they are, though one cannot be dogmatic about the relationship: particulars may be said to 'share in' Forms or resemble them imperfectly (74e), or Forms can 'be present in' or 'associate with' particulars (100d). (3) Hence one may distinguish between a Form in and by itself and its instantiation in a changing and perishable particular (102d). (4) There is a hint also of perfect instances of Forms, besides the Forms in physical beings, only mentioned in

[1] This is plainly what S. means, though he has been thought to be denying *any* combination of Forms. τὰ τοιαῦτα are pairs of incompatible Forms like Unity and Plurality. Cf. Hicken in *SPM* 191.

[2] For Z. see *Phdr.* 261 d–e and Cornford, *P. and P.* 67f. (Note S.'s little joke at 128b: Z. denies the existence of many, and brings forward *many* arguments to prove his case.) For Parmenides, note S.'s expressions at *Tht.* 183e and *Soph.* 217c modified by his fears in *Soph.* (216b) that an Eleatic will be a 'god of refutation', and the Eleatic's own criticisms of his master at 241 d and 242 c. (Vlastos in *JHS* 1975, 150–5, sees rather differently the implications of *Phdr.* 261 d–e.)

[3] The latest of many theses about the apparently severe criticism of the Forms in the *Parm.* is Zekl's of 1975. He holds that what is offered for criticism is not the genuine theory but a 'pale copy' of it, the immature effort of a not very bright pupil. The criticisms therefore do not touch the genuine Platonic teaching.

connexion with mathematical concepts ('the equals themselves' 74c), which is taken up at *Parm.* 129b, 'the similars themselves'.[1] (5) The Form itself has the character which it implants in particulars. Beauty, for instance, is also 'the Beautiful itself', the very perfection of beauty, and of Largeness it is said that 'being large, it cannot bear to be small' (102e). (6) The extent of the world of Forms is not discussed, but mention is made of Forms corresponding to value-concepts such as good and beautiful, relations (so that 'Simmias is taller than Socrates' is re-formulated as 'Simmias possesses Tallness in relation to the Shortness of Socrates', 102b–c), mathematical concepts like quantity, length or number (100e–101c), and physical substances like snow and fire (vol. IV, 357, 359).

All these aspects of the *Phaedo*-theory are discussed in the *Parmenides*, but the omissions are at least equally striking. In the *Phaedo* the doctrine of Forms is unthinkable without the complementary doctrines of the human soul (mind) as immortal, periodically re-incarnated, and an intermediary between the visible world and the intelligible Forms to which it is akin (79d). The problem of how our minds, tied to bodies and living in the physical world, can have any contact with the invisible and changeless, is solved by supposing that when out of the body we had complete vision of the Forms, of which we may therefore be reminded by their imperfect and impermanent embodiments on earth, at first dimly, but by perseverance in the philosophic life ever more clearly. Inseparable from all this is the constant association of the Forms with value. Not only do the moral and aesthetic Forms, as in many other dialogues, have pride of place, but the intelligible world is consistently lauded at the expense of the physical, and even in the case of Forms which might not seem to have any special value, such as equality or size, particulars are represented as 'wishing' or 'striving' to be as their Forms are, but remaining 'of less worth' (74d–75e).

---

[1] Identified by some with the Form, but cf. Bluck, *Phron.* 1957, 118, and Cornford, *P. and P.* 75: 'quantities defined simply as equal and nothing else'. See also vol. IV, 342–5.

Parmenides's questions and objections (130a–35b). With Parmenides in the lead, the discussion proceeds on Parmenidean lines, that is, by means of dilemmas, demanding a choice between two contradictory theses only, with no compromise or qualifications allowed. In the *Sophist* on the other hand it is led by an Eleatic *heretic*, who is not afraid to criticize this procedure of his master on the master's own ground, namely the alternatives 'being' and 'not-being'. This is the first hint that the *Parmenides* is intended as a stimulus to further thought, offering no positive result but leading to the *Sophist* which seeks a solution to the difficulties raised by Parmenidean logic.

(i) *Of what things are there Forms? (130b–e).* When Parmenides has verified Socrates's theory as 'making a division between Forms on the one hand and the things that share in them on the other, so that there exists a "Similarity itself" separate from the similarity which we possess, and a One and a Many' and so on (130b), his first question concerns its *scope.* Apart from 'what Zeno mentioned', Socrates agrees that there are Forms of such attributes as beautiful and good. Concerning natural species and substances like man or fire he hesitates, and when it comes to 'undignified and worthless' things like hair, clay and dirt he feels that to posit Forms of these, besides the visible substances, would be absurd. He is, he admits, troubled by the thought that the same rule should cover all cases, but retreats to things of whose Forms he feels sure, and confines his study to them. Parmenides however attributes this to a youthful lack of confidence in his own opinions: as his philosophy matures he will cease to despise any of these things.

In view of the uncertainty surrounding the extent of the world of Forms, we may take this as representing Plato's own attitude. Since hair and clay are classes of substance with a recognizable form or nature,[1] it would be only logical to assume a separate Form of each. Doubtless there is, but the Forms which interest him as a philosopher are not these, but the moral and mathematical, and those of the widest

---

[1] It may be that, as Crombie says (*EPD* II, 330), P. regarded clay and hair as 'indeterminate objects', 'matter left to its own devices', corresponding to 'no definite and intended character'. But (*a*) he would probably not have ascribed so sophisticated a view to the young S. of this dialogue; (*b*) that the point lies in worth or dignity is suggested by repetitions of the same criticism at *Soph.* 227b and *Pol.* 266d; (*c*) in any case clay is definable at *Tht.* 147c. (On Forms of clay and hair see also vol. IV, 549.)

concepts like Being, Sameness, Difference, Motion, Rest, which he deals with in the *Sophist*.[1] The comment allowed to Parmenides hints for the first time at something which acquired greater prominence as Plato re-thought the theory of Forms in his later dialogues, namely a doubt about its universally teleological orientation. Two passages will illustrate this. (i) *Soph.* 227b. Dialectic or philosophical method, in its quest for understanding through the detection of affinities, holds all pursuits in equal honour. Either generalship or de-lousing may be adduced as a species of hunting with no hint that one is more contemptible than the other. (ii) *Pol.* 266d, after a reference back to the *Sophist*, says: 'A philosophical enquiry like this one is not concerned with degrees of dignity and does not despise the smaller more than the greater, but makes straight for the truth every time in its own way.'

When Parmenides's questions become critical, they do not bear at all on the *existence* of the Forms, but only on their relationship to this world and to ourselves (as objects of our knowledge)—a reminder that we are listening to a man whose own philosophy allowed the existence of the intelligible only, and denied any connexion between it and the sensible world. Judge by reason alone: human senses and opinions have no validity at all. (Parm. fr. 7, 3–7.) This then is the line of his attack.

Once again he restates the doctrine, with an actual quotation from the *Phaedo*:[2] there are certain Forms, and other things which share in them and are called by their names. What shares in Similarity is called similar, in Largeness large, in Beauty and Justice beautiful and just. Then come the difficulties.

(ii) *What shares in a Form must contain either the whole of it or a part (130e–31e)*. (*a*) How can it be as a whole in many separate things,[3] when it is a unity? Why not (says Socrates) as a day is in many places

---

[1] On the extent of the world of Forms, a question which as Goldschmidt truly said 'ne paraît pas admettre de solution satisfaisante' (*Essai* 201), some remarks have been made already. See vol. IV, 359 (*Phaedo*), and 548–51 (*Rep.*), and this vol. 22 (*Crat.*). For assessments of the evidence in both P. and Aristotle see Ross, *PTI* ch. 11, Joseph, *K. and G.* 65 ff. and the writers to whom they refer. In the late *Philebus* (15c) P. mentions as examples Man, Horse, Beauty, Goodness. From Aristotle we learn that the subject was still unsettled and under lively discussion in the Academy. For the pronouncement on it in the Seventh Letter see pp. 407f. below.

[2] 130e. Cf. *Phaedo* 102b.

[3] The question whether a Form can either be parcelled out among its instances or exist in each as a whole is posed again in *Philebus* (15b).

at once without losing its unity or becoming separated from itself? Ignoring this analogy, Parmenides counters with another: you might as well spread a sail over a number of people and say that it is one whole thing over many. The young and inexperienced Socrates has no reply to this, though in fact a material object like a sail is very different from a period of time,[1] which provides no bad analogy for a relationship which, as Plato saw and Aristotle deplored, can only be described analogically or metaphorically.[2]

(*b*) Assuming that he has proved his point that a Form must be divisible and each particular possess a part, Parmenides goes on to draw from it a string of absurdities. Each large thing will be large by having a portion of largeness smaller than Largeness itself, *x* will be equal to *y* by receiving a portion of Equality less than Equality itself, and finally if the explanation of a man being small is that he possesses a portion of Smallness, (i) Smallness ('the Small itself')[3] must obviously be larger than its part, (ii) an individual is made smaller than before by having something added.

The examples are taken from the *Phaedo* (102b–103a), where it is said that if Simmias can be called both big and small, being bigger than Socrates but smaller than Phaedo, the explanation is that he possesses both Largeness and Smallness, the one in relation to the Smallness in Socrates and the other in relation to the Largeness in Phaedo.

Plato may well have thought that the theory in this form needed re-thinking, or at least re-formulating, and especially that the notion of immanent Forms laid itself open to misinterpretation.[4] But Parmenides's

[1] I have no doubt that ἡμέρα in ordinary usage meant this, and that references to light or the sun are irrelevant. A Greek could of course say ἡμέρα ἐξέλαμψε (see LSJ) as we speak of daybreak or broad day, but in either language, unless the context demands it, a reader would think of it in the sense in which we say that two events happened in different places on the same day. Mrs Sprague not unfairly compares Parmenides's argument here with Dionysodorus's analogy between Beauty and an ox in *Euthyd.* (vol. IV, 278).

[2] See further on this Crombie, *EPD* II, 330f., 333.

[3] Parmenides uses the abstract noun 'Largeness', but the adjectival forms 'the Equal' and 'the Small'. This is not sharp practice on his part, for Plato has always treated the two expressions as identical; and it is essential to his theory in the *Phaedo* that 'the Small' (or the Form Smallness) cannot become large in any respect or in relation to anything else.

[4] I cannot here attempt a critique of Fujisawa's thoughtful and challenging article on "Εχειν, μετέχειν and idioms of "Paradeigmatism" in Plato's Theory of Forms' (*Phron.* 1974), in which he argues that a distinction between immanent character and separate form, and so between ἔχειν and μετέχειν, 'is and will remain ultimate and fundamental in Plato's theory', and that Parm's. point depends on confusing them. It would take an article of at least equal length. (But I do not

criticisms are based on the assumption, drawn from a crudely materialistic analogy, that an intelligible Form can be cut up and divided like a cake, whereas Plato had written in the *Symposium* (211b) that a Form is eternal and single, and that particulars share in it in such a way that while they come into being and perish, it does not increase or decrease or change in any way.

(iii) *First regress argument: the largeness of the Large (131e–32b).* Parmenides suspects that the reason for Socrates's belief in a unitary Form was this: experiencing a number of things as large, he thought he detected a single character in them all, and therefore that 'the Large' was a single thing. A glance back at the *Meno* or *Euthyphro* shows that this is a fair enough summary of the origin of the theory of Forms, but what follows? If 'the Large itself' is large—and this seems obvious—it must belong to the same class as the visible large things, and so it and they together share the same characteristic, which on the theory will exist separately; but it will also be large, and so *ad infinitum*. Each Form will not be single, but an indefinite plurality.

This is the argument which has become known as the 'Third Man', being one of the arguments described under that title by Aristotle,[1] in which 'man' is substituted for the 'Large' of the *Parmenides*. It involves the notion of the self-predication of Forms (as it has been called), and (especially since Vlastos's article in 1954[2]) these two, often under their abbreviated titles TMA and SP, have become a battlefield for commentators. Every possible view has been both asserted and denied by scholars modifying not only the views of others but also their own, and

think he is right in attributing to P. himself the extreme flux-theory of the *Tht.*, p. 53, n. 58.) In vol. IV, 353–6, I tried to defend the view that in *Phaedo* it is the Forms themselves that enter into things.

[1] So at least it is generally thought, though Leisegang denied it (*RE* 2485). For Aristotle's evidence see Ross's ed. of the *Metaph.*, vol. I, 194–6, or Cornford, *P. and P.* 88–90, and on the possible Megarian origin of the argument see Taylor, trans. pp. 21–3, v. Fritz, *RE* Suppl. v, 722, Cornford, *o.c.* 89, Burnet, *T. to P.* 253f.

[2] Repr. in Allen's *SPM*. Even then V. could begin by saying that hardly a text in P. had been discussed as much in the last forty years as the two passages in *Parm.* invoking the TMA. He lists there 9 'major contributions'. Returning to the subject in 1969 in *PQ*, he gives 16 (including 4 of his own), and this article has already been replied to by S. Panagiotou in *PQ* 1971. Add Teloh and Louzecky in *Phron.* 1972, and Clegg, *Phron.* 1973, and a reader will be reasonably well equipped to pursue this topic, though he should look also at Crombie's review of Allen's anthology in *CR* 1966, 311f. The standard works on P. should of course also be consulted. (Vlastos's latest and longest list is in his *PS*, 1973, 361f. Later come S. Peterson, *JP* 1973 and (also relevant) D. M. Armstrong, *Aust. J. Ph.* 1974.)

must be borne in mind by anyone reading the necessarily brief account offered here.

That in Plato's eyes Justice itself was just, Piety pious and Beauty beautiful, both before he came to separate Forms from their instances and in his statements of the theory of separate Forms in the middle dialogues, has been noted more than once (see vol. IV, 119f., 223, 359f.), and is inherent in his indifferent use of the substantival and adjectival forms.[1] This is a survival of the ambiguous Greek use of article with adjective whereby 'the hot' appears to refer both to heat and to that which is hot, with, in Anaximander at least, a distinct bias towards the latter. In any case, whether as paradigm or as 'shared in', it is by imparting its own characteristic that a Form is the cause of particulars being what they are, and it must, therefore, possess this characteristic itself.[2]

According to the same middle dialogues, however, it possesses it in a peculiar way. In *Rep.* 5 (vol. IV, 487f.) Beauty is distinguished from its instantiations in this world—sights, sounds and so forth—as being the unchanging reality which they fitfully and in a relative sense imitate. It is beautiful always, everywhere and absolutely, not beautiful in comparison with this but not with that. The Form of Beauty (*idea*, 479a1) is unambiguously characterized by—is the perfect exemplar of —itself. Nevertheless there is this great difference. The ordinary man, trusting to the senses, sees only the many beauties of this world, for Beauty itself can only be perceived by the mind. So too in the *Symposium* the goal of the philosopher's pilgrimage is itself something unchangingly beautiful, in no respect ugly, not to be grasped by the senses but only in a flash of mental vision supervening on a strenuous course of dialectic. Only that brings knowledge of the truly beautiful.[3] In *Phaedo* and *Phaedrus* it is the cause of the beauty of earthly things

[1] For the persistence of this identification of 'universals' with 'perfect types' Miss Hicken aptly refers to *Soph.* 256aff., where P. illustrates the point that no Form can stand in a relation of sheer identity with its opposite by saying that Movement does not rest.

[2] Ross (*PTI* 86 and 88) says that the cure is to realize that the Form is not another thing, but an attribute. This would abolish the most distinctive character of the theory of Forms, their independent existence, and it is at least doubtful whether P. was ready to do that. That *some* Forms are predicated of themselves is undeniable; e.g. 'the One itself', or Unity, is one. See Crombie, *EPD* II, 347, n. 1, *CR* 1966, 311. Weingartner makes the point over again, *UPD* 193.

[3] 'True beauty' if you like (and so it is often translated), but only if it is understood that it is itself beautiful.

by being beautiful itself, but its beauty is not of this world nor perceptible to the senses, and this is true of Largeness or any other Form.

Largeness indeed is a particularly good example, because, as a purely relative term, it could never be mistaken for a sensible attribute. Indeed absolute largeness strikes us as an impossibility: one can speak of some thing purely red, but never purely large. We can call a girl beautiful meaning only that we admire her looks, with no thought of comparison, but if we speak of a large dog or a small elephant we must always have in mind a comparison with other members of its class. Comparing the dog to the elephant we at once call it small. Yet largeness is a general term which can be consistently used in the sense that a speaker and hearer understand each other because it conveys the same concept to both. In *Phaedo*-terminology the largeness in both dog and elephant is the same, though the dog possesses smallness in relation to the elephant. There is a Form of Largeness in which both share, and though perfect justice in this world is, if not attainable, at least not inconceivable, unqualified Largeness as a physical attribute is an impossibility. Since however it is a legitimate concept marking 'natural divisions', there exists a separate Form of it accessible to reason. Obviously, however, it is not anything that can be seen, cut up or distributed as the Form Whiteness might (erroneously) be thought to be.

When Plato wrote these dialogues he clearly believed that a Form, being incorporeal, was not large in the same sense as a large physical object, and its relationship to particulars was not subject to the materialistic criticism of Parmenides. This, however, does not settle the question whether he has seen logical difficulties in his earlier metaphysical doctrine and is expressing his own doubts through the mouth of the Eleatic. Is he saying, let us strip off the mystical language of *Symposium* and *Phaedrus*, the talk of a revelation vouchsafed only to initiates, and of the Forms as divine and apprehended by intuition, and see what is left if we stick to a logical analysis alone, as the only method proper to a philosopher? Certainly the *Parmenides* breathes an entirely different spirit from the central dialogues, but we had better go a little further before deciding.

(iv) *Can the Forms be thoughts?* (*132 b–c*). Defeated again, Socrates is driven to try the anti-Platonic solution of Antisthenes (vol. III, 214): a Form can retain its unity because it is a thought, occurring nowhere but in our minds. Parmenides first meets this with an argument from his own poem:[1] a thought must have an object, and that object must exist. When therefore we think of a group of things as having a certain common character, there must be not only a universal concept in our own minds but a single reality corresponding to it, the character or Form (*idea, eidos*) itself. By this argument Parmenides answers not only Antisthenes but also, in advance, the long line of interpreters who have supposed the Platonic Forms to be thoughts in the mind of God.[2] Even God can only think of the Forms because they are there. This is unambiguously stated in the *Timaeus*. So far, the Parmenidean position was adopted by Plato himself, as appears from *Rep.* 476e: 'Does a knower know something or nothing?' 'Something.' 'Something that exists, or not?' 'Something that exists. How could he know anything non-existent?' It is therefore to him a legitimate proof that the Forms are not *mere* concepts, but exist independently of our thought of them. His modification of it, as we have seen (vol. IV, 487ff.), was to allow for particulars as a class between existence and non-existence and cognized by a faculty (belief or opinion) between knowledge and ignorance. On the view taken by Parmenides here, Forms exist, each with the properties of his own One (eternal, changeless, single, indivisible, isolated, grasped by thought alone), but nothing else exists, and if it did it could enter into no relation with such an intelligible unit.

Parmenides also produces a second objection. If, as Socrates says, 'the other things' partake of the Forms, either each will be composed of thoughts, and everything thinks, or else they are unthinking thoughts. One's immediate reaction is to say that it is not a thought (concept) that thinks, but the mind which forms it. If I think of something existing outside me, there are three factors involved: a thinking mind, the concept which it forms, and the reality of which it is the concept. Parmenides has used the Greek word *noëma*, in form a passive noun from the verb *noein* (to apprehend by thought), but from Homer onwards commonly used in an active sense, to signify an act of thought

[1] Frr. 3 and 8, 34–6 DK. On these see vol. II, 14, 39–41.
[2] See Audrey Rich, 'The Platonic Ideas as Thoughts of God', *Mnem.* 1954.

or even the thinking mind.[1] As Grote truly said, the argument is not easy to follow. It can hardly be reproduced in English, but to a Greek it could seem a fair objection to the view (which Plato had no wish to defend) that the Forms are no more than concepts in the mind.[2]

(v) *Second regress argument: Forms as patterns or paradigms (132c–33a).* Baffled again, the youthful Socrates tries the other main explanation of the relationship which was accepted without question in the *Phaedo*. The real meaning of 'participation' is[3] that Forms are a sort of patterns fixed in the real world and particulars resemble them and are made in their image. Parmenides replies that this relationship is reciprocal: in so far as a particular resembles the Form, the Form must resemble the particular; but if two things resemble each other they do so by sharing the same character, and what is this character but a Form? It follows that nothing can resemble a Form, nor a Form resemble anything else. Otherwise a second Form immediately appears, and if it resembles anything, then another, and this series will be endless.

This argument depends for its force on the question whether the resemblance assumed between particular and Form must be symmetrical, as are resemblances between particulars. If *a* is like *b* in being large, *b* must be like *a* in the same respect. If the explanation of their resemblance is that both resemble the Form of Large or Largeness itself, does it too resemble them in the same way? There has been much dispute over this. Taylor and Cornford (following Proclus) said no. The relation of sensible particulars to a Form is that of copies to an original, and that is not simply one of likeness. The reflection of a face in a mirror is both like the face and a copy of it: the face is like the reflection but not a copy of it. Others (e.g. Hardie, Ross, Ryle, Owen,

---

[1] In Greek his alternatives are ἢ . . . ἐκ νοημάτων ἕκαστον εἶναι καὶ πάντα νοεῖν ἢ νοήματα ὄντα ἀνόητα εἶναι. Both νόημα and ἀνόητα are in form passive, but as commonly used active, ἀνόητος meaning 'unthinking', not, as its form suggests, 'unthought'. In many places νόημα could as well be translated 'mind' as 'thought'. See Xenoph. fr. 23, Parm. 7.2 and 16.4, Emped. 105.3, 110.10, Aristoph. *Clouds* 229.

[2] Of several interpretations Peck's in *PR* 1962, 174–7, is especially interesting, though in view of 132b4–5 it is difficult to agree with him that S. is not temporarily abandoning the transcendence of the Forms. Cf. Johansen, *Cl. et Med.* 1957, 7 n. 14.

[3] This disposes of the idea that 'participation' and 'imitation' might be different relationships, upheld by P. at different stages of his thought. Cf. Cherniss in *SPM* 362–4, and especially Arist. *Metaph.* 991a20: 'To say that they are paradigms and that other things share in them is empty talk and poetic metaphor.'

Runciman) think this reply vitiated by its reliance on the words 'simply' and 'merely'. Granted that the relationship is not *merely* one of likeness, it still *involves* likeness. A model and its copies *are* related by resemblance even if that is an incomplete account of their relation.[1] I believe myself that Plato did not admit the objection, and that his defence would lie in the non-sensible nature of the Forms. I have referred to this already in the context of the somewhat mystical language of the *Symposium* or *Phaedrus*, but in the *Cratylus* he has given more philosophical expression to this essential difference between a Form and its physical manifestations. Runciman has written (in *SPM* 158f.) that the paradigm-theory reduces a Form to the logical status of a particular. 'If whiteness is white (which must follow if white objects are white by resembling it) then whiteness is one of the class of white objects.' Now in the *Cratylus* Socrates's position is that we must know the Forms of things, through which they have their being or essence (*ousia*), before we can communicate by applying names to them (p. 28 above). At 423c–e he says that the art of naming does not consist in trying to reproduce in words actual sounds, shapes and colours. That belongs to music and the graphic arts. But sound, shape and colour each have an *ousia* in contrast to their visible and audible manifestations.[2] Ontologically at least, the Form is not reduced to the status of a particular. It may be, as the same scholar remarks with Aristotelian austerity, that nothing could resolve the difficulties raised in the *Parmenides* because 'the theory of forms is logically unsound', but for Plato at least, the status of an intelligible could never be on a par with that of a sensible.[3]

[1] Taylor, *PMW* 358; Cornford, *P. and P.* 93f.; Hardie, *Study* 96, Ross, *PTI* 89; Ryle in *SPM* 105; Owen, *ib.* 319f.; Runciman, *ib.* 158.

[2] It is perhaps useful to remind oneself here of the course of the discussion in *Meno*. For *ousia* as a transcendent Form see *Parm.* 133c. It was one of Aristotle's objections to the theory of Forms that it made the substance of things exist apart from as well as within them (*Metaph.* 991b1).

[3] Cf. my review of Wedberg's *Plato's Philosophy of Mathematics*, *Philosophy* 1957, 370. I hope I have now answered Weingartner when he writes (*UPD* 192): 'The unacceptability of SP is even more obvious when we consider such forms as that of Noise (listen to it!) and of Visibility (look at it now!).' It should give some support to Peck's view in *PR* 1962 'that Forms are ontologically superior versions of a quality which should be referred to as, for example, the large (intelligible), while a particular should be referred to as the large (visible)'. I take this summary from Clegg's article in *Phron.* 1973, 35. His own opinion on p. 37, that 'Participation in a Form guarantees that what does the participating is without class-membership' because it is imperfect, seems topsy-turvy. Class-membership is just what participation in the same Form does

A few more words are needed on transcendent and immanent Forms. When we first met them in the *Phaedo* (and I intentionally repeat here a part of vol. IV, 354f.) I took the view that the Largeness in us was the Form itself which also existed beyond, and that there was no need to posit a third ontological level between Forms and particulars. This seemed confirmed by the fact that it is purely large, never admitting any admixture of its contrary as concrete individuals do, and so (one would think) in no way imperfect. Ross however supposed the immanent qualities to be themselves imperfect copies, and more recently Rist has written that the largeness in the particular is 'of an ontologically defective kind'. He adds later that 'Whiteness is the cause of white in white particulars; it is not itself the whiteness in those particulars.'[1] Yet the *Phaedo* says it is by its *presence* in particulars that the Form can act as a cause.

When writing the *Phaedo*, as I have said, Plato may not have been clear in his own mind about this, but the nearest approximation to his thought at that stage seems to be as follows: Whiteness is an intelligible (not visible) Form. When it enters a material object (say a face), its *combination with* body produces visible whiteness, an imperfect imitation of the transcendent Form in the only medium in which material objects can reflect it. The face, which was never perfectly white, may turn red by 'receiving' (*Phaedo* 102 d–e) Redness instead of Whiteness, but Whiteness, whether 'by itself' or in us, will always be Whiteness and nothing else.

It may be said that this is not 'self-predication': the Form has not the quality that it *is*, for invisible, intelligible whiteness is not white in the only acceptable sense of that word, if indeed it means anything at all.[2] That has at least the advantage that it relieves Plato of the 'Third Man' argument.[3] Nevertheless, as we have seen time and again, for him

guarantee. One might almost say that to explain class-membership, to answer the question by what right we group certain individuals together in a class and give them the same name, is a *raison d'être* of the theory of Forms.

[1] Ross, *PTI* 30, Rist, *Philologus* 1964, 221 and 223. Likewise Cornford says (*P. and P.* 78) that the tallness in a person 'is not exempt from all change'. This directly contradicts what S. says in *Phaedo*. It is its possessor who is not exempt from change.

[2] Nor is it simply the concept of whiteness, 'a thought in the mind'. That interpretation, already rejected in this dialogue, is not Plato's.

[3] The main thesis of J. N. Findlay's book *Plato, the Written and Unwritten Doctrines* is that Plato's ontology is not in fact dualistic. There are not two parallel kinds of being: only the Forms exist. Consequently, he argues, all arguments of the 'Third Man' type must fail.

Beauty was the perfection of what is always and in every respect beautiful, Largeness the large *par excellence* and so on; and he is beginning to see that such a doctrine has certain logical drawbacks.

(vi) *The Forms unknowable to us and we to God (133b–34e)*. Following up his rejection of any kind of participation of sensible particulars in a Form, Parmenides's next point is that it would be difficult to argue against anyone who claimed that Forms, 'being what we say they must be', will be unknowable. If they exist 'by themselves', i.e. not in our own world (a genuine tenet of the theory of Forms to which Socrates immediately agrees), they must be related only to each other, not to the copies —or whatever we like to call them—in our world. Similarly, things in our world which indicate a relationship, though named after the Forms, can only be related to each other. Asked to explain further, he offers the illustration of a master and his slave. The one is not slave of the Form of Master, nor the other master of the Form of Slave.[1] Each is a man, and his relationship is with a man. But Mastership itself exists in relation to Slavery itself, a relationship entirely within the world of Forms.

Now knowledge (as Aristotle said, *Cat.* 6b 5) implies a relationship, being necessarily knowledge *of* something. In and by itself, then, Knowledge will be of Reality itself, and its branches, the Forms of the sciences, will have as their objects the varieties of Reality. Therefore if we have no part or lot in the Forms, which are not in our world, and every Form is known by the Form of Knowledge, none of the Forms— the Beautiful itself, the Good itself and the rest—can be known by us. Worse still, no god or gods can have knowledge of us and our world nor be our master. Knowledge itself is perfectly accurate, and if any being has it, it must be a god, but from what we have agreed about Forms having no reference to our world, it follows that Knowledge in the gods' world cannot be knowledge of us,[2] nor their Mastership exercised over us.

This argument is generally dismissed as fallacious, especially the part

---

[1] αὐτοῦ δεσπότου, ὁ ἔστι δεσπότης, but in the next sentence we find the abstract noun, αὐτὴ ἡ δεσποτεία. P. intended no distinction between these expressions. All occur interchangeably elsewhere as synonymous with a Form (εἶδος).

[2] That God, the ultimate cause of everything in the physical world, had no knowledge of that world, was the serious view of Aristotle. It would detract from his perfection, and the world was sustained in being (not brought into being, for it was eternal) by its own inner drive towards the perfection of form represented by God.

about the gods' knowledge ('unwarranted' Ryle, 'meaningless . . . a worthless fantasy' Ritter). Cornford said it confused a Form with a perfect instance of it. 'The form itself . . . cannot know anything.'[1] This reopens the whole question of 'self-predication'. If Plato said that Beauty was perfectly beautiful, he was bound to say that Knowledge was knowing, and he could only avoid these errors by the dualistic metaphysics of the *Phaedo*. Such a two-world theory was impossible for Parmenides, for whom the only alternatives were 'It is' or 'It is not', and the latter was inconceivable. He is speaking in character. His pressure all along has been against any sort of connexion between the real world and the sensible, which in his eyes of course was non-existent. So now he uses his familiar weapon, the 'either–or' dilemma. Either Forms are outside our world and ourselves or they are within: there is no middle course. One misses immediately Plato's conception of the human soul as the epistemological link between the visible and intelligible orders, as 'akin to the Forms'. For Parmenides there are only two faculties: *logos* or *nous* which grasps the unity of reality, and the sense-organs whose fantasy of a world of plurality and variety is utterly unreal. Plato's suggestion that the senses might take us the first steps on the way to an understanding of the intelligible (*Phaedo* 74a–b), the idea in the *Phaedrus* that the human mind can grasp the unity in the plurality, the universal in the particular, and so begin the process of recollection of the Forms—all this is foreign to the elementary logic of Parmenides, who is arguing from his own premises.[2]

Conclusion on Part One

Why did Plato write it? Because in the first place, I suggest, his own system, with its equation of the real with the intelligible, was firmly rooted in the Eleatic's. He had however introduced substantial modifications, not glancing back to Parmenides as he did so, but seized by the inspiration which fired him to the amazing intellectual and imaginative flights of the *Phaedo* and *Phaedrus*. Now he feels the necessity to pause and take stock, to clarify once for all his position *vis-à-vis*

[1] Ryle in *SPM*, 105, Ritter, *Essence* 124, Cornford, *P. and P.* 98f. For an able defence of the argument see Bluck, *CQ* 1956, 31–3.
[2] A different approach to this argument has been made by J. W. Forrester in *Phron.* 1974.

Parmenides. Parmenides had oversimplified and his conclusions could not be the last word. But Plato himself had perhaps ignored this simple logic too much, and his own doctrine of Forms, and especially the questions of their relation to particulars and of our knowledge of them, needed a sober reappraisal and overhaul.

Being Plato, he puts the critical part of the task in the dramatic form of a personal encounter with his great predecessor. Chronology demanded the fiction that his mouthpiece Socrates had evolved the full Platonic theory as a very young man, but this had the advantage of offering Parmenides only the mildest opposition. Before it is rethought, the theory of Forms must be submitted to the most rigorous examination compatible with the fundamental assumption (which he shared with Parmenides) of a stable and intelligible reality. Here he points out difficulties. The positive side of the process is left to the later dialogues in the group. For instance, in the *Sophist* (249 c ff., pp. 142 ff. below) the soul is restored to its place in the real world, but in terms very different from those of the *Phaedo*.

On the unknowability argument Parmenides chooses his words carefully. He does not say it is irrefutable, but only that to show that it is wrong would need a long and abstruse argument with an opponent both experienced and gifted: and he concludes by saying that in spite of this and many other difficulties, and though it may need a genius to maintain the existence of Forms, to deny it would rob thought of all direction and make rational discourse impossible.[1] The bafflement which

---

[1] Rist (*CQ* 1970, 227) says that the only demand here is for Forms as class-concepts or universals. 'Philosophy . . . operates with general propositions, and if particulars cannot be classed . . . (whether or not the classes are Platonic Forms), then thought is at an end.' 'There is no assertion by Parmenides that philosophy is impossible without separate Platonic Forms, there is an assertion that philosophy is impossible without εἴδη.' Weingartner makes a similar point (*UPD* 149) as an argument that P. in *Parm.* abandons the notion of Forms as paradigms. Cornford on the other hand (*P. and P.* 100) saw Parmenides as accepting the full Platonic view. Since Forms are necessary as 'objects on which to fix our thoughts, and as constant meanings of the words used in all discourse', they 'must not be wholly immersed in the flow of sensible things. Somehow they must have an unchanging *and independent* existence, however hard it may be to conceive their relation to changing individuals' (my italics).

I believe Cornford is right. That 'an essence all by itself' (οὐσία αὐτὴ καθ' αὑτήν 135 a) should be nothing more than a 'common factor' in particulars (Rist 229) is utterly at variance with the way the phrase has so far been used in the dialogue. (Cf. esp. 133 c 2–6.) I cannot think that P. would suddenly have expected his readers to see that Parmenides was now abandoning the sense given to εἶδος in all his previous arguments, which depended for their force on its separate and independent existence.

Socrates now feels is simply evidence that he has tried to run before he can walk. He cannot expect to seize the truth about Forms like Beautiful, Just and Good unless, before he is much older, he submits to a tedious training in what is commonly dismissed as useless talk.[1]

Transition to Part Two (135d–37c)

What manner of exercise is needed? asks Socrates. The manner exemplified by Zeno's arguments which they have just heard, with one difference. Socrates himself had suggested confining the discussion to Forms, objects of reason, and ignoring the objects of sense ('Yes, because I don't see any difficulty in sensible things having contrary properties'), and they should continue to do so.[2] Also, one must consider the consequences not only of any hypothesis being true, but also of its being false, e.g. in Zeno's case not only the hypothesis 'if there is a plurality', but also 'if there is not a plurality'. One must ask what are the consequences in either case for the many, the one, and their mutual relationships; and so also with similarity and dissimilarity, motion and rest, birth and destruction, and being and not-being themselves.

'In a word, whenever you suppose that anything exists or does not exist or has any other character, you ought to consider the consequences with reference to itself and to any one of the other things that you may select, or several of them, or all of them together; and again you must study these others with reference both to one another and to any one thing you may select, whether you have assumed the thing to exist or not to exist, if you are really going to make out the truth after a complete course of discipline.'[3]

Socrates, appalled at the magnitude and difficulty of this programme, begs for an illustration of the method at work, and Parmenides is prevailed upon to apply it to his own postulate 'about the One itself' and consider the consequences of the existence or non-existence of its sub-

---

[1] ἀδολεσχία, a charge brought against both Socrates and Plato. See vol. IV, 431 n. 3, 499 n. 4. P. is probably thinking of Isocrates. Cf. his *In soph.* 8, *Antid.* 262.

[2] Taylor, Cornford and Runciman (*SPM* 161) speak of *not confining* discussion to visible things, but the Greek plainly says that they are to be excluded altogether. This would naturally be approved by Parmenides.

[3] 136b–c, trans. Cornford. I should prefer to render the last few words: 'if you are going to carry out a complete course of training preparatory to discerning the truth properly'. The aorist participle, as often, carries the weight of a main verb.

ject. This examination occupies the whole of the rest of the dialogue, which from now on changes its character completely. It proceeds by question and answer, but the youngest present (Aristoteles) is chosen for respondent as 'likely to give least trouble', and the exposition could as well have been continuous. The narrative form is quietly dropped.

With what expectations should we approach this second part? First, it is offered simply as one example of a series of dialectical exercises which Socrates should undergo while still young (135d5–6). As verb or noun, the word 'exercise' (γυμνάζω, γυμνασία) is used five times to describe it, and it is strange that some have seen in the coming section a promise of more. It is to be a training through which Socrates must 'drag himself' (135d3) before he can hope to see the truth.[1] Secondly it is said to be of the same type as Zeno's. His procedure was to assume that only two opposed hypotheses are conceivable, and leaving one aside, defend it indirectly by showing that the other led to absurd consequences. The flaw in this was that both hypotheses might be untenable, being wrongly or incompletely formulated (as indeed were the 'It is' and 'It is not' of Parmenides; see vol. II, 73 f.), and as an exercise they are now to apply the deductive procedure to *both* sides of the Parmenidean antithesis, the hypothesis of the One as well as its contradictory. It can best be described as an exercise in dialectic in the Aristotelian sense, useful primarily as mental training, secondly to meet opponents on their own ground, and finally for progress in philosophy itself because 'the ability to raise difficulties on both sides of a question makes it easier to detect truth and error in every case'.[2] It is in this sense that Plato's Parmenides says exercises like this are necessary if the truth is not to escape Socrates. That he should simply raise the *aporiai* is

[1] It may seem presumptuous thus summarily to take one side in a dispute which was raging in the time of Proclus and has on the other side such names as Hegel, K. F. Hermann and Zeller, as well as many more recent scholars. (See Friedländer, *Pl.* III, 504f., n. 23.) A good defence of the view that Part 2 is more than mental gymnastics is Runciman's in *SPM* 168–71 (against Robinson), and it is also Cornford's position in *P. and P.* What seems to me incontrovertible is that 135c–36c contain a promise of γυμνασία and nothing more, not for instance (as Brumbaugh puts it, *P. on One* 189) 'an indirect proof that the theory of forms is a necessary presupposition of understanding anything at all'. If I understand Zekl's work rightly (his long and complex sentences can be hard going for a non-German) this is his conclusion too, that (as he says at the end of his introduction, *Parm.* p. 14) properly analysed and assessed, the dialogue 'becomes decidedly what its second part expressly claims: a lesson and an exercise in thinking'.
[2] See Arist. *Topics* I ch. 2.

appropriate. To tackle them is left to his 'more moderate' follower (*Soph.* 216b) in the *Sophist*.

Part Two (*137c–66c*)

The plan of the exercise is to take the Eleatic hypothesis of Unity and follow out the consequences of its being (*a*) true and (*b*) false, in each case considering the effects on the One itself and 'the Others'.[1] Its final conclusion is (and these are the last words of the dialogue):

Whether One is or is not, it and the others, in relation both to themselves and to each other, are and are not, and appear and do not appear, everything in every way.

This sentence is reminiscent of nothing so much as the riddle of the eunuch and the bat in the *Republic*, nor is the resemblance fortuitous. The riddle was quoted as an illustration of ambiguity, and of the unreal dilemma brought about by asking the incomplete question 'Is it or is it not?', without allowing for a middle status between being and not-being which is in fact that of the whole sensible world. (See *Rep.* 479b–d.) By laying the emphasis on the *Unity* of the One, Parmenides deduces that neither it nor the Others can have any properties, be in any state, or in any relation to themselves or anything else, or even exist. By starting from its *existence* (which immediately introduces a duality, Unity and Existence) he deduces that both it and the Others are an infinite multitude, with both of any pair of contradictory attributes, in both of any pair of contradictory states (e.g. at rest and in motion), and in contradictory relations (same and other, like and unlike, equal and unequal etc.) to themselves and anything else. Equally disconcerting conclusions are drawn from the hypothesis that 'the One is not' and 'it is not one'.[2]

---

[1] Burnet (*T. to P.* 262) writes that 'the discussion is about forms alone, and we are expressly warned against the idea that "the rest" of which he speaks are the things of sense (135e). They are just the other forms.' For Cornford the terms 'One' and 'Others' are 'blank cheques' (*P. and P.* 113) until a particular hypothesis makes clear the sense in which they are there being used. Thus in the first two hypotheses they are 'sensible appearances', 'physical bodies' (pp. 157, 203 f.). This variety of views emphasizes the studied vagueness of the language which alone makes the contradictory conclusions possible. Similarly some (Ryle, Runciman) have thought that 'the One' is throughout the Platonic Form of Unity, others that it is not.

[2] A full summary of the 8 (or 9) arguments will be found in Burnet, *T. to P.* 264–71. Brief and clear is Hamlyn in *PQ* 1955, 298 f. Burnet's section on *Parm.* makes perhaps the best case for regarding part 2 as a polemic against the use of Parmenidean postulates by the Megarians. A 'map' of the arguments is also provided by Owen in *Ryle*, 349–62.

'The key to the understanding of the second part must be sought in the unmistakable ambiguity of the hypothesis, "If there is a One".' So Cornford, and Crombie emphasizes 'the complete vagueness with which the topic to be discussed is introduced'. 'The meaning of the essential terms shifts as the argument develops.' Without this ambiguity and lack of precise definition the arguments could not proceed to their mutually contradictory conclusions. We may note, first, that this lack of definition, the incompleteness of the predicate in pronouncements like 'It is', was a mark of Parmenides himself.[1] Secondly, as Plato showed in the comedy of *Euthydemus*, it was adopted by the Sophists as the basis of the logical trickery by which they confused their opponents and upheld the rhetorical thesis that 'on every topic there are two arguments contrary to each other'.[2] 'Both and neither', the triumphant cry of Dionysodorus (*Euthyd.* 300d), is the conclusion which Parmenides is made to reach in this dialogue.[3] Gorgias in *On the Non-existent* showed that by Parmenidean logic one could as easily prove 'It is not' as 'It is'.[4] The ambiguities were perfectly plain to Plato,[5] yet on that very ground Cornford denied that he was 'consciously playing on these ambiguities to construct a string of sophisms'. 'The student is expected to infer' the ambiguity, and on this understanding the arguments 'cease to be either fallacious or meaningless', being in fact a valid, indeed brilliant, refutation of Eleaticism. As evidence that Plato would deem it beneath him to construct sophisms of this sort, Cornford quotes the expression of contempt for them in the *Sophist* (259b–c). The fact remains that some of the arguments as presented do play on

[1] Vol. II, 73 ff., comments on this and on Plato's criticisms and more advanced position.

[2] Vol. III, 50 f., 316. That the thesis owed its origin to Parmenides is none the less true because he himself would not have approved it. Cornford admits both that Parmenides himself confused the two senses of 'If One is' and that the eristic Sophists used the ambiguity 'to entangle disputants in contradictions or paradoxical nonsense' (pp. 109, 111).

[3] Noted by Grote (II, 290 f.), who adds that if the demonstrations in Part 2 had come down under the name of Protagoras, Gorgias or Euclides, critics would probably have called them poor productions, worthy of men who made a trade of perverting truth.

[4] For Gorgias's work see vol. III, 192–200. A close parallel occurs in *Parm.* at 162a. It is noted by Cornford (p. 226), who thinks of it as 'answering' one of G.'s arguments, but perhaps it would be fairer to say that it makes use of it. Brumbaugh (*P. on One* 21 f., 22 n. 4) sees a complicated relationship, a 'double irony' showing that the joke is on G., not Parmenides.

[5] Though there have been sceptics, e.g. Grote (II, 297) and recently Runciman (in *SPM* 180): 'It seems improbable that Plato saw at all clearly where and why the arguments of the exercise are fallacious.'

ambiguities and are therefore fallacious and sophistic; and if Plato was aware of this, so, one would assume, were Euthydemus and Dionysodorus. It seems more likely that the visitor in the *Sophist* can speak as he does just because the exercise in such sophistry provided by the *Parmenides* has already shown up the absurdities to which it leads. The one dialogue is certainly a preparation for the other. Readers are intended to detect the fallacies, but as a training in how to avoid them, and as Parmenides himself put it in introducing his account of men's false beliefs, 'that no judgement of mortals may outstrip thee'.[1]

Some object that to make Parmenides propound arguments which are in any case fallacious but, if valid, would undermine his own philosophy, is incompatible with the respect in which Plato held him. I have remarked already that this respect was not unqualified; and the point on which the Eleatic visitor in the *Sophist* feels bound to contradict his father in philosophy, even at the risk of being thought unfilial, is the one which is so conspicuously lacking in the *Parmenides*, namely that 'is' and 'is not' are not absolute: 'what is not in some respect is, and what is, in a way is not' (241 d). Since all that Parmenides offers is a training exercise, one out of several necessary before the positive search for truth can begin, one might even conjecture that Plato is paying him the compliment of himself seeing through the sophistic abuses of his central dictum. The dialogue ends abruptly at the conclusion of the exercise, and whatever moral Parmenides might draw from it remains unspoken.

A point remains which has been made by Ross (*PTI* 100), that to treat the second part as 'gymnastics' does not imply that nothing of value emerges from its arguments. Ross speaks of 'positive ideas which will fructify in his later thought'.[2] We have noticed, too, in the earlier

---

[1] Parm. fr. 8.61. I differ from Cornford reluctantly, and would direct a reader to Allan's defence of him against Robinson in *PQ* 1955, 373 f. Important for his denial of sophistry in the arguments is the statement on p. 110 that 'Plato usually indicates clearly enough where he is passing from one to another sense or aspect of "the One" or of "the Others". But contrast p. 217: the contradictory conclusions of hypotheses 1–4 'can be stated thus only because the different meanings of the supposition [that there is a One] have been disguised'. For a full critique of C. see Robinson, *PED* 268–74. R. adopts the 'gymnastic' view, as does Ross (*PTI* 99–101). Both acknowledge their debt to Grote (*Pl.* II, 293 n. *h*, which also contains an interesting discussion of still earlier views).

[2] *PTI* 100. Perhaps even in later centuries. Cf. Runciman on the mathematical proofs that can be discerned at 143a–44a and 149a–c (*SPM* 165). For Plato one might instance 158d:

dialogues, a puckish habit of interspersing serious Socratic or Platonic ideas with otherwise *ad hominem* arguments, though the interlocutor or audience is unlikely to appreciate them, and they are not followed up. On the negative side, 'Parmenides enunciates his contradictory demonstrations as real logical problems, which must exercise the sagacity and hold back the forward impulse of an eager philosophical aspirant' (Grote II, 301).

Conclusion

To understand the purport of the *Parmenides* is very difficult indeed. Every possibility has been put forward and rejected in turn, so that any interpretation must be offered with great diffidence.

My own starts from the conviction that if Plato chose to make Parmenides the leading figure in a discussion of the Forms, it was because he wanted to clear up the relationship between his own doctrine and the Eleatic thesis of One Being. To exalt the intelligible as alone fully real was an achievement for which, he believed, philosophy must be for ever grateful, but at the same time, stated in Parmenides's terms, it would have brought philosophy to a halt. Hence his own efforts to provide a bridge between being and not-being, knowledge and ignorance. Somewhere the two doctrines had to be brought face to face. I have tried to show that this is happening here, and it will continue in the *Sophist*. Direct confrontation with the old man himself leads to an impasse, but Plato's debt to Eleatic thought appears when he is replaced by a less uncompromising representative of the same tradition. Parmenides attributes Socrates's discomfiture to immaturity and lack of training in argument, and offers a demonstration. For one thing, Socrates was certain that Forms could not admit contrary predicates or combine with each other. The demonstration 'proves' that they can do both. In this and other ways Parmenides performs the necessary preliminary operation of reducing Socrates to perplexity (*aporia*) as the mature Socrates did to people like Meno. And like Meno he is the better for it. Only in the *Sophist*, under more sympathetic Eleatic tutelage, do we proceed to build on the ground thus cleared, and learn, for instance,

the unlimited Many acquire limit through association with the One. This suggests the Pythagorean notion which according to Aristotle P. adopted in calling his first principles 'the One and the great and small' (or 'indefinite dyad'). See *Metaph.* 987b18ff. and other passages cited in Ross ch. 12.

that some Forms can combine and others not. A short paragraph from the Sophist will illustrate the point that in the *Parmenides* Plato states dilemmas resulting from the original Eleatic thesis and in the *Sophist* suggests solutions on his own lines.

We must admit that motion is the same and not the same, and we must not be disturbed thereby; for when we say it is the same and not the same we do not use the word in the same sense. When we call it the same, we do so because it partakes of the Same in relation to itself, and when we call it not the Same we do so on account of its participation in the Other, by which it is separated from the Same and becomes not that but other so that it is correctly spoken of in turn as not the Same.[1]

The Parmenidean confusion between identity and attribution is cleared away in terms of the doctrine of Forms, and by the realization that a word may be used in more than one sense.

On this interpretation the *Parmenides* is an aporetic dialogue with a difference. The early dialogues showed Socrates skilfully reducing a respondent (and as he would say, himself as well) to *aporia*, thereby exposing the confusions of thought underlying the popular use of language. In the meantime he has become a teacher with elaborate positive doctrines about Forms, soul, the physical world and their mutual relations. With astonishing artistry as well as flexibility of mind Plato now transforms him again, this time into a young man, keenly intelligent and eager for truth yet in argument no match for a great philosopher, in order to subject these positive doctrines to an examination from the other's point of view.

Prima facie at least, the first part makes some telling criticisms of the doctrines in question, and they are never answered. In face of this, some commentators have argued that they are not in fact serious, others that they are fatal to the *Phaedo* doctrine and Plato must have known it (or alternatively that he failed to realize how damaging they were), others

---

[1] *Soph.* 256a–b; see p. 152 below). The translation is M. G. Walker's (*PR* 1938, 513; I have supplied capital letters for Forms), whose thesis is that P. arrives at his solutions in *Parm.*, and *Soph.* is only conveying the same lesson. She quotes Morris Cohen to the effect that P. avoids 'the indecent confusion at which we arrive if we violate the principle of contradiction and try to wipe out the distinctions of the understanding'. I should have said that he intentionally does *not* avoid it in *Parm.*, but does in *Soph.*, and I claim no originality for this. Cf. Brochard, *Éts. de Phil. Anc. et Mod.* 167: 'Le *Parménide* pose le problème dans toute sa difficulté, le *Sophiste* et le *Politique* en donnent la solution.'

again that they did not touch the essence of the doctrine but called for a modification which Plato later effected. Most who take the last view see the change as a renunciation of the idea of the Forms as transcendent paradigms in favour of regarding them as no more than universals, stable general concepts.[1] Ackrill, upholding this view, says honestly that it would be more natural to call it jettisoning the theory than revising it. The remark at 135b, he says,

strongly suggests that what he is now sure of is *not* that there must be Forms as conceived in the middle dialogues, Forms as ethical ideals and as the metaphysical objects of intuitive and perhaps mystical insight; what he is now sure of is that there must be fixed things to guarantee the meaningfulness of talk, *fixed concepts—the meanings of general words.*[2]

That Plato, as a result of his own criticisms here, gave up the doctrine of transcendent Forms, is disproved by many references to it, in dialogues universally agreed to be later than the *Parmenides*, which contrast, in the terminology of the *Phaedo*, a world of realities—eternal, unchanging, perfect, bodiless—with the visible world of change and becoming. It is true that a list of references only (like Runciman's in *SPM* 152) needs careful checking, for a die-hard believer in Forms as concepts or common properties might interpret the language of some of them in that sense. At *Laws* 965b–e, for instance, Saunders in the 'Penguin' translation gets on well enough with a vocabulary of 'concept', 'notion', 'common element' (p. 379 n. 3 below). But one can add 859e, where the language of 'association' and 'sharing' is more strongly reminiscent of the *Phaedo*. The *Philebus* has several decisive passages, as have *Sophist* and *Statesman*, and of course *Timaeus* (if one accepts the traditional dating). It is also explicit in the Seventh Letter.[3]

---

[1] An early and formidable champion of a change of doctrine after *Parm.* was Henry Jackson in his series of articles in *J. of Philol.* on 'Plato's Later Theory of Ideas'. His conception of the nature of the change, however, was different, and based on an interpretation of the *Phil.* which has not found general favour. For a criticism see Ross, *PTI* 133f.

[2] Ackrill in *SPM*, 206 (my italics). For Rist's view see p. 51 n. 1 above. Abandonment of paradigmatism is also argued by Weingartner (*UPD* ch. 3), and denied by Cherniss (*SPM* 361f.). Ross (*PTI* 86) thought P.'s doubt concerned the 'Largeness is large' form of expression. That P. did not realize the damaging effect of the criticisms is the view of Runciman (*SPM* 151–3). Those who think that he neither regarded nor should have regarded them as serious include Taylor (*PMW* 350), Grube (*PT* 36), Cornford (*P. and P.* 95), Field (*Phil. of P.* 110f.), Crombie (*EPD* II, 332ff.).

[3] *Laws* 859e ὅσονπερ ἂν τοῦ δικαίου κοινωνῇ κατὰ τοσοῦτον καὶ τοῦ καλοῦ μετέχον ἐστί. (For the bearing of the *Laws* on this question see also Runciman, *PLE* 54f.) See also *Phil.*

Two passages are especially interesting as explicitly meeting objections raised in the *Parmenides*. One has been mentioned already. *Soph.* 248 e– 49 d, in coming to terms with the 'friends of Forms', restores soul to its place among the real and explains thereby the possibility of our knowledge of a changeless reality. *Phil.* 15 a–b takes up the question whether a unitary and eternal Form can be scattered among an infinite number of generated individuals, or alternatively be somehow separated as a whole from itself. It may be added that Aristotle, in his various accounts and criticisms of the doctrine, never suggests that Plato altered it in this way. Had he done so, the sting would have been removed from most of Aristotle's attacks.[1]

Having noted all this we may justifiably remind ourselves how much of his own doctrine—call it metaphysical, religious, mystical or what you like, but at any rate genuine Platonic doctrine—Plato has omitted for the purpose of the experiment with Parmenides (pp. 38, 43, 50 above), and we need feel no compulsion to suppose that he has abandoned it.[2] Some changes might be needed (e.g. in the language of 'self-predication' or the status of a Form when it has 'entered into' a particular), but the cornerstone of the whole, the transcendent, eternal, ideal character of the Forms, remained in place. The challenge of Parmenides was how to reconcile this transcendence with a form of 'association' (κοινωνία) both with the sensible world (said in the *Parmenides* to be a prerequisite of knowledge) and with each other (declared at *Soph.* 259 e–60 a to be essential if discussion is to be carried on at all). The casual allusion to both in the *Republic*,[3] compared with their serious examination in these dialogues, shows how far Plato has come from the easy, dogmatic assurance of his golden period. The old

15 a–b, 58 a, 59 a–c, 61 d–e, 62 a; *Pol.* 269 d, 285 e–86 a; *Soph.* 248 e–49 d, 254 a; *Ep.* 7, 342 a–d. Kucharski's article 'La "théorie des Idées" selon le "Phédon" se maintient-elle dans les derniers dialogues?', in *Rev. Philos.* 1969, is mainly concerned with *Philebus*.

[1] Chung-Hwan Chen, so far as I know, is alone in doubting that Aristotle attributed χωρισμός to Plato; and he seems to have misunderstood the attitude adopted in *Soph.* to the 'friends of Forms'. (See *CQ* 1944, 101 with n. 3.) It may be helpful to compare vol. IV, 117 f., 118 n. 1, and p. 47 n. 2 above. Ross notes (*PTI* 99) that *Parm.* is the one important dialogue to which Aristotle never refers.

[2] Some have supposed that the dialectic of the later dialogues replaced the belief in knowledge as recollection. But see Gulley in *CQ* 1954 (esp. pp. 209 ff.) and Rees, *Proc. Ar. Soc.*, suppl. vol. 1963, 172 ff. (against Strang).

[3] 476 a. See vol. IV, 498. Similarly at *Phaedo* 102 d it is clearly stated that a Form must be both transcendent and immanent, with no suggestion that this involves any difficulties.

Greek problem of the One and the Many—and we must never forget that Plato was in this tradition—was not to be so easily conquered. 'How', as the Orphic Creator asked, 'shall I have all things united yet each one separate?'[1]

(2) THEAETETUS[2]

Connected with this is the hardest and most urgent of all problems, to which the argument has now brought us. If nothing exists except individuals, and there is an infinite number of them, how can one attain knowledge of the infinite? We know things in so far as they are one and the same and possess some universal attribute.

Aristotle, *Metaph*. 999a24–9

Date. The introduction tells of Theaetetus being carried home dying of wounds and dysentery after a battle at Corinth. Two such battles come into question, one about 394 or not much later, the other in 369. Campbell (*Tht*. lxi f.) argued for the earlier, but the later is generally favoured today and much the more probable. The *Theaetetus* is a tribute to his memory, and probably written not long after his death, i.e. shortly before Plato's second visit to Sicily. The majority would now agree on 369/7.[3] In spite of its close connexion with the *Sophist* and *Politicus* (p. 33 above), some are still so impressed with the novelty of the method of collection and division in the *Phaedrus* that they regard its absence from the *Theaetetus* as sufficient evidence of earlier composition. I have already given my opinion that the novelty of the method has been exaggerated (see vol. IV, 430 f. and p. 28 n. 1 above), and can only record a personal impression that the *Phaedrus* is lit by the same glow as *Phaedo* and *Symposium*, a glow which has faded by the time of *Parmenides* and *Theaetetus* and is not recaptured even in the *Timaeus*. Unless the *Theaetetus*, as a Socratic and aporetic dialogue, is to be put in the early group (and few would wish to do that today), I would say, on partly subjective grounds certainly, that all four

[1] Kern, *O.F.* 165. Cf. vol. I, 132.

[2] For a full discussion of philosophical questions raised by *Tht*. a reader may be referred to McDowell's edition.

[3] E.g. Taylor, *PMW* 320, Field, *P. and C.'s* 70, Jowett's edd. III, 392 n. The case for the later battle was first argued by Eva Sachs, *De Th.* (1914), 22–40. (Cf. vol. III, 499 and vol. IV, 52.) For earlier disputes about the date see her notes to pp. 18 and 19. Diès remained agnostic (*Autour de P.* 247).

dialogues in this chapter were written after the great middle dialogues which include the *Phaedrus*.[1]

ADDITIONAL NOTE ON DATING THE THEAETETUS

Some would explain the Socratic character of the dialogue by the theory that most of it was written comparatively early and what we have is a revision by Plato of an earlier edition. It is largely a matter of internal indications and personal impressions, and was conjectured even before the discovery of part of a papyrus commentary published by Diels and Schubart in 1905 which has been thought to furnish some external confirmation. This rests on the fact that the commentator mentions the existence of another, 'rather frigid' proem beginning 'Boy, are you bringing the dialogue about Theaetetus?' If this opening also is by Plato (and who would forge it?), the most obvious occasion for replacing it by the proem in our manuscripts would be the death of Theaetetus, from which it is concluded that the main dialogue, or much of it, was written before he died. (See Cornford, *PTK* 15.) The best defence of this theory is by Popper (*OS* 321 f.), who sees signs in the dialogue itself that it was written earlier than the *Republic*. It may be correct, and should certainly not be passed over even if I am not personally convinced. Popper adduces a number of arguments in its favour, of which I will only point to two that seem to me dubious.

(1) He takes two passages of Aristotle, which ascribe to Socrates the invention of induction, and mention his profession of ignorance, to be allusions to the *Theaetetus*. But both these historical facts may be illustrated from other dialogues. The profession of ignorance suggests most strongly the *Apology*, but also *Symp.* 216d, *Charm.* 165b and other places.

(2) In the proem Euclides says that Socrates repeated to him the conversation with Theaetetus, that as soon as he got home he made notes of it, and that on subsequent visits to Athens he verified some points with Socrates himself. Popper claims that this contradicts the statement at the end of the dialogue that Socrates's trial was already imminent, which would leave no time for such visits, and suggests that it is a relic of the earlier version overlooked or ignored by Plato in his revision. As to that, however, see p. 64 n. 1 below (written before I looked at Popper's arguments).

---

[1] Of recent writers, Robinson (*Essays* 58) and De Vries (*Phdr.* 11) agree with Von Arnim that *Tht.* is earlier than *Phdr.* Stylometry may be a fickle guide, for reasons given by Cornford, *PTK* 1. It led Campbell (*Tht.* lv) to put *Tht.* 'between the *Phaedrus* and *Republic*', a result which modern admirers of his pioneer work in this field seem content to ignore. On some points the 'infinitae disceptationes' which Apelt noted in 1897 are still with us; e.g. on whether *Tht.* was completed long before *Soph.* was composed, contrast Cornford (*l.c.*) and Ritter (*Essence* 28). That *Tht.* itself was composed over a considerable period is of course possible.

Theaetetus

Dramatic date. At the very end of the main dialogue Socrates casually mentions that he must leave for the King's Stoa in connexion with the indictment of Meletus. The date is therefore 399, and his trial and death are near. (Cf. vol. IV, 102.) His hearers would soon see in reality what is described in the dialogue (173 c–75 b), the relation of the philosopher to the practical world and his behaviour in a court of law.

Characters. Euclides and Terpsion from Megara were intimate friends of Socrates, present at his death (*Phaedo* 59 c). Of Terpsion nothing more is known. For Euclides and his philosophy see vol. III, 499–507. That such an intimate friend of Socrates should be keenly interested in one of his conversations as recorded by another is natural, and need not mean that the main dialogue contained reflections on Megarian doctrine, but for internal evidence see Campbell's edition, xxxv–xxxviii.

Theaetetus of Athens, a friend of Plato, became one of the most brilliant mathematicians of his generation. Only a boy at the time of the dialogue, he receives unstinted praise for his intellectual curiosity and promise from both Socrates and his master Theodorus. His death of wounds and illness must have struck him at the age of 48–50. Of the older mathematician *Theodorus* of Cyrene, who taught both Plato and Theaetetus, the dialogue itself tells us much: his work on square roots, his early abandonment of general philosophy to concentrate on geometry, his friendship with Protagoras.[1] The presence of the *Younger Socrates* is also mentioned, though he remains silent—an additional indication that *Theaetetus, Sophist* and *Statesman* are to be read as a continuous series, for his presence is again mentioned at *Soph.* 218 b, and in the *Statesman* he replaces Theaetetus as chief respondent. He too is a historical figure, criticized by Aristotle for treating physical beings like mathematical abstractions,[2] and pretty certainly the Socrates mentioned in the Eleventh Letter (358 d) as prevented from travelling by ill

[1] For Theaetetus see Sachs's dissertation already mentioned, von Fritz in *RE* 2. Reihe, x. Halbb., 1351–72, or more briefly Taylor, *PMW* 322; and for his mathematics M. Brown in *JHP* 1969, 362 f. Brown refers to earlier studies and gives the evidence for T. having written most of Euclid Bk 10. His connexion with the construction of the regular solids is mentioned in vol. I, 268 f. For Theodorus, von Fritz, *ib.* 1811–25.

[2] *Metaph.* 1036 b 25 ff. 'He thought that man could exist without his parts as the circle without the bronze.' It sounds as if Y.S. was using a mathematical analogy in support of the full Platonic theory of transcendent Forms. For further details about him see Skemp, *P.'s Statesman* 25 f.

health. Socrates makes much of the fact that both the boys have something in common with himself, one being his namesake and the other resembling him in appearance, but if this has symbolic significance it is hard to discover.

Prefatory conversation. This takes place in Megara, where Euclides tells Terpsion how he met Theaetetus, barely alive, being carried home from the Corinthian battlefield to Athens. They grieve at the approaching death of a man so talented and in every way admirable, and Euclides recalls how Socrates had prophesied a brilliant future for him when, shortly before his own death, he met and talked with him—still a mere boy—at Athens. Terpsion would like to hear what they talked about, and this is still possible, for as soon as Euclides got home after hearing it all from Socrates he made notes which he afterwards wrote up at leisure, checking the details with Socrates on further visits to Athens.[1] They therefore settle themselves, and a slave reads the manuscript. This is the only dialogue which is represented as actually read, though in the introductions to *Phaedo, Symposium* and *Parmenides* Plato has been at some pains to authenticate the record, at least dramatically. Also of interest is Euclides's remark that he has written it not in narrative form as Socrates told it, but leaving out the connecting 'and I said', 'he agreed' and so on as tiresome, and casting it into direct dialogue form. This is a form which, as we know, Plato sometimes used in earlier dialogues, but from now on he gives up the narrative form altogether. The *Parmenides* showed a transitional stage, in which the narrative form is tacitly dropped half way through, and it is a fair inference that, as has been assumed on other grounds, it slightly preceded the *Theaetetus.*

Introduction to main dialogue. The *Theaetetus* is a brilliant adaptation of the manner and plan of the earlier dialogues to the more critical and probing approach to knowledge of Plato's late maturity. The restoration of Socrates to his earlier role, with much of his original personality,

---

[1] S.'s trial was already imminent, but the *Phaedo* (59d) tells how his friends used to visit him in prison during the month which intervened between trial and execution. As E. was in Athens for the final farewell, he would certainly have made several previous visits. For the practice among S.'s admirers of recording his conversations see vol. III, 343 f.

shows Plato still anxious to be regarded as the true heir and continuator of Socratic teaching.[1] In this respect it is a complete contrast to the *Sophist*. Socrates is not just a thinking-machine like the Eleatic visitor, but Plato has brought out his character by a number of dramatic touches, e.g. the Socratic humour of the midwife analogy, the seriousness with which his confession of ignorance is followed up in its consequences and the positive value of teaching from that position explained. This accords with the philosophical purpose of the two dialogues, the one aporetic, setting forth problems, the other didactic, solving them.

Reminders of the earlier dialogues are many. Socrates is still seeking out the most promising of the young (143d; cf. *Charm.* 153d), and is introduced to one whose name he does not know (144d; *Lysis* 204e). The aim is to define a given concept, the respondent at first offers instances instead (*Laches, Hipp. Maj., Meno, Rep.* 1), after which several suggestions are considered and rejected and the dialogue ostensibly ends in failure. The difference lies in the choice of subject. In the previous dialogues certain moral or aesthetic concepts have been examined—Goodness, Self-control, Beauty, Justice. As to knowledge itself, the current puzzle of whether one can learn either what one does not know or what one knows has been made fun of in the *Euthydemus* and answered in the *Meno* by reference to reincarnation and recollection. The *Charmides* even raised the question whether there can be knowledge of knowledge (vol. IV, 160f., 169f.). In *Meno* and *Republic* the distinction between knowledge and true belief is drawn and is seen in the latter to depend on the supposition of the changeless Forms: knowledge is the philosopher's recovery of the eternal realities with which we all had direct acquaintance before birth, and the existence of which is simply assumed. Now for the first time Plato has chosen to make knowledge itself the main subject of enquiry, setting aside for the purpose all preconceived ideas such as appear unchallenged in the *Phaedo–Republic* group. Nevertheless he still *has* his own standpoint, and it cannot but show itself occasionally. At one point he even turns aside, in what is formally a pure digression introduced on the flimsiest pretext, to remind his readers that neither the attack on worldly success

---

[1] This is perhaps also the purpose of emphasizing, in the preface, the pains taken to ensure the accuracy of the report. Cf. Stoelzel, *Erkenntnisprobl.* 6–8.

in the *Gorgias*, nor the eschatological beliefs of the *Phaedo*, nor the divine Forms of that dialogue and the *Republic*, are to be regarded as superseded. Yet as we saw from the *Parmenides*, new problems have arisen for him, and in his search for knowledge and its objects he shows far more interest than previously in the individuals of the phenomenal world. The enigma of the *Theaetetus* may be illustrated by two quotations. To Stoelzel it seemed a work that might have been written for his own time (1908) 'as a weapon in its fight against materialism, sensualism, empiricism and positivism'. Richard Robinson on the other hand cites its 'empiricist and subjectivist tone' as something 'definitely unfavourable to the theory of Forms'. Against this one may note that all the empirical and subjective theories discussed are shown to fail, and the dialogue could be regarded as a demonstration of their inadequacy.[1]

The question: What is Knowledge?[2] 'This is just the question that baffles me: I cannot sufficiently grasp in my mind what knowledge is . . . Speak out like a man: what do you think it is?' (145e, 146c). Here Socrates lays down the topic of the whole discussion. But what are the

[1] See Stoelzel, *Erkenntnisprobl.* v, Robinson, *Essays* 42. Although P.'s attitude to the Forms when he wrote *Tht.* is much debated, so far as I know no one believes that he had abandoned them. Cooper in *Phron.* 1970 is emphatic that they are not in *Tht.*, but is not there concerned with the wider question. In the past Campbell wrote (*Tht.* liii) that 'Plato's ideal theory, so far as it is allowed to appear in the *Theaetetus*, deals not with hypostatized entities, but rather with necessary forms of thought, which are as inseparable from perception as from reasoning.' But he excepted the digression, and even Robinson, who so vigorously opposed Cornford's thesis in *PTK* that the Forms are deliberately held back to show that knowledge was impossible without them, grants that there may be allusions to them. (See his *Essays*, 48. McDowell similarly sits on the fence, p. 174.) Miss Hicken in *SPM* argues that Plato is genuinely baffled, convinced of the necessity of Forms yet no longer able to distinguish knowledge from belief by their aid. (Cf. Raeder, *PPhE*, 1905, 283: 'Platon versteht nicht mehr das Band zwischen Idee und Wirklichkeit zu knüpfen.') Most however would agree with the view put forward long ago by Schmidt in his commentary of 1880: 'Since neither sense-perception nor true belief nor finally determination of the concept (*Begriffsbestimmung*) prove to be adequate definitions [of knowledge], nothing else can be in Plato's mind, as alone in conformity with his philosophy, but a definition directed to the Idea, i.e. the reality of the concept or the real and true Being on which it is founded.' Among more recent scholars one may cite Ross (*PTI* 101, 103), Fowler (Loeb ed. 4), Solmsen (*P.'s Th.* 76), Hackforth (*CQ* 1957, 53 ff., a reply to Robinson), Grube (*P.'s Th.* 36–8), Cherniss (*SPM* 7), Llanos (*Viej. Sof.* 35), Runciman (*PLE* 28 f.), Sprute (*Phron.* 1968, esp. p. 67). For references to Platonic Forms in dialogues believed to be later than *Tht.*, see above, p. 59 with n. 3.

[2] An observation of Th. Ebert is worth quoting (*Meinung und Wissen* 9, n. 15). Scholars speak of P.'s 'theory of knowledge' (or epistemology, *Erkenntnistheorie*), but 'the inappropriateness of the title lies in this, that with it the *genetic* interest of modern philosophy in the problem of knowledge—that is, the question of the *sources* of our knowledge . . . replaces the question of *what* it is' (in German its '*Wesen*').

criteria that an answer must fulfil? We are up against Meno's pertinent question: how do we know what we are looking for before we know what it is? Unfortunately it is not the way of Plato's Socrates to lay down criteria before beginning the discussion—they are treated as self-evident—but just as the *Meno*'s enquiry into *aretē* turned out to be based on the hypothesis that whatever *aretē* was, it must be something unfailingly good and beneficial in its effects (87d–e), so certain criteria, by which candidates for the name of knowledge are being judged, may be gleaned as they are casually dropped in the course of the discussion.[1] Without criteria the suggestions could not be tested and rejected. Thus we learn that knowledge must be true and infallible (152c, 160d, 200e, 207c–209b) and its object existing (152c, 186c) and stable (there cannot be knowledge of the ever-changing, e.g. 182e). It must be the result of first-hand experience not hearsay (201b–c), and it must *include* (though the dialogue ends with the admission that these are not *sufficient* to constitute knowledge) true belief (or recognition) plus the ability to give an account (*logos*) of what one believes or recognizes. What has no *logos* cannot be known (202d, 205e).

For comparison, one may quote what has been called 'the classical definition of knowledge' in modern times. Though expressed in various terms, it amounts to this: A man knows that *p* (*p* being any proposition) if (*a*) he believes *p*, (*b*) he has adequate evidence for *p*, (*c*) *p* is true. Thus 'according to the classical definition, knowledge is justified true belief, or true opinion combined with reason'.[2] This is closely similar to the third of the three definitions which Plato here discusses and ultimately rejects, but there is a difference in that the modern definition speaks only of knowledge in propositional form (knowledge of facts) whereas in Plato it is more like knowledge of things, not 'knowledge that' but knowledge with a direct substantival object—knowing a syllable, the notes of a scale, a waggon, Theaetetus.[3] In fact three kinds of knowledge

---

[1] Late in the dialogue, at 196d, S. asks permission to do something 'shameless', i.e. disobey his own rule in *Meno* (71b) and claim to state a property of something whose definition is as yet unknown.

[2] Hilpinen, *Synthèse* 1970, 109f., *q.v.* for reff. to various twentieth-century formulations.

[3] Cf. vol. IV, 493. It is well known as the difference between Fr. 'savoir' and 'connaître', Germ. 'wissen' and 'kennen'. Once English too could mark in words the difference between 'D'ye ken John Peel' and 'He wist not that it was true' (Acts 12: 9). Some have thought that P. marked it by his use of εἰδέναι, ἐπίστασθαι and γιγνώσκειν, but this is not so; e.g. in the short

are commonly acknowledged today, the two just mentioned and 'knowing how',[1] as in knowing a game or knowing one's craft, which involves a large element of acquired dexterity, skill or technique, or in morals, knowledge how to behave. Such knowledge however is never entirely divorced from the other two kinds.[2]

These distinctions have not fully come to the surface in Plato, who throughout the *Theaetetus* tends to speak of knowing in terms of a verb followed by a direct object—a concrete individual thing or person —rather than by the equivalent of 'how to' or a proposition expressing a fact.[3] For this there were more reasons than one. First, he was the heir of Socrates, the kernel of whose teaching was that the knowledge on which all human excellence depended was knowledge of what something *was*. To 'know justice', in the sense of being able to define it, was the only guarantee of leading a consistently just life. (Even now Plato preserves the substantival expression so unnatural to us: a definition of knowledge is desirable because 'the knowledgeable are knowledgeable by knowledge'.[4]) Here (as Aristotle saw) lay the originality of his message, for from Homer onwards Greeks had used the words in question (ἐπίστασθαι, ἐπιστήμη) to denote practical abilities or skills, even bodily skills, rather than intellectual understanding.[5] For Socrates, as for them, knowledge was the basis of both technical skill and general excellence, but whereas others had thought of this *technē* and *aretē* as simply knowing how to act, he believed that

---

space between 192d and 193a he has used all three for the same sort of knowledge, namely direct acquaintance. The point has been noticed in connexion with *Charm.* in vol. IV, 169 n. 1. Cf. Runciman, *PLE* 34f.; Sprute, *Phron.* 1968, 58–60.

[1] The terminology is Ryle's in *The Concept of Mind*.

[2] Cf. Runciman, *PLE* 11f.

[3] A rare exception is ὅτι ἐστόν at 186b.

[4] σοφίᾳ σοφοὶ οἱ σοφοί (145d: S. has already equated σοφία with ἐπιστήμη, on which see vol. IV, 265). For this form of expression cf. *ib.* 118f. (*Euthyphro* and *Phaedo*) and 189 (*H. Maj.*).

[5] See vol. III, 450 n. 2, and foll. pp. Examples are collected by John Gould, *P.'s Ethics* 7ff. He errs however in supposing that because this use existed earlier it is also the basis of the Socratic conception of knowledge. The end (right action) is the same, but the knowledge leading to that end has become something different. G. points out also that Hdt. uses ἐπίστασθαι of being convinced of something which is untrue (p. 10), but this only shows up another difference. For S. and P. the object of knowledge must be ὄν or ἀληθές. (Cf. *Gorg.* 454d.) More to the point are expressions like εἰδὼς δίκαν in Simonides (Pl. *Prot.* 346c) and the Homeric ἄγρια οἶδεν (*Il.* 24.41) etc. but these, as Dodds says (*G. and I.* 17), illustrate the Greek intellectualist approach to an explanation of behaviour (making the Socratic doctrine less paradoxical) rather than a 'behaviourist' explanation of knowledge. For criticism of Gould see Vlastos, *PS* 205ff.; Kuhn, *Gnomon* 1956, 339f.

one could only know how to act if one first understood the nature and function of the thing to be made—shoe or shuttle—or the moral ideal (e.g. justice) to be pursued. Plato started at least from this Socratic idea that knowledge is of 'things' (universals), whether justice, courage or clay (mentioned *exempli gratia* at 147a–c), and that what one knows one can *define* by stating its *eidos* (specific character) and so placing all instances of it in their proper *eidos* (class).[1]

Other temptations to extend the model of perceptual knowledge or direct acquaintance beyond its proper frontiers arose from Plato's native language. One has been referred to already (vol. IV, 493 n. 1), namely the interchangeability of the Greek words which without context we translate 'true' (*alēthes*) and 'being' (*on*), though the first may qualify a thing, a being, a substance or the like as real or genuine and the second a statement as true.[2] We may occasionally, and rhetorically, speak of 'a true Englishman', but we would not say of imitation mink that it is not true, or of a liar that he says what is not. Even the *Sophist*'s clarification of 'being' and 'not-being' did not remove this particular temptation. Another lies in the fact that 'I know what *x* is' could be idiomatically expressed in Greek (as Plato often expresses it) in the form 'I know *x* what it is'.[3] In the course of the *Theaetetus* itself difficulties (doubtless real to Plato) begin to come to light in the conception of knowledge as of things rather than facts.

ADDITIONAL NOTE: EXEMPLIFICATION AND DEFINITION

It is now commonly believed that Socrates was mistaken in claiming that one cannot know what *x* is without being able to produce a definition of it: that even if a definition could be produced it could not be a *means* of knowing what *x* is since, to take the example of knowledge, 'one would need to have a complete grasp of all the cases of knowledge, and of their relations to each other and to everything that is not knowledge, *before* one could know that the definition was correct'. (Quotations are from Bambrough, *Reason, Truth and God* 14f.) Wittgenstein is thought to have delivered a fatal blow at Socrates's demand for definitions in *The Blue Book* (p. 20), by turning the

---

[1] See further on this pp. 112f. below.
[2] E.g. τὸν ἐόντα λόγον λέγειν, Hdt. 1.95.116; τὰ ὄντα ἀπαγγέλλειν, Thuc. 7.8.2.
[3] See also McDowell's remarks on pp. 188 and 192f. of his *Tht.*

tables on him. Socrates will not accept, even as a preliminary answer to the question 'What is knowledge?', an enumeration of cases of knowledge, and the commentators (adds Bambrough) support him. But 'when Socrates asks for a definition instead of mere examples, and Theaetetus asks for an explanation of what a *definition* is, Socrates does not *define* definition: he gives *examples*. And now the commentators are silent.' (Italics are Bambrough's.)

I would rather not be completely silent, for this does not seem to me quite fair. To begin with, and most important, Theaetetus has not asked Socrates to define a definition. On the contrary he says that he understands and agrees with Socrates's demand for universal definitions and claims to have produced them in his own subject, mathematics (147 c–48 b). It is only in the special case of knowledge that he has experienced difficulty, though he has given much attention to it and cannot get the question out of his mind. He has no doubts as to the legitimacy of the question itself. Mr Bambrough, agreeing that it was not quite fair to cite *Theaetetus* in this connexion, has suggested to me that Wittgenstein would have done better to refer to *Meno* or *Laches*. (On the usefulness of definition in *Laches* see vol. IV, 244 f.) That he does seek to make his point through *Theaetetus* is surely quite a serious fault.

Next, though in the particular case of the *Theaetetus* Socrates simply gives an example sufficient to remind Theaetetus, who has heard reports of the sort of questions he asks, one may make two further points. (1) This is not true as a generalization about him. At *Gorg.* 463 c he refuses to say whether rhetoric is good or bad 'until I have answered the question *what* it is', and this he proceeds to do. (2) He has in many of Plato's dialogues, both early and late, answered quite explicitly the specific question what a definition is. The following sentence does not occur *totidem verbis* in any one passage, but adds nothing to what Plato has repeatedly affirmed: ὁρισμός ἐστι λόγος τῆς τοῦ προτεθέντος πράγματος οὐσίας [or τοῦ. . .εἴδους], τοιοῦτος οἷος περὶ πάντων τῶν ἐκείνου ὀνόματι καλουμένων ἀληθὴς εἶναι καὶ ἀφαιρεῖν αὐτὸ ἀπὸ πάντων τῶν ἄλλων εἰδῶν. (See *Meno passim*, *Pol.* 258 c and many other places. I am not saying here that the Platonic Socrates was *right* to offer universal definitions, only that he sometimes does so.)[1]

Plato himself has anticipated his modern critics by saying later in the *Theaetetus* that the idea of knowledge as true judgement plus a λόγος is unsatisfactory if λόγος expresses a mark or sign (ὅρος) by which the object of enquiry differs from everything else, because one cannot state such a λόγος unless one already knows what knowledge is, and is bound to commit the error of including the definiendum in the definition (208 c–10 a). I doubt in

[1] Cf. the quotation from Russell in vol. IV (244 n. 1) on the advisability of defining wisdom before taking practical steps in connexion with it.

any case if the Platonic Socrates ever spoke of definition as a *means* to knowledge, rather than as evidence that one already possessed it.

Plan of the enquiry. In spite of some digressions, the *Theaetetus* pursues a more orderly and systematic course than many dialogues, and this may be briefly outlined without forgetting Stoelzel's warning that 'it is immensely difficult to force a work of art like the living Platonic dialogue into a rigid schematic arrangement'.

When they have settled the difference between a string of instances and a universal definition, and Socrates has explained his art of intellectual midwifery, three suggested definitions of knowledge are tested and found wanting.

1. *Knowledge is sense-perception* (151d–86e). This is rejected on the ground that to grasp a thing's being or essence, as well as concepts such as similarity and dissimilarity, good and evil and the like, the mind must go beyond sensation and use its peculiar powers of reason and reflection. Without Being, no one can reach the truth, and a man who cannot reach the truth cannot be said to know.

The section includes a discussion of two particular theories which according to Socrates are closely related and both imply that sensation is the same as knowledge:

(i) Protagoras's 'man the measure' theory of knowledge.

(ii) A remarkable theory of perception based on the view of extreme Heracliteans that the only reality is perpetual motion, change, process.

Interlude (172c–77c). A reminder that, whatever the conclusions of this dialogue, the philosopher knows of another world than this, one purged of evil, to which he may aspire through 'imitation of God' in righteousness and wisdom. 'But', Socrates abruptly concludes, 'that is not our present business.'

2. *Knowledge is true belief* (187b–201c). Rejected very briefly on the grounds that one can have a true belief without knowledge, as when the account of a witness rightly persuades one of its truth, though only personal experience of the events described can properly be called knowledge.

In proposing this definition, Theaetetus says that he cannot simply suggest 'belief', because there is false belief as well as true. This leads at once to a discussion of how false belief, or error, is possible, which occupies most of the section ostensibly devoted to true belief.

3. *Knowledge is true belief plus an account*, with the corollary that only that can be known of which an account or description (*logos*) can be given (201 c–10 b).

This raises the question what can be the subject of a *logos*, and they examine a theory that only compounds can be described, whereas their simple elements can be neither described nor known but only perceived and named. However, reason and experience, it appears, both show that a compound cannot be more knowable than its elements or parts.

Three possible senses of *logos* are then discussed, to see if they could turn true belief into knowledge:

(i) Speech in general, the expression of thought in words. This is dismissed as much too general.

(ii) Enumeration of parts or elements. But addition of this to true belief will not give the guarantee of future correctness which is demanded of knowledge.

(iii) Ability to name a mark by which the thing in question differs from all other things. This proves to be circular, for it amounts to saying that knowledge is true belief plus *knowledge* of what makes the object unique.

So we end. The dialogue has not achieved its object, but has not (says Socrates) been fruitless, for if Theaetetus should have other brain-children they will be the better for the present scrutiny, and if not, he himself will be a better and more amiable man for no longer thinking he knows what he does not.

Introductory conversation. With his usual skill, Plato leads us gently into the discussion by letting the speakers make themselves known. Theodorus, 'expert in geometry, astronomy, calculation, and a man of general culture' (145 a), introduces Theaetetus to Socrates as a youth of quite exceptional intellect and character, and moreover one who resembles Socrates in physical features. Typically, Plato adds the purely personal detail that his father left him a fortune but it has been squandered by trustees. Socrates quickly puts his question about the nature of knowledge, and Theaetetus reveals his own bent when, to show that he has grasped the difference between exemplification and universal definition, he illustrates it by a point in mathematics that had occurred to himself and a fellow-student, namely that the geometrical equivalents of what are now called surds could be grouped in one class and given a single name ('powers') by virtue of their common character of irrationality or incommensurability.[1] He cannot as yet, however, find a similarly universal formula to cover the different kinds of knowledge or skill, though the question is always in his mind. This shows that his mind is pregnant, indeed in labour, with some offspring, and needs the aid of that mental midwifery which Socrates, though barren of knowledge himself, knows how to practise on others.[2] Let Theaetetus only say boldly whatever he can, and Socrates will assist him, not least in judging whether his idea be a proper child or a changeling.

(1) *Knowledge as perception* (151 d–86 e)

Thus emboldened, Theaetetus replies that, as far as he can see at present, knowledge is nothing but perception (*aisthēsis*): whoever knows something is perceiving it.

[1] For literature on the mathematics involved in Tht.'s example see Friedländer III, 488 n. 16. Cf. also M. Brown, 'Plato disapproves' etc., *P.'s Meno* 236ff. It is simply explained by McDowell, *Tht.* 116. The general definition arrived at is, in effect, 'a power is the square root of a non-square integer'. It is a good illustration of how mathematics can be propaedeutic to philosophy, as P. teaches in *Rep.* 7.

[2] On S.'s midwifery see vol. III, 444f., 378 n. 1. P. may have connected it with *anamnesis*, the ideas brought to birth by S. being innate (Cornford, *PTK* 27f.), but cf. Hackforth, *Mnem.* 1957, 128f. The passage contains a spirited defence of S.'s annoying habit of continually questioning while refusing to give his own opinion. Cf. esp. 150b–c, 151c5–8, *Rep.* 336c, 337a. The possible connexion with *anamnesis* is denied by McDowell (*Tht.* p. 117) on two grounds which make one, if anything, more inclined to believe in it than before. He says : (1) 'The "offspring" delivered by Socrates are just as likely to be incorrect as correct'; (2) 'Second, the Theory of Recollection contains nothing corresponding to the barrenness of Socrates himself.' Comment: (1) In *Meno*, the *locus classicus* for the theory of recollection, the slave does give several incorrect answers. True, each wrong answer brings him nearer the truth, but so do the formulation and discarding of three wrong answers in *Tht.* (See 210c.) (2) In the *Meno* too, S. says that Meno's question 'Is virtue teachable?' implies the prior question 'What is virtue?', and that to that he does not know the answer (71b). *Anamnesis* in fact provides the solution to the problem of how one can look for something that one does not know. How this would work out in terms of a metaphor of pregnancy and giving birth, it might be hard to say, and since that metaphor is not used in *Meno*, it would be wrong to try.

What is included in aisthēsis (*usually in this chapter 'perception'*[1])*?* It was a wide term, for the Greeks had no single words to distinguish sensation from perception, i.e. mere awareness of sense-data (colours, sounds etc.) from the perception of external objects which derives from it. It was used of a single sense, and in the plural of the five senses, but also much more widely, as when Thucydides (2, 50) says that the dogs of Athens, by refusing to touch the corpses of those who had died in the plague, provided the best *aisthēsis* (visible evidence) of its effect on animals. Plato does not confine it to a single technical use. Even when using it narrowly, he includes pleasures, pains, desires and fears along with sight, hearing and smell as *aisthēseis*,[2] adding that there are innumerable others, named and unnamed. But he can draw the distinction when he wishes, even inventing a word (ποιότης 182a) to distinguish a sensible quality (or sense-datum) from the object that it qualifies, e.g. whiteness from a white stone (156e5).[3] In general however what we receive through the senses includes any direct or unbidden experience, as distinct from the results of rational reflection;[4] and the latter are confined to highly abstract concepts like existence, unity, sameness, dissimilarity and their opposites (185c). Things white, hot, sweet, or hard the mind perceives through the senses, and though the neuter plurals point to things rather than qualities, it is extremely doubtful whether at this point Plato had the distinction in mind. (See 184c–e; but 'sound and colour' at 185a.) Fine distinctions are well enough when they affect the immediate argument. Otherwise, to depart from the

[1] A word 'now normally restricted to sense-perception—to the discovery, by means of the senses, of the existence and properties of the external world' (Hirst in *Ency. Phil.* VI, 79).

[2] 156b. For P.'s views on the status of pleasure and pain see *Tim.* 64d–65b: pain results from a sudden and violent disturbance of the bodily condition, pleasure from its sudden restoration to normal.

[3] Nakhnikian (*R. of Metaph.* 155–6, 129f.) usefully draws attention to these passages, and mentions as a second criterion for distinguishing them that sensation is private and irrefutable, perceptual reports are public, objective and testable. Together, he considers, they justify him in treating the theories of sensation and perception separately in discussing the whole of 151d–86e. Cooper's article 'P. on Sense Perception and Knowledge' (*Phron.* 1974) is an interesting discussion of this subject from a modern standpoint.

[4] At 185a–b not only δοξάζειν but also οἴεσθαι and διανοεῖσθαι and a 'that' clause ('that they are gods') are used of perception (αἴσθησις). This might have given more support to Gulley's claim (*PTK* 77) that αἴσθησις includes δόξα (judgement or belief, clearly distinguished from it in other dialogues) than the passages he actually refers to. Of these, 161d speaks of 'what a man judges *by means of* sensation' (cf. the distinction between ᾧ and δι' οὗ at 184c), and 179c actually distinguishes αἰσθήσεις from judgements based on them.

usages of ordinary Greek is ungentlemanly pedantry (184c). Thus at
Rep. 608d Socrates asks, 'Have you not *perceived* (ᾔσθησαι) that the
soul is immortal?' One must also remember Plato's dichotomy of
everything conceivable into sensibles and intelligibles (*aisthēta* and
noēta). The latter are eternal, invisible and wholly real. *Aisthēta* include
our whole world and whatever happens in it, the whole realm of
Becoming as opposed to Being.

Protagoras and his 'secret doctrine' (151e–55d). Socrates immediately
says that Theaetetus's suggestion is identical with the implications of
Protagoras's famous dictum that 'man is the measure of all things',[1] by
which he meant that everything is for any individual exactly what he
perceives it to be, so perception is always infallible—is knowledge in
fact.[2] This was doubtless based on a theory of perception held by the
great man as a secret to be divulged only to his pupils. (The irony is
obvious, especially when one remembers that Protagoras only took
paying pupils.) It holds that all things are in continuous movement and
mutual mixture, to which they owe what is wrongly called their
existence. Nothing should be spoken of as *being*, either absolutely ('in
and by itself') or in the sense of having a definite property,[3] being large
or small or white, but everything is *becoming*, a product of flux and
motion. Motion is the universal creator and sustainer: life, like fire,
comes from friction, and depends on the movement of the sun, exercise
preserves the body, processes of learning and practice the mind. Motion,
as preservative, is good, stagnation destructive and bad.[4] What we call
colour is not a separate thing, whether inside or outside our eyes, but
arises from the meeting of our eyes with the appropriate motion. It is

[1] 152e. He 'put the very same thing in another way'. Yet it appears later that he did not *confine* knowledge to perception. See p. 86 n. 3 below.

[2] 152c5–6. Cf. McDowell's trans. I see no reason to adopt White's desperate expedient of excising ὡς ἐπιστήμη οὖσα (*Phron.* 1972). A full account of Prot.'s doctrine will be found in vol. III, 171–5 and 183–92.

[3] 152d. Cf. *Crat.* 439d: on the flux-theory one cannot say of anything that it is either 'that' or 'suchlike' (τοιοῦτον).

[4] At 152e this theory is sweepingly ascribed not only to Prot. but to all previous thinkers except Parmenides. Though the Ionians and Empedocles taught of generation through mixture of opposites, P. is obviously thinking primarily of the flux-doctrine of Heraclitus, as suggested e.g. by the association of fire and life (153a–b) and the idea of motion as not only universal but *good*. (Cf. vol. I, 454, 462, and Heraclitus A 22 DK.)

neither what meets nor what is met, but an event occurring between them, peculiar to each percipient. We cannot affirm that a colour appears the same to us as to another man or animal, or even to our changing selves; and this could not be so if what we perceived were *itself* large or white or hot.

There follow (154b–55d) certain paradoxes concerning relative size and number which have been thought both unreal and irrelevant,[1] and Theaetetus himself cannot see their connexion with the present topic (155d). Six dice are more than four, but put them beside twelve and they will be fewer. Socrates is taller than Theaetetus, but when Theaetetus grows he will be shorter. But how can fewer become more, or a taller man become shorter, without changing his size? This question of relational properties was explained in the *Phaedo* by reference to the Forms (102b–103a), but from the *Parmenides* (131c–e, p. 41 above) it could appear that Plato saw difficulties in that, as well he might. Here Socrates himself enlarges on the difficulties: the question seems to hint at inconsistency[2] in three statements on which they both agree, namely (1) nothing becomes greater or less in size or number so long as it remains equal to itself; (2) whatever has nothing added to or taken from it remains equal (the same in amount); (3) what formerly was not cannot later be without a process of becoming. To find the connexion of all this with Protagoras, Socrates proposes to examine the mysteries of certain unnamed 'cleverer' or 'subtler' thinkers.[3]

[1] So Cornford (*PTK* 41), and Russell (quoted by Brown, see below) dismissed the trouble as 'an infantile disease of philosophy'. Its relevance to the argument has been defended by Bluck (*PCPS* 1961, 7–9), and M. Brown explains the point as a mathematical one (*JHP* 1969, 373 ff.). S. does not simply say that 6 is greater than 4 and less than 12; it exceeds 4 *by a half* and falls short of 12 *being half*, i.e. the difference between 6 and 4 is the same fraction of 4 as the difference between 6 and 12 is of 12 (harmonic mean). This links up with Tht.'s work on irrationals, and Brown sees P. as influenced by these mathematical advances and problems to see difficulties in his own epistemology as hitherto conceived. For some earlier opinions on the significance of the puzzles for P.'s thought see Cornford, *PTK* 43–5; Ross, *PTI* 102; Runciman, *PLE* 18.

[2] On μάχεται αὐτὰ αὑτοῖς see Hackforth in *Mnem.* 1957, 130f.

[3] Actually the puzzles about relative predicates are never returned to, nor is it absolutely clear that 'S. promises that the theory of perception he is about to expound will contain the solution' to them. So McDowell (*Tht.* 135), but I am not entirely happy about either his or Cornford's translation. More literally S. says (155d5–e1): 'Do you understand why these things being as they are follows from the doctrine of Protagoras?' (Tht.: 'Not yet'.) 'Then you will be grateful to me if I examine with you the hidden truth of the thought of a famous man—or rather, famous men.' He does not explicitly promise a solution, and we are left to infer that in a world where all is change and becoming, the problem of something being now small, now large, without an intermediate process of becoming, loses its meaning.

The cleverer theory of sensation (156a–57c). This is in fact a refinement on the 'secret doctrine' of Protagoras, and together they present an astonishingly advanced and imaginative theory. Two accounts are given, because Theaetetus does not follow the first, and it is a pity that Socrates did not start with the second, fuller one, as they are not in every detail easy to reconcile. In the first, all is motion, but motion is of two sorts, active and passive. From intercourse and friction with each other these two motions (i.e. sensible object and sense-organ) give birth to twins, an act of perception and a percept (colour, sound etc.). The second account is in several stages. (i) Motions are now re-divided into quick and slow. Both motions in the previous account are slow, and move always in the same place.[1] (ii) When one of them—e.g. an eye—and an object structurally adjusted to it[2] come near enough, they engender the quick motions which traverse space, i.e. a colour and the sensation of that colour, unique to the particular pair that engendered them. Then, as (iii) 'vision'[3] from the eyes and colour from the other parent traverse the space between,[4] (iv) the eye becomes filled with vision and sees, becoming not sight but a seeing eye, and its partner is suffused with colour and becomes not colour but coloured, whether stick or stone or anything else.

All other sensations work in the same way.[5] They have no being of their own, but arise from intercourse and motion: nothing is an agent until it meets a patient, and what is agent in one encounter may be

[1] Of course an eye or ear, or skin sensitive to touch, moves around, but only as Aristotle would say *per accidens*, because moved by the person, not by any motion of its own. Its proper motion is alteration, included in κίνησις at 181 d 5.

[2] σύμμετρος, lit. 'commensurate'. The terminology is from Empedocles's theory of sensation by pores and effluences, for which see vol. II, 231 f., 234–7 (sight).

[3] Presumably a sort of ray, or Empedoclean effluence. Cf. *Tim.* 67 c.

[4] This hardly seems to fit the immediately preceding description, though no commentator that I know seems worried about it. There the active and passive motions must be in actual contact and generate quasi-sexually by friction between them. Here however the slow motions (which one must assume to be the same things, namely percept and percipient) need only 'approach' (πλησιάζειν, 'come within range' Cornford, adopted by Nakhnikian; a very different metaphor from Plato's of copulation!), and they give birth although a space remains between them into which the offspring are projected. Crombie says without apparent unease 'that when *contact* is established between subject and object, a twin progeny is begotten . . . and that these *travel between* the two parties' (*EPD* II, 10 my italics; cf. p. 7).

[5] 156e7. P. does not explain how this mechanism can account for desires and fears. For guesses see McDowell 137 f.

patient in another.[1] Nothing *is*, everything is in process of change, and ideally the verb 'to be' should be excised from our vocabulary, along with other 'static' words like 'this' or 'something'.[2]

The theory seems to borrow features from both Heraclitean flux and the atomism of Democritus. He too taught that sensations are a momentary product of physical contact, that sensible qualities have no independent character (*physis*), sensation being a result of alteration in our bodies caused by the impact of a stream of atoms thrown off by the object perceived, and moreover that our bodily conditions are in any case changing through age or other causes, so that the effect will be different not only on different people but on the same person at different times. (Cf. *Tht.* 159b–d.) He too quoted sweet and bitter as examples of the relativity of sensation. He even added the refinement that in the case of sight the atoms from the object do not enter the eye directly, but meet effluences from the eye itself and form jointly with them an image which does enter it. We need not deny a debt here because Socrates distinguishes the theory's authors, as 'much subtler', from those who 'only admit the reality of what they can get a grip of with their hands, not of actions or comings-to-be or anything invisible' (155e). These, commentators argue, are the materialists, and Democritus was a materialist. Nevertheless he did posit continuous motion and did deny reality to all sensible qualities, the only realities being atoms and void, neither of which could be seen or grasped with the hand. Even if he 'made all sense-objects tangible', he did so only in the sense that 'most of the natural philosophers' did (Arist. *De sensu* 442a29–b1), and this did not give the sense of touch any advantage over the others. It appears with them in fr. 11 as one of the untrustworthy, 'bastard' faculties.[3]

---

[1] 'The eyeball can be seen by another eye, the flesh touched, etc.' (Cornford). S. gives no examples.

[2] Is 157b (habit makes us use these words, though wrongly) another reminder of Empedocles? Cf. fr. 9.5 (on γενέσθαι) ἦ θέμις οὐ καλέουσι νόμῳ δ' ἐπίφημι καὶ αὐτός.

[3] For another view see Campbell, *Tht.* xli–lv, and for a detailed account of D.'s theories of perception vol. II, 438–49. The theory of the κομψότεροι has been attributed in modern times, not very compellingly, to Antisthenes and Aristippus. (For some reff. see Friedländer, *Pl.* III, 488 n. 20.) It is also held that P. himself either constructed the theory or at least believed it. So McDowell, *Tht.* 130, preceded by Friedländer, Cornford, Jackson, Burnet, Stenzel, Ritter, Nakhnikian and others: *contra*, Taylor, *PMW* 329f. Runciman (*PLE* 19) argued that it could not be P.'s because he never held a Berkeleian theory of sensation, which would have conflicted

In summing up the theory to test Theaetetus's assent, Socrates says at 157d: 'Tell me whether you like the idea that nothing *is* good or beautiful or all the things we have just spoken of, but all are *becoming*.' The sudden introduction of 'good' and 'beautiful' into what had been a list of sense-perceived properties like white and hot may sound odd, but for Plato all alike belong to the sensible world. What he has in mind is the 'many beautiful things' of *Rep.* 5, which are recognized by the 'lover of sights and sounds', and in fact are no more beautiful than ugly, in just the same way as large and small, heavy and light things (both in the *Republic* and here) can appear as their opposites. There too, exactly as here, he says that none of the many phenomena are, rather than are not, what they are said to be. (See *Rep.* 479a–b.)

Status of the sensible world. A point vital to Plato's philosophy arises here. It is pressed home at 182cff.: on the theory that everything is in unceasing change (flux) we cannot even say that a thing 'flows white', for the whiteness itself is flowing and shifting into another colour. We cannot name anything with any assurance that we are naming it rightly, or even say that perception is knowledge any more than non-knowledge. In short, the theory makes all discourse impossible.

Now in the *Phaedo* and *Republic* Plato teaches that sensibles are always changing but at the same time can 'remind' us of the changeless Forms—the only realities—because they resemble them or in an imperfect and timebound manner 'share' their natures. But if we assume (as many do) that Plato accepts for the sensible world the extreme form of the flux-doctrine which we have here, then, as Gulley writes (*PTK* 74),

What becomes of the doctrine that sensible characteristics are 'copies' or 'images' of Forms, that they are recognisable and hence are able to prompt the recollection of Forms? This doctrine clearly assumes that there are determinate and recognisable sensible characteristics; indeed it is a doctrine *that* sensibles are determinate and recognisable in so far as they 'participate in' and hence 'resemble' Forms. There is a serious inconsistency, then, between this doctrine and the consequences drawn by Plato from the fact that sensibles are in flux.

with the theory of Forms, but Cornford (*PTK* 50f.) seems to have thought it not exactly Berkeleian. (For comparison and contrast with the Berkeleian phenomenalist tradition see McDowell 143f.) In fact it could not be P.'s for the reasons given on the next few pages, and is plainly the neo-Heraclitean doctrine referred to as such at 179dff.

Others have expressed similar views,[1] but the point is, I suggest, that Plato here describes the sensible world *as it would be if there were no Forms*. Neither supporters nor opponents of this explanation have appreciated that their existence *changes the nature of the sensible world*. This indeed was a main reason for their introduction. Parmenides had denied all reality to the sensible world on the ground of his exclusive dichotomy 'is or is not'. The Forms, and the admission of 'becoming' as an intermediate stage, were designed, not to depress the sensible world but to save it from annihilation. Somehow the Heraclitean and Parmenidean views of reality must be reconciled. The Platonic universe is an integrated whole consisting of intelligible and sensible spheres. As the *Timaeus* teaches—that triumphant vindication of order, regularity and value in the movement and change of the sensible world—what gives it such order and stability as it possesses is the fact that it is modelled on the Forms.[2] It is true that for Plato 'sensible things are forever flowing, and there can be no *knowledge* of them'; but there can be true opinion because, Aristotle continues, there are also what he called Forms, with reference to which the sensibles can be spoken of because Forms are their *causes*, that is, they impart definite characters to the sensibles.[3]

Contemporary Heracliteans were like their master without his Logos, the universal law governing the continual flux of change,[4] and Plato had no thought of following them in their fantasy of a world adrift on a sea of indescribability. We may recall the outburst against them of Theodorus, an authoritative and sympathetic voice in the dialogue: you might as well, he says, talk to maniacs; they are living examples of their theories, always in motion, incapable of staying still a moment to listen to a question or an argument. They own no masters or pupils, it's a case

[1] Cornford held that the extreme flux-doctrine was P.'s own theory of the sensible world: having proved by its means that knowledge cannot be perception, he leaves us to infer that it depends on the Forms. This would certainly make him guilty of the inconsistency which Gulley finds. If Forms existed, yet in no way moderated the utter instability and disorder of our world (an inconceivable situation), knowledge would be as impossible as if they did not.

[2] Cf. esp. 52a. On the 'cleverer' theory, of course, one could not speak of a sensible as coming to be 'in a certain place' (ἕν τινι τόπῳ). Cf. also *Gorg.* 507e–508a.

[3] Arist. *Metaph.* 987a32–b9. The causal aspect of the Forms has been prominent in many places in dialogues already discussed. See on it vol. IV, 350–2.

[4] For a summary of H.'s conception of the Logos see vol. I, 434. His distance from his rabid followers is also indicated by fr. 55, where he makes a point similar to that made later (186d) by P. himself, that the senses are 'bad witnesses' which cannot yield knowledge without a mind to interpret them.

of spontaneous generation, and each thinks the other an ignoramus (179e–80c). Theirs was the position of Cratylus, who outdid Heraclitus by saying that one could not step into the same river *once*, and ended by taking Plato's hint and abandoning speech altogether (Arist. *Metaph.* 1010a12–15).

At the end of the *Cratylus* (439b ff.) Socrates demonstrates to Cratylus that on his extreme flux-theory, allowing no permanent entities at all, verbal communication and knowledge would be impossible. If not only beautiful things but the very property of beauty were under constant change, there would be nothing to which one could apply noun or adjective, as having either identity or qualities. This does not show that Plato 'does accept that the sensible world is in flux' (in the extreme sense) and so 'at the same time he asserts that Forms exist and denies that the sensible world has any determinate characteristics. This' (Gulley goes on to claim) 'is in itself implicitly to acknowledge that the argument that "being in flux" is incompatible with "being determinate" is equally valid whether or not it is assumed that Forms exist.'[1] All it shows is that the neo-Heraclitean theory that *everything* is in incessant flux and change is inconsistent with the existence and effect of the Forms. Finally, in the *Timaeus*, in which the Forms are assumed from first to last, it is said, in contrast to *Crat.* 439d9, that whereas physical bodies such as fire and water, being mutable and unstable, cannot be called 'this' or 'that' (τοῦτο), they *can* be said to possess certain qualities (τοιοῦτον) by virtue of the penetration into their habitat of copies of the Forms.[2] In their causal capacity the Forms

---

[1] Gulley, *PTK* 83. On p. 72 he admits that this thesis involves rejecting the 'grammatically more obvious interpretation' of 439d4. Even if (which I do not believe) P., never a precise writer, had been betrayed into giving the impression that the existence of the Forms made no difference to the nature of the sensible world itself, the weight of evidence on the other side would far outweigh it. Runciman saw the point. See his *PLE* 21 on the argument of the *Cratylus*. On G.'s views see also vol. IV, 493 n. 1. I believe that what I say here is also relevant to the remarks of Robinson in *Essays* 48, and Owen in *SPM* 323.

[2] *Tim.* 49d, 50c. This should be read in conjunction with Cherniss's acute arguments in *SPM* 355–60, though I do not necessarily follow him in all their subtleties. The late dialogue *Phil.* (59a–b), though it puts the contrast between being and becoming in strong terms, only repeats the point made in *Rep.* 5 that precise truth cannot be found within the changing sensible world, and therefore δόξα is different from ἐπιστήμη. I hope the last few pages answer the point raised by McDowell, pp. 180–1, para. (ii), and I believe I am in substantial agreement with the extremely close-knit argument of Cherry in *Apeiron* 1967.

rescue the sensible world from the meaningless chaos to which the neo-Heraclitean maniacs would consign it. Truly, as the *Parmenides* repeats (135 b–c), if you deny the existence of Forms you will have nothing on which to fix your mind and will destroy the possibility of rational discourse. To suggest that their existence and presence could leave the flux of becoming unaffected shows a fundamental misunderstanding of Plato's position.

Dreams and hallucinations (157 e–60 d). This theory (continues Socrates) can withstand the objection commonly made, that in dreams, madness or illness we have false perceptions, so that perception is not infallible after all. We cannot even give certain proof that we are not at this moment asleep and dreaming our conversation,[1] and the answer to the objection lies in the theory's assertion that sensation is nothing more than an interaction between two constantly changing things, and exists (or rather 'becomes') only in relation to both. One must always add the Protagorean 'for him', 'for me'. There is then no such thing as an illusory sensation. If wine sweet and pleasant to a healthy man tastes sour to the same man in sickness, the explanation in terms of the theory is that he has become a different subject, which together with the drinking of the wine produces different offspring, namely the sensation of sourness on his tongue and a 'moving and changing sourness' in the wine (159 e), which has no qualities 'in itself' but only 'for somebody'. Thus Protagoras is vindicated, and each man is the sole judge of what is for him; and the name of knowledge cannot be denied to a state of mind impervious to falsehood or error about what is or becomes.

---

[1] This was asserted independently by Descartes (*Meditation* 1, trans. Haldane and Ross pp. 75 f.). For Moore's and Russell's positions see Newell, *Concept of Phil.* 56–8. J. L. Austin (*S. and S.* 49 n. 1) says it is absurd because (for one thing) we describe some waking experiences as 'dream-like', and if Descartes (and P. whom neither mentions) were right, 'if dreams were not "qualitatively" different from waking experience, then *every* waking experience would be like a dream'. I do not believe P. was right, but I doubt if it is possible to refute him so easily. An experience which we call dreamlike is one which we believe to be real (not imaginary like a dream), but which gives an impression of the unreality which, *in our waking hours*, we ascribe to our dreams. While we are dreaming, our dream-experiences seem real (witness the way we may wake up laughing, crying or in a state of fear), and it is by no means inconceivable that in a dream we might speak of our experiences as dreamlike though (like the man awake) we believed them to be real. Somewhat similar is Tht.'s point that we can dream we are narrating a dream, a thing which I myself have often done. P. too could speak of a waking experience as dreamlike (*Meno* 85 c).

Theaetetus

Examination of the theory that knowledge is perception. Thus Theaetetus's firstborn has been delivered after a difficult labour. The next job is to examine the baby and see if it is worth rearing. I have said that the *Theaetetus* pursues on the whole a systematic course, but it preserves the natural turns of a genuine conversation, with short interludes, a longer digression, and shifts from one aspect of the subject to another and back again. This realistic style is particularly marked in the next few sections.

(i) *Return to Protagoras* (161 b–162 a). If knowledge is perception and every man has his private and unassailable truth (and on this supposition why confine it to man among sentient creatures?), what right had Protagoras to set himself up as a teacher? Can he have seriously meant that no man is wiser than another, or even than a pig or tadpole? Having said this, Socrates immediately turns round and denounces it in Protagoras's name as cheap rhetoric. Without refuting it, he insists they must attack the question in a different way, and passes to a new point.

(ii) *Foreign languages and unlearned letters* (163 b–d). Assuming that knowledge is sense-perception, what happens in the case of an unknown language? Do we not hear what is said, or do we both hear and know it? And again, before learning to read do we not see letters, or do we see and therefore know them? Theaetetus replies judiciously that we know just as much as we see or hear, the sound of the voices and the colour and shape of the letters; but we neither perceive nor hear what an interpreter or schoolmaster could tell us. Socrates congratulates him on this piece of clear thinking, which he will not dispute for fear of stunting his growth. He could of course have replied that to admit that language, besides its audible or visible symbols, has a meaning which an interpreter or teacher could convey, is to admit that perception is not the whole of knowledge. But this *coup de grâce*—the indispensability of mind and ratiocination in the acquisition of knowledge—is not to be administered until much later (184 b–86 d), to allow for further criticism of both Protagoras and the flux-theory.

(iii) *Memory* (163 d–64 b).[1] Knowledge, we say, is perception. Then

---

[1] Gulley (*PTK* 77) refers to this passage as evidence that in the claim of perception to be knowledge, perception is meant to include memory-images. This, surely, would reduce the

he who, for example,[1] sees something knows that thing as long as he sees it. Are we then to say that when he goes away or shuts his eyes, he necessarily forgets it, or alternatively that though he still remembers it clearly, he no longer knows it because he does not see it? Either alternative strikes Theaetetus as 'monstrous', and he admits that the limitation of knowledge to sensation apparently leads to impossible consequences.

(iv) *The 'knowing and not-knowing' dilemma* (165 b–d). This sounds final, and Socrates's next move is surprising. Without refuting the last argument, he declares that Protagoras would have put up a better fight for his theory. They have been quibbling like contentious Sophists, not true philosophers. He must try to come to the aid of the dead Protagoras. But far from defending the thesis that knowledge is perception (which he has all along said is included in Protagoras's), what he does first is to attack it once more by an ultra-sophistical argument. If you look at something with one eye closed, do you see (and therefore know) it or not? Answer yes or no—no nonsense about seeing with one eye but not with the other. Under such pressure Theaetetus agrees that the only possible answer makes his thesis self-contradictory. Many other questions might be asked, continues Socrates: for instance, can knowledge be keen or dim (like perception)? Then, throwing this argument aside, he goes straight on to ask how Protagoras would defend his position.

The argument is identical with some of those used by the fighting brothers in Plato's farcical exposure of eristic in the *Euthydemus*. It depends on demanding a simple answer in the terms of a question using an incomplete predicate or in some other way unanswerable without

argument to nonsense. Cornford (*PTK* 65) says S. breaks it off because to save the definition of knowledge as perception that term must be stretched to include memory (true enough), and 'there would be no objection to that'. For all P.'s variations on the scope of αἴσθησις, I think he would strongly object to calling memory a sensation or emotion (156b), or anything else but an act of the mind. In terms of the modern distinction between potential and actual remembering (for which see Broad, *Mind and its Place in Nature* 222, Shoemaker in *Ency. Phil.* v, 271), according to which one can say that a man remembers an event in his childhood even when he happens to be asleep or thinking of something else, P. seems to be considering memory-acts only, not memory-powers.

[1] Seeing is of course only one example of perception: P. could equally well have spoken of remembering a tune one has heard. (Cf. vol. iv, 508, n. 5). But in speaking of memory, as most often of knowledge in general, he has in mind acquaintance with an object or person rather than knowledge of a fact.

qualification.¹ It cannot have been meant seriously by Plato, who indeed emphasizes his irony by describing its proponent as 'an imperturbable gentleman', 'a targeteer serving for pay in the army of words'.² Why should he produce this succession of arguments which Socrates either drops abruptly or himself dismisses as contentious? Because, I suggest, though he enjoys playing with the indefensible thesis that all knowledge is provided directly by the senses, and takes Protagoras seriously enough to want to examine him from every point of view, there is for him only one unassailable refutation of these theories, which he is saving for the end: the need for ⌈mind, which can go beyond the senses to use its peculiar power of reason, drawing its own conclusions from the data which the senses present but cannot interpret. Only mind can fulfil the essential condition of knowledge by reaching the essence (*ousia*) and the truth of things (186 c–d); and when *ousia* and truth are contrasted by Plato with sense-perceptions, this can only mean that the sensible world is to be interpreted and understood in the light of the Forms.⌋

(v) *Back again to Protagoras: the defence* (165 e–68 c). Most of the defence is delivered by Socrates in direct speech, as from the mouth of Protagoras, with plenty of scolding of himself for unfair tactics.³ 'Protagoras' deals first with the last two arguments against identifying knowledge with sensation, and then at greater length upholds his own (historically genuine) views.

(*a*) To the argument from memory he replies that the memory of a past experience is something different in kind from the original experience. This would meet the question whether a man remembering something that he has seen nevertheless does not know it: he knows the memory-impression but not the object of his sensation.⁴ (It could also raise the unmentioned question, what is a memory-impression if it is distinct from a perception and all knowledge is perception?)

¹ Examples are the familiar Parmenidean 'Can a thing both be and not be?' at 293 c and 'Who learn, the wise or the ignorant?' (275 d). See also the summary of the *Euthyd.*, vol. IV, 268 ff., and 276 f.

² This character will ask an ἄφυκτον ἐρώτημα, reminding us of the boast of the brothers, πάντα...ἐρωτῶμεν ἄφυκτα (*Euthyd.* 276 e).

³ The dramatic and other significance of S.'s elaborate and entertaining impersonation of Protagoras has been vividly brought out in E. N. Lee's article, *Exegesis*, 225–61.

⁴ For a recent discussion of this argument see E. N. Lee, *l.c.* 235.

(*b*) The question whether someone can know and not know the same thing is meaningless, for in a world where both subject and object of perception are continually changing, one cannot speak of the *same* person or the *same* thing at all. Socrates might have added here what he says later (184d), that this theory treats a man as a collection of separate sense-organs, with no *psyche* (mind or personality) to unite them. On that hypothesis it could be legitimate to say that one eye sees and knows, the other not, but *psyche* is not to be mentioned yet.

(*c*) 'Protagoras' now returns to his own 'man-the-measure' statement (which clearly does *not* involve confining knowledge to perception),[1] and Socrates's 'vulgar and unscientific' objection that it would preclude any man from being wiser than another, or even than a beast. None can dispute that my beliefs are *true* for me, but it may be *better* for me that other things should both appear and be to me true. Just as the doctor with medicines alters a patient physically to give him pleasant sensations instead of painful (his indubitably sour wine appears and so becomes for him sweet again), so a Sophist can with persuasive words change a man mentally so that he has thoughts which, though not truer than formerly, are more profitable. Even the customs and laws of a state are always right and proper for it so long as it thinks them so, yet may in practical terms be harmful, and a statesman (or Sophist in his political capacity) can work on it by his oratory until useful and valuable practices both appear and are so for it. The test of truth or falsehood is replaced by the pragmatic one of future benefit or harm.[2]

(vi) *Protagoras continued: criticism of the defence* (170a–72b). (*a*) Everyone except Protagoras thinks false beliefs possible.[3] By his own doctrine he must concede that their belief is true for them, and it is therefore more false than true by as much as the rest of mankind outnumber his single self.

This argument is perhaps not very serious, but at least it is not, as one might suspect at first sight, contradicted by Socrates's insistence elsewhere that truth is not to be decided by a counting of heads, and that for his own part if he were convinced that something was true the fact

[1] Cf. vol. III, 186 n. 2.

[2] For a full account and discussion of this curious doctrine see vol. III, 171–5, 267f.

[3] Here S. frankly carries Prot.'s doctrine beyond the field of sensation, using the words δοξάζειν, κρίνειν, οἴεσθαι (170d).

that no one else believed it would leave him unmoved.[1] He would simply say that the others were wrong, but Protagoras cannot do so, and as a preliminary dig it is well enough to say that according to him there must be x-thousandfold more truth in the denial of his doctrine than in its assertion.

(*b*) Protagoras refutes himself. When he admits the truth of his opponents' contrary belief he is himself agreeing that his own is false, i.e. it is untrue that any man, however ignorant, is the measure of truth (171 a–c). This refutation was neatly summed up by Sextus, who attributes it also to Democritus (*Math.* 7.389): 'If everything that appears is true, the belief that *not* everything that appears is true, being based on what appears, will itself be true, and so the belief that everything that appears is true will become false.'

The simple syllogism: 'Every belief is true; some men believe that not all beliefs are true; therefore some beliefs are false' sounds cogent, and strongly suggests that the dictum of Protagoras, like the paradox of the Liar (vol. III, 499), involves a vicious circle. In the past, commentators have either passed over Socrates's argument in silence (e.g. Campbell) or called it fair (Cornford). Lately, however,[2] attention has been drawn to the fact that Socrates has omitted the qualification hitherto scrupulously inserted, that the contrary belief of others is only true *for them*. Could not Protagoras reply that his doctrine remains true for him, though false for others? Against this it is said that the belief of others is not, like his own, that the doctrine is false *for them*, but that it is absolutely, or objectively, false, and this therefore is what he is acknowledging to be true.[3] Most recently E. N. Lee has maintained that it is still open to him to say: 'Certainly it is true for me that it is true for them that my view is simply false; but that is because they cling to the old vocabulary of objective falsehood which I have shown to be inadmissible. If I say their view is true for them, I am not committed to saying that it is true for me.'[4] On the other hand, while rescuing him

---

[1] *Gorg.* 471 eff., *H. Maj.* 298 b.

[2] See Runciman, *PLE* 16 and Vlastos, introd. to *Prot.*, xiv n. 27.

[3] The question whether Prot.'s dictum can account for second-order judgements (judgements of the truth or falsehood of other judgements) has been discussed by Tigner in *Mnem.* 1971, whose view is disputed by E. N. Lee, *Exegesis* 242–8.

[4] I am not quoting Lee verbatim.

from the toils of Socrates, Lee concludes that his immunity from refutation is bought at the price of showing that he is not really saying anything serious that can be significantly discussed or denied.[1]

(c) Grant that the doctrine is true in the field of sensation: each man is sole judge of what appears to him sweet, cold, hot etc. But even our defence of it showed that, in the matter of what is expedient because it will bring future benefits, one adviser *is* better than another *in respect of truth* (172a8). As a judge of what will be healthy for him, 'knowing within himself the healthy',[2] one man will not be as good as another, nor one state in judging what actions will benefit it, even admitting that what it lays down as just or unjust, holy or unholy, *is* so for it. As for such moral and religious concepts, 'men do assert' that these have no real, fixed nature, but are only a matter of agreement. This line is taken by those who do not accept Protagoras's theory completely.

The above is a paraphrase of 171d8–72b7. Unfortunately there is disagreement about the last sentence. First, the subject is changed from 'the argument' (*logos, sc.* of the defence) to an unnamed 'they', which some think only a stylistic variation, others a different reference,[3] and secondly there is doubt about those who 'do not accept Protagoras's theory completely'. On the evidence about the Sophists presented in vol. III, I believe that what Plato has in mind is this. The view that 'things just and unjust, holy and unholy' have no nature or essence (*physis* or *ousia* 174b4) of their own but are only matters of convention (*nomos*) or agreement was shared by Protagoras with the other Sophists; but whereas he argued that, on grounds of simple expediency, established laws and customs ought to be upheld, many of them saw in the merely conventional basis of law and current morality a reason for a man to flout them whenever it suited him.[4]

[1] *L.c.* 248. Cf. earlier Runciman, *PLE* 16: 'He can, in fact, only advance [his belief] at the cost of any standard by reference to which it could be demonstrated.'

[2] Another instance of a current expression which may be taken as implying the full theory of Forms or not, according to choice. Cf. vol. IV, 222f.

[3] Contrast Cornford, *PTK* 81 n. 1, with Hackforth, *Mnem.* 1957, 132f.

[4] See vol. III, esp. pp. 146, 268. It will be seen that I do not agree with Cornford (*PTK* 82) that in Prot.'s belief sensations, still less moral concepts, existed 'by nature'.

At this point the argument is interrupted by the famous Digression contrasting the life of the philosopher with that of the lawyer and man of affairs. Though Plato is unlikely to have placed it there without good reason,[1] it may be simpler to finish the discussion of Protagoras first.

(vii) *Final refutation of Protagoras* (177c–79b). For this Socrates has only to elaborate a point already made. The theory that perceptions and experiences are unchallengeably real and true for the experiencing subject may well be valid for the present and past, but it fails the test of prediction. Judgements of expediency concern the *future* effect of present behaviour, as to which there is no disputing that one man knows better than others what *will* appear and be to them. This applies to experts in many arts—doctors, vintners, musicians, cooks, legislators—and Protagoras himself earned large fees in the sincere belief that he knew better than others what would appear and be to them in the future.

This leaves the flux-philosophers, who since they confine their belief in the infallibility of sensations to the present, are not touched by this argument. Before finishing with them, we may turn to the Digression.

Digression: the philosopher and the practical man (172c–77c)

Summary. The pretext for this is slight, simply a remark by Theodorus that if the arguments look like multiplying and getting more formidable, after all they have plenty of time. This prompts Socrates to reflect how natural it is that those who spend much time in philosophy should cut ridiculous figures when they appear and speak in a court, and we are back at the *Gorgias* and the reproach levelled at Socrates by Callicles. Plato never tires of insisting that it is in fact a mark of Socrates's superiority. The truth is, he continues, that compared with those bred up in the law-courts philosophers are as free men to slaves, having leisure[2] to pursue any subject they like for as long as they like, with the sole aim of reaching the truth. The lawyer by contrast is tied to a topic

---

[1] On the Digression as taking up on a higher, more universal level the theme of the criticisms of Prot., see Lee, *l.c.* 238–41, 354f.

[2] *Scholē*, 'leisure'. But as used by P. and Aristotle the Greek word acquires much richer associations and names a typically Greek ideal, more like our 'culture'. It is not accidental that it has given birth to 'school' and 'scholar'. Its value and its association with philosophy and learning are especially emphasized by Aristotle. When he says that happiness lies in *scholē* (*EN* 1177b4, *Pol.* 1338a1) he does not mean idleness. Nature herself prompts us to use leisure rightly,

imposed by a watchful opponent and to a strict time-limit. He must learn the arts of flattery and deceit, clever in his own estimate but in reality twisted and stunted in mind.

The complementary description of the philosopher suggests a Platonic rather than a Socratic ideal. He is a stranger not only to the law-courts and Council but to the market place and dinner-parties. Only his body is in the city, while his mind is abroad seeking the true nature of all that exists. His interest is not in the doings of men around him, but in what man is, and how distinguished from other beings. Since birth, wealth, rank and power mean nothing to him, he appears both arrogant and in practical affairs helpless and ignorant. The position is reversed if the man of affairs can be persuaded to abandon personal questions of who has injured whom for the question of 'justice and injustice in themselves, what they are', and instead of calling rich men and kings happy, consider the whole nature of kingship and human happiness. Then it is he who will make a fool of himself.

Theodorus comments that if everyone believed this there would be fewer evils in the world, but Socrates replies that evils can neither vanish ('there must always be something contrary to good')[1] nor have any place in the divine sphere, so they haunt this world 'of necessity'. Hence one should make all speed to fly from here to there. This is done by becoming as like as possible to God, the perfection of righteousness, making oneself 'just and holy with wisdom' (or knowledge, φρόνησις). To understand this is true wisdom and excellence (*aretē*), as opposed to the world's conception of them. Those who aim not at *being* but at *seeming* wise in the eyes of the world, whether in a profession or craft or in politics, are low and vulgar.[2] Their penalty is inescapable. Of 'two

---

not squandering it in play. *Scholē* is the whole basis of life, the goal of all business, and carries its own happiness and pleasure within it. In eulogizing it in the *Ethics* as an end in itself, he like P. calls the life of the politician 'leisureless'. If states do not know how to live at peace, their lawgivers are to blame for not having educated them in the life of *scholē* (*Pol.* 1334a9). At *Pol.* 1323b39 'a different *scholē*' means a different branch of learning, and at 1313b3 *scholai* in pl. are the bane of a tyrant ('societies for cultural purposes' Barker).

[1] This is not explained. At *Lys.* 221b–c S. says (though how seriously seems doubtful) that if evil disappeared, good would lose its value. Or P. may have in mind the thought at *Pho.* 97d that knowledge of the best involves knowledge of the worse. Similarly at *Ep.* 7, 344a–b, virtue and vice must be learned of together. (Cf. Arist.'s oft repeated principle τῶν ἐναντίων ἡ αὐτή ἐπιστήμη.)

[2] The politician whose wisdom is counterfeit is φορτικός and the technician βάναυσος. The latter word commonly expressed an aristocratic contempt of handicrafts. Here P. seems to be

patterns established in reality itself', one of divine beatitude and one of godless wretchedness, their unrighteous lives assimilate them to the latter, and shut them out for ever from the place where no evil can come. Their penalty is to live for ever on earth lives such as they live now, in the company of others as bad as they. All this they will dismiss as foolishness, though when any of them have the courage to stand up to questions and examination, in the end they feel dissatisfied with their own arguments and are silenced.

The lesson of the Digression. This is plain. The attempts to define knowledge in the main part of the dialogue are carried out by every means short of the doctrine of Forms, and end in failure. The digression assures us that the teaching of *Phaedo* and *Republic*, *Symposium* and *Phaedrus* has not been abandoned, and that a successful search for the nature of knowledge lies beyond Plato's self-imposed limitations here. The whole spirit of the Digression sets it apart from the rest, as do many details within it. Like the *Gorgias*, it not only contrasts the characters of the philosopher and the man of affairs but speaks of another world in which both get their deserts, as in *Phaedo*, *Republic* and *Phaedrus*. The practical helplessness of the philosopher and the reasons for it were enlarged on at *Rep.* 487 b ff., and his neglect of the trivial and passing affairs of men to concentrate on universal questions of the being and nature of things recalls 500 b–c, where the objects of his contemplation are described as 'fixed and immutable realities, existing according to order and reason', by familiarity with which he becomes, as here at 176 b (and at *Phdr.* 253 a, *Tim.* 90 c; cf. *Pho.* 82 b–c), 'like the divine so far as a man can'. That there is no unrighteousness in a god was stated in the condemnation of traditional mythology in *Rep.* 2 (379 b–c). The contrast between popular *aretē* and *aretē* 'with wisdom (*phronesis*)' was drawn at *Phaedo* 69 a–c (where the popular kind is also called 'slavish'). That the righteous man is happy, and the unrighteous wretched, in *this* life is asserted at *Rep.* 354 a. The most striking use of the language of the middle dialogues is the mention of 'patterns fixed in reality' at

saying that whether an art is banausic depends on whether it is pursued in the awareness of a higher good, a possibility which he does not rule out. (Cornford's loose translation here gives a false impression.)

176e3, and reincarnation is clearly implied at 177a. As a final small point, the politician who submits to the Socratic elenchus, and ends by being dissatisfied with his own statements, so that his rhetoric fades away and he seems a mere child (177b), though veiled in a discreet plural, is surely *par excellence* the Alcibiades of *Symp.* 215e–16a1.

A critic might claim that for all their echoes of the middle dialogues, not all these passages, taken singly, necessarily imply the full Platonic theory of Forms. But some do, and I have quoted them all to emphasize how the other-wordly, religious spirit of the Digression transports us momentarily away from the prevailing analytical tenor of the *Theaetetus* to regions from which it is unthinkable that the Forms should be absent. The Forms, we may conclude, remain for Plato a datum, almost an article of faith, but he is now much concerned with problems of their mode of existence and their relations both with each other and with the sensible world, which had not occurred to him in the magnificently confident mood of his middle period. These new problems necessitate leaving them aside at times to examine other possibilities.

Excursus: Evil and its sources[1]

Evils, says Plato here (176a), can never be abolished, nor have they any place in the divine world. It may be a good moment to consider what we have so far learned of his ideas about the nature and sources of evil, with perhaps a forward glance at what is still to come, bearing in mind that we can only pick up references to it scattered here and there through the dialogues. He nowhere draws the threads together in a systematic account, and it cannot be assumed from the start that he had a final solution of this intractable problem or that his views on it remained consistent. Some see him as gradually shifting the responsibility from body or matter to soul, others have detected two irreconcilable concepts of evil existing side by side in his system, or declared that the problem never seriously concerned him at all.[2]

---

[1] Only the dialogues are considered here. On *Ep.* 7, 344a–b, and its possible connexion with the 'unwritten doctrine', see Krämer, *Idee u. Zahl* 119. For the dialogues see also the full treatment by Hager, *Die Vernunft und das Problem des Bösen*.

[2] For a summary of views and references for the debate see Cherniss in *Plato* II, ed. Vlastos, 244 n. 1, and bibliography on p. 258. His article is largely concerned with *Tim.* and *Laws*, and argues strongly in favour of a consistent account based on P.'s analysis of the phenomenal world as a moving reflection in space of immutable, non-spatial reality.

(i) *Evil as a negative conception.* The *Republic* (379 b–c) confirms that evil is prevalent in human affairs and cannot be attributed to God. 'Some other explanation must be sought.' The first thought that occurs is that nothing in the phenomenal world can be perfect because it contains only imitations of the Forms, and the mutable cannot attain the perfection of its eternal models. Evil appears thus as something negative, a shortfall from perfection and, since only the Forms are fully existent, from complete reality. The description of the Form of Good in *Rep.* 6 explains the inseparability of being and goodness, of both of which it is the cause.[1] This however does not give evil a wholly negative character, as I pointed out earlier (vol. IV, 508 n. 1). Things in the physical world, though short of perfection, have their functions and therefore their own excellence (*aretē*), the absence of which can be an active power for harm. In Plato's example of a pruning-knife (*Rep.* 353 e), lack of its proper excellence—sharpness—is a positive evil which can harm the vine.[2] Similarly man's moral evil, though a powerful force for wrong, results simply from a lack, for Plato never gave up the Socratic tenet that its source is ignorance and it is therefore involuntary. (It is repeated in the *Laws*, 731 c, 860 d–61 d.)

(ii) *Evil due to body or soul?*[3] Evil (*kakon*) for Plato exists both in humanity and in nature as a whole, and covers physical as well as moral

[1] *Pace* Cherniss (*l.c.* 253 n. 34), P. does say at 509 b 6–8 that the Form of Good is responsible for the existence and nature (τὸ εἶναί τε καὶ τὴν οὐσίαν) of the objects of knowledge (*sc.* the other Forms). His citation of 517 c 3–5 against it ignores the fact that ἀλήθεια can (and in this context obviously does) mean reality rather than truth (p. 69 above).

[2] The identification of lack of goodness with its direct opposite, badness, at *Rep.* 353 c may be instructively compared with its heir, the Aristotelian conception of 'privation' or lack of form (στέρησις) which though called 'what essentially is not' (*Phys.* 191 b 15), at the same time 'is in a way form' (193 b 19) and 'works harm' (192 a 15). In the first quotation 'is not' does not refer to existence but means 'essentially is not *x*': coldness being essentially (καθ' αὐτό) not hot can never become hot, but a cold particular may. Aristotle maintained the distinction between 'opposites' and concrete things which 'possess' the opposites no less than P. when he wrote *Pho.* 103 b–c.

[3] I do not think we should look for P.'s mature convictions about the relation between body and soul at *Charm.* 156 c. There S., to make the purely Socratic point that 'care for the soul' is more important than care for the body, quotes an imaginary Thracian sage, from whom he claims to have obtained a herb which will cure Charm.'s headache, as saying that 'all good and evil in the body and in the whole man spring from the soul'. P.'s touch here is light, and his point is simply to draw the familiar analogy between health and moral education. (Cf. vol. IV, 164.) The *Charm.* is a relatively early dialogue, and contains no trace of the developed doctrine of Forms. Nevertheless it is not inconsistent with the conclusion suggested here. Without soul, the body would be a lifeless lump, incapable of action of any kind.

defects, in sentient beings such phenomena as disease and pain, in inanimate objects lack of the power to function well (cf. the pruning-knife), and in the cosmos as a whole irregular motions leading to confusion and disarray. On the cosmic scale it is considered mainly in the later dialogues. The *Phaedo* teaches that men may commit sins but only because the soul is corrupted and made to forget the Forms by its association with the body, which is itself evil (66b–e *et al.*). In its discarnate purity, face to face with the Forms, soul is perfectly good. The effect of physical condition on moral disposition is graphically described in the *Timaeus* (86b ff.). The *Republic* develops the picture with the notion of internal conflict between three impulses in the incarnate soul, and in the *Sophist* (227e–28e) Plato posits two types of psychic evil, conflict and ignorance, which he compares to disease and deformity in the body. The latter call respectively for medicine and gymnastic, to which correspond, for the soul, punishment and instruction.[1]

So much for moral evil in the human sphere. The whole cosmos, though designed by divine reason on the model of the Forms and therefore as good as it can be, has the faults inseparable from physical realization in space. (So the *Timaeus*.) The myth in the *Politicus* (269c ff.) explains that, though it is the best and most regular of all living things, and therefore endowed with the most nearly perfect of motions, circular revolution in the same place, yet because it has a body its motion cannot continue the same for ever. When therefore it has revolved for aeons in one direction under the hand of God, he withdraws his control and it reverses its movement, following its own innate impulse as a living creature. Two possibilities are explicitly denied: that God could move it in opposite directions is not meet (θέμις) nor can the alternation be due to 'two gods of opposed minds'. When under its own control, it gradually forgets[2] its creator's teaching

---

[1] In the *Laws* (860c ff., pp. 376 ff. below) P. argues that the need for punishment does not invalidate the proposition that all wickedness is involuntary and due to ignorance. The seeming distinction between voluntary and involuntary wrongdoing must be explained in some other way (861 c–d). Even here he is careful to say that of the two kinds of badness one *is called by the many* wickedness while *they call* the other ignorance.

[2] λήθης ἐγγιγνομένης 273 c. Cherniss (*l.c.* 27) observes that in general it is forgetfulness of the Forms which causes a soul to do evil. One may perhaps recall that in the myth of *Rep.* 10 the souls make their choice of lives (in which some do badly) *before* drinking the water of forgetful-

'owing to the bodily element in its composition' (273b), and all sorts of evils spring up and threaten to destroy it, until God, to prevent this, takes control once more. Thus on the cosmic scale too Plato attributes evil and destructive influences to the body.

It is in his last work, the *Laws*, that his position seems to have changed. His purpose in bk 10 is to combat the lack of moral standards resulting from a current form of materialism and atheism which saw the whole world as a product of chance. Nature is inanimate and purposeless, gods are human inventions, law and morality artificial and unstable, and the best course is to get all you can at others' expense, by force if necessary —the familiar farrago which he has so often attacked before. Here however his attack culminates in a foretaste of the astral theology developed, whether by Plato or another, in the *Epinomis*. All that concerns us now is that he starts from the affirmation of the *Phaedrus* that *psyche*, soul or life, as the only thing capable of spontaneous motion, is the ultimate cause of *all* motion or action everywhere. As such it is the cause of 'all contraries, good and evil, just and unjust, fair and foul' (896d), and there must be at least two souls concerned, one working good, the other evil. (This is stated without argument, but follows from the fact that, as he will mention shortly, the souls of the astral gods are wholly good.) But the good and intelligent type is in supreme control, for the primary cosmic movements which govern all the rest, namely circular revolution, are the physical manifestation of intelligence (897c).

There is here no Zoroastrian or Manichean dualism of God and Devil.[1] Plato speaks of 'kind of soul' (ψυχῆς γένος 897b) interchangeably with 'soul', and thinks of the heavenly bodies as living creatures each with its own soul like earthly animals.[2] The denial of two opposed gods in the *Politicus* is not contradicted. Whether or not Plato has renounced his previous view that evil is due to the body, or matter, is a difficult question which I cannot claim to have decided. Cherniss's

ness. But (apart from the dangers of looking for allegory in every detail of a Platonic myth) the souls in question have all had a previous incarnation and are not fully purified. The effect of their former life still clouds their judgement. (Cf. vol. IV, 558f.)

[1] Cf. p. 365 below and Koster, *Mythe de P.* etc. 36f.

[2] 'Soul' is a generic or collective term as well as a singular one, and since Greek lacks an indefinite article P. was not obliged to mark the difference.

solution is the outcome of deep thought and a comprehensive survey of the evidence. He concludes that evil for Plato is of two kinds, negative and positive. Negative evil is of course the necessary consequence of the falling-off of the physical world from the perfect reality of the Forms. Positive evil is caused directly by soul acting intentionally but in ignorance, and indirectly by the unintended effect of the good motions which it imparts, and which accidentally, by the necessity inherent in physical bodies, act on other physical phenomena. Why soul should ever lapse into error and ignorance of the Forms is a question to which Plato cannot be expected to give an answer.[1]

I should be the last to claim that the 'problem of evil' can be solved in other than mythical language.[2] But is it too 'unitarian' a view of Plato to suppose that, in the *Laws* as in the earlier works, soul only works evil when corrupted by the body? The *Laws* agrees with the *Theaetetus* (and the myth of the *Phaedrus*) that there can be no evil among the gods. The gods there are sun, moon and stars, and their souls are perfectly good (899b). Though soul is the cause of all good and evil, the statement that only good soul is in complete control, and the description of the souls of the astral deities, show that it can only work evil in the sublunary world; that is, the world of transient, physical phenomena, where the infection of the corporeal brings on forgetfulness and tempts it to act wrongly.[3] When Plato says that at least two kinds of soul must be at work in the management of the *ouranos*, he adds at once that this includes earth and sea. It is in applying its psychical characteristics to the secondary motions of material substances—processes like growth and decay, mixture and separation, heating and cooling, qualities like hardness and softness—that soul may exhibit folly as well as wisdom and produce ill as well as good. It remains the moving force in everything, but the direction of the motion,

---

[1] See Cherniss's important article cited on p. 92 n. 2. It should be read in full.

[2] Cf. my essay on the soul in P., *Entretiens Hardt* vol. III, 14f.

[3] So *Tht.* 176a7–8, τόνδε τὸν τόπον. The 'visible gods' (*Tim.* 41a, *Epin.* 985d) too have bodies, but of a substance not subject to destruction (they are everlasting, *Tim.* 40b) or to any irregularity of motion. They move (P. believed) in perfect circles, the only motion that can continue indefinitely, and the analogy in the visible world to pure intelligence in the psychical; therefore they (that is, their souls) can be entirely rational. The *Tim.* explains all this at greater length. Cf. also *Epin.* 982c.

whether to good or bad ends, depends on how far it resists the corrupting influences of the body.[1]

(iii) *Are there Platonic Forms of evils?* This much-debated question is even less susceptible of an answer than the last. The dialogues are not systematic treatises, and there are limits to the extent to which they can legitimately be synthesized. But two things can be said at once: first, the question was of no great interest to Plato; second, at no period did he allow a place for evil of any kind in the realm of the divine, which was the home of the eternal, changeless Forms.

Plato disliked technical precision in the use of words (*Tht.* 184c) and even his key terms can be multivocal. In the unlikely event of a modern philosopher promulgating the Platonic doctrine, he would undoubtedly take pains, by using a different word or symbol, to distinguish the technical sense of Forms from that in which the non-philosopher naturally says 'There are many forms of evil.' Plato's thought may have been itself affected by the homonymity. At any rate he used the word *eidos* in both senses,[2] and it is not always easy to know which is intended. For instance, at *Rep.* 402b–c he says that an educated man must be able to recognize the *eidē* of self-control, courage, liberality and high-mindedness and their kindred, *and also their opposites*, as they go about everywhere,[3] and perceive both them and representations of them . . . believing them to belong to the same science. Although the Forms are prominent in later books, this need not refer to anything more than the 'dividing according to kinds' already attributed to Socrates, and several considerations suggest that the transcendent Forms are not in his mind here.[4] (*a*) He is describing the primary education of the *whole*

---

[1] For different views see Solmsen, *P.'s Theol.* 141f., Grube, *P.'s Th.* 146f. and the reff. they supply. That the bad type of soul is not (as G. thinks) confined to human souls should be obvious. Cf. also Dodds in *JHS* 1945, 21.

[2] Examples (among many) of εἶδος as sort or kind are: *Phaedo* 100b τῆς αἰτίας τὸ εἶδος; *Rep.* 434b (τὸ τοῦ πολεμικοῦ εἶδος), 440d–41a; 441c εἶδος used synonymously with γένος (see Adam on 435b); *Laws* 963c ἀρετῆς εἴδη. A good example of the ambiguity of the term is *Phdr.* 249b, where συνιέναι κατ' εἶδος λεγόμενον describes a purely logical process, yet to be capable of it a mind must have seen the Forms, and the phrase may mean either (as the continuation suggests) 'spoken of in generic terms' or 'called after a Form'. (Absence of τι makes the former more probable.)

[3] πανταχοῦ περιφερόμενα, not quite the terms in which P. would describe the behaviour of his Forms.

[4] Many scholars, from Zeller (II.1, 560 n.) onwards, have assumed that they are, e.g. in recent times Grube, *P.'s Th.* 21, and Cornford in his translation.

guardian class, if not, as many think, the whole citizen body. (Cf. vol. IV, 455–7.) Yet only a select few, after fifteen years of adult education, will advance to recognition of the Forms. (*b*) 'Representations' or 'images' (εἰκόνες) of *eidē* might suggest instances of courage etc. in action, which with physical phenomena are so often called copies of Forms, but as Adam saw (*ad loc.*) Plato's subject here is education in poetry and art and the reference must be to narrative or graphic representations inspiring emulation of virtuous action or visible beauty. Such representations do not copy the Forms themselves, but only their earthly manifestations.[1] (*c*) Even if the *eidē* were Forms, Plato need not have been thinking of their opposites as Forms, rather than simply the lack of a Form.[2]

Rep. 475 e–76a is more difficult. There ugliness, injustice and evil are called *eidē* along with beauty, justice and goodness. It would of course make sense to translate *eidē* as qualities or even concepts. Thus (to paraphrase): 'Beauty and ugliness are single concepts opposed to one another, and so are justice and injustice, good and evil. Every concept is single, yet they are associated with innumerable particular things and actions, as well as, in some cases, with each other. The philosopher is one who does not merely perceive the particulars but grasps the concepts.' The rest of the book, however, leaves little doubt that *eidē* here are Plato's independently existing Forms.[3] On the other hand, in the ensuing comparison between the lover of sights and sounds and the philosopher the *eidē* of ugliness and evil are simply ignored, though there are places (like 479a) where mention of them would be quite appropriate.[4] As to *Tht.* 176e, the expression 'patterns established in reality' (ἐν τῷ ὄντι ἑστῶτα) of godly happiness and ungodly misery seems to me to recall so strongly the language of Forms that Plato must

---

[1] This passage has been more fully discussed in its proper place, vol. IV, 545 ff.

[2] So Rist, *Phoenix* 967, 291.

[3] It is hard, as Rist (*l.c.* 291) has said, to see how a Form of Evil or Injustice by itself could exist at all, since the Form of the Good is cause of the existence of the objects of knowledge (Forms), so that in so far as they exist they must be good. (Cf. p. 93 above.) Yet it is equally hard to agree with him that we have here too nothing but a '"lack" of the Form of Good'.

[4] It is tempting to add that when beautiful particulars are said also to seem ugly, this is attributed to the fact that they are 'between being and not being', which might support the idea that evil and its kin are nothing positive but only a lack of goodness. But does this apply to one member of a pair like greatness and smallness, weight and lightness, cited as parallels to goodness and badness, justice and injustice? One hesitates, for fear of falling into S.'s 'pit of nonsense'.

at least be seeing both for the moment as absolute and changeless; but *paradeigmata* are not always heavenly like the Form of the State (*Rep.* 596b),[1] and Rist (*l.c.* 290f.) would confine 'reality' here to this world, on the ground that the man who models himself on the bad and godless pattern will be condemned to this world and never enter the divine one, which is 'a place pure of evil'. That, we must agree, is the 'place above the heavens' where the *Phaedrus* locates the Forms.

Again at *Rep.* 445 e Plato seems to slip from one of the related but not identical uses of *eidos* to the other, when he says that the Form of *aretē* is one, but those of evil are infinite in number. Virtue is a Form, and there are also Forms of the separate virtues. (In the *Laws*, 963 aff., he discusses the old question of the *Protagoras*, how it can be right to call Virtue one and four at the same time.) But he would hardly posit a Form of something that has an infinity of forms or varieties. Forms are above all knowable, and the infinite is unknowable.

There are two main reasons why it may have seemed logically necessary to Plato (when he remembered, and when he did remember he appears to have momentarily forgotten some of the most important aspects of his doctrine of Forms) to include evil among the Forms. (*a*) Forms, apart from their independent existence as steadfast goals of becoming, undoubtedly retained the functions of the universals, or common natures, which they originally (i.e. with Socrates) were. There is an *eidos* for every group of particulars which have the same name, because (as Socrates insisted) to use a single name is to assume a common nature (*eidos*) among the things it names, which in Platonic terms means that they share in the being of a single Form.[2] (*b*) Secondly, Plato shared the general Greek tendency to see the world in terms of opposites. This polarizing habit was common to the early Ionians, Heraclitus, Parmenides, Empedocles, Anaxagoras and the Pythagoreans, whose 'table of opposites' (vol. I, 245) may have influenced Plato directly; and it still prevailed in Aristotle, for whom the term 'opposites' was a frequent alternative to 'forms', since for him forms normally occurred

---

[1] The word is of course a common one. In Plato himself, S. as 'wisest of men' was held up as a παράδειγμα by Apollo (*Apol.* 23b), and he gave Meno a παράδειγμα of a definition (*Meno* 77a); a παράδειγμα of bad and good oratorical technique appeared in the speeches of S. and Lysias in *Phdr.* (262d), and so on.

[2] See *Rep.* 596a and vol. IV, 550.

in pairs of contraries like hot and cold. Moreover to know a form was to know its opposite.[1]

To sum up, we are left in much uncertainty, because the dialogues never squarely face the question of the status of evil *vis-à-vis* the Forms. Hints that Forms of evil and ugliness exist occur only in passing and always in a context of opposites. Plato's attitude is that of his Socrates when asked whether there are Forms of mud, hair and dirt. To suppose there are seems absurd, yet he is sometimes tormented by the thought that what is true for one should be true for all ('Forms of every named group'). But at that point he runs away,[2] and reserves his energies for what is worth while, the Forms of moral and aesthetic values, *summa genera* like unity, motion, similarity and their opposites, mathematical concepts and natural species—whatever in his view has a positive place in a system teleologically organized—reminding himself that Forms exist in a timeless, divine region to which evil has no access. These were quite enough to provide him with problems, as the *Sophist* will show.[3]

Return to (1)

Final attack on the theory of total flux (179 b–83 c). Having allowed ourselves our own digression, we must return to the present argument. Protagoras failed the test of prediction, but it may yet be true that immediately present sense-experiences, and the beliefs or opinions (*doxai*) based on them (179 c 3–4), are infallible and constitute knowledge. This therefore, Socrates continues, they must examine further, not forgetting that there is a school of thought (the Eleatic) which holds, in diametrical opposition to the Heraclitean, that any form of movement or change is impossible.

[1] Cf. p. 90 n. 1 above.

[2] φεύγων οἴχομαι (*Parm.* 130d) is a very strong expression.

[3] Cherniss (*l.c.* 27, n. 34) lists a number of passages in which he sees Forms of positive vices. Some of these have been discussed here, others by Rist, *l.c.* 289–93. On *Euthyphro* 5 d I hope I have shown in my ch. on that dialogue that the doctrine of transcendent Forms had not yet taken shape in P.'s mind. *Parm.* 130c5–e4 does not mention Forms of bad things but only of trivia, 'things undignified and worthless' (though hair and clay are useful enough, and certainly do no harm). I do not see Platonic Forms at *Soph.* 251a or *Laws* 964c. Bodily diseases—indeed, as we know, the body as such—can affect the soul (*Tim.* 86b ff.) and impede its thinking (*Phaedo* 66c1), but are not necessarily an evil (*Rep.* 496b–c). In any case Forms of diseases are not mentioned at *Tim.* 87b–c, to which, with *Phaedo* 105 c, Cherniss refers us. (Tailpiece: Asclepiades reports Aristotle as saying in his *Platonic Discussions* that 'we (that is, the Platonists) say that there are no Forms of evils', *Arist. Frr.* ed. Ross p. 113.)

Those who assert that all is motion include in that term not only local motion but also alteration,[1] for they will not concede that reality is static in any respect. Everything is always changing in every way (cf. p. 79). But then sensation is no more sensation than not sensation, so if knowledge is sensation, it is no more knowledge than not knowledge. If sensation changed its content but kept its character as sensation, it would be in at least one respect unchanging, and so transgress the neo-Heraclitean law of flux.[2] In fact any answer to any question will be both correct and incorrect, and no existing language can express their thoughts. On the 'cleverer' theory of how sensation works it cannot be supposed to be knowledge.

To the surprise of the others, Socrates, who himself introduced the Eleatics into the conversation, is unwilling to discuss their views (183 d–84 b). His early meeting with Parmenides left him with such an impression of intellectual depth and nobility that he fears to misinterpret him. Besides, it could distract him from their main purpose, to discover the essence of knowledge by assisting Theaetetus to give birth to the thoughts with which he is in labour.

Final disproof of the identification of sensation with knowledge: the role of thought (184 b–86 e). A man is not a kind of Trojan horse in which the sense-organs lurk as individuals, the eye seeing, ear hearing and so forth. They all converge on one thing—call it the *psyche* or what you will—which employs them as instruments in making the man aware of perceptible objects. Each bodily organ conveys only its own kind of object—the eye colours, the ear sounds—yet we can *think* of the objects of several at once, e.g. of sound and colour that they exist, are different, are two and so on. Such concepts—being and non-being, similarity and difference, same and other (and, adds Theaetetus the mathematician, odd and even and numbers in general)—the *psyche* perceives not through any bodily organ but by itself. The same applies to aesthetic

---

[1] No English word covers the same ground as *kinesis*, translated 'motion'. It includes every sort of change as well as motion in space. Aristotle recognized four kinds: local motion (φορά), qualitative change (ἀλλοίωσις), change of size (αὔξησις καὶ φθίσις) and fourthly coming-to-be and perishing (γένεσις καὶ φθορά).

[2] 182 d 8–e 1. The hypothetical objection stated and met by Cornford (*PTK* 98 f.) seems to depend on the concept of 'moments' of a discrete, Zenonian kind, which the 'flowing philosophers' would not admit.

and moral qualities ('fair and foul, good and bad', 186a8). It is not by passively receiving what the senses convey, as any child or animal can, but by actively comparing and reasoning about them—which demands effort, education, maturity—that the *psyche* (mind) grasps reality and truth, without which no one can be said to know. Therefore sensation and knowledge cannot be the same thing.

This account of the mind reaching knowledge of the truth (*aletheia*) by reflecting on sense-experience might suggest at first sight an empirical theory of knowledge, but that is far from Plato's thoughts. The language of the passage illustrates once again the use of *alēthes* and *on* (with the nouns *alētheia* and *ousia*) as practically synonymous, to signify what exists or is real. (See p. 69 above.) 'Sensation cannot reach truth because it cannot reach Being' (186e4). 'Being' (*ousia*) is the key word in the argument. 'The *psyche* will perceive through touch the hardness of one thing and the softness of another, but their *being*[1] —what they both are—their contrariety and the *being of the contrariety* . . . it essays to judge for itself' (186b). The distinction between a sensible quality and its *ousia* was made in the *Cratylus* (423e, p. 47 above): sounds, colours and tactile qualities are always changing, and hence, in the language of the *Republic*, 'hover between what is and what is not'. What fully exists is their essence or Form.[2] Similarly a hard and a soft apple exhibit in this respect a contrariety, as the mind perceives by going beyond the immediate sensations and comparing them (ἐπανιοῦσα καὶ συμβάλλουσα 186b8), but the hard one may become soft and that instance of contrariety vanish, whereas Contrariety remains an unchanging reality knowable through further operations of the intellect alone. If there were no other evidence that Plato retained the full theory of Forms when he wrote the *Theaetetus*, the use of *ousia* in this passage, and especially the duality of 'the contrariety and the

[1] I.e. the being of hardness and softness (McDowell 191). 'Existence' Cornford, but in this context οὐσία must bear its other sense of 'true nature', and probably, as McDowell suggests, ὅτι ἔστον means 'what they are' or 'that they are [hardness and softness]', καί being equivalent to 'i.e.'

[2] On P.'s belief in 'degrees of reality' see vol. IV, 487ff. On the view taken here, P. does not, in Owen's sense (*SPM* 324 with n. 1), 'ascribe οὐσία to objects of perception': he says (as in *Crat.*) that besides audible sounds there is the οὐσία of sound, and so on, and that οὐσία is what the mind seeks without the aid of the senses (186a–b). Bluck in *JHS* 1957 (bottom of p. 182) makes the same confusion.

ousia of the contrariety', would suffice.[1] As in the *Phaedo*, the senses can start the mind on its way to knowledge of reality, but not only must there be a mind to go further 'on its own'; it can only do so because there are unchanging realities to be known. Ontology and epistemology remained inseparable for Plato, and the ontology of the *Theaetetus* is that of the *Republic*.

(2) *Knowledge as true judgement* (doxa)

Convinced that knowledge is 'not to be sought at all in perception' (187a), Theaetetus suggests that it is true *doxa*, provisionally described as the activity of the *psyche* when it investigates things without the aid of the senses. More precisely (189e–90a), thought is silent speech, a debate of the *psyche* with itself, and its final pronouncement is its *doxa* —opinion, belief or judgement.[2] In discussing its relation to knowledge, Plato is resuming a theme already familiar from the *Meno* and *Republic*.[3]

The main question is quickly, indeed cavalierly, disposed of (200d–201c) by an analogy from the law-courts illustrating precisely the same truth as the analogy of the road to Larissa in the *Meno*, namely that knowledge must be first-hand, something *seen* by the knower, not merely reported to him. By his choice of analogy Socrates also gets in yet another thrust at his *bêtes-noires*, the forensic orators, in substance a repetition of the *Gorgias*. In the short time allowed them, they cannot *instruct* the jurors about the facts of a case, but only *persuade* them to certain *doxai* about it.[4] What they persuade them of may be the truth, but only an eye-witness could *know* that it was so. In the *Meno* (97a–b) the comparison is between a man who knows the way to a place be-

---

[1] It is of course perfectly possible to conceive the duality as simply that between the particular instance of contrariety observed in the case of the hard and soft apples and the *concept* of contrariety abstracted from that and other instances by the mind. That indeed is how it would appear to everyone today, and no doubt some will think that is how it must have appeared to P. I can only state my firm belief that for this to have happened to the author of the 'middle dialogues', he would not only have had to undergo a credible change of mind; he would have become an entirely different person. Nor does οὐσία mean 'concept'. If this is 'unitarianism', I am a unitarian.

[2] Gulley (*PTK* 87) prefers 'belief', McDowell (*Tht.* 193) 'judgement'. Both have their reasons. On retaining *doxa* see vol. IV, 262.

[3] See vol. IV, 256f., 261–4, 489–93.

[4] The distinction between instruction and persuasion, one giving belief, the other knowledge, was made at *Gorg.* 454cff., the point about shortness of time at 455a.

cause he has been there before, and one who guesses it correctly. Both will get there, but one through knowledge, the other through true *doxa*; and the difference is of practical importance, for belief may be shaken, but knowledge never.

I have called the examples both of the wayfarer and of the witness analogies,[1] but some think them actual *instances* of knowledge as opposed to *doxa*, indicating a renunciation by Plato of his conviction that the object of knowledge cannot be any thing or event in the sensible world. Thus Stenzel wrote (*PMD* 71): 'The reason why . . . they [jurors] can have only right opinion is not that they have no knowledge of Justice itself (which, at an earlier time, would have been the reason given), but that they were not eye-witnesses of the crime. So that even in ethics the same entire change in Plato's view of knowledge is noticeable.' So too Hicken (*Phron.* 1958, 140) adduces the eye-witness as evidence that Plato has so far changed his position from the *Republic* as 'to bring the perceptible world within the range of knowledge'. For Robinson (*Essays* 41) this apparent denial of the *Republic*'s view is either a slip or an unnoticed implication on Plato's part. For A. Rorty (*Phron.* 1972, 228) the eye-witness example suggests that the objects of knowledge and *doxa* may be the same.[2] This last suggestion is not quite true. The witness's knowledge is of the crime itself, the juryman's *doxa* is of the witness's *mimesis* of that crime in words, a good analogy for the difference between the knowledge of a Form and of its *mimesis* in a sensible object or action.

There is a way of allowing that Plato spoke of knowledge (*epistēmē*) of the sensible world without implying any *volte face* on his part, namely by assuming that he sometimes used the word more generally, or in two senses. Thus Runciman (*PLE* 38): 'Eye-witness knowledge is not, of course, an instance of that highest and truest knowledge which . . . Plato distinguishes from phenomenal knowledge as in the *Parmenides*, *Phaedrus* and *Philebus*. But it is a perfectly good example of the knowledge which can be acquired . . . within the ontological frontiers of the empirical world.' And Rist (*Phoenix* 1967, 284) cites the road to Larissa

---

[1] For the former cf. vol. IV, 240 n. 3.

[2] Similarly Stoelzel, 11 n. 2: Right *doxa* is distinguished from knowledge 'nicht so sehr durch den Inhalt als vielmehr durch die Art der Entstehung'.

and the witnessed crime as in Plato's eyes legitimate examples of *epistēmē*. The strongest evidence for this is *Philebus* 61 d–e:

We agreed that one pleasure is more truly pleasure than another, and one art more exact than another. And knowledge differed from knowledge, one directed to the things that come to be and pass away, the other to those that do neither, but exist for ever, constant and unchanging. Examining them from the point of view of truth, we concluded that the latter was truer than the former.

Plato, then, in the later dialogues occasionally spoke of two kinds of *epistēmē* corresponding to what he also called *epistēmē* and *doxa*: one directed to unchanging reality, the other to unstable phenomena, and one 'truer' than the other. Here is no 'entire change of view' or abandonment of the Forms. Similarly the whole tenor of the *Theaetetus*, the manner in which the claims of sensation are dismissed, and the aporetic ending, point to the abiding necessity of the Forms if 'true' knowledge is to be attainable. It makes no essential difference whether we call the state of mind of the eye-witness and the experienced traveller analogous to knowledge or knowledge of an inferior grade,[1] but I believe Plato's meaning has been best expressed by Bluck (*Mind* 1963, 260):

Knowledge is to true belief as the state of mind of an eye-witness is to the state of mind of a juryman who is won over by persuasion. We are inevitably reminded of the road-to-Larisa illustration in the *Meno* . . . Both analogies suggest that some sort of personal acquaintance is the mark of knowledge;[2] and as applied to a priori knowledge, the *Meno* illustration certainly meant that knowledge involved γνῶσις [cognition] of τὰ ἐκεῖ [the things beyond]. It is natural to suppose that the *Theaetetus* analogy, as applied to such things as existence and likeness, ought to mean the same. Furthermore, the *Timaeus* tells us that if knowledge and true belief are different, then there are Forms, whereas if they are not different, sensible objects must constitute reality (51 d). Even if the *Timaeus* preceded the *Theaetetus*, it would seem natural, in the absence of clear evidence to the contrary, to take the present distinction as implying that knowledge is of Forms.

---

[1] It is extremely important with Plato to distinguish confusion or change of mind from his simple dislike of technical or pedantic language. Just as he occasionally uses ἐπιστήμη in the late dialogues for what he elsewhere calls δόξα, so he uses ὄντα for what, were a philosophical point involved, he would call γιγνόμενα, e.g. at 188e7ff. (For this, see p. 232 below.)

[2] On the language of direct vision as applied to the apprehension of Forms cf. vol. IV, 252, 392, 507, 511. The soul *has* been an eye-witness of them.

When at *Tim.* 51d3ff. (wrote Ross, *PTI* 124f.) Plato says that the existence of the Forms depends on the difference between knowledge and true judgement, he is relying on the argument here in the *Theaetetus*, 'in which he claims to establish just this difference'. This shows a better understanding of Plato than Stenzel's.

But is false judgement possible? (187d–200d).[1] The notion of true judgement implies a contrast with false, and before dismissing its claim Socrates initiates a long, complicated and fruitless digression[2] on the nature and possibility of false judgement, only to conclude that it was wrong[3] to consider it before settling what knowledge itself is. Earlier Plato had been content, like anyone else, to accept the existence of false beliefs as an obvious difference between knowledge and *doxa*. (Cf. *Gorg.* 454d.) Now, with his shift of interest towards logical and epistemological problems, he feels that the paradoxes of men like Protagoras, Antisthenes and Cratylus[4] are not to be so lightly brushed aside. The solution is only reached in the *Sophist* (pp. 154–6 below).

(i) *False judgement as mistaking one thing for another* (187e–88c). Here Socrates deliberately adopts the Sophistic starting-point by ignoring 'for the present' learning and forgetting as intermediates between knowledge and ignorance;[5] and the question itself treats knowledge as confined to acquaintance with a person or thing. On these premises false judgement is quickly rejected on the ground that one cannot mistake

---

[1] W. Detel has devoted a monograph to the subject of false judgement, or false statement, in *Tht.* and *Soph.*, which begins with a useful survey of over a score of recent interpretations and has a full bibliography (*Platons Beschreibung des falschen Satzes im Theätet und Sophistes, Hypomnemata* 36, Göttingen 1972). His own thesis is that, contrary to the usual view, Plato did not see himself as faced simply with the same difficulties as the Sophists and others who denied the possibility of false judgement, but rather with difficulties arising solely from his own theory of Forms and the way in which, in consequence of that theory, he himself used the verb 'to be'. Detel posits a sharp distinction in Plato's mind between the first three accounts of false judgement and the last two (the similes of wax tablet and aviary). The last two dispose successfully of the others, which *are* those of the Sophists and other predecessors, but prove unsatisfactory for different reasons. Their problems, arising out of the theory of Forms, are solved in the *Sophist*.

[2] Not such a digression from the main question of the nature of knowledge (McDowell 194).

[3] (200d) An error of judgement? But this second-order difficulty, or virtual *petitio principii*, is (rightly enough) ignored.

[4] For these see vol. III, 182, 207, 210f.

[5] (188a) The tactic on which the fighting brothers relied in *Euthyd.* See 275d–77c, 277e–78b. Learning and forgetting are restored to their place in introducing the simile of the mind as a wax tablet (191c).

one person for another whether one knows both or neither or one but not the other.

(ii) *False judgement as 'thinking what is not'* (188 c–89 b). This suggestion takes us back behind the Sophists to their Eleatic original.[1] It fails because it is impossible to think what is not, as Parmenides had said (frr. 2.7–8, 8.8–9). Plato however goes beyond Parmenides when he adds to 'think what is not' the words 'whether about any existing thing or absolutely' (lit. 'by itself'). Parmenides could not speak of non-being in relation to 'any of the existing things' (τῶν ὄντων του) because only a single Being existed, 'one, continuous . . . by itself' (fr. 8.6, 29). However, this is not necessarily (as Bondeson suggested)[2] an anticipation of the distinction to be drawn in the *Sophist* between the two senses of 'what is not', the existential and the merely differentiating —'does not exist' and 'is not *x*' (*sc.* what it was wrongly thought to be). The present distinction is more probably between thinking 'it is not' within the Parmenidean scheme of one unique Being (that 'wholly undiscoverable path', fr. 2.5 f.) and thinking of one of the many commonly accepted existing things that it 'is not' in the same sense (i.e. does not exist).[3] Anyway, by explicitly refusing to question the Eleatic thesis (183 d 10 ff.), Plato has made it clear that this indispensable means to an understanding of 'what is not' is to be reserved for the *Sophist*, where 'father Parmenides' will be cross-examined and the conclusion enforced that 'what is not in some respect is' (241 d).

The argument here rests on a simple analogy between sense-perception and judgement: if one sees, hears or feels something, there must *be* something which one sees, feels or hears. Similarly if one judges something there must be something that one judges. One cannot therefore judge 'what is not', for one's judgement would then have no object, one would judge nothing, and so not be making a judgement at all.[4] This therefore cannot be the explanation of false judgement.

---

[1] They used it too, of course (*Euthyd.* 283 a ff.), but S. does not draw the Sophists' conclusion (189 b 4).

[2] *Phron.* 1969, 117 f. B.'s is a most interesting and suggestive article, though one would have liked to know what he made of Bluck's '"Knowledge by Acquaintance" in P.'s *Tht.*' in *Mind* 1963.

[3] Cf. Stoelzel's rendering (p. 86): 'sei es als das Sein eines Gegenstandes oder als das **Sein** an sich'.

[4] Cf. the similar argument about speech at *Soph.* 237 d–e.

The persistence of the problem discussed here by Plato is brought home by R. M. Gale's article on propositions and judgements in the *Encyclopaedia of Philosophy*, VI, 494–505, which is largely concerned with theories about whether what a person thinks of must have some independent reality, and what is the object of a false judgement. Thus Moore wrote (see *ib*. p. 496): 'In order that a relation may hold between two things, both the two things must certainly be; and how then is it possible for anyone to believe in a thing which simply has no being? . . . I confess I do not see any clear solution of the difficulty.' According to Gale, the false analogy in the *Theaetetus* (he quotes 189a3–b2) has haunted most modern theories of judgements and propositions except the behaviouristic. He distinguishes two classes of verbs: *propositional* (such as 'judge', 'think', 'believe') and what he calls *cognitive* (such as 'know' and the verbs of sensation, 'see', 'hear', 'feel', 'taste', 'smell').[1] Cognitive acts require objects, but propositional acts do not. If one sees a cat on a mat, or knows that it is there, there must be a cat, but if one only thinks there is, there may be none; which means, on this view, that there may be no object of a propositional act.

(iii) *False judgement as 'other-judgement'*[2] (189b–90e). Perhaps false judgement occurs 'when someone exchanges one real thing for another in his mind, and says it is that other. In this way he will always think what *is*, but one thing instead of another, and since he misses his aim can rightly be said to judge falsely.' This might be thought similar enough to (i) to be ruled out by the same argument,[3] but on the contrary Theaetetus hails it enthusiastically, and gives an entirely different kind of example, namely qualities: when someone 'judges "ugly" instead of "beautiful"', then his judgement is 'truly false'.[4] Graciously waiving the oxymoron, Socrates does not interpret this in the obvious

---

[1] He does not mean that the objects of cognitive verbs cannot be propositional in form.

[2] P. apparently coined the word ἀλλοδοξία for 'misjudgement' on the analogy of ἀλλογνοεῖν, used by Hdt. (1.85) of failure to recognize a person; perhaps also with the Homeric ἀλλοφρονέω in mind; its secondary meaning—to be knocked senseless—would appeal to his sense of humour.

[3] Ackrill has tried to show that the two arguments are not identical (*Monist* 1966, 388 ff.). His second point of difference at least goes against Cornford and R. Robinson. See the latter's *Essays*, 64 f.

[4] Both S. and Tht. take for granted the objective character of aesthetic and moral values as things about which one may be simply mistaken, on a par with odd and even, two and one. This I take to be the ordinary commonsense view, unrelated to the theory of Forms, that 'there is such a thing as justice'. Cf. vol. IV, 115 f., 223.

sense of judging a beautiful (fine) individual or action to be ugly (shameful). Instead, having established that judgement is the final stage of a mind's converse with itself (p. 103 above), he asks if anyone, sane or mad, has ever said to himself that beauty is ugliness, odd numbers are even, ox must be horse or two one. 'Never', replies the bemused Theaetetus.

There is surely some sharp practice here, exploiting ambiguities which cannot easily be reproduced in English. 'The beautiful' (τὸ καλόν), as we well know, may mean either what is beautiful or the quality of beauty (whether in the commonly accepted sense or as a Platonic Form). Theaetetus clearly had the former in mind, but one must assume that Socrates intends his examples to stand, primarily at least, for concepts or universals, partly because he speaks of 'the ox' also with definite article (as when one says 'the ox is a patient animal'), but mainly because it is obvious that a man might mistake an ox for a horse in the dark or a schoolboy mistake 29 + 38 for 66, an odd number for an even. On Socrates's present interpretation, to make a false judgement as now defined one must consciously entertain the nonsensical statement 'An odd number is even' or oddness is evenness. The *Theaetetus*, though its lateness is scarcely in doubt, resembles the early dialogues in being deliberately aporetic and in consequence Socratic, in the sense that Socrates speaks in character and uses his own teasing arguments to avoid reaching a positive conclusion which nevertheless the reader can divine.[1] His object, as with young Charmides, is not to teach but, by his art of mental midwifery, to elicit and test his interlocutor's own ideas. The gain lies, not in finding the right answer, but in purging the mind from error and the false conceit of knowledge (210c). To attain this end he is not above misrepresenting a young man's meaning, as in his shocking distortion of 'to do one's own' in the *Charmides* (161b; see vol. IV, 267). He does not shirk the real question in the end. Having enjoyed his little mystification, he pursues the problem of 'other-judging' more seriously in the similes of the wax tablet and aviary, where mistaken identity and arithmetical errors are taken into account and the sophistic exclusion of memory and forgetfulness is abandoned. At that later stage Plato allows Theaetetus to distinguish

---

[1] The most striking case of this is the search for courage in *Laches* (vol. IV, 132f.).

carefully the two cases here confused: 'Seeing or touching 11 objects', he says, 'a man might think them 12, but he will never make that judgement about the 11 and 12 which he has in his mind' (195e).

(iv) *False judgement as the misfitting of a perception to a memory: the mind as a wax tablet* (191a–96c). One may certainly see a stranger at a distance and mistake him for Socrates whom one knows. This was impossible under the Sophistic limitation that one must either know or not know, and cannot both know and not know the same thing. That is now removed, having served the purpose of showing up the inadequacy of the Eleatic-Sophistic epistemology, and memory and forgetting are reinstated. Imagine the mind as a wax block, on which we stamp what we perceive or conceive,[1] like the devices on seal-rings. So long as these memory-impressions do not wear out we know what we have perceived or conceived. Socrates lists exhaustively the cases in which, on this supposition, false judgement is impossible.[2] The upshot is that both a present perception and a memory-imprint or concept must be involved, since false judgement consists in matching the perception to the wrong imprint. Seeing at a distance two men of similar height and build, both of whom one knows, one may, in fitting the perceptions to the memory-imprints, transpose them, like putting shoes on the wrong feet; or if one sees a stranger, wrongly match the sight to the imprint of an acquaintance. Socrates concludes by fancifully attributing disparity of intellectual gifts to variations of quality in the wax. Minds too soft learn easily but forget quickly, and hard wax, taking shallow impressions, also causes poor memory. Blurred imprints may result from softness, from adulteration, or from overlapping in a 'small mind'. The best minds have large and deep tablets of smooth, well-kneaded wax, taking clear, lasting and well separated impressions. Such minds learn quickly, are retentive, and make true judgements, for they quickly assign the data of perception to the appropriate memory-imprints.

Having obtained Theaetetus's enthusiastic agreement to his carefully

---

[1] ἔννοιαι, ἐννοεῖν. 'Conceiving is evidently intended to be a relation like perceiving, but with objects which are abstract, e.g. perhaps numbers' (McDowell 215). This seems to fit the context, though at *Pho.* 73c ἔννοια as contrasted with the direct object of sight or hearing is the mental image of a person conjured up by the sight of one of his possessions.

[2] They are fully tabulated in Stoelzel (97) and McDowell (215). Cornford gives a clear summary on p. 122 of *PTK*.

built up thesis that false judgement only occurs at the conjunction of perceptions with thoughts,[1] Socrates proceeds to dismiss it as inadequate. True, we cannot judge that man is horse when perceiving neither, but we can confuse two unperceived concepts, e.g. numbers. To Theaetetus's sensible observation that one could mistake 11 objects for 12 but not the one number 'in his mind' for the other, Socrates replies that one can wrongly think $7 + 5$ (the numbers themselves, not 7 and 5 objects) $= 11$, and since $7 + 5 = 12$, this amounts to thinking 12 is 11, and entails 'knowing what one does not know' in the forbidden sense. The substitution of $(7 + 5)$ for 12 is unfair. It is rather a truncated question than something known; at least it makes sense to ask 'how many are $7 + 5$?' but not 'how many are 12?'.[2] Nevertheless it remains true that arithmetical errors are possible and are of a kind not allowed for on the wax-tablet model.

(v) *Knowledge potential and actual: the aviary* (197b–200c). To escape this difficulty, Plato adumbrates what Aristotle has taught us to call the distinction between potential and actual.[3] A man may possess knowledge in the sense that, having learned it, he has it stored in his mind, but not 'have it about him'. (He knows the names of his friends Taylor and Weaver, but with something else on his mind may refer to one by the other's name.) This suggests another metaphor. The mind is an aviary, full of birds of all sorts.[4] The owner *possesses* them all, i.e. has a certain *power* over them: he can enter and catch one whenever he pleases, and will then actually *have* it. The birds are things known (lit. 'knowledges'), to stock the aviary is to learn, and to catch a particular bird in the hand is to recall a thing once learned and so known in a potential

---

[1] διάνοια, as S. at 295d1–2 calls what he continues to call memory-imprints (196a3). 'At this stage . . . memory is made to do the work of abstraction' (Campbell on 196a3; cf. McDowell 215f.).

[2] 'How many beans make 5?' was a question with which my grandfather's generation delighted to puzzle small children.

[3] Aristotle too uses knowledge as an example of the distinction, which can be threefold, e.g. at *De an.* 417b21: First, a man is potentially knowledgeable simply as being a member of the human race, which is capable of acquiring knowledge. Secondly, a literate man has a knowledge of letters, still in a potential sense, meaning that he can read or write whenever he wishes. Finally his knowledge is actualized when he is actively exercising these skills. (Cf. also *Phys.* 255b2, *De an.* 412a10, *Tht.* 198e.) These correspond, in terms of Plato's metaphor, to having an empty aviary, stocking it, and holding a particular bird in the hand.

[4] Nothing certain can be made of the addition that some are flying in flocks, others in small groups, and others singly. See McDowell 220f. or Cornford 132 n. 2. It is not referred to again.

sense. Thus one can know (potentially) what one does not know (actually), and here lies the possibility of false judgement: a man may enter his aviary meaning to catch a wood-pigeon, but lay hands on another variety.[1] One who has learned the numbers 'knows' (is acquainted with) both 11 and 12. If, when asked what is $7 + 5$, he replies in good faith, '11', he has hunted in his memory for 12 but caught instead 11.

The distinction between 'possessing' and 'having' knowledge, between having learned one's letters and being engaged in reading, is a genuine advance, and resolves the unreal dilemma about knowing and not knowing the same thing. Yet the aviary model, with its 'knowledges' or 'pieces of knowledge' flying about like birds, is not a happy one, and is soon impugned by its author. Does it, he asks, make sense to say that, when it is a piece of *knowledge* that one has caught and is actually examining, one could fail to recognize it for what it is? In desperation Theaetetus suggests that 'pieces of ignorance' ('unknowings') may be flying about among the knowledges, and be caught by mistake. Then false judgement would consist in mistaking one thing for another, which is precisely what they have been trying, and failing, to explain from the beginning.[2] It is hardly worth while to go into the question what the 'pieces of ignorance' ('misapprehensions', Ryle) might be. Indeed the aviary as a whole gives some support to Aristotle's dictum: 'What is expressed in metaphor is always obscure.'[3]

It is often pointed out[4] that one difficulty in accounting for false belief or judgement is Plato's assimilation of belief and knowledge to seeing or touching. This is basic to both his and Aristotle's epistemology, for different reasons. Both thought of knowledge as acquired by a process resembling sensation in its directness, Plato because it consisted

---

[1] A φάττα ('ringdove' LSJ) for a περιστερά ('common pigeon or dove'). A dove instead of a pigeon, say Cornford and McDowell, but see the *Shorter O.D.*: a pigeon is 'a dove, either wild or domesticated'. The choice of varieties so closely related makes the mistake sound easy and natural.

[2] See (i) and (ii) above. At 200b there is an elaborate reference back to 188b–c.

[3] *Top.* 139b34. Sometimes, e.g. in trying to describe the nature of the soul (*Phdr.* 246a), or the relation between eternal Forms and their sensible instances, it may be the only resource available; but as an explanation of false judgement it is less appropriate. Two suggestions for the meaning of ἀνεπιστημοσύναι (the first is Cornford's) are mentioned by McDowell (p. 225), and Ackrill (*Monist* 1966, 400) tries to make sense of Plato's metaphor by yet another, of coloured and labelled cards.

[4] Recent examples are Sprute in *Phron.* 1968, 59, and Bondeson, *Phron.* 1969, 118. Cf. the phrase οὐσίας καὶ ἀληθείας ἄψασθαι at 186d.

in a sudden mental vision of a Form ensuing on the philosopher's reasoning about the objects of experience (p. 105 n. 2 above), and Aristotle because, after his abandonment of the transcendent Forms, the philosopher's grasp of immanent form or essence depended ultimately on the ability to make the first inductive (and rationally unjustifiable) leap from individual sensations to the lowest universal. This intuitive power he called *nous*, the highest of human faculties, yet at the same time the closest to sensation, or even identified with it.[1] I mention all this now, in spite of the impossibility of discussing it fully, to emphasize that very much more is involved in Plato's arguments here than a mere vulgar error of confusing 'knowledge that' with 'knowledge by acquaintance'.

Two further points before we leave the aviary. First, it offers, like the wax tablet, an empiricist, *tabula rasa* view of knowledge, leaving no room for *anamnesis* of the Forms: we start with our aviaries empty (197e). Secondly, Socrates describes teaching as 'handing over' knowledge and learning as receiving it (198b). Together these suffice to show that for maieutic purposes Plato does not feel bound to express his real opinions.

Socrates attributes their failure to explain false judgement to the error of attempting to do so before settling the question of the nature of knowledge itself.[2] Returning then to the main question, they reject its identity with true judgement for the reason we have already seen (p. 103 above). The rejection was in any case a foregone conclusion, for the distinction between knowledge and true judgement or belief was vital to Plato's thought from the *Meno* right through *Republic* and *Timaeus* to *Laws* (632c).

---

[1] *Metaph.* 1036a5–8: ' There is no definition of individuals, but they are cognized by sensation or intuition, and when we are not actually perceiving them it is not clear whether they exist or not. But they are always spoken of and known by the universal *logos*.' Cf. *EN* 1143b4–5: universals are made up of individuals. Of these one must have sensation, 'and that is *nous*'. Although the immediate object of sensation is the individual, sensation puts us in direct touch with the universal: seeing Callias we get our first awareness of *man* (*An. Post.* 100a16–18). To intuit something is to *touch* it (θιγγάνων καὶ νοῶν, *Metaph.* 1072b21).

[2] 200c–d. Cf. 196dff. on the 'shamelessness' of attempting to say what knowledge is like before knowing what it is in itself. This methodical error takes us back to the *Meno* (71b, ὃ δὲ μὴ οἶδα τί ἐστιν, πῶς ἂν ὁποῖόν γέ τι εἰδείην;, also *Prot.* 361c).

(3) *Knowledge as true judgement with a* logos (201c–10b)

Theaetetus now 'remembers having heard' that knowledge is true judgemen or belief accompanied by a *logos*, with the corollary that only that can be known of which a *logos* is possible. That true *doxa* is converted into knowledge when one can 'give an account (*logos*)' of it is Plato's own view as expressed at *Symp.* 202a; and *Meno* 98a suggests that this consisted in a 'reasoning out (*logismos*) of the cause', equated with recollection of pre-natal knowledge. Here that thesis is put to a searching test, and found wanting whichever of three meanings one gives to *logos*.

The theory dreamed by Socrates (201d–206b). Theaetetus remembers no further details, so Socrates obligingly supplies them by relating a theory which he once 'seemed to hear',[1] according to which the world ('ourselves and everything else' 201e) is composed of complexes and their elements. Complexes 'have a *logos*', namely a statement of their elements: elements have none, but can only be named. Speech reflects reality, and *logoi* are complexes of names corresponding to the complex objects which they define. Of an element it is not even legitimate to say 'it is' or 'it is not', for to add being, non-being or any other predicate to it is to make it complex. Elements cannot be accounted for[2] or known, but are perceptible. Complexes can be known because about them one can both have a true belief and give a *logos*.

The theory is clearly not Plato's.[3] It has a Sophistic ring,[4] and most closely resembles one which Aristotle ascribes in his own terms to Antisthenes and his followers. At *Metaph.* 1043b28 he says that accord-

[1] I.e. in a dream: he will offer ὄναρ ἀντὶ ὀνείρατος. Hence what follows is usually called 'S.'s dream', and its significance sought by comparison with other metaphorical references to dreams in P. (See Burnyeat in *Phron.* 1970, 103 and A. Rorty, *Phron.* 1972, 229f.) The phrase sounds to me proverbial, meaning something like 'My story is as good as yours' (not the same as τὸ ἐμὸν ἐμοὶ λέγεις ὄναρ at *Rep.* 563d).

For a comparison of the theory with the elementary propositions of Wittgenstein (who discusses the *Tht.* theory in *Phil. Inv.* p. 21, §§46ff.) see McDowell 233f.

[2] There is a play on ἄλογον, which in normal use meant 'irrational' or 'unintelligible', but in form is simply 'without *logos*'.

[3] *Pace* Hicken and Burnyeat, who have argued elaborately against Antisthenian authorship in *Phron.* 1958 and 1970. McDowell also thinks that Plato may have originated it (pp. 234, 237).

[4] Cf. the summary of fifth-cent. views in vol. III, 218f. Pp. 209–18 give some background to the present discussion. The prohibition of attaching any predicate, pronoun or epithet (202a) to something that one perceives is typical of sophistry.

ing to them you cannot define what a thing is, but only say what it is like: 'there *is* a kind of substance of which definition (ὅρος) or *logos* is possible, namely the composite, whether sensible or intelligible, but this is not true of its primary elements, for a defining *logos* predicates one thing of another'. His Greek commentator illustrates their difficulty. 'Man' is a name. We may say he is a rational mortal animal, but this again is only a string of names. Even if 'animal' can be divided into a further plurality of names, we shall finally come to a simple, elemental entity which cannot be so divided. This will be indefinable, and we cannot claim to have defined, or explained the essence of, something simply by describing it as composed of elements which are themselves indefinable.[1]

Theaetetus agrees that this is the argument he had in mind, and they proceed to examine it. True belief and a *logos* are at least necessary conditions of knowledge, but as usual 'one thing' bothers Socrates. The unnamed thinker used the example of letters and syllables: the *logos* of the syllable 'so', which says what it is (203a8), is '*s* plus *o*'; but one cannot give a similar *logos* of *s* or *o*, naming their elements.[2] They are mere noises, which can only be heard and named.[3] But, asks Socrates

[1] See Antisth. fr. 44b Caizzi. Hicken (*l.c.* 138) makes a point of the inconsistency between saying *all* definition is impossible and denying it only to simples. But since Aristotle himself with his ὅρον καί appears to attribute both to Antisthenes, unless one regards the ὥστε clause 1043b28ff. as no longer referring to him (which she does but I confess I find unnatural), I prefer to see in this addition an understandably careless expression such as Aristotle is often guilty of. The commentator's account (which she does not mention) is certainly that Antisthenes denied *all* definition.

[2] The word for letters and elements is the same, στοιχεῖα. (P. is said to have been the first to use it in the latter sense, Eudemus *ap.* Simpl. *Phys.* p. 7.13 Diels.) More strictly στοιχεῖα are the elementary sounds of which letters like sigma are the symbols. So Arist. *Metaph.* 1000a1–4, and in the *Poetics* (1456b22) he defines them (if ch. 20 is genuine; see Bywater *ad loc.*) as 'atomic sounds' (φωναὶ ἀδιαίρετοι). This they evidently are here, though neither P. nor Arist. always maintains the distinction.

[3] Burnyeat (*Phron.* 1970, 119) says that to be unanalysable is not the same as to be indescribable, and in fact Tht. describes *s* as 'a sort of hissing noise' (203b), which a pertinacious critic might even call an analytical definition by genus and species. McDowell (241) claims that a particular instance used in explaining the theory need not be an instance of ultimate, abstract elements as envisaged by the theory itself. Yet its author did use letters as paradigms (i.e. '*instances* of the sort of elements and complexes with which the theory is concerned', *idem* p. 240), and as Tht. says of letters (that is, of στοιχεῖα, 203b2), 'How can one state the elements of an element?' It must be admitted that letters (or rather the elementary sounds of which they are the symbols) are treated here as primary elements (201c1), which can only be perceived and named (202b). Incidentally the theory under discussion precludes what S. himself gave as a specimen definition at 147c.

(like his one-time follower Antisthenes), how can a complex of indefinable and unknowable elements be itself definable and knowable? Not
if it is simply the sum of its elements, nor yet if their collocation has
brought into being a new, unitary form,[1] for that in turn will be an
indefinable simple. In *Hippias Major* (301 b–c) Plato disproved the idea
that a group and its separate members must have the same properties,
by the example of numerical properties: neither *a* nor *b* separately is
two, both together are two. So he knows that if neither *s* nor *o* can be
known, there is no logical necessity that the two should be unknowable
in combination. Here he refines on that argument. There would be such
necessity if the complex were nothing more than the sum of its constituents (205 b). Only by assuming that the elements have fused into a
new, single 'form' or 'whole' can the conclusion be avoided, and the
singleness of that form raises in this context the further difficulty that it
too will be unknowable (205 e).

The weakness of the theory is also shown up empirically, by the experience of learning. The elements—letters, notes in music etc.—are
the basis of our knowledge of their complexes. In general, 'elements are
more clearly known than their compounds, and more effective than the
compounds towards a complete grasp of every subject', so that it is
absurd to say that a compound is knowable and an element unknowable
(206 b).

The 'dream-theory' interweaves what might appear to be two
distinct, if related, questions, the logical one of how we can have
scientific knowledge of individual members of a definable species and
another of the relationship, from the point of view of knowability,
between individual persons or things and certain postulated[2] elements

---

[1] μία τις ἰδέα 203 c, ἓν εἶδος 203 e 4, μονοειδές τε καὶ ἀμέριστον 205 b. The language is that
used of Platonic Forms in *Phaedo* (μονοειδές 78 d, 80 b, 83 e), but here P. is speaking of elements
in the phenomenal world, what the *Phaedo* (79 a) calls 'things that one can touch and see'. The
simplicity of an invisible, incorporeal form has up to now been the guarantee that it is not only
immutable but knowable. Cf. p. 120 n. 3 below. Stenzel (*PMD* 73) however thought ἰδέα and
εἶδος here were Platonic Forms. Contrast the doubts expressed by Wedberg, *PPM* 143 n. 8.
  The argument of 204 a–205 a involves persuading Tht. against his will—and fallaciously—
that a collection of parts is the same as a whole—as if, as McDowell says (p. 145), having all the
parts of a car were the same as having a car. At least their position makes a difference (Arist.
Metaph. 1024 a 1). 'So' is not the same syllable as 'os'.

[2] In a commentary on this passage (see p. 114 n. 1 above) Wittgenstein has drawn attention to
the difficulty (of which P. of course had no suspicion) of pinning down a single use of the terms
'simple' and 'composite'.

of which they are composed. Simples or elements are not the same as individuals (Socrates and the dog Tray are highly complex), and it is difficult to know exactly what they are. One might suppose them to be, as in Antisthenes, the logical constituents of a definition, like 'rational' and 'animal' in the definition of the species man. Yet Plato calls them perceptible to the senses (*aisthēta*),[1] which may remind us of (though different from) Aristotle's view (referred to above, p. 113 n. 1) that only universals can be defined and so known in the scientific sense, but individuals are recognized by sensation, on which all scientific knowledge is ultimately based. He distinguished 'more knowable in its nature' (or 'logically prior' *Metaph.* 1018b 32) from 'more knowable to us'. 'By prior and more knowable in relation to us I mean those things which are nearest to sense-perception, by prior and more knowable in an absolute sense, those which are further from sensation. Now the things which are furthest from sensation are above all the universals, and those nearest are the individuals.' (*An. Post.* 71 b 33–72 a 5.) The theory here refuted by Plato is concerned entirely with the sensible world (spoken sounds and musical notes are instances, not analogues), and we must suppose it to have taught that just as a symphony is composed of single audible units, so 'we and everything else' are composed of irreducible physical elements which can be perceived but not known.[2] If this sounds unsatisfactory, I can only repeat my conviction that it is not Plato's invention but an inchoate attempt at epistemology by some Sophist or Sophists in the late fifth or early fourth century. Whoever invented it, it is an empirical theory like all those examined so far.

Three possible meanings of logos (206c–210b). What then must *logos* mean if its addition to true belief is to produce perfect knowledge? Socrates sees three possibilities. First, it is the noun from *legein* (to speak), including any expression of thought in words. But this is open

---

[1] In spite of this, not everyone is convinced that this is all they are. See Bondeson, *Apeiron* 1969, 2, p. 7 and A. Rorty, *Phron.* 1972, 235. But for contrast Hicken, *Phron.* 1958, 130.

[2] Since much of Aristotle's work is a development or clarification of his predecessors', one might compare his distinction between ἀνομοιομερῆ (organs like eyes, ears, heart, lungs) and the ὁμοιομερῆ of which they are composed (flesh, blood, bone and so on). The latter he actually calls ἀσύνθετα (*H.A.* 486 a 5, cf. *Tht.* 205 c 7), even though absolutely speaking they are not.

in some degree to all except the dumb, so that anyone with a true opinion would have knowledge as well. This cannot be what the statement means. Secondly, to give an account of something may mean to enumerate all its parts or elements.[1] Hesiod said that a waggon contains a hundred pieces. Most laymen would be satisfied if they could name five. Knowing, as it were, the syllables but not the letters, they have a true belief about what a waggon is but not the complete account (i.e. enumeration) which would convert it to technical knowledge. Now if a boy spells 'Theaetetus' correctly, one might assume he knows that the syllable 'the' is spelt *theta epsilon*. But the same boy if asked to spell Theodorus may begin '*tau epsilon*', thus betraying that in spelling 'Theaetetus' his correct belief about the first syllable was not knowledge, though he listed the elements (letters) correctly. Evidently correct belief plus a *logos* in this sense cannot be called knowledge. They must try the third.

The requirement of knowledge unfulfilled here, though assumed rather than stated, is that it must be permanent and unfailing, guaranteeing the right answer in every case. A true belief may give one the slip, as the *Meno* said (98a), unless it is secured by the 'bond' or 'tie' provided by working out *why* the answer must be what it is. It must be *iustified* true belief. This sense of *logos*, though common in the phrase 'to give a *logos*', meaning an explanation or reason, has not been considered.

The last of the three meanings of *logos* allowed by Socrates is the expression of a mark or sign by which the object of enquiry differs from everything else, as when we think of the sun as the brightest of the heavenly bodies which circle the earth. But here again, the idea of knowledge as true judgement plus a *logos* dissolves under scrutiny. Someone has a correct judgement of, say, Theaetetus.[2] To become knowledge it must, we say, be supplemented by the ability to state a mark which distinguishes him from everything and everybody else. To

---

[1] The idea that complexes can be known and explained but their elements cannot has, after all, proved untenable (205e6–7). Friedländer (III, 152) identifies the fault in this second suggestion with the logical error committed by Tht. himself (146c–e), as by Meno and others in earlier dialogues, of enumerating instances of a universal instead of showing a grasp of the 'one in many', 'what is in all instances the same' etc. There is an affinity, but surely also a difference between this type of error and that of naming the parts of an individual syllable or material object.　　　　[2] That is, as usual in these arguments, of who Tht. is.

say that he is a man, and has a nose, mouth, eyes and so on, or even a snub nose and prominent eyes, will not do, for it will not distinguish him from Socrates and many others. But if we had not already in our minds the means of differentiating him from all other men, we could not judge correctly who Theaetetus is and recognize him next time we saw him. So to add a *logos* in this sense to true judgement is meaningless, for the *logos* belongs to the true judgement itself, and so cannot be knowledge. Nor would it help if we *could* say that it is *knowledge* of the difference, for to offer 'true judgement plus knowledge of a difference' in answer to the question 'What is knowledge?' is nonsensical, including as it does the definiendum in the definition.

The definition of knowledge as true judgement plus a *logos* has proved unacceptable on any of the three approved meanings of *logos*, and since Theaetetus has no further definition to suggest, the dialogue ends in failure to discover what knowledge is. Its achievement has been to rid Theaetetus of several false notions of it, so that if another idea comes to him it will be a better one, and if not, the awareness of ignorance is always better than fancied knowledge, as Socrates or Plato has repeatedly taught in the *Apology*, *Meno* and elsewhere.

As already noted (and often by others) the real—in Plato's eyes—relationship between true *doxa* and knowledge has been omitted. True *doxa is* converted into knowledge by the addition of a *logos*, in the sense of a statement of the reason *why* it is true, the cause (*aitia*), as the *Meno* puts it, of its being what it is. It is difficult to believe that the omission is accidental.[1] The main question throughout has been how we can have knowledge of individuals in the physical world—Theaetetus, the sun and so on—not of facts, nor of universal concepts like courage or justice.[2] This is perhaps the strangest feature of the whole dialogue. Certainly for Plato the hallmark of knowledge was the ability to say 'what *x* is', i.e. to define it, and we have seen historical and linguistic reasons why this should be so (pp. 68f.). But his *x* is always a universal or class-concept: justice, courage, or as in the immediately

[1] McDowell's only alternative suggestion (p. 258), that during the actual writing of *Tht.* P. lost interest in the definitional task he had set himself at the beginning, is not very plausible.

[2] Moreover the sign or token required is a *perceptible* one, by which the object can be recognized at sight. It is not mentioned that part of the *logos* distinguishing Tht. from others is that he is a mathematician.

following dialogues 'the Sophist' or 'the statesman', not Prodicus or Pericles. Here he spends his time in a vain quest for knowledge of individuals, doomed to failure for at least two reasons:

(i) It could never surmount the difficulty discussed at length by Aristotle that definition can only proceed by genus and differentiation down to *infimae species* but not beyond: individuals can never be the object of scientific knowledge.[1]

(ii) To summarize it yet again, Plato's own doctrine, at once epistemological and metaphysical (but are not all epistemologies based on a metaphysic, empirical or other?), was that (*a*) of objects or events in this world, where everything is mutable, there cannot be more than true belief;[2] (*b*) human reason can classify them and form concepts; (*c*) from the abstraction of concepts a philosopher may proceed to complete knowledge of the Forms, which *is* direct acquaintance, comparable to vision. These immutable and intelligible Beings[3] are the causes of whatever degree of being and knowability physical phenomena exhibit, whose status between Being and utter non-Being, corresponding to the position of belief between knowledge and complete ignorance (*Rep.* 475 ff., vol. IV, 487 ff.), they owe to sharing in, or imitating, the Forms. Knowledge of individuals, therefore, on any of the hypotheses here offered—knowledge as sensation, as true belief, and as true belief plus any of the three kinds of account mentioned—was bound to elude the searchers.

Conclusion

There is little to be said in conclusion that has not been said already. The puzzle of the *Theaetetus* is why, in trying to say what knowledge is, Plato should have made little or no use of the doctrine of Forms,

---

[1] Cf. the passages quoted on p. 113 n. 1 above, and at the head of this ch., p. 61. In arguing this Arist. rejects P.'s own definition of the sun as not conveying its essence (οὐσία, *Metaph.* 1040a28–b1). Yet P. was aware of it too. See Allan's introd. to Stenzel's *PMD*, xxxii f.

[2] That so much is possible, contrary to the extreme flux-theory of sensibles, through their relationship to the Forms, has already been explained (pp. 79–82 above).

[3] A Form, though its transcendence makes it individual, retains enough of the character of a universal (the *x in* things) to be intelligible and definable. Its ambiguous status is the theory's Achilles heel, thoroughly probed by Aristotle (e.g. at *Metaph.* 1040a8–9). The concepts of sharing and imitation he dismisses as 'empty talk and poetic metaphors' (*Metaph.* 991a20). When we find these concepts put through a gruelling examination in P.'s own *Parm.*, and in the present dialogue a lengthy attempt made to confine the discussion of knowledge to apprehension of the phenomenal world, we may be sure that the Forms were being freely discussed and criticized in the Academy.

which even in the critical *Parmenides* (135 b–c) he admitted to be indispensable to philosophical enquiry.[1] Has he in fact renounced them? I hope I have shown that, mainly in the Digression on the philosopher[2] but also elsewhere, he makes it clear that he has not. Cornford's solution, that the Forms are excluded from the main arguments with the sole motive of demonstrating the need for them, may be too narrow.[3] As in the *Parmenides*, Plato is clearly aware of philosophical difficulties, and shows an interest in problems, that are absent from the *Republic*.[4] Nevertheless I would not go as far as to say, with Runciman on the problem of error (*PLE* 28), that it is left unsolved because Plato at this time 'did not begin to understand the logical and ontological misconceptions which underlie the problem as discussed in the *Theaetetus*'. Socrates does not give the impression (especially if one remembers the other ostensibly aporetic dialogues) of being a genuinely tentative enquirer. His object, as he said, is maieutic, that is, educational. He is completely in command all the time,[5] drawing out his brilliant pupil and then very gently[6] indicating the flaws in his answers and getting him to consider points which had not occurred to him. The 'usual Socratic pose' as an ignoramus, which so enraged Thrasymachus, is well in evidence.[7] The claims of sense-perception (which ever since the *Phaedo* has provided the first step on the road to knowledge) and of true judge-

[1] The relation of *Tht.* to the earlier dialogues, and a variety of opinions on its character, have been discussed or referred to on pp. 64–6.

[2] Robinson's assertion (*Essays* 46) that 'The theory of Forms is the theory that there is a second world . . . and this theory is not implied by the *Theaetetus*' description of the philosopher' is mistaken. What else can the κακῶν καθαρὸς τόπος be (177a5)? And what else can ἐνθένδε ἐκεῖσε φεύγειν refer to? (176a–b). On Forms in *Tht.* see also pp. 102f. above.

[3] Yet so astute a scholar as von Fritz can say (in *Essays*, ed. Anton and Kustas, 435), with no mention of Cornford, that 'the *Theaetetus* tries to show the difficulties into which an empiricist theory of knowledge falls when it attempts to do without the Theory of Ideas'.

[4] For a list of these see McDowell 258. But if Cornford's thesis were correct, much more would be involved than 'the mere stipulation that the verb "know" is to take only Forms as objects'. Robinson similarly oversimplifies when he finds in C.'s interpretation the implication that the difference between knowledge and true opinion lies solely in their objects (*Essays* 56). To use the Forms in solving the problem of knowledge involves above all, as C. well knew and the *Parm.* emphasizes, the frightful problem, not of their existence, but of their relation to particulars. May Yoh's article 'On the Third Attempted Definition of Knowledge, *Th.* 201c–210b', in *Dialogue* 14 (1975), is a defence of Cornford's position against Robinson and Ryle.

[5] Campbell anticipated me here (*Tht.* p. 1): 'He is not himself groping his way. Each footstep is firmly planted, as by one who has tried every inch of the path and knows the country well.' The echo of the 'road to Larissa', whether intentional or not, is apt.

[6] See 163c5, 199e7, 205a1.

[7] *Rep.* 337a. Cf. *Tht.* 154c4–d2, 157c7–d1.

ment to qualify as knowledge must be taken much more seriously than hitherto, and cannot now be dismissed without a penetrating and exhaustive examination; but Plato was never in any doubt that in the end they must by themselves fall short of perfect knowledge.

(3) THE SOPHIST[1]

Introductory remarks. The company of the *Theaetetus* meet again 'according to yesterday's agreement', and are joined by a visitor[2] from Elea who undertakes to characterize three types which are often confused but which he believes to be distinct: sophist, statesman, philosopher. The question was vital for Plato, and it will not do to say that 'the argument is hung on the figure of the Sophist quite arbitrarily'.[3] Isocrates would in his view present a living example of the confusion: he thought of Socrates and Plato as sophists, and of himself as both a philosopher and an authority on politics.[4] And the superficial similarity between sophistry and Socratic philosophy is emphasized in the discovery of a 'nobly-born' variety of sophistry which 'purges the mind' of counterfeit knowledge, and which the visitor is doubtful whether to call sophistry or not (230d–231b). It is in fact the Socratic elenchus. Again, the *Gorgias* and *Republic* have given the impression that philosopher and statesman *are* identical, if one excludes contemporary politicians as not 'true' statesmen. In the present group of dialogues Plato is looking back more soberly and critically on his earlier enthusiasms, and here was a field in which clarification was clearly desirable. Once again he employs his unique skill in handling the dialogue form to interweave (his own favourite metaphor) more than one theme, and the fact that the *Sophist* uses its avowed subject as a means of advancing also the discussion of Being, Non-being and the possibility of error does not

[1] R. S. Bluck, who died in 1963, left an unfinished commentary on the *Sophist* which was published by G. C. Neal in 1975 after this chapter was written. It discusses the opinions of one or two scholars whom I have omitted (Kamlah, Moravcsik).

[2] Often called the Stranger, complete with capital letter, which besides its vague suggestion of the occult, does scant justice to the word *xenos*. One translator even imports a Western flavour by making Theaetetus begin a speech with 'Well, Stranger . . .'

[3] The quotation is from Edith Hamilton, *Collected Dialogues* 958, but others have said the same. Cf. on the other hand 216c–d.

[4] On Isocrates and Plato see vol. IV, 282f., 308–11, and Cornford, *PTK* 177 with n. 2.

make it a mere continuation of the *Theaetetus*. In fact the search for the Sophist cannot be separated from this discussion, because the arguments to be opposed are all of Sophistic origin.

In reading the *Sophist* and *Politicus* ('Statesman') we must never forget that they are only the first two parts of an unfinished trilogy. The visitor is to describe three types, and this is repeated at the beginning of the *Statesman*, where Theodorus begs him to take the next two in whatever order he prefers, and the visitor replies that he will not give up until he has dealt fully with both. *Soph.* 253e also looks like a reference to the intended *Philosopher*.[1] We cannot therefore expect all our questions to be answered in these two dialogues. Indeed it is likely that Plato would leave the most important to the *Philosopher*.[2] First he must finish his argument with the Eleatics, the opponents most worth his steel because they were so nearly right. It was Parmenides who opened a window on the truth by introducing into philosophy the notion of a changeless, intelligible reality as a prerequisite of knowledge. But their absolutism, their 'is-or-is-not' dichotomy with its outright rejection of experience, was not a philosophy that could be lived with. A middle way must be found between this and the doctrine of total flux, and for that no better discussion-leader could be found than one brought up in the school who is yet an independent thinker. With the difficulties about 'is-or-is-not' removed, the way would be clear for a positive restatement of Plato's own conception of knowledge, and it is a most attractive conjecture (it cannot, alas, be more) that for this the leading role was to be restored to Socrates himself.[3] Meanwhile hints are given,

[1] These passages leave no room for reasonable doubt that P. planned the *Philosopher*. Most scholars agree, and conjecture that he was prevented from writing it either by the current of his own thoughts (Cornford, *PTK* 323) or by circumstances such as his last visit to Sicily and consequent disillusionment (Wilamowitz, *Pl.* I, 558; Leisegang, *RE* 2354f.). Friedländer however (*Pl.* III, 281; 525 n. 5) thought the project impossible and P.'s references to it ironic. The Sophist is a counterfeit philosopher, but the true statesman is the philosopher himself. (I do not find this plausible.) Since antiquity unsuccessful attempts have been made to identify it with an existing dialogue. See Taylor, *PMW* 375 n. 1.

[2] Cf. p. 154 below. Wilamowitz maintained (*Pl.* I, 559f.) that the lack of the *Philosopher* has robbed us of what was to P. the main point, and caused scholars to assume that he had given up much which, because of its importance, he had reserved for the concluding dialogue. Thus of the two problems left unsolved in *Tht.*—the definition of knowledge and the possibility of error—the first is not taken up in either *Soph.* or *Pol.* because knowledge is the prerogative of the philosopher.

[3] At *Pol.* 258a S. proposes that his young namesake should be respondent, now to the visitor and later to himself, which Cornford (*PTK* 168f.) thought difficult to explain except on this

as in the Digression of the *Theaetetus*, of the sort of man the philosopher is. The visitor, as a philosopher himself, is, 'though not a god, godlike; genuine philosophers look down from a height on the life of those below' (216b–c); and whereas the Sophist takes refuge in darkness, the difficulty in discovering the philosopher lies in the very brilliance of the realm of reality in which his mind dwells, 'dark with excessive bright', for the eyes of ordinary souls cannot endure to look steadfastly at the divine (254a–b).

At 217c the visitor is given the choice between continuous exposition and question-and-answer, and chooses the latter, provided the respondent is 'docile and gives no trouble'. There is, then, to be no genuine argument, but the retention of spoken dialogue does permit the enlivenment of much dry logical argument by the humour, metaphors and other characteristic touches which we have come to expect of Plato.[1]

Definitions: the angler and the Sophist (218e–31e). The visitor and Theaetetus (his chosen respondent) both use the word 'Sophist' but do not yet know whether they have the same idea of what they mean by it (218c). The Sophist is in fact an awkward creature to track down, and the visitor suggests they try out his proposed method first on something simple and trivial, say an angler. With no preliminary explanation of what this method is, no laying down of principles or rules, he plunges at once into the demonstration by example, from which we see that the first step is to fix on a very wide class in which the subject can safely be included. No one will question that the angler practises an art (*technē*). Arts are then divided into two, in this case productive and acquisitive, with angling assigned naturally to the acquisitive branch, and acquisitive into peaceful (e.g. by persuasion, barter, purchase) and forcible. So the dichotomies continue, expressible in a stemma in which the right hand member is always chosen and the left discarded, until the subject

supposition. Of course the visitor has promised to deal with the philosopher too, but as in *Tim.* (17a) P. could easily invent a reason for his absence on a later occasion.

[1] It may amuse readers to check their own impressions with those of Thompson in the long paragraph quoted by Campbell (ed., p. xliii), which ends: 'If vivacity in the conversations, easy and natural transitions from one subject to another, pungency of satire, delicate persiflage, and idiomatic raciness of phrase are elements of dramatic power, I know no dialogue more dramatic than the Sophistes.'

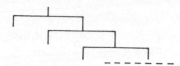 is defined by the original genus and a consecutive series of differentiae.[1] By this method the angler appears as a practitioner of acquisitive (not productive) art, forcible (not peaceful), by hunting (not fighting), of animals (not the inanimate) and water (not land) animals, fish (not fowl), by striking (not netting), with hook (not spear).

Not only is the method clumsy, but some of the divisions are questionable; all birds are apparently classed as the winged (as opposed to underwater) division of swimming animals. And though learning is undoubtedly the acquisition of knowledge, one wonders a little about a method that classifies it with trade, fighting and hunting as an unproductive art engaged in laying hands on what has been produced or preventing others from laying hands on it (219c). But before attempting a judgement let us see how it is applied to their real subject, the Sophist. Here a coincidence strikes the visitor: the Sophist is a kinsman of the angler, for he too is a hunter of animals. At this point however he diverges and takes up the left-hand alternative which he discarded in defining the angler; for the Sophist is a hunter of land animals (not water), tame (not wild). (Here he has to pause to win agreement from Theaetetus that man is a tame animal and is hunted.) After further dichotomies the Sophist's art is defined as acquisitive, hunting tame land animals, viz. men, privately for money, capturing youths of wealth and reputation under the pretext of education.

The definition is hardly a model of objectivity, and together with the pretended discovery that Sophistry is a kindred art to angling, ostensibly chosen at random simply to illustrate the method, shows from the start that, whatever Plato's opinion of the value of *diairesis* in general, what he is giving us here is satire not philosophy. Success in the method would demand a thoughtful and unbiased choice of genus and successive differentiae, not one designed to show the object in the worst possible light. In fact, with no other excuse than that the Sophist's art is

[1] A full table is given by Campbell (p. 24), Taylor (*PMW* 378), Ritter (*Essence* 238) and others. Bluck tabulated this and the other *diaireseis* in the dialogue on pp. 55–7 of his commentary.

formidably complex, six further definitions are given, each starting from a different genus. One metaphor retained throughout is that they are 'hunting' the Sophist, who, Proteus-like, in trying to escape their nets will assume all sorts of forms. By adopting different starting-points he is revealed in seven different guises. The first we have seen. Here are the next five.[1]

(2)–(4) (223 c–24 e). These are in fact three further varieties of the Sophist in his character as money-maker. Taking up the other main branch of acquisitive art, by peaceful exchange, and following it through three series of subdivisions, we find he is

(2) An inter-city trader in food for the mind concerned with the learning of virtue.

(3) A retailer of the same wares in his own city.

(4) A manufacturer of them for sale.[2]

(5) (225 a–26 a). Returning to the other branch of acquisitive art, acquisition by force, and that half of it which consists in open contest not stealth, we continue subdividing until we find the Sophist to be a pugnacious debater or eristic.

(6) (226 b–31 b). For this definition the original dichotomy of arts into productive and acquisitive is abandoned, and a new widest genus is selected, the arts of *separation*, in particular those which separate worse from better and so purify. Purification may be of body or of *psyche*.[3] Of the latter, the most important is that which purges the error of believing one knows what one does not, and for this the most

---

[1] In general I have followed P.'s own summary at 231 d–e rather than the details given earlier. Cornford (*PTK* 187) saw this as really a *classification* of Sophists, each definition referring to a different person or group, but this can hardly be maintained. He put Protagoras in the rhetorical group as distinct from the agonistic or eristic type represented by Euthydemus, and Hippias among the 'teachers of advanced subjects'. But Protagoras was a veteran in ἀγῶνες λόγων (*Prot.* 335a) and Hippias was undoubtedly a rhetorician. See vol. III, 44f. (following H. Gomperz and E. L. Harrison in *Phoenix* 1964, 190f.), and for Hippias *ib.* 280ff. But in any case rhetoric is excluded from Sophistic in this dialogue. See pp. 157f. below. F. Oscanyan (*Philos. Forum* 1972–3, 241–59) has made out an interesting case for assigning each definition to an individual, namely Gorgias, Protagoras, Hippias, Prodicus, Euthydemus, and finally (with qualifications) Thrasymachus as the 'nobly-born Sophist'.

[2] The notion of the Sophist as a seller of mind-food is repeated from the *Protagoras* (313c).

[3] Here P. divides the impurities of the *psyche* into wickedness and ignorance, corresponding to disease and deformity in the body, and to be cured by punishment and instruction respectively. Cornford (*PTK* 179) regarded this as going beyond S., for whom wickedness was identified with ignorance. However, in the *Laws* (860d, pp. 376–8 below) P. emphatically re-asserts the Socratic dictum that all wrongdoing is involuntary, but then argues with some subtlety that this does not

efficacious method is not chiding and exhortation (for all such ignorance is involuntary) but the elenchus, which by revealing inner contradictions makes a man aware of his own ignorance and prepared to receive positive teaching. To call one versed in this art a Sophist is questionable, but 'let it pass' (231 a 8–9). (More of this below.)

Comment on definitions 1–6. The production of multiple definitions by assigning the subject to different genera in turn may perhaps be justified in terms of general method (it is defended by Taylor, *PMW* 379), but Plato himself upholds it on the special ground that their quarry in this particular case is a slippery and many-sided creature who gives the appearance (φάντασμα) of belonging to more than one class.[1] The genera chosen without question—hunter, money-maker, dealer in unrealities—show the satirical, pseudo-scientific character of the exercise. Plato evidently had no individual Sophist in mind, but a combination of all that he found objectionable in the Sophistic profession. Only the sixth stands apart, and on this and no. 5 a historical note may be in place.

(5) In his summary of this definition at 231 d–e Plato stops at cristic, but earlier (225 d) he had added a further dichotomy: of eristics, one sort (the Sophist) debates for money, the other for its own (not its hearers') pleasure, neglecting its fortune to do so. These should be called chatterers or babblers (ἀδολέσχαι). Who are these? Cornford (*PTK* 176) chose the Megarians, against Campbell who thought Socrates himself a possibility. I should call it a certainty. Socrates impoverished himself in his zeal for the elenchus (*Apol.* 23 b, 31 b–c), his partners in argument certainly did not always enjoy it as much as he did, and his detractors called him 'chatterer' (ἀδολέσχης), a term which Plato defiantly adopted as the badge of true philosophy.[2] Cornford objected that he would not call Socrates an eristic, but that too he was called by others, and in the same ironic spirit Plato could enjoy a covert

for practical purposes invalidate the distinction between voluntary and involuntary misdemeanours as commonly accepted nor abolish the need for punishment, which may be the best cure for what is in fact a disease of the *psyche* (862c, as here at 222b8).

[1] 223c; ποικιλία again at 226a6, ὀλισθηρότατον 231a8. Cf. πολλὰ πεφάνθαι 231b–c.

[2] For reff. see Cornford, *PTK* 176 n. 3 (where however 'Statesman 270A' should be '299b'), and vol. IV, 431.

reference to him as an eristic of a different stamp from the Sophist. The point is not so much that he is called an eristic as that he is sharply separated from the Sophist, with whom he was so often confused. In the early dialogues Plato frankly demonstrated his use of eristic techniques [1]

(6) Here the visitor gives a precise and detailed description, not of Sophistry but of the elenchus as practised by none but Socrates himself. To confute the few who have thought otherwise,[2] one need only quote the passage at some length.

(230b4ff.) They [*sc.* the purgers of the mind otherwise than by admonition] cross-examine a man on a subject on which he thinks he has something to say though really saying nothing, and since such people are all at sea, have no difficulty in exposing their beliefs by putting them side by side in discussion and showing them to be mutually contradictory. When the speakers see this, they become vexed with themselves and more tolerant towards others. Thus they are delivered from pretentious and obstinate opinions in the way of all ways most enjoyable to the listeners [cf. *Apol.* 23 c, 33 c] and of lasting benefit to themselves. Their purgers treat the mind as doctors the body. As doctors hold that the body can get no benefit from food until some inner obstruction is removed, so these consider that a man's mind will not profit by an intake of knowledge until someone refutes and shames him, and by ridding him of the mental obstacles to learning purifies him and leaves him persuaded that he knows what he knows and no more ... For all these reasons the elenchus must be called the greatest and most effective kind of purgation, and he who has not undergone it, be he the Great King himself, is in the highest degree impure, ignorant and foul in the very respects in which to be genuinely happy a man ought to be purest and fairest[3] ... What shall we call those who practise this art? Personally I shrink from saying 'Sophists'[4] ... Nevertheless

---

[1] E.g. in *Charm.* and the Hippias dialogues. See esp. vol. IV, 159, 185 and 186, 195f.

[2] See the controversy between Kerferd and Trevaskis in *CQ* 1954 and *Phron.* vol. I, 1955, in which T. had the better of the argument. Burnet rather absurdly thought of the Megarians (*T. to P.* 276). The disguise of the plural can be disregarded.

[3] Cf. *Gorg.* 470e. This and the one mentioned at p. 126 n. 2 are of the sort of echo that scholars use in other cases as evidence that a dialogue is spurious, 'put together by a botcher'.

[4] Here follow the words μὴ μεῖξον αὐτοῖς προσάπτωμεν γέρας ('for fear of doing them too great honour'). The antecedent of αὐτοῖς is debated. Jackson, Cornford (*PTK* 180 n. 2) and Taylor (*PMW* 381 n. 1) thought it could not be the Sophists, and must be said ironically of S.: he only *sought* knowledge (was φιλόσοφος) and cannot compete with the man who has it (the wise man or σοφιστής). Kerferd and Trevaskis (*CQ* 1954, 85; *Phron.* 1955, 37) revived the contrary view, which is both possible and likely. In these descriptions of the Sophist P. uses the bludgeon rather than the rapier, and the elenchus, he goes on to say, can only be called Sophistry if we admit that it is a *superior* brand.

in our present discussion[1] let the elenchus of fancied knowledge be simply called 'Sophistry of noble extraction'.[2]

The elenchus as here described was not the procedure of Euclides (vol. III, 506), still less of the arrogant young followers of Socrates who brought his name into disrepute (*Apol.* 23c). It is an idealized picture of his own method and its effects, as described in the *Apology* and seen in action in many a Socratic dialogue—idealized because, unfortunately, in real life the adult and opinionated grew angry with him instead of themselves (*Apol.* 21 d–e, 22e–23a). Only initially modest and receptive young men like Charmides or Theaetetus could benefit from Socratic psychiatry. Indeed the parallel between this passage and the closing words of the *Theaetetus* is strikingly close. All his life Plato had in mind the tragedy that Socrates was commonly ranked with the Sophists. The inclusion of his elenchus among descriptions of Sophistry makes it stand out in vivid contrast to the rest, and Plato says in effect: 'Call it Sophistry if you like, but then "You and I have only the name in common, not the reality" [cf. 218c], unless we agree to include under Sophistry something entirely different in its aims and results from any other form of Sophistry, and of an altogether higher status; and personally I would rather not.'

Diairesis.[3] It is convenient to use this term, which is simply the Greek for 'division', for that division into kinds which was a part of Platonic method. Later in the *Sophist* he says (253d, exactly as at *Phdr.* 265 d ff.):

To divide according to kinds, not mistaking one form[4] for another, belongs to the science of dialectic. Whoever is capable of doing it distinguishes one

---

[1] LSJ offer no encouragement to follow Campbell and Cornford in translating παραφανέντι 'appeared *by a side wind*'. It simply means to appear or turn up. Cornford himself translates it 'coming in sight' at *Tht.* 199c8, and cf. Ar. *Poet.* 1449a2 παραφανείσης τῆς τραγῳδίας.

[2] Or 'of a noble kind'. English cannot reproduce the double reference of γένος: (*a*) family or descent, (*b*) kind, genus. Mortley's remark (*Eranos* 1969, 30) that 'it is difficult to see why a genus should be called noble' ignores this. His argument also suffers from identifying γενναῖος with γνήσιος.

[3] In a lucid and helpful account, Ackrill has defended against Ryle the standing of *diairesis* as 'a significant part or instrument of philosophy' both in P.'s mind and in fact. See his 'In Defence of Plato's Division' in *Ryle*, 373–92. *Diairesis* is taken up again in connexion with the *Politicus* on pp. 166ff. below.

[4] In using the small initial here I do not wish to prejudge the question whether the γένη or εἴδη referred to have the status of Platonic Forms. It should be noticed that γένος, εἶδος and ἰδέα are used interchangeably, as are γένος and εἶδος at *Pol.* 262d, not to distinguish genus from species.

form everywhere extended throughout many,[1] each of which lies apart, and many forms different from each other embraced from without by one; and again one form unified through many wholes, and many in every way distinct and apart.[2] This means knowing how to distinguish, kind by kind, how the several kinds can and cannot combine.

This dialectical skill, he adds, is the philosopher's.

This complex process, going beyond the simple dichotomous classifications of the early part of the dialogue, is the climax of a fairly long development, originating in the Socratic search for definitions (pp. 27f. above). That was carried out by 'dividing things according to their kinds' (Xen. *Mem.* 4.5.12), e.g. in defining courage by separating it from misplaced stubbornness or from rashness (*Laches*). An early form of the Platonic procedure also appears in the Socratic *Euthyphro* (12dff.), where to discover the nature of piety the whole field of right conduct is divided into conduct towards men and conduct towards gods. A more elaborate division is carried out in the *Gorgias* (464bff.), which Dodds sees as exemplifying the method of *Sophist* and *Politicus*, but (following Cornford) calls 'a Platonic, not a Socratic invention'.[3] It recurs in the *Republic* (454a), where eristics are distinguished from dialecticians by their inability 'to divide according to kinds'. The first formal description of the dialectical method occurs at *Phaedrus* 265 d–e, though earlier in the dialogue (249b) Plato has mentioned the universal human power of forming a general concept from a mass of individual sensations. First the dialectician, taking a synoptic view, brings many scattered kinds under a single generic form, including the subject to be

[1] I am in doubt whether to follow Cornford in taking ἑνὸς ἑκάστου to refer to Forms, or Runciman (*PLE* 62) who, observing acutely that if this were so, grammar would require μιᾶς ἑκάστης, concludes that particulars must be meant. Yet the whole context here is concerned with the relationship of Forms, which of them can and which cannot combine, and the rest of the sentence certainly suggests that ἕκαστα at e1 are Forms. Plato could be thinking automatically of the terms εἴδη and γένη which he has just used (d1), and commonly uses in this dialogue in preference to the quite exceptional ἰδέα. (Now that Bluck's *Sophist* has appeared, I see that he agreed with Runciman. Cf. his p. 127. On pp. 130f. he also offers a different interpretation of e1–2, taking ἕκαστα to be particulars.)

[2] Bluck (*Soph.* 127–31) criticizes several interpretations of the last part of this sentence, and offers his own.

[3] For criticism of this view see p. 28 n. 1 above. I am puzzled by Luce's remark (*CQ* 1969, 230) that Socratic definition puts forward a name and asks for its *logos*, whereas much of the procedure in the *diaireseis* of *Soph.* consists in putting forward a *logos* and asking for its name. Does it not put forward the names 'angler' and 'Sophist' and ask for their *logoi*?

defined (in this case love), thus marking it off from the members of other genera.[1] Secondly, the generic form is carefully divided 'at the natural joints' until by applying successive differentiae the *infima species* ('indivisible', *Phdr.* 277b7, *Soph.* 229d5) is reached.[2] Formally therefore the dialectical process is a double one, a collection or 'bringing together' (συναγωγή *Phdr.* 266b) followed by *diairesis*, and to this method Plato was faithful all his life. Not only does he honour, as well as practise, it in the *Politicus* (see especially 285a–b, 286d), but in the *Laws* (965c) he was still writing that there is no clearer or more accurate way of investigating anything than by pressing on from many different instances to a knowledge of the single form, and then ordering them all in relation to it. The first stage is not mentioned in the *Sophist* (which is singularly lacking in explanation of the method it employs), and little use is made of it. In the sixth definition 'separative art' is reached through the mention of various homely processes—filtering, sifting, winnowing, 'combing' (in weaving)—but in the others the generic form is taken to be self-evident. In the elaborate statement of *Soph.* 253d, the term *diairesis* seems to include the preliminary process of collection.

In the early part of the *Sophist*, Plato writes as if dichotomy were an integral part of the method, but as a classificatory tool its usefulness is obviously limited, and elsewhere he speaks of it only as preferable but not always possible;[3] Aristotle, in his work *On the Parts of Animals*

---

[1] Some have thought particulars are meant (or at least included: see Hackforth, *PEP* 142f.). But the method being described is purely the dialectician's (253d2–3), whereas generalizing from particulars is a universal human accomplishment. The generic form is that 'one form, the same in all', which S. wants Meno to identify in *Meno* (vol. III, 433 n. 1). There too the 'many' falling under the one form are universals (kinds of virtue), not 'individual things'. Contrast Cornford, *PTK* 185, 186; but the 'Socratic muster' was never of individuals. (He accepts *Meno* as Socratic, 184 n. 2.)

[2] Arrangement of these volumes by dialogues has the drawback (for which I hope the compensations are adequate) that it necessitates either repetition or the inconvenience of cross-references. P. of course chose repetition. I have attempted compromise. For Socratic *diairesis* see vol. III, 440, and vol. IV, 431 n. 1, for *Phdr.* vol. IV, 427–31, and for an outline of the method of *diairesis* vol. IV, 47f.

[3] *Soph.* 229a–b, instruction has 'more than one' kind, but two are especially important; *Pol.* 286d, if dichotomy is impossible one must (as in *Phdr.*) divide limb from limb 'like a sacrificial victim'; *Phil.* 16d, divide the one form into 2, or if necessary 3 or more. In *Phdr.* divisions into 2, 3 and 4 are used. (See tables in vol. IV, 429f.) That *diairesis* was eagerly carried on and discussed in the Academy is obvious from the pages of Aristotle. Speusippus is thought to have been one who defended dichotomy as by itself sufficient for classification. Details in Cherniss, *ACPA* 27–63; more briefly Skemp, *Politicus* 70–3. But see also p. 464 n. 5 below.

(bk 1, ch. 2), argues in detail against it as a method of classification in biology. Biological distinctions figure in Plato's definition of the angler,[1] and since we know that zoology and botany were zealously pursued in the Academy, it is probably in this connexion that the method of *diairesis* was developed. The parody by the comic poet Epicrates is well known, in which he depicts Plato, Speusippus and Menedemus teaching pupils to 'divide' animals, trees and plants and setting them to assign the pumpkin to its proper class. Of Speusippus we have a number of quotations from a meticulous work on classification and nomenclature, in which for instance he groups no less than six species of bivalves together, then oysters and limpets in a different sub-group, and distinguishes four species (εἴδη) of polyp.[2]

Jaeger's claim that biological classification was pursued by Plato only 'in order to learn the logical relations of conceptions' (*Arist.* 19) seems to confuse Plato's appreciation of the truth that science can never penetrate below the level of *infimae species* (which for him was based on the doctrine of Forms) with a complete lack of interest in the sensible world. The mode of existence of individuals, and the nature of our cognizance of them, were always in the forefront of his thoughts, as the *Theaetetus* has shown. (See further pp. 412–17 below.) This brings us to another much-discussed question: how seriously are the dichotomies of the *Sophist* intended? Leisegang (*RE* 2493) found the paradigm definition of the angler so capricious and absurd that it must be simply a mockery of the whole procedure. Apelt (*Soph.* 30f.) wanted to distinguish ridiculing the Sophist from ridiculing the method, and even held that the reason for offering half a dozen definitions was to give the reader plenty of illustrations of a procedure of which Plato thought so highly: it was a gross error to suppose that he would laugh at the method itself. That the divisions are biased and polemical is obvious. That they display wit, jest and lightheartedness is Apelt's own admission. Beyond that each must judge for himself, but it is at least possible that Plato is, as one might put it, being his own Epicrates, and having a little fun at

---

[1] Arist.'s objection to classing some birds as water-animals (642b10–13) looks like a reference to *Soph.* 220a–b or some Academic scheme on which it is based.

[2] Speus. frr. 8 and 16 Lang, pp. 463f. below. On pp. 8–15 Lang notes the close affinity between his classifications and Aristotle's. The Epicrates fr. comes from Ath. 2.59 (fr. 11, p. 287, Kock, 2, 354 Edmonds). Further reff. in vol. IV, 22 n. 2.

the expense of over-enthusiastic colleagues who were advertising *diairesis*, especially in its dichotomous form, as the universal key to the problem of knowledge. There may also be an element of self-criticism, as in the later argument against the 'friends of Forms' (pp. 141–3 below), for having spoiled a fundamentally sound thesis by over-extending its field of application.

The method of *diairesis* has often, and rightly, been praised as the foundation of scientific classification, and no doubt it was Aristotle's experience in the Academy, as well as his natural bent, that set him on the road to becoming a biologist, superior in Darwin's eyes to Linnaeus or Cuvier. Its usefulness extends also to mathematics, a subject nearer to Plato's heart. But as a general philosophical method it perhaps bears too clearly the marks of its inheritance in its conception of all philosophy as comprised in an answer to the Socratic question of what a thing *is*, culminating in the majestic doctrine of the objectively existing Forms as the explanation of all being and knowledge alike. As we have seen in the *Theaetetus*,[1] knowledge for Plato would always present itself as knowledge of some 'thing' rather than 'knowledge that' or 'knowledge how'. Moreover to grasp the one Form above the many is not simply the last stage in a process of thought but an achievement of direct acquaintance with the divine world in an act analogous to vision. This for many is the core of Platonism, and for this reason (to voice an unpopular view) his greatness may be thought to show itself most clearly in the dialogues written in full assurance that this was the truth, before the pristine vision was clouded by doubts—which in any case never led him to abandon the assimilation of all knowledge to knowledge by direct acquaintance of 'what is'.

Seventh and Final Definition: the Sophist as Illusion-maker (*nominally from 232 b to the end*). The first six *diaireseis* have really only revealed six aspects, or manifestations, of our elusive subject. To get him wholly in the net, says the visitor (following the procedure described in *Phdr.* 265 d but practised by Plato since the earliest Socratic dialogues), we have to find the common element in all of them. As always, the Socratic assumption is taken for granted, that a common name implies a common

---

[1] Cf. esp. pp. 67–9 above.

nature. To begin with, all set up as controversialists and teachers in controversy on any subject whatever, even writing books which profess to outdo an expert in his own field, from theology to physical science, politics or even wrestling.[1] Since no man can know everything, what they offer their pupils must be the appearance, not the reality, of knowledge. As an artist might deceive young children, if they were not allowed to approach too close, into thinking that a painted scene was real, so the Sophist exhibits simulacra in words (εἴδωλα λεγόμενα, 234c), which those far enough removed from the truth mistake for realities, and ascribe all wisdom to their authors.

So the Sophist is placed in his genus: he is an illusionist or imitator[2] of reality (234e–35a), and applying *diairesis* the visitor discerns two kinds of imitation. A modeller may either reproduce the original exactly, in its proper dimensions and colouring, or intentionally distort its proportions (as in designing an over-lifesize statue for a high building) to make them appear correct from a particular distance and viewpoint,[3] though if seen close at hand and at eye-level the deception would be obvious. The reader may feel pretty sure which division the Sophist will end up in, but at this point the division is broken off and not resumed until near the end of the dialogue, for in the character of imitator their cunning quarry has found a dark and obscure hiding-place. Just as in the *Theaetetus* the definition of knowledge as true belief raised the whole question of the possibility of falsehood, so here before one can brand the Sophist as imitator one must settle the same baffling problem: 'This appearing and seeming without *being*, and the saying of things but not true things, are now as in past time thoroughly perplexing. How one may say that there really is such a thing as false speech or belief, without being caught contradicting oneself, it is very hard to see' (236e).

---

[1] For wrestling Tht. mentions Protagoras. Cf. also the claim ascribed to Gorgias that the rhetorician's skill in persuasion could get him the job of public physician in competition with a doctor (*Gorg.* 456b–c). The criticism of the Sophist as offering δοξαστικὴ ἐπιστήμη also goes back to *Gorg.* Cf. 459c1, d6 (δοκεῖν εἰδέναι οὐκ εἰδὼς ἐν οὐκ εἰδόσι), e5.

[2] As has often been said, P. obviously intends to recall the derogatory description of *mimesis* in *Rep.* 10 (vol. IV, 545 ff.). Cf. esp. 233d–34a with *Rep.* 596b–e. Many other parallels are pointed out by Diès, Budé ed. 271.　　　　　[3] Cf. *Rep.* 602c–d.

The status of 'what is not' and the criterion of being (237a–48e)

(*a*) *The Sophist's reply* (237b–41b). To believe that falsehoods can arise is to believe that 'what is not is', which 'the great Parmenides' expressly ruled out as impossible. First, then (to 241b), the visitor simply states the Eleatic case, and his language, besides one direct quotation from the 'Way of Truth', is steeped in Parmenidean phraseology. 'What is not' is confined to 'what *in no way* is', i.e. the absolutely non-existent, for so Parmenides understood it. We utter this phrase, but to what can it refer? 'What is not' can be neither one nor many nor have any attributes at all, for if it had, it would in some way *be*. Even to deny 'its' existence is to call it singular. It simply cannot be thought or spoken of at all, as the great man said.

If, then, we call the Sophist a maker of verbal 'images'[1] he will immediately ask what we mean by an image, forcing us to say that it really *is* an image, but *is not* the 'real thing' whose image it is, and so contradict ourselves by saying that 'what is not in some way is' (240c4–5). Moreover, if we accuse him of deception, we can only mean that he induces false beliefs in others, and he will not fail to point out once more that to believe a falsehood is to believe that what is not is, which we have just agreed to be impossible.

The use of the Parmenidean dilemma for eristic purposes was a genuine mark of the Sophists. Plato had not forgotten the declared purpose of the dialogue, to get the measure of people like Euthydemus and Dionysodorus. But what he attributes to them here contains a few curious features. Theaetetus thinks the Sophist's imagined question— What do you mean by an image?—an easy one. 'Obviously we shall say we mean images in water and mirrors, also pictures, models and so on.' But the Sophist will refuse to look at these visible objects and demand an answer based on *logoi*. He will want to know (to translate 240a4–6 as literally as possible) 'what permeates all these many things in men-

---

[1] εἰδωλοποιόν 239d3. An εἴδωλον was anything which gave the appearance of something without being the thing itself—ghost, reflection, painting or statue. P. coupled it with 'false' at *Tht.* 150c, and it is usually synonymous with εἰκών (cf. *Rep.* 509e with *Soph.* 239d6–8), though at 239d3 it appears, in the light of the *Soph.*'s division between εἰκόνες and φαντάσματα, to stand for the latter, deceitful type of imitation. This division is of course *ad hoc*. If at *Rep.* 509e–10a P. calls reflections εἰκόνες, at 516b φαταντάσματα and at *Soph.* 239d εἴδωλα, that only illustrates his dislike of a technical precision of language (*Tht.* 148c).

tioning which you thought fit to call them by one name, "image", covering them all as a unity'. Now (i) this is the standard Socratic procedure for eliciting a definition,[1] which when it comes (in this case 'another thing of the same sort copied from the real thing') is shown to be untenable as in several Socratic dialogues. Theaetetus, it appears, has not profited by the lesson he was given on the previous day. (ii) It is a method of which, in the Hippias dialogues, a Sophist is proved to have no understanding. (iii) Stranger still, to refuse to look at visible things, and seek the truth about reality in *logoi*, is precisely what Socrates describes himself as doing in the *Phaedo* (99 d–e) when, baffled by earlier and contemporary efforts to discover reality and its causes within the sensible world, he postulated the doctrine of Forms.

The argument is genuinely Socratic, not a parody.[2] Plato (I surmise) found it amusing to make the so familiar point *ex persona Sophistae*, with the subtle justification that the visitor is still assuming the purely Eleatic premise, on which so many Sophistic paradoxes were based, that there is no third choice between 'is' and 'is not'. The full subtlety and skill of the composition are revealed when the Sophist has the ground cut from under his feet by the acceptance of what he called impossible, that 'what is not in some way is, and what is in a way is not' (241 d). To defeat the Sophist Parmenides himself must be called in question.

Another point should be noted. The *diairesis* was broken off because the visitor could not decide which of the two species of image to ascribe to the Sophist's art, the (as near as possible) replica or the distorted-for-effect, the *eikon* or the *phantasma*. (Cornford's terms 'likeness' and 'semblance' are convenient.) In what follows, however, it is simply assumed that he is a maker of semblances,[3] and when the *diairesis* is resumed he is at once placed in that division without comment or question (266e–67a). It is hardly fair argument, just a reminder of Plato's ineradicable conviction of the harmfulness of the Sophistic art.

---

[1] The phrases τὸ διὰ πάντων and ἐπὶ πᾶσιν both occur in *Meno* (74a and 75a) when S. is trying to get Meno to see the same point.

[2] Campbell *ad loc.* calls this passage a caricature of Socratic method, but though the Sophist's feigned blindness is amusing, the method is not caricatured. The 'imperturbable gentleman' of *Tht.* 165c is irrelevant, and C. does not mention the striking parallel with the *Phaedo*.

[3] 239c9, 240d1. P.'s incorrigible distaste for a fixed terminology appears again when, even after the *diairesis* of εἰδωλοποιική at 235c8–36c7, he uses εἰκών as equivalent to εἴδωλον in general (240b11–13).

(*b*) *From the unreal to the real* (242 b–45 e). After declaring that he must lay unfilial hands on his own 'father' Parmenides, the Eleatic does not immediately do so, but makes a fresh start. Since the notion of the unreal ('what is not') has led to perplexity, let them turn to the real. Are they so sure they know what they mean by that?[1] What have previous thinkers made of it? The natural philosophers talked of one or more 'real things', e.g. two physical opposites like hot and cold or wet and dry, or said that what is was both one and many, either successively or even both together. Whether right or wrong, they treated us like children, speaking in mythical terms of these real things as moved by hatred or affection, fighting, marrying and begetting. The Eleatics, going back at least to Xenophanes, wove their myth on the theme that all things (so called) were One.[2] None of them made their meaning clear. Those who declare that there are two realities, say hot and cold, must be asked what is this being (or reality) that they attribute to them[3] severally and together. Is it something else besides them, making three in all? They cannot identify it with either separately, for then there would be one reality, not two; but if they identify it with both, that too is to reduce both to one. The monists are in no better case. Is *being* the same as *one*? How can there be two names on the monist hypothesis? How can a name exist anyway? If it is different from the thing named, they are two. If not, it is the name of nothing. Again, it must be a whole of parts, for Parmenides compared it to a sphere with centre and circumference.[4] As sum of its parts such a whole can have unity of a sort, but cannot be 'the One' itself.

This rather strange language has been explained by Cornford (*PTK*

[1] As others have pointed out, the question 'What is Real?' is not answered in the *Sophist*. For P. as for Aristotle it was the fundamental question of philosophy, and it is reasonable to suppose that it was to be dealt with in the *Philosopher*.

[2] Only Xenophanes is named, and P. is not attempting a history of Presocratic thought. But one can recognize the Eros of Hesiod and the Orphics, and the biological analogies of the early Ionians, as well as the Love and Strife of Empedocles and the antinomies of Heraclitus. The proponent of a triad of beings (242 c 9) could be Pherecydes. See fr. 1 DK.

[3] Only the ultimate ἀρχαί were recognized by the *physikoi* as being (ὄντα). Other phenomena, as derivative and transitory combinations of these, had no existence of their own.

[4] The visitor quotes fr. 8 ll. 43–5 DK. Plato next considers the consequences if 'what is' is not a whole, but since it is agreed that the Eleatics do say it is a whole, we may perhaps spare ourselves his intricate reasoning on this point. It is analysed by Cornford, *PTK* 223. Taylor (*PMW* 283 n. 2) and Schofield (*CQ* 1974, 42) point out how this short section resumes arguments from the *Parm.*

222f.), though its point need not depend on the existence of Platonic Forms, of which Cornford makes much (and they were of course in Plato's mind). Earlier thinkers had not distinguished clearly between what *has*, or is characterized by, a quality and the quality itself. The ambiguity of the Greek article-plus-adjective idiom facilitated confusion between the two: 'the hot' denoted both a hot substance and the quality of heat.[1] Plato's own indifferent use of 'the beautiful' or 'beauty' for a Form shows him still haunted by the ghost of this misprision, even while thoroughly alive to the distinction between the one Form and the many things that 'share in it'. Thus Cornford translates the Greek for 'the One itself' (αὐτὸ τὸ ἕν) also as 'unity', and represents Plato as drawing the distinction impossible to Parmenides: 'If the Real is a whole of parts, it has the property of unity . . . but it cannot be identical with Unity itself' (p. 223). This point will concern us again a little later.

(c) *Materialists and idealists: the criterion of being* (245e–48d). From those who try to fix the precise number of real things, the visitor passes to 'those who have put the matter in another way'. He depicts a continuous Hesiodic battle of gods and giants: the giants will only admit as real what has tangible body,[2] whereas the gods confine reality to 'certain intelligible and bodiless Forms' and assign to material objects not being but only 'a moving process of becoming'. To make progress it must be assumed that some of the materialists (in reality a crude and violent lot) have reformed sufficiently to be open to argument. These

---

[1] Cf. vol. I, 79 (Anaximander) and 116 (Anaximenes), vol. II, 284f. (Anaxagoras). Though abstract nouns existed, the general term 'quality' (ποιότης, translated by Cicero as 'qualitas') was P.'s own invention (*Tht.* 182a).

[2] The obvious reference is to the atomists, for the objection of Wilamowitz (*Pl.* II, 245) and others that single atoms are not perceptible to the senses is beside the point. The atoms are corporeal and in bulk tangible and visible, and what is not corporeal (i.e., for the atomists, void) is μὴ ὄν. In any case they were materialists in P.'s eyes, which is all that matters (vol. II, 462). I cannot see a strong case for Antisthenes, whom Campbell thought possible (introd. to *Soph.* lxxiv, though seeming to deny it later, *Tht.* xl), and Apelt (*Beitr.* 70 n. 1) indisputable. Some think no particular person or school is intended: 'the materialistic tendency in contemporary thought' (Campbell), 'the crass unthinking corporealism of the "average man"' (Taylor, *PMW* 334, who for the atomists' view quotes only, without identification, Epicurus), 'die Masse' (Wilamowitz). P.'s language suggests that he had a particular school in mind, and my vote goes to Democritus. The 'reformed' materialist *could* be the ordinary man, who would certainly agree that 'there is such a thing as justice' (p. 108 n. 4 above).

will agree that a living creature consists of body and soul, that a soul may be just or unjust, and that it is so by its possession, and the presence, of justice or the reverse. The soul, they think, *is* corporeal, but of justice, wisdom and the like they cannot deny either their existence or their incorporeality. (Reformed characters indeed, if not rather puppets, these materialists who meekly acquiesce in the Socratic–Platonic language of virtues as entities possessed by, and present in, individuals.[1]) The question Plato is leading up to is this: If corporeality is not essential to existence, what criterion of reality can we adopt? Perhaps the reformed materialists would agree that whatever has the power or potentiality (*dynamis*) of acting or being affected by action, even to the slightest degree, exists, and accept as a definition of the real[2] that it is nothing but *dynamis*. On their behalf Theaetetus accepts it 'because they have nothing better to offer', and the visitor adds that both he and they may change their minds later.

The 'friends of Forms' on the other hand, who distinguish between being and becoming, will not admit the new criterion. All power, whether active or passive, they relegate to the realm of becoming. Yet in their view being can be known and the mind can know it, and if knowing is an action, what is known must be affected by that action. To be consistent they must deny this.

This passage raises two related questions: (1) Is the professed criterion of reality Plato's own? (2) Who are the 'friends of Forms'?

(1) Effectively it existed earlier. Qualities like hot, cold, bitter, salt etc. were known by their *dynameis*—the effects they produced, and (more rarely) their potentiality of being affected by others—so that *dynamis* practically became a word for quality, especially in the medical writers, at a time when 'the hot' etc. were also thought of as substantive

---

[1] ἔχειν and μετέχειν are too common to need illustration. For παρουσία see esp. *Lysis* 217b–18c (cf. Crombie, *EPD* II, 255f.), *Euthyd.* 301a, *Gorg.* 497e, *Phaedo* 100d (vol. IV, 278f.); also the curious argument at *Charm.* 158e–59c. I have remarked on these 'substantival expressions' on p. 68 above.

[2] Cornford (*PTK* 238) pointed out that a ὅρος ('mark') is not necessarily a definition, but the words τοιόνδ' εἶναι τὸ ἕν (247d6), taken with e4, ὡς ἔστιν οὐκ ἄλλο τι πλὴν δύναμις, seem to justify regarding it as intended for a definition here. (Owen also takes it as such in Vlastos's *Plato* I, 230, n. 14. I find it natural to take τὰ ὄντα as subject of ἔστιν, against Cornford and Runciman, *PLE* 77 n. 1.) On the meaning and history of δύναμις see Cornford's account (*ib.* 234–8), which draws largely on Souilhé's *Étude sur le terme Δύναμις*, summarized in Diès, *Autour de P.* 367–75.

entities.[1] It is reasonable therefore that Plato should propose it *ad homines*, for the acceptance of men with materialistic tendencies, who 'have nothing better to offer' (247e). A passage in the *Phaedrus* (270d) does suggest that he at one time thought these 'powers' at least the most important factors in determining a thing's nature (*physis*): in studying a simple object (or the parts of a complex) one must look first for its natural *dynamis*, 'what power it has in relation to what, either to act on or be acted on by it'. However, (*a*) this is not the same as laying down this power as a test of the thing's existence; (*b*) he appeals by name to Hippocrates, and the medical writers were especially concerned with *dynameis*;[2] (*c*) the argument is *ad hoc*, the subject is oratory, and the moral drawn is that to be successful an orator must know what the mind can do to what, and by what it can be affected, a thesis that can hardly be denied. The phrase '*dynamis* of acting and being acted on' occurs also at *Tht.* 156a, where in their theory of sensation the believers that all is motion postulate two kinds of it, having respectively these two *dynameis*. As to this, (*a*) in their account the perceiving sense-organ is the passive partner, the *sensum* the active, whereas in the *Sophist* the knower acts (and the theorists of the *Theaetetus* equated sensation with knowledge) and the known is acted on; (*b*) the 'all-is-motion' school are explicitly distinguished from materialists as a 'cleverer' group (*Tht.* 155e–56a); (*c*) they are in any case not Plato.

Plato's conversations are separate and artistically composed wholes, and appeals from one to another, though often helpful, indeed necessary, call for careful attention to the context in each case. Nothing in the last paragraph should make us ignore Plato's explicit warning that this mark of the real is provisional only ('both we and they may change our minds later', 147e), or think of it as anything more than a dialectical device to help on the argument,[3] his purpose being to bring materialists

---

[1] See Cornford's account just referred to, and vol. ii, 286 n. 1.

[2] With the *Phdr.* cf. the conjunction of δύναμις and φύσις in *Morb. Sacr.* 13 (i, 600 Littré).

[3] 'Only a step, though an important step, in the dialectical progress of the argument' (Campbell 124). So also Diès, Budé ed. 288, but only Apelt, to my knowledge, has made out a detailed case for taking it as such (*Beitr.* 70–7). Aristotle, without mentioning P., cites this definition as exhibiting the same flaw as a parallel one in *H. Maj.*, where, we may note, P. points out the flaw himself. (See *H. Maj.* 297e ff. and Ar. *Top.* 146a21–31. I do not follow Apelt's treatment of the latter passage, *o.c.* 75.) Others adopting the 'dialectical' interpretation of the definition include Cornford and Taylor. The view that it is P.'s own is mainly that of an older generation, Grote, Zeller, Lutoslawski, Ritter. (Some reff. are in Runciman, *PLE* 77 n. 2.)

and idealists closer together: the former must admit an element of the non-material into their world and the latter give up their rigid insistence on the immobility and immutability of the completely real. But when, a little later, the necessity for motion is to be argued, he adopts quite a different approach.

(2) The 'friends of Forms' are those who 'separate Being from Becoming and say that we are in touch with Becoming by means of the body through sensation, and with real Being by means of the mind (*psyche*) through reason; and that Being is always in the same unchanging state, whereas Becoming changes' (248a). These distinctions, both ontological (sensibles denied the status of Being) and epistemological (sensibles apprehended through bodily organs, Being by the mind alone using independent reasoning), agree exactly with the teaching of Socrates in the *Phaedo* and *Theaetetus* (184b–86b).[1] As for the impossibility that Being ('the things that are') should suffer any change, this was and remained a pillar of Plato's philosophy from *Phaedo* to *Philebus*. It is applied to the Forms, and they are repeatedly said to be the only realities. The phrase used here, 'always in the same unchanging state',[2] is his favourite description of them, and in the *Symposium* (211b) he says of 'the Beautiful itself' that it is 'never in any way affected'. In the *Cratylus* (239d) it is only because it remains 'always what it is' that it can be the object of knowledge. His language there and elsewhere shows that he did not think of being known as being acted on (πάσχειν) in any way.

Faced with this (and I have multiplied examples in text and notes to bring the point home), I do not see how anyone can doubt that Plato is preparing the reader for a modification of his own metaphysics.[3] It remains to see what form the modification takes.

---

[1] To be strictly accurate, P. says in *Tht.* that sensation as well as thought is a function of the *psyche*, though in sensation it must make use of the body and its organs (184d); but no change of doctrine is implied. It is the doctrine of *Phaedo* 79a–d.

[2] 248a, ἀεὶ κατὰ ταὐτὰ ὡσαύτως ἔχειν. Cf. *Pho.* 78c–d (of ἕκαστον ὃ ἔστι, earlier οὐσία), ἀεὶ κατὰ ταὐτὰ ὡσαύτως ἔχει, *Rep.* 479a, 500c, *Tim.* 29a. At *Phil.* 61e, 'things that become and perish' are contrasted with τὰ κατὰ ταὐτὰ καὶ ὡσαύτως ἔχοντα. Cf. also *Pol.* 269d. The words at *Symp.* 211b are μηδὲ πάσχειν μηδέν, as in *Soph.* the friends of Forms deny them the δύναμις τοῦ πάσχειν. *Pho.* 78c–d and *Phil.* 58a show also that the Forms comprise the whole of reality: there are no 'things that are' except Forms.

[3] Yet it has been a matter of considerable controversy, a useful, but partial, summary of which is given by Jowett's editors, *Dialogues* III, 322–4. (See also Diès, ed., 292 n, 1.) To supplement

Motion has a place in the real world (248e–50e). At 248e the visitor bursts out: 'But by Zeus, are we to be easily persuaded that motion, life, soul and understanding have no place in the fully real—that it neither lives nor thinks, but stays still, august and holy, without wit (*nous*) or movement?' They agree that this would be a strange thing to say, and that, since thought is impossible without life and *psyche*, motion and what is moved must be allowed to exist.[1] On the other hand, if *everything* were in motion, intelligence would again be excluded, since its operation necessitates unchanging objects.[2] Reality therefore, philosophically considered, must contain both the unmoved and the moved.

But here a doubt arises. 'The whole sum of what is', they have agreed, must be 'both all that is unmoved and all that is moved' (249d3–4). But motion and rest are contraries. To say that they 'are' (exist) is not to say of either or both that they move or stay still. 'What is' must be a third category, embracing both motion and rest, which *are* by reason of their association with Being. The consequence drawn by the visitor is that reality ('what is') is 'by its own nature' neither at rest nor in motion, but this is baffling, for there is surely no third choice: what is not in motion must be at rest, and vice versa. The nature of reality is as obscure as that of unreality.

Plato's language here is bewilderingly loose, even for him, and makes it almost impossible to judge when he is talking of a state or attribute (or Form) and when of a subject in that state or characterized by the attribute, a distinction which he has always expressed in his own way as that between being a Form and possessing, sharing in or imitating it.

this, the friends of Forms have been identified with the Megarians (see esp. Zeller's long argument, II.1, 522–5), certain Pythagoreans (Taylor, *PMW* 385 f., Burnet, *T. to P.* 280; this goes back to Proclus; see Field, *P. and Contemps.* 227), disciples of P. who had misunderstood him (Campbell introd. lxxv, Ritter, *Essence* 176), and Academic opponents of Eudoxus (Cherniss, *ACPA* 439 n. 376). 'Don't knows' include Diès, Jowett (III, 337), Field (*P. and C.'s* 193 f.) and Runciman (*PLE* 76). Some of the above, like Diès, Taylor and Field, definitely exclude P., others think him a possibility. Some have tried to find a clue by combining the visitor's remark that he is acquainted with these people (248b) with the fact that he comes from S. Italy. I should not like to press this. As an admirer of Parmenides who has yet broken away from him, he is too plainly a mouthpiece for P. himself. Those who take a view similar to the one expressed here include Grote (*Pl.* II, 458), Friedländer (III, 265), Ross (*PTI* 107), Grube (*P.'s Th.* 41, 295 f.), Ritter *Essence* 175), Allan (intr. to Stenzel's *PMD*, xvii n. 1).

[1] *Psyche* has been defined in *Phdr.* (245 c, vol. IV, 419–21) as self-mover and source of all motion (*kinesis*; see p. 101 n. 1 above for the wide range of this word).

[2] This was demonstrated, against the neo-Heracliteans, at *Tht.* 181 d–83 c.

The confusion between the abstract nouns 'motion' and 'rest' (κίνησις and στάσις) and the verbs 'to be moved' or 'at rest' (κινεῖσθαι and ἑστάναι) with their participles, seems complete. (In the previous paragraph I have tried to give literal equivalents for Plato's Greek.)[1] At the moment Plato does not distinguish (i) 'x is neither A nor B' meaning 'x has not the property (or is not in the state) A or B' from (ii) 'x is not identical with A or B'; in this case 'what exists is neither at rest nor in motion' from 'existence is not the same thing as rest or motion'. Having said that both moving and unmoved things exist, he might be expected to ask, do we mean by this that they are (either one or both classes) moving or at rest? And although to say that they exist is not the same thing, it does not entail the absurd consequence that neither is either moving or at rest, which follows from the (surely unjustified) substitution of motion and rest for moving and stationary things. To the end Plato continued to believe that Forms were the supreme examples of their characters. (Cf. p. 43 above.)

Either Plato knew what he was doing, and this shifty behaviour[2] is practised on young Theaetetus (as his Socrates often uses fallacies for good ends)[3] to lead him on to the new and important doctrine of the combination of Forms, which at least tries to clear this confusion up; or he is once again allowing himself a carelessness of expression which in this case is hard to forgive. A similar vacillation in the description of reality as power, which if it does less harm is at least pointless, makes one's doubts difficult to dispel.[4]

The problem of motion and reality. Scholarship is sharply divided about Plato's meaning in this section. The main questions are: (1) Does he mean to attribute change to the Forms themselves,[5] or simply to enlarge

[1] At 250b7 Cornford calls τὸ ὄν 'realness', and he may well be right, though I have kept to 'what is'. Contrariwise γένεσις and οὐσία at 248a10–11 are used (as often) as collectives for τὰ γιγνόμενα and τὰ ὄντα.

[2] Mentioned but surely played down by Cornford, *PTK* 248f.

[3] Cf. pp. 41f. above.

[4] 247d8–e3 'Whatever *possesses* power really exists' and 248c 'Whenever power *is present to* something it exists'; but 248e7 'Existing things *are* nothing but power.'

[5] It is true that, as Diès pointed out (ed. 287f.), P. occasionally applies πάσχειν so widely as practically to eliminate any dynamic connotation. At *Pho.* 97c he speaks of ἢ εἶναι ἢ ἄλλο ὁτιοῦν ποιεῖν ἢ πάσχειν, and similarly at *Parm.* 136b ὡς ὄντος καὶ οὐκ ὄντος καὶ ὁτιοῦν ἄλλο πάθος πάσχοντος. If even to be is a πάθος, as well as to be known, one must agree with Runciman

the realm of Being to include life and intelligence which are not Forms? (2) Is he going even further in dissent from the friends of Forms and admitting what they called Becoming—changing and perishable objects of the physical world—as part of the realm of true Being?

Plato's language makes the second question almost if not quite insoluble. Cherniss affirms (*SPM* 352) that the motion (κίνησις) admitted is the *Form* of motion, and its manifestation in Being is the self-motion of life, a non-phenomenal motion which is entirely different from γένεσις (becoming), what Cornford and de Vogel call 'spiritual motion'. The disjunction between Being and Becoming is neither rejected nor qualified. This is eminently reasonable, and indeed the idea that Plato should ever have allowed the sensible world to cross the bridge between Becoming and Being is contradicted not only by the *Republic* but by every other dialogue early or late. Apart from the *Timaeus* one has only to look at *Philebus* 59a–c, where cosmologists are said to study 'not the things which always are but those which become', whose instability forbids any exact knowledge or thought about them.

Here however he says that Being includes not only the Forms Rest and Motion, but also 'whatever is unmoved and whatever is moved', which gives colour to the view of Diès, Solmsen, and more recently Keyt,[1] that it includes all or some things in the physical world. This would indeed be a recantation, and it is fair to recall what we have just noticed, that Plato can switch from motion–rest to moved–unmoved with a seemingly callous indifference to his readers' comfort. Plato, says Solmsen, 'would not easily allow himself to consign the Universe in its entirety', with all its qualities of order, structure and harmony, 'to

(*PLE* 81; cf. 23 n. 1) that there is 'a plausible sense in which P. can have thought that the Forms can change without forfeiting their changelessness'. Nevertheless since the decision that whatever exists is or possesses a δύναμις leads directly to the momentous discovery (so at least the visitor seems to announce it) of the presence of movement, life and intelligence in the realm of Being, the word here must surely have its stronger, more usual sense. In any case we have P.'s earlier statement that a Form does not πάσχειν at all. (See p. 141 n. 2 above.)

[1] Diès, *Autour de P.* 560 ('dans le visible même'), Solmsen, *P.'s Th.* 80–3 ('the Cosmos'), Keyt in *PQ* 1969, esp. p. 6 ('ensouled, living bodies': K. provides further reff. for the discussion). See also de Vogel, *Philosophia* I, 176–82, 194–209, Ross, *PTI* 108–11, Grube, *P.'s Th.* 295–7. I have not gone all the way with de Vogel, though her explanation is both attractive and well defended, namely that for P. the intelligible world was an articulate, organic unity and therefore a ζῷον, the νοητὸν ζῷον of *Timaeus* 39e1.

"non-being"'. Of course not. He assigns it to Becoming, having taken great pains (in the *Republic*) to show that the choice is not simply between the two contraries Being and Non-being. The *Timaeus* makes the position of the cosmos clear: the order which it undoubtedly exhibits it owes to its creation by the divine Mind as a *copy* (εἰκών) of the world of eternal Forms (28b), 'fairest of all things that become' (29a). Its status is laid down in the *Sophist*'s sequel, the *Politicus*:[1]

To be always the same and in the same unchanging state belongs only to the most divine of all things, and body is not in this class. What we call world and cosmos has received many blessed gifts from its creator, but all the same it partakes of body. It cannot therefore remain for ever changeless, though its motion is as far as possible uniform, invariable and in one place [i.e. circular].

The cosmos is alive (ἔμψυχον, 'ensouled', in Greek), and what Plato now admits to Being is not the revolving body of the cosmos or its contents but the element of soul in it ('life, *psyche* and understanding', 248e), reaching down to subordinate living creatures, and *a fortiori* the supreme Mind, the Creator, who made it 'as like as possible to himself' (*Tim.* 29a).[2] Previously, as we have seen, this status was reserved for the Forms alone, and in the *Phaedo*, though proclaiming the soul immortal, Plato ventured only to call it akin to the Forms, resembling them, and belonging to the same region (72d–e). From this to parity with them as equally belonging to true Being was not a long step—was perhaps implicit in the *Phaedo*—yet the visitor hails almost as a revelation his recognition of its full significance in introducing motion and activity into what had been a world of static and changeless Forms alone. Since the *Phaedrus* soul has been by definition the self-mover that initiates all other motion, and the *Laws* shows that, though it imparts physical motion to bodies by animating them, its own motions are spiritual. There the priority of soul to body, and its causal function, serve as evidence that psychical activities like wish, reasoning, memory, precede corporeal attributes like spatial dimensions and physical strength.[3]

---

[1] 269d–e, repeating in substance *Rep.* 530a–b. Even more telling is *Tim.* 38c: the world is γεγονώς, its model ὄν.

[2] The middle dialogues make no mention of a supreme Mind, and only once, in passing, of a creator (*Rep.* 530 a).

[3] *Phdr.* 245cff., *Laws* 895e–97b. See vol. IV, 419–21, but also p. 295 n. 3 below.

The Forms, as I have said, remain unmoved and impassive. Their causal function, in which some have seen a kind of motion,[1] resembles rather that of Aristotle's Unmoved Mover: the mere existence of their perfection excites the development of potentialities in physical things, which strive, in the *Phaedo*'s terms, to emulate them. This is perhaps to emphasize the 'paradigm' conception of the Forms at the expense of the notions of 'sharing' and 'presence *in*'. But of all the expressions with which Plato tried to convey the relationship between Forms and particulars, that of pattern and copy does seem to go nearest the root of the matter.

Note. I would be the last to claim certainty for what is said here. The temptation is always with us to adapt Plato's words to a preconceived idea of his philosophy, and readers will be well advised to study the interpretations referred to in p. 144 n. 2. Perhaps I might venture a few tentative comments on Keyt's.

(i) p. 4: 'It is only to bodies that the word ἔμψυχον can properly be applied.' But (p. 5) at 246e7 σῶμα ἔμψυχον describes a *mortal* creature (θνητὸν ζῷον), as at *Pol.* 261b ἔμψυχα (earthy animals) are a class of γιγνόμενα. τὸ παντελῶς ὄν is certainly not θνητόν, and nothing corporeal can be ἀθάνατον, not even the cosmos, which will last for ever only because its creator wills it so (*Tim.* 37c–38c, 41a–b). Language is not always perfectly logical, and I believe that at 249a10 P. meant by ἔμψυχα simply 'alive', even with the life of an incorporeal deity whose only activity is thought.

(ii) pp. 7 f. K. sees two paradoxes, depending respectively on the statements that Forms *become*, and that they *are*, known. I do not find this antithesis in the text (the present infinitive γιγνώσκεσθαι need not mean 'come to be known' any more than ὁρᾶσθαι need mean 'come to be seen') and we need not suppose (though it is possible) that P. has given up his faith that after the right intellectual preparation, Forms are known in a single instantaneous flash or vision, without any process of *becoming* known.

(iii) p. 10. K. claims that P.'s argument at *Crat.* 439e–40a does not prove that an object of knowledge must be completely changeless, but only that it must not be *always* changing. Proteus is changeable, but for so long as he chooses to remain, say, a tree or a leopard, I can, on K.'s argument, 'know this'. But (*a*) According to this reply, it is only so long as he is changeless

---

[1] For these and other theories, e.g. the 'animation' of the Forms as conscious and thinking beings, reff. will be found in Diès, *Soph.* 288 n. 1.

that he is knowable: an object is still only knowable in so far as it is change-less; (*b*) K. adds, 'In my example I am only interested in knowing what he is now, not what he is really', which surely abolishes any relevance to P., for whom to know something was to know its essence, 'what it is really', and nothing else.

The interrelationship of Forms (250e–54b). A little recapitulation may help. We call the Sophist a producer of counterfeits and falsehoods, unrealities in fact. He takes refuge in Parmenides's dictum that there is no middle way between 'what is' and 'what in no way is', 'non-being in itself'.[1] To catch him we have to show that Parmenides was wrong, that 'what is not in some respect is and conversely what is in a way is not' (240e, 241d). We started with an examination of past theories, of cosmologists who claimed that only very few basic constituents of the world exist and everything else has only a derivative status, becoming and perishing as the substantive elements combine and separate, and of Parmenides himself who allowed only one Being. Then, from another angle, we criticized the warring factions of materialists and idealists for their extremism. Reality, what *is*, must include both the unmoved and unchanging (the Forms of the idealists) and motion, at least in the form of life and intelligence. But what does it mean to say that Motion and Rest both *are*? Not that they are the same (for they are contraries), nor that either or both is the same as Being. Being is a third thing, but this cannot mean that it is neither in motion nor at rest, for that is nonsense. What is needed is a thorough investigation of the possible meanings of 'is' and 'is not'. So far, says the visitor, both have baffled us. As we proceed, one may throw light on the other, or if both elude us, we may hope to steer a course between them.[2]

So with characteristic skill Plato has taken us in living discussion from the Sophist's wiles, by way of early cosmology, monism, mate-rialism, and idealism, to an analysis of the concepts expressed indis-criminately by the Greek word for 'to be' as ordinarily used.[3] These were in the main three: identity (Tom is my son), attribution (Tom is

---

[1] 238d9 τὸ μὴ ὂν καθ' αὑτό, 240e2 τὰ μηδαμῶς ὄντα.

[2] 250e–51a, adopting Campbell's and Owen's rendering (*Plato* 1, ed. Vlastos, 230) in pre-ference to Cornford's.

[3] 243d. Tht. 'You mean we must first enquire what people who speak of "what is" think they are signifying.' Vis. 'You have taken my meaning exactly.'

tall), and existence (poor Tom is no more).[1] It has been commonly thought that in the *Sophist* Plato recognized all three. Cornford saw only two, existence and identity (*PTK* 296) and it has recently been claimed that he did not distinguish the existential sense from either of the other two.[2] What is certain is that the trouble started from Parmenides's assertion that 'is not' could only apply to the absolutely non-existent, 'what is not in any way at all', sheer nonentity.

Plato's new approach to the study of what is meant by being and not being starts from the age-old question, brought to a head by Parmenides, of the One and the Many. We habitually call a thing by many names, as when we say a man is pale, tall, good or bad; but, say some, you cannot make one thing many. Since man and good are different, you cannot legitimately say a man is good, but only 'man is man' and

[1] I do not think this classification will mislead us at present, though Kahn sees the primary sense of εἶναι as 'to be the case' or 'true' (an important sense to which I have referred more than once: see p. 69 above), with both existential and predicative senses as special cases of this. He maintains indeed that the Greek notion of being differs radically from ours of existence. For present purposes at least I regard usages like Homer's and Hesiod's θεοὶ αἰὲν ἐόντες and the famous ἔστιν θάλασσα (Aesch. *Ag.* 958) as both existential and primary, but Kahn's article ('The Greek Verb "To Be" and the Concept of Being', *Foundations of Language* 1966) should be required reading for any student of Greek thought.

[2] By Malcolm in *Phron.* 1967, 130ff., Owen, *Plato* I, 223ff., and most recently Gosling, *Plato* (1973), 213ff. M. cites also Runciman, *PLE* 84, but R.'s position, if one reads on to p. 90, is a little delicate. 'P. does not consider the problem of existence as such. He establishes only that everything must have some sort of Being; but this cannot be said to be the same thing.' 'In two places the purely existential sense does appear to be what is meant . . . P. is *deliberately* [my italics] using εἶναι in a sense where it is legitimate and complete without the addition of anything to convert it into an identitative or copulative use.' Yet 'he still did not specifically distinguish the existential sense as such'. On p. 102 R. calls it the principal achievement of Plato's analysis that 'it shows how negation need not involve an assertion of non-existence'. I am not sure how this could be achieved otherwise than by drawing the distinction between the copulative and existential senses of εἶναι. Bluck, I now see, held that 'Plato assimilated to each other the existential and the copulative senses of "to be".' See his *Soph.*, published 1975, 62–7, 119. At the risk of over-simplification (certainly not a fault of P.'s recent interpreters) I suggest that when P. asserts that Motion and Rest both *are* (254d10), but are not identical, he shows himself aware of the distinction between the 'is' of existence and of identity ('identity and existence cannot be the same thing' is a fair translation of 255c3); and by introducing the asymmetrical relationship of one Form to another (p. 117 above: μετέχειν is the verb commonly used of the relation of particulars to Forms) he draws attention to the third use of 'to be', the attributive, predicative or copulative. (I have been encouraged here by the lucid and convincing article of Ackrill in *SPM* 207–18.)

R. Robinson is of course right to remind us that for P. all this was not grammar or logic but ontology (*Essays* 37). 'He is talking about Being, not the word "being".' But this need not convict of error those who (like Shorey and Taylor) have ascribed to him the discovery of the copula or claimed that he distinguishes meanings of 'is' and 'is not'. Cf. also R.'s next para.: P. 'gives us an account of what he calls the "form" of the Other; there is no such form; nevertheless, all that he says about it is true of something else, namely the word "other"'.

'good is good'. This however is quickly dismissed as 'entertainment for boys and stupid old men'.[1] It had of course been settled by the doctrine that one individual could partake of, or be associated with, many Forms.[2] The philosophical question (as it is called later) is whether Forms themselves can associate or combine with each other, a question foreshadowed by the *Parmenides*, where Socrates said it would at least be a marvel if contrary Forms could combine, Similarity with Dissimilarity, Plurality with Unity, Rest with Motion and the like.[3] Now the doctrine of Forms enters a new stage with a full consideration of all possibilities: no Forms can combine, all Forms can combine, some can combine with some others, some can combine with all others. To disentangle their various relationships is the subject of a special science, dialectic.[4] But good Heavens! (says the visitor), in pursuing the Sophist we seem to have stumbled first on the philosopher, whose province it is. Well, he must wait his turn.[5] Just now the Sophist remains the quarry. His hiding-place is in the darkness of not-being, and to find him necessitates going into the question for at least some of the Forms.

[1] The argument against all except identical predication is generally attributed to Antisthenes, but I have expressed doubts about this in vol. III (214, 216–18).

[2] (That the arguments of *Parm.* do not imply abandonment of the earlier theory of Forms I have ventured to maintain on pp. 58–61 above.) Note the wording of 252b9–10. The opponents of non-tautological predication 'do not allow anything, by partaking in another property (κοινωνίᾳ ἑτέρου παθήματος), to be called that other'. Though this makes for awkward English, I doubt if the genitive ἑτέρου depends on παθήματος (Cornford, Owen in *Plato* I, 251 n. 48, 256), which would be decidedly awkward Greek. A man may not share in a property (goodness) which is other than himself (man) and so be called 'good' as well as 'man'.

[3] Similarly at *Pho.* 102d–e, S. says that Largeness will never 'admit' Smallness. For δέχεσθαι cf. *Soph.* 253c1. The various terms used to describe the relationship between Forms in *Soph.* (κοινωνεῖν, μετέχειν etc.: full list in Cornford, *PTK* 255) are mostly those which P. regularly employs for that of particular to Form. Now at least there is no doubt that Motion, Rest and so on are Forms, not moving etc. *things*, though we have to wait for a general term until 235b8 (γένη), d5 (ἰδέα) and 254c2 (εἴδη).   [4] For its full description at 253d–e see p. 129f. above.

[5] Peck (*CQ* 1952, 45) took this as a warning that the arguments which follow will be sophistic, not philosophic, thus supporting his general thesis that the γένη or εἴδη in this dialogue have nothing to do with Platonic Forms. But it does not appear that P. first puts forward sophistic arguments and then corrects them. The γένη belong to the main line of reasoning by which the Sophist is finally run to earth, and e.g. the proof that ταὐτόν and θάτερον are γένη in their own right (Peck 46f.) does not commit the fallacy of Dionysodorus. The dropping of the predicate in (2) (see *ib.*) is immediately put right by (4). To rely on unsound argument to this extent would be no way to define a Sophist, a philosopher or anything else, nor is P. hinting that he will do so. Cherniss in *JHS* 1957 (1), 23 n. 57, points out that οὐσία, ταὐτόν and θάτερον appear as Forms in *Tim.* (35a, 37a–b), which Peck thought later than *Sophist* 254b3 is another pointer to the intended dialogue on the philosopher.

In later terminology, that a Form (*A*) 'shares in' another (*B*) means that it has *B* as an attribute, so that *B* can be truly predicated of it, just as an individual, Socrates, can share in wisdom and so be wise. The relationship may be reciprocal, in which case the verbs 'combine' or 'associate' (μείγνυσθαι, κοινωνεῖν) are apt, or it may not. Motion shares in (μετέχει τοῦ) Being (for there is such a thing), but not Being in Motion, which would mean that whatever *is* (exists) moves.[1]

It cannot be either that no Forms can combine, or that all can combine with each other. The former would mean that no Form could even exist (that is, in Form-language, partake of Existence). Later he says that it would abolish all discourse, which consists in weaving Forms together. But if all Forms could combine, even self-contradictory statements would be true, such as that Motion is at rest or Rest in motion (252d).

It might well be said that the Form Motion must be unmoving (= unchanging), for all Forms are. I do not myself see that Plato ever completely overcame this difficulty, which is bound up with his indiscriminate use of abstract noun ('Motion', κίνησις, or 'Being', οὐσία) and participle ('the moved', τὸ κινούμενον, or 'what is', τὸ ὄν). Forms impart their qualities to whatever shares in or combines with them by virtue of being themselves the supreme and perfect examples of those qualities. It is curious how this hiatus in Plato's thought is ignored by Cornford, Ross (see *PTI* 112f.) and others. Plato may possibly have had in mind that contrary Forms cannot mingle in (enter simultaneously into) the same individual, as the *Phaedo* explained (102d–e); but that is not what he says. The doctrine of Forms independent of their instantiations had originally a strong metaphysical or religious flavour (they are 'divine') necessitating liberal use of metaphor, and as purely logical tools they play an uncongenial role—those Forms of which the Platonic Socrates said 'in his simple, unsophisticated way' that by *some* sort of attachment to things (and he could not safely say *what* sort) they gave them the character they had (*Pho.* 100d).

[1] P. also marks the difference by using κοινωνεῖν and its compounds with genitive or dative. See Ross, *PTI* 111 n. 6.

Five of the greatest Forms: Parmenides refuted (254b–59b). The only remaining possibility is that some Forms can, and some cannot, combine. In this they resemble the letters of the alphabet, and perhaps also in that some of these (the vowels) blend with all the others and make possible their union with each other (253a, 254b–c). Such all-pervading or penetrating Forms would be either bonds enabling others to combine or conversely in some cases responsible for keeping them apart.[1] The next step is to examine the relations between actual Forms in the light of these generalities, and since to review them all would be impracticable, the visitor picks out 'some of those recognized as the greatest' (254c),[2] which are especially relevant to a clear understanding of 'what is' and 'what is not'. Three are already familiar: Motion, Rest and Being, of which the first two will not mix, but the third mixes with both, for both *are*. Further, each is the same as itself and different from the others, and since none is *identical* with the Same (the Form Sameness), Same and Different are two more Forms, in which the first three share.[3] In demonstrating that Being and Difference are not identical, Plato draws the distinction between a thing's being 'in and by itself' and being relative to something else. The Form Being includes both, i.c. Socrates *is* (exists, or is himself)[4] and Socrates is . . . (e.g. shorter than Simmias) but Difference is always relative (πρός τι).

Attention is now concentrated on Difference, because the Sophist relied for his escape on the impossibility of saying of anything that it 'is not', and Plato wants to show that it may be equivalent only to the perfectly permissible statement that it 'is different' from something else.

---

[1] 253b–c. See Cornford, *PTK* 261f.

[2] For the translation 'greatest' rather than 'very great' (Cornford) see Ross, *PTI* 113 n. 6. Peck (*CQ* 1952, 45) says 'the meaning of μέγιστον is not explained'. Presumably it means, as usual, 'largest', i.e. widest. Each of the γένη Being, Same and Other includes everything, and Rest and Motion divide the whole field between them. Why should this need explanation? Cf. also Ackrill in *Ryle*, 391. Others (Leisegang, *RE* 2495, Trevaskis in *Phron.* 1962) render it 'most important' or 'basic', because these are the γένη to which earlier philosophers had paid most attention, asking 'What is Being?' and answering 'It is motion' (Heraclitus) or 'rest' (Parmenides).

[3] That 'Motion is different (from Rest)' does not mean that Motion and Difference are the same thing seems obvious enough, but P. defends it by quite a complicated little argument, explained by Cornford, *PTK* 280 n. 1.

[4] Owen has suggested that the contrast is probably not between the complete and incomplete uses of εἶναι but between two incomplete uses, in statements of identity and of predication (*New Essays*, ed. Bambrough, 71 n. 1). It may, however, distinguish the absolute use from use as a copula.

Difference is a 'vowel' Form which 'pervades' all the others (255e), for each is different from the rest without being Difference itself. We are now getting to the heart of the matter. We can say Motion is both the same and not the same because *we are not using the word in the same sense in both cases* (ού ... ὁμοίως εἰρήκαμεν 256a11). Our sentence is in fact incomplete. Properly speaking it should run: It is the same (partakes of Sameness) with reference to itself by being the same as itself, but not the same in that it partakes in, or combines with, Difference in relation to everything else. Thus the principle that whereas a particular could possess contrary qualities by partaking in contrary Forms, this could scarcely be true of the relationships of Forms to each other (*Parm.* 129d–e, p. 37 above), is modified. A Form cannot mix with its own contrary, but any Forms, say *A* and *B*, can partake of others *X* and *Y*, *X* and *Y* being contraries, if the concepts of which *X* and *Y* are prototypes are relative and with the proviso that *A* and *B* cannot partake of both in relation to the same thing. Completed and philosophically analysed, sentences like '*A* is the same' and '*A* is different' become '*A* partakes of Sameness with reference to itself' and '*A* partakes of Difference with reference to *B*.' And it both 'is' (partakes of Being) and 'is not' (is different from Being itself). Even Being 'is not' in the sense that it is different from the other Forms (257a).

Perhaps the great contribution of the *Sophist* to philosophy lies in the statement that I have italicized, that a word can be used in more than one sense.[1] The whole challenge of Parmenides, and many of the arguments of Sophistic, rested on the assumption that the verb 'to be' meant one thing and one thing only. Once it had been shown that the same word was not always used to express the same concept—that for instance existence, identity and attribution were not the same, though expressed by the same word 'is'—Greek thought was freed from a whole host of unreal (and at this distance of time almost incomprehensible) problems. Aristotle could start where Plato left off, with the simple pronouncement that 'there are many ways in which a thing is said to "be"', and proceed without further ado to enumerate them,

---

[1] Cf. also 259c–d, where the visitor speaks of the importance, 'when anyone says that something different is somehow the same, of being able to determine in what sense and in what respect he means it is one or the other'. He adds that this, in contrast to the trivialities of eristic argument, is a task both difficult and worth while.

discarding the clumsy language of Forms which had served its purpose in the pioneer work of Plato.[1]

As with knowledge (257c) and its different departments, sciences or crafts,[2] 'the nature of the Different' is divided into 'parts', the not-beautiful, not-tall, not-just and so on. These are contrasted with their opposites the beautiful and so on, and exist no less than they.

The not-beautiful obviously includes everything that is not beautiful, the not-just everything that is not (is different from) just (thus disposing of the fallacy committed by Socrates at *Prot.* 331a: the difference between contraries and contradictories has just been cleared up at 257b). Whether 'everything' should be 'every Form' the fatal ambiguity of 'the beautiful' makes it difficult to decide.[3] Probably the not-beautiful is, as Cornford said (*PTK* 293), 'the collective name for all the Forms there are, other than the single Form "Beautiful"'. Each of them partakes of the Different with reference to the others. This has a bearing on the warning in the *Politicus* to divide according to true kinds or classes. To divide mankind into Greeks and barbarians is bad classification because 'barbarian' is simply a name covering all the heterogeneous races which are not Greek—Lydians, Phrygians, Persians, Egyptians and so on. It signifies a part or portion (μέρος) of humanity but not a true species (εἶδος) with its own character. In the language of the *Sophist* it applies to all races which participate in Difference with reference to Greeks.[4]

---

[1] Τὸ ὂν λέγεται πολλαχῶς are the opening words of *Metaph.* Z, and in his glossary of philosophical terms in bk. Δ he can begin each section by saying that 'cause', 'nature', 'quality', 'state', or whatever it may be, is in one sense (lit. 'way of speaking') *x*, in another *y* and so on.

[2] Cf. *Rep.* 438c–d: 'Knowledge as such is of subject as such, but a particular science is of a particular subject, e.g. there is a knowledge of building, set apart from the others by the name architecture, because it has a character different from the others.'

[3] It is not always easy to share Cornford's optimistic view (p. 292) that though P. uses τὸ ὂν etc. ambiguously (sometimes as 'Existence itself', sometimes as 'the existent' or 'that which is so and so'), he himself was always aware of the ambiguities. Was Cornford himself always clear? In his translation of 258c ('that which is not . . . *is* what-is-not, a single Form') should not either τὸ μὴ ὂν be 'Non-being' or alternatively ἓν εἶδος 'a single class', with no overtones of capital-letter Forms?

[4] *Pol.* 262c–63b, pp. 168, 293 n. 3 below. As an illustration P. also cites Number, of which subordinate Forms (Odd and Even) are species or parts (εἴδη: every subordinate εἶδος is a μέρος, though not every μέρος is an εἶδος, 263b). Schipper's statement that a Form has no parts (*Phron.* 1964, 43) is erroneous. The language of the early dialogues (the Pious a part of the Just, Courage a part of Virtue, *Euthyphro* 12d, *Lach.* 199e) was not abandoned when the doctrine of Forms developed further. Cf. p. 276 below.

It looks as if the chase is over. By noting the all-pervading nature of Difference Plato has been able to maintain against Parmenides that what is not really *is*, though contrasted with what also is, as the non-Beautiful is contrasted with the Beautiful but exists no less than it (258d–e). Non-being need not mean absolute non-existence, but simply Difference in relation to *x*, so that 'there is much that each Form is, but an infinite number of things that it is not' (256e). 'And this is the non-being which our concern with the Sophist led us to seek' (258b6). When we accuse him of creating misleading copies that 'are not' the originals, we only mean that they differ from them.

Speech and thought: the nature of falsehood (259b–264b). But the visitor is not yet satisfied. The Sophist, it has been said, deceives us, that is, makes us believe falsehoods (240d), but thinking what is not true is thinking what is not in yet another sense more difficult to explain.[1] The difficulty here arises from the Greek equation of truth with 'being', referred to several times already. A Greek spoke not only of saying or believing a falsehood (*pseudos*) but equally idiomatically of saying or believing what is not.[2] So far the argument has not accounted for falsehoods as satisfactorily as for negative statements.

The Sophist had two escape-routes. First, he denied that he could be a deceiver or illusionist because it is logically impossible to speak or conceive of what is not. This is the difficulty stated and left unsolved in the *Theaetetus*, and the reason given for the failure was that they were wrong to discuss false judgement before deciding the prior question of the nature of knowledge. It is at least possible that the *Theaetetus* as well as the three following dialogues formed together a single plan in Plato's mind. The stages would be: (1) Preliminary: to raise the question of knowledge, explore its difficulties, and reject some inadequate answers (*Theaetetus*); (2) Destructive: to expose as fraudulent the Sophists' claim to knowledge (*Sophist*); (3) Positive: to answer the question and describe the state of mind of the possessor of genuine knowledge (*Politicus* leading up to *Philosopher*). The *Politicus* fills some

[1] The impossibility of false statement or judgement has been amply illustrated in the *Euthyd.* and is also asserted by Cratylus at *Crat.* 429d (p. 12 above). That its object cannot be 'what is not' was affirmed in *Tht.*, where the problem here tackled was shelved (p. 107 above).

[2] 240d λέγεις ἄρα τὰ μὴ ὄντα δοξάζειν τὴν ψευδῆ δόξαν; Cf. p. 69 above.

gaps in the right method of acquiring knowledge and describes the true statesman, who is in fact the philosopher in one of his aspects, and the series would have been crowned by a description of philosophy and the philosopher as such.

Now however it has been shown that 'is not' may mean only 'is different from'. This the Sophist must accept, but he may still hold out by suggesting that, since it also appeared that not all Forms can combine, Speech and Belief may be of those that cannot combine with Not-being, which again would make falsehood and deception impossible. To counter this new wile will necessitate an investigation into the whole nature and status of *logos* (here significant speech, statement or continuous discourse), *doxa* and *phantasia*. *Doxa* (belief or judgement) is the outcome of thought, which is simply a *logos* carried on silently by the mind with itself (263e–64a; *Tht.* 189e–90a), and when it depends on sensation is called *phantasia*. *Logos*, therefore, is basic to all three, and a study of it will be rewarding for its own sake, since without *logos* there could be no philosophy.

In this connexion the visitor says that those who deny any combination of Forms annihilate all *logos*, 'for the *Logos* owes its birth to the weaving together of Forms with each other'.[1] If there were no blending of Forms, *Logos* could never combine with Being, i.e. could not exist.[2] Having removed that initial difficulty, we have now to consider its nature, in the hope of discovering whether or not it will blend with Not-being, so allowing for 'a *logos* of what is not', or falsehood.

A *logos* consists of words, which are of two sorts, nouns and verbs.[3] Like the realities which they express, some words can combine and others not. The simplest *logos* must 'weave together' (262d4) one of

[1] The context shows that at 259e the 'things' separated (no noun is used) are in Plato's eyes Forms. The reference is to the foolish people of 251b who delight in allowing none but identical predication, and the question at 251d: 'Are we not to attach . . . any Form to any other, but to treat them all as incapable of mingling or partaking in one another?'

[2] See additional note on p. 161 below, and cf. 260a: 'See how pertinently we opposed such men [*sc.* those who separate everything from everything else] and forced them to allow one thing to mingle with another.' 'Pertinently to what?' 'To the thesis that the *Logos* was one of the kinds (γένη) of things that are.'

[3] ὀνόματα (lit. names, cf. *nomen*, 'noun') is first used generally for 'word' (261d2), and subsequently (262a1) confined to nouns, words being defined as 'vocal signs concerned with being' (οὐσία, 261e5). On the meaning of ῥῆμα see p. 11 n. 4 above and cf. Luce, *CQ* 1969, 229 n. 1. Here it is confined to τὸ ἐπὶ ταῖς πράξεσιν ὂν δήλωμα (262a3).

each class, for only so can one 'say something' (*legein*, i.e. make a significant statement) rather than merely naming.[1] Being about something, it will be either true or false; which it is depends on the relation between its parts. Once again the idea, already established, that 'to be' expresses relation as well as existence, provides the key. The conditions for a false statement like 'Theaetetus is flying' are two: (1) that the subject must be real (Theaetetus, not Mr Gradgrind),[2] (2) that the predicate must also be real (flying occurs), but not applicable to the subject. As a negative statement like 'Socrates is not a Spartan' or 'Clinias is not wise' expresses not non-existence but difference, so the false statement about Theaetetus expresses not 'what is not' absolutely but 'what is other than' the things that are concerning Theaetetus. The true one states 'the things that are about him as they are' (263 b–d).[3]

The extent of Plato's achievement here is well summed up by Ackrill (*Monist* 1966, 383 f.). He

makes clear the special grammatical and logical complexity of the sentence, a unit which interweaves a *naming* part (ὄνομα) with a *saying* part (ῥῆμα). A statement must be about something, and it must say something about it. But it can assert a real property of a real subject when that property does not in fact belong to that subject.

It is obvious that Plato's brief discussion in the *Sophist* does not say all that needs to be said about false statement. For example his account does not cater for the possibility of false existential statements. Nor does he make clear in what sense each part of a sentence must stand for something 'real'. Nevertheless he certainly makes an important advance in the *Sophist* by recognizing the special type of complexity which a sentence enjoys, and by tying the notions of truth and falsity to these specially complex units.

Return to dichotomy: the Sophist finally captured (266c–268d). The visitor now sums up the position. The aim was to define the essential nature of the Sophist by the dialectical method of *diairesis*, but when

---

[1] On the question whether this is consistent with the treatment of names in *Crat.*, see Luce 229. In general, their treatment there should be kept in mind. Cf. pp. 19–23, 25–9 above. That a λόγος consists of ὄνομα and ῥῆμα is repeated both there (425 a) and in *Ep.* 7 (342 b).

[2] The status of statements about fictional characters and mythical creatures is still under discussion. Strawson favours the view that they are neither true nor false (*Introd. to Log. Theory* 69), others that they are true and others again (including Russell) that they are false. See H. G. Blocker, 'The Truth about Fictional Entities', in *PQ* 1974.

[3] Cf. Ctesippus at *Euthyd.* 284c, vol. IV, 271. There the Sophists were allowed to triumph: here their crudity is revealed.

they had reached the point of seeing him as 'image-maker', offering the appearance of knowledge without the reality (pp. 133 f. above), they were diverted by the need to analyse and justify the concepts of imitation and deception. This done, they can return to their dichotomies.

However, instead of continuing from the division of images into likenesses and semblances at which they broke off, the visitor goes right back to the very widest genus, art, under which the Sophist's occupation, like the angler's, could be brought (p. 124), and from which therefore the classification had to begin. This is reasonable, because imitation or image-making had not been reached by the strict method of dichotomy. That had been used to elicit each of seven varieties of Sophistry, and its essential nature as imitation ('what a Sophist really is', 231 c) had been discovered in the more familiar Socratic way of achieving a definition by abstracting the common element from a number of diverse instances.[1] It is now to be given its place in a complete series of dichotomies.

As image-maker the Sophist belongs to the other main subdivision of the arts, productive not acquisitive, though admittedly the acquisitive branch did show up certain genuine aspects of him (265 a). To pursue the dichotomies, his art is productive (not acquisitive), human (not divine), of imitations (not originals), which are semblances (not likenesses: see p. 134 for the distinction), mimetic, i.e. in his own person (not produced with tools),[2] in ignorance (not with knowledge), insincere (not naive), in personal encounters, using brief arguments to make an adversary contradict himself (not using long speeches). Here at last we have the Sophist, rightly called by a derivative of *sophos* to indicate that, though not himself wise, he is an imitator of the wise man. So the dialogue ends.

The last dichotomy repeats one in an earlier *diairesis* (225 b–c). Plato is evidently considering the Sophist purely as an eristic, disregarding his epideictic displays. At 223 b, where he is seen as a 'hunter of men

[1] It may also be described as the collection that precedes division (p. 131). The above considerations make it unnecessary to suppose with Cornford that Plato's is 'consciously shelving the *eidola* problem' because he cannot yet solve it ('If he had thought it was already solved, he would have taken up the Division of Image-making at the point where it was dropped', *PTK* 323), and the ontological status of sensibles in *Rep.* 5 seems irrelevant. As C. himself says, 'the only *eidola* we are now concerned with are those which the Sophist is accused of creating'.

[2] The distinction is between acting a part and representation in sculpture and painting.

privately', Cornford (*PTK* 174) supposed that his displays before an invited audience are included in contrast to forensic and political oratory. But (apart from the fact that the Sophists gave them at the Panhellenic festivals) they can hardly be included in the 'private controversy chopped up into questions and answers' of 225 b, where Sophistic is classified under agonistic. That only referred to one aspect of Sophistic, but now we meet the same thing in its universal definition. This is curious when one remembers how the Platonic Socrates complains of the way that Protagoras will not stand up to short questions and answers but prefers to launch out into long speeches, or conversely Hippias is unhappy because Socrates will not allow him to explain himself at length instead of replying briefly to questions. Here long speeches are assigned to the demagogue, expressly distinguished from the Sophist with his contradictious brachylogy. The type seems to be that of Euthydemus and Dionysodorus rather than Protagoras. Plato's reasons for limiting Sophistic in this way are a matter of guesswork,[1] but with the 'Sophistry of noble extraction' in mind (pp. 128 f. above), we may suspect that he still felt the need to distinguish Socrates from the kind of Sophist with whom he was most easily confused.

If in some things the *Sophist* seems to reveal a changed Plato, the final *diairesis* reminds us that in at least two fundamental points he did not change. First, in clarifying the division of imitation into knowledgeable and ignorant, and of the latter into naive and insincere, he shows himself still mindful of the Socratic search for moral truth, for he takes as his illustration those who appear to others to exhibit in themselves 'the shape of Justice and the whole of Virtue', 'seeming to be, but in no way being, just', because they have no knowledge of what Justice is, but only *doxa*. Some are simple souls who genuinely mistake their *doxa* for the truth, but others are experienced debaters with a shrewd suspicion that what they give out for knowledge is not knowledge at all (267c–268a). These of course include the Sophists, and the passage would be quite at home in the *Gorgias* or *Meno*.

---

[1] Campbell (ed., p. xlviii) says P. is describing the ideal Sophist rather than any individual. Ritter comments simply that the eristic aspect is singled out as the most dangerous: compared with it mere loquacity is harmless (*N. Unters.* 65). In Taylor's view (*PMW* 376, following Schleiermacher as do many others) the solution was obvious: for 'Sophists' read 'Megarians'. I would not go bail for this, even though the latter are credited with maintaining τὸ ὂν ἓν εἶναι καὶ τὸ ἕτερον μὴ εἶναι (vol. III, 500).

Secondly we have the division of production or creation into human and divine. To justify it the visitor is at pains to insist that what are called the works of Nature must not be looked on as the product of some automatic and mindless force, but as the work of a craftsman-god, acting with reason, art and knowledge (265 c). The *Phaedo* had upheld a teleological view of the universe based on a development of Anaxagoras's brilliant but unexploited pronouncement that all things were ordered by Mind, and the *Timaeus*, whether written before or after the *Sophist*, expounds in detail the creation of the living cosmos by a divine craftsman[1] after the pattern of the Forms. In traditional Greek religion none of the gods, not even Zeus, created the world, and the combination of supreme god with creator may fairly be credited to Plato among philosophers, even if he had learned something from the Orphic writers to whom he frequently shows himself indebted.[2] It is interesting to find it in a predominantly critical and analytical work like the *Sophist*.

The Sophist *and the Forms*. The view adopted here of the role of the Forms in this dialogue should have emerged plainly enough by now, but it is a question that has caused considerable bewilderment. Richard Robinson for instance speaks sadly of 'the dreadful question of whether the μέγιστα γένη of the *Sophist* are Forms, on which I have not yet succeeded in reaching a confident opinion', and Peck denied that they were. Terminology does not help: εἶδος and γένος (used synonymously, e.g. at 254b–c) are frequently given by Plato their common meanings of 'character' or 'class'. We have also had to face the helpless feeling induced by the indiscriminate use of abstract noun and adjective (or participle) with the article (pp. 142f., 150 above).

Where Forms appear with capital initial in this chapter, it is assumed that Plato thought of them as Platonic Forms, not merely concepts of the mind but realities with an objective and independent existence. He even remembers their exalted status, for at 254a he says that the philosopher, through his devotion to the Form of Being, dwells in the brightness of the divine, and just before this the philosopher's ability to

---

[1] δημιουργός. Cf. δημιουργοῦντος at *Soph.* 265 b 4 and δημιουργός at *Pol.* 273 b and of the creator of the stars at *Rep.* 529 e 1.
[2] For Zeus as creator in Orphic literature see Guthrie, *OGR* 106f.

distinguish *eidē* aright, and the ways in which they can and cannot combine, is called dialectic, and though the description of dialectic as discrimination between *eidē* goes back to Socrates (p. 27 above), its goal since the central books of the *Republic* can only be Forms. A moment later he as good as tells us that this is matter for the *Philosopher* (254b).

Yet this aspect of the Forms merits, and finds, no place in the logical problems of the *Sophist*, and their solution is none the better for metaphysical props. Indeed the paradigmatic character of the Forms, involving the belief that they are perfect instances of themselves, only causes trouble. At 255a10 Plato meets an argument by rejecting as absurd the idea that Motion can be at rest. This ought to show either that Motion is not a Form or that motion and change have been not only accepted as realities but introduced into the Forms themselves. Yet it is hard to believe that Plato intended to imply either conclusion. The metaphorical language inseparable from the doctrine of Forms—sharing, binding, running through and so on—and especially its undue reliance on substantival expressions,[1] were unsuited to exploring the fields of logic and language. Difference is for Plato not simply a relation but a relational property (and so a Form), which leads to the clumsiness of analysing 'Motion is not Rest' into 'Motion shares in Difference with respect to Rest', instead of the simpler 'differs from'. It is said that he was hampered by the resources of language available to him at that time, but there was no difficulty about saying 'motion differs from rest' in contemporary Greek. What hampered him was his faith in the all-sufficiency of the doctrine of Forms, and the undoubted logical advances of the *Sophist* were gained in spite of that faith, not through it. By his definition of a *logos* he confined propositions to the subject–predicate type (the predicate at least being for him a Form), which persisted in Aristotle (*Rhet.* 1404b26) and dogged the footsteps of logic until the twentieth century. Like everyone else, he could not escape completely from his historical situation. Parmenides had compelled him to argue at length a case for 'is' not always meaning exists, and faced with this necessity he thought of the Forms, which he had first evolved in response to the Socratic faith in absolute values, as

[1] Commented on in vol. IV, 226.

suitable instruments for the purpose. They do play a role in the *Sophist*, but philosophy might have progressed more easily if they had not.

ADDITIONAL NOTES

(*i*) *On* 259*d* (*p.* 155): '*The Logos has its birth through the interweaving of Forms with each other*'

References: Cornford, *PTK* 300f.; Ackrill, *SPM* 199f., Hackforth, *CQ* 1945, 56–8; Bluck, *JHS* 1957, 181–6; Peck, *CQ* 1952, 32–56 and *Phron.* 1962, 46–66; Lorenz and Mittelstrass, *AGP* 1966, 113–52; Hamlyn, *PQ* 1955, 289–302; W. and M. Kneale, *Development of Logic* 20.

This sentence has caused great difficulty, for at 263a the statement 'Theaetetus is sitting' is given as an example of a *logos*, yet it exhibits a combination not of Forms but of a single Form with a particular. There have been many attempts to solve this problem, and others are referred to in the discussions mentioned above. Cornford took P. to mean that 'at least one Form' must be used in every statement or judgement, but Ackrill was quick to point out that this is not what he says. Hackforth suggested that συμπλοκὴ εἰδῶν was different from κοινωνία γενῶν and that the εἴδη here are parts of speech, but neither Peck, Bluck nor Lorenz and Mittelstrass could believe this, the last-named pointing out that συμπλοκή has occurred earlier, at 240d 1, where it is applied to the Forms Being and Not-being. Bluck, taking it as axiomatic that if all *logos* consists of a weaving together of Forms every statement must somehow involve at least two Forms, even if it is about an individual, concluded that the specimen *logos* about Theaetetus wove together the two Forms Man and Sitting. Hamlyn's solution is similar: Theaetetus 'unpacks' into a list of all the Forms in which he partakes. So too Lorenz and Mittelstrass, but this is to treat rather light-heartedly the most puzzling feature of the passage: Theaetetus is not the Form of Man. '"Theaetetus is sitting" can be true', says Bluck (p. 182), 'because men are in fact capable of sitting.' But Plato says it *is* true, though it is not true either of all men or of the Form Man: to sit is neither an essential nor an exclusive attribute of mankind and has no place in its definition. The statement refers to Theaetetus alone. Peck was probably justified in calling Bluck's 'a desperate expedient', though it is interesting to note by the way how close it would bring Plato to Aristotle's epistemological theory of the perception of the universal (or specific form) through the individual. 'Though it is the individual that is perceived, perception is of the universal, e.g. of man, not Callias *a* man' (*An. Post.* 100a 16–b1).

Peck reversed Bluck's argument by laying it down that since the statement

'Theaetetus is sitting' clearly does not make use of a combination of Forms, the sentence under discussion cannot mean that every *logos* is constructed by weaving Forms together. It only means that the combination of Forms is a necessary precondition of the existence of *Logos* because, to exist, it must combine with Doing, and it is itself a Form (260a5). The sentence is not intended as a definition, for at 260a7 the visitor says that having established, by the doctrine of the blending of Forms, that *Logos* can exist, it remains to agree on *what* it is. And when the definition comes, it is in terms of a combination of words, not of Forms. I have adopted Peck's interpretation as the least open to objection, though it may seem a little extravagant of Plato that in order to defend the possibility of *Logos* existing, he should cite the general conditions which secure the existence of anything at all. ('This συμπλοκή includes the συμπλοκή of οὐσία (or τὸ ὄν) with all other εἴδη or γένη (259a)', Peck, *Phron.* 1962, 57.) If unsatisfied, one can, I suppose, fall back on the simple admission of Martha Kneale that Plato 'never dealt clearly with the distinction between singular and general statements'.

(*ii*) Republic 5 *and the* Sophist

Stenzel represented a fairly widespread view with his statement (*PMD* 53) that when we find in *Soph.* that false opinion exists because '"Not-Being", to which it is related, exists', 'This is in direct conflict with *Republic*, 478 B, and *Theaetetus*, 189 A, B, where Not-Being was declared to be, not only unknowable, but inconceivable, because nothingness cannot be conceived.' (Cf. Grote, *Pl.* II, 455 and Apelt, introd. p. 40.) But where is the conflict? In *Rep.* 5 we have at 477a: 'What fully is is fully knowable, what in no way is is entirely unknowable.' In *Soph.* (238c) Plato says (Cornford's translation): 'One cannot legitimately utter the words, or speak or think of that which just simply is not; it is unthinkable, not to be spoken of or uttered or expressed.' He removes the difficulty there by pointing out that the choice is not a simple one between 'is' and 'is not', because the verb 'to be' is used in different senses. In *Rep.* 5 he is facing quite a different problem, the onto-logical status of the sensible world. Nevertheless he solves it similarly by positing an intermediate category which 'shares in both being and non-being, and which it is not right to call purely and simply either' (479e). This is the object of *doxa*, lying between the known and the unknown (478e). Plato has already escaped the Parmenidean dilemma. The *Sophist*'s concep-tion of τὸ μὴ ὄν as θάτερον is no doubt an advance, making possible the claim at 258d that 'we have not only demonstrated that "things that are not are", but have brought to light the real nature of "what is not"'. This is of interest from the point of view of Plato's development, but the context is quite different and there is certainly no conflict.

(4) POLITICUS[1]

Introduction, outline and general remarks

The position of the *Politicus* among the dialogues is plain: it is a continuation of the *Sophist* (p. 33). Some have attempted to date its composition by relating it to Plato's activities in Sicily. This is at best uncertain, though the date arrived at (between 367 and 362) is likely enough.[2] The company is unchanged, but as respondent Theaetetus is replaced by the younger Socrates (to be referred to here as Y.S.).[3]

For those tidy minds (mentioned in vol. IV, 130) which like every dialogue to have one single aim, one 'real subject', *Hauptzweck* and so on, Plato has for once provided an explicit clue. He describes the *Politicus* as primarily an essay in method: 'Has our search for the Statesman been proposed for its own sake, or rather to make us better reasoners on any subject?' 'Clearly the latter.' (285 d) Again at 286d: 'Reason requires that we are content to give second place to an easy and quick solution of the problem we have set ourselves: our first and greatest care must be for the method itself, that is, learning to divide according to kinds.' A thorough examination of the method is indeed important, for as Plato will show, it can trap the unwary who apply it too mechanically, and demands an alert mind and constant use of good judgement if it is to be successful. On the other hand he does not say that the ostensible aim of tracking down the statesman is unimportant, only that in dealing with this or any other subject our natural desire for a quick and easy solution must not be satisfied at the expense of correct method, which would only mean that the answer when it came was wrong. One can understand therefore, what the dialogue shows plainly enough, that the primacy of method does not mean that the enquiry into statesmanship is a mere logical exercise, an illustrative example on a par with weaving here and angling in the *Sophist*. Rather it emphasizes

[1] The *Pol.* contains many interesting reff. to Athenian political, legal and economic practices, on which Skemp's introduction and notes may be recommended.
[2] See Skemp 14–17, with Tate's criticism in *CR* 1954, 115. (Reff. to Skemp are to his translation of the dialogue.)   [3] On Y.S. see p. 63.

the supreme importance of getting the definition right. Nor is the lesson of the *Republic* irrelevant, that the master of dialectic and the statesman are the same man.

The *Politicus* has been called a 'weary' dialogue, but is not so for those who enjoy Plato's mastery of the art of weaving (the word imposes itself) different topics together, not offering us dry little treatises on logic, political theory or ethics, but passing from one to the other and back again in a natural process of thinking aloud, with the guiding mind of the discussion-leader not avoiding digression but ensuring that each topic has had its due before the end.

An outline of the dialogue's structure will exhibit this. It sets out, like the *Sophist*, to define its subject through a *diairesis*, starting from a different division of knowledge. In the course of this, Y.S. is given a lesson in the dangers of a lopsided principle of division. It proceeds to its conclusion, which however is *declared unsatisfactory* because it has not distinguished the statesman from his nearest rivals.

Next comes a *long cosmic myth*, introduced as 'relaxation' (*paidia*), but also to reveal the errors of treating the statesman as if he were a god, a being of a superior order to his charges, whereas he is only a man among men, and of failing to make a proper *diairesis*.

A revised division follows, but is also rejected. To explain his objection the visitor will use an analogy, first however *explaining and illustrating the use of analogy itself.* The chosen analogy is weaving in wool, which is *now itself defined* by a long *diairesis*, invaluable to those interested for its detailed information on Greek weaving technique.[1] *This is rejected* on the same grounds as the analysis of statesmanship itself (thus showing up a defect in the latter), namely that it does not cut off weaving from some closely allied arts. A further, successful attempt introduces a *distinction between principal and ancillary arts*,[2] one sort directly produc-

---

[1] Wilamowitz's remark is just (*Pl.* 1, 576 f., apropos of this and the passage on angling in *Soph.*): 'It must not be forgotten that Plato had more observation at his disposal than he displays in his writings.' The other *locus classicus* on weaving for students of Greek technology is Aristoph. *Lys.* 567–87, the point of which is that weaving is an entirely feminine art; so it is all the more impressive that Plato should have the technical details at his finger-tips.

[2] αἴτια and συναίτια 281 d, 287 b. In this connexion the distinction between causes and necessary conditions at *Pho.* 99 a–b is often quoted. Closer in language at least are *Phil.* 27 a and *Tim.* 46 c, d.

tive, the other providing instruments or means for the production. That all this is in fact analogy (rather than merely an example of correct division exercised on a simpler subject), because the weaver turns out to be cousin to the statesman as the angler was to the Sophist, will be explained a little later.

The only part of the dialogue which could be called 'weary' is the long-drawn-out series of divisions leading to the definition of weaving,[1] and for this the visitor immediately apologizes. But Plato has more than apologies in mind. In the guise of defending this wordiness he introduces the *concept of the right mean*. This in turn leads to yet *another reminder of the importance of dialectic*, the science of discerning both differences and affinities between groups of Forms or kinds (*eidē*).

Return to the statesman is effected (287b) by an application of the new distinction between directly productive and instrumental arts, and an acknowledgement that *dichotomous division is not always adequate*: the division of instrumental arts must be sevenfold, and even then, the statesman's rivals are found elsewhere, among politically minded Sophists. *The theme is now political theory.* Statesmanship being a science, constitutions are classified according to the amount of knowledge they display. Ideally a state should be governed by a man or men of genuine knowledge, and nothing else would matter. Failing the ideal, a city's best safeguard lies in laws strictly enforced, but these remain a second-best because, being universally binding, they cannot do justice to the infinite variety of people and circumstances. As a 'side-issue' (302b8), the imperfect constitutions are ranked according to the tolerability of life under each.

The final stage, to separate the statesman's art from others even closer to it than its counterfeits, is reached by *yet another primary dichotomy of arts* into (*a*) an art itself, e.g. rhetoric, the art of persuading, (*b*) a master-art of knowing whether an art should be learned and how and when applied. The statesman's knowledge gives him this priority over kindred arts also necessary to good government—generalship, the administration of law and justice, public speaking, education. These he will guide and direct towards his own end, which is to weave the whole

---

[1] It is conveniently tabulated by Ritter, *Essence* 239.

state, with all its institutions and every citizen—the bold and high-spirited with the quiet and gentle—into a close, firm and durable fabric.

I have called this method of presentation enjoyable, but it is more. It points to connexions in Plato's mind which we might otherwise miss, especially those between method and subject-matter. The definition of weaving shows up a fault in the logic of *diairesis* but is also a metaphor for the essential work of the statesman. The dichotomy of measurement into comparative and evaluative is an example of, and encouragement to, correct *diairesis* according to real kinds (285a–b, 286d), but the principle of division is axiological, a reminder that the Forms discovered by *diairesis* itself are not merely genera and species but patterns or norms.

With so much established, we may look at certain topics in more detail, fortified against supposing that they were as segregated in Plato's mind as we now regard them for expository purposes.

(1) *Logic and method*

(a) *Collection and division.* This is how the dialectical method of collection and division, already known from the *Phaedrus* and *Sophist*, is described once more in the *Politicus*.

The proper procedure is, when perception first presents the common features of a number of things,[1] to press on until one can see all their specific differences; and conversely when in a multitude of objects all sorts of disparities are detected, not to be shamed into giving up until one has penned all that are cognate into a single enclosure of similarity and included them within a genuine genus. (285 a–b)

---

[1] In the passages descriptive of this method here and at *Soph.* 253 d it is not easy to know whether Plato has in mind Forms or particulars as the starting-point. Perhaps he is not discriminating, as Hackforth suggested was the case at *Phil.* 16d. (See his *PEP* 23 n. 2.) Here however I have opted (unlike Skemp) for particulars, which are strongly suggested by the combination of πολλά with πλῆθος. (Cf. *Phil.* 16d7.) Even the dialectician must start (as in the *Phaedo*) from the evidence of his senses, making use of the universal human capacity to form elementary general concepts, and even at this early stage the non-philosopher may make mistakes, grouping, say, flowers by obvious but inessential differences which the trained botanist would ignore. I therefore give αἰσθηται at b1 its ordinary reference to sense-perception, which is of course natural and easy, though not absolutely necessary. (At *Soph.* 253d7 διαισθάνεται is used with ἰδέα as its object.)

This is a somewhat clearer exposition of the method than that at *Soph.* 253 d, quoted above on pp. 129 f. It is applied to 'the way of statesmanship' at 258 c: 'We must discover it, and separating it from other ways, stamp upon it its unique form.' In the *Sophist* the practice definition of the angler preceded that of the Sophist himself. Here Plato begins with the real subject, and only after failure turns for help to a parallel case. In the course of the long first *diairesis* the statesman appears as the nurturer of a hornless, wingless, tame two-footed herd incapable of interbreeding with other species. The *summum genus* chosen is again art (*technē*, dependent on knowledge), but a new initial dichotomy is adopted, into theoretical and practical. The statesman is assigned to the theoretical, not in the sense of being pure scientist or mathematician but like a master-builder who designs a house and supervises its construction, a worker with brain not hand. The risk of confusion is removed by dividing theoretical knowledge into critical (involving judgement alone with no action following) and directive. Knowledge is the sole qualification, and the man who has it deserves the title of statesman or king even if he remains a private citizen and only advises the actual ruler—the position Plato thought proper for himself and his associates.[1]

The *Politicus* brings out even more clearly than the *Sophist* how far *diairesis* is from being a merely mechanical process. It is indeed 'easy enough to indicate but extremely hard to practice' (*Phil.* 16b–c). From the initial dichotomy onwards, every step involves personal judgement and choice, and in spite of apparent trivialities, sometimes introduced only to show how the inexpert may go astray, the continual watchful insight required to keep on the right track makes credible Plato's claim that dialectician and trained philosopher are one and the same. Both, one might say, are far advanced along the road to 'recollection' of the Forms. 'Acquisitive and productive' and 'theoretical and practical' are in his eyes equally legitimate divisions of the genus 'art', but not equally suitable for the investigation of a particular subject. It may be necessary to proceed quite far with the successive subdivisions before it becomes evident that something is wrong, that divisions are not

[1] 259a. Cf. vol. IV, 23. He must also have remembered that in the *Gorg.* (521 d) he had described Socrates as the only one to practise the real art of politics. True, S. did not even advise the governing element (*Apol.* 31 c), but in his eyes as in P.'s, where power lay with the *demos* there was no genuine ruler to accept advice.

being made 'at the natural joints' but haphazard, revealing only parts that do not correspond to genuine Forms (262a–b). Then the successive steps must be retraced, to see at what point the error occurred (275c–d). In the first *diairesis*, the rather laboured humour of hinting that man's closest competitor is the pig, and likening his mode of walking to 'the two-foot potency of the diagonal' (266b c), as well as the ridiculous definition itself, are probably intended to emphasize the pitfalls of amateur dialectic. The failure of this first attempt is obviously contrived by the visitor with deliberate pedagogic intent.

The most important rule is that the divisions of dialectic must correspond to reality, i.e. to the ontological distinctions between Form and Form. They are discovered, not imposed.[1] The opposite fault comes to light when Y.S., in their search for the objects of the statesman's care, suggests dividing off men from beasts. This is to contrast a single species (Form) with an unanalysed aggregate. To put the whole non-human animal kingdom on one side of a dichotomy is not dialectical 'division according to kinds' but the severance of a part which exemplifies no specific Form. Every Form is a portion of a wider genus, but not every portion is a Form.[2] The visitor compares the Greek habit of dividing mankind into Greeks and foreigners (*barbaroi*, lit. 'inarticulate'), and the imaginary case of dividing number into 10,000 and the rest, inventing a collective name for numbers other than 10,000. On this principle cranes, who are reported to possess intelligence, might divide living creatures into cranes and beasts, including mankind in the latter.[3]

---

[1] εὑρήσειν γὰρ ἐνοῦσαν, *Phil.* 16d.

[2] 262b1–3: 'Not to separate one small part over against many large ones, nor without regard to Form: the part must at the same time have a Form.' The second condition disposes of scholars (mentioned by Runciman, *PLE* 60 n. 1) who believe that P. rejects a division like that into Greek and non-Greek on purely extensional grounds.

[3] Many believe that besides the methodological point, P. here gets in a forceful criticism of the Greek attitude of superiority to the rest of mankind. Skemp (131 n. 1), though Tate (*CR* 1954, 116) thought his view exaggerated, has the support of Friedländer (III, 287f.), Ritter (*N. Unters.* 77) and others. Field on the other hand denied it (*P. and Contemps.* 130n.). Skemp's view certainly goes dead against *Rep.* 470b, as he admits, but he also points out that a different attitude was gaining ground among intellectuals of the fifth and fourth centuries. If there is a moral point intended, one would expect it to apply also to the example of the cranes, which would become a rebuke to mankind as a whole for vaunting its superiority over the beasts. A modern reader might naturally see it in that light, but for Plato man, with his immortal mind, his divine gift (*Phil.* 16c) of forming general concepts, making it possible for him to work his way up to recognition of the Forms that he once saw, was indeed set apart from the beasts through his affinities with a higher world.

(b) *The two types of measurement.* 'More and less must be measured not only in relation to each other but also with a view to the achievement of a norm' (284b).[1]

This is introduced as a principle of great importance, on a par with the distinction established in the *Sophist* between negative predication and denial of existence. It is no merely logical pronouncement, but reflects the whole Hellenic ethos of 'nothing too much' and anticipates Aristotle's doctrine that goodness lies in a mean. It is 'what especially distinguishes bad men from good' (283e).[2] The word *metrion* (translated 'norm' above), from *metron*, measure, is basically what is within measure, sometimes 'average' (Hdt. 2.32.6), but generally used approvingly of what is in *due* measure, moderate, sometimes almost a synonym for 'good'.[3]

The first sort of measurement, Plato goes on, is sufficient for purely theoretical studies (284a). The pure mathematician calculates the relation between numbers. (Ratio was basic to Pythagorean mathematics.) He works with arithmetical, geometrical and harmonic means, but there is no question of a *right* mean because he has no ulterior purpose in view. But both are demanded by pursuits which, like statesmanship, have a practical aim. Plato goes so far as to say that without the skill to judge excess and defect, politics, weaving and every other art would be destroyed (284a), for all have to consider 'what is in due measure (*metrion*), what is fitting, what opportune, what has to be done', and these are never found among extremes (284e).

All this has an oddly familiar air. In the *Protagoras* (337e–8b) Hippias recommends a moderate (*metrion*) length in speeches, as opposed to long harangues or excessive brevity. Prodicus laughed at orators who boasted of making very short or very long speeches at will: a good speech should be neither long nor short but *metrion* (*Phdr.* 267b).

---

[1] πρὸς τὴν τοῦ μετρίου γένεσιν. There can be no philosophical significance in the change to γένεσις from φύσις at 283e3, though φύσις there must mean real nature or essence. Ritter perhaps goes too far in claiming that the phrases τῆς γενέσεως οὐσία and ὄντως γιγνόμενον at 283d8 and e5 imply a deliberate modification of earlier doctrine about the opposition between being and becoming. (See his *Essence*, 183.) In its context the first phrase simply means that if anything is to be brought into being, then in the nature of the case the second kind of measurement is required. For a fuller comment in connexion with the *Phil.* see p. 233 n. 3 below.

[2] ἀγαθοί are distinguished from κακοί by their attainment of ἡ τοῦ μετρίου φύσις. At Arist. *EN* 1096a25 ἀγαθόν in the category of quantity consists in τὸ μέτριον.

[3] A typical example is Soph. *O.C.* 1212.

Conversely, when Socrates himself in the *Protagoras*, ostensibly advocating a hedonistic ethic, says that the good life can only be assured by a science of measurement able to estimate excess and defect,[1] he confines his advice to the first kind of measurement, of pleasures and pains against each other, a process expressly condemned in the *Phaedo* (vol. IV, 234). Has not Plato himself asserted that the attributes of anything in this world (and it is with this world that the practical arts must come to terms) depend solely on its relation to other things? 'Large and small, light and heavy, can equally well be given the opposite epithet', what is double is also half and so on (*Rep.* 479b).

These statements need some sorting out. The Sophists were following the everyday use of *metrion* to mean not simply medial but of the *right* length. In a loose way it does measure things not against each other but against a standard, but they could not have defined their standard nor would they, with Plato at 286d, have rejected pleasure as a legitimate consideration. The Sophists were relativists,[2] and Ritter[3] does not fail to point in this connexion to Protagoras's teaching that the only *metron* is what appears to the individual (though according to the *Theaetetus* (p. 86 above) even he admitted that in practical judgements an individual man or state may be at fault). For Plato the standard is obviously provided by the changeless and definable Forms, culminating in the Form of the Good. After explaining the twofold division of measure, he immediately links it with *diairesis*, which, he repeats, is the method that enables one 'to divide according to Forms' (286d), and he

---

[1] See 356d–57b. μετρητική . . . ὑπερβολῆς καὶ ἐνδείας at 357b especially resembles the phraseology of the *Pol.* Cf. 283c11 and e3, 285b7–8.

[2] For the two kinds, or degrees, of relativity in values see vol. III, 166, and for a modern treatment of the distinctions between objective and subjective, absolute and relative, Flew, *Introd.* 81 ff.

[3] *N. Unters.* 87. All scholars except Ritter (including Skemp, p. 174 n. 1 and p. 79) have taken the κομψοί at 285a1 to be the Pythagoreans, but there is a strong case for R.'s belief that P. has in mind followers of Protagoras who upheld his doctrine of 'man the measure'. The case is strengthened (though R. does not mention it) by what we find at *Rep.* 454a about the ἀντιλογικοί, not dialecticians but eristics, who speak as they do διὰ τὸ μὴ δύνασθαι κατ' εἴδη διαιρούμενοι τὸ λεγόμενον ἐπισκοπεῖν. (At *Pol.* 285a the κομψοί go wrong διὰ τὸ μὴ κατ' εἴδη συνειθίσθαι σκοπεῖν διαιρουμένους.) And the κομψοί here could well hold the theory of the relativity of sensation ascribed to κομψότεροι at *Tht.* 156a (pp. 77 ff. above). The Pythagoreans would then be those who *rightly* employ the first standard because as mathematicians they are concerned only with 'all arts which measure number, lengths, depths, breadths and velocities by relative standards' (284e). From them the Sophists are distinguished as those who wrongly confine themselves to it in making practical and moral judgements.

warns that what has been said here will be needed when the time comes to demonstrate the very nature of truth.[1]

But this is not the whole story. Though not Sophistic, the message of the *Politicus* is not an extreme absolutism.[2] The discovery of the second type of measurement does not entail abandonment of the first (283e10–11), and the enlargement of the due measure to include appropriateness, opportunity (*kairos*), what the situation demands,[3] vividly recalls Gorgias and his fellow-orators, for whom *kairos* in particular, the sense of occasion, was a prime requirement of successful speaking (vol. III, 272). In the middle dialogues the exaltation of the divine Forms, and man's status as an immortal soul acquainted with them in another existence, had thrust into the background an essential ingredient of Platonism and in particular of its legacy from Socrates, which leads here to a conception of the statesman and his task more realistic than the visionary creation of the Republic.[4] In equating goodness with practical benefit Socrates saw that in ordinary life the good was always relative to a particular end, and as situations differed so did the good. Plato still shows him saying this in the *Phaedrus*: knowing how to administer different treatments does not make a man a doctor unless he also knows when and for which patients they are appropriate. In the *Meno* even virtues can be unwisely practised and lead to harm.[5]

In the *Phaedrus* it is the rhetoricians who resemble the quack doctor, and their fault is the same as that of those in the *Politicus* who fail to use the second principle of measurement, namely ignorance of dialectic, which prevents them from even defining their own art and so knowing its true purpose (*Phdr.* 269b). Now the strands begin to combine. Central is the concept of purpose, function, an end (*telos*) to be achieved—it is to practical arts that the second principle applies—and the end exists objectively and determines the means. If you want to

[1] 284d. Skemp's expansion of the untranslatable πρὸς τὴν περὶ αὐτὸ τὸ ἀκριβὲς ζήτησιν is 'to give a full exposition of true accuracy in dialectical method'. Lit. 'to seek to demonstrate the accurate (or true) itself'. Presumably the reference is to the *Philosopher*.

[2] Cf. Flew, *Introd.* 83: 'someone who believes that ethical values are objective can, with entire consistency, insist that the courses of conduct which these values determine must vary partly according to the particular occasions; and hence be relative to them'. Or Bambrough (*RTG* 143): 'The objectivity of morality is compatible with its "situational relativity".'

[3] τὸ πρέπον καὶ τὸν καιρὸν καὶ τὸ δέον, 284e.

[4] This is expanded on pp. 183ff. below.

[5] *Phdr.* 268a–c, *Meno* 88a–c. This side of S. has been treated fully in vol. III, 462–7.

produce a well-governed city or a woollen coat there are certain things you must do. It is 'in the necessary nature of production' (283 d). It was Socrates's insistence that the *telos* must first be understood, and as proof of understanding defined,[1] that led to the doctrine of Forms. They were and remained Ideals or standards to be aimed at (*paradeigmata*), even though human attempts must always fall short of their perfection. The further point that these standards lie in a mean between contraries is illustrated by the *leitmotif* of weaving with its firm warp and softer, more pliant weft, culminating in the final description of the statesman's own skill as that of reconciling bold and rash with quiet and peaceful temperaments; and that no earthly state can reach the ideal appears in the necessity for a permanent system of laws in default of the perfect ruler.

Plato did not give up his belief in a universal Form of Good. Even Aristotle, who argued against it, could not believe that carpenters and shoemakers, and even parts of the body like hands and feet, should have their proper function and activities yet humanity as such have none, and he went on to describe this universal and exclusively human end. (See *EN* 1097b 28–98a 20.) Conversely Plato is coming closer to the Aristotelian position that for practical purposes knowledge of the highest Good is insufficient unless one knows what means to it (subdivisions of it?) are immediately applicable. The philosophic ruler, while not losing sight of the ultimate goal, must also be able to think things through to the proximate step 'which he himself can take'.[2] His course resembles the 'downward path' of *Republic* 6, with the all-important difference that that 'involves nothing in the sensible world, but moves solely through Forms to Forms, and finishes with Forms' (511b–c). The statesman must continue until he can grapple with situations in this space- and timebound world. To this development Plato's increasing use of the method of *diairesis* made an obvious con-

---

[1] The process in the practical arts is well expressed by Aristotle in the *Ethics* (1111b23): 'The last step in the analysis is the first in production', and illustrated at *Metaph.* 1032b6–10: 'Health is produced by a train of thought like this: "Since this [of which I have the form (*eidos*) in my mind] is health, *this* must be present for the subject to be healthy, e.g. an equable state of the body; and if that, then warmth." So the doctor goes on thinking until he finally reaches a step which he himself can take... So in a way health is brought into being by health and a house by a house, the material from the non-material. For medicine and architecture are the form of health and house, and what I call substance without matter is the essence.'

[2] See previous note, and cf. *Phil.* 62a–b on the plight of the man who knows the Form of Justice but cannot use the tools of a trade or find his own way home.

tribution by bringing down the Forms as nearly as possible, within the necessary limits of knowledge, to the individual level.

(c) *The use of paradigm.* To begin once again with Plato's own definition, a paradigm is used 'when one thing is rightly divined in another, separate thing and being brought into connexion with it brings about a single true opinion of each separately and both as a pair' (278c).[1]

His own use of the method makes this general statement clearer. Wool-working is obviously 'other than' statesmanship, yet after recognizing within wool-working the contrasting arts of separation (carding) and combination (weaving) one can detect their reappearance in the organization of a community. It consists in a preliminary 'carding' or combing-out of bad citizen-material from good through tests, followed by 'weaving' the rest together into a unified whole (308d–e). Thus *paradeigma* here, though often translated 'example', bears neither of the two usual senses of that word. It is neither an instance (as in 'an example of the classical style') nor a pattern to be followed ('he is an example to us all').[2] Nearest to it is 'analogy'. In offering a 'paradigm of a paradigm' at 277d9–278c2 Plato employs two senses. What he gives is an *example* of paradigm in the new sense in which he proposes to use it, taken from children learning their letters. They first learn to recognize them in short, easy syllables, then are shown others which they fail to read correctly. Then the teacher puts the familiar syllables besides the new ones, and points out where the same letters recur. This is precisely what Plato now calls the method of paradigm: the detection of common elements in different compounds.

That he attaches great importance to it appears from 277d:

V. 'It is difficult to demonstrate anything of importance without the use of paradigms. I suspect that in a dreamlike way we know everything, yet know nothing in reality.'

Y.S. 'What do you mean?'

V. 'In an odd way I seem at this point to have raised the question of how we experience knowledge.'

---

[1] Reading καὶ at 278c6 with Friedländer (*Pl.* III, 527 n. 19). ὡς Skemp, following Campbell, Burnet and Diès. Both words have some MS authority.

[2] The meanings of *paradeigma* have been distinguished in vol. IV, 118 n. 2.

So paradigm has some relevance, albeit 'in an odd way', to the supreme question of philosophy, pursued in so many dialogues: What is knowledge and how do we know? Nor should this surprise us. Knowledge depends on the discovery of Forms, in which the first step is to recognize and isolate a common element, the 'single form' or 'one in and through all' of a number of different objects.[1] The contrast between dreaming and waking was used in the *Republic* (476c) to distinguish the mass of mankind, who are only aware of sensible things, from the philosopher trained to see beyond them to the Forms whose being they share; and again in the *Meno* (85c) to describe the state of mind of one whose progress from belief to knowledge is still incomplete. There and in the *Phaedo* the progress was towards recollection of pre-natal knowledge, and the fact that Plato can remind us so unmistakably of these dialogues without mention of this once central doctrine is symptomatic of the shift of interest in the present series towards a less metaphysical treatment of epistemological questions.[2]

The method as Plato introduces it here could be disconcerting, for if it were intended to serve the same purpose as definition in the *Meno* we should have to suppose that combination and separation represented the actual *eidos* (form) of weaving and government, which would therefore belong to the same *eidos* (species). This would hardly conform to a dialectical collection followed by division 'according to Forms', nor would *paradeigma* be a suitable term for that. Plato warns us that its relation to the acquisition of knowledge is 'curious' or 'unexpected' (μάλ' ἀτόπως 277d6). But something essential to a certain art can, *mutatis mutandis*, be revealed by an analogy taken from a quite different genre; and 'analogy' is the English word which comes nearest to *paradeigma*

---

[1] For these and similar expressions in *Meno* see vol. III, 433 n. 1.

[2] Ritter's explanation of P.'s silence about ἀνάμνησις was that he had always intended it metaphorically and found that he had been grossly misunderstood. (See his *N. Unters.* 80–2, and for the metaphorical interpretation *Essence* 121–3.) Others have argued that he once believed in it but dialectic has now replaced it. Yet as Rees pointed out in *Proc. Ar. Soc.*, Suppl. vol. 37, 172ff., the two combine happily in *Phaedrus*, and we should not assume that P. has abandoned the doctrine altogether, any more than he has abandoned the conception of the Forms as 'bodiless, fairest and greatest' (*Pol.* 286a). See Gulley's cogent arguments in *CQ* 1954, 209–13.

In the section on collection and division I have already spoken of 'Forms' to emphasize P.'s point that the method must have an ontological basis; but he says nothing there inconsistent with supposing that the objective realities which he insists on might be within the nature of the phenomena themselves.

in this context. Perhaps one might say that the paradigmatic method itself provides a paradigm of (i.e. is analogous to) the philosopher's pursuit of knowledge, and is itself a valuable epistemological tool.

(2) *Forms in the 'Politicus'*

The words *eidos* and *idea* existed before Plato appropriated them for his transcendent, intelligible patterns of sensible things and actions, and he himself continued to use them frequently to mean no more than kinds or species, and sometimes even in their root meanings of outward appearance. Hence the question whether, in using these or analogous terms in the later dialogues, he has at the back of his mind the exalted, other-worldly beings of the earlier, is and will probably remain a matter of controversy. In passages exemplifying the method of *diairesis*, the status of the *eidē* in the phrase 'to divide according to *eidē*' is not easy to decide. To treat them as nothing more than kinds or varieties certainly suits the context. Has Plato then ceased to believe in those divine entities on which he lavished such eulogies in *Phaedo* and *Phaedrus*? Has he, as it were, lost his faith in the 'place beyond the heavens', or is it simply that this aspect of the *eidē* has less relevance to his present concern for correct philosophical method?[1] This is the nub of the controversy between the so-called unitarians and their opponents, and such is the spell of Plato that an element of apriorism inevitably, if sometimes scarcely consciously, enters the argument: Plato was a great philosopher, and this he could not have been if all his life he believed (or alternatively did not believe) this or that, according to the interpreter's notion of what in a philosopher is sensible and desirable. My own position should be clear by now. Plato *was* one of the greatest philosophers, and that largely because he combined, simultaneously and uniquely, dialectical skill with a metaphysical, indeed religious belief in a supra-sensible realm of divine essences, and came nearer than anyone else to relating it rationally to the world of human experience.

Two passages have been thought specially relevant to the discussion.

(i) 278c–d. This immediately follows Plato's explanation of the use of paradigm by the example of teaching children to read, and he

---

[1] I have suggested that in the *Soph.* it was even an impediment. This section should be read in conjunction with pp. 161 f.

continues the metaphor[1] whereby letters and syllables stand for elements and compounds. With some hesitation I offer my own rendering of this difficult passage.

Should we be surprised then if our mind naturally undergoes the same experience [*sc.* as children learning to read by the paradigmatic method] in connexion with the elements [letters] of all things, and at one time, and in certain cases, guided by the truth, stands firm about each single one of them, but again, in different cases, is confused about them all? Some of the constituents it somehow guesses correctly in the compounds themselves, yet it fails to recognize the very same elements when they are transferred to the long and difficult syllables of everyday life.[2]

Skemp and Campbell (*ad loc.*) both take 'the elements of all things' to be the Forms.[3] They are certainly abstractions like combination and separation, but an opponent could justly claim to find no evidence here of the Forms of the middle period. Plato is now bringing the method of paradigm, just as he has illustrated and described it, to bear on his present subject. That subject is the practical arts (*technai*), and he is making the point that there are certain basic and elemental skills which enter into widely different occupations. These are the elements referred to here. In some cases (weaving) they are obvious, but in others, amid the distractions of ordinary practical life with which a complex art like politics is concerned, analogous skills are overlaid and concealed. If the would-be statesman can grasp the connexion—see, that is, through the simpler analogy of making a cloth of warp and woof, that his primary task is to reconcile contrasting human temperaments in a stable community based on consent (cf. especially 310e)—he will tackle the confusion of day-to-day political life with an eye fixed on the essential, ultimate aim. Such is the use of paradigm. It calls for no overt reference

[1] If it was a metaphor. Aristotle (*Metaph.* 998a23) speaks of φωνῆς στοιχεῖα, i.e. the simple sounds composing vocal utterances (of which letters are the symbols); but P. was said by Eudemus (*ap.* Simpl. *Phys.* 7.14 Diels) to have been the first to apply the word to the elements of physical and generated things. Skemp *ad loc.* (p. 161 n. 1) produces no solid evidence that it had been so used earlier.

[2] τῶν πραγμάτων. This can mean concrete things, or alternatively circumstances, affairs (especially political affairs), and trouble or annoyance (285e3).

[3] C. compares *Tht.* 201 ff., where however στοιχεῖα are the elements of physical things as Cornford said (*PTK* 143 n. 1).

to transcendent pattern-Forms, and Plato makes none.[1] Here he is primarily concerned with the application of a certain type of intellectual insight to the achievement of practical goals, and his discussion of statesmanship is on a more mundane level than that in the *Republic*. The absence from it of the Forms need not necessarily imply their abandonment if evidence can be found to the contrary. Indeed I have ventured to suggest that in extending the use of paradigm (unnecessarily for his present purpose) to the whole problem of knowledge Plato has in mind the existence of Forms as its basis. But if not denied, neither is this confirmed by the present passage.

(ii) 285 d–6b.[2] This follows Plato's assertion that the object of their enquiry is not merely to define the statesman but equally to assist their mastery of dialectic in general.

And as for weaving, no one in his senses would want to pursue its definition for its own sake; but there is something which I believe has escaped most people's notice. Some real things have perceptible likenesses which can easily be grasped.[3] There is no difficulty in pointing them out when one is asked for a definition and wants an easy and trouble-free method of exhibiting them without words. But the greatest and most precious things have no image so wrought as to be manifest to men, which the man who wants to give his questioner full satisfaction can point out to him, and by impressing it on one of his senses adequately satisfy his mind. Therefore we must train ourselves to be capable of giving and accepting a verbal account of everything; for the things that are bodiless, being the finest and greatest, can be clearly shown in words[4] alone—nothing else—and everything that we are saying now is said for their sake. But practice is always more easily exercised on the lesser than on the greater.

[1] Skemp assumes (p. 162) that P.'s thought here is metaphysical as well as logical: Statesmanship and Weaving, as Forms, are the complex 'syllables' whose 'letters' are 'the more general and universal Forms in which they partake', e.g. Combination and Separation. I sympathize with this view, but on the strength of the passage here quoted it cannot be said to be proved.

[2] For an alternative version see Owen in *Ex. and Arg.*, 350f.

[3] Reading ῥᾳδίως with the MSS. See Skemp's and Owen's notes (the latter in *Ex. and Arg.* 350 n. 3). Skemp's choice of ῥᾳδίοις is surprising. He believes τὰ ὄντα to be the Forms, but it is hardly Platonic to call these ῥᾴδια καταμαθεῖν. To grasp the Forms is reserved for the few, after arduous philosophical preparation. The balance of the sentence is also against the emendation.

[4] The Greek word is *logos*, with all its manifold meanings: statement, definition, argument and much else. Perhaps Campbell's 'rational account' or Owen's 'explanation' would be better, but here P. seems to have had especially in mind the distinction between visual representation and verbal description.

It has been generally assumed (and certainly by myself) that this passage contained a clear reference to Plato's 'middle-period theory of paradigm-forms'. Recently however G. E. L. Owen has denied this in a closely-reasoned article of which all unitarians must take note.[1] Plato, he argues, is still defending the tedious length of his analysis of weaving. At 277c he has emphasized the superiority of verbal explanation to visual aids whenever a pupil is able to follow them. Here he simply adds that the most important subjects cannot be shown in visible images at all. This is meant literally. The images are still man-made: weaving can be exhibited pictorially but statesmanship cannot. The words 'bodiless, finest and greatest' at once suggest Forms to one acquainted with the *Phaedo* or *Symposium*, but Owen notes that at *Rep.* 599c 'greatest and finest' is applied to 'wars, military commands, the government of cities and the education of men'.[2]

Others have seen this passage as an obvious parallel to *Phdr.* 250b–d, where Plato says that whereas earthly copies of the Form Beauty are visible, Justice, *Sophrosynē* 'and other things precious to the soul' produce no such immediate sensuous impressions, and only a few can apprehend the originals through such images as we have. Owen's reply is to dismiss the *Phaedrus* passage as mere myth and poetry, not seriously meant (p. 349). He points out that Socrates himself, in his concluding prayer to Eros (257a), describes the language of his whole palinode as poetical and says that, except for its introduction of the method of collection and division, it should be regarded as *paidia*. Plato's use of this word has been discussed in vol. IV,[3] and here it is sufficient to note that at 278b he applies it to their whole conversation,

---

[1] 'P. on the Undepictable' in *Exegesis and Argument* (Studies . . . Vlastos, 1973). I must omit many interesting points not central to the present argument, but pp. 354f. on the meaning of πεφυκέναι should not be passed over. In *Crat.* the object described as τοιοῦτόν τι ὃ ἐπεφύκει κερκίζειν is not a tool made by man. If it were, the operator would model his new shuttle on the broken one, which he is expressly said not to do. He models it on τὸ εἶδος, which deserves the name of 'really existing shuttle' (αὐτὸ ὃ ἔστιν κερκίς) more than any shuttle ever made. I cannot agree that O.'s point 'is unaffected by this' (355 n. 14).

[2] Not, however, ἀσώματα, and O. passes rather lightly over this word on p. 356. Cf. not only *Symp.* 211a5–7, 211e–12a (where moreover εἴδωλα is used of the earthly imitations of Beauty), but also the *Politicus* itself, at 269d. If however *Rep.* may be cited in evidence that middle-period Forms are absent from this particular passage, it is no evidence that they have been abandoned, for the existence of transcendent Forms is a central feature of that dialogue.

[3] See especially pp. 60–3, and for my own interpretation of the *Phdr.* as a whole, ch. VI(3) of that volume.

including the 'practical psychology of rhetoric' with which Owen contrasts the more lyrical portions. It is in the same dialogue that he extends it to every written composition (276 d, 277 e). Even at 265 b his Socrates says (with his usual *eironeia*) that the myth 'may have attained a measure of truth' and that 'blended with it was a *logos* that had some claim to credibility'. He adds (265 d) that the myth itself has exemplified the dialectical method, thus giving 'clarity and consistency' to the definition of love which it contained. To understand Plato one must recognize that he may present the same doctrine in myth and again in dialectical argument. If one denies that the poetical and religious language of the myth conveys philosophical truth for Plato, where is one to stop? Much of the *Symposium*, and what is given as argument in the *Phaedo*, will have to be discarded. What of immortality itself, the basis of all the rest,[1] which has been seriously propounded outside the framework of a myth in both *Phaedrus* (the argument from self-motion) and *Phaedo*?

Owen lays stress on the context of our passage, but the immediate context is the admonition that the aim of the enquiry is not even to define statesmanship (let alone weaving) but to become better philosophers. This is surely a warning that what follows will for a moment lift the argument from its immediate subject to a reminder of first principles, which if Plato still believed in them would be the Forms. All this does not prove that the Forms are referred to here, but if I am wrong and they are not (as I have argued may be the case at 278 c–d),[2] this in turn is no proof that Plato no longer acknowledged them. They are plainly referred to, in their 'middle-period' form, at 269 d:

To be always unchanging and constant[3] belongs solely to the most divine of all things, and body is not in that class. What we call the universe or cosmos has received many blessed gifts from its creator, but nevertheless it partakes of body and cannot therefore be utterly exempt from change, though its motion is as far as possible constant, uniform and in the same place.

If this occurred in a 'middle' dialogue it would be taken for granted

---

[1] For the intimate connexion between the immortality of the soul and the existence of Forms, see *Pho.* 76 d–e.

[2] May one occasionally leave a decision to the reader? It is certainly to be hoped that all readers of this volume will be readers of Plato.

[3] τὸ κατὰ ταὐτὰ καὶ ὡσαύτως ἔχειν, P.'s regular description of the Forms. See p. 141 n. 2.

that it described the divine (*Pho.* 80b etc.) and unchanging realm of Forms, and its relation to the physical world, so why not now?

Another pretty clear reference to Forms as paradigms is at 300c. In an ideal world a philosopher-statesman would act on his own initiative, in the light of his knowledge, without written laws. Next best however is a written code to which everyone must conform. 'These written laws would be in each case copies of reality,[1] if they are composed on the instructions of those who know.' The philosopher, that is, will model the laws on the changeless, perfect moral Forms which he alone remembers. They will be direct copies, not at two removes like the copies condemned in the discussion of mimetic poetry in *Rep.* 10. Plato still thinks of the philosopher-statesman as he did in *Rep.* 6 (500c, d) as one who 'beholds things that are unchanging . . . completely orderly and rational'. 'These he imitates' and 'studies to implant them in human behaviour both private and public.' With this must be taken the references to the one true, right or godlike constitution, the paradigmatic Form of a state of which all human states are imitations, some better, some worse (297c). Plato is explicit that the perfect statesman, and therefore the ideal state, do not exist on earth.

Since there is nowhere to be found, as we assert, a Royal Being in our cities like the Queen in a hive, one man outstanding both in body and mind, we must, it seems, meet together and draw up laws, pursuing the tracks of the true constitution. (301 d–e)

And at 303b: 'For that city is to be distinguished from all others, as god from man.' Finally, *Sophist* and *Politicus* are undoubtedly products of the same stage of Plato's development, and it would be strange indeed if a renunciation of the Forms came between them. Yet I hope it has been shown in the previous chapter that the Forms are still present in the *Sophist*.

(3) The myth[2]

Something has gone wrong with the definition of a statesman, and as a respite from strenuous dialectical exercise the visitor undertakes to

---

[1] μιμήματα τῆς ἀληθείας. The best expansion of this brief expression is in Aristotle's *Protrepticus*. See vol. IV, 548. οἱ εἰδότες would be people like P. himself and the members of the Academy who did in fact act as legislators for a number of states (vol. IV, 23).

[2] I have collected in an appendix (pp. 193–6) some evidence for its sources, which may interest the historically-minded. Skemp has a long excursus on the myth (pp. 81–111) with many reff. to modern writings.

uncover the mistake through a story.[1] Many ancient myths, he begins, contain a dim folk-memory of the same historical event. He instances the reversal of the course of sun and stars by Zeus in the myth of Atreus and Thyestes,[2] the age of Cronus, and the earthborn men. All these reflect the fact that the universe suffers a periodical reversal of its rotation. In one era God controls the motion, but he cannot do so for ever because its material embodiment prevents it from either being motionless or enjoying a perpetual, single and perfect motion. He does his best for it, being perfectly good himself, nor must we suppose that there are two opposed gods turning it in opposite directions. What happens is that when God lets go, it begins to turn itself in the opposite direction, for (as in the *Timaeus*) it is a living and thinking creature.[3] The moment of reversal brings terrible convulsions, destroying much of the human race.

Then (1) in the period opposed to ours, when the sun travels from west to east, the sequence of life is first halted, then reversed. Men and animals grow younger, white hair darkens, adults dwindle to infants and finally disappear into the earth, whence the next generation are born fully adult.[4] This is the fabled age of Cronus, with all its traditional features: no fierce beasts, no wars or factions, earth yielding food untilled, perfect climate making clothes and shelter unnecessary. Moreover, to each tribe of animals, including mankind, is assigned a

---

[1] For its serious purpose see 274e: 'Here we may end our story, and turn it to account in discovering what a mistake we made when we demonstrated the royal and statesmanlike character in the previous argument.'

[2] Known from Euripides, *Or.* 1001–6, *El.* 726–44, *I.T.* 192–5.

[3] 269d7–c2. The motion is not mechanically caused, as 'momentum' in Skemp's translation of 270a5–7 might suggest, though physical characteristics—size, equilibrium and a tiny pivot—provide the necessary conditions like the bones and sinews of *Pho.* 98c–99b, or the συναίτια of the present dialogue.

[4] A nice point: are they born old or in the prime of life? The evidence is conflicting. If the course of life is reversed, they should logically start in old age; and at 271b4 P. says τοὺς πρεσβύτας ἐπὶ τὴν τοῦ παιδὸς ἰέναι φύσιν (though this might refer to the generation already old at the transition). So Frutiger, *Mythes* 242, and Koster, *Mythe de P., de Zurathoustra et des Chaldéens* 45: 'on naît vieillard'. On the other hand Skemp has (p. 153) 'stalwart in their prime of life' (which however is not in the Greek he is translating), 'in the prime of adult life' (110) and 'in P.'s era of Kronos there were no old men' (111). This would correspond to the earth-born warriors in the traditional myths of Cadmus and Jason, and to the Giants. Moreover Adam (*Rep.* vol. II, 297), who favoured the other view, supports it by a mistranslation of πολιὰ φύντα at 273b (which however he had strongly defended in *CR* 1891, 445), where P. is in fact describing the beginning of the other era (our own). Yet Hesiod spoke of a time (surely not unconnected with the source of P.'s idea) 'when men are born grey-headed' (*Erga* 181).

minor god,[1] under whose direct supervision no political organization is necessary. Nor was there marriage or begetting when all were born from the earth. At this point the visitor pauses to enquire whether the men of this (as it was usually thought) golden age were in truth happier than ourselves. The answer is Platonic. Yes, if they used their leisure and other advantages (including the gift of conversing with the animals) to acquire wisdom, but not if, as the legends suggest, they filled themselves with food and drink and wasted their time in idle talk.[2]

(2) With the world's latest reversal, ushering in the present era, 'the purpose of the story' comes into view (272d5). God relinquished his control, and the subordinate deities followed suit. After the inevitable upheavals and loss of life the universe settled down to guide itself on the lines which it had learned from its maker, but the imperfections inherent in corporeality have caused it to forget these more and more, and disorder and chaos are growing as the era approaches its end. Then God will again take charge and save it from complete destruction. However, our present concern is with mankind and the ideal ruler (273e5). After the cosmic reversal, life progressed from infancy to old age and conception by sexual means replaced birth from the ground. '*Now comes the point of the whole tale*' (274b1). Bereft of divine care, and with nature turned hostile, men became a prey to wild beasts, and were without arts or tools to provide for themselves the necessities which the earth once yielded spontaneously. Their miseries[3] were lightened only by the divine gifts and instruction of which tradition tells: fire from Prometheus, technical skill from Hephaestus and Athena, agriculture from other gods. Above all, from then to now mankind has been left to manage its own affairs and look after itself.

The declared lessons of the myth (apart from relaxation) are (i) that our statesmen are only human: the days are past when we were ruled by gods; (ii) that the assimilation of statesman to herdsman had led to

---

[1] Adam's 'God himself was the shepherd of the earth-born' (*o.c.* 296) must rest on a mistranslation of 271e5–6, which means '*A* god supervised them personally.' The supreme god has oversight of the whole cosmic motion, and allots to each subordinate his province, as in *Timaeus* (41bff.) he leaves to them the creation of mortal beings.

[2] A number of jokes in Aristophanes show that 'Cronian' could mean old-fashioned to the point of stupidity. For reff. see Baldry, *CQ* 1952, 85.

[3] Described in greater detail in Protagoras's myth of human progress, where too emphasis is laid on the lack of the political art (*Prot.* 321d4–5, 322b5).

a faulty *diairesis*, which by implying responsibility for the actual nutriment of his flock, failed to divide him off from such classes as farmers, traders, millers and bakers, doctors and trainers. To many the length and elaboration of the story have seemed disproportionate to this simple task, and they have sought something more recondite. Best is the conclusion of Solmsen,[1] which not only takes into account the doubts cast on the wisdom and happiness of life under Cronus, but is in keeping with the ethos of this whole group of dialogues. The myth shows that change and even deterioration are essential phases of a corporeal world, and that 'the philosopher who confines his attention to the Permanent and Unchanging misses a great deal, and cannot arrive at an integrated picture of the world'. In saying this we need not quarrel with the dictum of Wilamowitz (*Pl.* 1, 576) that though in the circumstances to look for hidden meanings is pardonable, it is more cautious and truer to content ourselves with the welcome fact that Plato still takes pleasure in telling stories.

(4) *Political theory*

(*a*) Politicus *and* Republic. Reading the *Politicus* cannot fail to bring to mind the earlier *Politeia* and the question how far Plato's standpoint has changed between the two dialogues. Both are based on the fundamental Socratic principle that government is an art, a *technē* dependent on knowledge,[2] which few if any can master (297b–c). The familiar Socratic analogies with other *technai* are prominent, for instance in the statesman's[3] attitude to rules or laws: the skilled captain needs no rules but his own *technē*, his *technē* is superior to rules (297a); the doctor may do better for his patient by relying on his own *technē* than by sticking to what the books prescribe (296b). Yet with this insistence on an art to be learned, the *Politicus* is silent on the all-important subject of education for statesmanship which occupies the central place in the *Republic*. Evidently Plato had no wish to change the programme there laid down,

---

[1] *P.'s Th.* 85 f. I admit to having slightly altered it, preferring not to speak of change and deterioration 'in Reality'.

[2] Socratic: see vol. III, 409 ff. For the repeated use of τέχνη in this connexion, e.g. 297a and b, 300c10.

[3] Or 'king'. In this dialogue 'statesman' and 'king' are convertible terms for the ideal ruler (276c8, e13). The king, of course, is at the opposite pole from the tyrant, who governs for purely selfish ends.

and saw no point in repeating a task already done. Knowledge of goodness, to be imparted to others as true belief (309c), is a prime requisite
in both.

The *Politicus* reaffirms the *Republic*'s distinction between a single
ideal polity and all others, but whereas the *Republic* concentrates on the
ideal, whether or not Plato thought it could ever be realized, the
Politicus recognizes that it is not of this world. The best of our statesmen are only human, and the present aim is, without losing sight of the
'one true constitution' as standard and guide, to plan a society as like it
as human imperfections allow. Plato sometimes seems to have three
levels in mind: (i) the ideal statesman, god rather than man, whose en-
lightened will is his only law; (ii) the best sort of human statesman or
political reformer (who himself has not yet appeared), whose qualifications and policies form the main subject of enquiry in the *Politicus*;
(iii) the political Sophist or spurious statesman, who pretends to the art
and passes himself off as a statesman instead of the mere party-hack that
he is (303b–c). This includes all contemporary politicians.[1] But the
distinction between (i) and (ii) is not always clear, and he admits at
301a–b that he uses the same title for both. 'When one man rules
according to laws, imitating the one with knowledge, we call him king,
making no distinction of name between monarchy with knowledge and
constitutional monarchy with right belief.' This leads him into at least
apparent contradiction on the use of a written code of laws and the
desirability of government by consent of the governed. More points for
comparison with the *Republic* will arise as we proceed.

(*b*) *Rule by force or consent.* After the myth Plato points out certain
grave defects in their previous *diairesis*. One is that by omitting the
distinction between enforced and willing submission they confused two
very dissimilar types, the king and the tyrant. Oversight freely accepted
belongs to 'the genuine king and statesman' (276d–e). According to
Xenophon, this distinction went back to Socrates:[2] 'In his view the rule
of men with their consent and according to the laws of the state was

---

[1] The *Critias*, which has several elements in common with the myth of the *Pol.*, casts a similar
threefold classification into mythical form. See Campbell, *Pol.* xlviii.

[2] Xen. *Mem.* 4.6.12 (vol. III, 412). According to this passage Socrates foreshadowed the
division of constitutions at *Pol.* 300eff. (p. 188 below).

kingship, but rule over unwilling subjects, not according to law but at the whim of the ruler, was tyranny.' Somehow Plato must have reconciled this in his mind with what he says after enumerating the recognized types of constitution—constitutional monarchy and tyranny, aristocracy and oligarchy, democracy—distinguished by the number who govern, their wealth, and the consent or otherwise of the governed. Since government is a branch of science, he goes on (292b–c), the criterion should be none of these, but solely the mastery or otherwise of that science. Given the requisite knowledge, which few if any can attain, it makes no difference whether the subjects bow willingly to his rule, or whether it is with or without a code of laws. He may at his discretion purge the city by banishment or executions, or increase it by immigration. Where cautery or surgery is needed, the doctor will best serve his patient's interests by carrying on regardless of his cries and protests. Even before starting his reforms the statesman will, like a good craftsman, reject any bad material. That is, after a series of tests he will put to death, expel or degrade any who prove incapable of acquiring the social virtues (308c–309a). This corresponds to the 'cleaning of the canvas' in the *Rep.* (501a) and, interestingly enough, to what Protagoras laid down in the *Prot.* (322d) as a prerequisite of life in a *polis*. Any laws will have been drawn up by the scientific statesman himself and may be altered as he thinks fit. The current assumption that he must first gain the agreement of the citizens, though admittedly plausible, is wrong. It seems a far cry from the *Crito*, where Socrates, whom Plato regarded as the one scientific statesman, laid down as the only allowable alternatives obedience to the laws or their amendment by peaceful persuasion.[1]

It is, however, the ideal statesman who is here portrayed. The only modification required in the earlier statement is that the essential difference between him and the tyrant is one of motive. The statesman pursues justice, truth and the welfare of society, the tyrant his own and his friends' aggrandisement and the destruction of his personal enemies. Since this is what men have learned to associate with absolute power, they will entrust it to no one. Nevertheless if the one true statesman should ever appear they *would* recognize and welcome him and leave

---

[1] *Crito* 51e–52a. For S. as sole practitioner of the art of statesmanship see *Gorg.* 521d.

him to inaugurate unopposed the one true and happy form of society.[1]
The question of force or consent would not arise.

(c) *The role of law in government.* When the visitor maintains that the
perfect state, whose ruler acts with knowledge and justice, will need no
laws, and that law-abiding states, though better than some, are only
imitations, even the docile Y.S. rebels ('The rest of what you say sounds
reasonable, but that one should rule without laws is a hard saying'),[2]
and the visitor agrees to discuss further the rightness of ruling without
laws. He is emphatic that the scientific ruler will often be guided by his
knowledge without paying attention to any written code. Any code
must be universal and indiscriminate, a blunt instrument (παχυτέρως
295a) which can never provide for the individuality and variety of
human personalities, needs and circumstances. 'It cannot be right for
what is everywhere uniform to deal with what is never uniform' (294c).
This is followed by a violently sarcastic attack on laws and their universal enforcement. Admittedly a ruler who was a law to himself could do
great harm. So too a doctor might poison his patient for money, or
a captain maroon his passengers or throw them overboard, and Plato
amuses himself with a satirical picture of what it would be like if for
that reason medicine and navigation were entrusted to untrained men
following a code of legally binding instructions. The Assembly would
welcome the advice of laymen on the use of medical drugs and ap-
pliances and on seamanship, and officers would be appointed annually
by lot to perform cures and command ships strictly by the book.
Further provisions include a ban on research into medicine, navigation
and their ancillary sciences. Anyone undertaking it will be denounced
as a chattering, star-gazing Sophist, and may be brought to trial as
a corrupter of the young. In this caricature of Athenian democracy,
with its obvious references to Socrates,[3] he carries to its logical conclusion the soberly critical description of it in the *Protagoras* (319b–d).

---

[1] A similar hope was expressed in *Rep.* about the public's reception of the philosopher-king,
a phenomenon as yet beyond their experience (498d–502a).

[2] 293a. The Greeks took pride in owning no master but the law. (See vol. III, 69f.) Y.S.'s only
other doubt concerns the idea that the laws might be altered without popular consent (296a),
another affront to Athenian democratic theory.

[3] For Socrates as a 'star-gazing Sophist' see vol. III, 364 and 374; IV, 431 n. 3 and 499 n. 4.

Since the Assembly listens to the pronouncements of laymen on the supreme and all-important science of statemanship, why should it not pay equal heed to their views on other arts and sciences?

After this outburst Plato unexpectedly turns round and declares that after all we cannot have the ideal. No ruler can be everywhere at once and attend to every case. (He always speaks in the singular. The possibility of delegating legislation to subordinate ministers or committees is ruled out by the impossibility of finding enough men qualified in the political *technē*.) Therefore written laws with all their defects must be adopted as a second-best. Here is another departure from the *Republic* in the direction of practical politics. There he had dismissed detailed legislation as useless in either a well or a badly constructed state (427a). Here he argues that although a burden of petty legislation might destroy all arts and make life intolerable, there is something worse still, namely that the official charged (perhaps by lot) with administering it should prove corrupt as well as ignorant, and abuse his position to gain personal power. Plato's lasting idealism is at odds with his present determination to be practical. He has just argued that fear of tyrants should not debar the expert statesman from dispensing with laws, any more than the occasional appearance of an unscrupulous doctor justifies replacing the expert's knowledge by a state code of therapeutical practice. Now he says that disobedience to the laws, founded as they are on long experience and public approval,[1] would inflict much more harm on society than the existence of the laws themselves. The *Politicus* forecasts the detailed legal enactments of the *Laws*, where they are still described as a second-best for the same reasons as are given here. (See *Laws* 875 c–d, translated on p. 335.)

The true statesman, then, will be right to draw up a scheme of laws, which will at least copy the truth directly (300c), and to impose the severest penalties on their infringement. But he himself will act like a doctor who goes abroad,[2] leaving written directions for his patients to

---

[1] 300b. Contrast 296a–d. The resemblance between this teaching and that attributed to Protagoras in the *Prot.* is remarkable. See vol. III, 136–8.

[2] 295b–e. P. may have in mind himself and his colleagues, who visited several cities to draw up constitutions for them (vol. IV, 23 f.) and then left, though Campbell refers it in two different places to (*a*) gods who once looked after us but have now left us to ourselves (p. xlv) and (*b*) Solon (p. 141). More probably the going abroad refers only to the doctor in the simile.

follow. If he returns earlier than expected, and finds the condition of a patient changed, he will not hesitate to cancel his own earlier directions and take the case into his own hands again. So the statesman, who is his own legislator, will alter laws and customs as he thinks fit, his only criterion being the furtherance of justice and social benefit.

As a tailpiece the known forms of constitution, excluding the 'true' one, are ordered according to the quality of life offered by each (300e–303b). Government may be by one man, by a few, or by the whole people (democracy). Only through laws strictly enforced can any of them emulate the one true state ruled by the one scientific or truly kingly statesman. Democracy, being the weakest, has least power either way, for good or evil, monarchy is best of all if under law (kingship), worst if lawless (tyranny), and in between come aristocracy and oligarchy, rule of the few under law and without it.[1] But, he concludes, one can only wonder at the natural stamina of communities which survive under any of them, administered as they are by unscrupulous party-leaders with no understanding of the principles of government.

(*d*) *Final isolation of the statesman* (303b–305e). By a series of *diaireseis* Plato has now marked off the statesman and his function from

    (i) others who might be called 'nurturers of mankind', such as farmers, bakers and traders (276e);

    (ii) superhuman beings (274e, 275b–c);

    (iii) tyrants (276e);

    (iv) producers of various material goods (287b–89b);

    (v) subordinate ranks in the community's hierarchy: servants, wage-earners and minor state functionaries or civil servants, including religious officials (289d–90e);

    (vi) bogus politicians, the statesman's closest imitators and rivals (291a–303d).

There remains one class especially difficult to sift out, for their functions are much closer to the statesman's, nor are they fraudulent impersonations of him but perform a valuable as well as a leading role in the community. Such are the masters of the arts of strategy or military

---

[1] This brief note may be instructively compared with the long description of the imperfect types of polity in *Rep.* 8 and 9, for which see vol. IV, 527–37.

command, of the administration of justice, and of oratory when it shares with kingship the task of persuading men to just ways.[1] The problem is solved simply enough by yet another dichotomy of arts into an art itself—music, say, or a handicraft—and the superior art of knowing whether such an art is worth learning and how and when it should be employed.[2] The commander's *technē* tells him how to conduct a campaign but not whether or not his country should go to war.[3] The magistrate or juryman does not make the laws. His job is only to see that in any particular case they are administered without fear or favour. Oratory is in a similar position. All three, though genuine arts related to government and autonomous in their own spheres, are subordinate to the statesman's or kingly art which makes the supreme decisions.

(e) *The essence of statesmanship* (305 c *to the end*). The aim of the discussion, we have been told, is first to isolate its subject, then 'to stamp upon it its unique form' (p. 167 above). We now enter the last stage. The form or essence of statesmanship is found in the art of 'kingly weaving', understood as combining disparate characters into the firm fabric of a stable community. When the bad material has been eradicated (p. 185 above), the acceptable citizens will fall into two main psychological groups, one marked by courage, boldness, enterprise and vigour, and the other by moderation, gentleness, the spirit of compromise. In private life, Plato notes, it is only amusing to see how the epithets change according to the natural affinities of the speaker (307d): the 'brave and energetic' become in the mouths of the others 'hard, insolent, manic', while they for their part convert 'gentle and moderate' into 'tardy, soft, cowardly'. But if either gains power their virtues may

[1] In *Gorgias* P. had condemned rhetoric outright. In *Phaedrus* he ridiculed contemporary rhetoricians but spoke of a 'true oratory' based on knowledge. Here we have an intermediate class of those who, without possessing philosophical knowledge themselves, act under the instructions of the one who does and in the light of the 'true belief concerning what is just and good and their opposites' which he imparts to them (309e–d) as the philosopher king imparts it to the subordinate guardians in the *Republic*. I hope this answers Skemp's question in n. 1(iii) on p. 219. His description of the orator as a '"goverment spokesman"' is apt.

[2] When it is a question of *defining* the statesman P. of course reverts to the perfect embodiment of the art. He is not pronouncing on ethical problems arising from actual historical events, e.g. whether it was right for a doctor to obey a Nazi order to conduct experiments on human beings or for technologists to make the atom bomb possible but have no say in the decision to drop it.

[3] There is a parallel to this at *Euthyd.* 290c–d (noted by Skemp, 220 n. 1).

indeed turn to excess, and this is serious. One party, in its zeal for peace and quiet, may follow a policy of appeasement which may lay the country open to aggression by sapping its will to resist. The more militant sort may rush it into a series of rash ventures which by arousing the hostility of powerful neighbours lead to the same result.

These are the main contrasting elements which the statesman must weave into his web as the firm, hard warp and softer woof. They will remain after the preliminary rejection of threads either too hard or too soft and weak to stand the strain, indeed both are necessary for the wellbeing of the state; but like the guardians of *Rep.* 2 they will be educable in the *virtues* of both courage and gentleness as distinct from their vicious excesses. They can be reconciled by bonds both spiritual (indeed divine, for men have a divine element in their souls) and natural or human. The first consists in education inculcating a true sense of values, a 'true belief' soundly based on the knowledge which only the statesman is qualified to impart. This will purge the courageous type of any tendency to violence and turn gentle temperaments from a foolish softness towards moderation and good sense. Given generous natures to work on, the laws can foster a spirit of unity between virtues of opposite tendency. The more earthly bond is eugenic: check the tendency of similar types to marry, and encourage[1] opposites to intermarry and so produce children with the virtues of both. This will be easy once the higher bond has been forged and all share the same standards and values. Then authority will be given to men of the mixed type, and when several act together the king will see that both types are represented, for the moderates are cautious, fair-minded and safe but deficient in drive, whereas the other set, though less careful and balanced, excel in getting things done.[2]

So by his weaving the king unites individuals and the whole community, bond and free (311c4), in lasting concord and friendship, 'and

---

[1] There is no mention of legal enforcement as with the more drastic provision for community of wives among the guardians in *Rep.* (See 457c.) Here P. speaks only of common ideals reinforced by honours, reputation and mutual pledges (310e). This advice on marriage recurs in *Laws* (773a–d), where the idea of legal enforcement is explicitly rejected as productive of resentment and ridicule.

[2] Anyone with experience on committees may question Plato's optimism about the possibility that anything will be accomplished by this carefully planned collaboration between progressives and conservatives.

in his oversight omits nothing conducive to such happiness as it befits a human society to enjoy'.

(5) *Ethics and psychology*

The last few pages of the *Politicus* contain clear reminders of earlier dialogues, and have been seen by many as deliberately repudiating doctrines fundamental to the *Protagoras* and the *Republic*.[1] The *Protagoras* is a full-dress defence of the Socratic thesis that the so-called different virtues are identical, to the extent that no one can possess one without the others and all alike are reducible to knowledge of good and evil. No 'part' of virtue therefore can conflict with another. In the *Republic*, as Skemp says (223 n. 1), all the virtues are harmonized and integrated in 'justice'. In the *Politicus* Plato goes out of his way to say that his present contention, that virtues can be in conflict, is something strange and surprising (306a), though no ordinary person would have been surprised to learn that, as Protagoras maintained, a man might be brave but lack self-control or piety. Is this a signal that Plato is abandoning his own earlier teaching? According to Skemp, 'the new statement . . . is equivalent to declaring eternal conflict between the warrior and civilian classes'. But the lesson of the new statement is precisely that the possessors of opposing virtues can and must be reconciled by wise government, and the *Republic* itself declares that 'a gentle nature is opposed to a high-spirited',[2] but that the guardians must combine both. Naturally high-spirited or gentle temperaments are the raw materials of virtue on which the statesman-educator works, for both must be guided by reason (virtue, after all, is knowledge or wisdom) and the means to this is 'the one big thing', education,[3] in *Republic* and *Politicus* alike. The *Politicus* repeats that they can be combined in one man, who should be given a position of authority, like the guardian. Harmony is achieved in both dialogues by recognizing that

---

[1] E.g. Skemp 222 n. 1 and 223 n. 1: 'the new statement must necessarily destroy the *Republic* psychological scheme'. Cf. Gomperz, *GT* III, 184: 'a notable piece of self-criticism . . . breach of Socratic intellectualism' (somewhat weakened by an uncalled-for reference to 'a breath of the Baconian, or modern inductive spirit'). Von Fritz (*P. in Siz.* 127) says P. departs from the Socratic principle enunciated in *Prot.* that you cannot have ἀνδρεία without σωφροσύνη or vice versa, but adds that an inclination to bold precipitancy (*darauflosgehen*) or cautious holding back is expressly differentiated from the ἀρεταί of ἀνδρεία and σωφροσύνη.

[2] ἐναντία γάρ που θυμοειδεῖ πρᾳεῖα φύσις, 375c.   [3] *Rep.* 423e, 441e–42a and elsewhere.

the state will contain contrasting psychological types and teaching them to live together. Neither the rash or violent, nor the foolish and weak, possess the *virtues* of courage or moderation, but aberrations from them. All excess is bad. Not for nothing has the *Politicus* given a homily on the importance of 'right measure'.[1]

I would therefore suggest, without dogmatizing, that if one forces the comparison, there is no direct contradiction between the *Politicus* and the *Protagoras* or *Republic* on the unity of the virtues or the scheme of psychology,[2] although Plato speaks in simplified language of 'virtues' as conflicting, instead of the more precise 'qualities which when moderated and controlled by reason and education are parts of virtue'. There are of course differences, and Plato is not pressing us to take the two dialogues together. There is no one-for-one correspondence between the 'parts' of the soul and the two opposed temperaments, and the three social classes based on three psychological types are dropped. The careful education to ensure that reason predominates has been extended from 'guardians' to the whole citizen body, and so on.

Conclusion

This strange and fascinating dialogue is as much a work of art, or philosophical tapestry, as any other work of Plato's. He could have made his points that rulers must not be thought of as divine beings, or described as nurturers of a flock, or even the more general point that ours is an age of deterioration, without an elaborate cosmic myth; but he happens to like myths. He could have chosen another—perhaps more suitable—art than weaving to illustrate some principles of correct *diairesis*, but his fancy was caught by the idea of an inner affinity between weaving and statesmanship, just as in the *Sophist* he chuckled over the thought that the Sophist was first cousin to the angler.

The *Politicus* does much to 'bring philosophy', in the shape of the *Republic*, 'down from the skies'. Its central topics are the art of government at the human, 'second-best' level and the correct application of the method of later dialectic. In spite of the myth, the other great sub-

---

[1] Already in *Rep.* (423e5) μέτριος is the epithet for the properly educated.

[2] Cf. Tate in *CR* 1954, 116. Courage and σωφροσύνη are still 'parts' of virtue at 308b, and the idea of virtue and the virtues as a unity in diversity is still maintained in the *Laws*, at 963c–d.

jects of the *Republic*—the relation between knowledge and true belief, the education of the philosopher-statesman in mathematics and dialectic culminating in the vision of the Good and the whole hierarchy of Forms beneath it, the nature of poetry, the divinity and immortality of the soul—get little or no mention. In its content the *Politicus* combines the ideal and the practical in a unique and puzzling way which probably reflects a transitional stage of indecision in Plato's own thought. Is it the ideal or the possible statesman that he has in mind in the final section on royal weaving? Presumably he is the one who has to use laws, and one remembers qualifying phrases like 'at least so far as possible in a polity' applied to the moderate character educated to a true belief, and 'as much as it befits a society to be happy', at 309e and 311c. But apart from the language of perfection used elsewhere, are the preliminary purging and the divine and human bonds meant seriously? One cannot be sure,[1] but the licence to kill, banish and enslave makes one think it is perhaps just as well that the true statesman has not yet appeared, and one may even hope that, if he should appear, that well-founded fear of the abuse of absolute power of which Plato speaks at 301c–d may make people more chary than he expects of granting it to the superstatesman to inaugurate his reign of perfect felicity and righteousness.

APPENDIX

Elements of the myth in Plato and elsewhere[2]

To judge by other examples, Plato in his myths took over much traditional material from earlier mythology and science, but built it into a new structure and drew his own moral. Here he openly acknowledges his debt to the stories of Atreus, the earth-born and the reign of Cronus, and mentions the services of Prometheus and Hephaestus. Apart from the reversal of cosmic motion, the following interrelated elements may be distinguished.

1. The idea, familiar from many cultures, of the cyclic recurrence of historical events, credited in Greece to the Pythagoreans.[3]

---

[1] The elimination of bad material, or unfit stock, is discussed at greater length in *Laws* (735a–36c), where both drastic and milder measures are described. The subject is shelved, however, by the observation that if their theoretical plans for a Cretan colony should ever materialize, they could solve the problem simply by refusing entry and citizenship to unsuitable applicants.

[2] Skemp discusses the myth and its sources on pp. 82–108.

[3] See in general M. Éliade, *Le mythe de l'éternel retour* (1949, Eng. tr. 1954). J. A. Philip's denial that Eudemus fr. 88 Wehrli shows it to have been Pythagorean seems to me wrong, in

2. The Great, or Complete, Year, defined by Plato as the period required to bring sun, moon and planets back to the same relative positions (*Tim.* 39 b), a matter, it was thought, of some 10,000 years, though theories of its conditions and duration varied considerably. For information about it see my *In the Beginning* 64 f. and 134 n. 2, and vol. I, 282 f. and (in Heraclitus) 458 with notes. Here it is strongly suggested by the description of the cosmic reversal as 'the greatest and most complete of all *tropai*', *tropē* being the word for solstice, applied by Plato also to the planets (*Tim.* 39 d).

3. Connected with these was the belief in recurrent catastrophes by flood or fire (*Tim.* 22 c), destructive of all civilization. Floods are linked by Aristotle to the notion of a Great Winter, corresponding on a far larger scale to the annual winter (*Meteor.* 352 a 28 ff.), from which only a few ignorant hill-dwellers survived. In Plato these natural disasters reappear in the *Timaeus* (22 c) and *Critias* (109 d), and their effects are described in the *Laws* (677 a–b, p. 330 below), and Aristotle takes seriously the belief that all knowledge and arts have been repeatedly lost and recovered. With the story of Deucalion (mentioned by Aristotle, *l.c.*), we may assume it to have been part of the common stock of Greek lore. For details see *In the Beginning* 65–9.

4. The age of Cronus, or golden age, was familiar from Hesiod and others. Empedocles had linked this with the cyclic theme in his doctrine of the alternate cosmic cycles, of increasing Love and increasing Strife, which put the golden age of innocence and happiness at the beginning of our own, when the power of Love was stronger. For this see vol. II, 248 f. Besides the *Politicus*, the rule of Cronus occurs in Plato at *Laws* 713 a–b. There too Cronus appointed *daimones* to look after man. (The parallel with *Pol.* 271 d–e is close, and cf. *Critias* 109 b.) In general see Baldry's article 'Who Invented the Golden Age?' in *CQ* 1952.

5. The earth-born. In early Greek accounts, both mythological and rational, of the origin of life, the conception of the earth as literally the mother of the human race was widespread. It is fully treated in *In the Beginning*, chh. 1 and 2. For its place in the cosmic theory of Empedocles, see vol. II, 206. Plato mentions the earth-born again in the 'grand myth' of *Rep.* 3 (vol. IV, 462 f.), the *Protagoras* (320 d), the *Sophist* (247 c) and the *Critias* (109 d). A variant occurs at *Symp.* 191 c (men beget children themselves, but on the earth, not on women), reminiscent of the story of the birth of Erechthonius (Eur. fr. 925 N., Rose, *Handbook* 110).

6. The strange reversal of individual life, from age to infancy, occurs in a

spite of the approval of de Vogel (*JHS* 1969, 164 f.). For the same idea in recent times see vol. I, 282 n. 1.

line of Hesiod, *Erga* 181, where he says that the present wretched 'age of iron' will be destroyed when men and women are born grey-headed. This, the only known reference before Plato, is not explicitly connected with a cosmic reversal, but its mention in the context of a succession of races, beginning with the golden one ruled by Cronus, does suggest that Plato has worked another old belief into his framework. Some have also seen it in Heraclitus fr. 88 DK: 'Living and dead . . . are the same, for the second changes and becomes the first, and the first, changing again, the second.' But see vol. I, 478 f. Theopompus, a younger contemporary of Plato, wrote of a tree whose fruit made men's lives flow backwards from old age through maturity and childhood to its end, and it is a matter of opinion whether he is more likely to have borrowed this from the *Politicus* or used a common source. (Theop. *ap*. Ael. *VH* 3.18, text in Frutiger, *Mythes* 243 n. 1. See Skemp 111.)

7. The miseries of primitive life and the benefits of progress. This repeats the account in the *Protagoras* (321 c–22 c), which especially emphasizes the drawback of having no political art (322 b 5). The best pre-Platonic account is Aeschylus, *PV* 442–68.

Greek mythology and philosophy were divided between two theories of human development (described in detail in my *In the Beginning*, chh. 4 and 5). One saw it as a degeneration from a primitive age of innocence as well as happiness, the other more rationally in terms of progress and improvement both technical and social, from wretched, animal-like beginnings. It looks as if Plato had ingeniously reconciled the contradiction by the conception of a universe undergoing periodic reversals of its motion, with contrary effects on the state of mankind. His nearest predecessor is Empedocles with his alternating eras of Love and Strife. But in Empedocles, first, the world is utterly destroyed at the end of both periods, which lead respectively to a complete, motionless fusion and a complete separation of the physical elements which by their partial mixture constitute a cosmos; no deity intervenes to save it at the last moment. Secondly there is no hint of the strangest feature of Plato's account, the reversal of cosmic revolutions. In this he has no Greek precursor, unless one regards as such the information acquired by Herodotus (2.142) from Egyptian priests that during the 11,340 years of Egyptian monarchy the sun reversed its course four times. The priests expressly said, however, that the changes brought no abnormalities or disasters on Egypt.[1] This does not, any more than the Atreus portent, imply

---

[1] They also said that there were no gods in human form. I do not see how, as Skemp thinks (p. 91), this contradicts P.'s statement that a god, 'a different and superior being' (*Pol.* 271 e), once looked after mankind.

14-2

Plato's extraordinary story of God turning the world for thousands of years and then 'letting go the rudder' (272e) and leaving it to its own devices. Reitzenstein long ago suggested an oriental source, Zoroastrianism, but this has not stood up well to examination.[1] The most natural conclusion is that this remarkable 'single fact' behind the variety of traditional lore was the product of Plato's mythopoeic imagination.

[1] Reitzenstein and Schaeder, *Stud. z. ant. Synkr.* (1926). For criticism see reff. in Leisegang, *RE* 2500 (1941) and Koster, *Mythe de P.* etc., ch. VII (1951). The point that P. expressly denies the theological dualism basic to Zoroastrianism (270a), though not overlooked by R. (see Koster 42), certainly did not strengthen his case. See also Skemp 92–5 and 146 n. 1.

III

PHILEBUS[1]

> We are speaking to men, not gods, and the most natural concerns of human kind are pleasures, pains and desires.
>
> Plato, *Laws* 732 e

Date.[2] The *Philebus* is generally held, on grounds of both style and content, to be one of Plato's latest dialogues. Bury (1897, p. ix) could call this 'the verdict of the most recent critics', and it is still that of the majority, e.g. Crombie (1962): 'It is certainly one of the latest group of dialogues.' Ryle however (1967) placed it in the middle group, though later than the *Timaeus* for which he adopts Owen's dating. Some close parallels between the two dialogues strongly suggest proximity in time, of which anyone attempting to date either must take account, whether he believes, with Ryle, that *Philebus* 'echoes' *Timaeus*, or with Leisegang, Diès and Hackforth that it leads up to it.[3] It will be treated here as a late work, following on those in the previous chapter.

Characters. Socrates again leads the debate, probably because the subject is pleasure, about which he has so often expressed strong views in earlier dialogues, but his manner is more like that of the Eleatic visitor than of the ironic Socrates we know. To lend credibility to this, Plato makes Protarchus, in the name of all the young men present, demand

---

[1] Besides the published sources mentioned, I wish to acknowledge a debt to Cornford's MS notes for a lecture-course on the *Philebus*. Gosling's *Philebus* (1975) appeared after this chapter was written, but I have added a few references to it.

[2] The authenticity of the dialogue is no longer in doubt. In the last century Schaarschmid and Horn denied it on the ground that it ignored the theory of Forms and was in other respects unplatonic. See Bury's ed., p. lxiv, and for a point-by-point refutation of Horn, Rodier's chapter on the *Phil.* in his *Études*.

[3] Bury, ed. p. ix, Crombie, *EPD* I, 252, Ryle in *Ency. Phil.* VI, 320 and *P.'s P.* 251 and 285, Leisegang in *RE* 2505, Diès, Budé ed. cii, Hackforth, *PEP* 3. In putting *Phil.* after *Tim.* Ryle follows Wilamowitz, *Pl.* I, 628, 635. To put it nevertheless in an earlier group is to revive a still older view. For details see Bury lxxxvii–lxxxi. It should be added that Owen, though assigning *Tim.* to the middle group, still regards *Phil.* as late and as representing a changed Platonism. See his 1953 article reprinted in *SPM*, 315, 321, 324 and (especially) the final paragraph on 338.

that he abandon his practice of getting everyone into difficulties by asking unanswerable questions. This time *he* must resolve their difficulties, and they will follow him as best they can. (19e–20a. Cf. 28b–c.) It is one of few personal touches in a dialogue on the whole lacking in dramatic interest.[1]

The name Philebus is unknown to history. Some have thought it invented: he is simply the embodiment of a dogmatic hedonism.[2] This would certainly fit his role. After being introduced as maintaining that 'gladness, pleasure, enjoyment and all that go with them constitute the good for all living creatures',[3] he turns his back on the discussion named after him, and leaves it entirely in the hands of Protarchus.

Protarchus is called son of Callias and a follower of Gorgias (19b, 58a), and could be the man mentioned in Aristotle's *Physics*, 197b 10. This suggests a historical figure, though some think him imaginary. Callias was a common name, but there is no reason why he should not have been one of the two sons of the well-known Sophist-fancier (vol. IV, 216).[4] Though calling himself a hedonist like Philebus, he is a very different character. He may stick to his guns on a point like the non-existence of false pleasures (p. 218 below), but agrees without argument to some fundamental Socratic theses, such as the government of the universe by divine Reason (28d–e), which make his ultimate conversion certain. He is young (16b).

[1] Nevertheless Hackforth (*PEP* 7) mentions a number of places where S.'s familiar traits come through. Wilamowitz (I, 628) took the *quantum mutatus* view: S. has turned into a 'thesis-defender'.

[2] Wilamowitz I, 629, Friedländer III, 309, Leisegang, *RE* 2502, Hackforth p. 6 with n. 3. As to his name (φιλ-ηβος), S. is surely witness that a 'lover of youth' need not necessarily be a champion of extreme hedonism. Nor need a φίλος be an ἐραστής. Gosling's 'Loveboy' is ambiguous: cf. 'playboy'.

[3] Philebus has maintained not only that 'good' is rightly predicated of pleasure (as 11b alone might suggest), but that 'pleasant' and 'good' have the same denotation (are properly used of one single φύσις: see 60a).

[4] Taylor (*PMW* 409) thought it impossible because *Apol.* 20a represents them as boys at the time of S.'s trial; but S. specifies no date for his conversation with Callias about their education. Among previous scholars Wilamowitz (I, 629) and Friedländer (III, 310) thought Protarchus historical, Hackforth (p. 7) imaginary.

Pleasure and good. Since Plato's subject is the place of pleasure in the good life, something must first be said about the two key-concepts, of pleasure and 'the good',[1] as he uses them in this dialogue.

Pleasure. Plato nowhere defines pleasure, and indeed the word's field of reference changes during the discussion. The Greek word '*hēdonē*', like the English 'pleasure', was applied widely.[2] A glance at the lexicon shows that it was not confined to sensual pleasures or what are called here the pleasures of 'replenishment', the sort to which, as in the *Protagoras*, one 'yields', which one 'cannot resist', which 'defeat' one. Yet this was the most popular usage, which Plato adopted without examination when in the *Gorgias* he wanted to combat hedonism in its most extreme form. According to its champion Callicles, pleasure attends the *process* of satisfying wants like hunger and thirst: with their satisfaction the pleasure ceases, and since pleasure and good are identical —there are no bad pleasures—happiness lies in letting the appetites grow as big as possible and ensuring the means of feeding them (494a– 95a). It is from this simple conception of pleasure that the *Philebus* starts,[3] when it is sharply opposed to intellectual activity as its rival for the title of 'good'. As the discussion proceeds, however, we find that one of Plato's main aims is precisely to analyse the concept of pleasure as a necessary preliminary to estimating its value in human life. Hedonism in various forms was being actively preached by Plato's acquaintances, including Aristippus representing the extreme, Calliclean type, and Eudoxus who, says Aristotle, combined it with a life of unusual temperance and self-control.[4] It badly needed the attentions of

[1] I have omitted pleasure's rival, intellect, as to which only a reminder should be needed of how Plato associates various terms covering thinking, the mind, and knowledge (φρόνησις, νοῦς, ἐπιστήμη and others) more closely than we do. ἐπιστήμη is at one moment *what* is known, the content of knowledge including practical crafts, and at another equated with νοῦς, the mind that knows. As opposed to pleasure it must be thought of as mental activity, yet in the classification of what is called νοῦς καὶ ἐπιστήμη at 55c ff. all the emphasis is on the subjects known, from husbandry and building to pure mathematics. If the Greek assimilation of these terms is not familiar by now, see vol. III, 501 n. 3 and IV, 265.

[2] Nor is the discussion confined to this word, but τὸ χαίρειν and τέρψις are thrown in as working equivalents (11b). Cf. S.'s depreciation of Prodicean niceties at *Prot.* 358a. Thus pleasure and enjoyment are not separated in Plato as they are, for instance, by a modern philosopher like Bernard Williams in *PAS* suppl. vol. XXXIII, 67.

[3] As an argument *ad hominem* this is fair enough, for it is Philebus's conception of pleasure.

[4] Arist. *EN* 1172b9–16. For Eudoxus see pp. 453–5 below, for Aristippus, vol. III, 490–9. On the relation of P.'s discussion of pleasure to current debates in the Academy see Jowett's editors, vol. III, 532f., n. 1.

a skilled dialectician to clear up the confusion caused by the use of a single term to cover a complex of different, even incompatible experiences. Pleasure, Plato claims, may be 'true' or 'false', and 'true' or 'pure' pleasures turn out in the end to be closely related to wisdom and knowledge (63 e). In this way pleasure as such can before the analysis be characterized as *apeiron*, without bounds or measure (27e, 31 a), whereas later 'pure' (opposed now to 'intense') pleasures are *emmetra*, bound by measure (52c); and again at 65 d pleasure (glossed as *excessive* enjoyment to show that the word is used in the old sense) has relapsed into the measureless. The crude question: 'Is pleasure good or bad?' is unreal until one has answered the further questions: 'What sort of pleasure?' and 'Pleasure in what?' This is a big advance on the *Gorgias* and *Protagoras* and even on the more elaborate treatment of pleasure in *Republic* 9; and it owes much to that 'gift of the gods' (16c), the dialectical art of collection and division evolved, from a hint of Socrates,[1] in the other dialogues of Plato's late maturity.[2]

The good. In defending the identity of pleasure with goodness[3] before the dialogue began, Philebus has said that by 'good' he meant what is good for every living thing (11a, 60a), as in real life Eudoxus had included 'creatures both with and without reason' (Arist. *EN* 1172b 10). Socrates on the other hand, by his original claim that it resides in intellectual activity, or as he modifies it in the dialogue, that thought is the superior element in the mixed life which is the best, has immediately confined it to the human race.[4] 'Pleasure must be the good because every creature pursues it', said Eudoxus. 'Pleasure is not the supreme good, though every ox and horse and other beast proclaim it by their

[1] See p. 27 above.

[2] A. Hermann in *Untersuchungen zu P.'s Auffassung der Hedoné* pursues the conception of pleasure through the dialogues and concludes on p. 77 that they show 'a planned and systematic development'. The obscurities of *Phil.* are reduced if one can see it historically, taking into account the contemporary controversies in which P. was involved. If this chapter has not said enough about them, Thompson's lecture 'Introd. Remarks on the *Phil.*', printed in *J. of Philol.* 1882, should still be read for its information on the Cyrenaics, Cynics, Megarics and Pythagoreans.

[3] That ἀγαθόν at 11b means not only 'good' but '*the* good' is clear from the context and confirmed by the substitution of τἀγαθόν in the recapitulation at 60a.

[4] The necessity of thought must clearly override the few passages in which, whether from indifference to detail or a willingness to humour the hedonists where the distinction was less important, S. uses their expressions. See 60c, 22b. At 22b the addition of φυτοῖς is remarkable, and was arbitrarily excised by Badham.

behaviour' is Plato's reply (67 b). Thought and its congeners—memory, right belief, true reckoning—are better than pleasure for all capable of engaging in them (11 b). What they seek is 'a habit (*hexis*) and disposition of the soul capable of making the life of all *men* happy', elsewhere expressed as 'the best of human possessions' (11 d, 19 c); and it amounts to asking the old Socratic question posed in the *Gorgias*: 'How ought one to live?'

In the *Republic* too (505 d) the good was described as 'what every soul pursues, for the sake of which all its actions are performed', but the *Philebus* offers not the slightest hint of a culmination in any mysterious Form of the Good, transcending knowledge, truth and even existence. What it offers is far less open to Aristotle's criticism of 'a Good solitary and apart, which even if it exists can clearly never be practised or possessed by man' (*EN* 1096b 32). Rather does it resemble Aristotle's own teaching, that human excellence (*aretē*) is a *hexis*, and the good for man (which both philosophers identified with *eudaimonia*, happiness) an activity of soul dependent on that *hexis* (*EN* 1106b 36, 1098 a 16). Here again we notice that tendency away from the ideal to the practicable, the humanly attainable, which marked the *Politicus*. It is a fine thing to know the divine Form of Circle, but it will not help us to find the way home (62 b). As we shall see later, this by no means implies cutting off humanity from what is above it, the eternal Reason which controls the cosmos, and of which man's own reasoning powers are a part. Nor need it involve sacrificing the belief in transcendent Forms, even if they no longer occupy the centre of the stage (p. 237 below).

Three criteria are mentioned by which any candidate for the title 'the good' must be judged: it must be perfect (complete in itself, fulfilled),[1] adequate (so that whoever possesses it needs nothing besides) and the universal object of choice. (See 20 d, 22 b, 60 c, 61 a.) The nearest to a definition of it comes near the end, at 65 a, where Socrates says that it combines three forms: beauty, symmetry or proportion, and truth or reality. These, they agree, are furnished by mind (*nous*) rather than by pleasure. Nevertheless mind by itself is not in human life either

---

[1] τέλεον, having achieved its *telos*, i.e. not only full internal development but purpose or aim. Similarly its contradictory ἀτελές meant not only incomplete or imperfect but ineffectual, a failure.

the sole or the supreme good. It has already been agreed that no one would choose either pleasure or intellectual activity *alone* (21a–e, 60d–e), and in the final five-fold classification of human 'possessions', intellect and thought are placed third in order of merit. Further comment on this must come later.

Subject and scope. Most commentators at some stage emphasize the obscurity of the *Philebus*.[1] Plato's principle of going 'wherever the wind of the argument blows' leads to some disconcerting transitions, and the doctrines themselves, while reminding us of those in other dialogues, give them at the same time a new twist and are bafflingly complex. This chapter cannot hope to solve all the problems, but will try to set them out fairly and assess the various solutions which have been proposed.

Let us first of all be clear what is the subject under discussion. It is not what Taylor said it was (*PMW* 408), 'a straightforward discussion of whether the "good for man" can be identified either with pleasure or with the life of thought'. That has been argued out (evidently to a stalemate) before the dialogue began. The dialogue opens when Philebus, exasperated perhaps like Callicles by Socrates's 'fiddling little questions', hands over his part to Protarchus. After a brief recapitulation Socrates radically changes his ground with the suggestion that perhaps neither pleasure nor thought in isolation can provide a happy life. Both have their place, and the question he wishes to discuss with Protarchus concerns their relative importance. First prize for goodness must go to the 'mixed' life, and what remains to be decided is whether pleasure or thought shall have the second. By this dramatic device of a dialogue before the dialogue Plato shows plainly that he has no intention of treating us to yet another refutation of the naive hedonistic equation of pleasure with good which he had already dealt with amply in the *Gorgias* and *Republic*. With the question 'what place can be assigned to pleasure in the good life, and what sorts of pleasure can there find admission?' he breaks new ground.[2] This explains both his

[1] A good example is Grote: 'It is neither clear, nor orderly . . . Every commentator of Plato, from Galen downwards, has complained of the obscurity of the Philebus.' This 'remains incorrigible'. (*Pl.* II, 584 with n. *u*.)

[2] The above owes much to some remarks of Hackforth's on p. 112 of *PEP*, from which I have quoted the question above. Among previous discussions of pleasure, perhaps that in

reason for writing another dialogue about pleasure and the complexity of its argument.

One must also note at the outset a premise on which Plato's whole case rests, that is, his conviction that the world is rationally ordered by a divine Intelligence which, as he argued in the *Phaedo* (97c), naturally aims at the best. Its effect has been to introduce order, harmony and measure, and through them beauty and goodness. This runs right through his thought from *Phaedo* and *Republic* to *Laws*, and is the main theme of the *Timaeus*. Its evidence, he thought, is daily before our eyes in the order, beauty and regularity of motion of the sun, moon and stars,[1] governed by mathematical ratios and giving birth to time, the uniform succession of days, nights and seasons on which the life of all creatures depends. Thus Plato's exalted view of measure, proportion, symmetry and so forth is governed throughout by a universal teleological hypothesis: what makes any mixture good is, as in the macrocosm, a due measure and proportion among its ingredients. He is emphatic about this. (See 64d–e.) The *Philebus* is an excellent illustration of Plato's talent for combining the ethical and the metaphysical, the human and the cosmic.[2] The whole of reality is his province, and he is unwilling to separate any of its parts since for him they are parts of an organic whole. Man's soul is a fragment of the universal soul (30a), order is the same in individual souls, in the city-state and in the universe at large. The *Philebus* treats of it in the individual, the *Politicus* in the state, and the *Timaeus* in the universe at large, but all alike are at pains to put mankind in his setting as an integral part of the cosmic order.

The argument. A brief outline may help to keep the connexion of thought in mind when we turn to details.

In pitting pleasure against thought as 'the good', Socrates and Philebus may have been wrong. What if it is some third thing, with pleasure and thought competing only for second place? Both are genera

---

Protagoras comes nearest to *Philebus*. Whatever view one takes of the seriousness of S.'s hedonistic thesis in that dialogue, the 'pleasure' which he advocates contains a strong admixture of thought in its 'art of measurement' and canny foresight.

[1] Mentioned at *Phil.* 28e. For the divine mind see, besides 28c–e, 22c and 30a–d.

[2] For the Victorian rationalist, George Grote, 'the forced conjunction of Kosmology and Ethics' was 'the one main defect' pervading the dialogue (*Pl.* II, 611).

containing dissimilar species, certain pleasures may be good, others bad (though at this stage Protarchus maintains that any pleasure, *qua* pleasure, must be good).

But this raises the old question of one and many, how a single Form can exist, retain its unity, and enter into its many transient instances.

To answer this Socrates describes a method resembling the dialectic, or division into kinds, of *Sophist* and *Politicus*.[1] Protarchus and Philebus doubt its relevance, but if Socrates proposes to investigate the different kinds of pleasure and wisdom, well and good. He replies that the task may be unnecessary, because neither pleasure nor thought by itself satisfies their agreed criteria of goodness, which demand a 'mixed' life containing both. No one would wish for a life of pleasure devoid of all thought, memory and kindred faculties, nor one of cerebration with no pleasures. Yet either pleasure or wisdom may win second prize by being the element which *makes* the mixed life good, and this he claims for wisdom.

In all that exists four forms, or kinds, can be distinguished: the unlimited, limit, their mixture and the cause of the mixture. 'Unlimited' designates what admits indefinitely of more and less, like size or speed, 'limited' includes proportionate relationships expressible numerically (half, double etc.), their mixture results in goodness and harmony, and the cause, or maker of the mixture, is reason, supremely manifested in the divine Mind that regulates the universe. Pleasure belongs to the unlimited because, as its advocates themselves say, it always admits of more. But that cannot be a reason for its goodness, for it is equally true of pain.

Pleasure in fact cannot be considered apart from pain. Pain occurs when the internal harmony of a living creature (belonging to the mixed class) is disturbed, and pleasure accompanies the process of return to its natural condition. That is one kind,[2] but there are also pleasures of anticipation, i.e. mental pleasures. But anticipation may be disappointed, and its pleasure dependent on a false belief, in which case Socrates maintains that the pleasure itself is false, which Protarchus stoutly denies: beliefs can be true or false, but not pleasures. In a long discus-

---

[1] Cf. 23 c 4 διχῇ διαλάβωμεν, 12 εἴδη, d 2 κατ᾽ εἴδη διιστάς.
[2] So pleasure is to be analysed after all.

sion, Socrates suggests other ways in which a pleasure may be false. First, as with vision, in judging pleasures from a distance one may be deceived about their magnitude (intensity), and the amount by which a present pleasure exceeds or is exceeded by the pleasure of anticipation may be called false pleasure. Secondly, one may confuse absence of pain with positive pleasure, in which case the impression of pleasure is false.

This reminds Socrates of thinkers who claim there is no such thing as pleasure, but only escape from pain. They go too far, but their reminder that many pleasures are not pure pleasures, but mixed with pain (as drinking with thirst), is salutary. Yet pure pleasures there undoubtedly are. They include appreciation of form and colour, many sounds, and even scents; and lastly the pleasures of learning. None of these is preceded or accompanied by any painful sense of want. Further, 'unlimited' applies only to the mixed pleasures going with bodily replenishment; the pure should be classed with limit or the measured; and the truth (reality) of pleasures is decided by their purity.

Pleasure is a *process*, not a finished state, or product, and processes are means not ends, as shipbuilding is for the sake of the ships. Therefore not pleasure, but a higher end, should be called 'good'. Is it not unreasonable also to admit that the good resides in soul rather than body yet confine it to pleasure and deny the title 'good' to wisdom, courage and other virtues? Is one to equate the suffering of pain with lack of virtue?[1]

Now it is the turn of wisdom and knowledge to be analysed and tested. Knowledge is divided into practical, or technical, and cultural, and the former judged by the extent to which it uses exact canons of measure and number, that is, approaches pure knowledge. The study of number is itself twofold, philosophical, operating with abstract, equal units, and popular, whose units are unequal—encampments, cows, anything whether large or small. The purest, truest knowledge is dialectic, whose objects are the 'really real', 'always the same, unchanged and unmixed', and their closest kin.

Both ingredients of the best life having been analysed separately, it

[1] Even in the loose construction of *Phil.* these arguments are exceptionally isolated from any context, and one would hope too that, as Hackforth says (*PEP* 111), they were not intended to stand on their own feet as a serious refutation of hedonism.

remains to consider how to mix them, and in particular which species of each should be included. As to knowledge, to live a human life at all one cannot confine it to dialectical philosophy. Not only the Forms, but their imperfect embodiments must be studied, even those arts which rely on empirical guesswork rather than calculation. Of pleasures, the true will be admitted, and any others that may be either necessary (presumably as attending the satisfaction of basic physical needs) or compatible with health, temperance and the other virtues. But Intelligence itself will reject the intense pleasures which go with folly and vice, for the simple reason that they would make its own operations impossible.

Finally there is a third ingredient to add, namely truth or reality, for the best life must be capable of realization.

The good for man, then, does not lie in either pleasure or intellectual life alone, but is a blend of both, containing all kinds of knowledge, and the better kinds of pleasure. One last question remains: What is the most valuable element in the mixture, that which *makes* it so desirable? When they know this, they can consider whether pleasure or knowledge comes closest to it.[1] But what makes any mixture good is its formula, the proportion in which its ingredients are blended. It is due measure that imparts goodness, and beauty and truth as well; and Protarchus needs no persuading that the achievement of measure and proportion is due to rational activity rather than pleasure. So intellect gets second prize. The dialogue ends with a list of five 'human possessions' drawn up in order of merit.

The One-and-Many Problem (14c–16a). At 12c Socrates declares that though pleasure is one thing it takes many forms, unlike and even opposed to each other, as black and white are contraries though both embraced by the same genus, colour; so one pleasure may be good and another bad. By allowing that his own favourite, wisdom, is in the same case, he gets Protarchus to withdraw his objection that though pleasures may arise from different *causes*, in themselves they cannot be opposed.

Protarchus perhaps gave up too easily. Socrates is treating pleasure as a genus: there are different *kinds* of pleasure. In illustration he cites

---

[1] So in spite of intervening turns and twists, the original plan has been faithfully executed. See 11d–e, and the careful recapitulation at 66d–67a.

the pleasures of the licentious and the temperate, the foolish and the wise. This, as Protarchus says, is to differentiate them by their *objects*, by what induces the pleasures. He himself understands by pleasure the subjective feeling alone. The gluttony or lechery, the knockabout farce or the improving book which *give* pleasure to different people are not a part of the pleasure itself. This was the view of the Cyrenaics. According to them 'pleasure does not differ from pleasure ... Pleasure is good even if it arise from the most unseemly sources ... Even if the action be unacceptable, the pleasure by itself is choiceworthy and good' (D.L. 2.87–8). This is relevant to the later question of true and false pleasures, and it would have been interesting to have it thrashed out.

They are now faced, says Socrates, with the whole troublesome question of how one thing can also be many, not as it applies to physical objects, either as wholes of parts or in their mutual relations (one thing both large and small etc.), but as it arises when one posits single Forms like Man, Ox, the Beautiful or the Good. The points of doubt are three:

(1) Should one accept such monads as really existing (ὄντως οὔσας)? (2) As an immutable and eternal *unity*, how can each Form *be* this one thing [i.e. contain both Unity and Being]? (3) What is its relation to the infinite multitude of things that come to be [*sc.* in its image]? Does it become many by being distributed among them or does it achieve the apparent impossibility of getting apart from itself and appearing as a whole in one and many at the same time?[1]

The question of one thing being both large and small was mentioned in the *Republic* (524a–b) as a useful propaedeutic and stimulus to thought, and dealt with in the *Phaedo* by the concept of participation (102b–103a). More generally, to puzzle over one thing having many attributes was dismissed in the *Sophist*[2] as due to 'poverty of intellect'. More relevantly to the present passage, participation is the first solution to the one-and-many problem offered, and subsequently criticized, in the *Parmenides*, where also all the three 'serious' questions raised here were debated.[3]

---

[1] 15b. Some have seen only two questions here. But πρῶτον μὲν ... εἶτα δὲ ... μετὰ δὲ τοῦτο makes P.'s intentions clear, and the three are not hard to distinguish. I am not convinced by Striker's arguments (*Peras u. Apeiron* 14 n.) for a different interpretation of μετὰ δὲ τοῦτο in this context. Crombie (*EPD* II, 362 n.) resorts to emendation.

[2] 251a–b; see pp. 148f. above.   [3] See pp. 36f., 40f., 54 above.

It is tempting to translate the questions into modern terms as asking how one subject can have many predicates (trivial) and how one predicate can have many subjects, or what is the relation between a universal and its particulars (serious). But these would be different questions. The 'serious' questions would today be treated purely as questions of logic, but for Plato the so-called 'predicate', or 'universal', *existed* in a supersensible world. It is not a question of logic but of the structure of reality. So his first question is: Do such monads as the Forms exist? The second is Parmenidean: Since Unity and Existence are two, not one, how can a unit both exist and maintain its unity? It would already be a combination of more than one Form, as the *Sophist* says.[1] The third was raised at *Parm.* 130e–31e and never directly answered.

A brief addition, difficult to translate,[2] shows that in Plato's mind the question is closely bound up with speech and its mental counterpart.[3] The enquiry, it says, must start from the admission that one and many become the same *through discourse* (ὑπὸ λόγων). Their identity pervades *everything that is said*, is a permanent feature of speech and thought and something inherent in our own nature, and a young man's first awareness of it is an intoxicating experience. From this point the argument goes on to show, first, that our understanding must be disciplined by dialectic, and second, that, so disciplined, the form of our sentences and thoughts does reflect the structure of reality and is not *only* something 'in us', i.e. subjective.

Dialectical solution of the one-and-many problem (16b–18d).[4] There is a method 'easy enough to indicate but hard indeed to practise', to which Socrates is devoted though it has often left him deserted and helpless,[5] a veritable gift of the gods, to which, he claims (16c2–3), is owed every

---

[1] *Parm.* 142b–c, p. 54 above. Cf. *Soph.* 250a: If Motion and Rest exist, there must be τρίτον τι παρὰ ταῦτα, τὸ ὄν.

[2] Cf. the renderings of Hackforth (p. 22), Bury (xxxv) and Ackrill, introd. to Stenzel's *PMD*, xxxi.

[3] λόγος covers both speech and thought, conceived of as an internal dialogue of the mind with itself (*Soph.* 263e).

[4] Anyone who reads the following pages on dialectic and the Fourfold Analysis must be directed also to Crombie's long and meticulously careful discussion of them in *EPD* II, 359–70 and 422–40, which differs on several important points.

[5] P.'s insistence on the extreme difficulty of success in the dialectical method is noteworthy. Cf. p. 167 above. 16b6 ἐραστής, as at *Phdr.* 266b.

discovery of art and science. It is based on the truth that 'all things that are ever said to be consist of one and many, and combine in their nature limit and unlimitedness'.[1] So (16c10),

> Things being thus ordered, we must assume a single form for every thing and look for it—for we shall find one there—then after one form two, if there are two, or else three or some other number; then do the same with each of these units until we discover that the original unitary form was not simply one, many, and an infinite number, but *how* many. We shall not introduce infinity into the plurality until we have seen the whole number which lies between infinity and the one. Only then shall we release each unity in every thing into the infinite . . . But our clever men of today posit their one arbitrarily and their many too quickly or too slowly.[2] They leap straight from the one to the infinite multitude, and the intermediates escape them. This is the difference between eristic and dialectical discussion.[3]

This is a more elaborate and obscure description than those in the *Sophist* and *Politicus* (pp. 129f., 166 above), but the upshot seems to be roughly similar. With them also in mind, we may say that any group of phenomena to which we rightly give the same name will be found to have a common nature or form.[4] With 'every thing' (περὶ παντός) at 16d2 I take it Plato has chiefly in mind sensible particulars, also called 'the unlimited'. Even the philosopher or scientist must start from these,[5] though scientific thinking is concerned with the higher levels.[6]

---

[1] *Peras* (limit) and *apeiron* (infinite, indefinite or unlimited in number, quantity or degree). For their meanings and strong Pythagorean associations (well known to Plato) see index to vol. I, *s.vv.* and p. 532. (Gosling uses 'determinant' and 'indeterminacy'. See his note on 16c10, p. 84.) It may be confusing, but must be accepted, that P. here uses *apeiron* numerically, for the uncountable multitude of particulars in a species, and in the Fourfold Classification qualitatively, to signify the indefinite possibilities of variation in temperature, strength, speed and so on. (For a rather different possibility, see Gosling, *Phil.* xiii, xvii.)

[2] βραδύτερον has been found strange, because P. has only mentioned the fault of jumping too quickly from a genus straight to particulars. But it is an equally possible fault in classification, which he presumably mentions for the sake of completeness. One may wrongly interpose what are not true species, because their differences are non-essential, as for instance with biological 'sports'. See also Rodier, *Études* 76f., and for Gosling's interpretation his *Phil.*, p. 85. H. Maier, *Syll. des Arist.* 2. Teil, 2. Hälfte, pp. 5f., interpreted this sentence as an attack on the Megarians.

[3] The same distinction between eristics and philosophers goes back to the *Rep.* See 454a.

[4] See *Rep.* 596a and vol. IV, 550. Names depend on forms or essences, not vice versa (pp. 27–29 above).

[5] Cf. 18a ὅταν τις τὸ ἄπειρον ἀναγκασθῇ πρῶτον λαμβάνειν.

[6] This perhaps needs a little enlargement, since it has worried commentators. Neither P. nor Aristotle differentiates between the relation of genus to species and that of species to individual. It is only that beyond a certain point philosophical knowledge cannot penetrate. It must go as

The first step, then, is to identify a generic form in a multitude of instances;[1] then to work downwards, dividing it into species, and those into sub-species, until the lowest definable class is reached. Beyond that the philosopher cannot penetrate. There remains only the unlimited and not further definable mass of individuals from which we started. Plato would have agreed with Aristotle that 'there is no definition of them but they are known by perception and intuition' (*Metaph.* 1036a5). Nevertheless, though we perceive the individual, perception is in a sense of the universal: seeing Callias gives us our first impression of the species man, to which Callias belongs (*An. Post.* 100a16). There is this unique human faculty, described by Plato at *Phdr.* 249b, of advancing 'from many sensations to a unity pulled together by reason'.

Socrates follows this description with two[2] illustrations, of which the second at least does not seem to exemplify the method of genus–species division,[3] However, we shall shortly see it applied to the concept of pleasure, for the sake of which it was introduced. People experience on innumerable occasions feelings which they deem sufficiently alike to be given a common name, 'pleasure'. It is 'one in genus', but its 'parts' differ widely.[4] But it cannot be evaluated by saying simply that it is a unity with many parts and innumerable instances: the species must be

far as it can, e.g. in 'dividing' animals one must not stop at dogs, but continue to divide into Alsatians, spaniels, fox-terriers etc. These still present specifiable, or intellectually separable, differentiae (in Platonic-Aristotelian language, they have a comprehensible *eidos*), but the two King Charles spaniels Fido and Bruno no longer do so, though the senses can tell one from the other. At this point one must, for scientific purposes, let things 'slip away into the *apeiron*'. For Aristotle this was philosophy's greatest crux, for he had to reconcile two theses, both of which he believed to be profoundly true: (1) The philosopher's task was to explain substance or reality (τίς ἡ οὐσία, *Metaph.* 1028b4), (2) the primary realities are individuals. For his statement of the dilemma see *Metaph.* 999a24–9. But this is not the place to pursue Aristotle's full solution.

1 P. says nothing here about definition, but what we have is the first stage described at *Phdr.* 265d as 'bringing the dispersed plurality synoptically under one form, in order to define . . .'. P. never gives as much attention to collection as to the subsequent division, but it is mentioned by name (συνάγειν) at 25d.

2 Generally reckoned as three, but see below.

3 See Hackforth 24f. and Ackrill in *Ryle*, 380. Trevaskis in *Phron.* 1960 has made out an interesting case, based on the illustrations, for holding that the method described is not that of division at all. But one may agree with Runciman (*PLE* 61 n. 2) that 'it is perhaps more appropriate to see it as a further development of the method of diairesis'.

4 12e. For 'parts' = species cf. *Pol.* 262b, *Euthyphro* 12c–d, and p. 153 n. 4 above. All members of the same genus must have at least one feature in common (or so it appeared to Plato and Aristotle), even though in other respects opposed. In S.'s example of colours, black and white and all the rest possess visibility, as all animals resemble each other in being alive, though as different in other respects as tiger and mouse.

enumerated and defined. We are indeed spared the successive dichotomies of the *Sophist* and *Politicus*, and the classification may not seem so methodical, since by the adoption of different principles of division[1] some classes overlap or even coincide with others, as pure with true and mixed with false. The outcome, however, is clear and instructive as Socrates proceeds to distinguish pleasures of replenishment, of anticipation, of body, soul, and both together, pure pleasures and mixed, true and false, and subdivides false pleasures into three. Dialectical method is no bed of Procrustes, forcing every subject into a single rigid framework. Its general rules leave plenty of scope for philosophical initiative, which is why it is so difficult.

Note on the 'third illustration'. At 18 a Socrates says he will add one further point before returning to the subject of pleasure. Just as one must not leap straight from the single generic form to the infinity of particulars, so on the contrary (οὕτω καὶ τὸ ἐναντίον) when starting (as one must) from particulars one must not go straight to the one, but (in a clause admittedly difficult to translate and possibly corrupt; see Bury *ad loc.*) first grasp the number of its species, and come to the one last of all. What follows is therefore not, as many call it, a third illustration of the process already outlined. It refers to the reverse process, and moreover seems to contradict the earlier instruction to start by identifying the generic form and only then go on to distinguish the species within it. The example tells how Theuth, reputed inventor of the alphabet (*Phdr.* 274 c–d), faced with the infinity of vocal sounds, first distinguished within them vowels, semi-vowels and consonants and their subdivisions, and finally reached the genus which he named 'letters', uniting all the sounds into one. Bury *ad loc.* says only 'as in the analytical or deductive process, so likewise in the synthetic or inductive', but the simple antithesis between deduction and induction hardly fits. Stenzel gives the fullest explanation, but unless I have misunderstood Plato (which is not impossible), it does not quite correspond to his text.

Let us assume men capable of articulate speech but not yet of writing. Theuth's first step was to find the largest group or species in the infinite number of phonemes (not necessarily of different *kinds* of phoneme, but including the daily repetition of what kinds there were: the *apeira* are individuals); his next, to divide these groups into their several components (e.g. vowels into a, e, i, o, u) until he 'grasped the number of them and gave the name *stoicheion* [meaning both element and letter, p. 176 n. 1 above] to

---

[1] Analogous to the choice of different genera to produce different definitions of the Sophist.

each and all' (18c6). The letters, into which the groups are divided, are, one would think, *infimae species*, and it is to them that Theuth's method finally leads, not to the generic conception 'utterance' (φωνή) or its definition. To them he gave the generic *name* 'elements', and this is evidently the 'one' to which one should come last. It conveys a clear conception, that speech is reducible to a limited number of atomic forms; but Theuth must have had this conception of *stoicheion* in his mind from the start. It was not the last arrived at. Though Plato does not seem to see it, there is no real reversal of the original procedure. At the very least one must say that Theuth *assumed* (the θέσθαι of 16d2) a single generic notion to begin with, though only after he had seen that we cannot know a single set of letters on its own (18c7) did he *discover* (εὑρήσειν 16d2) the nature of *stoicheion* as a bond. (I make these comments with diffidence, but cf. Hackforth, *PEP* 26.)

The fourfold analysis of everything (23c–26d). After satisfying Protarchus that the good life must be 'mixed', including both pleasure and knowledge, Socrates says that to justify his claim that intellect, knowledge and their kin deserve second prize he needs fresh resources. With a little self-mockery about his passion for 'dividing according to kinds', he lays it down that everything in the world has a fourfold explanation. There are the unlimited and limit, already mentioned at 16c, third the mixture of the two, and fourth the cause of their mixture. Unlimited includes qualities exhibiting an indefinite more or less, e.g. hotter–colder, stronger–weaker, lighter–heavier. Over against them are set the limiting factors of measure, proportion, ratio: double, for example, does not admit of more or less. All these involve *number*, and the imposition of the right numerical limit on an indefinite continuum (in Plato's terms their 'mixture', 25e7) reconciles opposites and produces harmony. Examples are health,[1] music (in the ranges of pitch and tempo), equable climate and so on. By slipping in the word 'right' (ὀρθή, 25e7) Plato virtually excludes from the category of limit the abstract, value-neutral concepts of pure mathematics, and confines it to the second of the two kinds of measurement described in the *Politicus* (pp. 169f. above), though obviously a medicine with three ingredients which

[1] P. has in mind the orthodox Greek medical theory, attributed to Alcmaeon, that health depends on a proper balance (σύμμετρος κρᾶσις) of the opposites hot and cold, dry and wet, bitter and sweet etc. in the body. See *Symp.* 186d and vol. I, 346.

depends for its effects on their being mixed in the proportions 1:3:7 will not be improved if the proportions 1:4:16 are chosen because they represent a perfect geometrical progression.[1]

Much has been written in attempts to find a place for the Forms in the fourfold classification. They have been detected in every category except the unlimited, and even in all four together. Since however the phrase 'all things which there *now* are in the all', which designates the subjects of the analysis, in my opinion clearly excludes the Forms, I shall not continue the chase.[2] They might come under 'cause' (so Zeller), if the cause is to be thought of as external to the 'all',[3] were not the cause explicitly said to be mind. (Nor again, since the mixture *has* a cause, can the Forms, being uncaused, play any part within it.) True, the Forms had a causal role in the *Phaedo*, but the most hardened unitarian must agree that Plato's thought has developed considerably since then. The development has been in the direction of reducing the elements of metaphor, about which Aristotle complained, and of the vagueness of a sentence like 'Beauties became beautiful by the Beautiful, though whether by its presence or communion or how, I can't say' (*Pho.* 100d). The Forms have become patterns only, formal causes which can create nothing without an agent at work to reproduce them in a medium. Soul, life and mind were dramatically introduced into Reality in the *Sophist*, in the *Philebus* mind is assigned its function as active cause, and the whole scheme becomes clear in the *Timaeus*, where the divine Craftsman, who is also Nous, creates the cosmos by reproducing, so far as the nature of the medium allows, the eternal, uncreated

---

[1] Aristotle saw the flaw in this. See p. 277 below. To P.'s Pythagorean friends limit as such was in the 'good' list (vol. I, 245 f.), and words like μέτρον, μέτριον, ἔμμετρον regularly refer to due, or correct, measure. (See p. 169 above.) The association of measure and number with goodness was therefore natural to Plato, though if he had already drawn the distinction in *Pol.*, to ignore it here was a pity. The distinction between practical and philosophical arithmetic is introduced much later, at 56e, in a different connexion.

[2] πάντα τὰ νῦν ὄντα ἐν τῷ παντί (23c) cannot refer to τὰ ἀεὶ κατὰ τὰ αὐτὰ ὡσαύτως ἀμεικτότατα ἔχοντα (59c). Yet many have argued otherwise. For earlier views see Bury, lxiv–lxxiv and Ross, *PTI* 132–8, and cf. Rodier, *Études* 79–93, who found them in the mixed class, Friedländer, *Pl.* III, 324 f. and Grube, *P.'s Th.* 301–4, who both identify them with limit. Diès (Budé ed. xciv) and Gentile (see Friedländer, *Pl.* III, 537 n. 37) saw them in all four. Hackforth (p. 34) and Rist (*Philol.* 1964, 227) agree that the classification excludes the Forms.

[3] This is at least doubtful. Cf. 64c: 'What is it *in the mixture* which is at the same time most valuable and in the fullest sense the cause of such an arrangement commending itself to all of us?' At 23d the cause is a fourth class (γένος) of the contents of the universe, and at 30a–b it is ἐν ἅπασι τέταρτον ἐνόν. See pp. 215 f. below.

Forms in the 'receptacle of becoming', variously described as a plastic material and as space.[1]

Finally we have the application of all this to the case of pleasure. Its lack of limit (of which Philebus will boast), its encouragement of appetite to seek insatiably for more and more, is not a recommendation but a source of wickedness, and the imposition of limit, law and order, far from spoiling it, gives it a saving grace.

The cause: cosmological and teleological arguments (26 d–31 a). The mixture of the unlimited with limit is a 'being that has become' (27 b, i.e. something in this world as opposed to the eternal Forms). It is accepted as axiomatic that nothing can be generated without a cause, and that 'becoming' and 'being made' are the same. What, then, is the cause or maker of the mixture and the becoming? This question is highly relevant to the main aim of judging between pleasure and wisdom for second prize. The first goes to a life in the mixed category, pleasure falls within the unlimited, and a reader needs little perspicacity to see that Socrates will place wisdom (mind, thought, knowledge) in the remaining one. Since he has already emphasized the good effects of limit and its correlates measure, proportion, number, the competition is already virtually won, and from now on we are like readers of a detective story who have already guessed the outcome. The prime question, he continues, is whether the universe is at the mercy of chance, some random, irrational force, or guided by the regulating wisdom of Mind. Protarchus is shocked. The first alternative is sheer profanity, if not insanity. One has only to look at the cosmos, with its circling sun, moon and stars—responsible, as Socrates adds later, for years, seasons and months—to be convinced that it is the work of reason. This reply is a little unexpected from a man who has undertaken to defend hedonism. The view

---

[1] ἐκμαγεῖον 50 c, χώρα 52 a 8 (p. 265 below). The theme of Rist's article in *Philol.* 1964 is that in *Phil.* copies of the Forms, corresponding to the 'largeness in us' of *Pho.* 102 d, and not the Forms themselves, enter the physical world and constitute the element of limit. (If, as appears likely, the Forms are already acquiring the numerical character which Aristotle ascribed to them, this would strengthen the identification.) The divine Mind is like a painter who paints many pictures of the same scene. The scene may be said to be in the pictures, but still remains unique and apart from them. R. claims that with this conception P. has solved the problems about Forms raised in *Parm.*, and he may be right, though I have queried some of his points on the *Pho.* in vol. IV, 354 f.

that 'Reason is King of heaven and earth', which Socrates complacently attributes to 'a consensus of all the wise', was not without powerful rivals among the natural philosophers, nor does Plato underrate them in book 10 of the *Laws*. Even the admired Theaetetus had his doubts (*Soph.* 265 c–d). By enthusiastically espousing it Protarchus has given away his case from the start, and one can imagine a satirical smile on the face of the listening Philebus.

Microcosm mirrors macrocosm. Our bodies are composed of small portions of the same four elemental masses—fire, air, water and earth—as the universe, and draw on the body of the universe for their sustenance and growth. Likewise we have souls, and we cannot suppose that the Supreme Mind should have provided them for us yet failed to give soul as well as body to the macrocosm. Our souls indeed, like our bodies, are derived from their universal counterpart.[1] After repeating that mind is the fourth kind, the cause, Socrates continues (30c): 'But mind and the power of thought cannot come into existence without soul, so you must say that in the nature of Zeus there appears a royal soul and mind by the power of the Cause.' This is not immediately clear, but Zeller and Hackforth have explained it well.[2] Whichever came first, the *Philebus* and *Timaeus* expound the same cosmology and theology. Here there is an almost word-for-word coincidence,[3] and we may make use of the fuller account at *Tim.* 29d–30b. The supreme Cause is the divine Mind or intelligent Craftsman who created the cosmos. Knowing that nothing mindless would be as good as something intelligent, he gave it a mind. But nothing can have mind without soul, so he placed mind in soul and soul in a body. Soul (*psyche*) here is simply life, animation. The beasts have *psyche* without intelligence, and man cannot have intelligence without physical life. It is corporeal, visible nature, not the First Cause which is pure intellect, that cannot have mind without *psyche*.[4] Zeus in the *Philebus* passage is a literary

---

[1] This was a belief of Socrates himself according to Xen. *Mem.* 1.4.8. It can be traced back at least to Diogenes of Apollonia, who held that the soul is air and the air in us is 'a small portion of the god' (vol. II, 373 f.).

[2] See, for both, Hackforth 56 n. 1.

[3] *Phil.* 30c σοφία μὴν καὶ νοῦς ἄνευ ψυχῆς οὐκ ἄν ποτε γενοίσθην. Cf. *Tim.* 30b νοῦς δ' αὖ χωρὶς ψυχῆς ἀδύνατον παραγενέσθαι τῳ. That the elements of our bodies are 'borrowed' from the universe is also stated in *Tim.* (42e).

[4] Cf. p. 275 n. 1 below.

variation for the living and intelligent cosmos, borrowed from a pantheistic Orphic cosmogony.[1]

Mind, then, may be said to be both immanent and transcendent, but the cosmic mind is only a self-projection of the other, who 'being good and free from all envy, wanted everything to be as like himself as possible' (*Tim.* 29e).

In all this Plato's debt to the Pythagoreans is obvious. Among notions which may fairly be ascribed to them, one may mention Limit and the Unlimited as primary principles and respectively good and bad, the importance assigned to number, ratio and harmony, the cosmos as a living and intelligent creature, and men's souls as fragments of the soul of the universe.[2]

The psychology of pleasure, pain and desire (31 d–36 c). I avoid the heading 'classification of Pleasures', though that may be said to start here, because, true to the conversational genre, Plato is very casual about his classifications. What he now calls pleasure covers only one kind, the 'mixed'. Later come 'pure' pleasures, which even include the pleasures of learning.

Pleasure occurs during the process of restoration or replenishment following on a disturbance of the bodily harmony causing pain. Examples are drinking when thirsty, cooling down when suffering from heat.[3] Anyone experiencing neither deterioration nor restoration will feel neither pleasure nor pain. This state (which Socrates mentions here by the way, to be kept in mind for their future judgement of pleasure) would accompany the life of pure thought, which however is a life for the gods. To return, pleasure also accompanies the anticipation of something pleasant, as fear of something unpleasant may be called painful. This is a second kind, felt by the *psyche* independently of present bodily affections. To understand it calls for consideration of the nature of sensation, memory and desire, which are all involved. Some bodily

---

[1] See Guthrie, *OGR* 81.

[2] See the account of Pythagoreanism in vol. I, especially pp. 201, 207, 248, 289.

[3] In this account P. is unusually reticent about the pleasures of sex. τἀφροδίσια are mentioned at 65c, and doubtless hinted at among the 'unseemly' pleasures of 46a–b with its tactful reference to Philebus, the 'shameful' of 66a and the 'greatest and intensest' of 63d. In the most general sense they satisfy a felt want, but would not be so appropriate to his description of physical pleasure as accompanying the 'refilling' of a deleterious 'emptiness' in the body.

changes do not reach the level of consciousness,[1] but when soul and body are moved together in a common affection, this motion is called sensation. Memory is 'the maintenance of sensation',[2] and recollection the process whereby a lost sensation is recaptured without further recourse to the body.

The remarks on desire aim at proving, in a bafflingly roundabout and obscure way, that it is a purely psychical phenomenon. ('The argument denies that desire belongs to the body', 35 d.) Desire—thirst is the example—is for replenishment of what one lacks ('is being emptied of', 34e11), and is therefore for the opposite of what one is at the moment experiencing. Yet one must be aware of what one desires, and this can only be by *remembering* a previous experience of fulfilment, which, as we now know, is an activity of the *psyche* alone.

There is an apparent contradiction here. To paraphrase 35 a–d more fully, when the body is for the first time depleted, one cannot conceive of replenishment either by present sensation or through memory, since we have never experienced the pleasure of replenishment which the desire is for. Yet something in the thirsty (desiring) man must apprehend it (35 b 6), and this must be his *psyche*, which can only do so by memory. How then, one must ask, does the *psyche* apprehend the object of its desire through memory on the occasion of the first emptying? Plato says nothing, but it can only do so if its memory is the pre-natal memory described in *Meno*, *Phaedo* and *Phaedrus*. This is not explained, nor is the difficulty seen by Protarchus, but I suggest it as a possibility because no alternative so far proposed seems satisfactory,[3] and Plato does at least hint in this passage at the exalted

---

[1] In a repetition at 43 b, P. instances growth. *Tht.* 186c also defines the objects of sensation as ὅσα διὰ τοῦ σώματος παθήματα εἰς τὴν ψυχὴν τείνει, and cf. *Tim.* 64a–c.

[2] Or preservation (σωτηρία). P. has dealt with sensation and memory in *Tht.*, and allows himself here a misleading brevity. He appears to be asserting the absurdity that the sensation itself persists, but cf. *Tht.* 164a10: a man remembering what he has seen μέμνηται μὲν οὐχ ὁρᾷ δὲ αὐτό. It is rather the image imprinted on the soul in the wax-tablet simile of *Tht.* 191 d. On the scope of αἴσθησις, which I have rendered 'sensation', see pp. 74 f. above.

[3] Many of course believe either that the doctrine of *anamnesis* was never intended seriously (notably Moreau in *IPQ* 1959, 485), or that P. had by now abandoned it. Jowett (III, 533) thought its omission a sign of progress, 'rendered all the more significant by his having occasion to speak of memory as the basis of desire'. Horn used the contradiction to support his attack on the dialogue's authenticity. Apelt thought that what is remembered is not the pleasurable process but the original bodily equilibrium (the state, one may add, in which neither pleasure nor pain is felt). But the use of πλήρωσις, and the context, are strongly against this. As in *Gorg.* (496e), the

position of the soul as it has been described elsewhere. 'The argument, by demonstrating that it is memory that leads us to the objects of desire, shows that every impulse and desire, and the source and principle (*archē*)[1] of every living creature, belong to soul' (35 d).

Thus besides feeling pain when the body is depleted, and pleasure while its balance is being restored—processes closely connected with the destruction or preservation of life (35 e)—there is an intermediate state[2] in which we feel the pain of depletion but remember the pleasure which goes with replenishment. The memory gives pleasure if there is hope of future replenishment but doubles the pain if hope is absent.

False pleasures (36 c–44 a).[3] 1. Pleasure may result from a hope, or belief, which turns out to be false.[4] Socrates wishes to call this a false pleasure, but Protarchus objects. A belief may be true or false, but not a pleasure, because no one can think he feels pleasure without really feeling it. At first sight this seems irrefutable. 'Pleasure cannot err since it is not cognitive.' 'The predicate is altogether inapplicable to the subject.' The pleasure that a man feels at the news that he has been appointed to an honourable and lucrative post is real, though if the news is false it will be short-lived. 'The pleasure of hope is just as much pleasure when the hope is ill-founded, and due to false opinion, as when it is well-founded and based on right opinion.'[5] This is exactly

pleasure for which the desire is felt is the 'mixed' pleasure of drinking when thirsty. Hackforth (anticipated in this by Rodier, *Études* 98) simply says that desire *does not occur* at the first κένωσις, which appears to me to be ruled out by 35 a–b. (For Apelt and Hackforth, see the latter, p. 66 n. 1.)

1 Jowett (III, 590) renders ἀρχή by 'moving principle'. Cf. *Phdr.* 245 c–d.

2 ἐν μέσῳ 35 e7. To be distinguished of course from the middle state of feeling neither pleasure nor pain because the body is in equilibrium (32 e–33 a).

3 Gallop's remarks on this section in *PQ* 1960 are refreshingly independent and critical.

4 The possibility of false belief was fully discussed in *Tht.* (pp. 106–13 above). Since P. is now after a different quarry, he accepts like anyone else the obvious fact that it occurs. Philosophers who earnestly discuss the existence of tables do not in fact doubt that they exist; they readily assume it when not philosophizing about it. For a modern discussion of the relation between pleasure and belief see the papers by Williams and Bedford in *PAS* vol. XXXIII.

5 A. Brémond quoted by Friedländer, *Pl.* III, 539 n. 58; Grote, *Pl.* II, 603 f., Horn as cited by Bury, 206. Friedländer, Bury, Diès, Budé ed. ciii–cv, Taylor *PMW* 421 f., and Rodier, *Études* 113–28 are among P.'s defenders. More recently the question has aroused an extraordinary amount of interest. See Gosling in *Phron.* 1959 and 1961, Kenny in *Phron.* 1960, Gallop in *PQ* 1960, McLaughlin in *PQ* 1969, Dybikowski (1) *Phron.* 1970, (2) *PQ* 1970, Penner in *Phron.* 1970. One or two additional items are in the bibliographies of Dybikowski (1), 147 n. 2 and Penner 167 n. 3, and Gosling has resumed the discussion in his *Phil.*, pp. 214–20. The criticism goes back to Theophrastus, who, says Olympiodorus, 'opposes P. on the existence of true and false plea-

Protarchus's contention. As with beliefs, a man may be mistaken about the object which gives him pleasure, and the pleasure cannot then be called 'right' or 'good' (χρηστή), but what is *false* is only the belief on which it is founded, not the pleasure itself (37e–38a).

One or two points from the text should be noted at once.

First, at 36d and 38a Protarchus denies the existence of false pleasures. At 40b–c he admits it. So Socrates must have said something in between to make him change his mind. Second, Socrates himself asserts at 40d that anyone who feels pleasure, however groundless, always really (ὄντως) feels that pleasure, though it may be based on no actual facts, past, present or future. Evidently the difference between them has been one of terminology: he and Protarchus meant different things by the word 'false'.

The analogy with belief is central. The beliefs 'infect' the pleasures with their own condition (42a). Beliefs have qualities, of which truth and falsehood are two. Pleasures can also be qualified: they have just been speaking of great or intense pleasures and their opposites. Now a belief, whether true or false, is none the less truly (ὄντως) a belief (37a11). That is, a belief is judged true or false not in so far as it is or is not a belief, but with respect to the truth or falsity of its object. Why then should it be illegitimate to judge a pleasure by the same criterion? This is what Socrates proposes to do. By a false pleasure he does not mean an unreal one but one which arises from a false estimate of the situation, past, present or future. Belief and pleasure alike will be falsified in both senses when their falsehood becomes apparent, for they will cease to exist. Plato is using his own terminology, but has been at pains to make his meaning unambiguous.

The account of pleasure in *Republic* 9 (583b–87b) makes many of the same points as the *Philebus*, but here the *Philebus* shows an advance. At 585d–e Plato insists that the reality of a pleasure depends on the reality of its object: pleasure felt in the acquisition of what is more real (τὰ μᾶλλον ὄντα, i.e. the objects of knowledge) is 'more really and truly' pleasure[1] than pleasure felt in the less real. In the *Philebus* the reality

---

sures. All are true, for if there is a false pleasure, he says, there will be a pleasure that is not a pleasure.' (Text in Rodier, *o.c.* 123.)

[1] ὄντως τε καὶ ἀληθεστέρως χαίρειν . . . ἡδονῇ ἀληθεῖ (585e1).

of the pleasure is clearly distinguished from the reality of its objects, while the words 'true' and 'false' are retained in the specified sense, that is, with reference to the reality of the objects.

Additional note. In discussing this type of false pleasures I have said nothing about the metaphor of the internal scribe and painter, or the idea that bad men are most likely to have their pleasures of hope falsified because the gods dislike them. Both have been discussed by others, and their introduction would only obscure what I hope has been a clear as well as brief indication of the main point. (i) The metaphor is not directly relevant to the problem of false pleasures, but to that of false beliefs. As such Runciman found it 'more illuminating and more sophisticated than the unsuccessful analysis proffered in the *Theaetetus*'. But the question of *justifying* error is not raised here: its existence is admitted from the start (37b and e, 38b). See also Friedländer (III, 335 f.), who compares the treatment of false belief in *Theaetetus*, but adds that the possibility of error is a problem outside the scope of the *Philebus*, which need not be explicated there as it was in *Theaetetus* and *Sophist*. (ii) The immorality of the disappointed is in my opinion (not everyone's) a complete red herring. The argument requires only the fact of disappointed hopes, but we have seen more than once how characteristic it is of Plato's Socrates (and surely of the real one) to slip in, half humourously, a moral of his own. McLaughlin (in *PQ* 1969) says that 'for Plato, falsity has definite moral implications'. In a somewhat specialized sense of 'falsity' this is true (*Rep.* 382a), though one cannot help recalling with some uneasiness the justification and extensive use of ψεῦδος as an educative and political device in the *Republic*. (See vol. IV, 457 f., 462.)

2. At 41a Socrates suggests a second way[1] in which pleasures (and pains) may be false. Again we are concerned with feelings of anticipation. The question is put: since pleasures (and pains) belong to the 'Unlimited', i.e. admit of indefinite variation of magnitude, degree or intensity, is there any way of comparing them in these respects? It has been agreed that pleasures and pains are induced by a state of the body, that when its state occasions pain the soul desires the opposite pleasure which it is not experiencing, and the anticipatory pleasure exists simultaneously with the present pain. Now the distance in space at which an object is seen distorts our impression of its magnitude, and this is even more true of the temporal presence or distance of a pleasure

[1] He calls it the reverse of the first, presumably because in the first the pleasure was 'infected' by the belief, whereas in the second a false belief is the result of an illusory feeling of pleasure.

or pain. The amount by which the anticipated pleasures exceed or fall short of the actual (τῶν οὐσῶν, 42b8) must be reckoned unreal.

In this highly artificial argument Plato is not expressing his full thoughts. The distortion due to distance is made to sound inevitable, and there is no mention of counteracting it by an art of measurement. Contrast the hedonistic argument in the *Protagoras* (357a–b), where also the analogy with spatial distance has been invoked: 'Since our salvation in life lies in the correct choice of pleasure and pain—more or less, greater or smaller, nearer or more distant—is it not in the first place a question of measurement, consisting in a consideration of relative excess, defect or equality?' So to live a successful life on hedonistic principles demands the acquisition of a *technē*, that is, of knowledge, which transforms it into something very different from hedonism as vulgarly understood. Later in the present dialogue the importance of measure and *technē* will loom large, and be the means of putting pleasure in its proper subordinate place.

3. The third type of false pleasures mentioned does involve the 'impossibility' that one can suppose one is feeling pleasure when one is not. 'False' here means unreal. The inconsistency is probably due to Plato's wish to account for all current theories about pleasure which he thought wrong. One of these was certainly the belief that the *pleasantest* (ἥδιστος) life was one of calm and tranquillity undisturbed by either pleasures (in the commonly accepted sense) or pains, the state which Democritus called *euthymiē* and Epicurus would soon make famous as *ataraxia*. It may have been more widely known as a bit of proverbial wisdom.[1] Socrates adapts it to his physiological explanation of pleasure by calling it the state in which the body is undergoing neither of the processes of deterioration and renewal, or at least (if as the Heracliteans say such stability is unattainable) not to a perceptible

---

[1] For Democritus see vol. II, 492f. Antisthenes has also been suggested, for whose condemnation of pleasure see vol. III, 307. But one recalls also the reported contentment of the aged Sophocles at his release from the tyranny of sexual desire (Plato, *Rep.* 329c), and especially the sentiments of Amphitryon in Euripides, *H.F.* 503–5:

μικρὰ μὲν τὰ τοῦ βίου,

τοῦτον δ' ὅπως ἥδιστα διαπεράσετε

ἐξ ἡμέρας εἰς νύκτα μὴ λυπούμενοι.

Cf. *Phil.* 43d ὡς ἥδιστον πάντων ἐστὶν ἀλύπως διατελεῖν τὸν βίον ἅπαντα and 44b τὴν δ' ἀπαλλαγὴν τῶν λυπῶν ... ἡδὺ προσαγορεύεσθαι.

degree. People do say and believe that in such a state they are feeling pleasure, but since positive pleasure and absence of pain are two different things, their belief that they are feeling pleasure must be false (44a9–10).[1]

Socrates's constant reference to pleasure as such as if it consisted solely of physical pleasures and their anticipation is an irritating feature of the *Philebus*, scarcely redeemed by the partial justification suggested on behalf of the anti-hedonists at 44e–45a (that the nature of anything appears most plainly in its extreme or intensest forms and bodily pleasures are the commonest and greatest) or by the fact that Socrates will shortly show that he himself does not so limit it.[2] One may guess that the explanation is again historical. Current controversy between hedonists and anti-hedonists did concern indulgence in physical pleasures, and the conception of these as disturbances lay behind such dicta as the 'give me madness rather than pleasure' of Antisthenes.[3]

Are there any true pleasures? Description of pleasure–pain compounds (44b–50e). Considerations like the foregoing have led certain philosophers[4] to deny the existence of pleasures altogether. There are not, they say, three states, painful, neutral and pleasant, but only two, pain and relief from pain. Though this is not quite true, they show a severely puritanical zeal[5] which is commendable in its detestation of the un-

---

[1] A repetition of the argument of *Rep.* 583c–85d.

[2] It is fascinating to compare Ryle's essay on pleasure in *Dilemmas* (pp. 54–67) with some ancient views. For instance he agrees with Aristotle against P. that pleasure is not a process (p. 60). Of pains he too speaks apparently universally as 'the effects of such things as the pressure of a shoe on a toe', and the sense of 'pains' at the top of p. 67 appears to be the same. Yet he would not have denied us the right to speak of the pain of bereavement or parting, and the Greek λύπη had similar scope.

[3] Fr. 108 Caizzi. Notice the connexion between profligate pleasures and madness at 45e.

[4] Described as 'recognized experts in the study of nature' (44b9). Opinions as to their identity have differed widely. (Bignone's argument for Antiphon in *Studi* 221–6 is one that seems to have been forgotten.) Perhaps the *non liquet* of Wilamowitz (*Pl.* II, 272), Jowett (III, 542) and Hackforth (p. 87) must be accepted, but more recently M. Schofield has vigorously revived the case for Speusippus, whom some earlier critics had rejected (*Mus. Helv.* 1971, 2–20 and 181), though Taylor too thought the description 'exactly fits Speusippus' (*Timaeus*, 456). K. Bringmann, on the other hand, in *Hermes* 1972, has argued equally vigorously for Heraclides Ponticus.

[5] Not, I hope, too wide of the mark as a translation of δυσχέρεια φύσεως οὐκ ἀγεννής in this context. I now see that 'Puritan spirit' occurred to Bury too. (But Schofield suggests a reason why δυσχέρεια might be peculiarly appropriate to Speusippus.)

healthy power and 'witchery' of pleasure. They concentrate on bodily pleasures as the most obvious and greatest. Of these in turn the greatest are those preceded by the greatest desires, and are therefore felt predominantly by the ailing in body or mind, in the satisfaction of the morbid desires of the sick or those who lack all self-control. Starting with the relief of an itch by rubbing, Socrates calls all such pleasures 'unseemly', and without specifying its causes vividly describes the mad delight of the fool or profligate, 'dying with pleasure' and calling himself the happiest of men.

Such pleasures are inevitably mixed with pain, and originate in the body alone. A second type of mixed pleasures, Socrates recalls, has been discussed already, namely those where a single pleasure–pain complex is formed from the pain felt in a present bodily depletion combined with the pleasure of the mind (*psyche*) in anticipating future replenishment. Thirdly, there are mixtures of pleasure and pain in which the *psyche* alone is concerned. These are the emotions—anger, fear, longing, grief, love, emulation, malice (47e). They are pains, yet also fraught with immense pleasures, as Homer speaks of wrath as 'sweeter than honey in the human breast'. Even grief and longing, Socrates claims, are mingled with pleasure, and he instances the effect of hearing a tragedy, or, in the case of malice at another's ridiculous misfortunes, a comedy, with no hint of any difference between personal and vicarious experience of tragic or comic situations. He goes on to analyse the psychology of the pleasure–pain combination arising from such causes as a malicious sense of the ridiculous or the *Schadenfreude* which we cannot help feeling when even our friends make fools of themselves. Then realizing that he has got into a digression, he sets aside an examination of the other emotions until they have settled the main question raised by Philebus's attitude to pleasure.

Puzzles. At places in the *Philebus* the threads get bewilderingly entangled, and Plato's application of the same descriptions to ideas which sometimes are, but sometimes are not, the same is certainly no help in unravelling them. Nor can one resist a sneaking doubt whether in every case the attempt is worth while. His language seems almost intentionally mystifying, and moreover what he is really driving at only becomes fully clear in the concluding part of the dialogue. As far as I can see, in the most recent sections there are two outstanding difficulties.

1. What is the relation between various states described as neutral, or as 'intermediate lives'?

(*a*) 32c. Anyone undergoing neither deterioration nor restoration of body feels neither pleasure nor pain. A life of uninterrupted thought would be of this kind, and would be fit for gods.

(*b*) 35b–36b. When one experiences a present pain of depletion but entertains a pleasurable hope of repletion, one may be said to be pained and pleased at the same time.

This is obviously different from the neutral state of feeling neither pleasure nor pain, but like (*c*) is called an intermediate sort of life, one 'in the middle'.[1]

(*c*) 42e. If no perceptible depletion or replenishment is taking place in the body, people feel neither pleasure nor pain, but *think* they are feeling pleasure. This is a case of false pleasure, and is called the intermediate, or middle, life.[2]

Setting aside (*b*), there is nothing in the descriptions to suggest a difference between (*a*) and (*c*). Yet (*a*) is exemplified by a life of pure thought unmixed with pleasure, which, it now appears, was only rejected as the best for man because it is beyond his reach, whereas the false pleasure of (*c*) sounds more like the sensation of a once-hungry man of sound digestion peacefully relaxing after a good meal. (*c*) refers to the common man, (*a*) to a super-philosopher who has succeeded in the philosopher's aim of 'assimilation to God' (*Tht.* 176b).

2. How do the 'puritans' deny the existence of pleasure and at the same time detest its evil influence?

Their introduction at 44b–d is made to sound like a straight follow-on from what has preceded. These 'enemies of Philebus' assert that what he and his like call pleasures are simply escapes from pain. One expects this to refer to case 1(*c*), where neither pain nor positive pleasure is being felt because the body is in a state of equilibrium. Yet they go on to say confusingly that the very attractiveness of pleasure is not

---

[1] βίου εἶδος 35d9, ἐν μέσῳ e7.

[2] ὁ μέσος βίος, 43e8. At 55a the life without pleasure or pain becomes once again the life of pure thought as in (*a*).

pleasure (*sic*, 44c–d) but illusion, and take as their examples not the placidity resulting from this physical balance, nor the quietist ideal of a life without pain, but the most violent and profligate of pleasures, which certainly fit Socrates's initial description of pleasure as accompanying the process of satisfying what is felt as a bodily need. Socrates goes on to describe these, not as states neither pleasurable nor painful but on the contrary as mixtures of pleasure and pain.[1]

The upshot of it all is perhaps no more than this. 'Pleasure' stands for what worldlings like Philebus call pleasure, that is, the physical pleasures only, whose character has been more fully expressed through the mouth of Callicles in the *Gorgias*.[2] Our severe moralists refuse it the title of pleasure and condemn its false allure: its devotees are not enjoying pleasure but endlessly seeking relief from the tyranny of their pathologically inordinate desires. The unmarked transition from 'relief from pain' as a calmly neutral state to 'relief from pain' as indulgence in the most intense and exciting of pleasures seems monstrously illogical today. It is probably to be explained, though hardly excused, by the familiarity of Plato and his original readers with current ethical theories and controversy. He has already said in the *Republic* (584c) that 'most—and those the most intense—of the so-called pleasures that reach the *psyche* through the body, are of this kind, relief from pains'.

True pleasures (50e–53c). Socrates does not conceal his sympathy with these opponents of vulgar hedonism. Their only mistake was to confine the whole concept of pleasure to what is in fact a travesty of it. Pure pleasures, unmixed with the body's pains and ailments, do exist and truly deserve the name of pleasures.[3] They include the enjoyment of

---

[1] One is tempted to throw back at S. the question he himself asked in *Rep.* (583e): 'Is it possible that what is neither of two things should be both?' It is difficult to decide at what point he ceases to speak for the puritans and reverts to his own views, but they are at least credited with the advice to seek the true nature of anything not in a mean but in its extreme forms, e.g. if you want to know what hardness is, take the hardest thing you can find (44d–e).

[2] It is the life of the *charadrios*-bird, continually eating and excreting. (At *Tim.* 72e–73a the coiling of the intestines is explained teleologically as a device to counteract the natural human propensity to overeat. See pp. 313f. below.) In connexion with *Phil.* 46a one may note the transition from scratching an itch to sexual activity. See *Gorg.* 494b–c.

[3] Throughout this passage S. uses 'pure' or 'unmixed' (καθαραί, ἄμεικτοι) and 'true', 'genuine' or 'real' (ἀληθεῖς) as synonyms. He argues briefly for this at 52d–53c. Taylor's 'true to type' comes close to what P. has in mind (*PMW* 427).

beautiful colours, shapes, and sounds, and even, though on a lower level, scents.[1] The shapes must not be those of representational art, but abstract geometrical forms, either plane or solid, and the sounds a series of single pure notes, for there must be no element of association or comparison in a pure pleasure. Such pleasures approach the divine. It is the apotheosis (or would an art critic say the *reductio ad absurdum?*) of the peculiarly Greek preference, exemplified *par excellence* in the Pythagoreans, for 'the intelligible, determinate, measurable',[2] the keen appreciation of mathematical form, symmetry and proportion which pervades classical architecture, sculpture, pottery and literature, and which made such a tremendous appeal to Plato that he prescribed a long and arduous course in mathematics as an essential part of a statesman's training. (Politics, one must admit, was the field in which the Greek instinct for due measure and avoidance of excess was least conspicuous.)[3]

These contemplative pleasures satisfy two conditions: they are untainted by the pain of a previous perceptible lack, and the beauty of their objects is intrinsic. The description of these as beautiful 'not relatively, in comparison with others, but in and by themselves' (51c, d) is interesting, and led Hackforth to suppose them to be 'perfect particulars of the Idea of Beauty, its fully adequate expression to sense' (*PEP* 99). I do not see that his second designation coincides with the first, nor did Plato ever think of visible surfaces and solids, 'produced by the carpenter's lathe, rule and square' (51c), as perfect. At 62b he actually calls these 'human' circles and straight-edges 'false'. The language, it is true, resembles that reserved elsewhere for Forms, and may be another indication that in these later dialogues Plato shows more respect for the sensible world than previously. Hackforth reminds us of what the *Phaedrus* says about visible beauty, but that contains no suggestion that earthly objects can be anything but imperfect copies of

---

[1] '*Most* scents', says S. (51b4). Hackforth suggested that those excluded were only enjoyed by contrast with preceding unpleasant odours, Taylor that 'of course' he was excluding smells of food or the scent of the female perceived by the male (*PEP* 98 n. 1, *PMW* 426 n. 1). At *Rep.* 584b odours are mentioned without qualification as an outstanding example of pure pleasures, and I doubt if πλείστας here has any special significance. Unpleasant smells naturally do not give pleasure.

[2] The words are from E. Fraenkel's inaugural lecture *Rome and Greek Culture* 25.

[3] Aristotle is a true follower of P. when he castigates those who deny that mathematics has anything to say about goodness and beauty. 'The chief forms of beauty are order, symmetry and limit, and these the mathematical sciences demonstrate to an especial degree' (*Metaph.* 1078a31).

the Form of Beauty. In any case the present concession to the sensible world is minimal. We are not to admire a beautiful landscape or girl (who may be beautiful compared to a monkey but not to a goddess, *H.Maj.* 289a–b), but solely mathematical drawings and models, or series of 'single pure notes', whose pitch the Pythagoreans had shown to be essentially a matter of number. And mathematics is the study by which the philosopher 'rises out of this transient world to a grasp of reality' (*Rep.* 525b).

Pure pleasures include also those of learning (51e). The lack of knowledge, which learning fills, or the loss of it through forgetfulness, are not perceived as painful (though pain may be caused incidentally by the practical consequences of forgetfulness, 52b1). These pleasures are only for the few.

Having distinguished pure from impure[1] pleasures, Socrates, reverting to his earlier *diairesis* of all things, assigns the impure, which (following the diagnosis of the puritans) he now also calls vehement, to the Unlimited, subject to the measureless range of more and less, and the pure to the Limited or measurable class. Measurable pleasures are evidently to be regarded as stimulated by measurable objects.[2]

Finally, anything in its purest, least adulterated form is more truly that thing than even a larger quantity of it contaminated with something else. So the pure pleasures felt in the beauty of geometrical shapes and in acquiring knowledge are more truly pleasures than those, however intense, that are mixed with pain.[3] This is illustrated by an analogy: Even a small patch of pure white colour is more truly white than a large surface on which white is mixed with some other colour.[4] Given Plato's presuppositions this seems fair enough, and one cannot read the *Philebus* at all unless one accepts that it is an exposition of his credo rather than a defence of it. A question that one *can* legitimately

[1] Instead of simply 'mixed', at 52c Plato uses for the first time the adjective ἀκάθαρτος with its rhetorical overtones of physical, moral or ritual uncleanliness or *miasma* (*Pho.* 80b).
[2] Though how scents, as well as spheres and cubes, can be measured is not explained. (In fact they cannot. See *Tim.* 66d–e.)
[3] There is no change here from the *Republic*, where any pleasure except the wise man's is οὐδὲ παναληθὴς οὐδὲ καθαρά.
[4] In the case of colour this seems to be true, and I do not see the relevance of Gallop's introduction of parti-coloured objects in *PQ* 1960, 340 n. 6. Crombie's complaint (*EPD* I, 260) is that it is not a valid analogy to pleasure.

ask, because it falls within the framework of Platonism, is: if the pleasure of learning is not preceded by any sense of lack, what has become of the philosopher's *eros*, his passionate longing for truth? Jowett (III, 53) speaks of its absence as marking a different stage of Plato's thought from the *Symposium* and *Phaedrus*, but it is not absent: love of, or longing for, truth (ἐρᾶν τοῦ ἀληθοῦς) is mentioned as a natural faculty of the *psyche* at 58d.

Socrates is now beginning to unmask his batteries, and we can foresee the inevitable outcome of the fight. In introducing the topic of the place of pleasure in the good life, he started from the conception of it held by a hedonist like Philebus, which enabled him to place 'pleasure' in the Unlimited class. Now he has made it clear that these are not the only, nor even the genuine and desirable pleasures (though he will shortly switch back, without warning, to the earlier use of the term!). True pleasures belong to Limit, they observe due measure and are better (καλλίων 53c2) than the others, and chief among them are the pleasures of contemplating geometrical forms and acquiring knowledge. The original admission that pleasure as well as intellectual activity must play a part in the good and happy life takes on a rather dubious air when the pleasures that contribute to it turn out to be the pleasures of intellectual activity.

Pleasure as process and means (53c–55c). This is an unsatisfactory little argument, soon to be refuted by Aristotle. That pleasure is a process (*genesis*, a coming or bringing into being as opposed to a completed state of being) is not argued but laid down as a premise on the authority of certain pundits, 'to whom', says Socrates, 'we should be grateful'.[1] No doubt for Plato it seemed a necessary consequence of its association with processes of bodily restoration and its cessation when restoration was complete. A generative process, he goes on, like the instruments it uses, is never an end in itself, nor good for its own sake: the goodness is in the product at which it aims. So pleasure, being a process, can never be good in itself, and Socrates's informants laugh at

---

[1] Various guesses at their identity have been made (e.g. Speusippus, Hackforth, *PEP* 106), but as S. goes on they come to sound suspiciously like his troublesome relative in *H.Maj.* or Diotima in *Symp.*, i.e. nothing but a vehicle for his (or P.'s) own views. See vol. IV, 176 and 385.

its devotees, who are happy to put up with hunger and thirst in order
to enjoy what they regard as the pleasure of eating and drinking, a life
of continual demolition and rebuilding, rather than the life of the purest
possible thought containing neither pleasure nor pain.

Plato's thought is less confused than his exasperating language.
'Pleasure' has jumped back to mean the Phileban pleasures which we
have now been taught to regard as no true pleasures, while the Socratic
pleasures of the mind, just represented as the purest and best, revert to
being no pleasures at all. But with this sorted out, it does not follow
that because the satisfaction of hunger is a process, occupying time, and
approaching its fulfilment by stages, the pleasure accompanying it is
also a process (presumably progressing inversely, since it ceases at the
end, as if one were bound to enjoy the hors d'oeuvre more than the
sweet). Rather, as Aristotle was quick to point out, pleasure is not any
sort of motion or change 'because no change is complete at any and
every moment . . . whereas the form of pleasure is complete at any time'.
'It is a whole. You could never find a pleasure such that if it lasted
longer its form would be brought to completion.'[1]

Analysis of knowledge (55c–59c). After pleasure, it is only right that
reason and knowledge should be scrutinized, to discover whether some
kinds are truer or purer than others. For this purpose 'knowledge', like
'pleasure', is given its widest application, even including guesswork and
doxa, which in earlier dialogues have been strongly contrasted with
knowledge. No change of doctrine is involved, for considered as
knowledge they are soon shown to be neither true nor pure; but as with
pleasure, for dialectical purposes Plato needed a single general term to
be the subject of division. The whole field of knowledge is first
divided into practical, or technical, and educational or cultural. Of the
former, some branches (e.g. building) make great use of measuring aids
and instruments, whereas music,[2] medicine and others rely on trial and

---

[1] See Arist. *EN* 1174a13–b14, 1152b12–15, 1153a12–15. The allusions to P.'s *Phil.* are
unmistakable.

[2] It may seem surprising to find music in this category, in view of the Pythagorean success in
demonstrating the mathematical basis of music, and P.'s own teaching about *harmonia* involving
measure and its exploitation in *Tim.* But apart from the fact that he was not entirely uncritical of
Pythagorean methods (*Rep.* 531b–c), he is here speaking of execution, not theory; and 56a
shows how much room there still was for a hit-or-miss technique in contemporary musical

error and guesswork. So the arts themselves subdivide into the more and less exact. Most exact of all is arithmetic, with its kindred, measuring and weighing. But must we not divide this art of number in its turn, into practical and philosophical? The man who uses number in his practical work must take as his units physical things like cows or bricks which are never precisely equal (nor of course are they in philosophic eyes purely unitary), whereas the pure (philosophic) mathematician deals solely in abstract units all absolutely equal and identical.[1]

Once again (cf. p. 167 above) we see that the dialectical framework is no unrealistically rigid one. It would be difficult to make a straightforward tabulation of these divisions on the lines of the *Sophist* (pp. 124 f.). Perhaps Plato had come to see the inevitable disadvantages of such a stringent scheme, 'easy to indicate but hard to practise' (16b). Here arithmetic turns up on the practical side of the dichotomy, but one of its subdivisions clearly belongs to the theoretical, and Socrates adds for good measure that there are plenty more such 'twin pairs' among the arts, though united under a single name.[2] Yet regarded not as a *diairesis* but as a single scale of ascending degrees of precision the passage is perfectly in order: music and its kin, building, practical calculation, pure arithmetic or theory of numbers, dialectic.

It only remains to equate the precision or exactness of a science with the degree to which it is 'purely and truly' a form of knowledge, and this is soon done. If after attending a meeting I said 'I know there were at least 100 people there', Plato would say that my knowledge was not only less precise, but less properly to be termed knowledge, than if I knew there were 106 because all present voted and the voting was 60 to 46. It might therefore appear that mathematics or any science carried on in its philosophic mode is the most exact form of knowledge. But this,

---

performance. Cf. *Rep.* 531 a–b. On medicine Plato is in line with some contemporary medical opinion. The author of *On Ancient Medicine* writes (ch. 9, i. 588 L.): 'A certain measure must be the aim, but you will not find any weight, number or other standard, reference to which will make knowledge precise; there is nothing but the body's sensations.'

[1] On this see vol. IV, 523 n. 1, where a reference to the μονάδες ἄνισοι of 56d10 might have been apposite.

[2] This is further evidence, in conjunction with the *Crat.*, that the statement at *Rep.* 596a, about positing a single form for every set of things to which we give a single name, was not intended to be taken *au pied de la lettre*. For this see pp. 25 f. above and vol. IV, 550.

says Socrates, would be to neglect dialectic, the truest and most exact of all. It is the old story. No science can be exact which deals with ever-changing material, and only dialectic has for its objects the absolutely real, unchanging and separate. Only in them, and what is most akin to them,[1] can we find stability, purity and truth: in other words, the transcendent Forms which we have known since the *Phaedo*.[2]

If the conception of 'twin arts', and their relation to dialectic, is at all obscure, one has only to turn back to some pages of the *Republic*, of which this passage is no more than a brief summary. (Plato lived up to the proverb he is just about to quote, that what is worth saying is worth saying twice or thrice.) There in book 7, 523a–32b, we have a full description of the two sorts of arithmetic, geometry, astronomy and harmonics, one directed to practical use—in commerce, war, navigation, agriculture and so on—and the other leading the mind upwards to perfect and changeless entities like numbers, regular figures, the mathematical relations embodied in the notes of a scale, and the ideal motions of which the revolutions of the heavenly bodies are the physical counterpart. There, as here, all are propaedeutic to dialectic, the study whose final aim is nothing less than a grasp of the Form of the Good through pure thought (532a–b).[3]

A short digression on rhetoric sparked off by Protarchus, who like many young men has been impressed by Gorgias's claim that it is the finest of all arts, is the occasion for Plato to repeat his criticism of it elsewhere as relying on probability instead of truth, and to give a brief reminder of the concept of *doxa*. Not only rhetoricians, he says, but even natural philosophers rely on this, for of the changing world of sense there can be only opinion, not knowledge. Even when, in the *Timaeus*, he himself thought it worth while to devote a long and

---

[1] Hackforth thought (*PEP* 122 n. 2) the 'closest kin' were the objects of astronomy. But P. is talking not of astronomy, even in its philosophical form, but of the objects of dialectic. If the insertion is significant at all, it probably refers to souls, or rather minds, described as akin to the Forms in *Pho.* and admitted to the realm of the completely real in *Soph.*

[2] τὰ ἀεὶ κατὰ τὰ αὐτὰ ὡσαύτως ἔχοντα (59c4) is the familiar formula. (Cf. 58a, 61d–e and p. 141 n. 2 above.) With καθαρόν, εἰλικρινές, ἄμεικτον cf. the same words used of αὐτὸ τὸ καλόν at *Symp.* 211e. See also additional note on p. 232.

[3] Though the objects of the other philosophical sciences are also fully real and changeless their practitioners differ from the dialectician in that they do not use pure thought alone, but are still dependent on objects of sense (visible figures, stars and the like) to set them on their way. For the contrast see *Rep.* 510c–11c, and cf. vol. IV, 509f.

detailed disquisition to the natural world and its creatures, he never lost sight either of its subordinate place on the ontological scale or of the goodness which it nevertheless exhibits through being modelled on the Forms by the divine Mind—another point emphasized in the present dialogue.

ADDITIONAL NOTE ON BEING AND BECOMING IN THE 'PHILEBUS'

At 16c9 I have translated τῶν ἀεὶ λεγομένων εἶναι 'all things that are ever said to be' (p. 317), and taken it to refer to the phenomenal world. Plato uses εἶναι loosely of γιγνόμενα when he is not emphasizing the distinction. As I remarked in connexion with *Tim.* 52a (vol. IV, 495), it is a difficult word to get rid of. In *Phil.* we have also the phrases γένεσις εἰς οὐσίαν (26d) for the coming-to-be of a thing in this world from the blending of limit and unlimited, and γεγενημένη οὐσία at 27b; and at 64b he says that without an admixture of reality nothing 'can truly become nor be a thing that has become' (οὐκ ἂν γίγνοιτο οὐδ' ἂν γενόμενον εἴη). Hackforth is right in saying (*PEP* 49 n. 2) that we should not read too much into such expressions. Of the other examples which he quotes, *Tim.* 35a (οὐσίας . . . γιγνομένης) is particularly apposite (and cf. 31b3 γεγονὼς ἔστιν καὶ ἔτ' ἔσται), for in no other dialogue is the contrast between Being and Becoming so uncompromisingly drawn (27d–28a). One cannot agree with those who see the expressions as marking a radical change in Plato's philosophy, putting sensible things on the same ontological level as the Forms. At the same time Bury too was right to remark, on p. 211 of his edition, that this apparent weakening of the barrier between Being and Becoming occurs especially in the later dialogues (note the sources of Hackforth's parallels), where it seems to be a question less of contrasting Being with Becoming than of distinguishing grades of Being. This accords with the shift of interest towards the temporal world which became noticeable in *Pol.* and reaches its climax in *Tim.* I suspect however that the linguistic variations were largely unconscious. But see also Solmsen's judicious note in *Aristotle's System*, 39 n. 79, and p. 233 n. 3 below.

Composition of the mixed life: pleasure loses second prize (59d–66a). The mixed life of knowledge and pleasure is, as they agreed at the beginning, the best, rather than a life of either alone,[1] as Socrates and Philebus had

---

[1] Enjoyment of pleasure with no trace of mental activity, neither remembering past nor looking forward to future pleasure, nor even able to reflect that one is enjoying it (21b–c), sounds like a

earlier been contending. Its ingredients being now prepared, it remains to decide how to blend them, and award second place to one or the other. Each has been found to admit of several varieties, some more genuine and true to type, others adulterated. The question as Socrates sees it is whether all kinds of each should be admitted to the good life, and if not, which. Take knowledge first. The thought of a man knowing the true nature of Justice and the other Forms, but none of the practical arts, makes Protarchus laugh. Life itself demands that the doors be flung open and all forms of knowledge allowed to pour in, the inferior with the pure. Is it the same with pleasures? The answer, given as a reply by Pleasures on the one hand and Thought and Intelligence on the other to the question whether they would like to live together, is that the Pleasures would welcome all knowledge, both in general and of themselves,[1] whereas Thought would recoil from any pleasures which were not pure and true, or at least attendant on health, temperance and all virtue. The vehement and intense pleasures that go with folly and vice simply harry and destroy it with their frenzy.[2]

The 'necessary' pleasures which Plato (somewhat grudgingly, one feels) admits (62e) will be those that go with nourishment and procreation. These cannot be ensured without pleasure, and the life being prescribed for is that of a 'living *body*' (64b7), but he has not concealed his view that if we could rid ourselves of the body and live by thought alone we should be as gods. The emphasis may have changed, but the doctrine is still substantially that of the *Phaedo*.

As a third and final ingredient Socrates adds reality to the blend. To treat it as a component sounds odd, but his next sentence makes the meaning clear: 'Anything in which we are not going to mix reality will not really come into being nor be a thing that has come to be' (64b).[3]

purely logical construction. Yet Aristippus seems to have come near to recommending it as a practical aim. He is said to have defined the goal of life as momentary experience of pleasure with no thought of past or future. Memories and hopes were alike irrelevant, for the past no longer existed and the future might never be. Only the present moment was ours. (Frr. 207 and 208 Mannebach.)   [1] This is probably aimed at Aristippus. See previous note.

[2] A repetition of the teaching of the *Phaedo*. Cf. especially what is said about bodily desires at 64d and 65b–d. Again at *Tim.* 86b–c excessive pleasures and pains are called the greatest diseases of the *psyche*, under whose influence a man cannot see nor hear aright and is incapable of reasoning.

[3] To translate γίγνεσθαι and its inflections without clumsiness is always a problem, for there is no corresponding single English word. Jowett has 'nothing can truly be created or subsist',

This is probably intended as a reminder of Plato's increasing concern, manifested also in the *Politicus*, that his principles must be capable of being put into practice.

The good then is in the mixed life. That is its dwelling or lair (61 a–b, 64c), but we must still ask what is the most valuable element *in* the mixture, and *makes* it universally desirable, and after that, whether it is more akin to pleasure or intelligence in the whole scheme of things (ἐν τῷ παντί, 64c9). But this is easily answered. Everyone knows that the goodness in *any* mixture depends on correct measure or proportion. This at once unites goodness with beauty, for that too is a matter of measure and proportion like any kind of excellence (*aretē*).[1] Reality[2] too is in the mixture, and without further ado is declared to be part of that which makes it good; so the good is a trinity in unity, combining beauty, proportion and reality.[3] All these are present in intelligence and thought, whereas pleasure is a cheat (in love, reputed the greatest pleasure, even perjury is forgiven) and unmeasured in its intensity, and the greatest pleasures are either ugly or ridiculous, banished for shame from daylight to the hours of darkness. Clearly pleasure cannot be given second place as more responsible than intelligence for the goodness in the good life.

In this brief argument, if such it can be called, the reader is rushed breathlessly along to the ultimate Q.E.D. of the whole dialogue. Why does it follow that because reality is in the mixture it should be part of that which makes it good? What about those pleasures which are no less in it? Protarchus's by now enthusiastic cooperation makes it clear that in deciding the issue between pleasure and thought only the 'false',

a better rendering than Hackforth's. P. has in mind of course his standard contrast between γιγνόμενα and ὄντα, impermanent physical things and the eternal Forms. The former are not μὴ ὄντα, they have a share in reality through participating in the Forms. Without any reality at all, a man (say) would never be born, nor grow to be that transitory thing (γενόμενον) which we call a man. Phrases like γενόμενον εἴη, γένεσις εἰς οὐσίαν (26d) and γεγενημένη οὐσία (27b) certainly do not indicate that P. is now promoting γιγνόμενα to the full status of ὄντα. The difference between them is emphasized throughout the dialogue. (See additional note on p. 232.)

[1] This, like so much else, is repeated in *Tim.* (87c): πᾶν δὴ τὸ ἀγαθὸν καλὸν τὸ δὲ καλὸν οὐκ ἄμετρον.

[2] ἀλήθεια again, usually translated here (64e9) as 'truth'. I have thought it better to make it uniform with the occurrence at b2 to which P. is referring, where the meaning 'reality' is uppermost.

[3] Dr G. E. R. Lloyd has suggested to me that the impossibility of looking for the good in a single form, though doubtless not to be directly related to the single Form of the Good in *Rep.*, is nevertheless a further indication of the tendency towards increased flexibility in P.'s dialectical method.

most vehement pleasures are being taken into account. What has happened to those 'consistent with health and virtue'? Well may Protarchus feel a residual twinge of doubt when Socrates has pronounced the inevitable verdict. 'Well', he says cautiously, 'so it appears at least from what has now been said' (66a9).

The five possessions (66a–c). We have been told so far that the best life contains three elements: intelligence (including knowledge of any kind), pleasure (strictly limited in kind) and reality. To conclude, Socrates divides what he calls 'possessions'[1] into five, on a scale of decreasing value. To determine the difference between the first two has been a standing puzzle with scholars for many years, intensified by an unsolved textual crux.[2] There is also the old difficulty of the article-plus-adjective construction. Are 'the symmetrical', 'the beautiful' etc., here things of a certain character, the character they have, or Platonic Forms? The relevant passage may be approximately rendered thus (66a5–b3):

Pleasure is not the first nor yet the second possession. The first is found somewhere in the region of measure, what is within measure (τὸ μέτριον) and appropriate,[3] and everything that must be thought to be of this sort . . .[4] The second is in the region of the duly proportioned (or symmetrical, σύμμετρον) and beautiful, what is complete in itself and adequate to its purpose[5] and everything of that kind.

It is hard to believe, with some scholars, that no distinction of value or pre-eminence between these two is intended. In determining it we must, I think, limit the fivefold assessment to good things within human life, in view of the word 'possession' as well as the tenor of the dialogue as a whole. This excludes the Forms themselves, though Plato will have in mind that goodness for man, inseparable as it is from due measure and

---

[1] κτῆμα 66a5. Cf. 19c τί τῶν ἀνθρωπίνων κτημάτων ἄριστον.

[2] Bury discusses the problem fully in his App. B, 164–78, with copious reference to previous views. One may add Rodier, *Études* 134–7, Jowett III, 544, Friedländer, *Pl.* III, 350 with notes, Hackforth, *PEP* 137f.

[3] τὸ καίριον, a reminder that we are dealing with human life. Cf. p. 171 above.

[4] There follow the doubtful words, which *may* mean, if φύσιν is retained, that measure etc. 'have taken on the nature of the eternal'. The passage is discussed by Gosling, *Phil.* 137f.

[5] τέλεον καὶ ἱκανόν. Cf. 20d, and for the distinction Bury 177.

moderation, mirrors that of the cosmos ordered by the divine Mind.[1]
In spite of Rodier's criticism, there may be something in Zeller's suggestion that the first 'possession' represents participation in the Form
Metron and the second its effects, the elements of moderation and the
like in human life.[2] But nothing is certain save that the two together
exalt the primacy of measure, moderation, the right mean, on which
Plato expatiated at greater length in the *Politicus* (pp. 169–72 above).

Third in the list come intelligence and theoretical knowledge,[3] on the
human level one must assume (p. 238 below); fourth, practical knowledge and true beliefs; fifth, the pure pleasures enjoyed by the mind
alone, though some are occasioned by the senses.[4] Enigmatic to the last,
Socrates ends with a tag from an Orphic theogony: 'But in the sixth
generation cease the order of your song.' Does this mean 'Do not go
beyond the fifth' or 'End with the sixth'? The former has been maintained,[5] nor does Plato say what the sixth would be. Nevertheless the
Orphic poet did include the sixth,[6] and the reference is probably to the
necessary and temperate pleasures which have been admitted to the
good life on sufferance.

There follows the *coup de grâce* and the dialogue ends. Victory in the
contest for the title 'the good' goes to the mixed life of reason and
pleasure together, but 'reason is a thousand times more closely akin to
it than pleasure'.

[1] Cf. *Rep.* 500c. The words ἐν τῷ παντί at 64c9, and ἐν ἀνθρώποις τε καὶ θεοῖς at 65b2, if
significant at all, will not imply more than this.
[2] Zeller ΙΙ.1. 874f., Rodier, *Études* 134–7. There are difficulties, as Z.'s long note shows,
especially in agreeing with him that though no. 1 is not the Form itself, only in no. 2 do we get
the 'projection into reality' ('Einbildung in die Wirklichkeit') of the Form. It is hard to see just
what P. would have had in mind as a third stage between a Form and its instantiation in the
world, unless (which I do not advocate) it is something like the 'tallness in us' of the *Pho.*,
interpreted in a somewhat Aristotelian way. (Cf. vol. ιv, 354–6 and Archer-Hind on *Tim.* 50c.)
[3] νοῦς καὶ φρόνησις, φρόνησις being, as often, interchangeable with ἐπιστήμη (vol. ιv, 265).
[4] These correspond to the pure pleasures earlier described. There is some doubt about the
text, on which see Rodier, *Études* 132. On the order of merit Crombie writes with his usual
illuminating good sense, though confessing himself puzzled as everyone must (*EPD* ι, 264f.).
I have felt some doubt over his point that intelligence would be placed third because responsible
for the first two. One would expect an αἴτιον to be *prior* to its effects. However, 22d may justify
the supposition that P. had some such notion in his mind.
[5] E.g. by Jowett ΙΙΙ, 535: 'The fifth [place is assigned] to pure pleasures; and here the Muse
says "Enough"', and further on p. 545.
[6] See Guthrie, *OGR* 82 with n. 4.

The philosophy of the Philebus

1. *The Forms and the sensible world.* Plato's two-world scheme, of Being and Becoming, is basically unchanged. This is indisputable, though the phraseology of Being may have infiltrated into the purlieus of Becoming. (See additional note on p. 232 above.) At 61e1 we have the familiar antithesis between 'the things that come to be and perish' and those that 'neither come to be nor perish', which are the subjects of different kinds of knowledge. We have also met other unmistakable references to the unchanging, absolute realities. Philosophical dialectic is still concerned with these (57e–58a), and the pleasures of knowledge remain highly exclusive, 'by no means for the *polloi*, but for the very few' (52b). At 62a Justice serves as a typical example, though at 15a we have besides the moral and aesthetic Forms those of natural species.

The eternal realities, however, are not the subject of the dialogue. Plato may be repetitious, but not so much so as simply to enlarge once again on the metaphysical theories of the *Phaedo, Republic, Symposium* and *Phaedrus*. They can now be taken for granted. Like the *Politicus*, the *Philebus* is concerned with life in the body, and how to live it as well and happily as possible. 'The good' in several places may recall what we have learned of the Form of the Good, but I think this would be misleading, even in the phrase 'the good itself', as at 61a and 67a. 'The good' is the goodness in human life, which, life being a mixture, consists not in the actual ingredients but in the correctness of the formula to which it is made up. If the proportions are right, the mixture will be good.[1]

2. *Theology: microcosm and macrocosm.*[2] As *diairesis* has been said to overshadow the nominal theme of the *Sophist*, so theology, the concept

---

[1] It has been objected that a mixture compounded strictly to rule could as well be a poison as a healthy drink. Plato could with consistency reply that it did indeed owe to its proportions the achievement of its *telos* and so was a good poison. Whether or not it ought to be administered to an insect-pest or a person, or neither, is a question which does not concern the dispenser. In the same way a captain does his job well if he brings his ship and passengers safe to land. For a particular passenger drowning might have been better, if a worse fate awaits him at his destination, but that is not the captain's business. (See *Gorg.* 511e–12a.) This is not inconsistent with disapproval of Gorgias's contention that a teacher of rhetoric is not responsible for the use of it made by his pupils (*ib.* 457b). Arts concerned with material production, health or safety are subordinate and morally neutral. It is in their use by a higher art that good or evil enters in; and rhetoric is an art (or pseudo-art) with a moral influence as strong as that of the statesmanship which it mimics.

[2] Something has been said about this already, on pp. 203, 213–16.

of a divine Mind penetrating the universe and all things in it, is basic to the *Philebus*. Only on that basis can Plato's theory of the place of pleasure in the good life be justified. [Mind is the fourth kind of being, the cause of the combination of Limit with the Unlimited which ensures that the cosmos shall exhibit the supreme merits of order, right measure and proportion (30a–c). It is of course an extra-cosmic God, yet there is no real problem in reconciling this with the statement that the cause is something within the mixture (22d1, 64c5), for the cosmos itself is living and intelligent and so, within it, is man, possessing 'fragments' (as the Pythagoreans said) of the divine Mind, timebound and restricted by association with the body.] (As the *Timaeus* teaches, the Creator is not omnipotent, and can only impart his own nature to his creation as far as the irrational force of Necessity, or brute matter, allows.) Considered as possessions of mankind, mind and thought may be given only third place because the first two are concerned with the divine gift of due measure, proportion, the right mean which he shares with the cosmos. [But universally speaking primacy belongs to Mind or Reason in its purity, 'King of heaven and earth', giver of beauty, symmetry and truth which are the marks of goodness.] For full understanding, the *Philebus* must be read in the light of its sister-dialogue the *Timaeus*, which Plato may well have written first. The same applies to the *Politicus*, where the nature and importance of *metron* and the *metrion* are more fully and clearly explained, though without the theological overtones. (See pp. 169–73 above.)

Conclusion. To be subjective in my turn, if Plato ever wrote a 'weary' dialogue (p. 164) it is not the *Politicus* but the *Philebus*. This is not the fault of its main subject, the central importance of which he rightly emphasizes in the *Laws*. 'Human nature involves above all things pleasures, pains and desires. Every mortal animal is so to speak hung up on them and kept dangling like a puppet.' 'When men consider legislation, practically the whole enquiry concerns pleasures and pains, in both communities and private individuals.'[1] What tries the reader is a certain untidiness, and a lack of that precision which Plato himself singles out as the mark of real knowledge. Outstanding is his unqualified

---

[1] *Laws* 732e and 636d. For the language of 732e cf. what is said of the πάθη at 644e.

use of the word 'pleasure' to mean sometimes all that he most disliked in the popular notion of pleasure, and sometimes what Philebus and his like do not admit to be pleasures at all. He is at pains to show that the only pleasure worth having is the pleasure attendant on mental exercise —neither, that is, what others call pleasure nor he himself in other parts of the dialogue, both before and after his demonstration that they are falsely called pleasures. He admits 'necessary' pleasures to the good life, which can only be the pleasures of moderate eating and drinking and of sex within marriage, on which the preservation of individual and race depends. (Cf. 35 e.) But one feels he would have been happier if these ends could have been achieved without pleasure. Eating, drinking and sex, after all, provide the measureless, the 'greatest and most intense' pleasures which cannot be admitted at all.[1] More generally, much of the dialogue repeats obscurely what has been more fully and clearly explained elsewhere.

The whole question at issue is really settled from the beginning. It is a statement of belief rather than a genuine argument. Socrates makes a series of dogmatic pronouncements which go unchallenged and which, once granted, make the victory of philosophy over pleasure a foregone conclusion. For a defender of hedonism it is absurd that Protarchus should agree to them as he does (with the temporary exception of the existence of false pleasures). This, I surmise, is why the hard-line hedonist Philebus had to be replaced by a pliable youth who only thought he was a hedonist. In the *Protagoras* Socrates himself demonstrated how the art of measurement was reconcilable with hedonism, indeed essential to it; but not here. The whole argument is based on premises both intellectual and moral which a Callicles or Philebus would deny. Perhaps this is a reason for its obscurity: it is not genuine argument but a façade for dogma.

Another reason may be that it is a compromise. Plato retains his conviction that the philosophic life is the best, but knows that very few can practise it at all, and those not all the time. He is in the ambiguous position so strikingly brought out by Aristotle, who shared it. Perfect human happiness and self-sufficiency, he says in the *Ethics* (bk 10 ch. 7),

---

[1] Cf. *Laws* 782e–83a: The appetites for food, drink and sex are all distempers (νοσήματα), to be held in check by fear, laws and sound reasoning, together with the moderating influence of the arts.

lie in intellectual activity, but to spend a whole life in it would be superhuman. A man will live it not *qua* human being but in so far as he has in him something divine. In the very next sentence we are exhorted not, as the poets recommend, 'being mortal to think mortal thoughts', but to aim at immortality as far as we can and live according to the best in us, which would even seem to *be* each one of us. The dilemma is patent. In the same breath Aristotle can speak of the life of reason as too high for men and exhort us to pursue it as really and truly our own. Man's position in the world is unique, because like no other creature he houses reason, which is divine, in a mortal body. All Plato's inclinations were towards cultivation of the divine part, and when, as in these later dialogues, he determined to allow full weight to the necessities of our incarnate state, the resulting tension led to an unevenness, and even downright inconsistency, disturbing to a reader but rendered more comprehensible by Aristotle's prosaic assessment of their common position.[1]

[1] P.'s own clearest statement of it is at *Tim.* 90b–d. Aristotle's ἐφ' ὅσον ἐνδέχεται ἀθανατίζειν is practically a quotation of 90c2–3, καθ' ὅσον δ' αὖ μετασχεῖν ἀνθρωπίνῃ φύσει ἀθανασίας ἐνδέχεται. In *Phaedo* the word 'man' (ἄνθρωπος) is reserved for the compound of body and soul (95c6, 76c11), but in *Alc. I* we have ἡ ψυχή ἐστιν ἄνθρωπος (130c).

VI

TIMAEUS AND CRITIAS

Introduction

It must be admitted that few books created so much intellectual evil as
the *Timaeus*; the only one which created a greater perversion of thought
in the Christian world was the revelation of St. John the Divine.

G. Sarton

Our illustrator of the atomic model [in a school text-book of physics]
would have done well to make a careful study of Plato before producing
his particular illustration.

W. Heisenberg

The influence of the *Timaeus* down to the Renaissance was enormous,
and interest in it has continued unabated, if from different motives, to
the present day. One of its most perceptive commentators, Th. H.
Martin, called it 'the most quoted and least understood' of Plato's
dialogues. Plato's younger contemporaries were already disputing its
meaning. Aristotle cites it more often than any other dialogue, and
thought it worth while to write an epitome. Whatever he may have
known of any 'unwritten doctrines', he took the *Timaeus* as a serious
exposition of Plato's own philosophy and science. The first commentary
was written by Crantor, a pupil of Xenocrates, about the end of the
fourth century B.C., and the Hellenistic and Roman periods saw contributions by Stoics like Posidonius and Panaetius, Cicero (who translated
it), Plutarch (in his *On the Generation of Soul in the Timaeus* and
Platonic Questions) and others. The Christian world received a portion
of it in the fifth century in the Latin version of Chalcidius (to 53c),[1]
through which alone it was known until the twelfth. Klibansky's comment might surprise some critics of Plato, that in an age marked by an
attitude of contempt for the world, it was he who kept alive 'the
Hellenic appreciation of the rational beauty of the universe'. For that
reason the *Timaeus* deeply influenced the philosophers of the Renais-

---

[1] The date of Chalcidius is controversial, but Waszink, the editor of his *Timaeus*, thinks he
wrote it a little after 400.

sance. Later, as scientists increasingly followed Bacon's advice to detach physical science from final causes, talk of which, 'like barnacles on a boat, holds up the voyage of science', its study was left increasingly in the hands of historians and scholars. Most recently however, in spite of its lack of experimental method, its geometrical theory of the world has come into its own again as evidence of a brilliant natural insight into the structure of matter. Whitehead had already written in 1929 that 'Newton would have been surprised at the modern theory and the dissolution of the quanta into vibrations: Plato would have expected it', when authorities like Jeans and Singer were still describing the influence of the *Timaeus* as a scientific disaster and a degradation of knowledge. Now we have Popper's claim that the geometrical theory of the world's structure, which makes its first appearance in Plato, has been the basis of modern cosmology from Copernicus and Kepler through Newton to Einstein, and Heisenberg's opinion that the tendency of modern physics brings it closer to the *Timaeus* than to Democritus. Yet Democritus had for long been hailed as the true precursor of scientific atomism, partly perhaps because, as Bacon said in his praise, he assigned the causes of things to material necessity *sine intermixtione causarum finalium*.[1]

However, our present task is not to consider later developments, but (to quote Rivaud) 'de nous mettre en présence du texte même et de tenter de l'entendre'. So after a few remarks on date and personalities, we shall start by considering the general purpose and framework of the *Timaeus–Critias* ensemble.

[1] Rivaud has a brief summary of the influence of *Tim.* on pp. 3–5 of his introduction. For the Middle Ages see Klibansky, *Continuity* 28f. (quoted by H. D. P. Lee, *Tim.* 23f.). Aristotle's epitome is mentioned by Simpl. *Cael.* 379.16 Heib., Crantor's exegesis by Procl. *Tim.* 1.76.1 Diehl. For Cicero's translation, of which fragments are preserved, see F. Pini, *M.T. Ciceronis Timaeus* (1965) and R. Giornini, 'Osservaz. sul testo del *Timeo* ciceroniano' in *Riv. di Cult. Class. e Med.* 1969. Bacon's *De augm. sc.* bk 3 ch. 4 (Spedding, Ellis ed., 1, 568–70), quoted here in translation, is a powerful indictment of the introduction of final causes into physics. For reff. to modern scientific opinion see Friedländer, *Pl.* 1, 264ff. with notes. Add Sarton in *Isis*, 1952, 57; Heisenberg, *Physicist's Conception of Nature* 60f. and 'P.'s Vorstellungen von den kleinsten Bausteinen der Materie und die Elementarteilchen der modernen Physik' in *Im Umkreis der Kunst* (Festschr. Pretorius); Singer, *Short Hist. of Sc. Ideas* (1959), 40; Popper, *Conj. and Ref.* 88 n. 45, 89–93. But Democritus had a stout defender in Schrödinger. See his little book *Nature and the Greeks* (1954), esp. p. 82: 'Democritus was intensely interested in geometry, not as a mere enthusiast like Plato; he was a geometer of distinction.'

Introduction

Date. It should perhaps be said first that Morton and Winspear claim to have established, by stylometric tests with a computer, that the first 300 sentences of the *Timaeus* are by Speusippus, not Plato.[1]

Until 1953, the *Timaeus* and its sequel the *Critias* were universally believed to be, with the possible exception of the *Philebus*, the latest of Plato's works except the *Laws*. In that year G. E. L. Owen published his now famous article designed to show that on the contrary it belonged to the middle group of *Republic* and *Phaedo* and preceded the 'critical' group. This has aroused a great deal of comment, mostly but by no means entirely adverse, and there is no point in adding to it,[2] but the importance of Owen's thesis must not be underestimated. It carries with it a radical change in previously accepted ideas of Plato's development and a re-assessment of the philosophical basis of the critical dialogues (including the *Philebus*), which in Owen's judgement 'gain in philosophical power and interest when they are read as following and not paving the way for the *Timaeus*' (*SPM* 313). So read, they can be interpreted as teaching a more sophisticated metaphysic based on renunciation of the doctrine of paradigmatic Forms and the opposition between Being and Becoming. Since I have tried to show at several points that these doctrines still make their appearance in *Theaetetus*, *Sophist*, *Politicus* and *Philebus*, I naturally find this view difficult to accept, but Owen's arguments must be read for themselves before anyone decides which course will lead him to the true mind of Plato.

[1] *Gk to the C.* 13. They do not say to what point in the dialogue this brings us, and I confess to not having counted up the sentences to find out.

[2] Owen, 'The Place of the *Tim.* in Plato's Dialogues', *CQ* 1953, repr. in *SPM* 313–38. (Before Owen wrote, the arguments in favour of the late date were summarized in Rivaud's edition, pp. 21–3.) The first notes of misgiving were sounded by Vlastos in 1954 (see now *SPM* 245 n. 3 and 247 n. 4) and by Field in a communication to the Classical Association (*Proceedings*, 1954, 52). Cherniss published a long rebuttal in *AJP* 1957, supported by another in *JHS* 1957 (1). See also Skemp, *P.'s Statesman* 237–9, A. and P. in *Mid-Fourth Cent.* 201 f., *TMPLD* 68, de Vogel, *Philosophia* Pt I (1964), 190 n. 2 and 237 f. and Cherry in *Apeiron* 1967.

Among brief or occasional criticisms that I have seen are D. Tarrant, *CQ* 1955, 224; Runciman, *SPM* 152 (1960); Reiche, *Empedocles' Mixture* 87 f.; Herter, *Rh. Mus.* 1957, 347 n. 66 and *Palingenesia* IV (1969), 117 n. 35; M. A. Stewart, *PQ* 1971, 172.

In favour of Owen's re-dating have been Ryle, *P.'s P.*, ch. 7 and elsewhere, and *Ency. Phil.* VI, 320; T. M. Robinson in *AJP* 1967, p. 57 n. 1 and cf. Anton and Kustas, *Essays*, where on p. 353 n. 31 he mentions (with full reff.) John Gould, D. W. Hamlyn, D. A. Rees and C. Strang as also accepting it.

On the computer-based stylometric results of Cox and Brandwood (*J. of R. Statist. Soc.* 1959, 195–200) see Robinson (last ref.) and for a different estimate Stewart, *l.c.*

About the relation of the *Timaeus* to the *Philebus* one cannot be positive. I have been strongly tempted to put it earlier on the ground that doctrines elaborated at length in the *Timaeus* are briefly assumed in the *Philebus*, giving Ryle very good reason for saying that it 'echoes' the *Timaeus*. But for one who still inclines to the traditional date of the latter, there seems no possible reason why Plato should have broken off his grand trilogy (p. 246 below) to write a dialogue like the *Philebus*. That he should have abandoned it for the *Laws*, as a better treatment of the same subject, namely the best possible human society, is understandable, but for the *Philebus*—no.

Characters. Besides Socrates these are Timaeus, Critias and Hermocrates. The main part of the work is a continuous lecture by Timaeus, of whom we have no authentic information other than what is given in the dialogue, namely that he is a prominent citizen of Locri who combines statesmanship with philosophy and is especially well versed in astronomy and cosmology (20a, 27a). He may or may not be a historical figure (cf. Martin, *Timée* I, 50), but at any rate his Italian origin implies that his philosophical affiliations are with the West. Hints of the age of Critias make it appear that he is not the oligarch and second cousin of Plato, but his grandfather. Hermocrates is identifiable with the Syracusan general, highly praised by Thucydides, who foresaw and then defeated the Athenian aggression against Sicily. He was the father-in-law of Dionysius II.[1]

Framework and purpose

Socrates opens the *Timaeus* by repeating the main heads of a talk which he had given the day before to the three now present and one other,[2] on the best form of political association. This recalls many of the political and social provisions of the *Republic*. At his request, the others are now to bring the planned city to life and show it in action, and especially in the conduct of war and international relations generally. As experienced

---

[1] For further details of all these see Cornford, *PC* 1–3. Popper cites 'Plato's eulogy of an enemy of Athens like Hermocrates' as part-evidence of his hostility to contemporary Athens (*OS* I, 311). Similarly Rivaud, *Tim.* 15. On Critias I have given what is now the general opinion, instanced by (besides Cornford) Taylor, *Comm.* 24; but Vidal-Naquet thought it unnecessary to insist on such chronological niceties in Plato (*REG* 1964, 420 n. 3).

[2] There is no hint of the identity of this unnamed person, said to have been taken ill, nor of P.'s motive in mentioning him.

politicians they are better fitted for this than a theorizer like himself. They then unfold their plan. Critias will tell the story, preserved in Egyptian tradition, of the defeat of the aggressive power of Atlantis by Athenians of 9,000 years ago, whose institutions, by a providential coincidence, closely resembled those of the state imagined by Socrates. He will take this Athens of a bygone heroic age to have actually been that ideal state, thus illustrating its successful conduct of a war, and the others will follow him in a programme designed to satisfy Socrates to the full.

The self-criticism of Socrates as an impractical theorist is striking. For the Socrates of the *Republic* it was not important that his model state should ever be realized in practice; it remained as an ideal (*paradeigma*) to guide men's footsteps towards justice and the right (472 d– 73 b). But now he wants to know how it would fare in the rough and tumble of clashes with other states. This, surely, is the purpose of the opening reminder of some of the *Republic*'s measures. Plato is telling us explicitly that in the years since he wrote it his interests have veered from an idealistic view of society towards practical policy, as the *Politicus* has already shown.[1] Another lesson of the introduction is that Plato's talent for casting his ideas in dramatic form, the creative imagination that puts him in the front rank of poets and story-tellers as well as philosophers, is undiminished. The portrayal of Atlantis, when it comes, is so vivid that many scholars and geographers have supposed that it really existed. Most of it comes, however, not in the *Timaeus* but in the *Critias*. The opening of the *Timaeus* is an introduction not to that

[1] For the *Pol.* see pp. 171, 184, 187 above. Dramatically, P. differentiates S.'s exposition from the *Rep.* itself by making the narration take place on the day before the Panathenaea instead of the day after the Bendideia (κατέβην χθὲς . . .). The additional point raised by Rivaud (p. 3), Ryle (*P.'s P.* 230) and others, that the characters of *Tim.* are not those of *Rep.*, is strictly speaking irrelevant. However unrealistically, the *Rep.* is in form a continuous narrative by S. of his conversation in the house of Cephalus on the previous evening, and nothing is said of the audience to whom he is relating it. Of course, against the strange view of *Tim.* as a 'continuation' of *Rep.*, Raeder's objection on grounds of form is sound enough (*P.'s Ph. Entw.* 195), and to regard the characters in *Tim.* as the silent auditors of *Rep.*, though logically possible, is implausible. The passage has led to some curious theories, e.g. Rohde's invention (*Psyche* 477 f.) of an earlier, incomplete edition of *Rep.*, because only some of its tenets are mentioned and Timaeus agrees that S. has recalled in summary (ἐν κεφαλαίοις) the whole of 'yesterday's' speech— surely a minimal dramatic licence. The fact remains that he does list unmistakable excerpts from *Rep.*, and the motive for this I have suggested in the text. Only a few reminders were necessary.

dialogue but to the *Critias*, or rather to the whole trilogy[1] which Plato planned but for some reason abandoned after writing a small part of the *Critias*, so that we can never see it in its true proportions.

It is essential to see the *Timaeus* in this perspective. Plato has not abandoned human affairs for cosmogony and natural science. His purpose is to place man in his setting in the world and draw out the implications for human life and aims. The theme to be elaborated in detail is that taken for granted in the *Philebus* and already hinted at in the *Republic*, namely the close relations between microcosm and macrocosm. 'Familiarity with the divine and orderly makes the philosopher divine and orderly so far as a man may be ' (*Rep.* 500c). In the *Timaeus* this becomes: 'By learning to know and acquiring the power to compute them rightly according to nature, we may reproduce the steadfast revolutions of the universe and reduce to settled order the wandering motions in ourselves.' For Plato this is now the essential prelude to his new vision of the good society in action. Similarly in the *Laws* (bk 10), which appears to have replaced the rest of the trilogy, a conviction that the universe is rationally and divinely governed is the prerequisite for a moral human life. In the *Phaedo* Socrates abandoned natural philosophy altogether because its exponents asked only *how*, not *why*, things happened. This was true of the real Socrates, and at that time Plato followed his lead.[2] In the *Philebus* he says (58c–59c) that most arts are concerned only with beliefs (*doxai*). Even the students of nature confine themselves to this world, how it came to be and what goes on in it; but all this has nothing to do with what is real and unchanging, nor can its study by itself lead to knowledge of the truth. This contrast between changeless reality and changing phenomena, knowledge and belief, is the starting-point of Timaeus's discourse. Now however Plato has decided that it will not do simply to point out the physicists' error and

---

[1] That a third dialogue *Hermocrates* was planned is clear not only from the promise of Critias at 27d that all will take part, dividing the work between them, but from *Cr.* 108a: 'when it is H.'s turn to speak'. What it was to contain we are not told, but Cornford's guess is plausible (*PC* 7f.). Critias's story ends with one of those natural catastrophes mentioned in *Pol.* (270c–d) and here at 22c–d—in this case earthquake and flood—after which civilization has to start again from the rude beginnings of a few illiterate survivors in the hills. Just such an extinction and rebirth of culture are described in *Laws* 3 and 4, which may reasonably be supposed to replace what H. would have said when he took up the tale from Critias.

[2] For S.'s own attitude to natural philosophy see vol. III, 421–5, and for his belief that the world is divinely governed, *ib.* 442.

leave the subject. He must challenge them on their own ground by constructing his own *De rerum natura*, which on the level of physical causes will incorporate much earlier work but will relegate them to their proper place as secondary, necessary indeed but only auxiliary to the creation of a rational order modelled on the changeless Forms. Only in the light of the final cause can the *physis* of things be really understood. Like Anaxagoras, Plato starts from the axiom 'All things were in confusion, then Mind came and set them in order', but unlike Anaxagoras the Ionian he will continue to maintain it as the premise on which all conclusions about the physical universe must depend. It has been said that 'The basic question of philosophy is the question concerning the relationship between thought and being, between spirit and nature— which came first.'[1] The *Timaeus* is Plato's full and definitive answer to that question, and this must never be forgotten when we turn to the self-confessed obscurities and difficulties of his detailed account of the physical world.

One further point. In trying to interpret his thought, I shall not feel bound to follow the order of Timaeus's exposition. Plato has retained one feature of his conversational manner: even in a continuous account he still aims at the effect of an unrehearsed talk. Themes intertwine, one being pursued until Timaeus remembers something that he ought to have said earlier and goes back on his tracks to pick it up. (See Appendix, pp. 391f.)

Atlantis (*Tim.* 20d–25d, *Cr.* 108e–21c)

Few commentators spend much time on the marvellous story of Atlantis, and a general historian must certainly resist the temptation to do so. A bibliography of 1926 listed 1,700 items on the subject, and it would need little research to add another 50 or more.[2] There are those who believe, with Martin (p. 332), that 'elle appartient à un *autre monde*, qui n'est pas dans la domaine de l'espace, mais dans celui de la pensée', and those who fight hard to give it a terrestrial locality. It

---

[1] I. M. Bochenski, *Dogmatic Principles of Soviet Phil.* I, 13.

[2] No attempt at a bibliography will be made here. Martin (*Études* I, 257–332) deals comprehensively with the literature up to 1840. See also Rivaud's ed., 27–32. James Bramwell's *Lost Atlantis* (1937) gives a highly readable accounts of facts, theories and fancies from Crantor to the present century.

has been sought from the Arctic Ocean to North Africa, from America to Ceylon. Interest in its historical existence has now been given fresh stimulus by the discovery of Minoan remains on the volcanic islands of Santorin (Thera and Therasia), destroyed about 1500 B.C. by an enormous eruption. According to Plato Atlantis was swallowed by earthquake and floods in a single day and night, and the Greek seismologist Galanopoulos believes that the metropolis of Atlantis was on Thera itself. Others, notably J. V. Luce, identify it with Minoan Crete, which certainly suffered severely from the effects of the eruption.[1] It is certainly true that if the Atlantis story reflects a historical disaster, Thera provides the only known example on a sufficient scale to be taken seriously.

It must be remembered that Plato is our *only* authority for the story,[2] which he ascribes to Solon, who learned it from Egyptian priests and told it to his contemporary Critias, who at the age of ninety repeated it in the presence of his grandson the narrator in *Timaeus* and *Critias*, who was then about ten (21 a). Now Plato tells us two things: (1) Atlantis was a huge island, or rather continent, lying in the Atlantic Ocean just outside[3] the Straits of Gibraltar.[4] That a submerged land in such a situation is a geographical impossibility has been made a reason for finding it elsewhere, but is of course irrelevant if one regards the whole story as the product of Plato's imagination. (2) Its destruction took place 9,000 years before Solon heard of it (*Tim.* 23e, *Cr.* 108e). On the Santorin theory it should be about 900. Galanopoulos has attributed this to a mistranslation by Solon of the not very similar Egyptian symbols for 1,000 and 100;[5] but the mistake would have been the

---

[1] The theory that Atlantis is a memory of the Minoan civilization goes back to K. T. Frost in *JHS* 1913. See now A. G. Galanopoulos and E. Bacon, *Atlantis, the Truth behind the Legend* (1969), and J. V. Luce, *The End of Atlantis: New Light on an Old Legend* (1969).

[2] It is true, and I have not seen it mentioned, that Plutarch in his life of Solon (ch. 31) says that he left the writing of the story unfinished 'not, as Plato says (21 c), through other preoccupations but rather through old age'. This might suggest a second source, but in context sounds more like a personal surmise on the part of Plutarch's own authority.

[3] 'Before the entrance' (πρὸ τοῦ στόματος 24a) I take to mean that it was at no great distance, but the volcanic Azores have a better geographical claim to be the remains of Atlantis than any spot within the Mediterranean. They were first proposed in 1787 (Bramwell 137).

[4] As to the name, Herodotus called the sea beyond the Pillars of Heracles Ἀτλαντίς (1.202). Plato (24c) calls it τὸ Ἀτλαντικὸν πέλαγος. The Pillars were known also as τέρμονες Ἀτλαντικοί (Eur. *Hipp.* 3). All these names were presumably taken from the ὄρος τῷ οὔνομα Ἄτλας, the dwellers around which are called Ἄτλαντες (Hdt. 4.184).

[5] Besides G.'s book, cf. *The Times* for 13 Feb. 1962: 'Professor Galanopoulos told your correspondent: "Solon, in translating Egyptian texts, systematically mistook the symbol for

Egyptians' own. Solon did not try to decipher hieroglyphics: he was told the story by the priests (23 d ff.). A mere 900 years would also be a sad anti-climax immediately after the impressive testimony to the extreme, antediluvian antiquity of Egyptian temple records (22 b–23 b). Moreover at 111 a Critias says that many great floods have occurred in the 9,000 years since the time of which he is speaking.

But the most persuasive case for identifying Atlantis with Minoan Crete was presented after Galanopoulos and Luce by the Cretan archaeologist Nicholas Platon in ch. 35 of his book on *Zakros* (1971). Undue importance, he says, has been given to the fact that Plato places it beyond the Straits of Gibraltar (whereas I am inclined to think that this fact has been too much ignored). 'According to the earlier cosmographic conceptions' it was in the centre of the Mediterranean that Atlas supported the vault of heaven. Unfortunately he gives no references for this, and I have failed to find any hard evidence. In *RE* I, 2127, Wernicke certainly demonstrated that the earliest associations of Atlas the Titan were with Arcadia, and adds 'And so [or 'therefore', *also*] in Arcadia he supports the sky.' It follows that this belief will have been held by the pre-Greek dwellers in Arcadia. 'How natural it was for them . . .', he exclaims, and adds that they equated Atlas with the sky-god. Wernicke's article shows signs of the mythological theories of its time (1896), not all of which are acceptable today, and in classical times Atlas's task was certainly associated with the North African mountain. However that may be, the strength of Platon's case does not lie there. The historical coincidences which he reveals between Plato's description of Atlantis and the physical equipment, layout and institutions of Minoan cities as elucidated by excavation are both fascinating and impressive. Here, I should say, lies the strongest argument that besides Plato's own fantasy, old memories of the Minoan empire, perhaps preserved in Egypt as he says, have gone to build up his picture of Atlantis.

Though Bacon in his *New Atlantis* depicted the islanders as bellicose and imperialistic, and Ruskin told the tale of its destruction to the manufacturers of Bradford as a warning against materialism, Atlantis

'100' for that of '1000'".' (Would P. perhaps have replied in words like those he uses about Egyptian art in the *Laws* (656e), οὐχ ὡς ἔπος εἰπεῖν μυριοστὸν ἀλλ' ὄντως?)

has inspired generations of writers as an ideal, another Eden, Isles of the Blest, Paradise or Utopia. This is curious, because in Plato's story the Atlanteans are the imperialist villains, the Athenians the heroes who by 'going it alone' and repulsing them saved their fellow-Greeks and all the Mediterranean peoples from enslavement. Their success was due to the invincible spirit of unity resulting from an education and institutions miraculously like those of the 'best society' described by Socrates on the previous day. The Atlanteans on the other hand, though once virtuous, had degenerated into a covetous and power-seeking lot, ripe for divine judgement. Reading the last extant words of the *Critias* one does not need much imagination to see in them Plato's strictures on the Athenians of his own day, so different from those who beat back the Persian hordes at Marathon and Salamis.[1]

Whether or not Plato's tale of Solon is all imaginary, or dimly reflects a folk-memory of some past event or distant land, Atlantis has taken on a life of its own of which neither time nor scepticism can rob it. Perhaps John Masefield had the last word:

> The Atlanteans have not died;
> Immortal things still give us dream.

The 'probable account'

When Protagoras says 'I shall tell you no longer a *mythos* but a *logos*' (*Prot.* 324d), his meaning is clear. So far he has cast his view of human nature into the form of a fictional narrative: the rest he will impart as a straightforward statement of fact. Each conveys truth in its own way. In the *Timaeus* Plato does not even distinguish them. Timaeus calls his discourse a *mythos* or a *logos* indifferently, though more often the latter,[2] and regularly with the epithet 'probable' or 'likely' (*eikōs*). The first problem facing an interpreter is how far the account is intended as serious philosophy or science. In the nature of the case, the text cannot decide this for us, and opinions are inevitably coloured by the indi-

---

[1] The chief thesis of Vidal-Naquet's interesting and thought-provoking article in *REG* 1964 is that Athens' conquest of Atlantis was a conquest of herself. Athens and Atlantis represent two sides of the same city. Primitive Athens is the Athens of the land, of Athena and the olive, whereas Atlantis, founded by Poseidon, is the imperialistic sea-power which she became.

[2] See Vlastos's figures and reff. in *SPM*, 382 with notes. Note that at 56b he claims to speak κατὰ τὸν ὀρθὸν λόγον καὶ κατὰ τὸν εἰκότα.

vidual's impression of Plato as a whole, which in its turn will almost certainly be influenced by his own outlook on the world.[1] I claim no exemption for what I shall say in subsequent sections, but the text must have first consideration.

Introducing his theme, Timaeus says (29c–d) that one cannot hope to give a completely consistent and precise account of such subjects as gods and the origin of the universe, but must be content with a probable *mythos*. At 48d he speaks of 'maintaining what we said at first, the force of a probable *logos*', and at 47c of 'holding fast to what is probable'. By contrast, the poets have spoken of the gods '*without* probable and necessary demonstrations',[2] and our trust in them can only be based on their divine descent (40d–e). Whether or not this amounts to a dismissal of their claims,[3] it is clear that such methods are not going to be followed here. At 59c, after speaking of the composition of metals (hardly a mythological theme, as Vlastos remarked), he calls this sort of analysis 'pursuing the method of probable *mythoi*', and adds: 'When a man for relaxation puts aside *logoi* about what exists for ever and gets an innocent pleasure from the probable *logoi* of becoming, he will add a reasonable and sagacious recreation[4] to his life.' Here is the clue to an assessment of the 'probable *logos*'. Only of being can there be certain knowledge: of the natural world, as a world of becoming, we can only have belief. This is the basic distinction which Timaeus laid down at the beginning (27d). But even beliefs can be 'firm and true' (37b), though perhaps we cannot be sure of it. 'That what has been said about the soul is the truth, we could only assert if God confirmed it; but that it is probable we must venture to say now, and the more so as investigation proceeds' (72d).

---

[1] Cf. Tarán's remarks at the conclusion of his article on 'The Creation Myth in P.'s *Tim.*' (Anton and Kustas, *Essays* 392). The point 'cannot be settled by discussion, for what is in question is how one reads Plato, how one conceives Plato's role as a writer and as a thinker'; but the issues 'can be discussed and can at least be clarified by the use of argument'.

[2] 40e. Contrast 53d: the geometrical structure of the elementary particles is given κατὰ τὸν μετ' ἀνάγκης εἰκότα λόγον. Contexts like this tell strongly against Howald's assimilation of εἰκός in *Tim.* to the rhetorical εἰκός condemned by P. in other dialogues (*Hermes* 1922, 70f.).

[3] The difference is one of subject: cosmic and astral beings, or the denizens of Olympus. The passage is generally taken to be wholly ironical, but cf. Guthrie, *OGR* 240f.

[4] *Paidia*. On this word cf. vol. IV, 61. At 69a (see next page) this same study of nature has become the indispensable preliminary to the knowledge of divine causes which is the primary objective. Nor should we overlook the fact that the manuscripts are divided between παιδιά and παιδεία. See Burnet's app. cr.

The progress of Plato's thought is subtle. He has abandoned nothing of his conception of reality as incorporeal and supra-sensible, or of divine purpose as the ultimate cause of everything being as it is; yet his present view of science as advancing indefinitely through investigation of phenomena without ever reaching unquestionable truth has more in common with the twentieth-century than the Aristotelian conception of its progress. In the *Phaedo*, though the senses could stimulate the mind to search for the Forms, the instability of the world of change made it waste of time to study it in detail. Now it is only through that study that we can hope to attain the knowledge of divine and changeless reality, because even the divine Craftsman, in making the world as good as possible, availed himself of given material and secondary causes.

Therefore we must distinguish two types of cause, one necessary, the other divine. Divine causes we must ever be seeking in order to secure a life as blessed as our nature admits, and the necessary for the sake of the divine, reckoning that without them we can never apprehend in isolation those other things on which our mind is set, nor receive nor in any way have part in them. (68e–69a)

The reasons why only a likely account of the natural world is possible are twofold, objective or ontological, and subjective. (1) An explanation must be conformable to its subject. The world is only a changing *likeness* (*eikōn*) of an unchanging model (*paradeigma*), therefore its description can only be provisional and *likely* (*eikōs*), not final and immutable like a *logos* of the model. (2) Neither speaker nor listeners can transcend the limitations of human nature. (See 29b–d.)

The upshot is that Plato intends his account of the natural world to be as accurate as possible within the limits imposed by the subject-matter and man's powers of understanding.[1] Much of the contents bears this out. The human physiology and pathology, for instance, reflect the latest opinions of the Sicilian medical school. Yet this does not settle every question. What of the liver as literally a mirror of the mind (made 'solid, smooth and bright' for the purpose), with the function of induc-

---

[1] Note that in introducing the geometrical structure of matter Timaeus emphasizes that his *logos* is intended for experts. It is unfamiliar, he says, 'but since you are versed in the branches of learning which I must employ to demonstrate my thesis, you will follow me' (53c).

ing prophetic dreams (71 a–d)? What of the mixing-bowl in which God blends the ingredients of the souls of the world and of men (41 d)? Plato believed in transmigration, but did he believe that at first only men were created, and women originated from inferior males at a second birth? Hardly, yet this statement is accompanied by a solemnly scientific account of the physiology of sexual reproduction. On a higher level, some regard the Creator himself as mythical, identifying him with his model or the World-Soul—which according to the 'probable account' he brought into being—or both. How far the *Timaeus* is intended to be mythical, and what exactly 'mythical' means, will never be settled now by argument, if indeed Plato could have settled it himself. Jowett thought he could not,[1] and it is remarkable that Plato's own pupils, Aristotle and Xenocrates, differed over whether the temporal creation of the world was intended to be taken literally.

Maker, Model and Material

As Plato presents it, his cosmogony demands three, or perhaps four, ultimates: the Maker, his eternal Model, and the unformed material on which he worked, and which was pervaded by a restless, irrational motion from no other cause than necessity or chance (*Ananke*). Let us take these one by one.

The Maker. In the *Republic* Plato calls the maker of the heavenly bodies their *demiourgos*, and this word is used several times in the *Timaeus*. Consequently he is now usually known as the Demiurge, though Plato more frequently calls him God (that is, usually *theos* with the definite article, to distinguish him from the many derivative gods), and also Father and begetter.[2] In the latter metaphor his raw material is compared to a mother, according to the usual Greek beliefs about parentage.

---

[1] *Dialogues*, vol. III, 698: 'We cannot tell (nor could Plato himself have told) where the figure or myth ends and the philosophical truth begins.' Not surprisingly when Plato, like his Protagoras, used myth to convey philosophical truth.

[2] *Rep.* 530a, and cf. 507c, *Soph.* 265c, *Pol.* 270; δημιουργός in *Tim.* 41a, 42e, 68e, 69c (and verb δημιουργεῖν 37c); with πατήρ at 41a, ὁ τόδε τὸ πᾶν γεννήσας 41a, ποιητὴς καὶ πατήρ 28c (cf. *Phil.* 27a: τὸ ποιούμενον and τὸ γιγνόμενον differ only in name), ὁ γεννήσας πατήρ 37c. ὁ θεός is the most frequent title (30a, b, d, 31b, 32b, 34a, 55c, 56c, 69b, 73b). It is going too far to say with Cherniss (*ACPA* 608) that sing. and pl. are used 'practically without discrimination'.

However, the choice of Demiurge, meaning craftsman or technician, is sound. The spirit of Socrates still lives, with his endless talk of 'shoemakers, carpenters and smiths', and the word reminds us that a craftsman works in a given material and to a pattern or form, either before his eyes or reflected in his mind.[1] Similarly the Maker of this world is not omnipotent, but does the best he can with an already existing stuff, and creates the physical cosmos after the model of the eternal Realities. The metaphysic of the *Timaeus* is not monistic in the sense that One Being is primary and all else derived from Him. In the *Philebus* we have seen it put plainly and succinctly (23c–d): for anything in this world to exist, there must first be, as its constituents (27a11), an Unlimited element and the principle of Limit or proportionate measure to be imposed on it, and besides these a Cause to effect their union. (Cf. 30c.) The Cause does not create these two, but only blends them to make the concrete object. This supreme Cause in the *Philebus* is Reason, more fully personified in the *Timaeus*, where among the Demiurge's many titles is 'Best of causes'.[2]

It is the lesson of the *Gorgias* all over again (503e–504b):

The accomplished speaker who aims at the best result will not choose his words at random, but with his eye on something—just as all other craftsmen, each with an eye to his own work, do not pick out at random the materials they bring to it, but so that what they are making shall have a certain form. Look at artists,[3] builders, shipwrights or followers of any other craft, how each of them imparts a certain arrangement to what he is working on, and makes one part fit and harmonize with another until he has constructed the whole as a thing of system and order.

The goodness of anything, Socrates continues, whether house, ship, or the human body and soul, depends on whether it manifests order (*kosmos*). The world itself is a *kosmos*, as we know, and the action of the

---

[1] Cf. Skemp, *TMPLD* 109. The need for a pattern colours P.'s thought at all periods. Cf. *Crat.* 389a, *Euthyphro* 6e.

[2] *Phil.* 28d–e, *Tim.* 29a, 39e (νοῦς). Conversely the αἰτία of *Phil.* is τὸ δημιουργοῦν at 27b. νοῦν ... πάντα διακοσμεῖν at *Phil.* 28e, if the wording is pressed, might suggest that P. has not yet distinguished Demiurge from World-soul as he does in *Tim.* Cf. 30c–d and de Vogel, *Philos.* pt 1, 227; also Hackforth, *CQ* 1936, 7.

[3] It is interesting that Plato includes graphic artists (ζωγράφοι), for in one aspect the Demiurge is such an artist: the world is a copy (29b), and 'the artist, clearly, can render only what his tool and his medium are capable of rendering. His technique restricts his freedom of choice.' (See Gombrich, *Art and Illusion*, 56.)

Demiurge is sometimes described as 'making' or 'putting together', but also as 'ordering' or 'shaping' the elements which had hitherto tumbled in haphazard disorder.[1]

Plato's first lesson, then, about the Maker of the world is that, as a *demiourgos*, he is not in sole and absolute control, but must bend to his will a material that is to some extent recalcitrant. Otherwise, being wholly good himself, he would have made a perfect world (29d–30a). This is philosophy, not myth. Those who demythologize him away (and so to water down Plato's persistent theism seems to me quite unjustified[2]) are at least left with a universe whose fundamentally rational structure is infected by an irreducible element of imperfection and waywardness inherent in its bodily nature. But at this point modesty compels us to recall Plato's own words at 28c: 'The Maker and Father of this Universe is hard to find, and when found, impossible to describe to all and sundry.'

The model. Following, or preceding, the trend of the *Philebus*, the Forms are now (to use the familiar Aristotelian terms) formal causes only, having resigned to a separate power the quasi-efficient function which they, rather obscurely, possessed in the *Phaedo*.[3] This power,

---

[1] ποιεῖν 31b, συνιστάναι 29a and frequently, συντιθέναι 33d, the cosmos a σύστασις 48a et al., ἀπεργάζεσθαι 37c–d and 39e (with ἀποτυπεῖσθαι); but κοσμεῖσθαι and διασχηματίζεσθαι 53b, διακοσμεῖν 69c. Cf. 69b ἀτάκτως ἔχοντα ὁ θεός ... συμμετρίας ἐνεποίησεν. The function of the Cause is exactly the same as in *Phil.* Cf. κοσμοῦσα καὶ συντάττουσα at 30c. The associations and history of the word *kosmos* have been discussed in vol. I, esp. 110f. and 208 n. 1. Reference should also be made to the following modern authorities: W. Kranz, 'Kosmos als philosophischer Begriff frühgriechischer Zeit' in *Philologus* 1938–9, and 'Kosmos', *Arch. f. Begriffsgesch.* 1958; H. Diller, 'Der vorphilosophische Gebrauch von κόσμος und κοσμεῖν', *Festschr. Snell*, 1956; J. Kerschensteiner, *Kosmos: quellenkrit. Unters. zu den Vorsokratikern*, 1962; A. Lesky, *Kosmos*, 1963 (inaugural lecture); C. Haebler, 'Kosmos: eine etymol.-wortgesch. Untersuchung', *Arch. f. Begriffsgesch.* 1967; J. Puhvel, 'The Origins of Greek *Kosmos* and Latin *Mundus*', *AJP* 1976.

[2] Cornford wrote (*PC* 34): 'Plato is introducing into philosophy for the first time the image of a creator god.' Did he not learn it from Socrates? According to Xenophon S. distinguished from the other gods ὁ τὸν ὅλον κόσμον συντάττων τε καὶ συνέχων (*Mem.* 4.3.13). He spoke of ὁ ἐξ ἀρχῆς ποιῶν ἀνθρώπους and made Aristodemus admit that the economy of the human body betrays the hand of a wise and beneficent *demiourgos* (1.4.5 and 7).

[3] See pp. 213f. above. The separateness of the αἰτία is especially emphasized in *Phil.* It is always a τέταρτον besides the Unlimited, Limit and their mixture (23d, 26e, 30a–b, a point against those who would identify the Demiurge with his model, pp. 259–62 below). In these dialogues there is a notable absence of the term μέθεξις, a trouble-making metaphor even if P. only meant it as a variation for μίμησις (p. 46 above), and one which took a severe beating in the *Parm.* Its absence is only confirmed by Grote's attempt to deny it, for all he can quote is μεταλαμβάνειν τοῦ νοητοῦ at 51a, which he says is equivalent (III, 268 n.). It does not even refer to physical objects but to

being a *demiourgos*, must have worked to a model. Now at the very outset Timaeus reasserted, as the first essential to be grasped, the familiar[1] Platonic distinction between what exists ungenerated and eternal, and what suffers coming-to-be and perishing but never fully exists; the one comprehended by the intellect through dialectic, the other only an object of belief (*doxa*) through sensation without reasoning.[2] For Plato the question is: on which of these did the Maker fix his eye as model for the world? And one cannot claim that he makes much use of dialectic to settle it. 'If this world (*kosmos*) is fair and its *demiourgos* good, he clearly looked to the eternal: if otherwise, to what has become. But that would be a wicked utterance. It is obvious to all that he looked to the eternal, for the world is fairest of created things, and he the best of causes.' He need say no more at present. That reason alone lays hold of the perfect ungenerated Forms, and their function as paradigms of the whole sensible world, he has already taught in many dialogues; and that the world is a creation of intelligence is inferred, as in the *Philebus* (pp. 214f. above), from the regularity, beauty and evidence of purpose in the major cosmological events, night, day, the cycle of the seasons by which all earthly life is maintained, and the recurrent celestial movements on which they depend. This is expanded in the *Laws* (897bff.), the *logos* to Timaeus's *mythos*. The 'teleological argument', powerful through centuries of Christian apologetic down to the well-known hymn of Joseph Addison, stems from Plato no less than the psalmist. To both 'the heavens declare the glory of God, and the firmament showeth his handiwork'.[3] Plato's argument is not that there is no ugliness or disorder in the world, but that they are local and insignificant compared with the marvellous organization of the cosmos as a whole. Without a rational God to tame it, disorder would have been the rule, not the exception. As it is, he thought, a philosophic observer

the ὑποδοχή, and the meaning is quite different. It may seem strange that Aristotle condemns the Forms so severely for not being efficient causes, when a separate efficient cause is so carefully provided. He actually asks: What is it that does the work with its eye on the Forms? (*Metaph.* 991a20–2). But to him a personal demiurge was just one of those 'empty poetic metaphors' of which in the same passage he complains. His own God does not soil his hands with craftsman's work: his mere existence is enough to sustain the ungenerated universe in being.

[1] Especially from *Rep.* 5 (vol. IV, 487ff.).

[2] 27d–28a. The distinction is so important that it is elaborately repeated at 51d3–52a7.

[3] Also to Isaac Newton. See the impressive passage quoted by Cornford in *Princ. Sap.*, p. 21, and in n. 2 to p. 286 below.

cannot deny that the world is a product of intelligence and copies a perfect model as well as the limitations of physical embodiment allow.

For Plato the endlessly repeated and (as he believed) perfectly circular motions of the cosmos and heavenly bodies were not only produced by, but actually resembled, the operations of Mind. (More of this later.) Sambursky in his *Physical World of the Greeks* (p. 54) has a comment on the difference here between the ancient attitude and our own. We live in a machine-age, and the essence of a machine is to reproduce the same movements exactly. Consequently we associate the idea of exact repetition with 'soulless mechanism'. But in an age of handicrafts, any exact reproduction appeared as a sign of the artist's divine inspiration. It sounds an illuminating comparison, but our attitude would not have surprised Plato, for it was current in his own time. In the *Epinomis* (982c) we read that men ought to have regarded the uniformity of the stars' motions as proof of their divinity, but in fact 'most of us think the very opposite, that because they always do the same thing in the same way they have no life'. Could he question us now, he would, I think, ask: 'Do your machines, then, make themselves? Can they exist without a mind to design them?' Machines presuppose minds, however much the word 'mechanistic' may be misused to deny it.

At any rate in Plato's view regularity in natural processes implied purpose. Arguing against the primacy of chance in some of the earlier philosophies of nature, Aristotle (no friend to myth)[1] admits, strangely to our minds, only two alternatives: regular repetition demanding a teleological explanation, and chance events which are the exception. A hot day in the winter would be due to chance; hot days in the summer are produced by the normal natural methods; *therefore* nature is purposeful (*Phys.* 198b34–99a8). Here he agrees with Plato.

The concept of the Model raises problems which are probably insoluble. God, says Timaeus, made the cosmos a living, thinking creature (p. 275 below), and his next question is: 'In the likeness of what living creature[2] did he make it?' (30c). Not of any particular species.

[1] 'The sophistry of myth is not worth serious consideration: only demonstration can instruct us' (*Metaph.* 1000a18).
[2] Greek has the convenient word ζῷον, from ζῆν, to live, often rendered with perfect propriety 'animal'. But some of the associations of animality in our language seem inappropriate here. I have adopted 'living creature', but of course the Model is not a creature in the literal sense.

It must embrace all intelligible living creatures, as the cosmos includes ourselves and all other visible animals. The living world is the image, or projection into body, of the Form of Animal and all the subordinate Forms of Man, Horse, Dog etc. Cornford has explained this well (*PC* 40): The intelligible Living Creature 'is a generic Form containing within itself the Forms of all the subordinate species, members of which inhabit the visible world'. Its widest divisions are four (39e–40a), *sc.* the visible gods (stars, planets, Earth), birds, fish, land-animals.

These main types, as well as the individual species of living creatures and their specific differences, are all, in Platonic terms, 'parts' into which the generic Form of Living Creature can be divided by the dialectical procedure of Division. The generic Form must be conceived, not as a bare abstraction obtained by leaving out all the specific differences determining the subordinate species, but as a whole, richer in content than any of the parts it contains and embraces.[1] It is an eternal and unchanging object of thought, not itself *a* living creature, any more than the Form of Man is *a* man.

Cornford continues:

Plato does not say . . . that this generic Form of Living Creature contains anything more than all the subordinate generic and specific Forms and differences that would appear in the complete definitions of all the species of living creatures existing in our world, including the created gods. We have no warrant for identifying it with the entire system of Forms.

Yet the cosmos as a whole was made in the likeness of this supreme generic Form. Should it not therefore embrace the Forms of all that the cosmos contains?[2] Thus Lee (*Tim.* 10): 'Plato must mean a complex system of Forms, containing within itself all the subordinate Forms whose likeness we can trace in the world of Becoming.' He finds the conception of the 'intelligible living creature', and its place in the world of Forms as a whole, not easy to grasp, and suggests that 'its presence is perhaps due as much to the requirements of the craftsman analogy as to any philosophic principle'. Plato, as Archer-Hind says, has left his

---

[1] The Platonic dogma that the higher (more universal) Forms were also the richer and fuller in content and being (elaborated on pp. 432 f. below) was one against which Aristotle reacted vehemently. For him it was axiomatic that only the individual was fully real (*Cat.* 2a11–14), and the genus the comparatively unformed 'matter' or 'substratum' of the species. (*Metaph.* 1038a6, 1058a23 etc. See Bonitz, Index 125a, 787a.)

[2] Taylor's attempt to help by a reminder that ζῷα in Greek could mean 'pictures', whether of animals or not (*Comm.* 81, adopted by Grube, *PT* 169), does not seem apposite in the context.

intention uncertain, and the question is hardly to be decided now. At 39a Timaeus says that, wishing to make the world more like its model, God (or Mind, Noῦs) gave it the four kinds of living creatures, 'seeing what and how many are the Forms[1] in the Living Creature Itself'. This supports the more limited conception of it. Even so, in describing it at 30d he called it 'the finest and in all respects most complete of the intelligibles', which sounds more comprehensive.[2]

Relation of the maker to his model. Here is another crux on which opinion has been divided down the centuries. Is their differentiation only mythical? Wilamowitz identified the Maker and Father with the Form of the Good in the *Republic*.[3] Hager also, if I understand him, identifies God with his model, i.e. the Forms, but *not* with the Form of the Good, and de Vogel writes: 'He is, so to speak, the intelligible order turned towards creation and personified into a creating God and Father.' Archer-Hind, amid much un-Platonic language, asserted that 'all that exists is the self-moved differentiation of the one absolute thought, which is the same as the Idea of the Good', and 'the παράδειγμα [Model] is universal thought regarded as the supreme intelligible, the δημιουργός [Demiurge] represents the same regarded as the supreme intelligence'.[4] The most frequent claim is that the Forms are nothing

[1] Ιδέαι. The word by itself could mean only species or kinds, but since they belong to the intelligible sphere they are of course Platonic Forms.

[2] Cherniss however (*ACPA* 576) thinks Proclus right in supplying ζῴων after νοουμένων. He, like Cornford, favours the view that the paradigmatic Living Creature contains only Forms of the animate, which Archer-Hind (*Tim.* 34f.) also thought more reasonable. On the other side one may mention Taylor, *Comm.* 80f. ('the complete system of the Forms') and de Vogel, *Philos.* pt 1, 181 ('l'ensemble des Idées'). Another question which has troubled scholars is whether the Model, being a ζῴον (30c3), is itself alive. To answer this dogmatically, it is τὸ ὃ ἔστι ζῴον (39e8), i.e. a Form, through which living creatures have their οὐσία, and Forms do not have ψυχαί. For the sense in which Forms are self-predicable see pp. 43f. and 47 above, and for arguments favouring the contrary of what I have said, de Vogel, *Philos.* pt 1, 228f.

[3] ἡ τοῦ ἀγαθοῦ ἰδέα or τὸ ἀγαθόν (*Rep.* 508b and c etc.), so prominent in the *Rep.*, is not in fact mentioned in *Tim.*

[4] Wilam. 1, 605; F.-P. Hager, *Der Geist u. das Eine* 37–43; de Vogel, *Philos.* pt 1, 229; A.-H. *Tim.* 28, 95 n. How the intelligible order turned towards creation de Vogel does not explain. If the Forms made themselves sole efficient causes, P. would be more naively susceptible to Aristotle's criticism than he was.

Taylor saw in A.-H. a 'determination to force on Plato a philosophy of his own devising' (*Comm.* 38). It was a philosophy very much of his own time, but this conception of the two aspects of thought has persisted. Hager in 1969 (*o.c.* 39) wrote of 'das wahrhaft erkennbare, bzw. wahrhaft erkennende Sein'. (Cf. p. 40, where the puzzling phrase 'rein theoretisch oder der Möglichkeit nach' does little to modify his statement.)

but thoughts in the mind of God, who creates them by thinking of them. So said Philo of Alexandria and many Christian Platonists, notably St Augustine, and it has been affirmed by good Platonic scholars of the nineteenth and early twentieth centuries such as Ritter, Henry Jackson and Archer-Hind, and as recently as 1969 by Moreau. Yet the case against it, as put for instance by Audrey Rich in 1954 (and for that matter Martin in 1841), has never really been answered. Others who have denied it include Cornford ('The model, as strictly eternal, is independent of the Demiurge'); Skemp ('The δημιουργός is not to be confused with the αὐτόζῳον [Form of Living Creature], which is the object of his contemplation'); and Taylor, who also refused to regard the distinction as 'only part of the fanciful imagery of the dialogue'.[1]

In *Rep.* 6 it is said that the Form of the Good gives both existence and essence[2] to the other Forms, and this is often compared to the activity of the Demiurge in the *Timaeus* as only another expression of the same thing. But the two accounts have nothing in common. *Rep.* 6 says nothing of a planning Mind, and has no concern with the creation of a cosmos. There is no hint, there or elsewhere, that the Form of the Good, or any Form, is or has *nous*, which is the whole being of the creative Cause of the *Timaeus*. The centre of Plato's interest has shifted, and his metaphysical scheme is now that of the *Philebus*.[3] Another passage on which some have relied is *Tim.* 29a, where it is said that the Maker wanted all things to be like himself. But, runs the argument, he made it like the Model; *ergo* he and his Model are mythical expressions for the same thing.[4] In context, this stretches the words much too far.

---

[1] For the earlier scholars see Rich's neglected article 'The Platonic Ideas as the thoughts of God', *Mnemos.* 1954, 123 n. 1. Other reff. are to Moreau, 'The Platonic Idea', *IPQ* 1969, 509 f., which I find hard to reconcile with 511 n. 135, where he speaks of the Ideas within the archetypal Living Being as 'the very *object* of the Intellect', and of the intelligible order as *perceived* by God and become 'the rule (δεῖν) of his actions' (my italics); Cornford, *PC* 40 f.; Skemp, *TMPLD* 108, and cf. 115; Taylor, *Comm.* 81 f. Add Brochard, *Études* 95–7. Brochard criticizes Lutoslawski on the point in his *Études*, 166 n. 1.

[2] τὸ εἶναί τε καὶ τὴν οὐσίαν, *Rep.* 509 b.

[3] Cf. Thompson on *Phil.* 26 c (*JPh* 1882, 20): 'Those whom the magnificent language applied in the Republic to the Ἀγαθόν may have tempted to believe that the God of Plato was, if not a number, an Idea, will find I think a corrective to that misapprehension in the passage quoted from the Philebus (p. 26E seq.). The language is indeed so explicit as to seem designed for the purpose of obviating the very inference I have alluded to.'

[4] E.g. Hager's argument is (*o.c.* 43): 'Die Welt nach Platon nicht zwei verschiedenen Wesenheiten ähnlich sein und werden kann.'

The Maker, says Timaeus (29a–30b), being good, and so incapable of jealousy, wanted everything to be as like himself as possible. This is the true reason for the genesis of the world. Wishing everything to be good, and nothing bad, so far as might be, he took over matter with its restless and discordant motion and reduced it to order. Judging, moreover, that anything of a visible nature was better with reason than without, he made the cosmos a living, rational creature. That is all. The world resembles its Maker simply in being (a) good and (b) alive and rational. To achieve this end he modelled it on the eternal Forms (29a).

In describing the Forms as thoughts of God, some speak in terms of the Aristotelian concept of thought which thinks itself. So Archer-Hind: 'Thus does dualism vanish in the final identification of thought and its object . . . Thought must think: and since Thought alone exists, it can but think itself.'[1] Aristotle's supreme God, unlike Plato's, is wrapped in eternal self-contemplation to the exclusion of any providence or planning of a world, on the argument that the perfect being's thought can only be of what is best, and that is himself. How he does this is explained on the lines of Aristotle's general psychology. In sensation and thought the *psyche* assimilates the form (sensible or intelligible as the case may be) without its matter. (Form is of course internal for Aristotle.) Both are purely psychical functions, though in sensation the *psyche* employs the bodily organs as instruments. In sight the eye, a physical organ, becomes coloured, but the *psyche* becomes *aware of colour*. In thought the *psyche* assimilates directly the intelligible form, that is, the definable essence of the object. But taking on a form is not an indifferent act like putting on a coat. As the actualization of a potency it implies a change in the object informed. In thinking of something, the mind *becomes* that object in so far as it is an object of thought, i.e. assumes its intelligible form. That is why, as we think of things or people, we usually suppose thought to be of what is outside the mind, not identifying thought and its object completely, because there remains the material element which of course the mind does not absorb.[2] Consider however the special case of God. As perfect being, he is pure

[1] A.-H. *o.c.* 28. 'since Thought alone exists' is surely a perfect example of *petitio principii*, the assumption of what has to be proved.
[2] This applies even when we think about ourselves: αὐτῆς δ' ἐν παρέργῳ, *Metaph.* 1074b36.

actuality, with no unrealized potentiality at all. Hence the object of his thought (himself) has no matter,[1] and therefore only intelligible form. If the mind in human processes of thought becomes identified with the intelligible form of its object, the identification of mind and its object must in this case be complete. Add the fact that the act of thought is eternal, and there is no longer any distinction between thought and its object: their essence is one and indivisible.[2]

This being so, there is much to be said for Audrey Rich's suggestion in the aforementioned article (p. 260 n. 1) that the notion of the Forms as thoughts of God in Plato originated in the desire of later antiquity to reconcile the Platonic theory of independent Forms with the Aristotelian doctrine of immanent form.[3] Our excursion into Aristotle's psychology may have seemed out of place, and certainly its brevity does Aristotle scant justice; but I hope it has been clear, and it was needed to emphasize by contrast how impossible it would have been for Plato, with his different metaphysical and psychological assumptions, to reduce the Forms to thoughts in the mind of the Creator. In every dialogue in which they appear, their existence independent of any mind conceiving them is a leading feature. The craftsman analogy prevails; and whereas for Aristotle the form of his product must pre-exist *in the craftsman's mind*,[4] for Plato he looks (at two removes perhaps) to an external, fixed, objective standard or Form, which he attempts to reproduce, though with imperfect success. The last three words apply even to the divine Craftsman who made the world, for he too had to work with a material which he could only partially subdue. To this we must now turn.

The material (48 d–53 c). Many have bewailed the obscurity of much of the *Timaeus*. In this case the warning—a strong one—comes from Plato himself. At 48e–49a Timaeus says he must make a new start. Earlier it seemed as if it was enough to speak of a model and its copy, but now the *logos* demands something else, a 'dim and difficult concep-

---

[1] Matter *is* potentiality, and form actuality (*De an.* 412a9).
[2] For God's activity as thought of himself see *Metaph.* Λ, chh. 7 and 9. Ch. 9 alludes to the general doctrine of the nature of thought which is expounded in *De an.* For sensation see bk. 2 ch. 12 and for thought 3.4, esp. 430a2–9.
[3] R. M. Jones has also written on the origin of the notion, in *CP* 1926.
[4] *Metaph.* 1032b1 ἀπὸ τέχνης δὲ γίγνεται ὅσων τὸ εἶδος ἐν τῇ ψυχῇ.

tion'. Besides these two there must be that *in which* becoming takes place. To explain it is hard. After a first attempt he must 'try to put it still more clearly' (50a), but at 50c copies of the Forms enter into it 'in a strange manner hard to express'. Again it is 'invisible and shapeless, receiving all things, partaking in some most bewildering way of the intelligible and hard to capture' (51a–b); 'indestructible . . . touched without the senses by a sort of bastard reasoning, hardly credible' (52a–b). In the effort to portray it Plato resorts to simile after simile, and it will be prudent to marshal the various expressions used as he struggles to convey this mysterious notion from his own mind to ours.[1]

1. It is an ultimate, having existed, like Being and becoming, 'even before the world was born'.[2]

2. Its nature and function are 'to be the Receptacle and so to speak nurse of all becoming' (49b). There being no obvious similarity between a receptacle and a nurse, Plato might have done better to omit 'nurse' and keep to the mother-image. ('Nurse' recurs at 52d5.)

3. It is a plastic substance[3] capable of receiving impressions, moved and shaped by what enters into it (50c).

4. The previous image is both extended and illustrated. A soft material which is to have a device impressed on it must first be made as smooth as possible (50e). At 50a–b the illustration is gold, which a goldsmith fashions into many different shapes. If asked of any of them 'What is that?', it would be safest to reply 'gold', not 'a ring' or 'a triangle', for even as the words were spoken, he might be giving it a different shape. So with 'the nature that receives all bodies'. It is only itself, not any one of them. If it resembled any of the things it takes in, it would reproduce other things badly, intruding its own features as well.

---

[1] It has been an object of controversy down the centuries. Baeumker in his book *Das Problem der Materie* (2. Abschnitt, 110ff.) includes an extensive review of opinions from Aristotle through Plutarch and the Neoplatonists down to his own time.

[2] 52d. There was of course γένεσις before the γένεσις of our world: the act of the Demiurge was simply to introduce order into it. The question of the temporal origin of the world will come up later (pp. 299–305). For the present those who like may take 'before' as referring only to logical priority.

[3] ἐκμαγεῖον (50c2) is used at *Tht.* 191c of a smooth block of wax before impressions are stamped on it, but at 194d of impressions already stamped. This second sense, of 'moulds' or 'dies', recurs at *Laws* 800b, where certain typical cases are to be used as ἐκμαγεῖα for legislators, and is probably the commoner. Here however only the first sense is intended. The receptacle must be ἄμορφον ἀπασῶν τῶν ἰδεῶν ὅσας μέλλοι δέχεσθαι (50d). Cf. the use of ἐκτυποῦσθαι at 50d.

5. The same point is made by comparing it to the oils used as a base for perfumes. They must themselves be as far as possible scentless (50e5–8).

6 'The Recipient is fittingly likened to a mother, the model of becoming to a father,[1] and the nature that arises between them to off-spring.' It was a common Greek belief that the father was the sole cause of generation, the mother contributing only nourishment and a place for the embryo to grow in.[2] Hence 'mother and receptacle' at 51a go quite naturally together. There is also a distinct trace of the Pythagoreans, with their association of the unlimited with the female, and the unit, the principle of limit and order, with *sperma* (Arist. *Metaph.* 1091a16; vol. I, 245f., 278).

7. After all the foregoing, Plato refers to the Receptacle as 'space' (χώρα), and says that it provides a 'seat' (ἕδρα) for everything that becomes (52a8–b1). It is what we have regard to when we imagine[3] that all that exists must be in a certain place and occupy space (52a–b); and in summing up at 52d he refers to his three factors as Being, Space and Becoming.

8. It is in constant irregular motion, swaying and shaken 'like grain in a winnowing basket' by the 'powers' of the rudimentary elements or qualities that pervade it, and in turn reacting on them (52e3–5).

What are we to make of this dim and dubious something, scarcely an object of belief, let alone of knowledge? Its essence lies in the oft-repeated statement, backed by the similes of the wax for stamping and the base for perfumes, that in itself it must have no perceptible qualities. Because its function is to 'receive' sensible copies of the eternal realities, it must be without any form[4] of its own which would distort the image. It is the medium or material 'in which' (again a repeated phrase) all

---

[1] 50d. τὸ ὅθεν refers back to the previous sentence, and is, more literally, 'that whence anything that becomes has its development by being made like to it'. Surprisingly, those who maintain the identity of the Demiurge with his Model have not, so far as I know, availed themselves of this comparison of the latter to a father.

[2] Cornford illustrates from Greek literature, *PC* 187. Aristotle calls the menstrual fluid the 'matter' (ὕλη) of the child, whereas the semen provides the efficient cause and the form (*GA* 729a32, 738b20).

[3] ὀνειροπολοῦμεν. It is a 'dream' because of course what really exists (i.e. Forms) is not in space. For this figurative sense of dreaming cf. *Rep.* 476c, 534c. See also Baeumker, *P.d.M.* 139, and for the hyperbaton Cornford, *PC* 192 n. 2.

[4] μορφή, εἶδος and ἰδέα are all used in this non-technical sense (50c1, d7, 51a2, 7).

perceptible things or qualities come to be. 'Receive' (δέχεσθαι) here has a wide sense, especially that of taking an impress or assuming a character. Plato had not developed Aristotle's technical vocabulary of potentiality and act, but it is not misleading to say that the material has in and by itself (in which naked state it never occurs, any more than Aristotle's prime matter, of which, as in Plato, the simplest kinds of body consist[1]) the potentiality of being informed by the properties of fire, air, water or earth.[2] The phrase 'in which' certainly does not, as Baeumker claimed, confirm his view that the receptacle is merely 'empty space, sheer extension', for it is ambiguous in Greek as in English. A clay bust is in space, but it is also modelled in clay.[3]

The third postulate, then, is something that can be called a matrix (ἐκμαγεῖον) or alternatively space (χώρα).[4] Many good scholars, from Zeller onwards have insisted that Plato intended it to represent nothing but empty space, or extension, and some have compared it to the matter of Descartes.[5] 'That the so-called "primary matter" of the *Timaeus* is

---

[1] It is becoming fashionable to deny that Aristotle believed in a 'prime matter'. See e.g. Charlton's App. to his ed. of *Phys.* 1 and 2, pp. 129–45 (criticized by Owens in *Phoenix* 1971, 281 f.). But I continue to regard as such the ὕλη ... ἐξ ἧς γίνεται τὰ καλούμενα στοιχεῖα, also called τὸ δυνάμει σῶμα αἰσθητόν (*GC* 329a26 and 33). H. R. King's article in *JHI* 1956, 370–90, I find quite unconvincing; but these are matters for the next volume.

[2] Baeumker gives no grounds for his assertion that 'Der Begriff des bloss möglichen seins, auf den Aristoteles das Wesen der Materie zurückführt, ist dem Plato noch fremd' (*P.d.M.* 186). P. has no technical term for it, and confesses that he is trying to express a novel and difficult conception. In a different connexion he clearly conveys the distinction between potential and actual knowledge at *Tht.* 197b–d. (Cf. Arist. *EN* 1146b31 and Taylor, *PMW* 343.)

[3] Baeumker, *P.d.M.* 166. He was following Zeller (II.1, 734 n. 1) and has been followed by Solmsen (*ASPW* 122) and Cornford, who writes (*PC* 181): 'There is no justification for calling the Receptacle "matter"—a term not used by Plato. The Receptacle is not that "out of which" (ἐξ οὗ) things are made; it is that "in which" (ἐν ᾧ) qualities appear, as fleeting images are seen *in* a mirror.' But cf. 50e ἔν τισιν τῶν μαλακῶν σχήματα ἀπομάττειν, whereas ἐκ is used of gold to convey the same notion. (The false distinction is again drawn by Düring, *Aristoteles*, 31 n. 202.) The indifferent use of the two expressions in connexion with raw material is exemplified by their appearance together at *Phil.* 59e and *Pol.* 288d. Keyt too (*AJP* 1961, 298) thinks that comparison with a mirror 'best captures Plato's thought'. But it is noteworthy that although P. uses a rich variety of metaphors to convey his difficult conception, and although (as K. notes) the mirror-metaphor is one of his favourites, yet 'The third factor is never, in fact, called a mirror' (Keyt, *l.c.*).

[4] These are the only two words applied to it without qualification or hint of simile (such as καθάπερ, οἷον, προσεικάζειν). I would not mention something that may well be accidental, were it not that Baeumker (*o.c.* 184) claims it as conferring special status on χώρα without mentioning ἐκμαγεῖον.

[5] E.g. Baeumker, *o.c.* 187; Taylor, *Comm.* 312, 322, 387; Milhaud and Robin (Claghorn, *ACPT* 15 n. 19). But Brochard wrote (*Études* 108): 'Quant à voir dans Platon un précurseur de Descartes, ce n'est pas possible.' His reason is that there is nothing geometrical about Plato's

space in three dimensions and nothing else', declared Burnet (*T. to P.* 344), 'is really quite certain both from Plato's own language and from the statements of Aristotle.' But it is time to heed the advice of Timaeus (49 a–b), that to understand the Receptacle we first need a 'firm and trustworthy account' of fire, air, water and earth, which Plato, like Empedocles, regards as the primary *bodily* constituents of everything in the physical world. No one, he says, has explained their origin, and we talk of them as ultimates without knowing what they are. Far from being *stoicheia*,[1] they are even more complex than syllables. What, we must ask, were they like before the creation of the cosmos? (48 b–c.)

First, observation shows that they are unstable, constantly changing into one another by condensation and compaction and rarefaction or dispersion—the old Ionian view. We cannot therefore call any of them an existing thing, but only a temporary qualification, a 'such', not a 'this'.[2] But qualities presuppose something in which and from which they appear and disappear.[3] Plato, one may say, is struggling to express

Receptacle. This is certainly right, and Taylor wrong in calling it 'geometrical extension'. Popper gives a helpful summary of the Cartesian theory in his article in *Studies in the Philosophy of Biology* 1974, 262. Note (especially in view of what will come later) that he does not speak of Descartes reducing matter to pure extension but to 'extended substance'. Matter was not reduced to space, but '*space too was reduced to matter*, since *there was no empty space* but only the essential spatial extension of matter'. (My italics.) Popper sees Plato's Receptacle as similar, a 'liquid-like medium' in which vortical motion could take place without empty space (*C. and R.* 81 n. 22).

[1] Elements or letters, pp. 176, 211 above. Unlike Empedocles, the atomists did try to penetrate beyond the four elements, but in Plato's view gave the wrong answers. Serious students of *Tim.* should be warned that this passage (roughly from 49b to 50b) has been the subject of prolonged controversy. Cornford's interpretation in *PC* (178–80) was challenged by Cherniss in *AJP* 1954. Gulley in *AJP* 1960 found Cherniss's view 'self-refuting and incorrect' and in the same journal for 1960 E. N. Lee had something to say about both Gulley and Cherniss.

[2] Owen's objection (*SPM* 323) that even the word τοιοῦτον cannot consistently be used, and contradicts *Crat.* 439 d 8–9, has I hope been dealt with on pp. 79–82. (Cf. also next page, on *Tim.* 52 a 5.) We must not confuse the Heraclitean flux of a world with no unchanging Forms behind it ('if even Beauty itself gives us the slip', *Crat. l.c.*) and the same flux in a scheme (Plato's) including the Forms. Since this chapter was written, a new interpretation of the relevant passage and its context has been offered by D. J. Zeyl in *HSCP* 1975, with detailed criticism of other recent views.

[3] I have avoided the word 'substratum', just as P. lacks the Aristotelian ὑποκείμενον, but is not this what we usually mean by the word? Taylor (*Comm.* 387) forbids us to 'introduce from Aristotle the notion of "matter" as a substratum of events. Aristotle is quite explicit . . . that Timaeus knows of no "matter" distinct from χώρα.' He gives no reference, but may be thinking of *Phys.* 209 b 11, where A. says τὴν ὕλην καὶ τὴν χώραν ταὐτόν φησι εἶναι ἐν τῷ Τιμαίῳ. This means that (as is obvious) he identified matter and space, not that he replaced matter by space. It is an interesting coincidence of vocabulary that matter (ὕλη) is for A. 'in the strictest sense' the substratum which *receives* becoming and perishing (τὸ ὑποκείμενον τῆς γενέσεως καὶ φθορᾶς δεκτικόν, *GC* 320a2). The idea that Aristotle's equation of P.'s ἐκμαγεῖον with his own ὕλη

for the first time what Kant said in 1787 and William Whewell sixty years later.

If we remove from our empirical concept of a body, one by one, every feature in it which is [merely] empirical, the colour, the hardness or softness, the weight, even the impenetrability, there still remains the space which the body (now entirely vanished) occupied, and this cannot be removed. Again, if we remove from our empirical concept of any object, corporeal or incorporeal, all properties which experience has taught us, we yet cannot take away that property through which the object is thought as substance or as inhering in a substance.[1]

There follows immediately in Plato the simile of the gold wrought into different shapes. Like it, the 'recipient of all bodies', 'of everything generated and perceptible' (50b, 51a), remains itself, uncommitted to any of the properties which enter into it, and which Plato now reveals as copies of the eternal realities[2] (50b–c); for there is an intelligible Form for each of the primary bodies. Fire and the rest in the physical world take the names of their Forms and, though generated, in constant motion, appearing and vanishing in a particular locality, *resemble* these changeless realities.[3] Here we have the familiar relationship of imitation in the classical doctrine of Forms, which Plato never abandoned, but has refined in three ways:

(1) The dubious notion of 'sharing' is dropped.

(2) The anonymous questioner of the *Phaedo* is given a final answer. Opposite qualities cannot change into one another, nor is it exact to say,

---

rests on a misunderstanding is still strongly held. Cf. Solmsen in *Mus. Helv.* 1976, 27, citing Cherniss, *ACPA* 165 ff.

[1] Kant, *Crit. of Pure Reason*, Introd. to 2nd ed., § 2, trans. Kemp Smith. (The passage will be found in Edwards and Pap, *Mod. Introd. to Phil.* 3rd ed., 688.) Cf. Whewell, *Phil. of the Ind. Sciences*, 2nd ed. 1847 (new impr. 1967), 404 f. The notion of substance as a substratum of change is unpopular with most modern scientists as it was with Berkeley and Hume, and Dingle in an article in *BJPS* 1951 dismisses it as pre-scientific and childish. Von Weizsäcker however speaks more cautiously in *W.-V. of Phys.* 31–3, and in America E. J. Nelson undertook in 1949 an impressive defence of substance in this sense as indispensable to empirical knowledge. (See *Philos. for the Future*, ed. Sellars etc., 106–24.) Stebbing wrote of the permanent psychological need for such a conception in *MIL*, 404. Dr G. E. R. Lloyd has suggested to me that there is a distinction to be drawn here between the application of the idea of substance to ordinary perceptible objects (where without some such idea it would be difficult to make sense of our experience) and the physicists' researches into matter and energy, which have largely outgrown it. Dingle and Nelson could both be right.

[2] μιμήματα 50c5, ἀφομοιώματα 51a2.

[3] ὁμώνυμον ὅμοιόν τε 52a5.

as was said there, that 'things' (πράγματα) take on these qualities in turn.[1] A neutral substratum is called for, which by receiving the imprint of the Forms produces visible and tangible things or bodies.

(3) Interpreters of the *Phaedo* have differed over the status of 'the tallness in us' at 102 d, and the sense in which, in this and other central dialogues, the Form was 'present' in the particulars, about which Plato was deliberately vague (100 d). Some have taken the immanent tallness to be not the Form itself, but something lower in the ontological scale.[2] Timaeus is unambiguous. The Form 'neither admits anything into itself nor enters into anything else' (52 a); it is only images or copies of the Forms[3] that enter and leave the Receptacle, making it part fiery, part wet and so on.

Some of those who interpreted the Receptacle as 'matter' destroyed their case by equating matter with body (*Körper*), thereby ensuring that subsequent criticism would be misdirected. Of course it is not body (which has sensible properties) any more than Aristotle's 'prime matter' is body. It is an abstraction,[4] reached by analysing corporeal substance in a way deemed necessary by both philosophers to escape Parmenides and explain the fact of change. It suggested to Plato the concept of space, not empty space as some have thought,[5] but ever full of a primitive kind of bodies, moving in every sense of the word *kinesis*—changing, generated and perishing, toppling over each other in their lack of homogeneity and balance (52 c) and communicating this motion to the Receptacle itself. That the Receptacle itself should be agitated, and communicate its agitation back to its contents, is the strongest argument for supposing that Plato meant what he said when he called it not only space but a matrix, 'stuff without property', as Popper describes

---

[1] *Pho.* 103 a–c; vol. IV, 356.

[2] Thus Ross wrote (*PTI* 30): 'What is present in the particular thing is not, strictly speaking, the Idea, but an imperfect copy of the Idea', and Rist and Cornford have taken similar views. (See p. 48 with n. 1 above, and Cornford, *P. and P.* 78.) I myself see strong reasons against this, but have felt a doubt whether Plato's own mind was clear on the point (p. 41).

[3] τῶν ὄντων ἀεὶ μιμήματα 50 c 5.

[4] I.e. something which we abstract or separate in thought from that from which it is inseparable in fact, not a *mere* thought or product of the imagination, 'bloss einen vorgestellten oder logischen Raum' (Gauss, *Handk.* III.2, 198), nor yet an abstraction in Cornford's sense (*PC* 203).

[5] Especially in Germany: 'das Leere' or 'leerer Raum', Zeller II.1, 740, supported by Baeumker and others. But there is no void in the cosmos (58 a 7, 79 b 1, 80 c 3 and p. 290 n. 3 below), nor, I think we may assume, in the chaotic mixture which preceded it.

it, comparing Anaximander's *Apeiron* (*OS* I, 211). This chaos, disposed 'without reason[1] or measure', is what the Demiurge took over: 'fire and water, earth and air, showing traces[2] of themselves but in such a condition as might be expected of anything from which God is absent' (53b3-4). Of their container, so far as its nature can be grasped, one can only say that the ignited part of it appears as fire, the wet part as water and so on (51b); so it offers every appearance to sight (52e1), though considered in abstraction from the diverse properties that everlastingly pervade it, it is of course completely imperceptible.[3]

What exactly 'enters and leaves' the Receptacle?[4]

'No Form enters into anything else.' This accords with the purely paradigmatic role of the Forms in these later dialogues, but it is difficult to understand Plato's exact intentions. Has he really explained the relation between Forms and phenomena? What are the 'copies' which, by entering the Receptacle, impregnate it with fieriness, wateriness etc.? 'Not the qualities, but enmattered forms', said Proclus oracularly,[5] but this hardly sounds like Plato. With the Forms as patterns only, he premises both in the *Philebus* and here a separate efficient Cause to create a cosmos in their image. This is Mind or God, but so far there is no cosmos and God has not yet taken the chaos in hand. His confession that the copies of the Forms 'take their stamp from them in a mysterious and scarcely explicable manner' (50c) betrays his embarrassment as a philosopher. He has not lost faith in the transcendence of the Forms, a partly religious belief as above all the *Phaedrus* showed, but one may

---

[1] Or proportion, ἀλόγως. Cf. our use of 'irrational' to mean 'without ratio' (Popper *C. and R.* 84).

[2] ἴχνη, primarily footsteps, and so traces of what is past rather than, as here, the beginnings of future development. (But cf. the use at *Pol.* 301 e.) But Plato with his figure of the ἐκμαγεῖον in mind thinks of them as *imprints* on the Receptacle. With ἐκτύπωμα and ἀπομάττειν cf. Theocr. 17.122 ποδῶν ἐκμάσσεται ἴχνη (of dust). Of this inchoate state P. says at 69b that there was nothing then deserving the names we now apply—fire, water and the rest.

[3] This should make it clear that there is no contradiction, as some have claimed, between 'invisible', 'grasped without sensation' (51a7, 52b2), and on the other hand, 'appearing in every guise to sight' (52e1), together with the statement that God took over 'all that was visible' (30a2).

[4] τὰ εἰσιόντα καὶ ἐξιόντα. It is terribly difficult to avoid the word 'things', and once again one envies P. the Greek resource of using the neuter plural participle only.

[5] ἔνυλα εἴδη. See Cornford, *PC* 183. 'Enmattered forms' are an Aristotelian conception, though not as Cornford says an Aristotelian phrase. λόγοι ἔνυλοι occurs once, at *De an.* 403a25, of the πάθη ψυχῆς.

be excused for feeling that the time is ripe for Aristotle to come forward with his conception of form as the intelligible, definable element *in* things. It helps little to suppose that the pre-cosmic chaos never actually existed, but only depicts what the world *would* be like if it were not divinely ordered. The analysis leaves us with two categories, both resembling Forms, of which only one seems wanted: the copies (μιμήματα) whose presence in the Receptacle of Becoming gives it visible and tangible character, and the physical bodies, or 'things which become', also 'like' the Forms and named after them, compounded of the copies and Space together.[1] No doubt the copies would be in modern terms what Crombie calls them (*EPD* II, 303–5), property-instances as opposed to properties as such; but to Plato the Forms were never just properties, and I doubt if his mind was altogether clear on this point. Deprived of the almost mystical glow of conviction and the religious language that goes with it in the great central dialogues, and transferred to the ambience of an Anaximandrian *Apeiron*, the relation between the Forms and the natural world becomes difficult to explain. But Forms remain for Plato the only possible bridge between a Heraclitean lack of all stability and the immobile unity of Parmenides. Either of these by itself would make knowledge impossible and cannot therefore be entertained by a philosopher.

[1] Is this pressing analogies too far? Archer-Hind says simply: 'The sensible objects of perception *are* the εἴδη εἰσιόντα καὶ ἐξιόντα' (*Tim.* 45, my italics). This may be right, but P. seems to say that, then as now, perceptible objects are bodies, albeit in an even more fluid state, whereas the εἰσιόντα καὶ ἐξιόντα are only the formal characteristics of earth, air and the rest (μορφαί 52d6).

The ontology and cosmology of *Phil.* and *Tim.* undoubtedly shed light on each other, but— at least concerning the primitive chaos—I think it is a mistake to expect a one-to-one correspondence between the features of each. Archer-Hind's is a good attempt, but for one thing it is obvious from *Phil.* 23c9 and 24a2 that no difference is intended between πέρας and τὸ πέρας ἔχον. Further, the temporal aspect of creation (whether literal or mythical) colours Timaeus's account and forbids exact equivalence. If the element of πέρας is represented in *Tim.* by the infiltrating μιμήματα of the Forms, we have the problem that the marks of πέρας include measure, proportion and number. These are expressly excluded from the primitive chaos, to be added by God (53a–b), whether we think of it in P.'s terms as existing 'before the genesis of the world' or simply as an imaginative description of the cosmos minus its rational organization. For this reason Ross's idea that the εἰσιόντα καὶ ἐξιόντα are geometrical figures is impossible (*Arist. Metaph.* vol. I, 168).

What is the cause of the pre-cosmic motion?

Here is another question on which scholars are, and will remain, divided.[1] Timaeus's reason for the motion in the Receptacle of Becoming is purely mechanical (52e): 'Because it was filled with powers[2] neither alike nor evenly balanced, no part of it was in equipoise, but it was everywhere swung and shaken unevenly by them, and by its movement shook them in turn.'[3] Plutarch however attributed it to soul, because 'soul is the cause and origin of motion' (*De an. procr.* 1015e): the soul of the world was at first irrational, and until it was endowed with reason by the Demiurge its motions were disorderly. So Cornford (*PC* 205): 'Since no bodily changes can occur without the self-motions of soul, the other factor present in this chaos must be irrational motions of the World-Soul, considered in abstraction from the ordered revolutions of Reason.' But even a myth (if this is all mythical) should be internally consistent, and in Timaeus's story the disorderly motion was there before the world-soul was created.[4] Plutarch, like others, had in mind the *Phaedrus* (246c) and *Laws* (896a–b), where Plato says that soul is the cause of all motion whatsoever in the present world-order. With due deference[5] I would suggest that one should not try to press into literal agreement the words of three very different dialogues, in two of which at least Plato's fertile imagination is conveying his message through different pictures. Only in the *Timaeus* does he speak of a period before the cosmos was organized, and in both the others he is describing the nature of our world as if it had existed everlastingly. In the *Laws* (896e–97b) the motions of soul are all properly psychical, including wish, reflection, care, counsel, judgement true and false, and emotions. It may exhibit reason or folly, guiding things well or badly. In either case, with these and similar motions as primary, it 'takes over'

[1] To name only two examples, the view taken here agrees with Crombie's (*EPD* II, 227f.) rather than Skemp's (*TMPLD* 76, 111 n. 1).

[2] I.e. qualities, hot, cold, wet, dry etc. (vol. I, 325 n. 1). At 50a3 P. uses the old word 'opposites'.

[3] 57e στάσιν μὲν ἐν ὁμαλότητι κίνησιν δὲ εἰς ἀνωμαλότητα ἀεὶ τιθῶμεν seems to clinch the point. Cf. Spoerri, *R. de Philol.* 1957, 213.

[4] The above was written before J. S. Clegg's article 'Plato's Vision of Chaos' appeared in *CQ* 1976, but having read it, I see no reason to modify what I have said.

[5] Tarán has presented a detailed case for the contrary view in § v of his article in Anton and Kustas, *Essays.*

the secondary motions of bodies and brings about their growth and decay, temperature, textures, colours and flavours. But (his favourite plea) only a rational soul could produce the regularity of the celestial motions (cf. 967b). No great ingenuity is needed to translate this into the terms of a genetic account in which, just as there was a pre-cosmic period, so there was a period before physical motions were due to the wish or judgement of any soul, good or bad. Certainly the *Timaeus* contains no hint of any other doctrine. They just 'came about of necessity' (47e), whose 'nature it is to cause motion' (47e–48a).[1] Finally, that motion in the Receptacle should be due to inanimate necessity accords with the scheme of Democritus on which Plato based it (p. 274 below).

Plato's point is the same throughout, that our world is the product of reason and design, not chance. Here his target may be Empedocles, or possibly, as elsewhere, Democritus. It was Empedocles who attributed motion specifically to overbalancing.[2] But whereas Empedocles was describing the origin of day and night, which he attributed, like all phenomena of the present world, to chance,[3] for Plato no soulless process could produce such uniform recurrence. The sum of things must remain in turmoil and disorder until Mind intervenes to rescue it.

Necessity

We have seen that the Demiurge is not omnipotent, but must create his cosmos in a given material which cannot achieve the changeless perfection of the intelligible world.[4] This resistance to perfect ordering Plato ascribes to necessity (*anankē*), which he presents under two aspects, positive and negative. To take an example, God wished us to have sight so that by observation of the heavens we might be led to philosophy (46e–47c). That is its primary cause. But it was only possible through

---

[1] It is ἡ τοῦ ἀλόγου καὶ εἰκῇ δύναμις καὶ τὸ ὅπῃ ἔτυχεν of *Phil.* 28d.

[2] Emped. DK A 30 (vol. II, 186) τὸν ἀθροισμὸν ἐμβρίσαντος τοῦ πυρός. According to Aristotle (fr. 208 Rose, DK 68 A 37) Democritus used the more general term ὁμοιότης. Cf. *Tim.* 52e μήθ' ὁμοίων.

[3] Frr. 59.2, 103, 104 etc. See vol. II, 161–4. So of course did most of the earlier cosmologists except Diogenes of Apollonia (vol. II, 369), and above all Democritus.

[4] A point made in the *Pol.* (269d): 'What we call universe (οὐρανός) and cosmos has received many blessed gifts from its progenitor, but nevertheless it partakes of body, and so cannot remain for ever without change.' Cf. the γενέσεως ἀναγκαία οὐσία at 283d.

the eyes—parts of a body made from the four elements—and the behaviour of light-rays. This physical mechanism of sight Plato describes in detail (45 b–46 c), calling it and other organs and processes 'co-causes',[1] secondary and subordinate. The error of most earlier philosophers had been to regard them as primary. In the *Phaedo* he had castigated this neglect of final causation as 'absurd' and 'sheer laziness', and dismissed as waste of time the attempt to explain the world by 'airs, ethers, waters and other strange things'.[2] Now his attitude has changed. Under the title 'what happens of necessity', material conditions and processes occupy at least a third of the whole work, and detailed explanations are given of the ingenuity with which the Demiurge adapted them to good ends. The cosmos is 'the combined work of Reason and Necessity', Reason prevailing over Necessity, in Reason's way, by 'wise persuasion' (47 e–48 a). The personification of Necessity as 'persuadable' is apt. In Greek poetry, including the philosophical poets Parmenides and Empedocles, the goddess Ananke, true to her name, was inexorable, and 'of unconquerable might'.[3] Plato corrects this in its own mythical terms: for the most part she has yielded to the arguments of Reason.

But not entirely. In turning to the negative aspect of necessity, Plato drops the personification, which has served its allusive purpose. Necessity, 'the errant cause' (48 a 7), is of the kind which 'destitute of reason produces chance results, without order'. They are not designed, but just happen (46 e, 47 e). Matter has its necessary characteristics ('powers') indifferent to reason or values. Fire may warm a house and cook a meal, or destroy the house and kill its owners. The latter we call an accident, and it explains the close association of necessity and chance in the Greek mind.[4] The necessity is internal to one thing, as heat to fire, the chance lies in the proximity of two things, burning agent and combustible material. Although fire *must* burn, the craftsman by his

---

[1] συναίτια 46 c, the word used in *Pol.* of τέχναι subordinate to a major one, as the manufacture of spindles and shuttles subserves the art of weaving (281 c–e).

[2] *Pho.* 98 b–99 c; vol. IV, 330, 350. Contrast esp. *Tim.* 68 e–69 a, translated on p. 252 above.

[3] Aesch. *PV* 105, Eur. *Alc.* 965. For Ananke in Greek literature and Parmenides see vol. II, 34–7; in Empedocles, *ib.* 163.

[4] For necessity and chance as practically identical for the Greeks, see vol. II, 414 f., and cf. Cornford, *PC* 165 ff. In Plato it is best illustrated by the atheists' account of the fortuitous origin of the world at *Laws* 889 a–c, esp. in the phrase κατὰ τύχην ἐξ ἀνάγκης (c 1).

choice of materials and design can reduce the danger of accidents and direct its activity, so far as possible, to useful ends, thus 'persuading Necessity'. She symbolizes the ultimate intractability of matter, which no craftsman can overcome entirely. The cosmos is a magnificent creation, modelled on the Forms by divine Reason, but being corporeal it cannot *be* the Forms, any more than a block of marble can be— though it may be made to resemble—a human face. Pygmalion is a myth, and even God could only make the world 'as good as possible', 'to the best of his powers'.[1]

The central idea of a material chaos moved by a mindless inner necessity bears a resemblance to the system of Democritus which can hardly be fortuitous.[2] 'Democritus', said Aristotle, 'ignored the final cause and attributed all the operations of nature to necessity.' According to Diogenes Laertius he held that 'All things come about of necessity, for the vortex is the cause of all becoming, and this he calls necessity', and the *Placita* have it that necessity for him consisted in 'the resistance, movement and blows of matter'.[3] For Democritus this was all that was required to produce our world. In Plato's eyes its beauty, goodness and order could never have emerged from such a welter without an intelligent disposer. He therefore speaks of it as the state of things 'before the creation of the cosmos'. Hence his duality of primary and secondary causes, which whatever its difficulties does avoid the intellectual dilemma facing those who try to reconcile an omnipotent and benevolent deity with the manifest imperfections of the world.

[1] This is repeatedly emphasized: 30a3, 37d2, 46c8, 53b5.

[2] Few statements about *Tim.* are uncontroversial. Said Taylor in 1926 (*Comm.* 3): 'I believe I shall be able to show ... that there are no traces anywhere in Plato of a knowledge of Democritus, and that in the *Timaeus* in particular the whole plan of the dialogue makes such references impossible.' Contrast Jowett's editors (*Dialogues* vol. III, 1953, 669 n.): 'Most authorities would now agree that the *Timaeus* is in part directed against Democritus.' This is true, so there is no need to quote individuals. Many refer to the study of Hammer-Jensen in *AGP* 1910, who weakened her case unnecessarily by the unacceptable claim that P. only learned of Democritus's work when *Tim.* was partly written, and changed his mind in the middle. (For some criticism see vol. II, 406 n. 2.) Stenzel in his essays on P. and Democritus tends to exaggerate resemblances between them, but is helpful nevertheless.

[3] Arist. *GA* 789b2, D.L. 9.45, Aët. 1.26.2 (DK 68 A 66 and 1).

The creation of cosmos

Why it was created (29d–30b). This section is the starting-point of Timaeus's narrative. The reason for creation is religious. God is good, and it is not 'lawful' (or permissible, *themis*) for the Best to act otherwise than for the best. Being good, he had no jealousy in his nature (a criticism of current ideas of divine *phthonos*). He wished everything to be as good as possible, and so, finding visible nature in its state of restless and inharmonious motion, reduced it to order, which he deemed better than disorder. Reasoning further that anything in nature would be better with intelligence than without, and cannot have intelligence without soul, he put mind in soul and soul in body.[1] So by God's providence this world was created as a living and intelligent creature, modelled on the intelligible and all-embracing Living Creature itself.

Uniqueness of the cosmos (31a–b). Democritus had argued that since there exists an infinite number of atoms moving at random in an infinite void, it was unreasonable to suppose that the chance collisions which have produced a cosmic system in our part of the void would not have led to the formation of similar systems elsewhere.[2] What is at stake therefore is not only the number of worlds, but the fundamental question of chance or design as the originating principle, and Plato's reply is in terms of purpose: '*In order* that it might resemble . . .' The cosmos must resemble its model in every way possible, the model is unique, therefore the cosmos must be unique. How the uniqueness of a physical world can be ensured is explained later (32c–33a, p. 279 below).

The case for the uniqueness of the model is more complex. Plato has argued in different ways in different dialogues that every form is unique, but the present argument is tailored to the Form in question, namely the Form of Animal, and is perhaps not exactly like any of the arguments for the uniqueness of a Form in general. There are in fact three

---

[1] Where *nous* and *psyche* are distinguished, *psyche* signifies what for P. are the lower parts of the tripartite soul, the life of an animate body with the capacity for sensation, desire and emotions such as anger and fear. Although it would be nonsense to say that God is not alive, I think, as I have said on p. 215, that *in the context of the distinction* God, having no body, has *nous* without *psyche*. It is τὰ κατὰ φύσιν ὁρατά that cannot have one without the other (30b1).

[2] Some at least, he thought, would not repeat the features of our world exactly. For innumerable worlds in Democritus see vol. II, 405, 406 n. 1.

arguments which have sometimes been taken as one and the same,[1] and have generated much comment. They are, besides the present one, the argument about the 'three beds' at *Rep.* 597c and the 'Third Man argument' of the *Parmenides*. I have tried to disentangle these in vol. IV, 552, and will only repeat here the gist of the one which now concerns us, at *Tim.* 31a. It runs as follows.

The Form of a *genus* (in this case Animal) must contain the Forms of all the species subsumed under it. In Plato's terms, they are 'parts' of it.[2] If there were two, each would contain *some only* of the relevant species, and there would have to be a more all-embracing Form containing both of these with the species which each embraces. They would be like the Forms of vertebrates and invertebrates, each containing a large number of species of animal but not all.

The body of the cosmos (31b–34b). The early Ionians had assumed one primary substance in the cosmos, Parmenides two,[3] and Empedocles four, fire, water, earth and air. Plato agrees with Empedocles, but unlike him offers reasons. Like everything generated, the cosmos must have body and be visible and tangible (solid). This demands two bodies, fire (which includes light, 45b) and earth. So much the Demiurge must accept, but now he gets to work himself. Two things cannot be 'well' (*kalōs*) combined without a third to bind them together. This is because the strongest bond is geometrical proportion, which cannot exist between fewer than three constituents. The fourth is added because the cosmos is to be three-dimensional, and whereas for a plane surface (i.e. to link two numbers) one mean proportional suffices, a solid body requires two.[4] We begin to see what Timaeus meant when he said that

---

[1] E.g. by Adam in his note on *Rep.* 597c.

[2] μέρη 31a6. Cf. p. 153 n. 4 above.

[3] In the 'Way of Seeming', of course. In fr. 8.53 the two are light and night, but he seems in some way to have identified night with earth. Aristotle says four times that his two primary substances were fire and earth, Theophr. repeats it, and Alex. Aphrod. adds explicitly that he called the earth darkness. (See vol. II, 58 with n. 2.) These commentators had the complete poem, and even in the surviving frr. (*l.c.*) he calls night 'dense and heavy'. Plato's start from fire and earth may reflect once again his great respect for Parmenides.

[4] P. is speaking in terms of square (or rectangular) and solid *numbers* (Taylor, *Comm.* 97f.). His last statement is not universally true. See Grote, *Pl.* III, 252 n. *a*, Taylor, *Comm.* 97f. and on these mathematical passages in general Cornford, *PC* 45–52 (with his quotations from Heath) and Archer-Hind, *Tim.* 97–9.

his listeners would follow his demonstrations because they were experts, trained in the requisite sciences (53 c). 'Plato is compressing his statement of technical matters to such an extent that only expert readers would fully appreciate his meaning' (Cornford, *PC* 47). Apart from that, his Pythagorizing synthesis of the mathematical and the physical may seem strange today.[1] If a medicine which requires ingredients mixed in the proportion 1:3:7 is made up in the proportion 1:10:100, it will not console us to be told that the latter is a perfect geometrical ratio. It was too much for Aristotle's common sense. 'One might also ask', he protests (*Metaph.* 1092b 26), 'what good things get from numbers by their mixture being in accordance with a number . . . Honey-water is no more wholesome if it is mixed in the proportion of three times three: it would do more good if it were in no particular ratio but well diluted than if it were numerically expressible but strong.' Nor is it obvious why two elements (water and earth, say, to make clay) should need a separate third to 'bind' them. Cornford says nothing of this, and Taylor (*Comm.* 95) treats it as a special condition for earth and fire: they need a mediating element because their own characters are so strongly opposed. This will not do. The condition, laid down at 38b8–c1, is purely general: 'It is impossible for two things to be well combined without a third.' Plato is using the language of mathematics, not of chemistry or any science which takes account of the physical properties of different kinds of body.

The *Politicus* and *Philebus*[2] have accustomed us already to the importance in Plato's eyes of measure, limit and proportion as essentials of goodness (fitness for function). He does not say that two elements by themselves cannot mix: the emphasis is on *kalōs*. The cosmos, though not perfect, is the best and most lasting of all created living things. It cannot therefore have been thrown together haphazard, but was planned as an organism in which the various components are blended

[1] For the Pythagorean derivation of bodies from geometrical solids, and ultimately from numbers, see vol. I, ch. IV(D), esp. pp. 229–73.

[2] Not to mention *Gorg.* 507e–508a, which applied the laws of mathematical proportion to cosmic structure and human conduct alike. The same association of them with values permeates the *Rep.*, but it reaches its climax in *Tim.*, both here and later in the construction of the geometrical particles. 'Of course', says Taylor of the present passage (*Comm.* 98), 'this is not given by Plato as a *demonstration*' that there are exactly four 'roots'. 'It is simply a play of mathematical fancy.' I suspect that for P. it was more than that.

with the most exquisite delicacy and precision. This proportionate blending ensures its wholeness and unity (32d9–33a1), knitting its parts together in bonds of amity[1] indissoluble save by its author. In the *Phaedo* Socrates demanded an explanation of the world which would demonstrate that what binds and holds it together is the power of the good and right.[2] Here where Plato gives the full answer, the binding force is expressed in terms of *analogia*, geometrical proportion. No reader of the *Gorgias* and *Republic* will be surprised.

God, then, made the elements 'as far as possible proportionate to each other, so that as fire is to air, so air is to water, and as air to water, so water is to earth' (32b). This is usually, as by Cornford,[3] referred to their respective quantities, but with the description of pre-cosmic chaos fresh in our mind, some questions must suggest themselves, perhaps unfairly, to the literal-minded. The Receptacle of Becoming itself had a fiery part, a watery part and so on, and it was also said that fire, water, earth and air, though 'without proportion and measure', already possessed traces of their distinct natures. Those four, and no others, were *data*. The Demiurge only imposed order on them through number (53a–b). We are about to learn also that, for excellent reasons, he incorporated *all* the fire, water, air and earth into the cosmos. How then, first, was it in his choice to have, for mathematical reasons, four elements rather than two, and how, secondly, if he used all there was of them, making no selection, was it open to him to relate the quantities in geometrical proportion?[4] One might also wonder, thirdly, since the creation is cast in narrative form, whether we are to imagine that he has already organized each element, whose quantities are here decided, into

---

[1] P. uses φιλία (32c2), the Empedoclean term for the unifying force. Empedocles, a westerner like Timaeus, also introduced the idea of definite numerical (if not geometrical) proportions, at least for organic compounds, though in a less advanced way and without P.'s teleological implications. See vol. II, 211–16.

[2] 99c. English cannot reproduce the affinity of the Greek words in τὸ δέον συνδεῖν.

[3] *PC* 43: 'All that the Demiurge does now is to fix their quantities in a certain definite proportion.' Cf. 51: 'Plato has not indicated what are the quantities between which his geometrical proportion holds . . . It may be conjectured that the quantities in question are the total volumes of the four primary bodies.'

[4] I might mention R. J. Mortley's alternative suggestion, in a note in *Hermes* 1969, that 'The numbers that could be used in a proportion such as this would not represent relations between elements, but cosmic forces existing as Forms and affecting the sensible world in the same way as other Forms.' I do not feel able to comment on this, but some may find it helpful.

minute corpuscles of geometrical shape.[1] This is not mentioned until much later, after the description of pre-cosmic chaos, where it certainly appears as his first step in the introduction of order. It seems possible that the randomness of Timaeus's discourse and his repeated fresh starts, which he puts down to human weakness, besides conveying an air of spontaneity, have the ulterior purpose of making these discrepancies less noticeable. Certainly they do not seem to have occurred to previous commentators, who have followed Plato's order of exposition rather than what he himself says is the right one. If so, one can only sympathize and agree with his reasonable plea that on a subject like the origin of the whole universe one should not expect an account in every way self-consistent and precise (28c).

To make the body of the cosmos, the Demiurge used the whole quantity of all four primary bodies (32c), thus ensuring first its unity (there was nothing left over from which a second might arise, 33a1) and secondly its permanence. This has already been attributed to the 'amity' brought about by the proportions between its elements, but Timaeus now adds that the only causes of sickness and senility in living creatures are attacks from heat, cold and other 'powers' of extraneous bodies.[2] Immune from these dangers, although material it can last as long as God wills; and since God himself says later (41b) that only an evil being would wish to dissolve what is good and well constructed, it will last for ever; but its preservation lies in God's hands, not in its own nature, for nothing bodily can be intrinsically indestructible. Certain other consequences flow from its completeness, and differentiate it from any of the living creatures which it contains. It needs none of their organs or limbs, for there is nothing outside for it to see or hear, nothing to eat or excrete—it is entirely self-sufficient—or grasp with hands, nowhere to go on legs and feet. So he made it a sphere, the best of all shapes, which contains all others[3] as the cosmos

---

[1] If, as Cornford seems to have thought (*PC* 223), the mention of numbers (πλῆθη) in the summing-up of God's work on the corpuscles at 56c, refers to the relative quantities of each kind, this would seem to be so.

[2] In case we should fail to take the animation of the cosmos seriously, this is an effective reminder of its affinity to the rest of animal life. 'Analogy' would be too weak a word.

[3] It is the only figure in which all five regular polyhedra can be inscribed, and these underlie the structure of the primary bodies (pp. 282ff. below). Inscription is mentioned at 55a. This is given by Proclus as the more probable of two explanations (*In Tim.* 2, 71 and 76 Diehl).

contains all living creatures, and gave it as sole motion revolution about its axis, the only motion which a body can perform within its own limits.

In this, and especially its psychological connotations, Plato owes something to Alcmaeon, but more to Parmenides, especially in the denial of some features of Pythagorean thought with which they were both familiar. He takes over the One Being of Parmenides, 'complete', 'like the mass of a well-rounded sphere', 'equal every way from the centre' (fr. 8.42–4), with nothing outside it.[1] Even when he allows for Becoming by restoring motion and heterogeneity, he continues to respect Parmenides's next dictum, that it 'keeps evenly within its limits' (*v.* 49). Nor can Empedocles have been far from his thoughts, who describing the sum of things in the reign of Love wrote (fr. 29): 'No twin branches spring from its back, there are no feet nor nimble knees, but it was a sphere and in all directions equal to itself.' He even contributed the conception of a great Mind pervading the whole cosmos (fr. 134). Cosmogonical theory is not Plato's *métier*, and he does not hesitate to hark back to earlier leaders in the field if he can adapt them to his demonstration that the world is born of design not chance; for on that, as he makes even clearer in *Laws* 10, depended the existence of objective criteria for human behaviour. He regrets therefore the view common to the Milesians and Democritus that the cosmos is surrounded by a mass of bodily substance out of which it had arisen and into which it would some time disintegrate; for that was linked to the conception of it as a product of mindless physical forces alone.

Construction of the primary bodies (53c–57d)

So far Timaeus has described the body of the cosmos in fairly general terms, apologizing at the same time for not treating first of the soul, which was created first. The heavenly bodies, on the other hand, are

---

[1] For Alcmaeon see vol. I, 354; for Parm. vol. II, 47f. Plato even recalls his language. Cf. *Tim.* 33b4–6 σφαιροειδές, ἐκ μέσου πάντη πρὸς τὰς τελευτὰς ἴσον ἀπέχον ὁμοιότατόν τε αὐτὸ ἑαυτῷ σχημάτων with Parm. fr. 8.42–4 (which he quotes verbatim at *Soph.* 244e):

τετελεσμένον ἐστί
πάντοθεν εὐκύκλου σφαίρης ἐναλίγκιον ὄγκῳ,
μεσσόθεν ἰσοπαλὲς πάντη.

Mortley has drawn attention to the meaning of ὁμοιότατον and its connexion with Parm. in an article on Plato's choice of the sphere in *REG* 1969.

displaced from the account of the world's body and brought in after its soul in explanation of time, which depends on their revolutions (37 d ff., pp. 299 below). His order has indeed something of a casual air,[1] and just as he described the creation of cosmos before the pre-existing chaos, so he defers the structure of the elements of which the body of the cosmos consists until after the account of its soul, of time, the heavenly bodies, and even the creation and destiny of man. It arises, naturally enough, out of the description of the pre-cosmic chaos, in which 'traces' of the elements tossed about 'without proportion or measure' (p. 269 above). To reduce them to order, the Demiurge 'fashioned them by shapes and numbers'. We have already examined their previous state, and since they are the constituents of the world's body (31 b–32 c) their formation may best be taken here.

The geometrical basis of matter. If the world is the work of reason, rationality (displayed in measure and proportion) must be detectable in the ultimate and most elemental forms of which it is built up; and these, he has warned us (48 b–c), are not simply the earth, water, air and fire of Empedocles. Those are more complex than syllables, and to find the actual 'letters' of the universe one must probe deeper. The atoms of Democritus were of all kinds of irregular shapes and sizes, which suited his general view of the world as a product of undesigned coincidence. With an infinite number of irregularly shaped atoms colliding and becoming entangled in infinite space, it was inevitable (*anankē*) that somewhere, some time, they should build up into a world like ours. Implacably opposed to such a view of its origin, Plato was bound to carry his opposition into the ultimate structure of matter and show that even an atomic theory need not be atheistic. Against the Democritean jumble he set the Pythagorean idea that number and measure entered into everything. The Pythagoreans, said Aristotle (*Metaph.* 985 b 32, and similarly in many places), since the nature of everything else seemed to be entirely assimilated to numbers, and numbers to be primary throughout the natural world, supposed the elements of numbers

---

[1] I hope this will not be taken to imply anything but the most artful composition on Plato's part, appearing not least in the impression he conveys of an expert giving an impromptu talk to friends rather than a formal lecture.

to be the elements of all that exists, and the whole universe to be a *harmonia* and a number.[1]

The details, as Timaeus says, are for mathematicians. The general scheme is based on the five regular solids or polyhedra: tetrahedron (three-sided pyramid), cube, octahedron, icosahedron, dodecahedron.[2] Their regularity, and doubtless also the fact that they can all be inscribed in a sphere,[3] gave them, at least in Pythagorizing eyes, a peculiar perfection and beauty. Plato calls the first four 'the four surpassingly beautiful kinds of body' (53e7). The pyramid, as the smallest, most mobile and sharpest of these regular solids,[4] is assigned to fire, the icosahedron to air, octahedron to water and cube to earth. These shapes and sizes are connected with their physical qualities, the destructive power of fire, the stability of earth and so on. So far the theory may be called particulate if not atomic, for the solids are bodies too small to be seen, though visible in the aggregate (56b–c). As bodies they cannot be geometrically perfect, but have been made by God as accurate as the nature of Necessity would allow. They are not strictly atomic (indivisible), for they can be actually divided (not merely analysed by the philosopher) into yet more elementary forms. One of the objects of Plato's theory of matter was to allow for the mutual transformation of certain elements. Both he and Aristotle rejected the theory of Empedocles who, under the direct influence of Parmenides, had denied the change of any of the four 'roots' into another: all phenomena were accounted for by their mingling and separation (fr. 21.13–14; vol. II, 148). In combination they retained their individual identities, though these might be imperceptible.

[1] Some scholars who deny that P. had Democritus in mind point as evidence to the fact that their theories are quite unlike in this respect, that P.'s atoms are geometrically constructed— as if any reference of P. to Democritus could be other than polemical.

[2] Owing to the fame of *Tim.*, the five regular polyhedra on which P. based his atomism became known as 'the Platonic figures', but he was certainly not responsible for their recognition, and the evidence that their connexion with the four elements and the cosmos as a whole was already a feature of Pythagoreanism is strong. It is fully discussed in vol. I, 266–73 (together with the date of the construction of the five regular polyhedra), and cf. the quotation from von Weizsäcker on pp. 225 f.

[3] Perhaps also the beauty of crystals. Ridgeway observed in *CR* 1896 that quartz crystals are pyramidal, iron pyrites cubical, and garnets dodecahedral. (There is a reference to inscription at 55a3, and it is probably also implied at 33b3–4.)

[4] A glance at scale models (of which I have a set in front of me as I write) or drawings brings home the relative smallness and sharpness of the pyramid, assuming (as one must) that all the figures have sides of the same length. (The drawings on p. 76 of Lee's translation are helpful but not to scale.)

Transformation of the primary bodies. To combat this view, Plato carries his analysis a stage further. The surfaces of three of the four polyhedra which he has assigned to the elements are triangular, and the square itself can be divided into two triangles.[1] For reasons not immediately obvious,[2] Plato does not take the equilateral triangular faces of the first three as ultimate, but divides them, as well as the square, into two right-angled triangles, scalene and isosceles respectively. These he posits as truly elementary, all other triangles being derived from them (53c–d). Since, then, the particles of three of the elements have identical surfaces, it is possible that, if they should be broken up, the surfaces will re-combine in different ways to form any other of the three regular solids so constructed. When for instance heat dries up a puddle of water, the small, sharp, mobile pyramids of fire have pierced and split up the water-particles, and the twenty faces of each have regrouped themselves as two octahedra (air-particles) and one pyramid (fire) (56d). Earth alone is not subject to this process of transformation, for its surfaces can only be reduced to isosceles triangles which cannot combine with the others. If earth is split by fire, its parts simply drift about until they meet others of their kind and can re-combine as earth.[3]

[1] Cornford (*PC* 211) said it is 'by no means obvious' why Plato does not take the square as one of his elementary plane figures. Others have also seen it as a problem. Surely the reason is that it is not an elementary plane figure. It can be analysed into triangles, but with triangles the analysis of a rectilinear plane figure must stop, as Plato noted (53c7).

[2] Cornford (212) attributed it simply to the choice of the regular solids. We cannot here pursue Plato's geometrical scheme through all its details, but mention must be made of Popper's brilliantly argued thesis that the special importance of these triangles lies in their incorporation of the irrational square roots of 2 and 3. Plato's main contribution to science, in Popper's view, sprang from his realization of the problem of the irrational (on which he lays such stress at *Laws* 820a–b), and his consequent substitution of a geometrical view of the world for the arithmetical outlook of early Pythagoreanism. See Popper's *C. and R.* 75–93 (repr. in Brown's *Meno* 143–73) and *O.S.* I, ch. 6 n. 9, 248–53. The thesis is summarized by Toulmin and Goodfield, *A. of M.* 80 (in both original and Penguin eds.: pp. 75–82 of this book give a lucid summary and appraisal of Plato's theory of the composition of matter). I was puzzled at first that Plato should introduce irrationals at the very heart of his scheme, when he has been so emphatic (here and in *Pol.* and *Phil.*) that the work of Mind was always characterized by measure and ratio (μέτρον and λόγος). But Popper's explanation of how, precisely because of this innovation, 'the existence of irrationals was no longer incomprehensible or "irrational"' has removed this difficulty. See *O.S.* I at top of p. 251.

[3] 56d. Aristotle, who believed that transmutation occurred between all four simple bodies, complained that in making earth an exception P. was exalting his own mathematical theory at the expense of observed facts (*Cael.* 306a5–9). This criticism has been repeated in modern times. Cornford (*PC* 216) thought it 'simply a consequence of the decision to assign the cube to earth', and Eva Sachs surmised that P. would have been happy if someone could have supplied a fourth

Fifth figure and fifth body. Of the five regular solids there remains the dodecahedron, whose surfaces are pentagonal. It was used by the Demiurge not for any of the simple bodies, but for the whole cosmos. This, as we know, was spherical, and commentators since Plutarch have aptly compared *Phaedo* 110b, where the spherical earth, seen from above, is said to resemble 'a ball (σφαῖρα) made of twelve pieces of leather' and to be 'picked out in various colours'.[1] This raises an interesting question in the history of ideas, namely the emergence of the notion of a fifth element, Aristotle's *aither*. Each of the other polyhedra is associated with a simple body. The dodecahedron is not. The heavenly bodies are said to be largely made of fire, while *aither* is simply the clearest form of air (40a and 58d). But the symmetry of a scheme in which all five figures corresponded to different simple bodies must have made a strong appeal,[2] and it is about this time, or a little earlier among the Pythagoreans, that the first hints of a fifth body appear. It is unambiguously present in the *Epinomis* (981c), and even in the *Cratylus aither* is expressly separated from air (410b).[3] Other evidence has been examined in vol. 1,[4] where it is suggested that the

regular body made up of triangles similar to those of the others. Others agree (Solmsen, *ASPW* 52 n. 124; G. E. R. Lloyd, *EGSc* 77), but Proclus (*ap.* Simpl. *Cael.* 643) defended P.: earth is never seen to change, though earthy compounds do when water or fire leaves them. In modern times Cherniss (*ACPA* 150) and Taylor incline to the empirical explanation: 'It is because of the irreducibility of earth that Timaeus needs *two* primary triangles' (*Comm.* 369). Cornford himself said earlier (213) that P. wished to explain transmutation, and '*for this physical purpose* all he needs is triangles which can be reformed into solids of a different pattern' (my italics). Though there can be no proof either way, this seems to me the more likely order of P.'s thought. If so, the words ὡς δοκοῦμεν and ὡς φαίνεται at 49b8 and c7 are to be taken seriously, which is reasonable. Cf. ἐφαίνετο, φανταζόμενα at 54b.

[1] ποικίλη, χρώμασι διειλημμένη. Burnet saw in these words the explanation of διαζωγράφων at 55c6, denying that it could refer to the signs of the Zodiac as usually supposed (*EGP* 294 n. 5). Cf. Cornford, *PC* 219: 'not only the twelve signs of the Zodiac, but all the other constellations'. On the sphere constructed out of twelve pentagons see further vol. 1, 268f.

[2] This is how Simplicius saw it (*Phys.* 1165,18): 'Why then does [Aristotle] calls the heavens a fifth body? Perhaps because Plato himself describes the substance of the heavens as different from the four sublunary bodies. After all, he assigned the dodecahedron to the heavens, and each of the four elements he described by a different figure.'

[3] In *Pho.* too, ὁ δὲ ἡμῖν ἀήρ, ἐκείνοις τὸν αἰθέρα occurs in the cosmological myth (111b1). The fifth body was ready and waiting, so to speak, in common belief and in myth, to be adopted into natural philosophy.

[4] Pp. 267–73. To the modern references given there may be added P. Moraux, art. 'Quinta essentia' in *RE* xlvii. Halbb. 1171–1263 with *Nachtrag* 1430–2; Harward, *Epin.* 125f.; Tarán, *AJP* 1962, 315f. (reviewing Novotný's *Epin.*), where the statement that Xenocrates 'located [*aither*] outside the sphere of fire' must be an inference from the order in which X. mentioned the five bodies. (In his *Academica* of 1975, p. 40, Tarán concludes from Simpl.'s testimony that

conception of a fifth element evolved gradually out of earlier cosmological presuppositions.

The remoter principles: geometry and physics. At 53d Plato hints that even his analysis of physical bodies into triangular surfaces is not complete: 'The principles more remote than these are known to God and such men as he favours.' Being concerned with the physical world, the *Timaeus* has no need to go further back than the surface, which as the boundary of the third dimension, depth, makes sensible body possible.[1] But the Pythagorean flavour of the whole makes it easy to guess what these remoter principles are. First come Limit and the Unlimited, equated with numerical oddness and evenness. They produce the unit, first imposition of Limit on the Unlimited, from which spring numbers. From numbers are derived geometrical figures by equating the unit with the point, two with the line, three with the simplest rectilinear plane figure. From plane figures come solids, and from solids sensible bodies.[2] Aristotle never tired of castigating the Pythagoreans for this derivation of the physical—visible, tangible—from mathematical abstractions. 'They assumed the principles of mathematics to be the principles of everything.' 'They suppose units to possess magnitude.' 'When they construct physical bodies out of number—things that have lightness and weight out of elements which have neither—they appear to be talking about some other universe and other bodies, not those that we perceive.'[3] In *De caelo* (299a1–300a19) he levels similar criticisms at the *Timaeus* itself.

As so often, opinions differ. Thus Cornford, *PC* 285: 'We must reject the view that Plato has reduced the bodily to mere empty space figured in the geometrical patterns which the Demiurge is now going to introduce'; but Burnet, *T. to P.* 344: 'Plato undoubtedly means to say that the corporeal can be completely reduced to extension geometrically limited.' The question is obviously bound up with the nature of the 'Receptacle of becoming', that 'dim and difficult' something which

Xenocrates 'identified the ether with the dodecahedron', i.e. believed that this was Plato's intention.)

[1] 53c, A. T. Nicol in *CQ* 1936, 125.

[2] Alex. Polyhist. *ap.* D.L. 8.24. For a full account of the Pythagorean theory, with authorities, see vol. I, 238ff. For Plato, Stenzel's discussion in *Z. und G.* 70–5, 'Das Ende der Teilung des Räumlichen im math.-physikalischem Atom', is relevant.

[3] For reff. and further quotations see vol. I, 229, 232, 234, 235.

neither senses nor mind can properly comprehend. The difficulty for Plato results, I suggest, from an attempt to reconcile two different types of cosmology: the Pythagorean, predominantly mathematical and paying the minimum of attention to physical substances or properties like fire or earth, hot, cold, wet and dry; and the Ionian or materialistic, culminating in the Heraclitean conception[1] of the world as a never-ending flux of change. Hot is continuously becoming cold and cold hot, water is drying up and turning to air, air condensing and becoming water, with never an instant's pause. We know what a tremendous impression this world-view made on Plato, but if absolute instability represented the true nature of the universe it could never be the object of scientific knowledge, for it could never be brought under general laws. When he wrote the *Phaedo* and *Republic* he appears to have accepted its consequences and abandoned hope of a science of the physical world. Knowledge is not of 'what becomes' but only of 'what is', the immutable world of Forms after the pattern of which the temporal world is formed. The *Theaetetus* probed the question further on the epistemological side, and now comes the *Timaeus*. Here he maintains as strongly as ever the distinction between 'what becomes' and 'what is', with its parallel epistemological distinction between belief and knowledge, and warns that any account of the physical world can be no more than probable; yet such an account has now become for him supremely worth giving, and he takes great pains to work it out in detail. His conclusion seems to be this. If Heraclitean flux or Democritean atomism has the last word, the world in which we live must be abandoned to chance. No other cause brought it into being or sustains it now. But this belief is both erroneous and (as he will argue at length in the *Laws*) morally disastrous. True, the creative Reason had to work on a given and to some extent recalcitrant material. Perfection is found only among the Forms, not in space at all; but even in this world Reason has overcome Necessity to a large extent, and the study of mathematics and above all of astronomy will quickly satisfy a thoughtful man that the primary impulse behind the creation of the universe is rational.[2]

---

[1] The conception of contemporary Heracliteans rather than of Heraclitus himself (p. 80 above).

[2] Cf. *Phil.* 28e, p. 214 above. The part of astronomy in the argument from design, which becomes one of the main themes of *Tim.*, was echoed in remarkably similar terms by Newton in

If, then, the cosmogony of the *Timaeus*, represented by Plato as the conquest of (Democritean) Necessity by Reason, may be crudely described as an attempt to impose the Pythagorean mathematical scheme of reality on the Heraclitean flux of becoming, we need not be surprised to find it less than wholly successful; and this is suggested by his hesitant and fumbling description of the Receptacle. It is better to appreciate his state of mind, and the philosophical situation which gave rise to it, than to try to force into clarity and consistency what was for its author himself 'dim, difficult, hardly to be believed'. We have seen that the rest of his description forbids us to think of it as mere empty space. It might be so if one could abstract from it the 'motions' and 'powers' which continually surge about in it, but not only does it never exist without them: it is inconceivable without them, for they are in a sense qualities of itself. True, it must be imagined as *per se* qualitiless, like the oil which must be odourless to serve as a base for perfumes. Yet, says Plato (51 b), one should not speak of fire, water and the rest being in it, so much as of the incandescent part of it, the liquefied part of it and so on. Even before the ordering by figures and numbers began, it contained inchoate forms or 'traces' of the four simple bodies. Physical matter, solid substance, did exist, but 'without proportion or measure', in fact as an unlimited awaiting the stamp of Limit.

The most probable conclusion is that the particles created by God's conversion of chaos into cosmos were genuine *corpuscula* in the shape, so far as Necessity allowed (56c5), of one or another of the regular polyhedra, which gave each of the popular elements its character as fiery, wet and so on. Unlike the traditional Pythagoreans, Plato could distinguish when he liked between mathematical figures and their approximations in material objects, models or drawings (*Rep.* 510c, *Phil.* 62a–b). Yet in this his most Pythagorean dialogue[1] he does not always observe the distinction. In more than one place he seems to

the *Principia* (ref. in Cornford, *Princ. Sap.* 21): 'It is not to be conceived that mere mechanical causes could give birth to so many regular motions . . . This most beautiful system of the sun, planets and comets, could only proceed from the counsel and dominion of an intelligent and powerful Being.' 'Counsel and dominion' almost translates *Tim.* 48a2 νοῦ . . . ἄρχοντος τῷ πείθειν.

[1] Though like everyone else I cannot accept Taylor's thesis that in *Tim.* P. does not give his own doctrine but only a historical account of fifth-cent. Pythagoreanism, the fact that so experienced a scholar could hold such a belief says much about the character of the dialogue.

assume that once a geometrical construction has reached the third dimension, one has immediately a perceptible body. 'Every kind of body has depth, depth includes surface, and every rectilinear surface is composed of triangles' (53c). Conversely at 53e–54a 'the four most beautiful bodies' appears to refer to the figures, including the triangles of which they are constructed. In the *Laws* he is even more definite (894a): 'What is the condition for the coming-to-be of all things? It occurs when a starting-point is extended to the second dimension and thence to the next, and having achieved three dimensions becomes perceptible to whatever has senses.'[1] This is pure Pythagorean doctrine as described by Alexander Polyhistor (p. 285 above) and criticized by Aristotle. It bears on a problem that has never been solved.[2] How can triangles float about by themselves, as the triangles of a disintegrated earth-particle are said to do, until they can re-unite with their own kind? Martin's conception of them as 'thin plates of corporeal matter' enclosing empty space (*Tim.* II, 241 f.) has found little favour.[3] The reverse is surely correct, that the triangles are surfaces bounding solid corpuscles, and so giving geometrical form to previously formless matter. This does not solve the problem of the drifting triangles. I would dare to say that it did not present itself to the Pythagorizing Plato of the *Timaeus*.

Particles vary in size. At 54d–55c the faces of three of the polyhedra are said to be further divided into six triangles instead of two, and those of the cube into four. No plausible explanation of this was forthcoming until Cornford (*PC* 234f.) connected it with the statement at 57c–d that the triangles exist in various grades of size, and that this explains the varieties to be found in each element. As Timaeus goes on to say,

[1] For the language (αὔξη = dimension) cf. *Rep.* 528b, which gives the cube as an example of the three-dimensional, and *Epin.* 990d τοὺς τρὶς ηὐξημένους [ἀριθμοὺς] καὶ τῇ στερεᾷ φύσει ὁμοίους. At 990a στερεόν is equated with ἁπτόν.

[2] Unless it is a solution to say with Cornford (*PC* 229f.) that it 'cannot be taken literally' (though later, on p. 274, he himself offers a tentative solution), or with others (Prantl, Luria, Friedländer) that P. had not bothered to think out the consequences because he was only playing or joking ('*Spielerei*', '*halb-scherzend*', 'playfully'; see Luria in next note and Friedländer, *Pl.* I, 256). The triangles recur at 81b–c in a passage describing the physiology of youth, old age and death (p. 314 below).

[3] It was also the view of Eva Sachs, and in ancient times of Proclus, Simplicius and Philoponus. Aristotle, as we have seen, interpreted them as ideal or purely mathematical surfaces, as in modern times have Zeller, Archer-Hind and E. Frank. See Luria, *Infinitesimaltheorie* 151 with n. 120.

elemental fire may appear as burning flame, glowing embers or light, bright without heat, air as the limpid *aither* or as fog, and water as liquid or equally as solid but fusible metals or ice.[1] He does not say explicitly that there was a strict mathematical relationship between the different sizes of triangle, but it was made clear at the outset and emphatically repeated in the summing-up at 69b that the Demiurge introduced proportion and conmensurability (συμμετρία) everywhere and in every way possible. Moreover if there were no such relation between the triangles forming varieties within the same element, one would have the curious situation that there could be no transformation between them, as there is between one element and another, though they resemble each other much more closely. Cornford's solution, whether correct or not, was beautifully simple, namely that in Plato's mind the triangles constituting the larger-grade solids are exact multiples of the smaller. Then the triangle of the smallest grade will be the highest common measure of the others, and will be the *stoicheion* proper, the irreducible element out of which they are built up. In mentioning six, Plato would be describing figures of an intermediate size to make it more immediately clear that the triangles can be put together in various ways (*PC* 234). The simplicity and rationality of this solution are attractive.[2]

[1] 45b, 58c–d. True to P.'s premises, melting and solidification of metals are not to be thought of as changes of 'water' into 'earth' (in Vlastos's phrase, fusible metals are 'liquids with very high freezing-points', *P.'s Universe* 84), nor even as mixtures of the two, though mixtures of the elements do occur, e.g. the warming property of wine is attributed to an admixture of fire with water (60a). They are due solely to differences of size between the octahedral water-particles, making them more or less mobile. Heat, the agent of melting, works by the action of fire-pyramids causing the preliminary disintegration of the icosahedra. (Details at 58e–59a; cf. 61a5–6.)

[2] Crombie finds it convincing (*EPD* II, 220), but Popper has rejected it, and it has been criticized in detail by Pohle in *Isis* 1971. (See however Vlastos, *P.'s Universe* 69. V. gives an excellent summary of the whole theory.) One argument of Cornford's I do find surprising, namely that if the simpler procedure were followed the particles would have increased so rapidly in size that they might cross the threshold of visibility. (See his diagrams on pp. 237 and 238.) One assumes that the ultimate elements of body are microscopic, and we can surely imagine them as small as we like. Popper himself is inclined (with due caution) to attribute the subdivisions of the square and polygonal surfaces into 4 and 6 triangles, like the original division into 2 and 4, to Plato's interest in irrationals, and more specifically to the use of $\sqrt{2}$ and $\sqrt{3}$ to achieve an approximate squaring of the circle. See *OS* I, 250–3.

Perpetual motion and warfare of the primary bodies (57c 1–6, d7–58a3).
By the axiom that like attracts like,[1] the main masses of fire, air, water
and earth collect in different regions, and would become wholly separate, and the universe completely static, were it not for the continual
warfare between their particles whereby they are broken up and re-
united in other shapes. Thus when sharp fire-pyramids attack an
octahedral particle of air, and it re-forms into two fire-particles itself, it
leaves the predominantly airy region to join the main mass of fire.[2] It is
a condition of motion that heterogeneous bodies should be in contact
in the same area, one to cause the motion and the other to be moved;
but given the fact of transmutation, even if they began like this, what is
to prevent them from becoming separated and quiescent in the end? The
cosmos, with all its movement and change, is to last for ever, and to
ensure this Plato reminds us that his cosmology denies another main
tenet of the earlier atomism, namely that the atoms had infinite space to
move in. Plato's cosmos is a revolving, finite sphere, 'the shape which
contains all other shapes' (33b). From this envelope the particles
cannot escape, but are turned back on themselves, jostling and thrusting
at each other unceasingly. The smaller penetrate the interstices between
the larger[3] and proceed to break them up, while elsewhere the larger
force the smaller to combine, and so the process of transmutation and
consequent local displacement swings this way and that for ever.[4] One
must remember the continuity between the pre-cosmic motions and
the same motions as ordered by the Demiurge when he took them
over. (See 53a–b.) Much of the description of the earlier state at 52d–
53a still applies, for the Demiurge turned to his own use, so far as

[1] Especially prominent in the atomism of Democritus (vol. II, 429f.), whom beyond reasonable
doubt P. has in mind. What he is describing now is the work of Necessity.

[2] Plato does not expressly state that the four main masses form concentric spheres, with fire
on the outside and earth at the centre, but it would be taken for granted. (See Cornford, *PC* 246.)
It must, one would think, form the background for the explanation of the popular terms 'heavy'
and 'light' at 62c–63e.

[3] P.'s denial of empty space within the cosmos at 58a7 is not therefore true in the strictest
sense: regular polyhedra in contact must always leave interstices. But none is *surrounded* by
emptiness; contact is never lost. At 80c the denial of void is repeated and motion accounted for
by the 'thrusting round' of the particles by each other. See further vol. II, 147 with n. 1.

[4] One must assume that beyond the cosmic sphere there is not even space. This was the belief,
not only of the pioneer Parmenides, but also of Aristotle, who added in astonishingly Platonic
language and in line with the *Phaedrus* myth, that whatever is there is ageless and changeless,
beyond place and time, in fact divine. See *Cael.* 279a11–33.

compatible with his purpose, the co-causes already furnished 'of necessity'.

Motion demands both mover and moved. In the course of making this point, Plato says (57e): 'It is difficult, or rather impossible, for there to be something that will be moved without something that will move it, and vice versa. In the absence of these there is no motion, and they cannot be on the same level.'[1] Here he lays down a law that for movement to take place there must be two things, one which moves and another which is moved. Nothing single and homogeneous can move itself. But was it not Aristotle who, for reasons connected with his distinction between potentiality and actuality, argued, against Plato, that a self-mover was impossible? Plato's new principle, if applied universally, would seem to contradict his definition of soul or life in *Phaedrus* and *Laws* as the first cause of motion by virtue of moving itself. All physical, mechanical motion, as of one billiard ball when struck by another, can be traced back to soul (in that case the player's intention), for only what lives can initiate its own motion and transmit motion to others. Here however the contradiction is only apparent, because the only motion in question *is* physical, mechanical motion. We are taken no further than the secondary causes whose author is Necessity, learning 'in what manner it is of the nature of the errant cause to produce motion' (48a). Plato does not go right back to the first cause of cosmic motion,[2] the gift to the whole universe of a self-moving and rational soul. When dealing with secondary causes he borrows freely from the earlier mechanistic cosmologies,[3] e.g. the collisions and blows

---

[1] ὁμαλά, not quite 'homogeneous' (Cornford, as if ὅμοια) nor 'in equilibrium' (Lee, as if ἰσόρροπα) but 'evenly matched'. The comparison is of power or strength, as in a tug-of-war. When motion and change occur, two parties have fought and one is beaten; it is a weaker fighting with a stronger (56e4 and 57a6). In the cosmos the stronger may be either a sharp and agile particle attacking a blunter, clumsier one, or a large force of bigger particles surrounding and crushing a few smaller ones. Homogeneity is of course ruled out *a fortiori*. The homogeneous and therefore motionless One of Parmenides still haunts cosmology. Cf. vol. II, 36.

[2] I say '*cosmic* motion' because I have argued, against others, that the irregular pre-cosmic motion in the Receptacle, caused ultimately, as motion in the cosmos is proximately, by heterogeneity and disequilibrium, has nothing to do with soul, either rational or irrational.

[3] At 58b4 he uses for 'compression' the word πίλησις, a technical term of felting which according to our sources had been used metaphorically by cosmologists from the early Milesians onwards. See vol. I, 90 (Anaximander), 121 with n. 3 and 133 (Anaximenes), 391 (Xenophanes), and for other Presocratics the word-index to DK.

of the atoms which Democritus had identified with Necessity (vol. II, 404). His criticism is directed not so much against their description of the processes of nature as against their confusion of processes with causes. What escaped them was the ascendance of Reason over Necessity.

Five worlds? At 31a–b (pp. 275f. above) Plato gave his reasons for believing the cosmos to be unique. Immediately after the description of the five regular polyhedra at 55c, he reiterates this and dismisses with contempt the idea of an indefinite number of worlds, but adds that someone might reasonably ask whether there were five. Nobody knows why. The conjecture of ancient commentators (for whom see Cornford, *PC* 220f.) that *kosmoi* refers to regions within our world seems ruled out by the context, which, however, strongly suggests a connexion with the five figures just enumerated. Yet even if the dodecahedron stands for a fifth element, there seems no reason to conjure up five worlds each composed of one element. Miss Nicol suggested to Cornford (see *PC* 221 n. 3) that since only four of the five solids are assigned to elements, leaving out the dodecahedron, five worlds could be obtained by including it and omitting each of the others in turn. Some member of the Academy might have suggested that there was nothing to prevent the Demiurge from creating elsewhere a cosmos in the shape of a pyramid, cube, octahedron or icosahedron (though Plato would have been quick with his objections). But would these shapes be supposed to retain their connexion with a bodily element? At this point one finds oneself beginning to wonder what it would be like to live in a world with an outer shell composed of earth, and it is time to dismiss the gentleman with his unspecified 'other considerations',[1] as Plato does without argument.

The soul of the cosmos (34b–36d)

In taking the world's body before its soul, we have given in to Timaeus's 'random' way of talking, for he is careful to point out that as senior partner the soul must have been created first.[2] The heavenly bodies, on

---

[1] Possibly Speusippus (H. A. S. Tarrant in *Phron.* 1974, 132, 137).

[2] Since the Greek word πρεσβύτερος is ambiguous between seniority of age and of rank or status, he goes out of his way to emphasize that soul is senior to body in both respects, καὶ γενέσει καὶ ἀρετῇ προτέρα (34c4).

the other hand, as already noted, are brought in after the soul in explanation of time.

As a created god, divine but embodied, the cosmos combines all psychic functions, self-locomotion (of the most perfect kind attainable), true *doxai* about the sensible, and full knowledge of the intelligible (37b–c). The account of its making is highly symbolic, and the key to understanding it lies in the old doctrine, so prominent in Empedocles (vol. II, 228f., 256) and still upheld here, that like is known by like.[1] The Demiurge proceeds in two stages.

(i) Preparation of ingredients. This is described in the most difficult and debated sentence in the whole dialogue (35a1–b3). However one reads and interprets it, further thought suggests unsolved difficulties. On the most probable interpretation, there are three entities, Being (οὐσία), Sameness (ἡ ταὐτοῦ φύσις) and Difference, each of which has two forms, 'the indivisible and ever constant' and 'the divisible which comes to be in bodies';[2] that is, the Form[3] and its copies in the sensible world. From the indivisible and divisible forms of each of the three, the Demiurge made an intermediate blend, then mixed the three intermediates to make the stuff of the cosmic soul.[4] The significance of this will emerge later.

---

[1] γινώσκεσθαι τὸ ὅμοιον τῷ ὁμοίῳ, as Aristotle phrases it with express reference to soul in *Tim.* (*De an.* 404b17).

[2] P. speaks here again of οὐσία γιγνομένη (35a2–3), but as in the *Philebus*, without promoting γιγνόμενα to the full status of unchanging ὄντα. See p. 233 n. 3 above.

[3] It must be so, and Cornford wrote (*PC* 64): 'The being of a Form is indivisible. A Form may indeed be complex and hence definable. But it is not . . . "put together" out of parts that can be actually separated or dissolved.' But P. does speak of the species contained in a generic Form as its parts (μέρη 31a6), and though the Form Man is thus a part of the Form Animal it has none the less a separate existence. As I have suggested before (pp. 150, 270), the magnificent conception of these divine, eternal realities, though never abandoned, does not always stand up well to the development of analytical methods in P.'s later period. (Form and particulars are again compared at 51e–52a.)

[4] So Proclus (whom Cornford followed, also Ross, *De an.*, p. 177, Jowett's edd. vol. III, 669 n. 3) and before Proclus Aristides Quint. *De mus.* bk 3 (p. 125 Winnington-Ingram), which I quote for its clarity: 'The divine Plato, too, says in the *Timaeus* that the Maker of the soul took a mean between the indivisible and the divisible Being and combined with the intermediate form of Being the intermediates between the divisible and indivisible forms of Sameness and Difference, making a blend of the three.' Taylor's explanation, which resembles Martin's, is simpler (*Comm.* 109; cf. Martin I, 346). He regarded Same and Different as equivalent to the two forms of Being, indivisible and divisible, and wrote: 'He first takes two ingredients *A* and *B*, and by blending them produces an intermediate *C*. He then makes a single uniform whole by blending *A*, *B*, and *C*.' On the other hand (*a*) In spite of Friedländer, *Pl.* III, 366, it is strange to speak of three ingredients in a mixture (τρία 35a6, ἐκ τριῶν b1) if the so-called third is a blend of the first two; (*b*) Later, at 37a, P. speaks in the plainest terms of 'the Same, the Different, and Being, these three'; (*c*) Being, Same and Difference figure prominently in *Soph.* as separate Forms (p. 151 above).

(ii) Construction (35b–36d). This is steeped in Pythagoreanism,[1] and its use of material imagery to represent the invisible *psyche* is not a little fantastic. The compound is treated as a sort of dough, to be kneaded, cut into strips and bent into circles. (Later, at 41 d, there is a reference to the 'mixing-bowl' in which it was blended) As in body, so in soul the primary requirement is proportion and harmony. The Demiurge therefore cuts off[2] seven portions of the soul-fabric—now, it would seem, imagined as a long strip—in proportion, beginning with 1 (outside the number-series according to the Pythagoreans) and proceeding in a series of square and cube numbers thus: 1, 2, 3, *4, 8*, 9, 27. He then inserts harmonic and arithmetical means between each term in the original series.[3] Squares and cubes suggest the three dimensions of body, which the soul in its cognitive aspect must recognize, but the numbers have also a musical significance. The harmonic mean was so called because it expresses the numerical ratios between what were for the Greeks the principal musical intervals.[4] The word *harmonia* combined so closely the ideas of numerical ratio and musical 'concord' (συμφωνία) that they could not be separated in Plato's mind. But the arbitrary range of the scale presented by his table—four octaves and a major sixth, much greater than any employed in the music of the day (Taylor 140)—led Cornford to suppose that the compass was solely due to Plato's wish to end the series with 27, the cube of 3, and 'this decision has nothing whatever to do with the theory of musical harmony' (*PC* 67). This goes too far. The soul is about to be distributed to move the stars and planets in their respective orbits, and as the *Republic* has it (530d): 'As our eyes are made for astronomy, so are our

---

[1] For the Pythagorean origin of P.'s amalgam of mathematics and music, and its cosmological significance, see vol. 1, ch. IV D, esp. pp. 206–14, 220–4.

[2] The procedure would be easier to visualize if he simply, as Taylor says, 'marked off' divisions as on a ruler or tape-measure. But P.'s word is ἀποτέμνων (36a2).

[3] The full scheme is set out by Cornford on p. 71 of *PC*. For the complex mathematical details of the passage see also Taylor, who quotes extensively from the ancient commentators, and Rivaud, *Tim.* 43–52. A. Ahlvers, *Z. und K. bei P.*, offered a new interpretation of the division of the world-soul, on which see Trevaskis, *CR* 1957, 31.

[4] The harmonic mean was defined by Archytas in his *De musica* (fr. 2 DK): it occurs when 'by whatever part of itself the first exceeds the second, the second exceeds the third by the same part of the third'. An example is 6, 8 and 12: $(12-8)/12 = (8-6)/6$. For further explanation and the connexion with musical notes see Taylor, *Comm.* 95 or Freeman, *Pre-Soc. Phils.* 115. Aristotle, though no Pythagorean, still defined συμφωνία as 'a commensurate numerical ratio in the sphere of high and low' (*An. Post.* 90a19).

ears for the movements of harmony, and these sciences are sisters, as the Pythagoreans say and we agree.' The 'harmony of the spheres', poetically described in the *Republic*,[1] was in Plato's mind even if not expressly mentioned.

The essential is that the world's soul, being good and wise and destined to be everlasting, displays inner harmony,[2] or due proportion and measure, which we know to be a prerequisite of goodness. It 'partakes of reason and harmony' together (36e). Having now used up the whole of his mixture (36b 5–6), the Demiurge continues his self-imposed task by cutting it into two strips, laying one across the other in the form of a chi (X), and bends them round to form two circles, an inner and an outer, lying obliquely to one another. The immediate references are now astronomical, but for Plato the soul of the cosmos retains its twin powers throughout, the merely motive and the rational. The circles, being each a portion of rational soul, are in rotatory motion,[3] which they will impart to the heavenly bodies when these are created.

The astronomical details are highly condensed, indeed elliptical, and Timaeus himself says later that to understand them properly would require a visible model (40c–d).[4] In outline the scheme is this.[5] There is

[1] *Rep.* 617b. For the harmony of the spheres see vol. I, 295.

[2] Perhaps a reminder is advisable that this is not the doctrine of soul as a harmony which was refuted in *Phaedo*, namely as supervenient on a harmonious disposition of the bodily parts. Soul is a harmony of *its own* parts. See vol. I, 307–17. Its priority to body could hardly be more strongly expressed than by saying, as here, that it was created before it.

[3] The strange conception of a soul performing locomotion has to be accepted. Soul is not simply the power of a living creature to move itself: soul *itself* moves, and *imparts* its own motion to the complex of soul and body. 'Only what moves itself is the source and cause of motion in others' (*Phdr.* 245 c, cf. *Laws* 896a). This evidently did not for P. carry any connotations of existence on a physical plane, like the air-soul of earlier thought, which he consistently denies. Sometimes, as at *Laws* 896e–97a, he speaks as if it initiated only the higher 'movements' of thought and emotion, but it includes every stage of animation. Aristotle criticized P. here for making the soul behave like an extended body (*De an.* 406b 26ff.). Skemp (*TMPLD* 83) tries to defend P., but has to admit on the next page that certain features 'do indicate localisations of ψυχή'. They are especially apparent in the distribution of soul through the human body (69d ff.). See also pp. 315–17 below.

[4] For the use of armillary spheres by P. and his contemporaries see Cornford, *PC* 74–6. It could explain the talk of rings rather than spheres. In any case, P. did not of course hold Aristotle's theory of the heavenly bodies as carried round in spheres of a tenuous matter (*aither*).

[5] For details and difficulties see Taylor and Cornford (72 ff.), and Dicks's criticisms of Cornford in his *Early Gk Astron.* 124 ff. An excellent account of P.'s astronomy, of the state of the science in contemporary Greece, and the effect of his metaphysical approach on its future development, is now available in Vlastos's *P.'s Universe*, ch. 2.

(1) a rotation of the outermost sphere, the motion of the fixed stars from east to west in the plane of the celestial equator, accomplished in 24 hours. It is called the motion of the Same, presumably (in this connexion) because it is also imparted, as the same motion, to the whole contents of the universe.[1] It is thus the 'dominating' motion (has κράτος, 36c7). (2) Contrasted with this is a revolution from west to east, and in the plane of the ecliptic, that of the Different, conceived both as a whole and as split into seven separate circles, those of sun, moon and the five known planets. All these bodies will share one general motion (besides, of course, its reverse, the motion of the Same), but some will also perform their own, differing from one another in speed and even direction. These proper motions counteract the common revolution of all, and explain why the planets do not all complete their orbits in the same time, the sun in one year, Jupiter in about 12 and so on. Sun, Venus and Mercury revolve only with the combination of the movements of the Same and the Different; Moon's extra motion is in the same direction as that of the Different but much faster; Jupiter, Mars and Saturn have extra motions in the opposite direction to the common revolution of the Different, which slow down, in varying degrees, their apparent motion round the circle of the Different. The whole scheme depends of course on the assumption, common to Plato, Eudoxus and Aristotle, that the apparently irregular paths of sun, moon and planets are reducible to a combination of perfectly circular revolutions.[2]

---

[1] Including perhaps the earth, but that is a notorious crux. See p. 306 n. 1 below.

[2] In a well known passage (*Cael.* p. 488 Heiberg) Simplicius says that P. himself set astronomers the problem of determining what uniform and regular (circular) motions must be presupposed to account for the apparent movements of the planets, and that Eudoxus was the first to solve it. (This appears, probably correctly, as a fr. of Eudemus in Spengel's collection, no. 96; but Grote, *Pl.* I, 124f., doubted the attribution to P., which he thought an embroidery by Sosigenes. For a full discussion of authorities and the historicity of the story, see now Vlastos, *P.'s Universe*, App. § L.) The faith in the perfection and circularity of the celestial motions haunted astronomy for the next 2,000 years. Even the young Kepler, with his deeply theological outlook, wrote that 'we chose the spherical surface precisely because it was the most perfect quantity'. His *Mysterium Cosmographicum*, published in 1597 when he was 26, is a defence of the Copernican system, and its second chapter (quoted in full by Heisenberg, *PCN* 78–83) both mentions and echoes the *Timaeus*. This persistent exaltation of circularity has been commonly regarded simply as, scientifically speaking, a nuisance, but has been put in a more favourable light by Dicks (*CR* 1969, 362, mostly repeated in his *Early Gk Astron.* 176): 'Particularly in astronomy, the Greeks wisely placed more reliance on their advanced mathematical techniques than on observational data obtained by necessarily crude instruments . . . Granted that circular motion for the celestial

Plato next mentions, in one sentence (36d), the contriving of the body of the cosmos within its soul, which envelopes it from centre to circumference, before passing to the cognitive aspect of the soul. 'Revolving on itself, it made a divine beginning of unending *and rational* life' (36e). Its reason is to be imparted to the stellar gods and man, and life to the lower creatures as well, though in less pure forms as it encounters grosser and more perishable forms of body. We now learn the effect of its construction and motions on its cognitive powers, in a passage (33a–c) which expounds what to us is perhaps the strangest feature of Plato's psychology, the association of circular motion with thought.[1]

Since then it is blended of the nature of the Same and the Different and of Being, these three, and is portioned out and bound together according to due proportions and turns round upon itself, therefore whenever it comes into contact with either something that has a dispersed existence or something that is undivided, being moved throughout itself it tells what something is identical with and from what it differs, and in what particular respect, in what way, how and when it happens that things are severally related to and acted upon by each other with reference both to what becomes and to what is always the same. When true and consistent discourse, alike about what is different and what is the same, is carried on without utterance or sound[2] within the self-moved, and the circle of the Different, running true, communicates it to its soul,[3] there arise firm and true judgements and beliefs; but when it concerns the intelligible, and the circle of the Same on its even course[4] declares it, the result must be intellectual apprehension and knowledge.

Besides exemplifying the 'like-known-by-like' principle, this passage brings into new company the logical distinctions established in the

bodies *did* become accepted philosophical doctrine, yet this was in the first place a wholly legitimate inference from the results of observation, since the stars *are* seen to move in circular orbits across the sky, and sun and moon *do* appear to go round the earth in circles. What is commonly overlooked is the mathematical utility of the concept of circular motion; reduce your observed periodic movements to circles and combinations of circles, and at once you make them amenable to calculation and predictable as to both spatial position and time.' Cf. Taylor, *Comm.* 102 (on 33b7).

[1] Here it is more or less assumed, but a demonstration is attempted in the *Laws* 897dff. It goes back to Alcmaeon, for a comparison with whom see vol. 1, 351–7.

[2] Cf. the definition of thought in *Soph.* (263e) as 'dialogue taking place in the soul with itself, without utterance' (and similarly *Tht.* 189e).

[3] I.e. the soul of the self-moved regarded as the whole cosmos, the ὁρατὸν ζῷον.

[4] I take ὀρθὸς ἰών and εὔτροχος ὤν at b7 and c2 to be only literary variants. Cf. the hindrances to true judgements of identity and difference experienced by the newly-incarnated soul, before its circles have settled into their proper courses (44a, p. 310 below).

Sophist.[1] These had been introduced to refute the primitive, but at the time troublesome reasoning of Parmenides that one can say nothing about anything except that it *is*, and what follows directly from that (its unity, continuity, changelessness). Plato showed that this limitation depended on confining the verb to one sense only, whereas in normal usage it had at least two: 'exists' and 'is identical with'. Similarly 'is not' might signify either 'does not exist' or 'is different from'. In the light of this advance he named Being (or Existence), Sameness and Difference as the three universal categories. (See pp. 151-4 above.) One other point made in these meticulously drafted sentences is that the mind of the physical universe apprehends both what is and what becomes, the intelligible and the sensible, objects of knowledge and objects of belief. As elsewhere, a leading motif of the *Timaeus* is Plato's dualistic ontology and epistemology, expounded and emphasized at 27d–28a and 51b–52a. The mind's faculty is one of discrimination.[2] Whatever it encounters, it can say not only that it exists, but that it is identical with *this*, and different from *that other*. More precisely, it is capable of determining the relations (*a*) between one particular and another and (*b*) between a particular and a Form.[3] We now see what was meant by making it a mixture of the indivisible and the divisible-by-bodies forms of its three ingredients (35a). It is still the *psyche* of the *Phaedo* (79c–d), 'akin to' the eternal realities yet not itself one of them. It is 'between the worlds of being and becoming, at once intelligible and generated, indivisible and divisible, simple and in another way compound'.[4] So constituted, it can apprehend both the intelligible and

[1] The relevance of *Soph.* is controversial. Cornford (*PC* 61) asserted it emphatically, but it has been denied by Owen (*SPM* 327f.) and queried by Manasse (*Bücher über P.* II, 83). Cornford perhaps went too far in saying that without *Soph.* the *Tim.* passage would be 'simply unintelligible'. It may be, as Crombie wrote (though such a generalization cannot be compelling) 'unusual for P. to write in one dialogue words that can only be understood by the aid of a *specific passage* in another' (*EPD* II, 262); but that the two are unconnected I cannot believe. Shorey was as emphatic as Cornford: 'It is impossible to explain the world-soul as Rivaud does without mentioning the *Sophist*, and it is idle to affirm . . . that the Same and Other of the *Timaeus* have nothing to do with the Same and Other of the *Sophist*' (*CP* 1928, 344f.). In *Tht.* (185a–e) it is noted that judgements of existence, identity and difference belong to the mind, not the senses.

[2] In Greek κριτική. Cf. Aristotle's description of sensation as δύναμις σύμφυτος κριτική at *An. Post.* 99b35, and Crantor *ap.* Plut. *An. procr.* 1012f.: the special function of the soul is τὸ κρίνειν τά τε νοητὰ καὶ τὰ αἰσθητά.

[3] κατὰ τὰ γιγνόμενά τε πρὸς ἕκαστον ἕκαστα . . . καὶ πρὸς τὰ κατὰ ταὐτὰ ἔχοντα ἀεί (37b2).

[4] Proclus, *Tim.* II, 117 Diehl, quoted by Cornford, *PC* 63. Cf. Plotinus, *Enn.* IV.2.1, μεριστὴ μὲν οὐ πρώτως ὥσπερ τὰ σώματα, μεριστὴ μὴν γινομένη ἐν τοῖς σώμασιν.

(through the medium of bodily sense-organs) the sensible, and can be dispersed in the bodies of all living creatures without losing its unity.

Time and creation

Nothing generated can be strictly eternal, that is, not simply everlasting but exempt from all distinctions of before and after, was and will be; but by introducing *measure* into the previous disorderly motions, the Demiurge effected 'a moving image of eternity, that which we call time (*chronos*), moving according to number', thus bringing the cosmos even closer to its pattern (37c–d). This distinction between the everlasting and the timeless may fairly be credited to Plato himself.[1] Parmenides (whom Plato practically quotes) had said of his One Being: 'It *was* not, nor *will* be, since it now *is*, all together' (fr. 8.5–6). But for him there was nothing else, and about nothing nothing can be said. Plato rejects this outright denial of the world of *doxa*, of temporal change or motion, and gives it a place, albeit a subordinate one, in a wider ontology. To this world *chronos* belongs. We translate it 'time', but the prevailing Greek conception of time was not ours. *Chronos* was cyclical and repetitive,[2] and identified with the celestial motions which produce the recurrence of day and night, months and years, which Plato calls 'parts of time' (37e3); so for time to be, the stars and planets had to be created and placed in their orbits. The sun, made brilliant for the purpose, demonstrates in its daily revolution the motion of the Same, and by its own independent motion marks the year, as the moon the month. The circlings of the other planets are less easily observed, 'indeed men scarcely know that their wanderings *are* time' (39d1), though there is in fact a 'perfect' or great year, marked by the time taken by sun, moon and the rest to return to the same relative positions.[3] Before the creation of these bodies, therefore, there could not be *chronos*, and to bring *chronos* into being was the motive for their creation.[4] We speak of

---

[1] See however the full discussion of time and eternity in P. by W. von Leyden, *PQ* 1964. Owen has discussed the passage in *Monist* 1966, 332–6.

[2] Cf. vol. I, 428–30 (where it is noted that the atomists were an exception) and Cornford, *PC* 103f.; also Arist. *Phys.* 223b23–33. This does not of course mean that Greeks generally held the Pythagorean doctrine of an exact repetition of history. The distinction between that and the cycle of celestial motions is clarified by Eudemus as 'numerical' and 'formal' identity respectively (fr. 88 Wehrli).

[3] On the Great Year in Plato and elsewhere see vol. I, 282 and 458, and Cornford 116f.

[4] ἵνα γεννηθῇ χρόνος 38c4.

making clocks to measure time. For Plato *chronos* itself is a clock, not mere succession or duration but a standard by which duration can be measured. In Aristotle's concise definition (*Phys.* 219b1) it is 'the number of motion in respect of before and after'. In the *Timaeus* the purpose of the sun is to provide 'a conspicuous measure ... in order that suitable living creatures [i.e. men] might possess number'.

Suddenly we are reminded that the whole cosmogony is being seen in its relation to man, who through its providential arrangement can not only tell day from night and observe the seasons, but learn the art of counting.[1] Through mathematics he can reach an understanding of the cosmic *harmonia*, and in this lies the secret of philosophy, by which the human soul itself is attuned to the divine music and achieves its chief end, 'assimilation to God as far as possible' (*Tht.* 176b; cf. *Tim.* 90c–d). The starting-point is observation of the celestial motions, and the sense of sight is singled out for praise in a characteristic passage (47a–c):

The sight of day and night, months and circling years, equinox and solstice, led to the contrivance of number, and gave us the idea of time and curiosity about universal nature, from which we have derived philosophy, the greatest gift of the gods that ever has or ever will come to mortal men . . . God invented and gave us vision in order that, by observing the circuits of intelligence (νοῦς) in the sky we might use them to the benefit of the revolutions of our own thought (διάνοια) which are akin to them, though disturbed while they are untroubled; and that by learning them thoroughly and being able to calculate them accurately according to their nature we might copy the unerring motions of the god [the cosmos] and give a firm basis to the errant motions in ourselves.

Hearing too, through speech and music, contributes to the appreciation of harmony and helps to combat the discords in our souls. In fundamentals, Plato's philosophy changed little. The *Timaeus* only gives a fuller explanation of how, as we were told in the *Gorgias*, 'heaven and earth and gods and men' are united in society and orderliness, whence the whole universe got its name of *kosmos*, order; and in the *Republic*, 'through association with the divine and orderly the philosopher

---

[1] Cf. *Epin.* 987b–e.

becomes divine and orderly as far as that is possible for a human being'.[1]

It is surprising how many have taken the statement '*Chronos* came into being together with the universe' (36b6) as conclusive proof that Plato's story of the creation is metaphorical. 'No sane man', said Taylor, 'could be meant to be understood literally as maintaining at once that time and the world began together, and also that there was a state of things . . . *before* there was any world.'[2] Space and becoming, Plato says (52dff.), existed 'even before the heavens came into being', and the contents of space, still untouched by the hand of God, were tossed hither and thither at random, in irregular and unbalanced movement without reason or measure. Without the heavenly bodies in their orbits, there cannot be *chronos*, but there can be what we must surely call time, that is, duration, a succession of before and after. 'Before and after', as Aristotle said (*Phys.* 223a28), 'belong to motion, but *chronos* is these *in so far as they are numerable.*' It provides the regular and periodic units of motion by which duration can be measured. Space and time are not correlative to Plato. Space, the Receptacle of Becoming, was always there as the matrix on which the Demiurge set the stamp of order, but time is a part of the divine creation itself, a feature of *kosmos*. No one has put it better than Plutarch (*Qu. Pl.* 1007c): 'So Plato said that time came into being with the world (οὐρανός), but motion even before the world's birth. There was then no time, for neither was there arrangement, measure or mark of division, only an indefinite motion, as it were the unformed, unwrought matter (ὕλη) of time.'[3]

---

[1] *Gorg.* 508a (vol. IV, 300f.), *Rep.* 500c–d. I make no apology for repeatedly drawing attention to this key passage (vol. I, 210, vol. IV, 500, 524f., and p. 246 above).

[2] *Comm.* 69. Cf. 67: 'That he did not mean to say that there was ever a time when the world did not exist is plain from the express words of 38b6 χρόνος μετ' οὐρανοῦ γέγονεν.' My point here was made by Hackforth (*CQ* 1959, 21f.), who refers to Skemp, *TMPLD* 77. But what Skemp says is: 'It may not be a literal description of what happened in the past, but it is a description of the actual process of the world in which we live', which sounds rather like the 'logical analysis' that he has just denied it to be. The removal of this particular argument does not of course settle the question whether the creation is intended mythically or literally; but many have thought that the mythical interpretation needed no other support. So e.g. Gauss, *Handk.* III, 2, 170.

[3] In any case, is the idea of a 'time before time' so inconceivable? Not to a nineteenth-century cosmogonist, C. S. Pierce, who wrote of 'the first stages of the development, *before time existed*'. 'Out of the womb of indeterminacy [the Receptacle as mother?] we must say that there would have come something, by the principle of Firstness, which we may call a flash. Then by the principle of habit there would have been a second flash. *Though time would not yet have been*, this

The question whether Plato believed the creation of the cosmos to have been an actual event, or simply wished to convey allegorically the idea that it depends for its goodness and order on the divine will, is endlessly debated and may be insoluble, though earlier sections of this chapter have hinted at a preference. Belief in a creation does not of course commit one to obviously symbolic details[1] like the mixing of Being, Same and Other in a bowl. On the other hand antipathy to the mythical interpretation could be in part an unjustifiable reaction from the unacceptable way in which the denial of a 'time before time' has been used by so many to prop it up. One can at least say something of the history of the debate and explain the alternatives further.[2]

The argument starts among Plato's immediate followers. Aristotle, who believed that everything generated must some time perish, took the creation literally, and criticized Plato for saying in the *Timaeus* that the world has been generated but will last for ever.[3] Elsewhere he says that Plato is the only philosopher to maintain that time had a beginning: 'for he says that it came into being together with the world, and that the world was generated' (*Phys.* 251 b 17). He also mentions the alternative view (*Cael.* 279 b 33–280 a 2):

The self-defence attempted by some of those who hold that it is indestructible but generated, is untrue. They claim that what they say about the generation of the world is analogous to the diagrams drawn by mathematicians: their exposition does not mean that the world ever was generated, but is for

---

second flash was in some sense after the first, because resulting from it.' (Quoted by Gallie in *Pierce and Pragmatism* 118 f., italics mine.)

[1] As Hackforth remarked in an article full of good sense (*CQ* 1959, 20).

[2] The most recent modern champions on either side are Vlastos, 'Creation in the *Timaeus*: is it a Fiction?' (printed with his earlier article, 'The Disorderly Motion in the *Timaeus*', in *SPM*), and Tarán, 'The Creation myth in Plato's *Timaeus*' (in Anton and Kustas, *Essays*), which is expressly directed against the literal interpretation of Vlastos. This with G. E. R. Lloyd's discussion in *P. and A.*, 279 ff., will provide orientation in the modern controversy, though I would also single out Hackforth, 'P.'s Cosmogony', in *CQ* 1959. (H. changed his mind: contrast his 'P.'s Theism', *SPM* 442.) Cornford (like Taylor) took the creation as mythical, while admitting that, since this left the Demiurge without a function, he must be mythical too. He therefore identified him with the reason *in* the world-soul (*PC* 97); but P. was no pantheist, and no γιγνόμενον, not even ὁ κάλλιστος τῶν γεγονότων (29 a 5), can be its own cause. (Cf. 28 a 4–6, as well as the *Philebus*.)

[3] *Cael.* 280 a, 28–32. As Martin points out in an interesting note (*Tim.* II, 195), this criticism is met in advance by *Tim.* 41 a, though Arist. would not agree. The world is by its own nature perishable, but preserved by the will of the supreme being who produced it (p. 279 above). This is what makes it an exception to the rule laid down by P. himself in *Rep.* (546a), γενομένῳ παντὶ φθορά ἐστιν.

instructional purposes, since it makes things easier to understand just as the diagram does for those who see it in process of construction.

For these men Plato's account of creation is no more than an analysis of the world's structure expressed in synthetic or genetic terms. Similarly a geometrician to describe the form of a cube may speak in terms of a square being constructed out of four equal straight lines, and then a cube out of six squares. He does not mean that lines exist prior in time to planes, or planes to solids, but has described the cube *as if* in the making, as a teaching device. On this view 'generated' means only 'derived from an external cause, not self-born nor self-substantial' (Procl. *Tim.* ii, 276 Diehl). It goes back to Speusippus, Xenocrates and Crantor,[1] and seems to have prevailed in the later Academy as among the Neoplatonists.[2]

Modern opponents of the literal interpretation of creation express themselves similarly, e.g. Hackforth:[3] Plato does not mean that either soul or the universe was created in time: 'The meaning in both cases is that they are derivative existents, things whose being depends on something more ultimate.' The Greek words for 'becoming' and 'to become' (γένεσις, γίγνεσθαι) had two senses: (*a*) coming into existence at a particular time, either suddenly or at the end of a process of development or manufacture; (*b*) in process of change, in which

[1] Simpl. *Cael.* 303 Heiberg (and cf. Vlastos, *SPM* 383 n. 1), Procl. *Tim.* 1, 277 Diehl. For Speusippus see fr. 54a and b and p. 31 Lang. Theophrastus was doubtful, but followed Arist. in maintaining that if P. did intend the world's construction only in the geometer's sense, the analogy was a false one. (Fr. 29 Wimmer, cf. Arist. *Cael.* 280a2–10.) (Here the comments of Taylor, *Comm.* 69 n., and Tarán, *l.c.* 390, are a little tendentious.) We have not Xenocrates's words, but the Theophr. passage tells slightly against the suggestion of Vlastos and Hackforth that he and others might have put forward their view not as P.'s meaning but their own. It *was* their own (see e.g. Plut. *An. procr.* 1013a–b), and Aristotle called it a *self*-defence (βοήθεια ἑαυτοῖς), but it is clear that, not wishing to go against Plato, they assumed that it was his too. This is what made Xenocrates, in the current phrase, 'overreact' (ὑπεραπολογούμενος, ps.-Alex. *in Ar. Metaph.* p. 819 Heib.). See Lang, *Speusippus* 30.

[2] Simpl. (*l.c.*) attributes it to 'Xenocrates and the Platonists'. Augustine too (*Civ. Dei* 10.31) says the latter believed that beginning means causal subordination, not an order in time, and it was the view of the middle Platonist Albinus (*Isag.* ch. 14; see Gauss, *Handk.* III, 2, 189). But the opposite view was held by Plutarch, by Albinus's fellow-Platonist Atticus, and according to Proclus (1, 276) by 'many other Platonists' (not therefore '*einzig* Plutarch und Attikos', as Dörrie in *RE*, 2. Reihe, xviii. Halbb. 1523). For Plato himself it may be relevant to notice that in the *Republic* (527a) he ridiculed the geometers' habit of speaking in terms of action, of 'squaring', 'applying', 'adding' and so on, 'as if they were *doing* something'. (I have not seen M. Baltes, *Die Weltentstehung des plat. Tim. nach den ant. Interpreten*, Teil 1, 1976.)

[3] *SPM* 442, i.e. before he changed his mind and wrote his 1959 article.

though something new is always appearing, something old passing away, the process may be thought of as going on perpetually. It does not then need a cause to start the process at one moment and complete it at another, but a *sustaining* cause, to keep it going endlessly.[1] The latter sense had a peculiar importance for Plato, whose talk of 'what is' and 'what becomes' marked a difference of ontological rather than temporal status. It should be observed, however, that Plato is aware of the ambiguity and more than once goes out of his way to remove it in favour of the temporal sense. The 'timeless dependence' explanation is not in Plato: it begins with Xenocrates.[2] Consider the way in which the question is first put and answered: 'Has it always been, having no beginning of its birth, or has it come to be, having started [aorist participle] from some beginning?'[3] And the answer is an emphatic perfect tense: 'It has come into being.' The reason is that it has a physical body, and such things 'can *and do* come into being'.[4] Another relevant instance has been referred to already (p. 292 n. 2): 'senior both in birth and in excellence' at 34c removes any misapprehension that 'senior' (πρεσβύτερος) might refer to status only.

Many more passages could be quoted,[5] but the case for denying literal creation does not rest on a claim that Plato avoids the *language* of temporal sequence.[6] That Plato speaks of God creating the cosmos

[1] In this explanation I have drawn freely on Cornford's phraseology (*PC* 24 f.). He goes on to say that for (*b*), which is his own interpretation of P.'s meaning here, 'both the images "father" and "maker" are inapprorpriate' (though P. uses both!), and we should rather think of 'some ideal or end, constantly exercising a force of attraction, and perhaps of some impulse in the thing itself, constantly aspiring towards the ideal'. He does not add that this is pure Aristotelianism. It accurately describes the action of Aristotle's god ('the Unmoved Mover') on the natural world, which excluded divine providence and so was quite foreign to P.

[2] A man pleasantly characterized by Martin (*Tim.* II, 195) as 'homme de bien, très-studieux, mais de peu de génie'. He was relying on D.L. 4.6, Aelian, *V.H.* 14.9, Plut. *De recta rat. aud.* 18, 47e.

[3] 28b6ff. Cornford translates ἀρχή 'source' at b6 and 'beginning' in the next line. It could mean either, but not both in this one short sentence. In defence of his view, C. (pp. 25 f.) emphasizes ἀεί in the phrase γιγνόμενον ἀεί at 28a, without noting that the authority for ἀεί in our printed texts is slender. See Hackforth, *CQ* 1959, 19 and Whittaker, *Phoenix* 1969, 181–5.

[4] γιγνόμενα καὶ γεννητὰ ἔφανη. Cornford translates 'become and can be generated', but I do not believe that the second epithet is merely pleonastic.

[5] E.g. τόν ποτε ἐσόμενον θεόν at 34a–b, which Proclus (II, 100 Diehl) does his Neoplatonic best to explain away, and the frequent use of aorist and perfect tenses: γενόμενον 28c, 31b, γεγεννημένος 29a, 39e, 31b; the stars ἐγεννήθη 39d. πρό and πρίν are used at 52d4 and 53a7. Cf. also δεύτερον κατὰ γένεσιν of air, 56b.

[6] Yet how easy it would have been to omit the words καὶ γενέσει at 34c! Nor does the phrase γενέσει προτέρα suggest myth. It is rather a technical philosophical expression for distinguishing

by stages out of a pre-existing disorder is certain, but he could still have deliberately chosen to cast an analysis of nature into a synthetic or narrative form. As to that, I can only refer to what has already been said about the intention of the 'probable *mythos* (or *logos*)' (pp. 250–3). In any case, the statement that the cosmos 'has come into being' belongs to the fundamental principles laid down before the 'probable story' is begun. But at this point the reader may be left to study the arguments and counter-arguments of Vlastos and Tarán (and Cherniss to whom both refer frequently) and make up his own mind.

Note. To compare the *Timaeus* with passages in other dialogues may savour of the use of biblical proof-texts, but one or two may be mentioned. If *Pol.* 273b ('The universe was in great disorder before it came to its present order') is disallowed as itself part of a myth, *Laws* 892a speaks of soul in the same temporal terms as *Tim.* 34c: it is older than body because it and its kindred 'came into being before bodily things'.[1] H. J. Easterling in *Eranos* 1967 maintained that *Timaeus* and *Laws* were consistent on the subject of causation, but has been criticized by Tarán (*l.c.* 403). Tarán however argues from the assumption that soul in the *Timaeus* is the ultimate cause of the pre-cosmic disorderly motion of the Receptacle.

Creation of living creatures: nature and fate of the human soul (39e–42c)

We might say that Plato's observation of four main types of living creature led him to assume the existence of as many archetypes. His argument is the reverse. Because the Model contained these types, the cosmos, to be complete, must contain them too. They are the race of gods (that is, principally, the stellar gods), the winged and airborne, aquatic and land animals. Each corresponds to one of the primary bodies. The divine race the Demiurge made mostly[2] of fire, for beauty and conspicuous visibility, and set them in the circuit of the supreme (that is, of the Same) to adorn it all round. (But Plato says 'set in the *intelligence* of the supreme' (40a5), so complete is his assimilation of

---

the senses of πρότερον. With Aristotle indeed it become wholly technical, and the antithesis of γενέσει and λόγῳ (or εἴδει) πρότερον is one of his favourites, e.g. *Metaph.* 1050a4, τὰ τῇ γενέσει ὕστερα τῇ οὐσίᾳ καὶ τῷ εἴδει πρότερα.

[1] See on this pp. 366f. below.

[2] Not entirely. With τὴν πλείστην ἰδέαν cf. *Epin.* 981d.

circular movement to reason.) Besides their common motion in this circuit each star performs a revolution in its own place 'as each thinks the same thoughts about the same things'. Earth is at the centre, and described as our nurse and guardian, maker of night and day, and more surprisingly, 'first and eldest (or most venerable, πρεσβυτάτη) of all gods born within the heaven'.[1] Timaeus then excuses himself from recounting the birth of the gods of ordinary Greek mythology. That is the province of the poets, who claim to be of divine descent and must know their own family history. This may be no more than half ironical —Plato was a staunch upholder of the established cults—but does show that traditional mythology is to play no integral part in the *Timaeus*.

As created beings, the lesser gods cannot be immortal, but will live for ever in dependence on the will of their creator. It is for them to make and nurture the three mortal kinds, which if made by himself would be as gods.[2] Only the divine and immortal part of the human soul will he make himself, then hand it over to them to 'weave mortal and immortal together', creating the mortal parts of the human soul and implanting the whole in bodies. It appears that, though birds, fish and animals will be needed to make the world 'complete', the gods will at first make only men. Women and lower animals are hastily dismissed in a postscript

---

[1] I shall not go into the vexed question of the possible motion of the earth. The different interpretations of the relevant passages in *Tim.* and Aristotle (40b–c, *Cael.* 293b30 and 296a26) have now been fully discussed by Dicks in his *Early Gk Astron.* (132–7), who concludes (with Cherniss) that A. does not attribute to P. a belief in a moving earth. There I must leave the matter, though with an uneasy feeling that this involves an unnatural rendering of A.'s Greek. It may seem odd that in P.'s cosmos the earth—heavy, solid, furthest from the heaven, home of transient beings—should be πρώτη καὶ πρεσβυτάτη. But one must remember the status of Gaia in Greek belief and cult. Sprung direct from Chaos and mother even of Ouranos (Hes. *Th.* 117, 126f.), 'first of prophets' (Aesch. *Eum.* 2) and original mistress of the Delphic shrine, she was indeed our nurse (Aesch. *Theb.* 16) and the first and most venerable of deities, and is about to appear as such in the summary of popular theogony which immediately follows (40e). Plato will not show disrespect to deep-rooted Hellenic beliefs, though concerned, as he showed in *Rep.*, to purge them of certain moral crudities.

[2] One might ask, 'And why not? Why must they be mortal?' Taylor says (*Comm.* 253) 'Death and generation are part of the original good plan of God.' This is wrong. The Model does of course contain eternal Forms of what in the cosmos will be mortal creatures (30c), but Archer-Hind was nearer the mark when he said that becoming and perishing belong to materiality (*Tim.* 140). God can only make from a given unformed material something as like as possible to the non-material Model, and the implanting of souls in bodies is one of the limitations imposed by Necessity (42a). Even the cosmos and the star-gods have bodies and are generated and not immortal, though the Demiurge has power to postpone their dissolution indefinitely.

Creation of living creatures

(90e–92c) after a reminder by Timaeus that he only agreed to take the tale of creation as far as the birth of mankind. According to the 'probable story' (90e8) the rest originated from souls of inferior men degraded by transmigration into lower forms of life: first women, then birds from harmless lightweights who thought it enough to study the heavens with the eyes alone. (Cf. *Rep.* 528e–30c.) Quadrupeds and reptiles come from men whose minds were subordinate to their animal desires, and fish from the stupidest of all, unworthy any longer to breathe the air and thrust into the turbid waters. Suitable bodies are devised by the lesser gods.

I should not like to say just how far this appendix is a mere *jeu d'esprit*. The closest parallel is *Phaedo* 81 d–82 b, but neither there nor elsewhere does Plato repeat this insult to women as originating from morally defective souls (90 c), which is scarcely compatible with their role in the *Republic* (though that has actually been recalled at the beginning, 18 c) or the *Laws*.[1] In the *Phaedo* the only degenerate forms of life mentioned are bees, wasps and ants, donkeys, wolves and birds of prey. Moreover Timaeus's words at 42 a, 'human nature being twofold, the superior part is the one later called "man" (ἀνήρ)', strongly suggest that both were there from the beginning. Perhaps the most likely explanation is that Plato does sometimes make Timaeus speak in his character as a Pythagorean, and for a Pythagorean the female came in the second column of opposites, along with evil, darkness and the unlimited.[2] The rest accords with the *Phaedrus* and *Republic* myths, though without mention of the choice of lives. What one can say is that the ethical implications of the Orphic and Empedoclean doctrine of the cycle of births and the means of escape gave it a strong attraction for Plato.

Making and destiny of human souls (41 d–42 e). The Demiurge now made a new soul-mixture, 'in the same bowl in which he had formerly mixed the soul of the whole', and using the remains of the same ingredients

[1] That women fall short of men in ἀρετή (*Laws* 781 c), and men are superior and stronger (*Rep.* 455 c, 456a), does not alter the fact that women are to be trained for and share all activities and duties with men, including government.

[2] For the table of opposites see vol. 1, 245 f. The above suggestion is made by D. F. Krell in *Arion* 1976, 401. (This does not imply that I agree with everything in his article.)

but less perfectly blended.[1] Then dividing it into separate souls equal in number to the stars, he set each one on a star 'as on chariots' (an echo of *Phdr.* 247b), and lectured them on the laws of the universe and their own destinies. Their implanting in bodies was a matter of necessity (42a3–4), but he himself would ensure a fair and equal start for all. If they yielded to the passions and desires that incarnation would bring, they, not he, would be responsible for the consequences.[2] Whoever followed the circuits of reason (that is, of the Same, 42c4–d2) would return to a blessed life on his appointed star. Once again Plato shows his skill in conveying the same truth in slightly different mythological form. In the *Phaedrus* (248a ff.) only souls which have seen reality from the rim of the circling heaven are born as men, for only human souls can pass beyond sensations to concepts and if philosophically inclined and trained retrieve their ante-natal knowledge and regain their wings. The actual connexion with stars is borrowed, like so much else, from popular tradition. (Cf. Aristoph. *Peace* 832f.)

What Plato is trying to describe in this imagery is an immortal soul (for the Demiurge himself is only concerned with the immortal part) which is yet in some way inferior to the cosmic soul because it is capable of being incarnated in mortal bodies. The bodies animated by the world-soul are those of the everlasting gods, sun, moon, stars and planets. The same contrast is pictured in the *Phaedrus* through the image of the charioteer and winged horses. This presents on the one hand the souls of the gods, a blessed throng who always remain on the outermost rim of the heavens; and on the other, those destined for incarnation in mortal bodies. The difference is symbolized by saying that in the souls of the gods all three constituents—driver and both horses—are alike good, whereas in the others only the driver (representing the philosophic *eros*) is perfectly good. The horses stand for the 'spirited' and appetitive parts in *Republic* and *Timaeus*, and the bad and unruly one finally brings about the fall of the soul to earth and its incarnation in a mortal body. Through this image Plato expresses a

---

[1] Other translators say 'less pure', and Jowett even adds 'diluted'; but with what could a mixture of Being, Same and Other be adulterated? ἀκήρατος (from κηραίνω, not κεράννυμι) means unspoilt or unharmed, and is explained by κατὰ ταὐτὰ ὡσαύτως. They are not mixed in such exact proportions.

[2] 42d3–4; as in *Rep.* (627e).

religious truth (the fall of a soul made in the image of God) which cannot be explained rationally.[1] In the *Timaeus* he tries what is surely a less happy metaphor, of the Creator stirring a sort of pudding in a basin. Human souls are made of the same mixture as the souls of the gods, but its quality has somehow deteriorated. Once the fall has occurred, Plato's dualistic philosophy can account for the evil in human life, as especially in the *Phaedo*, by the contamination of soul by body, but it can never explain how the divine soul came to be incarnated in the first place. The passions are definitely the result of incarnation: they do not precede it. It happens 'of necessity' (42a), not therefore expressly through a fault or flaw in themselves, as in the *Phaedrus* and Empedocles,[2] but through an external force or inevitability. At the same time Ananke does stand for the element of imperfection ('disorder' in Timaean terminology) *in* things, a certain intractability in their nature, so it is probably fair to connect this phrase with the imperfect *harmonia* in the material of souls destined to enter bodies.

The supreme Creator now retired from his work (42e), and the lesser gods turned to their appointed tasks. To make our bodies, they used portions of the four elements in the cosmos, as, for our souls, the Demiurge had used the remains of the cosmic soul-material. As in the *Philebus* (p. 215 above), the kinship between microcosm and macrocosm is emphasized at every turn. These portions are 'borrowed to be repaid' (42e), for mortal bodies are at death resolved back into the main masses of earth, water etc. from which they came. The details of our creation come much later in the narrative, at 69c ff. Taking over the immortal soul, the gods gave it a mortal body as a 'vehicle', and 'built on' another kind of soul, the mortal, containing the irrational feelings and emotions, headed by pleasure, 'the greatest lure of evil'. The complete soul of mortal man is, as in the *Republic*, tripartite, and each part

---

[1] This is elaborated in the section on *Phdr.*, vol. IV, ch. VI (3).

[2] The whole scheme of incarnation and transmigration is reminiscent of Empedocles, and the poetic picture at 43 b–c of the hostility of the several elements to the soul vividly recalls fr. 115, which describes the sufferings of *daimones* exiled from the company of the blessed and born into various forms of mortal life. 'The mighty air pursues them to the sea, the sea spews them out to the dry land, the land to the rays of the flashing sun, who casts them into the whirling air. One receives them from another, and all loathe them alike. Of these am I now one, an exile from the gods and a wanderer.' Behind both P. and Empedocles are the Orphic poems, if what I have said in ch. II of *G. and G.* is right.

is assigned to a specific part of the body.[1] The immortal part, the reason, resides in the head, separated from the others by the narrow channel of the neck, to avoid contamination. (This example may serve to illustrate the teleological character of all Plato's physiological descriptions.) Since the mortal part itself has a nobler and a baser half, another barrier is formed by the midriff. The 'spirited' part[2] inhabits the thorax with the heart as its organ, near enough to the reason to heed its behests, and the appetites are below in the belly, 'tethered like a wild beast, untamed but necessary to be fed if a mortal race were ever to exist'.[3]

The infant soul and the cause of error (43a–44d). When first the gods confined an immortal soul within the flux of a mortal body, it produced a horrific effect, repeated at every birth today (44a7–9). Plato's figure throughout is of something at the mercy of a raging torrent, or the ebb and flow of a tide. It is the Heraclitean world-picture which, as Aristotle said, he never gave up. In this welter of instability the circuits of the soul, though indissoluble save by him who made them, have their original motions twisted and disorganized, just as the human body rushes in all directions in contrast to the uniform revolution of the sky. Lacking the regularity of the turnings of Same and Other in the cosmic soul, newly incarnated souls cannot produce rational thought, but are full of falsehood and folly. 'When they meet something outside to which the name Same or Different applies, they speak of it as the same as this and different from that contrary to the true facts.' Plato's view of children ('harder to handle than any wild animal', *Laws* 808d) is the reverse of the sentimental or Wordsworthian. Our birth is indeed a forgetting, but far from 'trailing clouds of glory' until 'shades of the prison-house' descend with advancing years, the shock of birth and the flood of undigested and unclassified sensations, which play a far greater

[1] This is in conformity with the ostensibly scientific spirit of this part of *Tim.*, and leads to much psycho-physiological detail, e.g. the throbbing of the heart in fear and anger and the provision of lungs to relieve it (70c). Such localization seems to threaten the complete immateriality of the soul, but P. would still distinguish between any form of consciousness and the physical organs through which it is experienced. Cf. *Tht.* 184b–85e: the eye does not see; the *psyche* sees through the eyes as its instruments. Also pp. 314–17 below.

[2] The nature of this (θυμός or τὸ θυμοειδές) has been described in vol. IV, 474.

[3] 70e. 'Necessary pleasures' played a part in *Phil.* (62e, p. 233 above). On the position of sexual desire see Additional Note (i) on next page.

part in childhood than later, overwhelm the mind and drive from it all that it has seen and learned in its unbodied state. With advancing years the cessation of physical growth and development allows it comparative calm in which to recover its regular courses and a rational life becomes possible. With proper training a man may become wholly sound, but if neglected he will return to Hades after a maimed life with his imperfections and folly upon him.[1]

The problem of the possibility of error is a serious philosophical one, and as such Plato discussed it in the *Theaetetus*. Here it takes its place in the great myth of the creation of all things, and appears in symbolic guise. One has to remember that he thought it worth while to put the same problems in both a dialectical and a mythical setting, a feature which sets him apart from every other thinker. But in the *Theaetetus* and even the *Sophist* the question remained unanswered. Perhaps[2] it could only be answered in the light of a vast scheme of theology and cosmology, and man's situation within it, in which he believed none the less profoundly because it could only be expressed in the form of a probable account or *mythos*.

ADDITIONAL NOTES

(i) *The status of* eros

Of the appetites only those for food and drink are mentioned (70 d 7), and Cornford (*PC* 292 f.) suggested that the omission of sexual desire from the lowest part of the soul is deliberate and due to the exalted position of *eros* in Plato's philosophy, especially in the *Symposium*. In the strange amalgam of spiritual and physical which marks the *Timaeus*, the semen is a part of the marrow and through the spinal cord continuous with the brain, lodged in the seat of reason. (So 73 c–d. This was a theory of the Sicilian medical school. Some Hippocratics believed the semen to come from all parts of the body, solid as well as liquid: see Cornford 295 and Hippocr. *De genit.* 3, VII 474 L.) The lower organs only provide a receptacle and outlet for it. Aristotle also held that, as the producer of life, semen both has soul and is soul potentially (*Gen. an.* 755 a 7). I am doubtful of Cornford's point however because (a) sex, at least as a means of reproduction, is excluded because women are not

---

[1] As an example of how P.'s thought underwent development and substantiation rather than radical change, one may compare this with the *Phaedo*'s statement of our loss of knowledge at birth (75 e; vol. IV, 345).

[2] Perhaps, because we do not know what the *Philosopher* would have contained (see pp. 154 f. above); but the *Philosopher* was never written.

supposed to be yet created, and (*b*) when sexual reproduction is introduced, the male sexual organ is described as 'disobedient and imperious, like an animal heedless of reason, bent on mastery through frantic desires' (91 b). 'The *eros* of reproduction' (91 b 4) could easily have been mentioned here as belonging to the lower part of the soul; and in fact the phrase at 70 d, 'the part of the soul desirous of food and drink and everything of which through the body's nature it stands in need', is fairly inclusive. Cf. 69 d: in making mortals the gods included '*eros* that ventures all things'.

(*ii*) Extra-terrestrial life?

In his speech to the lesser gods, the Demiurge says at 41 c 8 that *having sown* the souls and made a beginning, he will hand them over for the creation of the mortal parts of soul as well as body. At e 4, telling the newly-created souls their fate, he says that '*having been sown* each into its proper instrument of time, they must be born as the most god-fearing of creatures'. After these two forecasts, the actual operation is described at 42 d 2:

> 'Having given them all these ordinances that he might be guiltless of the future evil of each one, he *sowed* them, some on the earth, others on the moon, and others on the remaining instruments of time [the planets], and *after the sowing* he handed them over to the young gods to mould bodies, to create the other parts of a human soul that needed to be added, and to govern and guide the mortal living creature as well as lay in their power, save in so far as it might become a source of evil to itself.'

I have put these passages together because it has become a matter of controversy whether the statement that souls are 'sown' not only on earth but also on the sun, moon and planets means that these as well as the earth are supposed to be inhabited. It is an exciting thought. Taylor believed it did (*Comm.* 258 f.), Cornford denied it (*PC* 146 n. 2), Hackforth in his lectures said that though it seemed absurd to think of human beings as living on the sun, one might conceive of some kind of embodied souls living there.

That men lived on the moon seems to have been a Pythagorean belief (DK 44 A 20; vol. I, 285), which has also been attributed, on doubtful authority, to Anaxagoras (Guthrie, *OGR* 247 n. 10; *HGP* II, 308 and 314). Of any similar belief about the sun or planets there is no trace anywhere in Greek thought. Nor should it be necessary to go into the question here, for the passages just quoted surely show that it is not what Plato meant to say. In all three, it is only *after* the Demiurge has sown the souls in the planets that they are to be provided with their lower elements and incarnated in bodies. Three stages are involved: (i) journey round the outer heaven on star-chariots to learn 'the nature of the whole', the knowledge which they may recover by their own efforts in the coming bodily life; (ii) 'sowing' in the instruments of time: still only the immortal soul is concerned; (iii) addition of other parts of soul and setting of the whole in a body. If this is right, the intermediate stage may symbolize, as Cornford suggested (*PC* 146), the intermediate status of the soul, partaking of both being and becoming, subjected to time and change yet essentially immortal; but one can only conjecture.

Necessity and design in the natures of men (61 c–90 d)

Teleological explanation. The rest of the dialogue deals in detail with the limitations imposed by necessity on the nature of human bodies and faculties, and the devices of the gods to overcome them in the interests of the immortal part of the soul.[1] Its subjects include anatomy and physiology, the composition of bone, hair, flesh and so on, the function of certain organs and of the blood, respiration and digestion, and also pathology, the diseases of both body and soul, their causes, prevention and treatment. Here we can only note a few general features and one or two particulars which have a wider interest.

Teleological explanation is universal, and sometimes carried to lengths which have aroused suspicion that Plato is only amusing himself. Wilamowitz was moved to write (*Pl.* I, 612): 'The description of the human body, its parts and their functions, would draw from an unprepared reader (if he had not thrown the book away at once) the cry: "This may be madness, but there's method in it." Sometimes he might feel doubtful even about the method.' As throughout the dialogue, Plato warns that no account of such matters can claim certainty (72 d), and we have to bear in mind both the inchoate state of medical knowledge in his time, as compared not only with today's but even with Galen's, and also how different was his purpose from that of the modern scientist. Aristotle too can surprise us with his unwavering adherence to teleological explanation. The idea that our makers lengthened and coiled the intestines in order that retention of the food

---

[1] 69 d σεβόμενοι τὸ θεῖον ὅσα μὴ πᾶσα ἦν ἀνάγκη. The creation of the body and the mortal parts of the soul have already been referred to (pp. 309 f. above). Often quoted as the best example of the tension between design and necessity is the thinness of the head and its covering of skin, necessary to it as a seat of intelligence but rendering it more vulnerable. The gods had to choose between making a dull but long-lived race or one shorter-lived but better and more intelligent (75 b–c; Lloyd, *EGSc* 73).

might check what they foresaw as our propensity to unreasonable greed (73 a) has been thought merely playful, but the connexion between a straight gut and an insatiable appetite is noted by Aristotle in a serious zoological work and moreover in a teleological context.[1] Many items in Plato's account of the body and its ailments can be traced either to Empedocles or to a writer of the Sicilian and Italian or Coan medical schools: Alcmaeon, Philistion, Diocles or a Hippocratic treatise.[2]

Physiology based on physics. At the same time Plato's physiology is firmly based on his physics. The strength of youth and wasting of old age are due to the condition of the elementary triangles, fresh and strong in youth to cut up and absorb those that come in from outside, but finally loosened and enfeebled by the struggle and themselves broken apart by the attacks of the environment. When these reach the life-giving marrow, death ensues. Apart from disease or violence, life has its natural term, determined by the length of time for which the triangles can hold together.[3]

Sensible qualities: body and soul.[4] First of all (61 c–68 d), Plato explains the sensible qualities of things in terms of the shapes and sizes of their

[1] *GA* 717a23, repeated at *PA* 675a18–21, b25f. (Taylor supposed that A. was joking too. See his *Comm.* 517.) 'An abnormally short gut is, in fact, a sufficient cause for a ravenous appetite' (Ogle on 675a in Oxford trans. vol. v). The gods have saved us from behaving like Callicles's ideal, the χαραδριός (*Gorg.* 494b). The prophetic function of the liver and its adjunct the spleen is a doubtful case (71a–72d), but at least P. makes it an opportunity to condemn as useless the regular practice of taking omens from the livers of sacrificial animals (72b). His belief in divination is sufficiently attested in *Phdr.*, and the necessity for a 'sane' interpreter of the inspired μάντις is typical (72a–b; for prophets who 'say many true things but don't know what they are saying' see *Apol.* 22b–c, *Meno* 99c).

[2] For Empedocles see Taylor 18, and for information on both him and the medical writers Taylor's and Cornford's notes on the relevant passages. Cf. Taylor 410, and his commendation of the 'amazing erudition' of Martin's notes on this section. Note also Hoffmann's appendix to Zeller II.1, §v, pp. 1070–86, 'P. und die Medizin'. Reff. to more recent discussions of P.'s relation to contemporary medicine are in Lloyd, *JHS* 1968, 84 n. 32.

[3] 81b–d and 89b. Triangles are also referred to at 73b and 82d. It will be remembered that the deathlessness of the cosmos was ensured by making it of the whole sum of body so that it could not be attacked from outside (p. 279 above). The span of human life is said to be εἱμαρμένον, which I take to mean resulting from necessity, not the planning of our makers. (In P. the preceding ἐξ ἀνάγκης need not rule this out.) For Democritus death was 'the outflow of soul-atoms from the body owing to pressure from the environment', and there was no immortal part to escape it. (Arist. *Parva Nat.* 472a14; vol. II, 434.)

[4] Sight and the visible have already been dealt with at 45b–46c, but colour is treated here (67c–68d). On a difficulty in the account (the uselessness of experimentation), see Lloyd, *JHS* 1968, 83.

constituent bodies. This is not intended as a complete explanation of sensation; he expressly says that the fact of sensation must be taken for granted, even though the creation of the body and the mortal parts of the soul have not yet been described.[1] Being thus limited to the physical qualities of sensa (their παθήματα, 61 c 5) his account sounds Democritean in its materialism, though based of course on atoms of regular geometrical shape. The sensation of heat from fire, for instance, being a piercing one, is effected by small, sharp-angled, mobile particles, hardness by cubes with their stable bases. But whereas the materialism of Democritus was consistent, the sensitive soul itself being a composition of exceptionally small, smooth, round atoms and sensation a direct result of their disturbance, Plato with his incorporeal soul (46d) has not that resource, and yet speaks as if the transition from physical to psychological motions presented no difficulty. For instance, speaking of sight at 45 c–d he has said that the *body* formed of light and the visual ray conveys motions 'to the whole body until it reaches the soul'. Similarly at 64b 'when anything naturally mobile is even slightly disturbed, it spreads the disturbance around, other particles (μόρια) passing it on to yet others, until it reaches consciousness and announces (ἐξαγγείλη) the effect of the agent'. If asked to attach a noun to 'the conscious' (τὸ φρόνιμον), what would Plato have said? Part (μόριον)? Faculty (δύναμις)? As it is, the passage might have been written by Democritus about soul-atoms.[2] The insensitiveness of bone and hair is ascribed solely to their material composition: they consist largely of earth with its motion-resisting cubes which do not pass on a shock (64c). Again, at 86e–87a, on the somatic causes of psychological disturbances, we are simply told that certain varieties of phlegm and bilious humours penetrate to 'the three seats of the soul' (so the effect is not confined to its mortal parts) and 'mingle their vapours with the motion of the soul'. Plato, one may fairly say, was not at his best when trying to graft an atomic physical system, hitherto associated with chance or necessity as sole causes, on to his own very different metaphysical and theological stock. One's questions, which would have seemed impudent

---

[1] 61 c6–d5. Cornford simply comments: 'The mortal part of the soul and the main bodily organs are reserved for the third part of the discourse, from 69A onwards' (*PC* 259 n.). But no explanation is given there of the relationship between body and soul that makes αἴσθησις possible.

[2] For D.'s theories of sensation and the soul, see vol. II, 430 ff., 438 ff.

intruders on the conversation in the *Phaedo*, become more pertinent when he sets himself up as a rival to the atomists.

Aristotle was the first to offer, through his doctrine of form and matter, a non-material explanation of sensation: sensation he defines as reception of the sensible forms of things without their matter. Faculty (*dynamis*) and organ of sense together form one concrete individual, a material object endowed with the power of sense-perception. A seeing eye is one thing, but like every separately existing thing can be philosophically analysed into two components. Its material constituents and qualities are defined differently from its form, the faculty of sight: numerically one, they are different in essence (*De an.* 424a25). Otherwise, he adds, what perceives would be body. This relationship exhibits in a single organ the relation of soul as a whole (of which sight is an activity) to body as a whole. ('If the eye were an animal, sight would be its soul', *De an.* 412b18.) Whatever we may think of this, we must admit that we are scarcely nearer than Aristotle to understanding the interaction (if there is interaction) between body and mind,[1] and he did at least see the problem and attempt to put an answer into words. Plato seems unaware of it. He himself, to use the modern jargon, was no reductive materialist.[2] When we say we see with our eyes and hear with our ears, we mean that our *psyche* sees and hears *through* these organs as instruments (*Tht.* 184b–d). In the *Phaedo* it is through the body that the *psyche* becomes acquainted with the sensible world, but the wise *psyche* will resort to it as little as possible, for the body and sensation are a hindrance to its philosophical quest for knowledge of the Forms (64a–66a). There however the soul is still a unity, the intellect alone, and immortal. Sense-perception, emotions and desires are assigned to

[1] Paul Edwards in *Mod. Introd. to Phil.*[3] 172ff. runs through the main conflicting theories (interactionism, reductive materialism, epiphenomenalism). Cf. W. A. Sinclair, *ib.* 577: changes in the retina cause changes in the nerves, which cause changes in the brain, 'after which, *in some way we do not understand*, we have the experience called seeing' (my italics). See now Popper and Eccles, *The Self and its Brain* (1977). To Aristotle goes the credit of being the first to separate the physical events (which he also describes) from the experience. In *De sensu* (438a10) he demands of Democritus, who had thought it sufficient to call vision a reflection of the object in the eye, why every reflecting surface is not capable of sight. For Plato plants, though created solely for the sustenance of man, have sensation and appetite, and feel pleasure and pain (77b), but for Aristotle they do not, precisely because they are only acted on by the matter, not the form, of an external object.

[2] He strongly disagrees with the 'Giants' of *Soph.*, who maintain that the soul itself has a body (247b).

the body. Now, in a development of its tripartite nature in the *Republic*,[1] it has acquired mortal parts created in conjunction with its incarnation and occupying different parts of the body. Plato clearly wished to maintain the *Phaedo*'s conception of it as belonging wholly to the realm of the invisible and unchanging, akin to the Forms, yet he sometimes comes perilously near to justifying Aristotle's criticism that he treats it as a physical magnitude.[2]

Pleasure and pain. These are treated as sensations, and with this limitation are accounted for in general much as in the *Philebus*, but linked with the particulate theory of matter. Any disturbance of our natural state is painful, and the return to normality pleasant, if they occur suddenly: what happens gently and gradually is not perceived,[3] and the nature of the change depends on the size and consequent mobility of the particles. One may enjoy replenishment, without having been conscious of a previous lack, as with the 'true' pleasures of the *Philebus*, which include those of scent (51 b; cf. *Tim.* 65 a6). 'Bodies [*sc.* organs] formed of larger particles yield reluctantly to the agent, and passing on the motions to the whole, have [*sic:* ἴσχει] pleasures and pains, pains when they are being shifted out of their normal state, pleasures when they are being reinstated' (64 e). These particles are presumably different from those just mentioned whose stability keeps their motion below the threshold of sensation altogether. There it was the most mobile particles, those of fire and air, which caused the keenest sensations. Again, the reason why the material sight-ray, though highly sensitive, gives us no pain when it is cut or burned (64 d–e), is that the smallness of its particles enables this to happen without violence.

[1] The analogy between the partition of the soul and the organization of a city is recalled at 70a–b.

[2] *De an.* 407a2–3. Cf. 406b26 and Cherniss, *ACPA* 393–5. It may be said that the limitation of the discussion to material *sensa* at this point is deliberate (61 c), but if so one would expect the problem of their relation to the perceiving soul, and the whole phenomenon of αἴσθησις, to have been recognized elsewhere. Note also the residence of the soul in the marrow at 73b–d, 73a5. When the triangles of the marrow break down, the soul (presumably here the immortal part only) is free to depart (81 d). On the other hand, what promotes 'the motions of the soul' is *musikē* and philosophy (88 c).

[3] This restriction does not appear in *Phil.*, and is perhaps an innovation due to the particulate theory.

Diseases of body and soul. The section on diseases is remarkable for its views on the physical origin of psychological disorders, disorders of the *psyche*.[1] Sexual incontinence results from superfluity of semen in the marrow, and a man troubled with this should not be reproached as wicked but treated as diseased. At this point (86d)/–e1) the Socratic maxim 'No one is willingly bad' is repeated: 'badness' is due to bodily defects and ignorant rearing.[2] Ill health can cause bad temper, depression, rashness, cowardice, forgetfulness and stupidity. If men with these initial disadvantages live in a badly governed community, the chances of amendment are still further reduced. This does not, however, imply a rigid determinism. Everyone's condition may be improved by education and training, study, and choice of pursuits, and these are the joint responsibility of parents, community and the individual himself. (But these, adds Plato at 87b8, are subjects for another occasion.) His aim, as always, is balance, symmetry, due measure and proportion. Soul (mind) must not be too strong for body nor body for soul. The remedy (which is relevant to the present discourse) is to give plenty of exercise to both. The naturally studious must not neglect physical training, nor the athlete mental culture. Even in sickness, exercise and diet are, except in the gravest cases, better than the use of drugs, which only upset the natural course of the distemper.

As for the soul itself, this calls, he says, for only a glancing reference to what he has said before. The three forms of soul in us, with their several motions, must be kept in proportion. Over-exercise of the appetitive and ambitious parts will fix our thoughts on mortal things, and the divine spark will fade. Our duty is, through the pursuit of knowledge and true wisdom, to cherish the divine and immortal part, placed at the summit of the body and raising us towards our heavenly kindred, a guiding spirit given us by God. In this way we shall attain the fullest immortality possible for the human race. Everything flourishes by exercising the motions proper to it, and the proper motions of

---

[1] On the extent of P.'s originality here see Lloyd in *JHS* 1968, 87. Note also the highly somatic description of emotions at 70a–d.

[2] τροφή probably refers primarily, as Taylor suggests, to bodily regimen, though it can cover education too. Cf. τροφή παιδεύσεως at 44c. For the Socratic paradox see vol. III, 459–62, and for P.'s retaining it while still maintaining a distinction between ignorance (cured by education) and wickedness (cured by punishment) see p. 126 n. 3 above.

the divine part of us are the revolutions and thoughts of the cosmos. By studying these we may repair the damage done to our own circuits at birth and bring our minds to resemble the Mind which is their object, so achieving the best life offered to us by the gods, now and for ever.

APPENDIX

The narrative order

By his own confession (34c), Timaeus's narrative has much in it of the casual and random, and follows neither the order of events nor a logical order. Beginning with the reasons for the world's creation and the nature of its model, he passes to consider the making first of its body, then of its soul, with the warning that as the soul is of higher worth than the body, so also it preceded it in the order of generation (34b–c). There follows the creation of the heavenly bodies (making time as we know it possible), of the stellar gods and mankind, including the nature and destiny of human souls and the effect on them of incarnation, and ending with an account of the purpose and mechanism of sight.

So far, he says (47e), he has spoken mainly about the work of Reason. Now he must begin all over again (48d–49a) and tell of the subordinate cause, necessity, and its effects 'before the heavens came into being' (52d). (These have therefore been taken before the creation in the present chapter.) There follows the description of the pre-cosmic chaos, the Receptacle and its tumultuous contents, 'without proportion or measure', which brings him back in a circle to the work of Reason, which was precisely to introduce the missing measure and proportion and produce the four bodily elements in their present distinct form by organizing them into microscopic particles of regular geometrical shape. So at 53c he picks up again the theme of the body of the cosmos, which he left at 34b. He describes the structure, varieties and combinations of the elements, and the sensible qualities that result from them. (We are asked at 61d to assume the faculty of sensation and its fleshly organs, though they have not yet been described, because one cannot, unfortunately, talk of both topics at once.)

The natures and effects of the physical elements are still partly determined by necessity. Timaeus now 'makes another fresh start' (69a) to remind his audience that 'these things' were in confusion until God bestowed measure and proportion on each one and on their mutual relations, so far as their nature allowed.[1] The rest of the dialogue (from 69c) tells how necessity was

---

[1] Cornford and Lee divide the dialogue into three main parts, classifying 27d–47e as the work of Reason, then the whole of 47e–69a as the work of necessity, and only what comes after that

subordinated to intelligence in the creation of human bodies and the mortal parts of soul, which God delegated to the minor gods, his offspring. It deals in clinical detail, from Plato's teleological point of view, with bodily parts and organs and their functions, and the cause and prevention of diseases. The dialogue ends with a hasty tailpiece on the origin of women, the physiology of sexual reproduction, the lower animals, and a final sentence summing up the excellence of the universe as a visible, perceptible god.

as the collaboration between Reason and necessity. They take 'All these things were so constituted of necessity' at 68e to refer to what has been described in the previous section, which however relates to the cosmos *after* the Demiurge had ordered the elements into regular geometrical shapes. Both scholars ignore the temporal force of τότε . . . ἡνίκα (68a1 and 3). All these things owed their condition to necessity *until* the Demiurge took them over and used their causes as accessories in creating the cosmos. In what preceded we were shown the limitations still imposed by necessity on the elements as constructed by Reason.

V

THE LAWS[1]

Introduction

Authenticity and date. 'Jowett opens with a proof, unnecessary today, of the authenticity of the *Laws* . . . The authenticity of the work . . . is no longer questioned.' So Jowett's editors in 1953, and most would agree today. The *Laws* contains infelicities of style, irregularities of syntax verging occasionally on incomprehensibility, repetitions and internal inconsistencies which some nineteenth-century scholars, on the familiar 'unworthy of Plato' argument, attributed to heavy posthumous editing on the part of Plato's pupil Philip of Opus.[2] External evidence they found in (i) D.L. 3.37: 'Some say that Philip of Opus transcribed (μετέγραψε) the *Laws*, which were on wax.[3] They add that the *Epinomis* is his work'; (ii) Suda, *s.v.* Plato: '[Philip] divided the *Laws* of Plato into twelve books, and the *Epinomis* is said to be his work.' These statements, even if based on a sound tradition, do little to substantiate a charge of extensive meddling with the *Laws*, which they clearly distinguish from the *Epinomis*, and which was known to Aristotle himself as Plato's.[4] Nowadays it is recognized that faults of the type found are more naturally explained by the unrevised state in which

---

[1] For bibliography see T. J. Saunders, *Bibliography on P.'s Laws* (1976).

[2] Tarán has performed the valuable service of collecting and evaluating the *testimonia* concerning Philip's work and activities. See his *Academica* (1975), § III, pp. 115–39. M. Krieg (*Überarbeitung d. 'Gesetze'* 1896) was one who argued that Philip made serious alterations and additions to Plato's text.

[3] Wilamowitz (*Pl.* 1, 655 n. 1), reasonably surmising that no one would write a work as long as the *Laws* on wooden tablets, took these words as metaphorical, meaning 'im Konzept' ('from the rough draft', Lesky, *HGL* 538). He was following Bergk, who explained the figure as taken from a model coated with wax for casting in bronze by the *cire-perdu* process. (See Morrow, *PCC* 515.) Tarán however (*Academica* 130 n. 542) doubts whether the expression is metaphorical. The most judicious estimate of the part played by Philip is that of von Fritz in *RE* xxxviii. Halbb., 2360–66. Raeder (*PPE* 398f.) went so far as to doubt the actual fact of a posthumous editing.

[4] See *Pol.* 1265 b 5 and Tarán, *Academica* 131 n. 548. As evidence of early circulation many scholars confidently cite Isoc. *Phil.* 12, which however speaks only of 'laws and constitutions written by the Sophists'. Isocrates may sometimes have hinted at Plato under the guise of a Sophist (vol. iv, 310f.), but the reference here could as easily be to Protagoras, who according to D.L. (9.55) wrote both a *Laws* and a *Constitution*, or Antisthenes (D.L. 6.16).

Plato had to leave this work of his old age, and their retention as a mark of the scrupulousness with which Philip carried out his work of copying. On the critical, or subjective, side, Ast (1778–1841) wrote: 'One who knows the true Plato needs only to read a single page of the *Laws* in order to convince himself that it is a fraudulent Plato that he has before him here.' Brochard in 1926, after claiming that Gomperz in 1902 had definitely established its genuineness, goes on to say that in spite of some *lenteur* and negligence, the unity of plan, the vigour of the general conception, the beauty of certain pages and the perfection of the *ensemble* show us Plato still in full possession of his genius.[1] For myself, coming to it (as the reader may grant) after a fairly close study of all the other dialogues, I feel no doubt that, to adapt the ancient critic's verdict on the *Odyssey*, it is a work of old age, but definitely—even if (as the content may occasionally make one think) regrettably—the old age of Plato.

The only early external evidence for the date of the *Laws* is Aristotle's statement in the *Politics* (1264b26) that it is a later work than the *Republic*. Internally, the defeat of the Locrians by the Syracusans mentioned at 638b is thought to be that of Dionysius II in 356 B.C.,[2] which means that bk 1 at least was written when Plato was over seventy. Evidence that bk 12 too was written after this date was seen by Grote at 944a. (See his vol. III, 443 n. *q*.) Plutarch (*Is. and Os.* 370f.) speaks of Plato being 'already an old man' when he wrote the *Laws*, and there is much in the tone of the work to suggest that he wrote it after the failure of his last visit to Sicily in 360.[3] If so, the composition of so long and detailed a work may well have been still occupying him at the time of his death, as tradition says.[4] Yet his disappointment never destroyed his faith in

[1] Ast quoted by Harward, *Epin.* 34; Brochard, *Études* 154, referring to Th. Gomperz's decisive article 'Die Composition der Gesetze' in *S.-B. Wien, ph.-hist. Kl.* 145 (1902). Not to leave modern technology unmentioned, according to Morton and Winspear (*Grk to the C.* 13, 78f.) bks 5 and 6 are stylometrically un-Platonic, revised by another, possibly Speusippus.

[2] Or 352: see Tarán, *Academica* 132 n. 554.

[3] This is largely a matter of general impression, but *Ep.* 3, 316a may indicate that his work with Dionysius II on that visit provided the prototype for the 'preambles' of the *Laws*. (So Harward, *Epp.* 179f. and others. For these προοίμια see p. 336 below.)

[4] Morrow, in his essay 'Aristotle's Comments on P.'s *Laws*' (Düring and Owen, *A. and P. in Mid.-4th Cent.* 145–62), argued that when Aristotle wrote *Pol.* bk 2 he only knew bks 3–7 of the *Laws*, and that this must have been in P.'s lifetime, before he wrote the rest. Ryle in *P.'s P.* (89, 257–9) makes much of this thesis of a '*Proto-Laws*', but see T. J. Saunders in *Rev. Belge de Philol. et d'Hist.* 1967, 497. Though Friedländer agrees that parts of the dialogue could be older than others, the whole of his ch. xxxi reads as a vindication of its essential unity.

what could be achieved if a young man, talented, brave and with the gift of self-control, should gain dictatorial powers and be fortunate enough to have at his elbow a legislator of the right sort. Teachable tyrant and wise adviser still constitute his recipe for a happy and well-governed state (709e–10b). As we know (see vol. IV, 23f.), several members of the Academy were invited by existing states to draw up or reform their laws, and in the *Laws* Plato lays down the principles on which they should act and offers a model of an actual constitution and legal code for their guidance.

Characters and setting. Three old men, as they frequently call themselves though still capable of walking many hours in the heat of a Cretan midsummer's day (683c), set out from Cnossus for the cave and shrine of Zeus on Mount Ida.[1] They are Clinias, a native Cretan, Megillus a Spartan, and an anonymous Athenian[2] who leads the talk. The little that is told of the other two is designed to indicate that they will make sympathetic and attentive listeners. Clinias has family connexions with Epimenides, the Cretan seer who encouraged the Athenians with his prophecies about the Persians, and has himself inherited feelings of goodwill towards Athens. As for Megillus, his family at Sparta were *proxenoi*[3] of Athens which he had been brought up to regard as a

---

[1] This is the cave to which the legendary Minos is said to have ascended periodically, bringing back laws which like his predecessor Rhadamanthys he claimed had been delivered to him by Zeus—falsely according to Plato's contemporary Ephorus. See Strabo 10.8, p. 476. For the Cretan therefore it would be a pilgrimage, and it makes the walk an especially fitting occasion for a discussion on lawmaking. On the Idaean Cave as their destination rather than other caves sacred to Zeus, see Morrow (p. 324 n. 3), 27f.

[2] At *Pol.* 1265a11 Aristotle makes a general criticism of 'all the discourses of Socrates', in which he includes the *Laws*. (He does *not* mention the name Socrates three times as the Oxford translation does!) The criticism seems intended for all Plato's dialogues, and the name may have slipped in inadvertently as Cherniss suggested. (See Morrow in Düring and Owen 146 n. 3.) At 1266b5 it is replaced by 'Plato in the *Laws*'. Some have thought however that A. is referring to an earlier version in which Socrates himself was the speaker. So Ryle, *P.'s P.* 258. Morrow however, whose suggestion it was that the *Laws* was only partially extant when A. wrote *Pol.* 2 (*PCC* 111 n. 44), does not believe this. See Düring and Owen 146. I cannot believe that P. ever made Socrates the speaker. Apart from the un-Socratic (sometimes even anti-Socratic) character of much of the work, a Socrates tramping the Cretan mountains is unimaginable (see especially *Crito* 52b and *Phdr.* 230c–d), and no one, I think, has suggested, on no evidence at all, that the scene too was altered during composition. 'The shift of scene to Crete and the introduction of the Athenian are to be thought of as a single creative act' (Friedländer, *Pl.* 1, 362 n. 9; cf. 111, 388f.).

[3] Citizens of one state who represented the interests of another in their own. The connexion was usually hereditary.

second fatherland (642b–d). He is not especially intelligent and maintains the Spartan reputation for brevity, to which he refers at 721e. Clinias has more to contribute, but both are completely overshadowed by the Athenian, Plato's own mouthpiece.[1] He is allowed long stretches of monologue, and there is no real argument. Together, the participants symbolize the system to be expounded, largely Athenian in origin, stiffened with Dorian, and especially Spartan, discipline.[2] The setting is not entirely forgotten as the dialogue proceeds (cf. 683c, 722c), but lacks that integration with the talk which the *Phaedrus* so skilfully and delightfully displayed.

Plan of chapter. The twelve books of the *Laws* include several devoted entirely to the exposition of a constitution and a legal code dealing with everything from subversion and treason to neighbourly disputes over drainage, enticement of bees or filching of fruit. To follow these in detail is neither possible nor, fortunately, necessary since their thorough analysis by Morrow.[3] But before the model city and its laws are reached there are three books of an introductory conversation on such topics as legislation in the Dorian states, the lessons of history, types of constitution, education and the arts. The recommendations for the city itself, apart from externals like town-planning (778a–79d, 848c–e), fall into two halves, the establishment of offices with the methods of election or appointment, and promulgation of the laws which the elected officials will be expected to enforce (735a). The necessarily curtailed treatment here will be divided into four main sections: (1) The introduction (bks 1–3), (2) The city of the *Laws*, (3) Life in Plato's city, (4) A few more general philosophical points. One aim will be to keep the other dialogues in mind and see how much of his earlier views Plato

---

[1] Gigon's observation, that it is a puzzle to know what an Athenian and a Spartan are doing in Crete (*Mus. Helv.* 1954, 207), is just, whether or not one accepts all the conclusions he draws from it.

[2] Some bibliography on P.'s attitude to Sparta will be found in Tigerstedt, *Legend of Sparta*, I, 544f., n. 202. His own estimate of Sparta's influence on the *Laws* differs markedly from Morrow's.

[3] G. R. Morrow, *P.'s Cretan City* (1960; hereafter simply 'Morrow'). See also Gernet, 'Les Lois et le droit positif', Budé ed. pp. xciv–ccvi, H. Cairns, *P. as Jurist*, ch. xxxi of vol. I of Friedländer's *Plato*, and for earlier reff. Leisegang in *RE* 2514. Saunders's translation has a full analytical table of contents (pp. 5–15). Special mention must be made of Jerome Hall's essay on 'Plato's Legal Philosophy' (*Indiana Law J.* 1956), a valuable appreciation of P.'s whole theory of law from the standpoint of a modern legal and political theorist.

has abandoned or retained. I hope that in spite of the necessary compression and omissions, what follows will succeed in preserving a proper balance.

(1) *Introductory conversation (bks 1–3)*

Aims and methods of education, with special reference to the use of drink (bks 1 and 2). The laws of Crete and Sparta (say Clinias and Megillus),[1] with their emphasis on courage and physical endurance, were devised on the assumption that cities are in a continual state of war. Conflict in fact is the keynote of life, from cities down through villages to families and individuals. 'And *within* an individual?' asks Plato (for surely one may give the Athenian this name), introducing at once the familiar theme of internal tension between a man's better and his worse self, of mastering or being mastered by oneself (*Gorg.* 491d, *Rep.* 430e, *Phdr.* 237d–e), in short of the virtue of *sophrosynē*. This internal struggle occurs also in states, where the worse element may rise to the top:[2] but laws should aim at reconciliation and peace, not war, and encourage *all* virtue, not just a part of it (courage), and that the least.[3] In any case, courage is shown not only in facing dangers and enduring pain but also in withstanding desires and pleasures—a reminder especially of *Laches* 191d–e, but also *Rep.* 413d–e. Spartan training hardened its youth in dangers and pains but offered no opportunity of testing their resistance to the seductions of pleasure. Quite right too, thinks Megillus. He has been shocked by the sight of drunkenness at parties and festivals in other states. Drink simply weakens a man's resistance to temptation, and its prohibition in Sparta has been a source of strength. The Athenian replies with an extraordinary eulogy, in several parts and at tedious length, of properly conducted drinking parties, not stopping short of intoxication, as a beneficent educational influence and test of moral stamina.[4] The argument is this. Wine increases passions and weakens

---

[1] For the traditional connexion between Cretan and Spartan Laws see Hdt. 1.65.4.

[2] The parallel is drawn all over again at 689b.

[3] Cf. the remarkable passage in bk 6, 803d–e, on the avoidance of war (cited on p. 352. below).

[4] The main passages are 639c–41d, 645d–50b, 671a–72d, 673d–74c. For P.'s sake one must hope those are right who attribute its length to the lack of opportunity for revision and excision. There are also a few other points to notice which may modify the impression given here. The need for νόμοι συμποτικοί (671c) reflects the practice in the Academy. (See vol. IV, 20f.) In the

judgement. It can make men childish and incapable of self-mastery. So something to be avoided at all costs? Not if it means accepting temporary incapacity to gain lasting good, as with some medical treatment and exhausting exercise. Fear is of two kinds: (1) of pains and the like, (2) of infamy, also called a sense of shame. This must be cultivated, and its opposite, shamelessness, avoided as a great evil. A man learns to overcome fear by being brought (as in the Dorian states) into controlled contact with danger and pain. Similarly he must learn to overcome the temptations of desire and pleasure by experiencing them under controlled conditions. The master of the revels must be of mature age (over 60) and remain sober (640 d, 671 d–e). Wine is a safe test of character. To discover whether a man is a cheat or a sex maniac, one need not have business dealings with him or put one's wife and children at risk: in his cups he will reveal his true nature. The educational object is to produce men like Socrates, who can expose themselves to the risks of drink and other temptations without losing self-command.

The importance of pleasure and pain in human life can scarcely be exaggerated. They may be 'witless counsellors', but are also the cords by which the puppet Man is manipulated. The study of law is almost entirely an investigation of pleasures and pains, and law itself may be defined as 'the public decision of a city on the relative merits of pleasure and pain'.[1] No one would voluntarily act in a way that brings him more pain than pleasure (663 b), but fortunately the virtuous life is the most pleasant. So the Athenian argues in bk 2, and in bk 7 (732 e–33 a) that it is natural to human beings to feel pleasures, pains and desires, and the best life is praiseworthy just because, if people will only give it a trial, it ensures a predominance of pleasure over pains for the whole of life.[2]

Platonic society no one under 18 may touch wine at all, and no one under 30 get drunk (666 a). The gift of Dionysus was not intended to madden us but to produce a sense of shame or reverence (αἰδώς) in the soul and health in the body (672 d). Its use must be state-regulated for these purposes, not solely for amusement. It is forbidden altogether to slaves, serving soldiers, magistrates during their term of office, jurymen and ships' steersmen; and 'licensed hours' are restricted: no one may drink until evening. In view of all these regulations viticulture will be strictly limited (673 e–74 c).

[1] See bk 1, 644 c–45 a, 636 d. (Law will have other definitions before the *Laws* is finished.) This is one indication that most of the *Laws* is concerned with 'popular virtue', not the philosophic virtue to which the calculation of pleasures and pains is irrelevant. They simply 'nail the soul to the body', escape from which should be its highest endeavour (*Pho.* 69 a–b, 83 d).

[2] In bk 7, 792 c–d, the Athenian declares that the right life must not pursue pleasures nor shun pains altogether, but accept a neutral state, which indeed is what the gods enjoy. This apparent

These considerations lead, at the beginning of bk 2, to a definition of education in general as inculcation of the right attitude to pleasures and pains, loving the good and hating the bad. It is best inculcated through music and dance, by which the natural restlessness of all young things is translated into the distinctively human gifts of rhythm and melody. The moral effect of these, for good or ill, is so strong that, as in the *Republic*, the composition of tunes and songs must be strictly controlled by law, and innovations frowned on.[1] Apollo's and the Muses' gifts are for our recreation and delight, but it is through play, song and dance that children can be educated to accept what the law approves. The lesson of the *Republic* remains valid.[2] Clinias claims that this is recognized only in Crete and Sparta, whose example other Greek states would do well to follow, and the Athenian innocently assumes his agreement that a man with every external advantage including tyrannical power is wretched and unhappy unless he is also just and good. Clinias does *not* agree. Such a life is morally reprehensible (*aischron*) but not bad, unhappy or unprofitable (*kakon*). So we are back at the argument with Polus in the *Gorgias* and the Socratic point, which the Athenian goes on to defend, that the most righteous life is also the pleasantest.[3] This is the truth, but even if it were not, a lawgiver's only consideration should be what beliefs in the young will most benefit the state. Again the ambivalent attitude to truth which we found in the *Republic*: the philosopher must pursue truth exclusively, yet the 'medicinal' use of spoken falsehood is recommended to the founding fathers (vol. IV, 456–9).[4]

inconsistency can hardly be understood apart from the analysis of pleasure and pain in *Phil.*, especially 32e. See p. 224 above.

[1] Later, in bk 3, 700a–701a, P. sees the first signs of the decline of Athenian morale in the innovations and decadence of Athenian music. The strict censorship of poetry, drama and music recurs in bk 7 at 801c–d. See also 817a and bk 2, 660a. Friedländer (*Pl.* III, 560 n. 29) has noted the close verbal parallel between 801e and *Rep.* 607a. To forbid innovation was a Spartan tradition according to Plut. *Inst. Lac.* 238c.

[2] See vol. IV, 450ff. for this and the general Greek association of aesthetic with moral values. On song and dance in the *Laws*, and their general importance in Greek life, see Morrow 302–18.

[3] For the *Gorg.* see vol. IV, 288f., and cf. *Crito* 49b. (Wrong-doing is κακόν as well as αἰσχρόν.) And of course the happiness of the just is a leading theme of the *Republic*.

[4] For truth as, in the *Laws*, the highest good for men and gods alike see 730c. The late C. D. Broad, one of the gentlest of men, expressed his full agreement with Plato that the political use of myth or fiction by governments was justified as an instrument for the promotion of good conduct. See *The Mind and its Place in Nature* 511f., of which I was reminded by Bambrough in *RTG* 85.

To return to music, choruses for song and dance will be divided according to age: children, under thirties, and the middle-aged from thirty to sixty. Since the last-named would feel a natural embarrassment at being detected in such activities,[1] they may perform at private parties, softened up and rejuvenated by their patron god Dionysus, tipsy and merry (671 a–b, 672 a) under the eye of a supervisor over sixty. A regrettable casualty of Plato's old age seems to have been his sense of the ridiculous.[2] The idea of this 'Dionysiac chorus' shocks Clinias, but the Athenian is undeterred. Its members will be better educated than others, including the song-writers themselves, to understand what rhythms, tunes and words are not only enjoyable but correct and salutary. Music and dance are *mimetic* arts (668 b), and besides pleasure and charm (χάρις) should aim at truth and utility. To judge a piece the elders must penetrate to its essence (οὐσία 668 c) and aim. So equipped, they will both enjoy a harmless pleasure themselves and instil virtuous habits in the young. Practised in this way, singing and dancing are not only a delightful recreation but may be equated, so Plato now claims, with the whole of education, divided according to Greek custom into 'music' and 'gymnastic'. In view of the importance assigned to all forms of gymnastic in the Dorian states (see 625 c), its virtual restriction to dancing here is surprising, and of course Greek *musikē* meant not only music but a whole literary education.[3]

Bk 2 ends with a return to the subject of drink, its uses and regulation, and bk 3 begins: 'So much for that. What are we to say about the origin of political organization?' There is no apparent connexion with the first two books. In the form in which we have the *Laws*, it looks as if Plato was dissatisfied with this treatment of education as a product of song, dance and intoxication. If so, one may sympathize. England regarded the disquisition on drinking as a general introduction to education,[4] and such indeed Plato calls it; but as it stands it is an odd, unsatis-

---

[1] There is some doubt about their age. At 670b they are 'the fifty-year-olds'.

[2] Aristotle, whose *Politics* contains many echoes of the *Laws*, assigns dancing to the young, and allows those of maturer age to sit as judges of it (1340b35–9). Nevertheless, apart from the festive details, the three choruses of boys, men in their prime, and the old were no fancy but existed in Sparta. Plutarch quotes from their songs (*Rep. Lac.* 238b, *Lyc.* 21).

[3] Cf. *Rep.* 376e. Admittedly music did play a larger part than with us, owing to the Greek belief in its moral effects. Still, we may be relieved to learn in bk 7 that education has other sides as well.   [4] *Laws* vol. 1, 340, and cf. 10 n. 1.

factory and inordinately long one.¹ The best points made in bks 1 and 2 are all repetitions of familiar Socratic or earlier Platonic tenets. Such are the need for self-mastery (where *symposia* could have been brought in briefly as an illustration); the difference between knowledge and true belief (632c); a hierarchy of goods as goods of soul (intellectual and moral),² of body (health), and lowest of the three classes, material possessions (697b); courage as not only physical but moral; the centrality of pleasure and pain in human life; the assimilation of a man to what he enjoys (656b, cf. *Rep.* 500c); the rigorous control of poetic subject-matter, education through play, the happiness of the good and misery of the wicked, the need to know what a thing is, and the equation of its essence with its purpose.³

The unity and multiplicity of virtue. One of these previously treated topics deserves special mention for its suggestion of a deliberate development from beginning to end of the *Laws*, and hence of its fundamental unity in spite of any disorder and untidiness of arrangement due to its unfinished state. I mean the relation of virtue as a whole to its parts. In the *Protagoras* Plato was at pains to show that the so-called virtues were not separate traits but only different aspects or 'parts' of a unity, the single virtue which was knowledge, source of all right conduct, whether in dangers (courage), temptations (self-mastery), relations with the gods (piety) or one's fellow-men (justice). To possess one was to possess all. In bk 1 of the *Laws* the Athenian speaks about courage and the other kinds or species (*eidē*) of virtue and virtue as a whole, and of treating courage first without the rest, with no suggestion that their relationship presents a problem. This is obviously right in its context. His aim is practical, to counteract the Dorian over-emphasis on physical courage, and his honest companions are no clever Sophists to relish a philosophical discussion of the unity of virtue. He therefore takes the commonsense view: courage is a species of virtue, attainable on its own, but a legislator ought to inculcate the whole (630d, 705d).

¹ It is only fair to add that he is aware of this and has his excuse. See 642a, and also p. 382 n. 2 below.

² To understand μετὰ νοῦ σώφρων (631c7), which offended Gigon (*Mus. Helv.* 1954, 225), I suggest one should look at *Meno* 88b7–8.

³ ὅτι ποτ' ἔστιν . . . τὴν οὐσίαν, τί ποτε βούλεται (668c).

One may use 'parts' or any other word provided the meaning is clear (633a). In bk 3 (696b) the possibility is envisaged that a man may be very brave yet wicked and licentious, exactly what Protagoras maintained in the *Protagoras* (349d) and the Platonic Socrates denied. When however in the last book Plato is describing the educational requirements of his supreme committee, the Nocturnal Council (also called Guardians and corresponding to the Guardians of the *Republic* in having not simply true belief but actual knowledge), he does put the question and his mature philosophy comes into view (963c–d). We speak of four kinds of virtue, as if each was a separate thing, yet we call them all by one name, 'virtue', as if they were not many but one. How is this? It is easy to see the differences, e.g. courage differs from wisdom by being a purely natural faculty found in wild animals and children. It does not need reason (*logos*), without which no soul can become wise.[1] But in what sense are they a unity? No answer is given (this was not the place for it), but it is said that to answer it calls for training in the dialectical method of collection and division, a method with which Plato has wrestled in the later dialogues from *Phaedrus* on. This will concern us further when we come to consider the purpose and training of the Nocturnal Council (pp. 371f. below).

The lessons of history (*bk 3*). How did political communities arise? Imagine life starting afresh after a great flood.[2] All civilization has been engulfed, and the only survivors are a few mountain herdsmen, good people but ignorant and illiterate. From separate families patriarchally governed they gradually form larger units, descend into the foothills and progress from stock-raising to agriculture. At this stage they would choose primitive legislators, to unify the different family traditions into a common code and also to appoint one or more governors to administer the new rules of behaviour, creating the first monarchy or aristocracy. (So the earliest legislators are already to be separated from the execu-

---

[1] This of course departs from earlier works, where P. follows Socrates in equating the virtue of courage with knowledge, and judgement based on knowledge. Unthinking rashness is no virtue, and may lead to harm. For this view see vol. III, 451–3 (Socrates), IV, 128 n. 1, 219–21, 228 (*Prot.*), and *Meno* 88e, *Rep.* 430b. Here P. is speaking of the 'demotic' virtues.

[2] For P.'s uses of the belief in recurrent natural catastrophes see *Tim.* 22c–e, *Critias* 104d–e, *Pol.* 273a and Guthrie, *In the B.* 65–9.

tive.) With the third stage, the foundation of cities in the plains, Plato moves into the light of history, starting with the fall of Troy, the exile of the Achaean victors from their homes, and their return under the name of Dorians.[1] This brings the trio back to their starting-point, the institutions of the Dorian states, the object being to appraise their merits and defects, to ask why some have survived and others not, and in general no less than to discover what changes would ensure the welfare and happiness of a city (683b).

From here Plato goes on to explain, on his own principles, the failure of the alliance between the three chief cities of the Peloponnese, the survival of Sparta, the defeat of Persia and the subsequent decline of Athens. The first was due to concentration on military strength and physical courage at the expense of a proper balance between the virtues. Undue subservience to the pleasure–pain standard and neglect of what is fine and good ruins state and individual alike. A soul whose grosser elements oppose the faculty of knowledge and judgement is like a city in which the mob refuses to obey its rulers and the laws. Internal concord is more important than professional competence, and no man who lacks it should be entrusted with government. In the Peloponnese (as usually in absolute monarchies) the rot started from above, in the discordant souls of the three kings, puffed with pride and greed, breaking their oaths and the laws. The remedy, discovered by Sparta alone, is constitutional reform. Irresponsible power inevitably corrupts, and the solution lay in Sparta's division of powers, exemplified in the dual kingship, the council of elders and the ephorate, introducing the invaluable element of measure and proportion.

Need for a mixed constitution. There are two extreme forms of government, absolute monarchy (or tyranny) and democracy, represented by Persia and Athens respectively. All others are modifications of these. For a state to be free, united and wise, it is absolutely essential that it combine elements of both.[2] By robbing the people of all liberty the

---

[1] For an appraisal of P.'s view of Greek history, see R. Weil, *L' 'Archéologie' de P.*, perhaps with the review by Kerferd in *CR* 1961, 30f.

[2] 693d. Cf. the warning against ἄμεικτοι ἀρχαί at 693b, and bk 6, 756e μέσον . . . μοναρχικῆς καὶ δημοκρατικῆς πολιτείας. For the theory of the mixed constitution, originated by P., see Morrow ch. x, von Fritz, *Theory of the Mixed Constitution in Antiquity*, and other works referred to by Morrow, 521 n. 3.

despotic and self-indulgent kings of Persia destroyed any sense of community in the state. In their wars of greedy aggression, they ended by being unable to rely on the loyalty of their own soldiers. The history of Athens on the other hand shows that excess of liberty is no less debilitating. When they threw back the Persian invaders, the people were the 'voluntary slaves' not of a tyrant, but of the traditional laws and their own moral sense (*aidōs*).[1] The falling-off from this admirable state showed itself first of all in music, with composers breaking the established rules and confusing the different genres to please uneducated and noisy audiences.[2] Thence it extended to general disregard for law and an impudent refusal to listen to good advice. In Sparta and early fifth-century Athens we saw how in a modified form authoritarianism and freedom alike lead to success and prosperity, but Persia and contemporary Athens show the disastrous effects of either when carried to extremes.

At this point the Athenian wonders what test there could be of the practical utility of their discussion, and Clinias suddenly reveals that he has been put on a commission to draw up laws for a new colony in Crete. Its population will be drawn from various cities, but Cnossus has been charged with the planning. He suggests that it will help him if they now plan an imaginary state on the basis of the points so far made.

(2) *The city of the* Laws

Was it intended to be realized in practice? The idea of starting a brand-new state with prefabricated constitution and laws is less familiar to Britons than it was to the Greeks, with their habit of founding politically independent colonies or offshoots of existing city-states. One might say that when the United States ceased to be a British colony it became a colony of Britain in the Greek sense. We have seen, too, in connexion with the Academy, how existing states would call in expert legislators from outside to reform their political and legal systems.[3] But how far did Plato intend or hope that his scheme for Magnesia[4] might

[1] Cf. the answer of Demaratus to Xerxes, Hdt. 7.104 (vol. III, 79). P.'s brief account of the spirit in which Athens met the Persian peril is in his best vein as a writer.

[2] 700a–701b. 700c closely parallels *Rep.* 492b–c.

[3] Vol. IV, 23, and cf. the pan-Hellenic colony of Thurii founded by Pericles (vol. III, 264). In some cases (cleruchies) the colonists retained citizenship of the mother-state.

[4] In the later books the citizens are several times referred to as 'Magnesians' (first at bk 8, 860e).

be realized in practice? In strong contrast to the *Republic* (a literal U-topia or Erewhon) it is located in Crete, named, and its site described: the deserted site of an ancient city Magnesia, some ten miles from the sea, with good harbours, self-sufficient in natural produce but with no surplus for export. The availability of timber for ships, and the advantages and disadvantages of a population of mixed origins, are also discussed.[1] In bk 5 Plato claims, with obvious reference to the *Republic*, that the ideal would be the abolition of all private ownership, in wives and children as well as goods. Perhaps some gods or sons of gods live under such a rule, but we must be content with human nature as it is, 'for we are addressing ourselves to men, not gods'.[2] We are no longer in the age of Cronus, when men were governed not by other men but by gods.[3]

In the *Republic* many things are left in the air which it would be essential to explain if it had been intended as practical politics. How the new regime would ever be brought into force is a question never seriously faced. In *Laws* 6 this is elaborately provided for. A mixed company of settlers from different states, strangers to each other, will not be immediately in a position to elect the best men to office (751 d).[4] The Cnossians must therefore appoint a commission of 200, selecting 100 of the best and most mature among themselves and 100, as far as possible similarly endowed, of the settlers, to choose the first officials. Pre-eminent among these will be the 'guardians of the laws', a board of 37 (initially 18 Cnossians and 19 settlers), aged between 50 and 70 (755 a), who besides their primary duties will keep the register of private property, each citizen having to declare his own. As time goes on and the constitution is established, this body, like the Council and other offices, will be recruited by internal election on mainly democratic lines, for which elaborate rules of procedure are laid down. The idea of a new

[1] In bk 3. We are here concerned only with the realism of P.'s picture. For a possible connexion with the Asiatic Magnesia on the Meander and an actual site at the W. end of the plain of the Messará in southern Crete see Morrow 30f., which may be called a defence of Plato's local knowledge against Wilamowitz and Taylor. (See Taylor's *PMW* 464.)

[2] 739c–e, 732e, 807b. At 739d ἐπὶ τοῖς αὐτοῖς χαίροντας καὶ λυπουμένους matches *Rep.* 464a. This remained a permanent ideal for P. Note that it is in both passages explicitly connected with the community of wives.

[3] 713c–d. This feature of the Cronus myth is repeated from *Pol.* 271e (pp. 181f. above).

[4] Against the idea that 751a–55b represents a conflation of two originally separate sets of proposals (Wilamowitz, revived by Morrow) see Saunders in *CQ* 1970.

colony has one advantage. The *Republic* was faced with the problem of what to do with adult citizens hardened in un-Platonic ways, and the simple remedy proposed was to send everyone over ten 'into the country' and educate the children away from the bad influence of their elders (540e–41a). Here, although Plato discusses dispassionately various forms of purge (καθαρμοί), with a preference for the more drastic,[1] he notes with relief that none will be necessary in the present case, only a rigorous examination of the candidates for admission. The risk of error will always remain, but an adequate period of trial and efforts at peaceful conversion should ensure rejection of the unworthy (736b–c).

The detailed nature of the legislation itself, and the fact that many of the institutions and laws copy or refine on those already in force at Athens or Sparta,[2] also point to a serious practical intent. We are far from the disdain expressed in the *Republic* for those who bother with laws about contracts, slander, assault, taxation and so on, which are unnecessary in a well-run state of properly educated citizens and ineffective in a bad one (425c–e, 427a). Both works insist that one should not try to legislate for everything—some things are better left to tradition and public opinion[3]—and the *Laws* (788a–b; cf. 773c) warns against making unenforceable laws which bring the whole system into disrepute, but at the same time seems to leave little outside the network of legal regulation.[4]

Certain phrases have sometimes been taken to indicate that Plato recognized his scheme as, like the Republic, visionary. Such are 632e, 'Let us refresh ourselves on the way with conversation', in conjunction

---

[1] Cf. *Pol.* 293d, 308–9, p. 185 above.

[2] Mainly Athens, in spite of the adoption of συσσίτια and certain other Spartan institutions. Morrow's book shows this in detail (see especially his pp. 232, 271 f., 295, 534f.), and cf. Grote, *Pl.* III, 427f. Jowett (IV, 15) gives a summary of Athenian and Spartan features. Yet one cannot read Xenophon's Spartan Constitution or Plutarch's *Lycurgus* without feeling that in spirit if not always in positive enactments, and in spite of his criticisms, P. found much to admire in the Lycurgan laws and their aims. See also Levinson, *Defense* 513–19.

[3] For the importance of ἄγραφα νόμιμα see 793a–d. They ought, P. thinks, to be put in writing as a code of approved behaviour, though without legal sanction. (793d, and cf. 822e8–23a1. The Greek conception of unwritten laws in general is discussed in vol. III, 118–31.)

[4] Private life—'how the individual spends his day'—must be regulated no less than public (780a). Cairns in Friedländer (*Pl.* I, 292) gives an impressive list of legally controlled activities, including marriage, procreation, distribution of wealth, price-fixing, shipping, merchandising, retail trade, innkeeping, the regulation of mines, loans and usury, farming, herding and beekeeping, appointment of magistrates, and funerals. I have omitted a few items, nor is Cairns attempting completeness. On the regulation of private life see also p. 350 below.

with 685 a, 'Let us relieve the tedium of our journey by playing an old man's sober game of legislation.' At 712, having stated the best conditions under which to launch a new state, the Athenian continues to Clinias, 'Let us suppose this fiction applies to *your* city, and like grown-up children invent its laws in our talk.' It is emphasized that they are under no obligation to legislate, and can take as much time as they want (857e–58c).[1] All this however does no more than reflect the dramatic situation. Our travellers are *not* sitting on a legislative commission but walking and talking in the mountains. No one can read the mass of detailed legislation proposed (and this must be emphasized here, where the omission of much of it might leave an unbalanced picture) without concluding that Plato is in deadly earnest about both the purpose and the content of his laws. The most reasonable conclusion is that he hoped to leave the *Laws* as a posthumous guide to members of the Academy in their business of legislation and to any rulers, such as Hermias of Atarneus, who were willing to listen.

Status and function of laws: the lawgiver as educator. Plato once taught that the philosopher, the man of natural wisdom perfected by a Platonic education culminating in mathematics and dialectic, should rule autonomously, unhampered by laws. In the *Politicus* we saw this still defended as the ideal, but replaced as a practical possibility by the admittedly second-best rule of law (pp. 180f., 183–8 above). The *Laws* takes the same position.

If ever by the grace of God a man endowed with a natural character equal to the test could take over the reins of power, he would need no laws to be his masters. No law or ordinance is superior to knowledge, nor is it right that wisdom should be a slave or subject. Natural wisdom, genuine, true and free, should be ruler of all. As things are, however, it is not to be found anywhere or anyhow, to any significant extent. So we must choose the second-best, ordinance and law, though they can only pay regard to generalities, not to every case.[2]

Today it is a matter of controversy whether law should concern itself with the positive inculcation of morality. Plato had no doubts: every-

---

[1] It is said more than once that at present their legislation is λόγῳ not ἔργῳ (736b, 778b).
[2] *Laws* 875c–d. With the last sentence cf. *Pol.* 294e–95a (p. 186 above) on law as a blunt instrument.

thing to do with laws has a single aim in view, and the right name for it is virtue (963 a). 'I liked the way you [Clinias the Cretan] embarked on explaining your laws. It was right to begin with virtue, and to say it was for the sake of virtue that your legislator laid down his laws' (631 a).[1] Law is in fact a form of education. 'Anyone who treats of law as we do is not laying down the law to the citizens but educating them' (857 e). 'I should like them to be as readily persuaded as possible, and this is clearly what the legislator will aim at in all his lawmaking' (718 c). To this end he proposes to introduce something for which he claims complete originality (722 d–e), the attachment of prefaces or 'preludes' (proems)[2] both to the code as a whole (and the Athenian claims that all this discussion so far, near the end of the fourth book, has amounted to a general preamble[3]) and to each separate enactment save the most trivial. It is tyrannical to impose law 'neat' (ἄκρατος 723 a), simply decreeing that this or that must or must not be done and fixing a penalty for disobedience, without an explanatory preface to enlist the cooperation of the citizens. The law must mix persuasion with compulsion (718 b).[4] To illustrate his point he immediately suggests an exhortation to be prefaced to a law imposing an annual fine on bachelordom after the age of thirty-five.

The role of punishment. So far it would seem that, in securing obedience to the laws, the consent of the governed is for Plato of primary importance. At 690 c, after what sounds a particularly authoritarian passage about the accepted right of parents to govern their children,[5] well-born

---

[1] For the contrasting view in Greece see vol. III, 139 f. P. was not in the line of Lycophron and Hippodamus, nor of J. S. Mill, Macaulay or most modern opinion, but might have found Lords Simonds and Devlin sympathetic. Cf. also Hall, *Indiana Law J.* 1956, 202, with his reference to 'the thoroughgoing social character of Plato's ethics'.

[2] In music a *proöimion* was a prelude to the main theme, and P. plays on the double meaning of *nomos*, law and tune. See 722 d. According to Pfister in *Mélanges Boisacq* 173–9, Plato's *proöimia* were not so original as he claimed.   [3] Cf. also the 'address to the colonists' at 715 e ff.

[4] This seems a praiseworthy idea, but is harshly treated by Versényi in his article on Morrow's book (*R. of Metaph.* 15, 1961–2, 69 f.). Why he thinks that P.'s preface contains no 'rational instruction' I do not know. It is not incompatible with persuasion, and the doctor of 720 d, whom he mentions, διδάσκει the patient, as good doctors do.

For a lawyer's opinion see Hall, *Indiana Law J.* 1956, 182 n. 52: 'The preambles in *Laws* include (1) references to the principles which supply the rational basis of the enactment and (2) exhortation to obey the law.'

[5] One would not expect P. to support the saying 'maxima debetur puero reverentia', especially in view of his characterization of children at 808 d as, owing to their still uncanalized powers of

the lower orders, elders their juniors, masters slaves, even of the stronger to rule the weaker,[1] he concludes that the strongest claim of all is that of the wise to rule the ignorant, and that this is achieved most naturally by the rule of law over willing subjects without force. But this again is not the last word. The lawgiver must not curry favour with the populace. To legislate for the people's pleasure would be like expecting medical treatment or hard training to be pleasant in itself (684c). This leads naturally to the role of punishment, though even to consider it, says the Athenian at the beginning of bk 9, is a kind of admission of failure in a city supposed to be founded on the right lines and to give every incentive to the practice of virtue. Laws are made for good men, to assist them to live amicably together, but some must be for those who spurn such instruction (880d–e). These the lawgiver hopes he will not have to use, but unfortunately human beings are not perfectible, and unteachable persons are bound to appear. In the event we find that every law carries its appropriate penalty, ranging from a vague 'reprimand' or 'loss of reputation'[2] through fines, loss of civil rights and exile, to death. On the one hand the aim is therapeutic, and in a remarkable passage (862d–63e) Plato says that it may be achieved not only by punishment but by talking with the offender[3] and even offering him pleasure, honours and gifts. *Any* means is right that will heal the criminal's diseased mind and bring him to hate injustice.[4] Only if he be

reason, 'Hardest to manage of all wild things . . . cunning, shrewd and insolent'. Yet Juvenal might almost have been translating his αἰσχύνεσθαι τοὺς νέους. Nowadays, he says (729b), admonitions to the young to be respectful are ineffective. 'A wise legislator would rather bid adults respect the young, and above all beware of letting their juniors see or hear them doing or saying anything disgraceful. Where the old have no shame the young will show no respect.'

[1] This may be a shock to those who remember their *Gorgias*. Clinias's rejoinder—'There's no getting away from that'—shows that he takes the words in their commonest sense, not as 'better' and 'worse'. One has to remember that P. has Pindar in mind (690b8), and take the passage with 714e, where he points out that some of the claims listed here are mutually incompatible, and 890a. (See England on 690b8.) The passage of Pindar has been discussed in vol. III, 131–4.

[2] Certain unspecified honours and awards for merit (ἀριστεῖα) are mentioned, from which an offender will be disqualified (845d, 935c, 952d). For the awards see also 961a, and Morrow 271 n. 65. Public opinion is often invoked against an offender, e.g. 762c, 880a, 914a, 917c, 936b.

[3] A good example of psychiatric talk is the preface to the law on sacrilege, 854b–c.

[4] Naturally this demands close attention to the circumstances of the crime and the criminal's state of mind at the time. Saunders (*CQ* 1973, 235; *PQ* 1973, esp. p. 353) refers to passages showing that P. was fully aware of this commitment. The conception of wickedness as a mental

judged incurable, then for his own sake (for life is no boon to such people, 862e) as well as the community's he must be put to death. In practice Plato by our standards make pretty free with the death penalty. It is exacted for instance not only in certain cases of deliberate murder[1] but for sedition (854b–c), open atheism (at the second offence, 909a), temple-robbery by a citizen (854e), persistent perjury in court (937c), acceptance of bribes when in office (955d), perversion of justice from motives of greed (938c), and disseminating harmful notions from abroad (952c–d).[2] For certain crimes a citizen must be put to death but not a slave or foreigner, because the citizen has had the right upbringing and yet proved incurable. The others may still be brought to see reason, and to this end they will merely be branded, given as many lashes as the judges impose, and cast naked over the frontier. They might well agree with Plato that death is preferable![3]

Imprisonment as a punishment or corrective[4] is occasionally resorted to, notably for atheism. As he explains in bk 10, Plato considers disbelief in the divine and rational governance of the world to be the root of most moral evil. Open atheists of otherwise blameless life are sent for at least five years to a kind of mental home (σωφρονιστήριον) where they will be visited only by members of the Nocturnal Council (pp. 369ff. below), who will admonish them 'for the salvation of their souls'.[5]

disorder raises the problem of how to reconcile punishment with the Socratic teaching that wrongdoing is due to ignorance and no one is voluntarily wicked. To this dilemma P. turns his attention in bk 9, and though it might be thought appropriate in the present context, I have deferred it to a final section on some philosophical points (pp. 376–78).

[1] The laws on homicide are complicated, as at Athens, by considerations of religious pollution (871a–d, 873b; cf. Grote, *Pl.* III, 404f.), and also by P.'s belief in posthumous punishment and reincarnation; e.g. a matricide will be reborn as a female (872e). In some cases where today capital punishment or life-imprisonment might be though suitable, purificatory rites are deemed sufficient, in others (murder of kin) purification plus a period of exile.

[2] The death penalty, at least for some offences, is to depend on a majority vote of the dicasts (856c), as at Athens in the trial of Socrates.

[3] But at 938c the foreigner will suffer only banishment for an offence for which a citizen must be put to death. Penology may well have been a subject which P. intended to revise.

[4] A thief will be detained in prison until he has paid twice the value of the theft unless excused by his prosecutor (857a). A citizen who illegally engages in retail trade will be imprisoned for a year in the first instance (919e–20a). See also 880c. Morrow points out (p. 294) that at Athens prison was as a rule only used for holding defendants for trial or the condemned until execution.

[5] 909a ἐπὶ νουθετήσει τε καὶ τῆς ψυχῆς σωτηρίᾳ. The dangers of such a system seem obvious today, when sinister analogies suggest themselves, and are pointed out by Morrow (491f.). Saunders however (*CQ* 1973, 235), though properly critical of P.'s assumptions, perhaps more justly calls the interviews 'serious philosophical discussions' and of all P.'s methods of assessing

Should the 'cure' prove ineffective after release, a second conviction carries the death penalty. Those on the other hand who, unbelievers themselves, prey on the superstitious fears of others, are condemned to solitary confinement for life in a remote part of the country.[1]

Emphasis is frequently laid on a citizen's duty to lay information if he knows a crime has been committed, and also (which sounds more dangerous) to carry out summary justice on his own account, inflicting physical punishment on anyone, slave or free, whom he sees misbehaving. 'He who commits no crime deserves honour, but doubly so he who checks the wickedness of others . . . by revealing it to the authorities; and whoever joins with them in punishing it is the perfect citizen and takes the palm for virtue.' Honours and punishments are assigned accordingly.[2]

To conclude, the severities of the penal code are due to Plato's keeping his principles as high as ever but at the same time trying to incorporate them in the institutions of a particular earthly state. Education, explanatory prefaces and the laws themselves are designed with one aim only, that conscious of the *underlying reasons* for the prescribed code of conduct the citizens will voluntarily adhere to it and serious transgression will disappear or be confined to a few perverted characters. If in spite of these exceptional advantages some do go seriously, even irreparably astray, their treatment must be correspondingly drastic. We must also remember that death in Plato's eyes was 'the least of evils' (854e), for exactly the same reasons as long before in the *Apology*: the good of the soul is all that matters, and for all we know, to meet the gods of the next world may be the best thing that could happen to us (727d).

Theory and reality. As enumerated by himself, Plato's aims could not be faulted by any modern democrat. They are to foster, besides good sense, liberty, equality, and the spirit of concord—the slogans of the

character 'certainly the one which approaches most nearly to modern psychological practice'. See also vol. III, 246.

[1] When they die they will be denied burial, but it is hard to see why they are not put to death at once. No hope of a cure is held out.

[2] 730d. For examples of summary punishment by private individuals see 762c, 914b (of slaves), 917c–d, 935c.

French Revolution.[1] How do these admirable ideals look when we examine his means of attaining them? The prime requisite is the mixed (or intermediate, μέσον) constitution already referred to (pp. 331f. above): neither unchecked dictatorship nor extreme egalitarian democracy. These are 'non-constitutions', implying simply the exploitation of one section by another. (Cf. 714d.) In his own state the law will ensure that no citizens interfere with any others and each has time and opportunity to pursue the best life.[2] There can be no friendship if rulers and ruled live like master and slave (hence liberty and friendship go closely together), nor on the other hand if good and worthless are treated alike, for 'equality between unequals is inequality' (757a),[3] and either extreme leads to discord. In what sense then is equality good? We have seen the answer in the *Gorgias*.[4] The word covers two contrasting procedures, the easy one of giving equal shares[5] to all indiscriminately (arithmetical equality) and the less obvious one of distribution in proportion to individual merit (geometrical equality). The second is the 'truest and best' because it secures *justice*, and justice is preferable to dictatorship and even to the power of the people.

In Magnesia the ideal of the mixed constitution will be achieved by providing that all magistrates, officials and members of boards charged with administering the laws will be elected by popular franchise and serve for a fixed term of years only,[6] after which, as at Athens, they will be called to account before a board of examiners, also popularly elected. The methods of election, age qualifications and length of service will vary with the office, and are prescribed in detail for each.

---

[1] 693b and d, repeated at 701d: (πόλιν ἐλευθέραν τε εἶναι δεῖ καὶ ἔμφρονα καὶ ἑαυτῇ φίλην), 757a5–6, 739d of the ideal state, οἵτινες νόμοι μίαν ὅτι μάλιστα πόλιν ἀπεργάζονται. The importance of φιλία is 'repeatedly emphasized' (Morrow 562 with 5 reff.).

[2] 832c–d. Cf. 712e–13a.

[3] 757a. At *Rep.* 558c he had described contemporary democracy as 'dealing out a kind of equality to equals and unequals alike'.

[4] Vol. IV, 301, where *Laws* 757b–d was quoted in explanation of the phrase 'geometrical equality' at 508a. The conception of geometrical equality, in both its mathematical and its political aspects, has been fully investigated by F. D. Harvey in *Class. et Med.* 1965. For the *Laws* see pp. 108f.

[5] Or chances. The Greek has no noun, and P. is here thinking of office rather than wealth. As an example of his meaning he mentions appointment by lot (757b).

[6] As Morrow says (162), we should regard this as truly democratic, but at Athens the requirements of democracy and equality seemed only to be satisfied by the use of the lot. This was of course entirely opposed to P.'s principle of giving office to the best qualified. Nevertheless he does allow for a strictly limited use of sortition, avowedly to avoid popular discontent. (For the

No man must be reckoned subject to another, but all alike will be subjects of the law. The doctrine attacked in the *Republic*, that to serve the interests of those in power is justice, is again rejected (741 c ff.). Laws must benefit the whole state, not a party, and office-holders like anyone else are their servants.[1]

(3) *Life in Plato's city*

Population. Before we go further, something must be mentioned which is of primary importance whenever Plato's social and political theories are compared—as they always have been and will be—with the theory and practice of more recent times. That is, the *size* of the community for which he is planning. Speaking as we do of democracy, aristocracy, oligarchy, tyranny, in terms taken straight from Greece (though to make it sound more modern we may replace the last by 'dictatorship'), we are apt to think that they originally stood for different forms of government in societies roughly similar to our own. We rarely pause to reflect on the difference of scale, sufficient to entail a difference in kind. We count our populations in millions—over fifty in the case of Britain —whereas Plato posits a community of 5,040 households,[2] each with its separate allotment of land. Morrow has estimated that this would mean 10,000–12,000 male citizens and a total citizenship of 40,000 to

---

details see Morrow 161–3, 233.) In some things he is indeed learning to come to terms with practical politics. (On the examination after laying down office see Morrow 220–7. It was especially directed against corruption.)

[1] ὑπηρέται, δοῦλοι τῶν νόμων. See 715 a–d. This rule of law, to replace irresponsible use of power, whether by a tyrant or the mob, is violently attacked by Versényi in *R. of Metaph.* 1971–2, 77 f.—curiously so for a scholar whose work is in general a model of restraint and fairness, as are the last two pages of the same article. As will appear, I cannot accept his statement that 'in Plato's Cretan state there will be no philosophers or philosophy'. Philosophy will of course be confined to a small number, as in *Rep.* and everywhere else.

[2] 737e–38a. It is typical of the difference between *Rep.* and *Laws* that in the former the state is simply to be 'of a size to which it can grow without losing its unity' (423b), with no hint of what that size might be, or how to ensure it. The expressed reasons for the choice in the *Laws* are purely practical, first generally (self-sufficiency, defence, 737c–d), then, in relation to the precise number 5,040 (ἀριθμὸς χρησιμώτατος 738a), the presence of a large number of consecutive divisors, useful for organization in war and peace, for contracts, taxation and distributions. Contrary to general opinion (cf. Taylor, *PMW* 477 n. 1, and Morrow 428) Kahn sees a deeper significance in it as an imitation of unity, and connects it with making the state 'as near immortality as possible'. (Cf. 739e and Kahn in *JHI* 1961, 422.) Bardies in Πλάτων 1971 thinks of the special status of the number 7. ($1 \times 2 \times 3 \times 4 \times 5 \times 6 \times 7 = 5040$.) But we may be content with what P. tells us.

48,000.[1] This is roughly the population of Farnborough or half that of Bath, distributed of course between city and countryside. In addition there would be 7,000–8,000 metics and perhaps 30,000 slaves. In a state of this size, as at Athens, important functions, including the election of officials and trials for offences against the state, could and would be performed by the whole body of adult citizens meeting in Assembly.[2]

Public before private weal. 'The law is not concerned to promote the especial welfare of a single class, but to ensure that of the city as a whole' (*Rep.* 519e; cf. 420b). This precedence of common interests over sectional or private is maintained in the *Laws*, even if as an ideal which admittedly can never be realized to perfection.

The first and best city, constitution and laws exist where the old saying applies universally, that the property of friends is truly common to all . . . where by every means the word 'private' is eradicated from life and things are as far as possible so contrived that even what nature has made one's own, like eyes, ears and hands, seem somehow to see, hear and act for the community. All praise and blame as one, and feel pleasure and pain at the same things. No one could propose better evidence of superlatively good laws than that they give to a city the greatest possible unity.

To this end both the laws and the educational system (to which in Plato's mind the laws belong) are principally directed. To take one or two illustrations, although the citizens will have their own plots of land, because farming in common would be too great a strain on men born and bred as they are now, each must regard his own plot as the common property of the state, cherishing his native land as a child its mother,

[1] See his *PCC* 128 f., 129 n. 105, for these figures and comparison with the population of existing Greek city-states. According to *Critias* (112 d), in the mythical and ideal primitive Athens care was taken to keep the population of military age, men and women, at about 20,000. The question how to maintain the population at the recommended size is not neglected. Each householder will have one heir and give his other sons for adoption to the childless. The birth-rate can be stimulated or reduced by educating public opinion through marks of approval and disapproval, and in the last resort excess of population can be checked by the old Greek device of colonization. See 740 b–41 a.

[2] Women can hold office (ἀρχάς 785 b), so *a fortiori* would be members of the Assembly. Aristotle defined a citizen as one who is eligible for deliberative and judicial office (*Pol.* 1275 b 18). Cf. *Laws* 768 b: 'Anyone debarred from taking part with others in judicial proceedings feels himself altogether excluded from citizenship' (Morrow 128).

indeed as a divine being.[1] Again at 923, in the preamble to testamentary laws, the citizens are told that they and their property belong not to themselves but to their families—ancestors, relations and descendants—and in turn the whole family and its property being to the community (923a–b). Even in marrying, the partners must consider the community's best interests, not their own preference. Here the point from the *Politicus* is repeated, that a union of opposite temperaments maintains the best balance of character, though it is natural for like to be attracted to like.[2] To put public good before private in this way is in the end best for the individual too, who cannot escape being a part of society, nor indeed of the whole cosmic scheme. In bk 10 the thoughtless youth who does not believe that God can care about the behaviour of a single individual is told that like a good craftsman God attends to details as well as the general plan. All have something to contribute. 'Creation is not for your benefit; you exist for the sake of the whole ... You grumble because you don't see that as far as you are concerned, what is best for the Universe is best for you, by virtue of your common origin.'[3]

Private property: the four classes. In the *Republic* (421e–22a) Plato was determined to keep riches and poverty out of his state, but gave no hint of how he would do it, save by forbidding the military and governing classes to have any possessions at all. Here again, the *Laws* reaffirms the goal (728e–29a, 744d) and fills in the practical details. The principle to be observed is that 'money must come last in the scale of values', after the proper care of soul and body (743e). All will live directly off the land. Gold and silver will be replaced by a token currency,[4] and the common coin of Greece reserved for military expeditions and officially

---

[1] 740a. This course is an appeal to popular religious belief in the Earth-Mother. Cf. *Tim.* 40b–c, and for the Athenian claim to be literally offspring of Attica, *Menex.* 237d–e, vol. IV, 315 n. 3, 463.

[2] 733a–e. Cf. *Pol.* 310b–11a, and p. 190 above. P. admits that legal compulsion here would be unpopular and ridiculous. Only by explanation, exhortation and reproach can people be persuaded of the importance of producing well-balanced children. Marriage itself however, by a certain age, is compulsory.

[3] *Laws* 903b–d. The 'common origin' has of course been explained in *Tim.*

[4] Another change from *Rep.*, where the possession of gold and silver will only be denied to the guardian classes (417a). P. is following Sparta's example. See Xen. *Rep. Lac.* 7.5, and for the iron currency of Sparta [Plato] *Eryxias* 400a, Plut. *Lyc.* 9.

authorized travel (741 e–42 c). Though it cannot be arranged that each citizen arrives with equal means (744 b), discrepancies of fortune will be strictly limited. Each citizen will be granted a holding of equal value,[1] which may not be sold or otherwise disposed of outside the family. Thus the poorest will have sufficient from their farms to support family and slaves, and at the other end of the scale no one may possess wealth exceeding four times the value of the plot.[2] (Wealth must be declared and registered, and any surplus handed over to the state, 744e–45a.) For administrative purposes, and in accordance with the principle that 'the truest equality is inequality in proper proportion', there will be four property-classes, and a man's class will make some, but not much, difference to his status and prospects. (There will of course be transfers as fortunes vary.)

In the filling of offices these property-classes play a very minor part. They are disregarded completely in the selection of the most important officers of the state, viz. the guardians, the euthynoi, the educator ['Minister of Education'; see below, p. 346] and the members of the court of select judges . . . also . . . generals and other military officers. All citizens are admitted to the assembly and to the popular law courts without consideration of property.[3]

The Council[4] will consist of an equal number from all classes, and in its election all citizens have the vote. However, at certain stages of the complicated five-day procedure, members of the lowest class, or the two lowest, are excused the fine imposed for not voting (756b–e). By provisions such as these Plato hopes to minimize any sense of grievance or unfairness between his citizens.

[1] By varying the size according to the quality of the soil. Further details of the elaborate pattern of allotment will be found at 745 b–e, e.g. each family is to have two homes, one in or near the city and the other near the frontier. In general, and for the historical precedents, see Morrow 103–12.

[2] There are four property-classes, but perhaps it is more accurate to say with Aristotle that the highest owns *five* times the minimum. See Morrow, *A. and P. in Mid-Fourth C.* 146 f.

[3] Morrow 133 f. Property qualifications are required for temple-treasurers and ἀστυνόμοι (city-wardens, Class I only), ἀγρονόμοι (country-wardens, I and II) and supervisors of athletic contests (I–III). For further details, and comparison with Greek practice, see Morrow 131–8. Public office carries no salary (Morrow 191).

[4] I.e. the *Boulē*, corresponding to that at Athens and not to be confused with the Nocturnal Council, which is called a σύλλογος (951 d, 961 a *et al.*).

Trade and labour. No citizen may engage in trade or ply any craft. These must be left entirely in the hands of resident foreigners, not as dishonourable but because no human being can carry on two callings efficiently, and a citizen's occupation is to maintain the social order (*kosmos*) which he enjoys, a task demanding his whole attention, with much study and practice.[2] In this the whole citizen body corresponds to the guardian classes in the *Republic*, but without being deprived of personal property and family life. For the same reason, though a householder will manage his farm and supervise the work, the actual labour will be undertaken by slaves.[3] At 806d–e Plato, raising the question of how his citizens will spend their time, notes that their basic needs have been provided for, manufacture has been left to others, their farms are worked by slaves who provide them with enough produce for men of temperate habits, and there are the common meals both for men and for women and children.[4]

Education.[5] In spite of its supreme importance for Plato, the subject of education is treated in a more rambling way, and with more irrelevant

[1] So it was in Lycurgan Sparta. See Xen. *Rep. Lac.* 7.2, Plut. *Inst. Lac.* 239d.

[2] 846d. It is the principle of 'doing one's own', declared in *Rep.* to be the essence of Justice. For the law relating to trade see 919d, 920a, and cf. Morrow 141–6, especially for the role of metics in historical Greek states.

[3] P.'s intentions are not altogether clear. ἐκδεδομένα and ἀποτελοῦσιν (806d–e) would normally refer to letting and paying rent, and are so taken by Taylor ('let out to villeins', trans. p. 101) and LSJ *s.v.* ἀποτελέω. The anachronistic 'villein' gives one pause, but P. may have in mind a status like that of the helots at Sparta, as Morrow and others have thought. See Morrow, *PCC* 149 (but contrast 150 and 151!) and *A. and P. in Mid-Fourth C.* 152. 'The helots worked the land for them', says Plutarch, 'paying the appointed tribute.' (See Plut. *Lyc.* 24 and other reff. in *RE* VIII, 205.) Morrow adds, however (*opp. citt.* 531 and 152), that in the farming laws of 842eff. 'Plato clearly implies that his citizens will be tillers of the soil'. I would say these laws imply no more than that they exercise supervision and give orders. At *Pol.* 1265a7 Aristotle says that they are free from all menial (ἀναγκαῖα) tasks, resembling in this the guardians of the *Republic*; and these, as he has just said, do not do their own farming but are provided for by the third class (1264a9 and 33; cf. *Rep.* 416d–e, *Critias* 110c–e).

[4] The Spartan institution of common messes for men is extended to women for reasons given at 781aff., but family life is not abolished as in *Rep.*: after the meal and due libations 'they all go home' (807a). How the συσσίτια are provided for is uncertain. The threefold division of household produce, for free citizens, slaves, and craftsmen or other foreigners in residence (847e–48a), leaves none earmarked as a contribution to the common table. See however Morrow 395f., and for the Spartan system of individual contributions Plut. *Lyc.* 12.

[5] For full details of the educational curriculum see Morrow ch. VII. Grote, *Pl.* III, 376–85, is also worth looking at. Bury's 'Theory of Education in Plato's "Laws"' describes P.'s educational aims in somewhat lyrical terms, with timely remarks on the relationship between παιδεία and παιδιά.

digressions, than any other major topic. Its purpose is defined more than once. In bk 1 (643e) it is 'that cultivation of excellence (*aretē*) which fills a child with eager desire to become a perfect citizen, knowing both how to rule and how to submit to rule with justice'. True education is contrasted with vocational or other training which is banausic, illiberal and unworthy of the name. Bks 1 and 2 showed the educational importance of play, song and dance. This is resumed in bks 6 and 7,[1] where also a more academic curriculum is mapped out. There will be a Director of Education, with assistants appointed by himself (813c), who must be considered supreme among the highest ministers of state.[2] Children from three to six years old attend village play-groups, at which, under supervision, they devise their own games. Schooling begins at six, and is compulsory,[3] because 'children belong to the community rather than to their parents'.[4] The teachers will be foreigners, paid by the state.[5] Boys and girls should have exactly the same education (including physical and military training, 804d–e), though segregated in different schools (794c–d). At first the chief part will be played by dancing and singing, about which bk 7 has a great deal more to say. Reading and writing will be learned from ten to thirteen, music (especially lyre-playing) from thirteen to sixteen. Basic literacy is essential, but high speed and calligraphy should not be demanded of slow learners (810b). At this stage the Director of Education will need to supply reading matter. Not all Greek literature is suitable, and Plato thinks his best guide will be the *Laws* itself.[6] Teachers should be told to study this

[1] What P. says about the psychology of Corybantic and Dionysiac frenzy, and its ritual indulgence as a homeopathic cure for irrational fears, is remarkable. See 790d–91b with notes in Saunders, Penguin trans. 274, and Grote, *Pl.* III, 376–8.

[2] 765e. For this office, its duties and mode of election, see Morrow 324–6.

[3] 794c–d. 'As far as possible', adds P.—further evidence that in the *Laws*, as nowhere else, he is conscious that politics is 'the art of the possible'.

[4] Sparta again. Cf. Plut. *Lyc.* 15: 'Lycurgus considered children not as belonging to their fathers but as the common property of the state.'

[5] 804c–d. The need for payment is probably, as Taylor says (*PMW* 484), the reason why citizens are not employed. Morrow (376 n. 102) remarks on the low esteem in which teaching was held in Athens as a profession for citizens. It is nevertheless surprising that P., for whom education meant above all inspiring the young with his own ideals of citizenship, should have entrusted them to foreigners in these impressionable years.

[6] 'The discussions which we have been having from dawn until now' (811e). These of course have not been written down, but on the side of dramatic plausibility it may be said that Clinias as a founder would certainly carry away a vivid impression of them, and the Athenian would no doubt help, as he will in the programme of higher education (968b).

and teach it to their pupils, together with such poems or prose-works as are in line with its precepts.

Other subjects to be taught (at what age is not specified) are arithmetic, mensuration and astronomy, not to a very advanced stage and with largely practical intent: letters and calculation for running a household, a state or a war, astronomy in order to understand the grouping of days into months and years for the organization of festivals and other honours to the gods (809c–d, 819c). Numbers are best taught from earliest years through play, sharing out apples between the children and so forth.[1] One thing they *must* learn. Ignorance of it is shocking, though even the Athenian (presumably Plato) only learned of it late in life and blushes for his former 'swinish' stupidity. This turns out to be the existence of incommensurables,[2] which he claims is not difficult to understand and may also be taught in play. Astronomical teaching too has its scandal to be removed, the heresy that the motions of the divine planets are irregular. This again the Athenian has only escaped at a mature age, but if he can prove the point it must find a place in the education of the young to save them from blasphemy. Instead of doing so however, he turns at this point from education to the laws on hunting. It would, after all, only repeat the *Timaeus*, and perhaps we may suppose that Clinias and Megillus would scarcely be capable at their age of taking it in.

Slavery.[3] In the *Republic* Plato says so little about slavery that some have thought he favoured its abolition. This is impossible,[4] and in the *Laws* he has given much thought to this firmly entrenched Greek institution. Slaves will be both public[5] and private. Ownership of slaves, he says (776b ff.), teems with difficulties. Slaves have been known to prove better than brother or son, the salvation of their master's

---

[1] Grote's note on method here (*Pl.* III, 383 f., n. *b*), though a century old, is still of interest.

[2] For the importance attached by P. to the discovery of irrationals or incommensurables see Popper, *OS* I, ch. 9 n. 6, pp. 248–53, already referred to in connexion with *Tim.*, p. 283 n. 2 above.

[3] This is an exceedingly complex subject. Besides Morrow's *PCC* see his 'P.'s Law of Slavery in Relation to Greek Law' and Gernet, *Laws* (Budé ed.) I, cxix–cxxxii; on Greek slavery in general, *Slavery in Class. Ant.* (ed. Finley) includes a 'Bibliographical Essay'.

[4] See vol. IV, 483 n. 1.

[5] τῆς πόλεως οἰκέται 794b. Privately-owned slaves may be requisitioned for public works, as far as possible when not required by their owners (760e–61a).

person, household and property. Yet some dismiss the whole class as depraved and untrustworthy and treat them like animals, making their souls a hundred times more slavish than before. The whole distinction between free man and slave is not easily maintained; witness the frequent slave revolts. The best policy is, first, to have slaves as far as possible of different nationalities and languages to make combination difficult,[1] and secondly to train them well both for their own sakes and one's own. For this the primary requisite is to treat them as humanely and justly as one would an equal, as indeed anyone in authority ought to behave to those weaker than himself, thus sowing the seeds of goodness in them by example. One should none the less be firm, punishing where punishment is merited (a rule which applies no less to one's own children, 793a–94a, 808e), and avoid familiarities, which only make life more difficult for slave as well as master.

The legal proposals sometimes shed a different light. Here are a few. Slaves may be freed, but retain fairly onerous obligations towards their former masters (915) and must leave the state after twenty years (i.e. are treated as metics). A slave (or foreigner) convicted of stealing public property will be fined (evidently slaves will possess money) or otherwise sentenced by the court on the assumption that he is probably curable, whereas a citizen who in spite of his upbringing commits robbery or violence against his country must be put to death as incurable (941d–42a). Murder of an innocent slave to conceal one's own crimes carries the same penalty as murder of a citizen (872c). A slave who murders a citizen will be delivered to the victim's family for execution in what manner they will.[2] In certain cases (e.g. neglect or illtreatment of parents) a slave will be freed for laying information and protected against retaliation.[3] Severe corporal punishment may be inflicted on a slave, e.g. for striking a citizen (882a–b), though a slave may be employed by the magistrates to mete out similar punishment to a free criminal (882a–b). Some proposals are both bizarre and brutal.

---

[1] No doubt P. would still forbid the enslavement of Greeks captured in war, as he did in *Rep.* (469b–c).

[2] 868b–c. That is, if the slave was carried away by passion. If the killing was cool and deliberate, he is to be taken by the public executioner within sight of his victim's tomb, scourged there, and if he survives the scourging, executed.

[3] 932d. In another case, his failure to inform carries the death-penalty (914a).

If a man strike his parents or grandparents, bystanders are bound to come to their aid. A slave who does so earns no less than his freedom, but if he does not, will receive one hundred lashes.[1] Such unfilial assaults, one imagines, are unlikely to occur often in public places, but Plato's language shows that the horror with which they inspire him is to a large extent religious. From 794 a–b it appears that infant slaves will share in the state-organized village play-groups for children between the ages of three and six,[2] though not in the later stages of state-education. There are laws to prevent the sale of unhealthy or otherwise inferior slaves (916a–b) and for dealing with the offspring of liaisons between slave and free (930d–e).

The whole conception of slavery has become so foreign to us that I prefer to give some information and leave moral judgements to the reader. He may care to consider Kahn's (*JHI* 1961, 424): 'There can scarcely be any doubt of Plato's natural humaneness: this is evident... even in his general remarks on the treatment of slaves (VI, 777d). Yet his humane sentiments are so utterly overruled by his sense for order and hierarchy that he proposes a slave legislation harsher and more retrograde than that of his own time.'

Daily life in Magnesia. Relieved of life's drudgery, are his citizens, asks Plato rhetorically (807b), to live like fattened cattle, at the mercy of any lean and spirited beast that comes along? Even the second-best state, lacking the perfect communism of the *Republic*, can do better than that. Since however a mass of trivial legislation on the daily round would be unseemly, he confines himself to a moral homily. Every day and night would hardly suffice for the mental, ethical and physical training demanded by citizenship, so from one dawn to the next a free man's life should run to a time-table. Body and soul need far less sleep than is normally taken, and much of the night should be spent on one's own or the state's business. Officials will be abroad in the city, feared by the wicked and admired by the just. The master of the house should be the first to be up and about, and the mistress should call the maids, not vice

---

[1] 881 c. Twice the legal maximum at Athens (Morrow, 'Law of Slavery' 69, Gernet, Budé introd. cxxv n. 2).

[2] This may be a misinterpretation, though understood in the same way by Morrow (*P.'s Law of Slavery* 44). See Saunders in *CR* 1961, 101.

versa. The days will be occupied either in public or legal business (for every citizen either is, or must be prepared to be, in office or on a panel of justice) or in healthy and pious enjoyment of the festivals dedicated to the gods. These are numerous,[1] and might be described as a sort of '*Kraft durch Freude*' institution, offering at the same time a rest from duties and an opportunity for self-improvement (653 d). Like all Greek festivals they included athletic contests as well as dancing and singing, the moral importance of which we have already noted. Second to divine favour, their organization has a definite social aim, 'to encourage mutual acquaintance and social contact of every kind' (771 d).

The above suggests that Plato would advocate more interference in private life than we should regard as tolerable,[2] and in fact he lays it down as a principle that 'without the proper regulation of private life it is vain to expect any firm foundation for the laws on public affairs' (790b). To make it a matter of legal compulsion, he continues, would be to invite ridicule and a flouting of the law, but the rules should nevertheless be spelt out without attaching any penalties, in the expectation that free men will treat them as laws and experience the happiness of having well-managed homes and city.[3] If moreover the state seems to intrude excessively into the private life of the citizen, he will at least be protected from annoyance by his neighbours. The non-interference of individuals in each other's lives will be secured by the provision for private suits in the courts (768b–c), the composition and procedure of which are laid down in elaborate detail and to a large extent follow Athenian practice. The brief preamble to the penalties for cultivating or grazing cattle on a neighbour's land, or enticing his bees away, is worth quoting for its human touch.[4] It runs (843b–c):

Next come the many petty injuries among neighbours. Their frequent repetition leads to considerable hostility and thoroughly embitters neigh-

[1] 'Everyone partakes in a lifelong round of sacrifices, festivals and choric song and dance' (835 e). See Morrow 353 f., and on the whole subject of festivals 352–89.

[2] Cf. p. 334 n. 4 above.

[3] 780a on the other hand does advocate the control of private life by actual legislation (in leading up to compulsory attendance at the common meals).

[4] For Plato, it would seem, *de minimis curat lex*. At 925 d ff., after some stringent marriage-laws, he adds that they will bear heavily on some people and the law must allow for hard cases. 'Some may think that these are not the legislator's concern, but they are wrong.'

bourly relations. Therefore everyone must take the greatest care not to offend his neighbour, especially in the matter of encroachment on another's land. It is easy to injure a neighbour—anyone can do it—but not everyone has the chance of doing him a favour.

Finally, something must be said about a passage on *discipline and command*, which has suffered from one-sided interpretations.[1] In bk 12, 942a–d, Plato returns to the subject of military service (στρατίαι 942a5). For this it is essential, he says, that no man or woman be without a superior (*anarchos*), whom he or she will obey in every detail, never acting independently. The soldier must be so habituated to acting as one of a group that the thought of doing anything on his own never enters his head, for this is the best and most efficient recipe for survival and victory in war. We recognize here the principle of discipline and the chain of command familiar in armies of our own day. In peacetime, he continues, from childhood upwards, we must practise this art of ruling others and being ruled by them in turn. The absence of a ruler (*anarchia*) must be wholly eliminated from the life of everyone.

Since the Second World War,[2] this passage has been branded as an outrageous example of totalitarian ethic. 'Like other totalitarian militarists and admirers of Sparta, Plato urges that the all-important requirements of military discipline must be paramount, even in peace, and that they must determine the whole life of all citizens', who must 'spend their whole life in a state of permanent and total mobilization' (Popper, *OS* I, 103).[3] Since this would be wholly opposed to Plato's recommendations elsewhere in the *Laws*, the passage must be looked at more closely. First, the total submission to orders is introduced as a necessity for military training and active service. The things to be done at command are enumerated: standing still, marching, physical training, washing, eating, night-duty as sentry or despatch-carrier, and in actual warfare pursuit of the enemy or retreat. Plato's love of analogy can mislead. He compares the legislator or *archōn* here to an army officer

---

[1] Dr Saunders when he read this chapter drew my attention to M. J. Silverthorne's article 'Militarism in the *Laws?*' in *Symb. Osl.* 1973. It does not conflict with what is said here, but makes some different points, and I think both accounts may be left to stand independently.

[2] And not only since then. Gomperz has some exaggerated and partial comments in *GT* vol. III, 262.

[3] See also Popper's 'Reply to a Critic' in later editions, pp. 338–42.

just as he compares him elsewhere to a doctor. Clearly it is army life in camp or battle that is being described. It has however, Plato believes, an analogy in ordinary life, part of which will in any case be spent in military training.[1] The analogy to indiscipline in the forces is anarchy[2] in civil life. There however the ideal is not for everyone to suppress initiative and blindly follow the orders of a superior. The art for a citizen to cultivate is '*how to rule and be ruled in turn*' (643e6, 942c7), for in Plato's state any citizen may be elected to administer the laws which are the only permanent rulers.[3] Far from following Sparta in this, Plato, as we have seen, castigated the Spartan and Cretan practice of directing all the energies of the state towards preparation for war. 'The greatest good is neither war nor civil strife . . . but peace and goodwill.' 'No one who makes warfare his sole or first concern can be a true statesman, nor legislate correctly unless his laws about war are designed to ensure peace, not his peacetime legislation as an instrument of war.' (628c, d.) People say they wage war for the sake of peace, but its results are not what they hoped. Genuine leisure and culture (on which, he says, we chiefly set store) are never a consequence of war. One should spend one's life in play of the right sort, sacrificing, singing and dancing, and so win the favour of the gods and repel our enemies (803d–e). In the *Republic* the guardian classes would spend their whole lives under the conditions of a military camp.[4] Now Plato has decided that such a life for his citizens would be neither practicable nor desirable.

Contact with the rest of the Greek world (949e–53e). The rules for foreign travel are among the least attractive features of Plato's state. As elsewhere, his general sentiments sound better than his practical proposals. He is of course convinced that unrestricted contact with

[1] Peacetime training is to be compulsory, and all will partake in a monthly field-day (829a–b). A Greek city-state had to be able to defend itself.

[2] P. uses the word ἀναρχία, which had the same associations with lawlessness (ἀνομία) as its English derivative. (See LSJ.) Its use after ἄναρχος at 942a7 is almost a play on words, as if wholly in the sense of Hdt. 9.23. Among the faults which P. saw in contemporary democrats was that 'they call anarchy liberty' (*Rep.* 560e). It leads to tyranny, which according to Aristotle apes democracy and courts popularity by allowing slaves, women and children the pleasure of ἀναρχία (*Pol.* 1319b27–32).

[3] In *Rep.* 8 (557e) one of the things that is said to make democracy popular in Greece is that 'no one is compelled to exercise authority, even if he is capable of it, nor to submit to it if he does not want to'.

[4] See 416e and vol. IV, 467.

foreigners is dangerous for a well-run state. (Most states, he adds, are badly run, so it makes no difference to them.) Nevertheless to expel foreigners and never go abroad, like the Spartans,[1] gives a state a bad name, and in fact to shut itself off from all contact with others, good and bad alike, will leave it immature and uncultivated. Even bad states contain outstanding characters, through converse with whom a visitor can confirm what is right in his home state and correct anything amiss. But what are the practical conclusions? First, no one at all, *in any circumstances*, shall go abroad under the age of forty, nor ever in a private capacity. (Military service does not count as travel.) Those who go in the state's interests will be carefully selected to make a good impression. Besides heralds and diplomatic missions, it will send teams to the Panhellenic festivals and contests.[2] In addition, citizens aged between fifty and sixty, approved by the *Nomophylakes*, may be commissioned to act as official observers, and spend as much time abroad as they wish. On return, a traveller must report to the Nocturnal Council, who will congratulate him if appropriate. But if his experiences appear to have corrupted him, he will be forbidden to speak to anyone as an expert on foreign affairs, for it is his duty to 'teach' his juniors that the ways of other states are inferior to those of his own.

Foreign visitors fare well enough, whether travelling officially or on business or simply to see the sights and attend the festivals. (It does not seem to have occurred to Plato that observation of the freedom accorded by other states to their citizens might arouse some envy in his own.) Provided that they do not try to introduce revolutionary changes, they will be hospitably and considerately received. Official missions are naturally guests of the state, but even the tourists are to be lodged near the temples and enjoy hospitality dispensed by the priests and temple staff.

Women. Their parity with men in education and physical and military training,[3] liability for military service, and eligibility for offices of state,

---

[1] The word ξενηλασίαι at 950b shows that Sparta is referred to. See especially Xen. *Rep. Lac.* 14.4, Plut. *Inst. Lac.* 238d, 239e, for both provisions.

[2] Unless the over-forty rule is broken in this case (and it is certainly presented as absolute), one would not give much for Magnesia's chances in the Olympic games.

[3] For their participation in military exercises and sports see 829b, 833c–d; for education 804d. Though women are liable for military service (with remission for childbearing) up to the age of

as well as their eating in public at common tables (with their children but segregated from the men, 806c),[1] have already been mentioned. Their participation in warfare is retained from the *Republic*, and just as their children were to be allowed to witness battles, so here they are taken along with their parents on the monthly field-days (829b). It is Plato's belief that both Sparta and Athens in their different ways (805 e–806a), by their waste of woman-power, have robbed the state of half its strength: 'The position in our parts of the world is utterly stupid, in that we do not have all men and women engaging with one accord and all their strength in the same occupations' (805a). Yet on feminine character he is somewhat equivocal. That it differs from the masculine he has no doubt. Characteristic virtues of the man are dignity and courage, of the woman orderliness and modesty.[2] At the same time the female sex 'because of its weakness is more given to secrecy and craftiness',[3] men are 'superior to' and 'better than' women (917a) and women 'of lesser virtue' (781c).

All that he says here simply works out in more detail the ideas of the *Republic*, except for the vital matter of community of wives and children, which, though he still maintains it as an ideal, he now admits to be impracticable. In the *Republic* women were to undertake the same duties as men (with allowance for their comparative weakness), and would consequently need the same education and training, including carrying arms and riding.[4]

Sexual morality and procreation. Plato's standards of sexual behaviour are strict. To overcome the temptations of pleasure is, as in the *Philebus*, the secret of a happy life (840c). Our pleasure in the sexual act has been

fifty, it will perhaps not be universally imposed. See 785b. Horse-racing and others of the more masculine sports are allowed but not mandatory (834d, 794c). For their education the model is of course Sparta.

[1] P. 345 n. 4. But 783b shows that the arrangements for συσσίτια are still fluid.

[2] 802e. τὸ κόσμιον καὶ σῶφρον cannot be precisely rendered in English. ('Modesty and restraint' Saunders, 'modesty and sedateness' Morrow p. 369, 'orderliness and temperance', *idem* 331.) In any case the terms are complimentary.

[3] 781a, though P.'s Amazons (the comparison to Amazons is his own, 806b) do not sound particularly weak, at least physically.

[4] See 451e–52c and vol. IV, 480. I have omitted the legal status and competence of women, which is dealt with by Morrow on pp. 121, 285 with n. 111. He notes that their privileges in the courts are to be wider than those they enjoyed in contemporary Athens, conformably to their greater responsibilities in public life.

bestowed by nature for the sake of procreation, which should be its sole purpose. It is, after all, nature's way of bestowing immortality on the human race.[1] That is why homosexual practices in either sex are an unnatural surrender to pleasure (636e). It is their *barrenness* that angers him (cf. σπέρματα ἄγονα at 841d), and he goes so far as to call sodomy 'deliberate murder of the human race' (838e). Scarcely less heinous is 'the sowing of unhallowed and bastard seed in courtesans'. Ideally therefore 'no citizen worthy of his birth should touch any woman but his own wedded wife'. We must not show ourselves inferior to the birds or other gregarious creatures who spend their whole lives with a single consort (841d, 840d). This may be only a romantic dream, adds the Athenian, but the climate of opinion *might* be changed, and if so, there is no limit to its influence, as the example of incest shows. However attractive a sister, brother or daughter, even a lawless man's lusts are checked, not by any law but simply because in this case their indulgence is universally condemned, not least by himself. The thought of it does not even occur to him (838a–c).

The first aim, then, is to secure complete abstinence except for the procreation of legitimate children. If this be unattainable, then as a second-best, while maintaining an absolute prohibition of homosexual intercourse, liaisons between the sexes must be surrounded with an aura of shame. The disgrace will be not in the act but in being detected. This should decrease the amount of indulgence, which in turn (says Plato optimistically) will reduce desire.[2]

The worst is to come. The chief object of marriage being to present the state with worthy children, a couple must approach this task with a fitting sense of responsibility(783d–84e: for instance, Plato has already said that a state of intoxication is prejudicial to the begetting of proper offspring, 757b–e).[3] To ensure this, female inspectors will periodically enter houses, and meet together daily in the temple of Eileithyia, god-

[1] 721b, in the preface to the law enjoining marriage.
[2] P. seems a little uncertain how much of this he wishes to secure by law and how much by his favourite method of education and persuasion. At 841b2–4 the citizens are to consider secrecy 'right and sanctioned by *usage and unwritten law*', and lack of it as 'disgraceful'; but very soon (841d–e) he is drafting a law that if any man have intercourse with a woman other than her to whom he is joined in holy matrimony, and fail to conceal it, he must be excluded from public honours and treated as an alien.
[3] Another Spartan touch (Plut. *Lyc.* 15).

dess of childbirth, to discuss their findings. Persistent offenders after admonition and threats will be reported to the *Nomophylakes*, who in the last resort will publicly post their names and (making the punishment fit the crime) forbid them to attend any parties to celebrate weddings or births. Home-inspections are to continue for ten years. If no children are born during that period the couple shall part on terms fair to both.

Conclusion: the ideal citizen. Plato never lets his readers forget that legal compulsion is to be the last resort, and if the rest of his plans work out properly, then even though 'we are talking to men, not gods', it should only be necessary in rare and isolated cases. The object is to produce a society of one mind, sharing the same ideals and united by bonds of real spiritual concord (συμφωνία 689 d). Many important precepts, as we have seen, cannot be embodied in law at all, but must rely for their observance on educated public opinion, and of the laws themselves the most important part is the first, which explains the benefits which will follow from their observance. What he could not see is that the best chance of obtaining general consent to his laws would lie, not in entrusting them to a handful of legislators, however determined to put persuasion before compulsion, but in allowing the democratic procedure of open debate on their content. In Plato's mixed constitution, any citizen may play a part in *administering* the laws, but to *create* them is the work of a superior few.[1]

In bk 5 (730b ff.) Plato outlines the characteristics of the ideal citizen. First comes a regard for truth. Anyone who does not tell the truth is either a liar or a fool, and one cannot make a friend of either. Next come self-control, good sense and other virtues which he not only possesses himself but can impart to others. He will be free from jealousy and a slanderous tongue, which discourage his fellows from goodness, and injure, so far as one individual can, the moral fibre and reputation of the whole state. He will combine a fierce spirit with gentleness (exactly like the guardians of *Rep.* 375 b–c), the first to assist in the stern repression of incurable crime, but the second also because he will know that

---

[1] This is clearly his intention, and appears to be the gist of the metaphor from weaving at 734e–35 a, with its distinction between electing people to office and providing those elected with a code of laws. ἄρξοντες at 735 a 3 cannot refer simply to office-holders.

most criminals are curable and no one sins voluntarily. He will avoid above all things self-love and a tendency to forgive his own faults rather than those of others. These are forms of stupidity mistaken for cleverness, and cloud one's whole judgement of where goodness and justice lie.

(4) *Religion and theology*[1]

State religion and ethics. Plato, as we have seen (pp. 350, 352 above), would promote the state religion by every means in his power, not only to secure the favour of the gods but because the sacrifices,[2] singing, dancing and athletic contests which made a religious festival were a source of recreation and pleasure, and through the promotion of social intercourse and good fellowship a contribution to the unification of society—apart from the educational advantages of rhythmic movement to music. Even the licence of the Dionysia was approved, and a festival was to be established by law for every day of the year, 365 in all,[3] 'so that there will always be at least one official sacrificing to some god or daemon on behalf of the city, its people and their property'. In addition to these public rites, each family's ancestral spirits will be annually honoured, with legally approved rites, in private homes.[4] Apart from this, private domestic rites and shrines will be strictly prohibited, in accordance with the principle that community life has everywhere priority over private, but also to discourage superstitious fears and hopes and the charlatans who prey on them.[5] In extreme cases the death penalty may be imposed. In matters connected with the public cults, Plato emphasizes the importance of heeding the oracles (738b–c, 759c, 828a), but is no longer content, as he was in the *Republic* (427b), to leave entirely to Delphi 'the founding of temples, sacrifices and other services to gods, daemons and heroes, the burial of the dead and the

---

[1] For a full treatment see O. Reverdin's *La religion de la cité platonicienne*.

[2] Sacrifices meant a feast of meat (rare in their homes) for the worshippers as well as the gods (Nilsson, *GPR* 87).

[3] 828a–b. P.'s assumption of a solar year is a striking improvement on the lunar year (with intercalations as necessary), which was still in use in Greece, though the Egyptians used the solar (Wilamowitz, *Pl.* 1, 687 n. 1). But he simply gives the number of festivals without comment.

[4] 717b (ἱδρύματα ἴδια πατρῴων θεῶν κατὰ νόμον ὀργιαζόμενα) evidently refers to deified ancestors, contrasted with γονεῖς ζῶντες. 723b mentions προγόνων θεραπείας. The dead tended κατ' ἐνιαυτόν 719e.

[5] The reasons for the prohibition are fully set out at 909d–10e.

tribute we must render to propitiate the dwellers in the other world'. Rules and regulations for all these, and the mode of appointment of priests and other religious officials, are set out in detail.[1]

This emphasis on the externals of religion does not mean that, like many Greeks, he divorced its practice from ethics. On the contrary, he insists on their connexion in language reminiscent of a Hebrew prophet (716c–17a):

What conduct is pleasing and obedient to God?[2] That alone which reflects the old saying that like loves like . . . He therefore that will be pleasing to God must do all in his power to resemble him, and accordingly the temperate (*sōphrōn*) man is dear to God, for he is like him, and the intemperate and unjust is unlike and at odds with him . . . It follows . . . that for the good man to sacrifice and approach the gods with prayers and offerings and every form of worship is above all else fine and good, conducive to happiness and especially fitting; but for the wicked it is the opposite. For the soul of the wicked is impure, but that of the righteous pure, and to accept gifts from polluted hands befits neither a good man nor a god. Therefore vain is all the labour of the impious to please the gods, but for the pious it is always in season.

Personal beliefs. In his own personal beliefs Plato shows that the immortality and reincarnation of the soul have not lost their hold. As in the *Symposium*, having children is called the 'natural' way for the human race to partake of immortality, but (as in the *Symposium* also) this does not exclude the belief in immortality as usually understood.[3] Pluto, lord of Hades, is a benefactor, for 'the union of soul and body, I say in all seriousness, is in no way superior to their separation' (828d). In line with earlier dialogues is 726–7, on the soul as the ruling element, to be held in honour above all else except the gods. We do it no honour by thinking that life is to be clung to at all costs, as if everything in the next world were evil, when for all we know its gods may have the best things of all in store for us. This seems to echo the ostensible agnosticism of the *Apology*, which in both dialogues is denied by the supreme importance attached to the soul and its 'care', and in the *Laws* by what

---

[1] Described by Morrow in chh. VII and VIII of *PCC*.

[2] On the whole this seems preferable to 'a god' for θεῷ, but note how easily P. slips from singular to plural.

[3] 721b, p. 355 above. For *Symp.* see vol. IV, 387ff. *Laws* 721b–c is referred to on p. 390, n. 5.

Plato says in other passages. As in the *Timaeus*, the intelligence is 'what we possess of the immortal' (713e). After some meticulous burial regulations,[1] his legislator will point out that the soul is far and away superior to the body. In this life it makes each of us what he is, while the body merely represents us visually, so we are right to say that a dead body 'looks like'[2] the man without being him. The real 'we', the immortal soul, goes to other gods to render its account. As part of the preface to the laws on wilful murder (870d–e), the legislator will tell 'what is firmly believed by many on the authority of those who have studied such matters in the mysteries', namely that criminals of this sort are punished in the next world, and when they return to this one will die at another's hands the death which they once inflicted themselves.[3] From these examples it might be argued that Plato's legislator is to exercise his privilege of using myths in which he does not himself believe, but besides being a complete reversal of what he has taught in other dialogues, this is excluded by his calling them 'most true' at 881a and by other affirmations. In bk 10 (903c) it is said that a soul is joined now with one body and now with another.

Theology. 'Virtue is knowledge', said Socrates, and it often seems to have been a corollary for Plato that the second was only desirable as a means of promoting the first.[4] That is true at least of the theology of bk 10, which in form is a lengthy preface to the law against impiety (887a3 and c1). 'The supreme decision is whether or not to have the

---

[1] E.g. no one to be buried in cultivable land, the epitaph not to exceed four hexameters in length and the tombstone to be of corresponding size.

[2] 959b2. I borrow these words from Saunders. Literally 'is an image' or 'phantom' (εἴδωλον). In Homer the ψυχή itself is the εἴδωλον (e.g. *Il.* 23.103–7, where note εἴκτο δὲ θέσκελον αὐτῷ) and Ast (see England *ad loc.*) was almost certainly right in saying that P. is here consciously contradicting that identification. At *Pho.* 81d it is continued pollution by the earthy matter of the body that renders ψυχαί visible as εἴδωλα (ghosts). P. enjoyed his skill at playing with ideas.

[3] With the mention of experts in *teletai* cf. in a non-legal context *Pho.* 69c: 'it looks as if our founders of *teletai* were no simpletons' etc. The eschatology of *Laws* 10, with its mention of posthumous punishments and reincarnation, is aimed at moral reform, but is not to be rejected on that account as foreign to P.'s genuine beliefs.

[4] Several dialogues could give this impression, but one must not exaggerate it to score a debating point. In the preface to a law P. is only trying to inculcate 'right opinion', not knowledge in his own stricter sense of the term. Moreover *aretē* is more than moral virtue. Mathematics, astronomy and theology will be carried much further by the highest Guardians of both *Rep.* and *Laws*. Yet the goal remains the same. These men and women 'must be better qualified than ordinary people both to expound and to practise virtue' (*Laws* 964d).

right ideas about the gods and so live well' (888b). The motive for proving that the cosmos is controlled by a good and rational god is that the contrary belief encourages wickedness. This has certain consequences: not that Plato uses any doctrine in which he does not himself believe, but it does lead to a curious incompleteness. For instance, it is enough to show that the motions of the heavenly bodies are due to soul. This might happen, he thinks, in any one of three ways. Take the sun (898e). Its soul might move it (i) as our souls move us, by inhabiting its body; (ii) by taking to itself an external body, perhaps of fire or air, and pushing body with body by force: (iii) by some other 'exceedingly wonderful' power of moving without body. Even if a reader is charitable enough to accept (iii) as a positive alternative,[1] Plato has no interest in deciding between the three. Again, how many of these souls are there? According to 898d each star or planet has its own as in the *Timaeus*. At 899b their motions are caused by 'a soul or souls', whereas at 896e he answers the question 'How many souls are at work in the heavens?' by saying that there must be at least two, a good and a bad. However, the prevailing regularity of the heavenly motions proves that the good soul is in control. That is all that matters to Plato. The question of monotheism or polytheism does not worry him so far as it concerns the actual existence of gods, but only one must have supreme control.

Young men (begins the Athenian) get infected with wrong beliefs about the gods, including actual atheism, and make them an excuse for evil living. If there are gods, either they take no thought for human affairs or a sinner can buy them off with sacrifices and prayers. These perverted minds can be compelled by threats and penalties to conform to the laws, but to persuade them by an appeal to reason would be very much better. This however faces us at once with a popular and powerful argument—and against this is directed the whole of the theology which follows—the argument that opposes *physis* (nature) to *nomos* (law, convention, the artificial).[2] According to it, the greatest and best things

---

[1] For instance Düring (*Arist.* 187) is confident that it refers to Arist. *Metaph.* 1073a3, i.e. to Aristotle's Unmoved Mover, a confidence against which G. E. R. Lloyd rightly protested in *JHS* 1968, 165.

[2] The *nomos–physis* antithesis is the subject of vol. III, ch. IV. The thesis which now follows is of such importance to the earlier history of thought that it has had to be referred to several times

in the world are the work of nature or chance (which is the same thing). The four elements, and the earth, sun, moon and stars which are made of them, are lifeless matter. Moving as their chance-got properties impel them, the elements somehow came together suitably—hot with cold, dry with moist, soft with hard—and combining 'by the inevitability of chance' generated the cosmos and everything in it. Animals, plants, and the seasons all owe their existence to these causes, namely nature and chance: no god, intelligence or art had any part in it. Art or design (*technē*) came later, a more insignificant force of human origin whose creations have little substance or reality. The only arts worth anything are those which, like medicine and agriculture, assist the powers of nature. Political skill has some slight connexion with nature, but is mostly a matter of art, and legislation has nothing to do with nature at all. It is entirely artificial and its postulates are untrue.

The gods themselves have no existence in nature, but are a product of human artifice, and vary according to local conventions. Goodness is one thing in nature and another by *nomos*, and as for justice, nature knows nothing of it. Men are for ever disputing about and altering it, and every change is valid from the moment it is made, owing its existence to artificial conventions rather than to nature. By theories like these agitators incite the young to irreligion and sedition, urging them to adopt 'the right life according to nature', by which they mean a life of ruthless ambition instead of service to their fellow-men and to law.

Many have sought to pin down this doctrine to a particular man or school.[1] The emphasis on the *nomos–physis* antithesis shows that Plato has primarily in mind the great Sophists and their followers. These in their turn invoked Presocratic natural philosophy, with its predominantly non-teleological theories of the origin of the world and life,

---

already, and I have taken the liberty of repeating the summary of it in vol. III, 115 f. Already in *Soph.* P. has mentioned as widespread the belief that nothing animate or inanimate is the work of a divine craftsman but that 'nature produces them from some spontaneous cause that generates without intelligence' (265 c).

[1] E.g. Tate in *CQ* 1936 argued that it probably belongs to (hypothetical) fourth-century followers of Archelaus, the reputed pupil of Anaxagoras and teacher of Socrates; but his interesting suggestion is purely speculative. Arguing that there were physical philosophers in the fourth century unknown to us he asks (p. 54): 'Who . . . were those mentioned in 899a as holding that the sun is moved by a soul not directly but indirectly through an intermediate body of earth or fire?' (Düring in his *Arist.*, p. 187, again proposed Aristotle, in *De caelo* and the Dialogue *De phil.*) Surely we need not look for anyone. P. is simply trying to exhaust the possibilities.

in support of their relativistic and in some cases self-centred views on human morality and institutions.[1] So behind the pernicious atheistic teachers of the young of Plato's day it is not difficult to trace the lasting influence of Empodocles, Democritus, Anaxagoras[2] and even Anaximander—doubtless also Archelaus—as well as contributions from Critias, Protagoras and Thrasymachus.[3] He describes a whole climate of thought, formed by the work of many original thinkers and seized on by a crowd of less talented or scrupulous hangers-on.

These arguments Plato counters by a thesis on the same general lines as the *Timaeus*, though more summarily expressed as befits its practical purpose.[4] He maintains that, far from there being any contrast between nature and art, nature and art are the same thing, and design is prior both in time and importance to chance, since it came first and the whole universe is rationally planned. Consequently to make any distinction between the life according to nature and the life according to law, and try to exalt one at the expense of the other, is nonsensical. Art, including law, is the product of intelligence, and intelligence is the highest manifestation of nature. Clearly a metaphysic which, if it can be proved, will have far-reaching effects on ethical theory as well. Our young men have got their causes the wrong way round (891e) by making an inanimate nature prior, and soul posterior. Hence their mistake about the reality of the gods. Soul and its kin, intelligence and art, must have come first, and what they wrongly call nature is later and subordinate. Soul is the truly natural thing, as will be obvious if we can only prove our belief in its priority. Being prior, soul is the cause of all

[1] For the debt of the Sophists to the Presocratics see vol. III, 45–8.

[2] 886d. Cf. *Apol.* 26d.

[3] For the Sophists as collectively champions of the *nomos–physis* antithesis see vol. III, 48 with n. 1, and for Archelaus and the link between it and the evolutionary physical theories *ib.* 58f. (The mention of 'prevailing by violence' at 890a5 is a paraphrase of Pindar. Cf. 715a and p. 337 n. 1.)

[4] On their relationship opinions differ. Burnet spoke of *Laws* as a 'matter-of-fact treatment' and 'an indication of Plato's mature thought on the soul': Plato's reasoning there was in his own eyes 'strictly scientific', whereas *Tim.* was at least partly mythical (*T. to P.* 334, 336, 337). Hardie (*S. in P.* 153) took Burnet to task, and according to Vlastos (*SPM* 392–3) the book is 'purely an exercise in apologetics . . . political theology', as opposed to *Tim.* which is 'esoteric philosophy'. We may notice one point. *Tim.* gives a narrative of creation, which many scholars, ancient and modern, have regarded as merely an instructional device, to be translated into terms of a static analysis (pp. 301–05 above). When therefore it speaks of soul being generated, they can discard this as part of the mythical apparatus. If we should find the language of generation applied to soul in *Laws*, that resource will be denied them.

movements of body, i.e. intelligent design, not chance, is the first cause.

The proof starts from an analysis of motion. It is first resolved into eight divisions, of which the most important, for Platonic reasons which should now be obvious, is revolution in the same place about a fixed centre, in which Plato finds it remarkable that points on the revolving object nearer to and farther from the centre complete the revolution in the same time, i.e. at different speeds. But these preliminary divisions are not mutually exclusive. There are cross-divisions, some include others, and the final result is to extract two main heads under which all motion may be brought and which are relevant to Plato's present purpose. These are *spontaneous and communicated* motion (894b). Here (let us say) are three billiard-balls. Ball *A* moves forward and strikes ball *B*, which moves forward and strikes ball *C* which moves forward. Evidently *A* by its own movement caused the movement of *C*. But *A* itself only moved because struck by a cue, which was propelled by a hand. Follow the chain back to its starting-point, and you will find it in the *intention* of the player to make that particular stroke; in other words, in a living soul. Lifeless matter is inert, and could never initiate motion, though it can transmit it. If the world were ever locked together at a standstill, as many say it once was, the deadlock could only be broken by self-initiated motion, which is therefore primary and the ultimate cause of all transmitted motion. The reference to the world being at a standstill clearly hints at Anaxagoras,[1] who however would seem to have anticipated Plato himself in attributing the original motion to Mind. But as we know, Plato condemned Anaxagoras for failing to exploit his great innovation and continuing to ascribe phenomena solely to material causes, 'necessary' not designed.[2]

Here some may see the weakest point in what has been unkindly called (though not for that reason) an 'inferior ancestor of Ontological Arguments'.[3] It is not now difficult for Plato to claim that whatever

---

[1] Compare the words εἰ σταίη πως τὰ πάντα (895a) with Aristotle's statement of Anaxagoras's theory ὁμοῦ πάντων ὄντων καὶ ἠρεμούντων τὸν ἄπειρον χρόνον κίνησιν ἐμποιῆσαι τὸν νοῦν (*Phys.* 250b25; also *Cael.* 301a12 ἐξ ἀκινήτων γὰρ ἄρχεται κοσμοποιεῖν). P. refers the theory to οἱ πλεῖστοι τῶν τοιούτων, an exaggeration, though Anaxagoras must have had other disciples besides Archelaus. He could not have meant to include the atomists. See vol. II, 396–9, and on Anaxagoras *ib.* ch. IV, esp. pp. 274f., 296.

[2] See *Pho.* 97b ff., vol. II, 274f.   [3] King-Farlow and Rothstein, *PQ* 1964, 18.

moves itself is alive (the Greek for which is *empsychon*, 'ensouled') and to define life or soul as 'the motion which can move itself' and so the ultimate cause of all motion, change and generation (895 a–96 b).[1] But soul in his eyes has a double function, as source of motion and as the seat of thought, deliberation and will. Now if soul precedes body its attributes will precede the bodily, from which he immediately concludes that 'manners, moral character, wish, calculation, true beliefs and memory are prior to length, breadth, depth and strength in bodies' (896 c–d).[2] One is tempted to remind him of his statement that even plants, let alone flies and worms, have life and even sensation (*Tim.* 77 a–b). It is possible to possess the lowest form of soul without the higher two, and this is all that is required for self-motion. Not that even the higher souls are all sweet reason and goodness. There are bad morals as well as good, and wishes and calculations may take a wrong turn. Hate as well as love is a property of soul, which may either 'take to itself reason' or 'consort with unreason' (897 a–b). 'We must admit that soul is the cause of good and evil, fair and foul, just and unjust and every other pair of contraries, if we are to maintain that it is the cause of everything' (896 d). Souls employ all the secondary physical motions and properties as instruments, the growth and diminution, separation and combination of bodies, heat and cold, weight, colours, flavours, texture. The existence of evil, and of irregular motions, suggests to the Athenian that there must be at least two souls concerned in the running of the universe, a good and a bad. Which is in control? Well, if the course of the whole cosmos proceeds in a way akin to that of intelligence he will ascribe it to the best soul, but if in a way akin to madness, to the evil. The *Timaeus* has told us what to expect. Here he takes the simile from his previous classification of motions. The ways of reason resemble axial rotation, proceeding with constancy on a single orderly plan and maintaining the same position in relation to other objects.[3] This granted, the general order, regularity and sphericity of the heavenly motions are

[1] For the wide sense of *kinesis*, translated 'motion', see p. 101 n. 1 above.

[2] This amalgamation of the motive with the cognitive and moral aspects of *psyche* is reflected in several dialogues and has had to be mentioned earlier. For *Tim.* see p. 293 above, and for other dialogues vol. IV, 347 f., 555, and (especially) 420 f.

[3] 898 a–b. The comparison he claims as a good specimen of the art of verbal imagery. On the Greek analogy between circular motion and reason see also vol. I, 356 f.

invoked to show that not only soul, but the best soul, is responsible for them. There follows the enumeration of the possible means employed in moving the heavenly bodies (mentioned on p. 330), including the statements that each has its own soul and these souls are gods.

A few points in conclusion. If the rebuttal of atheism leaves something to be desired, one must recall its purpose, to justify a law against impiety. Its persuasiveness must have an element of what Plato calls enchantment or spellbinding (903 b 1) as well as cold reason. It is as Vlastos said: for his philosophical theology one must look to the *Timaeus* rather than to the 'political theology' of the *Laws*. In his rebuttal of the other two heresies[1] the element of enchantment is even stronger, sprinkled with rhetorical questions about whether, granted that there are gods, they can be supposed either ignorant of anything or in the slightest degree neglectful of their duties as the supreme guardians of mankind. As the Athenian admits (907 b), he has spoken rather vehemently in his anxiety to get the better of the wicked. The case against divine neglect emphasizes yet again the effect of conduct in this life on the fate of souls after death. Our life is ours to live as we will, but how we live it determines our future place in the order of things, whether in the same phase, down to a lower place (popularly known as Hades), or upward to a better, holy region.[2]

The idea of two opposing souls, a good and an evil, contending for control of the universe, has naturally suggested to many a dualism of God and Devil, adapted by Plato from the Zoroastrian Ormuzd and Ahriman and flatly contradicting the denial in the *Politicus* (270 a) of 'two gods of opposite mind'. This has been challenged in a treatment of the general question of evil and its sources which it seemed appropriate to raise in connexion with the *Theaetetus*.[3]

---

[1] Mentioned on p. 360 above. For attributions of the 'Epicurean' heresy (Antiphon, Thrasymachus) see vol. III, 230 f. The other is obviously a matter of popular belief going back to Homer.

[2] 904 c–905 a. On the peculiarities of this passage see Saunders in *CQ* 1973, 233 f. As he says, the personal agency of the gods is reduced to a minimum, and the process 'seems to be automatic or semi-automatic'. One might add that though Homer's line about 'the judgement of the gods' is quoted, in Plato's language (904 c 8) it happens 'according to the ordering and law of fate'.

[3] Pp. 95–97 above. In fairness it should have been added that there is no reason to doubt P.'s knowledge of the Persian doctrine. On its attraction for the Academy see Jaeger, *Arist.* 131–5, who even includes *Laws* 10 among the evidence: 'The bad world-soul that opposes the good one in the *Laws* is a tribute to Zarathustra.' I do not find his reff. to *Epinomis* altogether convincing

The absence from the *Laws* of the Demiurge of the *Timaeus* is sometimes commented on, but should not be surprising in what is not, like the *Timaeus*, a narrative of creation. For Plato's present argument the primacy and overlordship of a good and intelligent soul are enough. Even so, we do find mention of 'him who looks after the universe, by whom everything has been arranged (συντεταγμένα) for the safety and goodness of the whole'. His work is even compared to that of a human *demiurgos*, he arranges his pieces like a divine draughts-player, and is also called 'our King'.[1]

ADDITIONAL NOTE: IS SOUL SOMETHING CREATED?

In ch. IV I ventured the opinion, not uncontested, that in the *Timaeus* the creation of the cosmic soul by the Demiurge was not to be dismissed as mythical, and the preceding disorderly motions of body were due to an inanimate necessity (pp. 271 f. above). What is the position in the *Laws*, where all the stress is on the ψυχή as first cause of all motion? The answer may turn on an oddity of Greek syntax. Usually the superlative of an adjective followed by a genitive case means what it does in English, e.g. 'Eve, fairest of women'. Occasionally however, in both Greek and Latin it is given the force of the comparative, as in Milton's imitation of the classical construction: 'Fairest of all her daughters, Eve'. (For Greek see Kühner–Gerth II, 1, 22–4.) A clear example of the latter use occurs in the *Laws* itself (969 a 7): ἀνδρειότατος τῶν ὕστερον ἐπιγιγνομένων. Now in bk 12 again, at 967 d, ψυχή is described as πρεσβύτατον ἁπάντων ὧν γονῆς μετείληφεν, and similarly at 966 d–e. 'Oldest of all created things' or 'Older than all created things'? England and Taylor chose the latter, and Saunders has followed them. If that is what Plato meant the question is settled, but since he could have meant either, one must look at any other evidence also. At 892 c 4–5 soul is 'preeminently natural' because ἐν πρώτοις γεγενημένη, which Saunders correctly renders, 'one of the first things *to be created*'. Similarly at 896 b 10 we have ψυχὴν μὲν προτέραν γεγονέναι σώματος, and at 894 d the self-moving motion, which is soul, is πρῶτον γενέσει τε καὶ ῥώμῃ, which reminds one of *Tim.* 34 c, καὶ γενέσει καὶ ἀρετῇ πρότερον καὶ πρεσβύτερον σώματος

(132 n. 2), but undoubtedly there is evidence enough. For further reff. see Morrow 448 n. 164. Leisegang is one who strongly denies any connexion with Persian belief (*RE* 2519), and cf. Koster, *Mythe de Platon* etc. ch. IX.

[1] ὁ τοῦ παντὸς ἐπιμελούμενος 903 b 5, 904 a 3–4; δημιουργός 902 e 5, 903 c 6; πεττευτής 903 d 6; ἡμῶν ὁ βασιλεύς 904 a 6. The last two echo (deliberately but not very seriously, I imagine) the mysterious fr. 52 of Heraclitus (vol. I, 478 n. 2). Nearer still to *Tim.*, in bk 12 (966 e), we hear of νοῦς ὁ τὸ πᾶν διακεκοσμηκώς.

(p. 304 above). At 892 a we are told that almost everyone is ignorant of the nature and power of the soul, 'especially about its birth, that it is one of the first, having come into being before all bodies'. *Laws* 10 makes no mention of the random motions in a 'Receptacle' which preceded the creation of a world-soul by the Demiurge who is pure Mind, but it does not profess to offer, like the *Timaeus*, a narrative of the process of creation or ordering. Even so, it tells (at 897 a–b, in an alarmingly complex sentence) that soul, which conducts (ἄγει) the primary physical motions, 'makes use of' them and of the secondary ones for which the primary are responsible. This it did, and does, through the agencies proper to soul—will, counsel, opinion, love and so on. (See 897 a–b. This supports the idea that the pre-cosmic motions in the Receptacle of the *Timaeus* were not caused by soul (pp. 271 f. above), since they were due to purely physical causes.) If therefore the *Timaeus* may be said to teach that the raw material of body existed, and was subject to a restless and confused motion derived solely from physical conditions such as lack of balance, before it was controlled by soul, there is nothing in the *Laws* to contradict it. The (to us) odd phrase 'raw material of body' is necessary because body as we know it is (for Plato) composed of the four elements, and it is these and their combinations that come later than soul. In the pre-soul, pre-cosmic state of things, they did not exist save in embryo. When Plato speaks of soul as prior to body, it is fire, air, earth and water that he is thinking of, not their formless predecessors in the Receptacle of Becoming, which do not yet deserve these names (*Tim.* 51 a–b). That is why he could say in both dialogues that soul came into being before body, though its birth was in fact prior only to the simple bodies of the cosmos and their compounds.

Perhaps it is going too far to attempt a reconciliation between two such different presentations of Plato's theology and cosmology. There is a further complication in that Νοῦς (or God, or the Demiurge) is indubitably ungenerated, and whereas in contexts where it is important he distinguishes Νοῦς from ψυχή, elsewhere he appears to say that it can only occur in ψυχή. I hope I have shown that the distinction was real and important for him (pp. 215 f., 275 n. 1), but we cannot be sure that it was always in his mind. Taking everything into consideration, it seems most probable that soul in *Laws* as in *Timaeus* is not uncreated but 'one of the first created things', brought into being by the divine King who ordered everything. But Plato himself would be the first to blame us if, in trying to push speculation back beyond the beginning of the universe, we expected to find 'accounts precisely wrought and everywhere in every way consistent' (*Tim.* 29 c).

(5) *Preservation of the laws: the Nocturnal Council*

The state must contain some element having the same conception of
organized society as you the legislator had when you made your laws.

Republic 497 c–d

The scandal of the *Laws* to many modern minds is Plato's ultra-
conservatism, which cannot be separated from its metaphysical background, especially the existence of the Forms.[1] He believed it to be
within human power to devise, at least in outline, the best possible
constitution and legal code and that thereafter any change of substance is
likely to be for the worse. This comes up in a rather sidelong way in
connexion with the regulations concerning sacrifices and dances.[2] He
begins by saying reasonably that many details can only be settled in the
light of experience by those who administer them. In the case of
sacrifices and dancing[3] ten years of annual revision should suffice for
this, in consultation with the original legislator if he is alive. After that
they must be regarded as immutable and 'applied along with the other
laws originally ordained by the legislator'. This is regularly taken to
imply that the whole legal system is immutable, though it would be an
oddly casual way of introducing such an all-embracing rule, and the
clause could mean only that the revised rules on sacrifices and dancing
will be incorporated with those on the same subject which have been
left untouched.[4] Even then Plato adds that if a change appears necessary
it may be made with the unanimous approval of office-holders, the
popular assembly, and the oracles.

His intentions emerge more clearly elsewhere. What must be preserved at all costs (he says in bk 6) is the moral aim of his original laws,
that everyone—male and female, young and old—should possess the
excellence of soul proper to human beings. But any mortal legislator is

[1] No one has done more to clarify this than Popper. See his *OS* I, especially pp. 35–8.

[2] 772a–d. This much-discussed passage must be here considered as a whole, since partial
treatment has led to differing conclusions in the past. Cf. also his eulogy of Egyptian conservatism
in the arts at 656d–57b, and arguments against innovation in education in bk 7, 797aff.

[3] ὧν πέρι, 772b6.

[4] In fact Morrow on pp. 200 and 270 mentions several other subjects on which the laws will
need to be supplemented or revised. There is no further mention of a ten-year limitation. Occasionally P. leaves blanks to be filled in, as at 721b: offenders against a marriage law will incur
fines and loss of privileges, χρήμασι μὲν τόσοις καὶ τόσοις, τῇ καὶ τῇ δὲ ἀτιμίᾳ.

bound to leave gaps and shortcomings in his work. His wish will be for successors who share his ideals and can correct any item which proves not to be furthering them. These in the present case will be the *Nomophylakes* (Law-guardians), who must therefore be sufficiently intelligent and educated to turn law-makers should the need arise.[1] It is not any particular law which must be preserved, but the philosophy of life which underlies the whole system. In the last book, explaining the functions of the Nocturnal Council (which will include the ten senior *Nomophylakes*),[2] Plato says (960b):

This pretty well completes our legislation, but a goal is not reached by simply doing, getting or founding something. You must provide for the full and permanent preservation of your creation before you can feel that everything necessary has been done . . . One thing seems to me to be missing from our laws, a means of making them so far as possible irreversible.

This means will be found in the Nocturnal Council, to which we must now turn.[3] It will act as the corporate mind of the state (965a), and its members will therefore be given a longer and more advanced education than the rest. They will in fact be philosophers, analogous to the Guardians[4] or philosopher-kings of the *Republic*. They will not have created the original constitution themselves, but if all that was wanted was a mechanical adherence to the letter of past enactments, a police force with 'true belief' would surely have been more useful than these intellectuals, who 'to be genuine guardians of the laws must know their true nature and be capable of interpreting it in words and following it out in practice, judging what is an intrinsically good or bad action and what is not' (966b). They must possess virtue whole and complete, understanding both its unity and its plurality, and so grasp the ultimate

---

[1] 769a–71a. For the *Nomophylakes* see p. 333 above, and for full details Morrow 195–215. Officials with that title existed in some contemporary states but not at Athens.

[2] Thus the entrusting of revision to the *Nomophylakes* is in part retained, but its transfer to the new and more complex body suggests an organizational change which has not been fully co-ordinated with bk 6.

[3] For further details see Morrow ch. ix. On p. 500 (and cf. 503 n. 6) he notes that to some scholars (not himself, p. 503) this Council has appeared as a kind of afterthought, tacked on by P., or perhaps even Philip of Opus, and impossible to reconcile with the constitution as hitherto described. I should say that on the contrary it represented for P. the crown and climax of the whole work. The problem of reconciliation with the rest has been adequately dealt with by Morrow.

[4] In fact P. slips easily back into the terminology of *Rep.* and calls them so (964c7 and e2, 965c10, 966b5, 968d1, 969c2).

purpose of the laws and pursue it single-mindedly. It is true that in practice this will mean leaving the Platonic laws largely unchanged, for he adds that diversity of laws and customs is due to differences of aim. Other governments may aim at power, or a so-called freedom, or even material wealth at the cost of freedom. Nevertheless the positive law remains a means only. It is to the end that the Guardians must look.[1]

The name of this Council is Plato's own, and less sinister than it sounds. He calls it this because it is to meet (not even at dead of night, but) from first light to sunrise, chosen as a time when its members will be least distracted by other cares, public or private. It will be composed as follows: (1) the ten senior *Nomophylakes*; (2) the present and former Directors of Education; (3) any who have won awards of distinction; (4) a selection, made by the others, from those who have travelled abroad to observe the institutions of other Greek states (p. 353 above); (5) a number of exceptionally promising younger men, aged between thirty and forty. Each member of classes (1) to (4) is to invite one of these to a meeting at which, unknown to himself, he will be scrutinized by the others.[2] The Council's business is to keep the current laws under constant scrutiny, with a view to possible improvements. Its terms of reference run thus (951e–52a):

The discussions at their meetings must always be concerned with the laws of their own city and anything important bearing on them which they may learn from elsewhere; and also with any studies which if pursued may be judged to assist in throwing light on this investigation, while their neglect will render the legal problems more difficult and obscure.

A state needs within it a body possessing full understanding of the *purpose* of statesmanship, the means of fulfilling it, and what laws, and after that what men, will best guide it to its end. Without such directors it will lack intelligence and perception and its undertakings will be at the mercy of chance (962b–c). Administrators, and the main body of *Nomophylakes*, can work by true belief, but only if there is in the back-

---

[1] This discussion owes much to Morrow, and as will be seen, agrees with his conclusion on p. 501 that 'the salvation of the laws implies something more than the preservation of a code rigidly and unthinkingly adhered to'.

[2] 951d–e, 961a–b. England (*Laws* II, 636) guesses the total membership at roughly 66. There is a slight discrepancy between the two accounts. At 951d class (3) is limited to *priests* who have been awarded ἀριστεῖα.

ground a body of philosophers whose guidance will be based on genuine knowledge.¹ Now the statesman's aim, they have already agreed,² is the promotion of *aretē*, distinctively human excellence. This therefore the supreme guardians must possess themselves (962 d, 964 d) and be able to grasp and expound its separate manifestations (as justice, courage etc.) and also the relations of these to one another and to the single principle which unites them and justifies applying the single name *aretē* to all alike.³ In other words, the members must know both the name and the definition of *aretē* (964a), transcending the popular conceptions of it.⁴ Only a body so qualified can guarantee the continuity of the political and social structure by acting as its soul and head, the seats of reason and sensation (961 d). The younger members, chosen for their outstanding natural gifts and powers of observation, will be as its eyes and ears. The older, as the intellect, will analyse and debate with their younger colleagues the reports from the city and environs which the latter provide, and between them they ensure the preservation of the whole state (964 b–65 a).

To fit them for this high calling the education of the Guardians (as the members of the Nocturnal Council are now called)⁵ must be carried further than that of the rest. Central is the application to virtue (*aretē*), goodness and beauty of the art which teaches 'not only to look at the many, but to press on to the one and grasp it, then having grasped it take a synoptic view of all the rest and relate them to it ... No one can find a surer way of investigating and viewing any topic than the power to look from many dissimilar individuals to a single form.' This is that

---

¹ ὄντως εἰδέναι 966b. Cf. bk 1, 632c: 'His system completed, the legislator will set guardians over it, some guided by wisdom, others by true belief' (interesting, incidentally, as an indication that P. has had the Nocturnal Council in mind from the beginning). The philosophic distinction between ὀρθή or ἀληθής δόξα and ἐπιστήμη is familiar from *Meno*, *Rep.* and other dialogues. See vol. IV, index *s.vv.* '*doxa*', 'knowledge'. (The latter entry was confused in the first impression. After the *Meno* references read '(*Phaedo*) 348 f., (*Symposium*) 386, (*Phaedrus*) 416 n. 2'.)

² 963 a; cf. 630 e–31 a, p. 335 f. above.

³ One should compare what is said on this topic in *Pol*. See pp. 191 f. above.

⁴ δημοσίαι ἀρεταί 968 a. Cf. the δημοτική καὶ πολιτικὴ ἀρετή of *Pho*. 82 a–b. 'the product of habit without philosophical reasoning'.

⁵ They are the *real* Guardians (τοὺς ὄντως φύλακας 968 b) of the laws, as distinct from the whole body of *Nomophylakes*. For the comparison with the Guardians of *Rep*. see Saunders, *Eranos* 1962, 44–6. At 965 c they are called τοὺς τῆς θείας πολιτείας φύλακας. Is this what is known as a Freudian slip? Contrast the insistence at 732 e that our state must remain on the human level: it is for men not gods. If ever P. was tempted to slip back into the idealism of *Rep.*, it would be in discussing the education of his new Guardians.

25-2

dialectic which we know from the *Sophist* to be the mark of the pure philosopher.[1] Next comes theology (966c). A Guardian must be able to demonstrate the existence and power of the gods, with particular reference to two points demonstrated in bk 10; (i) the seniority and divinity of soul and its superiority over every kind of body, (ii) the regular revolutions of the heavenly bodies as evidence of an all-controlling Mind.[2] This demands the mastery of certain ancillary techniques (not further specified, but from the *Republic* and *Timaeus* one can supply the necessary mathematics and harmonics).[3] He will then . . . and will use his knowledge to encourage moral and law-abiding habits.[4]

As founders, the main task of Clinias and his colleagues will be to recruit the first batch of Guardians, carefully selecting from those suitable in age, intellect and moral character. As for anything further, to discover what they must learn is difficult and to draw up a written time-table—how long and when each subject must be tackled—would be pointless. The students themselves cannot be expected to see what it will be opportune and relevant (πρὸς καιρόν) to learn until knowledge of a subject has sunk into their minds.[5] So without wanting to wrap it

[1] 965 b–c. Cf. *Soph.* 253 d–e, translated on pp. 129 f. above. For similar phraseology in *Phdr.*, at 265 d ff. and elsewhere, *Pol.* 285 a–b and *Phil.* 16c–18d, see vol. IV, 428 and pp. 166, 208–10 above.

[2] 966e. The *facts* may be taught to everyone as a part of secondary education (820e–22c, p. 346 above). But in Wilamowitz's words (*Pl.* I, 682), 'Hier sind es ganz elementare Dinge . . . Die Schüler lernen die Tatsachen als Dogmen, wie unsere Kinder; damit fertig.' They will then have a true belief about it, but the Guardians will have to demonstrate it from knowledge to people like the tough young atheists of bk 10. If P.'s lifelong interest in astronomy has been under-emphasized in this history, the neglect may be remedied by a look at E. Maula's *Studies in Eudoxus' Homocentric Spheres* 4–8, where the numerous relevant passages in the dialogues are collected together.

[3] For that matter μαθήματα at 967e2 is equivocal, being applied to mathematics as readily as to studies in general. So too at 968d2 μαθημάτων δυνάμεσιν, usually translated 'intellectual ability', may be intended to convey mathematical aptitude.

[4] I am following P.'s text closely here, and the words omitted (967e2–3) are obscure. 'Survey with the eye of a philosopher what they have in common' (Saunders); 'grasps the connexion between that study and the science of Harmony' (England); 'perceive the links that connect them with music' (Taylor). Crombie also (*EPD* I, 175) speaks of 'the relation of music to these things'. Probably the majority are right, though I do feel some uncertainty about both reference and syntax of τὰ κατὰ τὴν μοῦσαν. In translating μοῦσα by 'philosophy' Saunders is following Cherniss. It certainly has Platonic authority. See Saunders in *BICS* Suppl. 28 note 10, referring to Cherniss, *Gnomon* 1953, 377 n. 1.

[5] I translate P., though once again uncertain what was in his mind. He appears to say that no one can know when to study a subject until he has mastered it. Tarán sees the passage as less illogical (*Academica* 24).

in mystery, we must admit that no clear forecast can be made (968e). In popular phrase, concludes the Athenian, the whole business is wide open and they must trust to luck and the fall of the dice. He will share the venture by giving his own views on education, but the risk is formidable, indeed unique.[1] Now it is up to Clinias to get his colony founded. It will win him a glorious name, or at the worst a reputation for unsurpassed courage. What is certain is that if their body of philosophic counsellers, rigorously selected and suitably educated, can ever be set up, it must be entrusted with the oversight of the whole state. So the dialogue ends, with Clinias and Megillus agreeing that without the Athenian as their collaborator they might as well give up the whole project.

The Athenian has already offered to put his experience at their disposal in setting up the Council, 'and perhaps find other helpers too' (968b). No doubt Plato is thinking of the Academy, as Morrow says,[2] and certainly the last few paragraphs append, in Morrow's words, 'Plato's signature to the work he has completed'. No sensitive reader can doubt[3] that it is complete, and this is one of the best arguments for believing the *Epinomis* to be by another hand. The *Epinomis* purports to elaborate in detail the training in 'wisdom' to be given to the Guardians, though it concentrates on number and astronomy and passes over dialectic with a mere mention (991c), much more cursory than what it has already received in the *Laws*. Plato could not have said more clearly than he does at the end of the *Laws* that he does not intend to go any further into the education of the Guardians, as why should he? Some, misled no doubt by Plato's own disclaimer, write as if he had said little or nothing of its content, but what more could one want? If we may borrow Crombie's summary (*EPD* I, 175):

They learn the proofs of the existence of God; astronomy, as what is essential to true piety; the necessary mathematics; the relation of music to these things; and they are to use all this knowledge to understand the *rationale* of

---

[1] I suspect that in speaking of danger at 969a P. has in mind what he said in *Rep.* (497d, 537e), that it is difficult for a state to meddle in philosophy without destroying itself, and that dialectical expertise may lead to lawlessness.

[2] *PCC* 508. For his comparison of the Nocturnal Council to the Academy see also *ib.* 509f., 530, 571.

[3] It has of course been frequently doubted, and I fear the phrase only means, as I have found it to mean elsewhere, that the writer himself cannot doubt it.

human conduct and laws, and to be able to explain such matters as the way in which human goodness is a unitary thing.

To go further into details would only have meant repeating the education of the Guardians in the *Republic*, the theology and cosmology of *Timaeus* and *Laws* bk 10, and the descriptions of dialectical collection and division in *Phaedrus*, *Sophist*, *Politicus* and *Philebus*. Rightly seeing no necessity for this, Plato provides his Athenian spokesman with excuses for omitting it.[1]

To modern readers the functions and powers of the Nocturnal Council have seemed to be left rather vague. Its members as such have no direct hand in the business of government. All magistracies and offices for that purpose have already been provided for, and their various modes of election prescribed, in the earlier books, with far greater attention to detail than has emerged from the present short account. Nor does it impose penalties or in any way interfere with the processes of justice in the various courts of law. (Cf. Morrow 513.) A close link, however, between its deliberations and the administrative or executive side will be maintained through its carefully planned membership, including as it does the active Director of Education, who has been called 'the highest authority in the state' (765 e), and all his living predecessors, as well as ten *Nomophylakes*, who in their official capacity are charged with overseeing the working-out of the laws in daily life and practice.[2] These hold office for a maximum of twenty years, and the Director of Education has himself been elected from their number. All these therefore will be engaged in, or have had past experience of, government, and their age is noteworthy. The Director and his predecessors, other *Nomophylakes* and the returned travellers will all be over fifty, and the *Nomophylakes* may be nearer seventy. Even Ernest Barker, who held (erroneously) that by the introduction of this body 'the law-state is really destroyed', had to admit that its 'conservative composition' would probably mean little change in the law.[3] One wonders rather how these senior members would cope with the neces-

---

[1] This may even be the reason why the excuses seem a little lame and confused, if I am right in finding them so.

[2] These have been mentioned on pp. 333, 353, 369, but for their qualifications and multifarious responsibilities a reader may be referred to Morrow's index.

[3] Barker, *PTPA* 202. Cf. pp. 369 f. above.

sary astronomy and mathematics. In the *Republic* even the philosophers ceased their formal education at thirty-five, though of course in their maturity they would pursue philosophy from choice. Similarly in the *Laws*, the elderly and tested Guardians would not be submitting to education by teachers. There are strong hints in the final paragraphs that they will devise their own studies—research rather than a degree course. The whole scheme seems to be a revision of that of *Republic* 7 (for which see vol. IV, 526f.). The younger members replace the philosophers who from thirty-five to fifty must return to the Cave. Their place is among the rest of the citizens, becoming conversant with all that goes on, and they would be members of the Assembly, the regular Council (*Boulē*) and the law-courts, and eligible for a number of offices for which either no age-qualification or one under forty is prescribed. At the same time these exceptional young men will be pursuing the studies laid down by their seniors as conducive to their common aim.

(6) *The* Laws *in Plato's philosophy*

General. In his *Platon* (I, 655) Wilamowitz wrote of the *Laws*: 'In truth, anyone looking, as a philosopher, for Plato's philosophy, can spare himself the labour that this difficult work has in store for the reader.' He meant, I take it, not that Plato's philosophy is absent from the *Laws*, but that such of it as its books contain has been as well, or better, explained in other dialogues. Some examples have emerged in the course of this chapter, and a few are briefly listed on p. 329. To enlarge that list, we may observe the parallel between individual and state, 'a guiding principle here as in the *Republic*' (Friedländer, *Pl.* III, 391), introduced at 626e–27a in connexion with the Socratic concept of self-mastery, and again at 689b. Other Socratic notions persist, such as the happiness of the good man (so that even on the principle of the hedonic calculus he has the best life, 732e–33a). The argument that to live wickedly is to live miserably, whereas the good man is happy in any circumstances, that no unjust act can rightly be called profitable, together with Clinias's incredulous protest (661d–62a), takes us back to the dispute with Polus in the *Gorgias*, as the supreme importance of 'caring for the soul' (726a–28c) recalls the *Apology*. The concept of measure, proportion or limit as essential to goodness was worked out in detail in the *Politicus*.[1] In the *Laws*, like is attracted to like provided it is within measure: things lacking measure are dear neither to each other nor to the measured (or moderate, μέτριον 716c). The principle of the mean must guide the legislator in designing his mixed constitution and pervade every aspect of the city's life.[2] An isolated tirade in the eleventh book (937d–38c) shows that Plato's animosity against rhetoricians, especially paid advocates in the law-courts, has not lost its bitterness since his vehement attack on them in the *Gorgias*. Their practice is a filthy travesty of justice, falsely claiming the name of skill but really an unskilled empirical knack[3] of pulling off a victory whether right is on their side or not, and their speeches are available 'gratis to anyone who gives them money in return'. Greed is their motive, and so urgent is the need to stamp out this vice that where the motive can be proved, and if due warning has been given and ignored, Plato does not hesitate to prescribe the death penalty.

In closing this partial survey of a massive work, I choose two further topics for more than passing mention: the development of the idea that no one is willingly bad, and the presence or absence of the Forms.

The attitude of the law to the Socratic dictum that no one does wrong voluntarily (860c–64a).[4] There is no question of Plato having renounced this doctrine, which he must have heard from Socrates in his twenties if not earlier. He reiterates it at 731c2, 860d1 and again, an emphatic assertion, in the next sentence. In bk 9 he confronts the question how, if there is no such thing as voluntary wrongdoing, he can consistently admit such a distinction in law, with heavier penalties for voluntary than involuntary actions. A distinction *can* be drawn between injury, a morally neutral term, and wickedness, but not between voluntary and involuntary wickedness. Injury, damage, hurt of any kind (βλάβη) is

---

[1] Pp. 169ff. above. See also p. 234 for the notion in *Philebus*.

[2] 691c, 692a, 693a–94a, and 698b are only a few examples out of many. Besides its constitutional applications, this notion naturally figures especially in transactions directly involving number and quantity, e.g. profit on retail sales (920c).

[3] 938a, εἴτ' οὖν τέχνη εἴτ' ἄτεχνός ἐστίν τις ἐμπειρία καὶ τριβή. Cf. *Gorg.* 425c: rhetoric is to justice as cookery to medicine, an imitation; 463b, οὐκ ἔστιν τέχνη ἀλλ' ἐμπειρία καὶ τριβή.

[4] For relevant passages in *Soph.* and *Tim.* see pp. 126 n. 3 and 318 above. The passage in *Laws* 9 has been analysed by Saunders, Penguin trans. pp. 367–9. See also his article in *Hermes* 1968. It has been much discussed in the past, not always lucidly. M. J. O'Brien's article on it in *TAPA* 1957 has a bibliography (p. 81 n. 1).

frequently inflicted by one citizen on another, both voluntarily and involuntarily. An involuntary injury is not an involuntary injustice; it is not an injustice at all. Where injury alone is concerned, the duty of the law is to see that due compensation is paid and everything possible done to reconcile the parties. Unjust or malicious injuries (or benefits, for a man may be corruptly remunerated) must be treated as resulting from a disorder in the doer's soul, which if judged curable should be cured by the most effective remedies. These are not necessarily punitive and in any case will include instruction. If incurable, the sinner must be put to death, as the best thing for himself as well as the community.[1]

In answering a request from Clinias for a clearer statement of the distinction between injury and injustice (or crime)[2] and between voluntary and involuntary, the Athenian brings up the familiar Socratic division between 'single' and 'double' ignorance as one which a lawgiver should have in mind. Simple ignorance leads only to trivial faults, but ignorance of one's own ignorance, or false conceit of wisdom, if backed by strength and power, is a source of great and barbarous misdemeanours. (This is the state of mind of the tyrant, whom we remember from the *Gorgias* as, Socratically speaking, the most miserable of men, *and more wretched if his crimes go unpunished than if they do not.*) If lacking in power, however, this double ignorance, while still calling for the attentions of the law, should be treated by it with the utmost gentleness and understanding. Moral evil, then, is a sickness[3] of the soul, contracted when it has been mastered by anger, fear, envy, pain, pleasure, and desires. It may or may not result in the commission of crimes. If it does, they will be voluntary in the ordinary sense of being

---

[1] 862d. Cf. the section on the role of punishment, esp. p. 337.

[2] The Greek words βλάβη and ἀδικία probably convey the distinction intended better than the English. One might think of the difference in our own law between damage or injury with and without fault. But, first, without fault no compensation is due, whereas in P.'s scheme it is the one thing required, and secondly, fault includes negligence. P. does not mention negligence, but it could hardly be described as ἀδικία.

[3] The words νόσος, νόσημα illustrate the difficulty of conveying nuances of meaning from one language (especially a non-contemporary one) to another. It was used much more widely than 'disease', or, one might say, applied more freely in a metaphorical sense (but did the Greeks think of it as metaphorical?), e.g. to erotic passion or political disorder. In the *Laws* itself (782e–83a) the desire for food and drink is included among νοσήματα. (See Cornford, *PC* 346 n. 3.) In the *Prot.* (322d, Protagoras speaking) the man without sense of shame or justice must be killed as a νόσος of the city.

commmitted wittingly out of anger, lust, greed, envy and all the other impulses that commonly do lead to crime, but involuntary in the philosopher's sense that no one consciously[1] wills to have his soul corrupted and overmastered by such unhealthy impulses.

The Laws *and the theory of Forms.* By the theory of Forms I mean (to repeat) the idea that what we call universals are not simply concepts in the mind, but objective realities displaying their character to perfection and eternally, invisible to the senses but grasped after intensive preparation by a sort of intellectual vision, with an existence independent of their mutable and imperfect instances or copies which are all that we experience in this life.[2] Its importance in relation to the *Laws* lies in the circumstance that much recent discussion of Plato has been devoted to the question whether he abandoned this theory of paradigmatic Forms in the later, so-called critical group of dialogues from the *Parmenides* onwards; and the *Laws* is universally recognized to have been composed later than, or perhaps in parts concurrently with,[3] these dialogues.

Two scholars, Popper and Brochard, have each listed a number of passages as either referring to or implying the theory. Popper offers seven, Brochard four. Only one appears in both lists,[4] and between them they will offer an adequate basis for discussion. Since I shall do what I can to test them to destruction, I should state at once my belief that, as I have tried to show in connexion with the critical dialogues, though Plato may have modified the theory in non-essentials, the whole tenor of the *Laws* suggests that he never abandoned the central thesis of the existence and paradigmatic character of the Forms.

Popper (*OS* I, 215 n. 26(5)) lists, without quotation or discussion, references to passages which in his view show that Plato maintained in the *Laws* the theory 'in the sense in which it is maintained in the *Republic*'. The first is at 713b, where in adapting the old myth of the

[1] One might more properly say 'reflectively' or 'intellectually'. In translating ψυχή by 'soul', it is well to remind ourselves occasionally that for Socrates especially, but also for P., it represented first and foremost the human power of thought.
[2] It is a version of the theory commonly called realism (as opposed to nominalism). To avoid this misleading term, Popper has adopted 'essentialism' (*OS* I, 216).
[3] See Owen in *SPM* 334–6.
[4] Strictly speaking, Brochard's fourth (965a–d) embraces two of Popper's, who separates 965c and 965d.

age of Cronus, as he did in the *Politicus*, Plato attributes to those far-off days a system of government of which contemporary politics are imitations. With this goes 739d–e, where a completely communistic society like that of the *Republic* is said to provide the only pattern needed for our own states. I have ventured to argue (vol. IV, 486) that it would be wrong to suppose that in Plato's mind this society was a Form as the Good is a Form, and it is still more unlikely in the case of the Cronus myth. It would be difficult to maintain against an opponent that we have here any clear references to the theory.

962 f. says that the Nocturnal Council or supreme Guardians must possess 'all virtue', and emphasizes the need to pursue a single supreme aim. It has no indubitable reference to Forms. 963 ff. asks how one can speak both of four kinds (εἴδη) of virtue and of virtue as a unity, and the explanation given, so far as it goes (963 e), is purely one of logic or common sense. Following this up, 965c repeats from other dialogues[1] the description of dialectic as the enquiry which enables one to look from many dissimilars to a single *idea*. I have emphasized (on p. 175) that Plato frequently uses *idea* and *eidos* in their current meanings of 'sorts' or 'kinds', and when he continues that his Guardians must perceive the common element running through all four virtues— courage, self-control, justice and wisdom—which justifies our giving them all the single name 'virtue', his plea could be endorsed by anyone, whether or not a believer in Platonic Forms. Even Protagoras, in the dialogue named after him, talks freely about justice, piety and courage as 'realities' (justice is a πρᾶγμα, 330c) and is prepared to explain their relationship as 'parts' of virtue. Popper however evidently assumes that the single *idea* is such a Form, and Brochard's vigorous defence of this interpretation[2] should make if difficult, though doubtless not impossible, for an opponent to maintain that the Forms were not in Plato's mind when he wrote 965 a–d.[3] Popper's final reference is to 966a: the

[1] See reff. on p. 372 n. 1.

[2] Which is also Friedländer's (*Pl.* III, 442 f.), who speaks justifiably of the 'strong ontological-metaphysical hints that unmistakably call up the central part of the *Republic*'. Cf. also Cherniss, *Gnomon* 1953, 375–9. But neither Friedländer nor Brochard on his p. 161 strengthens his case by comparing *Protagoras* and *Meno*, at least if I have correctly followed the growth of the theory in P.'s mind.

[3] Saunders boldly translates τὸ ἓν at 965 b as 'the single central *concept*', and μίαν ἰδέαν at c2 'single *notion*' (my italics). The general colour of the language strongly suggests the ambience of

Guardians must understand the unity and plurality of beauty and goodness as of virtue. The continuation at 966b is perhaps even more telling: '*real* Guardians of the laws must *really* (ὄντως) know the truth about them . . . judging what is *naturally* (or intrinsically, κατὰ φύσιν) well done and what is not'. Knowing Plato as we do, we can confidently take the objective standards of reality and goodness, postulated in this sentence, to be Forms.

Brochard[1] conceded that the *Laws* contains no express mention of the theory of Forms, but saw good reasons for this both in the subject, which he says (with considerable exaggeration) is exclusively political, and in the intellectual limitations of the Athenian's companions. Not only are there no signs that Plato has abandoned it for a conceptualist theory, but reading 'entre les lignes' one can see that it is still the inspiration behind his reasoning. This, he claimed, is assured by the close examination of three or four passages.

The first is 668c ff.[2] Poetry or song is an imitation or representation, and to understand it one must know 'the reality, what it is aiming at, of what it is a representation'. This, said Brochard, is the doctrine of *Rep.* 10. So it is, but in that book poetry is at *two* removes from the Forms. The model which it directly imitates is not the Form but something experienced in this world. It is arguable that in the *Laws* we have only the advance from the lowest to the second stage of the *Republic*, from imitations of imitations (poems and pictures) to imitations of the Forms, i.e. the sensible world, here regarded as reality. After all, the recipients of the extra training (670e) needed for this discrimination are the third or senior chorus who sing under the warming influence of Dionysus and encourage the young in the virtuous types of music (p. 328 above). They are indeed called distinguished,[3] but they are not the philosophically educated Guardians of bk 12. (They need the good lawgiver to prevent them from becoming obstreperous in their

the Forms. Cf. ἀκριβής and ἀκριβῶς at 965 c 1 and 10; τί ποτ' ἔστιν εἰς ὃ βλεπτέον, 965 d 5; ὄντως εἰδέναι τὰ περὶ τὴν ἀλήθειαν, 966 b 6. On pp. 159 f. I have maintained that in *Soph.* the objects of dialectic are Forms.

1 'Les "Lois" de Platon et la théorie des Idées', *Études* 151–68, esp. pp. 154 ff. The whole essay is well argued and suggestive.

2 Better to start at the beginning of the discussion of 'music' as imitation, 668 a 6.

3 θεῖοι ἄνδρες (666 d 6), not 'divine'. The Athenian is talking to Dorians, and the Spartans applied the epithet to anyone whom they wished to praise as a good man (*Meno* 99 d).

cups, 671 c.) Any hint of the 'true' or philosophic poet, who composes with genuine knowledge, not just belief (vol. IV, 547f.), would be inappropriate in the context, and the case against it is strong.

Brochard next (p. 160) drew attention to 818b and e (actually from 817e onwards). All free men should learn sufficient arithmetic, mensuration and astronomy for practical purposes, but only a few, to be specified later (presumably the Guardians of bk 12), need pursue them in further theoretical detail. No other science is mentioned, and it does not seem necessary to read into this passage, as Brochard did, not only the mathematics (he refers to 525b ff.) but also the dialectic of *Rep.* 7. His final testimony, 965 a–d, has already been discussed.

As a final point, the survival of the Forms is confirmed by the distinction between wisdom (or knowledge) and true belief at 632c, noted on p. 371 n. 1 above. From the *Meno* onwards, and especially in *Rep.* 5, the objects of knowledge have been Forms, recovered by the intellect through *anamnesis*, and those of belief their changing copies in this world. The distinction was made most emphatically in the *Timaeus* (27d–28a), and could scarcely have been retained if Plato no longer believed in the existence of transcendent Forms.

(7) *Conclusion*

The *Laws* as we have it is an unwieldy production which does not lend itself easily to a general summing-up, and none will be attempted here. The best assessment is probably that of H. Cairns,[1] who draws a distinction between Plato's concrete proposals, to be understood only historically, in terms of the problems created by the age in which he lived, and his philosophical statements about law in general, as to which any validity and truth they may possess is independent of their temporal and local setting. Here, in the opinion of this critic, 'the questions raised by Plato have been among the most useful ever formulated for jurisprudence'. Others condemn the dialogue as being harshly, even cruelly, authoritarian and dogmatic, and as setting far too high a value on permanence rather than change. One thing is certain: its leading motive is to replace the arbitrary rule of men, whether an individual dictator, an aristocratic group, or the common people, by the rule of law, which

[1] See the first and last pages of his essay on 'Plato as Jurist' in Friedländer's *Plato*, vol. 1.

everyone has a chance to administer but only a few may create or alter. These few will be distinguished not only by exceptional ability, and a seniority which will itself incline them to conservatism, but by a philosophical training designed to reveal the ultimate aim of all law, namely the maintenance of a morally stable, happy and united community. Concord is the mark of wisdom, and the best laws rely not on force but on willing consent (689 c, 690 d). The law itself is analogous to gymnastic, law-courts and their procedure to medicine; that is, the purpose of the law is to keep minds healthy as physical exercise does bodies. Trial and punishment, and litigation between citizens, need only be called in, like the doctor, when something has gone wrong. The use of punishment corresponds to that of painful surgery or unpleasant drugs. 'In short, legislation is a constructive, educational process, implementing the ideal pattern, whereas adjudication is only remedial.'[1] The *Laws* is the culmination of the progress which we have already observed in other late dialogues, from the unfettered rule of the wise man in the *Republic*, that city 'laid up in the heavens', to the rule of law as the only safeguard against abuse of power in the world of fallible human beings.

In selecting from the mass of material in the *Laws*, I have tried to present a balanced account which may stimulate a reader to go through the whole work and form a judgement for himself. I hope at least that it will prevent him from being discouraged at the outset, as for a long time I was myself, by the obstacle which Plato himself has put in our way: the lengthy and humourless disquisitions in the first two books on the moral and educational advantages of drinking-parties.[2]

[1] See J. Hall in *Indiana Law J.* 1956, 189 f. The provision of an educational system as the most vital of all the functions of law, though perhaps the hardest for us to remember, is at the heart of the whole work. Everything else depends on it.

[2] My friend Dr T. J. Saunders and I have agreed to differ on this point, and I must record his contrary conviction that the *Laws* is full of humour, and that the long sermon on drinking-parties is written with tongue in cheek.

VI

DOUBTFUL AND SPURIOUS DIALOGUES

Introduction

A brief guide to these may be of some use.[1] The division into doubtful and spurious is adopted by Souilhé.[2] To the first class he assigns *Alcibiades II*, *Clitophon*, *Hipparchus*, *Minos*, *Rivals* and *Theages*, all of which are included in Thrasylus's tetralogies of the works of Plato; to the second, *Axiochus*, *Demodocus*, *Eryxias*, *Sysiphus*, *On Justice* and *On Virtue*. Of this class the first four, according to Diogenes Laertius (3.62), were unanimously rejected in antiquity, and the last two he does not even mention, though, short and feeble as they are, they have somehow crept into the medieval manuscripts.

Most scholars reject all of both classes. Friedländer stoutly defends *Hipparchus* and *Theages* as most probably by Plato, and devotes a chapter to each (*Pl.* II, chh. VIII and XI). Of the others, I shall for the moment only say that though they may not be genuine, some of the arguments brought against them could well predispose one to admit them to the canon.[3] Some critics are content to point to repetitions of matter or phraseology occurring in other Platonic dialogues, and dismiss them all without further ado as imitations. Some are admittedly inept (e.g. most of *On Virtue* is lifted from the *Meno*), but the principle is a dangerous one in the case of a writer who repeats himself so often as Plato.[4] This was probably an inescapable consequence of writing

---

[1] See also vol. IV, 39–41.

[2] J. Souilhé, *Dialogues suspects* and *Dialogues apocryphes*, introductions, texts and translations, vol. XIII, parts 2 and 3, of the Budé series (1930). He omits the *Epinomis*, on the grounds that (a) critics are tending more and more to regard it as genuine, (b) in any case it is best studied in connexion with the *Laws*. For earlier bibliography it should suffice to refer to this edition and to Leisegang in *RE*, 2365–9 (1950). I shall not say anything about the *Definitions*, which can also be found in Souilhé's edition. All the texts are included in Burnet's Oxford text of Plato. C. W. Müller, *Die Kurzdialoge der Appendix Platonica: philol. Beiträge zur nachplat. Sokratik* (Munich 1975) only came to my notice when this volume was in proof.

[3] I had written the above before I looked again at Grote's *Plato* and found this (*Pl.* I, 452): 'And when I read what modern critics say in support of their verdict of condemnation, I feel the more authorised in dissenting from it.'

[4] For an instance to show that even verbal coincidence need not mean imitation, see p. 376 n. 3 above.

dialogues rather than treatises on separate subjects. In general these short pieces have been a playground for ingenuity and conjecture on both sides. For instance, the *Clitophon* looks superficially like a condemnation of Socratic method. Against the objection that Plato would not have treated his hero in this way, its defenders have assumed it was never completed: Plato had to break off because he could not answer his own criticisms, so he substituted *Republic* bk 1, and the *Clitophon* was published after his death.[1] Further constructions will meet us as we look at the dialogues separately.

If they are not by Plato, the motives of their authors can only be surmised. Souilhé (Introd. p. ix) distinguishes the two classes. Those included in the ancient catalogues, in so far as they are not by Plato, were written (he suggests) by members of the Academy for whom the use of Plato's name was both a naive tribute to him and a source of pride if their efforts could be mistaken for his. The others, ranging from the fourth to the first centuries B.C., could have been forged for gain. There is evidence that the great Hellenistic libraries paid high prices for anything that could be passed off as by Plato or other great men.[2] Souilhé does not at this point mention a third possibility, exercises on the Platonic model by pupils of Sophistic or Socratic schools, which would fit little pieces like *On Justice* and *On Virtue*. In any case they are a reminder of the continuance of Socratic literature as a special genre, and *On Virtue* and *Demodocus* savour strongly of the Sophistic 'Double Arguments'.[3] The fact that Plato and other followers of Socrates used the same titles could have caused confusion of authorship. One thinks of the *Alcibiades* and *Axiochus* of Aeschines, and the *Menexenus* of Antisthenes.

I turn now to the separate works.

[1] Grote and Gomperz following Boeckh. 'It might seem as if Plato . . . finding that he placed Socrates under too severe pressure, had abandoned the project, and taken up the same subject anew, in the manner which we now read in the *Republic*' (Grote, *Pl.* III, 25).
[2] For a different view of the origin of these dialogues see Field, *P. and C.* 198 f.
[3] For the Socratic *logoi* see vol. III, 330–3, and for the 'Double Arguments' *ib.* 316–19.

Epinomis

I have already expressed the opinion that the *Epinomis* was not written by Plato, and shall not describe in detail this mainly astronomical and mathematical work.[1] Diogenes's statement (p. 321 above) is evidence of a clear distinction in antiquity between the *Laws* as transcribed by Philip of Opus and the *Epinomis* as his own work,[2] though he would naturally be fully cognisant of the studies in the Academy at the time of Plato's death and would use his knowledge in all good faith to compile what in his opinion Plato would have written had he survived (or alternatively had he seen fit) to describe in more detail the studies of his Nocturnal Council. Even Raeder, an upholder of Plato's authorship, said (*PPE* 413): 'The *Epinomis* appears as a continuation of the *Laws*, but nevertheless falls outside the framework and was obviously not yet planned when Plato composed the *Laws*.' Raeder also admits that although the *Epinomis* takes up the question what the members of the Nocturnal Council have to learn, this is not the way the author introduces his theme. In fact the Council is only mentioned in the very last sentence, and the stated aim is to discover that true wisdom, separate from all the special arts, 'which will make a man a good citizen whether he be governing or governed' (976d). This is immediately

[1] Those to whom Tarán's book on the *Epin.* (1975) is available will need no earlier reff., for they are amply provided in his text and 14-page bibliography. I will just mention a few contributions to the prolonged discussion of its authorship. A full defence of authenticity is in Harward's introduction, 26–58 (1928). Taylor also defended it more briefly in *PMW* 497f. (followed by a summary of contents) and in his *Laws*, lxiii f., with the warning that it is 'not the accepted view'. His earlier article, 'P. and the Authorship of the Epin.', is in *Proc. Br. Acad.* 1929. A. C. Lloyd in his introduction to Taylor's translation (1956) fully summarizes the debate. Von Fritz in *RE* xxxviii. Halbb. 2360–6 (1938) is judicious as always. Against P.'s authorship may be mentioned Solmsen in *P.'s Th.* (where note his ref. to two articles by Einarson), Cherniss's review of G. Müller's *Stud. zu den plat.* 'Nomoi' in *Gnomon* 1953, 367–79, Einarson on the Budé text and translation by des Places, *CP* 1958, 91–9. The last two are mentioned in Tarán's review of Novotný's ed. in *AJP* 1962, 313–17. Not to omit the computer's contribution, Morton and Winspear conclude, after a summary of past controversy, that it is not by P. (*Gk to C.* ch. 7). For affinities between *Epin.* and Xenocrates see Krämer, *Plat. u. hell. Phil.* 126 n. 88.

[2] It seems to me superficial to dismiss this clue as many have. So Burnet wrote, with singular lack of discrimination, that the spuriousness of *Epin.* 'is based solely on a statement of Diogenes Laertius, which seems to apply equally to the *Laws* as a whole' (*Platonism* 85; cf. Grote, *Pl.* 1, 167 n. *f*, Raeder, *PPE* 30). Despite one's suspicions of subjective judgements on stylistic grounds, it is difficult to resist quoting that of Wilamowitz. Defending the authenticity of *Epp.* 7 and 8, he says (*Pl.* 1, 300) that they are in P.'s style, and 'to imitate this style is given to no one: witness Philip's *Epinomis*, which makes the attempt with lamentable results'.

declared to be the science of number. As Raeder truly says, 'The same significance is attached to knowledge of number as previously to dialectic.' With all their emphasis on measure, this could not be said of Plato's later dialogues, including the *Laws*. (Cf. pp. 371f., 373 above and Tarán, *Academica* 27 32.)

In the *Epinomis* we at last have the statement that there are five, not four, primary kinds of body, fire, water, air, earth and *aither* (mentioned in that order at 981c). This in itself, as I hope I have shown (pp. 284f. and vol. I, 268–73), is no obstacle to believing it to be Plato's last work, but there are oddities. Each element, as in the *Timaeus*, contains its particular form of life. Highest is that of the stargods, with bodies of fire, though in the *Epinomis* the fire is said to be mixed with small portions of earth, air and everything else (981d–e). Earth is represented by the creatures that live on land, in which the *Epinomis* includes plants. However, in the *Timaeus* the denizens of the intermediate regions remain, as one would expect, in the natural world, in the air birds and in the water fish, 'the most mindless and stupid of creatures'.[1] In the *Epinomis aither* appears as a sort of fifth wheel as well as a fifth element, with no specific position or function.[2] Its inhabitants are combined with those of air to form 'the intermediate race' of invisible spirits (*daimones*), who know all human thoughts and as they pass between earth and heaven act as interpreters to the gods of all that goes on (984d–85b), like the *daimones* of the *Symposium* (202e). Moreover those who live in water are also demigods, sometimes visible and sometimes not. These are 'of course' nymphs, says Harward's note, but they are a far cry from Timaeus's stupid fish. It is hard to believe that all this was written by the author of the *Timaeus*.[3]

---

[1] 92b. The *Laws* retains the same classification at 823b.

[2] It does not seem strictly correct to say with Cherniss (*Gnomon* 1953, 372) that *Epin.* contradicts Xenocrates who said that P. assigned the dodecahedron, and therefore the outermost position, to αἰθήρ. Simpl. quotes the passage of Xenocrates verbatim no less than three times, and it contains no mention of the dodecahedron, or of the position of αἰθήρ in the cosmos. At *Cael.* 12.26 Simpl. adds on his own that therefore (ὥστε) the dodecahedron was also for P. the shape of a cosmic body which he called αἰθήρ, and at *Phys.* 1165.20 he writes τῷ μὲν οὐρανῷ τὸ δωδεκάεδρον ἀποδέδωκε σχῆμα. Doubtless he was right, but he did not find this in Xenocrates.

[3] From 990c to 991b the *Epinomis* outlines a course of mathematical study as a necessary propaedeutic to astronomy. The passage is difficult, indeed obscure, and has led to many attempts at elucidation. As I shall not go over its problems once again, a pointer to the main modern discussions may be helpful. We may begin with Toeplitz, 'Die mathematische Epinomisstelle' in *Quellen u. Studien* 1933 (who speaks of his predecessors Stenzel and Taylor), and continue with

Second Alcibiades[1]

The theme is that prayer is not to be entered on lightly, but only after careful reflection. A foolish man is in danger of having his prayers answered to his own hurt. (The same moral is drawn at *Laws* 688b.) The over-ambitious (μεγαλόψυχος) Alcibiades runs this risk. It is interesting that this characteristic appears here as a euphemism for folly or madness (140c, 150c), whereas for Aristotle it was a virtue, lying in the mean between vanity and meanness of spirit (*EN* 1107b22, 1123a34ff.). A subsidiary theme is that without knowledge of the Good, all other knowledge is worthless or harmful (146d–47b).

The genuineness of this dialogue was not doubted in antiquity, but is now thought to be excluded by certain post-Platonic turns of phrase (Souilhé 7, Leisegang 2366). Souilhé regards it as an imitation of the first *Alcibiades*, probably to be dated in the late fourth or third century. The German scholar Brünnecke (I take this on trust from Souilhé 17) concluded from certain 'veiled allusions' that it belonged to the period of open Athenian hostility to Macedon, and that in the warnings to Alcibiades the author might have had Alexander in mind. The reason for not naming him could have been that the events were too topical. One wonders how the author could have named him and still expected to pass off his opuscule as Plato's. However, its spuriousness seems certain.

Clitophon

Clitophon himself was a historical character, a supporter of the moderate democrat Theramenes in the political quarrels of 405 B.C. (For the evidence see Souilhé 165f.) He figures momentarily in the *Republic* (340b), where he tries unsuccessfully to get Thrasymachus to modify his identification of justice with the interest of the stronger. Here, he vigorously repudiates a report that he has expressed hostility to

---

Lacey in *Phron.* 1956 (and cf. Booth, same periodical 1957), and Novotný's commentary (thought by Tarán to give 'the definitive interpretation': see his review already referred to). The treatment of des Places, van der Waerden and others can be traced through these. Finally we have Tarán's commentary of 1975 in his *Academica*, 330ff.

[1] I have to confess to a certain neglect of the *First Alcibiades* in these volumes on Plato. It appears however in vol. III as a source of information on Socrates, which it mainly is. See the index of passages in that volume, and especially pp. 470–4.

Socrates's teaching, and expresses to Socrates himself his enthusiasm for its moral impact, which he appraises in some detail. He finds it, however, incomplete. What is this 'art of justice' which Socrates equates with the political art? When he urges men to 'care for their souls', it is like urging them to care for their bodies without telling them anything about the arts of physical training and therapy. He uses the *name* of justice, but does not make clear what it is and what is its effect.[1] Some of his disciples call it the beneficial, others the necessary, or the useful, the profitable or what they will. But these are common to many arts. What is the special function or product of justice? 'Friendship and concord in cities', said one, but again, further questioning revealed differences of opinion between them. Then (he goes on) he asked Socrates himself, who said justice was 'to harm one's enemies and benefit one's friends',[2] though later it appeared that the just man would harm nobody. In his bewilderment he will have to turn to Thrasymachus unless Socrates can show him that he is not only a master of moral exhortation (as Clitophon fully admits) but is able and willing to instruct his converts how to set about achieving the excellence which is now their goal.

The Platonic authorship of the *Clitophon* is still disputed. The strongest argument against it is probably not that most frequently used, namely that Plato would never have written such an attack on Socrates.[3] More suspicious is its attribution to him of a style reminiscent of Sophistic artificiality and tricks of speech. (For these see Souilhé 177f.) But Plato himself was a brilliant imitator and parodist. (Think of the *Menexenus*, or of Prodicus and Hippias in the *Protagoras*.) He is giving Clitophon's version of Socrates's homilies, not his own. The criticisms themselves are not offered in the contentious spirit of Thrasymachus in the *Republic*, but only after Clitophon has expressed an obviously

---

[1] *Ergon* (409b). This is a nice (Platonic?) touch of irony, for of course it was Socrates himself who was always asking 'What is *x*, and what is it *for*?', equating *ergon* with essence. See vol. III, 442, 466f., and cf. *Charm.* 165e, *Euthyd.* 291e, *Euthyphro* 13e.

[2] This is attributed to Socrates in *On Justice* (374c) without the correction. It looks as if some Sophists, or their pupils, chose to foist it on him. For the Socratic view that the just man will harm nobody see *Rep.* 335d–e, *Crito* 49c (vol. III, 113).

[3] Taylor (*PMW* 12) would have greatly liked to believe it genuine, but was troubled because 'It is hard to think of Plato as thus playing critic to one of his own writings.' Not more surprising, surely, than his self-criticism in the *Parm.*

sincere admiration of Socrates as an inspiring teacher. He does not want to go to Thrasymachus. It is Socrates to whom he has returned in his perplexity (ἀπορῶν 410c8), to see if he will even now answer the question which, as Plato knew and we know, the historic Socrates never did answer: What is the ultimate aim of life, or the good for man?[1] If the little work is by Plato, it need not even be incomplete, as most scholars have thought. It is an aporetic dialogue, and the *aporia* is the one which Socrates bequeathed to Plato, who devoted his life to solving it.

Hipparchus

This is of the Socratic, definition-seeking type, on the subject of avarice (love of gain, τὸ φιλοκερδές), the characteristic ascribed in *Rep.* 9 to the lowest part of the individual soul, and to oligarchy among political organizations. Its authenticity is almost universally denied by scholars (including Souilhé), though defended by Friedländer. It includes a fanciful eulogy of the tyrant Hipparchus, son of Peisistratus, who is said to have set up hermae in the streets inscribed in his own name with moral maxims such as 'Think just thoughts' and 'Do not deceive a friend'. With these he hoped to outdo the famous Delphic precepts in the minds of his subjects. The eulogy is clearly ironical, but in the rest of the dialogue Friedländer perhaps exaggerates the elements of irony and banter. The dialogue is of no great importance, and its content is fully described in Friedländer's chapter (*Pl.* II, ch. viii).

Minos

Like the *Hipparchus* this opens abruptly with a definition-question— 'What is law?'—and in both dialogues Socrates is talking to an un-named pupil. The pupil falls into the trap and asks, 'Which law do you mean?', to be told that laws do not differ *qua* law, and the question is: 'What is law in general (τὸ πᾶν)?'; and in the manner of Socratic dialogues, it breaks off without a satisfactory answer.[2] Its conclusion does indeed embody the paramount lesson of the *Laws*, that the aim of law should be to improve the soul, but what it is that the good lawgiver must impart to achieve this desirable end, as nourishment and exercise

---

[1] See vol. III, 486 f.
[2] Morrow regarded it as unfinished (*PCC* 36).

improve the state of the body—this they fail to discover. The dialogue includes an ingenious explanation of the contradictory characters assigned to Minos by legend, which had a great influence on later writers:[1] he was indeed a great lawgiver and a good man, but he made the mistake of attacking Athens and incurring her lasting antagonism. As a result her poets, and especially the tragedians, set out to blacken his character, and such was their influence in Greece that he acquired a totally undeserved reputation for ignorance and cruelty. Shorey found it hard to believe that anyone but Plato could have written this fantasy, and Morrow as inclined to accept the whole dialogue as authentic.[2] Critics, he thought, made the mistake of supposing that, if genuine, it must have been an early work, whereas its strongest affinities are with the *Laws* and it 'clearly' belongs to the same period. He suggested that it may be an abandoned introduction to them, replaced by the first two books, in which some of its content has been incorporated.

The *Minos* makes a number of Platonic points, some of which certainly sound like imitations rather than Plato himself, e.g. 'the wise are wise by wisdom, the just are just by justice', and so on.[3]

The Rivals

The discussion is narrated by Socrates, who describes the scene, which is in a school. The title[4] refers to the other speakers, who are rivals for the affections of two of the boys. The opening brings to mind both *Lysis* and *Charmides*, and 133a3–5 reads like a reflection of (or an early attempt at?) the effect of youthful beauty on Socrates at *Charm.* 155c3ff. The author has made a real effort to introduce some literary and dramatic interest, but falls short of Plato's best in this respect. Thrasylus himself may have[5] had doubts of its authenticity (D.L. 9.37), though he included it in his tetralogies, and Souilhé (107–10) has put the case against it. It is not, however, without originality, and it should be noted that Souilhé cannot point to any post-classical features in the

---

[1] For examples see Morrow, *PCC* 38f.

[2] *PCC* 35–9, against Souilhé and most of his predecessors. He quotes Shorey on p. 37.

[3] For an appreciation of the *Minos* as a contribution 'not unworthy of the founder of jurisprudence' see H. Cairns in *Washington & Lee Law Rev.* 1970, 193–222.

[4] Ἐρασταί or Ἀντερασταί. See Burnet's crit. n. It is therefore also known as 'The Lovers'.

[5] But see Grote, *Pl.* 1, 452, on the meaning of εἴπερ in D.L.

language.[1] Each critic must rely on his own impressions of what is, or is not, 'worthy of Plato'.

Whoever the author, he did not lack boldness. The question raised in his few pages is nothing less than 'What is philosophy?' (133c1).[2] The interlocutor's first reply is that it is polymathy, or knowledge of all arts. Told that this is impracticable, he limits it to 'those that a gentleman should know, requiring intelligence, not manual dexterity'. Persuaded that to master even two arts is impossible, he replies that the philosopher (whom he evidently equates with the Periclean ideal of the man of general culture) need not be a professional or expert in any one art, but should be able to follow the experts' talk better than the average man, and make an intelligent comment himself. This makes him like a *pentathlos*, who can come in second in all five events, but is first in none.[3] They agree, however, that philosophy is good, and therefore useful, but of what *use* is, e.g., a knowledge of medicine inferior to the doctor's? The sick will summon the doctor rather than the philosopher every time. Socrates now takes the lead, and using analogies from animal-rearing shows that the art of making men better depends first and foremost on knowing which are good and which bad, including oneself. This amounts to possessing the virtues of justice and *sophrosynē*, which is self-knowledge. On these virtues depends all good government, whether of cities or households. They may therefore be called political, but not exclusively so. In fact we may say that king, statesman, householder, master (of slaves), the *sōphrōn* and the just man are one and the same, and practise the same art. It is this art alone in which the philosopher, if he is to be any use, must be not a runner-up, but indubitably first.

If one admits (as everyone nowadays does)[4] the presence of certain indications that this is not a prentice work of Plato's early years, it is

---

[1] Schleiermacher himself, who started the fashion for rejection, appraises the style of the *Rivals* thus (quoted by Grote, *Pl.* I, 452): 'genus dicendi habet purum, castum, elegans, nihil ut inveniri queat quod a Platonis aut Xenophontis elegantia abhorreat.'

[2] Merlan has made a study of the dialogue from the point of view of this question: 'Das Problem der Erasten', in *Essays . . . Baumgardt* 1963.

[3] The events in the *pentathlon* were running, jumping, discus, javelin, and wrestling.

[4] But Grote did not. See his *Pl.* I, 452f. He defended the authenticity of the whole Thrasylan canon, and his critical review of previous scholarship in ch. v (esp. pp. 206–11) is still abundantly worth reading.

only with reluctance. Its message is genuinely Platonic (of the more Socratic type), and the parallels with other dialogues could be reasonably explained on the supposition that he later made use of and developed the idea adumbrated in this short sketch.[1] The *Charmides*, for instance, of which according to Souilhé (110 with n. 1) the *Rivals* is an imitation, is definitely an expansion and deepening, and could be a criticism, of its theses. The equation of 'good' with 'useful' is of course typically Socratic (vol. III, 462 ff.), the impossibility of knowing an attribute of something before knowing its essence (133 b) is enlarged on in the *Meno*, and the contention that no one can adequately master more than one skill is basic to the *Republic*, which also tells us that philosophical wisdom does not reside in any of the special crafts (428 b–c). Souilhé (110) denies that Plato would have identified philosophy with justice and the government of cities and households.[2] This is extraordinary, for that is just what he did in the ideal of the philosophic ruler, and moreover saw them all united in the single person of Socrates. If the dialogue were Plato's, one could even, without straining probability, guess that the title and speakers contained a hint of the philosopher (i.e. Socrates) as, on top of everything else, the ideal lover.[3] Souilhé guesses it to be a product of the Academy under Polemon, when it turned from pure speculation to practical life. But when was Plato uninterested in practical life?[4]

Theages[5]

Asked by Demodocus for advice on the education of his son Theages, Socrates questions the boy about what he wants to be. Like Alcibiades and so many others, he aims at political power—not by force like a tyrant, he concedes, but as a democratic leader. He will not, however, seek advice from successful politicians themselves because Socrates, or

---

[1] Socher in the last century had a similar theory about the dialogue on Virtue, that it uses a preparatory sketch for the *Meno*. This seems to me utterly incredible, and the comparison serves only to emphasize the vast difference between that dialogue and the *Rivals*.

[2] Both are included in the single art of πολιτική, which covers both government and good citizenship (*Prot.* 319 a).

[3] See vol. IV, 164, 395 f.

[4] Not much notice is taken of the dialogue nowadays, but one should mention the short appendix on it by Rosamond Sprague in her *Plato's Philosopher-King* 119–21.

[5] Note G. Krüger, *Der Dialog Theages*, Greifswald 1935, and the edition of G. Amplo, Rome 1957.

so he has been told, maintains that they cannot pass on the secret of their success even to their own sons, and it seems to be true. What he would like best is to be taken on by Socrates himself. His father enthusiastically supports this request, but Socrates demurs: the boy would do best to go to one of the Sophists, the professional teachers in such matters. For himself, it is not in his power to say whether a pupil will improve under his care. If the association is forbidden, or not actively encouraged, by his divine mentor, it will not be successful. He adds instances of its intervention in both the educational and other fields. Theages, however, is willing to take the risk, and having uttered his warning, Socrates consents.

Theages son of Demodocus is mentioned at *Apol.* 33e and *Rep.* 496b–c, in both places as an associate or pupil of Socrates. In the *Republic* Socrates says that it was only ill health that prevented him from deserting philosophy for politics.

Souilhé (137 n. 5) mentions (apart from himself) twelve scholars, from Schleiermacher on, who denied the authenticity of the *Theages*, and four who have favoured it.[1] It was never questioned in antiquity. No serious linguistic arguments can be brought against it.[2] There are some close parallels in other dialogues, to support the theory of imitation. The description of the Sophists' procedure (128a) clearly resembles *Apol.* 19e–20a, and in substance *Prot.* 316c; the assertion that politicians cannot teach their own sons (126d: actually 'that their sons turn out no better than the sons of cobblers') occurs at *Prot.* 319e–20b and *Meno* 93b–94e; and of course the divine sign is mentioned frequently by both Plato and Xenophon, and with specific reference to the performance of pupils at *Tht.* 151a. In the last case there is the difference that according to the *Theaetetus* unless the *daimonion* has expressly warned Socrates, a pupil does well, whereas in the *Theages* (129e6)

[1] Friedländer's 2nd vol. was originally published (in German) in the same year as Souilhé's ed., and he may be added to the supporters of authenticity, as Taylor (*PMW* 12), Rist (*Phoenix* 1963, 17), Ritter, and doubtless others, to its opponents. Rist cites Pavlu and Souilhé for evidence of its spuriousness.

[2] Ritter, it is true, names it in a list of dialogues which he claims to have proved spurious by *Sprachstatistik* (*Neue Unters.* 217, but cf. the reference to his *Untersuchungen* in Souilhé, 138 n. 1). On Demodocus's opening speech, condemned by Shorey, see vol. III, 400 n. 2. I there quoted Friedländer, unaware that its defence goes back, through Grote (*Pl.* I, 430), to Dionysius of Halicarnassus.

even without expressly prohibiting it, the divine power may withhold its co-operation, so success can never be guaranteed.

It is against the *daimonion* that critics direct their heaviest fire. Souilhé devotes over six pages to it, the upshot of which is that when the *Theages* was written Socrates had already become a figure of legend like Pythagoras, a magician or thaumaturge. Friedländer has answered this adequately in his chapter on the dialogue (*Pl.* II, ch. xi), and I have said all I have to say in vol. III.[1] The prize for ingenious conjecture must go to 'le critique allemand' (Souilhé 141) for the idea that the *Theages* was written (not by Plato) before the *Theaetetus*, which is a polemic by Plato against its distortion of Socrates's character.

The next four dialogues are survivors of Diogenes's list of 'universally rejected', nor have they any defenders today.

Axiochus

In the manner of several Platonic dialogues, the locality is fixed. Socrates is on his way to the Cynosarges gymnasium, and has reached the Ilissus, when Clinias accosts him and begs him to address some words of comfort to his father Axiochus, who is near to death and feels a fear of it which he had formerly despised. Socrates returns with him, and offers in consolation a scarcely reconcilable mixture of Platonic with what sounds like Epicurean teaching. Axiochus, he says, speaks as if he would still be there to lament his fate, but in fact the dead no longer feel, no longer exist at all. 'You lament the loss of your senses, but at the same time grieve at the thought of mouldering away and being deprived of pleasures as if you were dying into another life, instead of becoming completely insensible as you were before birth.' Just as past history did not concern you, neither will what happens after your death, for there will be no 'you' to be concerned (365 d–e). From there he goes on to talk of the soul leaving behind the 'earthly and mindless' body, which is not the real man,[2] and settling in its own place. We are

---

[1] Pp. 399–401, and on the *daimonion* and the less rational side of Socrates in general 402–5.

[2] So also *Alc. I* 130c and *Laws* 959a–b. Death as separation of soul from body is of course thoroughly Platonic. Besides *Phaedo* (esp. 64c) and other places cf. *Gorg.* 524b.

our soul, 'an immortal being confined in a mortal prison', 'longing for its kindred *aither* and the heavenly delights that await it'.[1]

The immortal soul cannot of course be expected to regret the pleasures of bodily life, yet to mention the immortality of the real Axiochus in the same breath as telling him emphatically that after death he will no longer exist is a maladroit kind of consolation. Socrates even returns to the idea of utter extinction, which he attributes to the Sophist Prodicus,[2] after recalling a disquisition by Callias on the trials of this life. He ends with an eschatological myth of Platonic type (371a–72a).

Apart from its inferior merit, the exceptional number of words otherwise unknown, or attested only for Hellenistic times, would suffice to stamp the *Axiochus* as post-Platonic. But if it does not concern the student of Plato as such, it has some interest for the historian of religion. Souilhé and others would place it in Neo-Pythagorean circles of the first century B.C., but by no means all Souilhé's quotations support the thesis. He mentions banquets in the next world as a favourite image of that period, but the author probably took them from Plato.[3] The 'springs of pure water' at 371c recur on the Orphic gold plates in verses taken from a fifth-century or earlier poem, as also does the idea of the thirsty soul.[4] Minos and Rhadamanthys, the judges whom no soul can deceive, are of course classical, and figure in the *Gorgias*. In the *Axiochus* the good souls enjoy music and dance in flowery meadows, and perform sacred rites. All these activities are celebrated by the chorus in the *Frogs* of Aristophanes, where they are the privilege of the initiated. (Cf. *Axiochus* 371d.) The meadows appear in Plato (*Rep.* 614e) and on an Orphic plate.[5] The well-known sinners of Homer make their obligatory appearance at 371e, and the climate of heaven resembles that of Homer's Elysian plain. Souilhé mentions none of these classical references. The myth of the *Axiochus* relies almost entirely on Plato and the sources, Homeric and especially Orphic, on

[1] For the prison cf. *Pho.* 62b, *Crat.* 400c. Euripides (*Hel.* 1015) speaks of the mind of the dead as 'immortal plunged in the immortal *aither*'. For this idea and other Euripidean quotations see Guthrie, *G. and G.* 263. It is the *aetherius sensus* of Virgil, *Aen.* 6.747.

[2] The reference at 366c to Prodicus as selling his wisdom for money is crude indeed compared with the mild irony of *Crat.* 384b.

[3] *Ax.* 371d, Souilhé 135. Cf. *Rep.* 363. The same word συμπόσια is used in both dialogues.

[4] Not to mention Plato's 'parching heat' at *Rep.* 621a. For the gold plates see Guthrie, *OGR* 171–82.   [5] For Plato and the Orphic literature see vol. IV, 338f., and reff. there.

which Plato himself drew. That Orphic and related ideas were wide-spread in the Hellenistic age is true, but they existed earlier.

A final note. Herodotus (4.33) tells that certain 'sacred offerings' wrapped in straw, still came to Delos from—as the Delians believed—the mysterious Hyperboreans. What these were, he does not say, but according to *Axiochus* 371a the original offerings were bronze tablets inscribed with the fate of souls after death. One would like to know the source of this information, if indeed the author did not invent it.

Eryxias

The attention paid to literary and dramatic elements make this a readable little work, though containing occasional awkward expressions and clumsy sentences. The talk is narrated by Socrates, and the subject is led up to, quite in the Platonic manner, through Erasistratus's impressions of the situation and intentions of the Syracusans, and the character of one of their envoys to Athens. The main discussion concerns the nature and purpose of wealth. There are reminders of the *Meno* in the impossibility of knowing whether a thing is useful until one knows *what* it is, the equation of 'good' with 'useful', and the argument that nothing is useful save to the man who knows how to use it. Socrates however meets considerable opposition to his characteristic argument that therefore wealth, in so far as it is useful, really consists in knowledge or wisdom. Various points are made by the way. What gives a witness credibility is not what he says but his reputation for virtue or the reverse, and an example is Prodicus: he is not believed, though he says the same thing as the 'upright' Critias, because people regard him as 'a Sophist and a crook' (again a crudity unlikely for Plato). The elementary lesson given to Euthyphro on genus and species (*Euthyphro* 11e ff.) is repeated at 401b–c: all money is useful, but not everything useful is money, just as all men are animals but the converse is untrue. 405a offers a new development of the distinction between means, or *sine qua non*, and final cause drawn in *Phaedo* and *Timaeus*. Not everything which must exist beforehand if x is to come into being is a means to x. Otherwise it would be true to say that because ignorance must precede the acquisition of knowledge, ignorance is a means of acquiring knowledge.

Here again one observes exaggerations in those who would detect specifically Hellenistic doctrines in these writings. Souilhé (86) even claims that the aphorism 'only the wise man is rich' (μόνος ὁ σοφός ἐστι πλούσιος) is 'strictement Stoïcien', though in the *Phaedrus* 279c Socrates prays 'May I count the wise man rich' (πλούσιον δὲ νομίζοιμι τὸν σοφόν). The 'contempt for riches' he regards as due to Cynic influence, referring as evidence (without quoting) to the same prayer, in which Socrates asks for 'only so much gold as a temperate (*sōphrōn*) man can bear'. The final conclusion of the *Eryxias*, that the most wealthy are the most wretched because they have so many material wants, reminds Souilhé of a remark of Diogenes the Cynic that to have few wants is to come nearest to the divine. Surely nothing could be more genuinely Socratic and Platonic than the need to reduce the desires of the body so far as is humanly possible for the sake of the divine and immortal soul. It is the foundation of the opposition to the ideal of Callicles in the *Gorgias*, 'to let one's desires grow as big as possible and have the means of satisfying them'. The Cynics too were disciples of Socrates.

Demodocus and Sisyphus

These two unimportant Sophistic exercises in paradox may be taken together. The first (which does not mention Socrates) has four un-related themes: (1) What is the use of deliberation? (2) Should one condemn a man after hearing only his accuser? (Answer: yes.) (3) If A cannot persuade B to lend him money, which of them is at fault? (Answer: A.) (4) Whom should one rather trust, strangers or relations and friends? (Answer: Since the same people, whether trustworthy or not, are strangers to some and known to others, the question of relation-ship is irrelevant.) The *Sisyphus* is entirely on the subject of deliberation.

Both are in places reminiscent of the 'Double Arguments', and ex-ploit Sophistic 'either–or' dilemmas like those with which Socrates has to contend in the *Euthydemus* (whereas in the *Sisyphus* they are put into the mouth of Socrates himself). The question 'Does one seek what one knows or what one does not know?' (*Sis.* 388b) recalls especially Meno's challenge at *Meno* 80d, but also *Euthydemus* 235d (vol. 1, 238, 269). Another pleasant sophism is at *Sis.* 390d. One deliberates, or takes counsel, about the future. But the future does not yet exist, so what is in the future has at present no reality or character (*physis*). Hence deliberation is pointless, for about what does not exist one cannot be either right or wrong.

Though some[1] have seen in these exercises traces of the Stoa or the New Academy, they may well have been written before the end of the fourth century.

On Justice and On Virtue

These dialogues are hardly worth mentioning. It is ironic that amid the loss of so much Greek literature these trivial schoolboy efforts should somehow have floated down the centuries. *On Justice* is a brief and jejune exercise in Socratic definition. *On Virtue* raises the popular question[2] whether virtue (or however one renders the current meaning of *aretē*) is teachable, but can do nothing better than copy out a few passages from the *Meno* almost word for word, while avoiding any reference to the deeper philosophical matters to which it led Plato, and with no trace of his masterly characterization of speakers and their dramatic confrontation.

---

[1] See Souilhé 64, and for linguistic criteria 41, 64–5. Souilhé himself is inclined to place both in the fourth century.

[2] See vol. III, ch. x, where something is said of its social background. For further evidence that it was a popular theme in the fifth and fourth centuries see Souilhé (p. 24); but apart from *On Virtue*, only the *Meno* and ch. 6 of the 'Double Arguments' have survived. Its treatment in the last-named is summarized in vol. III, 317–19.

VII

LETTERS[1]

We possess a collection of thirteen letters to various correspondents, which were included by Thrasylus in the ninth tetralogy of his collected works of Plato.[2] Their authenticity has been endlessly discussed, and the pendulum has swung from an extreme scepticism prevailing in the nineteenth century (which also deprived Plato of some of his best dialogues; see vol. IV, 40) to a more genuinely critical and selective attitude in recent times. Shorey wrote in *What Plato Said* (1933, p. 41) that acceptance or rejection of some of them was not so historically important as it might seem, because the two most important, the Seventh and Eighth, if not by Plato himself, must have been composed not later than a generation or two after his death by a Platonist who knew the facts (i.e. about Plato's life and involvement in Syracusan politics) and was himself so steeped in Plato's later writings that he could plausibly imitate their style.[3] Many would agree, but if this is so, it would hardly seem worth while to invent this shadowy figure. That these more personal documents should throw an unexpected, even occasionally a disturbing, light on Plato's character is not surprising when one con-

[1] For general orientation, including information about the controversy over their authenticity, it will suffice here to refer to Morrow's *Translation with Crit. Essays and Notes* (1962). He gives a selected bibliography on pp. 271 f. Note however a second edition of Pasquali's *Lettere* in 1967, and a German edition of the Letters by W. Neumann and J. Kerschensteiner published in the same year. Friedländer writes of the Letters in vol. I, ch. XIII, of his *Plato*. To bring us nearer the present, in the Vandoeuvres symposium published in 1972 (Fondation Hardt, *Entretiens* vol. xviii), the two speakers on the Letters came to opposite conclusions. N. Gulley argued that all are spurious, G. J. D. Aalders that the Seventh and Eighth are genuine and the rest either by P. himself or by a contemporary or near-contemporary.

[2] For Thrasylus see vol. IV, 39 n. 2. That the letters are those we possess is confirmed by the fact that his catalogue mentions the names of the recipients and the number addressed to each. Aristophanes the librarian of Alexandria lists 'Letters' in the same trilogy as *Phaedo* and *Crito*, but no details are reported in our source (D.L. 3.61–2). If (as is surely probable) they were the same as those in Thrasylus, this would carry the list of the collection back to the third or early second century B.C. They are not mentioned by Aristotle.

[3] Shorey, *WPS* 1933, 41. Cf. Finley, *Aspects of Antiquity* (Pelican ed.) 80: 'If P. did not write them [*sc. Epp.* 7 and 8] himself, then they were written not long after his death by one of his disciples, possibly Speusippus.'

siders how completely he has excluded from the dialogues any reference to himself except for two small factual points (*Apol.* 38b and *Pho.* 59b). Field remarked (*P. and C.'s* 197) that the main justification for suspecting the whole collection was, as with all Greek letters, the common practice of forging letters to sell to the great libraries in the Alexandrian age. He found it 'a psychological curiosity' that those who believed that they must, though not by Plato, have been written close to the time of Plato himself 'have continued to cling to their faith in the spuriousness of the letters, when they have themselves abandoned the original grounds for that faith'.

A few of the letters (in particular the First) are doubtless spurious, and some, whether spurious or not, tell us nothing important about Plato. Seven (nos. 1–4, 7, 8, 13) concern the Syracusan troubles and the relations between Plato, Dionysius and Dion, and are mainly of historical rather than philosophical interest. So far as was necessary for an introductory biography of Plato, the more reputable of them have been used in vol. IV, ch. II. The Second however throws some light on the relation of the dialogues to Socrates, and the Seventh contains a long, difficult and extremely interesting passage on the subject-matter and nature of philosophy. Of the Second I have spoken in vol. IV, 65 f., and the philosophical part of the Seventh must occupy us here. In connexion with the Fifth there is a small point of historical interest. It is a recommendation to Perdiccas, King of Macedon, of one Euphraeus, whom Plato is sending to him as an adviser. According to Carystius of Pergamon, a historian of probably the second century B.C., the sending of Euphraeus was mentioned by Speusippus, who said that by a chain of circumstances it was to Euphraeus that Philip owed his succession to the throne after the death of Perdiccas.[1] The Sixth[2] is addressed jointly to Hermeias, ruler of Atarneus in N.W. Asia Minor, and Erastus and

---

[1] One should perhaps add that the speaker in Athenaeus, who tells the story (11, 506e–f), comments: 'But whether this is true, God knows.' If it is true, history took an ironic turn. (See pp. 491f. below.)

[2] Mentioned in vol. IV, 23 and 62. (The tyrant's name is spelt both Ἑρμίας and Ἑρμείας.) In the oath at the end, which Plato himself says is not to be taken too seriously, the 'divine leader' seems to be the World-soul of *Tim.*, and its father the Demiurge. (See Morrow *ad loc.* and the article of Raeder there referred to.) It was interpreted in a Christian sense by some of the early Fathers, but to suppose it a Christian interpolation, as some have done, is perverse. (See Leisegang, *RE* 2530.)

Coriscus, two members of the Academy whom he had invited to his court. The association, Plato thinks, will do his colleagues good, since they have been educated in the 'noble doctrine of the Forms' but lack experience to defend themselves in the wicked world of men. Here speaks the man who in his late maturity could gently mock the idea that one could face this earthly life with a knowledge of the divine Forms of circle and straight line, while lacking the practical common sense and skill to build a house or even find one's own way home (*Phil.* 62a–b). The letter throws an attractive light on the personal relationships of all concerned, but is especially interesting for its connexion with the early middle age of Aristotle who, with Xenocrates, joined the group round Hermeias later.

Statistical note. Purely for amusement, I have compiled lists, including everyone whose verdict I happen to know, of those who do, and those who do not, accept particular letters as by Plato. In addition I could mention 24 who deny that he wrote any of them, and 8 who accept them all. Some others accept all but the First. These have been omitted, as have those who suspend judgement. (The number of 'don't-knows', as well as the unimportance of some letters, helps to account for the comparative shortness of some of the lists.) The figures are not offered as a guide to the probability of genuineness. They are incomplete, and they ignore chronology, e.g. most of the wholesale rejections belong to the past. Still, one can probably say that they represent a larger proportion of the field than most opinion polls. They demonstrate only the extent to which the authorship of the letters has been and is a matter of controversy, and suggest that subjective value-judgements have played a considerable part in it.

Letter	Pro	Con	Letter	Pro	Con
I	0[1]	22	VII	36	14
II	8	22	VIII	22	3
III	14	8	IX	6	8
IV	9	9	X	8	8
V	6	13	XI	11	12
VI	14	5	XII	5	16
			XIII	14	15

[1] Morrow (*Epistles* p. 14) says that 'even the First has found an occasional defender among recent critics'. I regret that I have not tracked these down.

Letters

The philosophical section of the Seventh Letter[1]

> There is much wisdom in the letter, but it is the wisdom of the philosopher, not of the man of the world.
>
> F. M. Cornford

The letter is addressed by Plato to the friends and associates of Dion after Dion's assassination, in response, so it says, to a request for his co-operation; but it is clearly an open letter addressed to a wider audience, and perhaps as much to Athenians as to Syracusans. In fact he uses the opportunity to offer a general defence of his political convictions as they have arisen out of the events of his own life and the development of his philosophy. (See vol. IV, 16–18, 24 ff.) He does not neglect the request for immediate counsel, but his answer, he says, can only be appreciated within this larger framework. In narrating the Syracusan episodes, he has occasion to make some severe criticisms of Dionysius II, who was not without a talent for philosophy and wished to stand well in Plato's estimation, but whose wayward, tyrannical and pleasure-loving charac-ter made his studies spasmodic and ineffectual. When Plato tried to stir him to further efforts (says the letter) he replied that he already knew the most important points through listening to others. It has now reached Plato's ears that he has written a book putting forward as his own the results of a single talk that they had together (345 a). Angry

[1] Ritter, while accepting the rest of the letter as by Plato, rejected this section as a later insertion by another hand (*Neue Unters.* 423, cf. 404). Against him Stenzel (*Kl. Schr.* 85) mentions Pohlenz, *Werdezeit* 113, and Wilamowitz, *Pl.* II, 281 ff. E. Hoffmann thought that this same section provided the real proof of the genuineness of the letter, since no one but P. himself could have written it. For Stenzel it is 'the only place where he speaks to us of philosophy out of his own mouth'. (See Stenzel, *OC* 68 with n. 1.) Computer-based studies led Levison, Morton and Winspear to reject it in 'The Seventh Letter of P.', *Mind* 1968, but on this see the comments of T. M. Robinson in *Cl. Notes and News* 1967, 49 f. Robinson (most surprisingly) speaks of 'its ultra-naive version of the Theory of Ideas'. He surely cannot have read the far-from-naive efforts which Stenzel has to make to explain it. On the letter in general, it is interesting that Robinson, a keen student of computerized stylometry, wrote in *Univ. of Toronto Qu.* for 1967–8 (p. 96), 'Until the Seventh Letter is demolished with arguments considerably superior to those put forward by the late Professor Edelstein in his recent book, most scholars will quite properly remain unconvinced.' Cf. also W. C. Wake, *J. Roy. Statist. Soc.* (ser. A) 1957, 343, and P. Deane ('Stylometrics do not exclude the Seventh Letter'), *Mind* 1973; also Solmsen's review of Edelstein in *Gnomon* 1969. Throughout the literature on the letters one is baffled by the way in which Dr *A* will recognize unmistakably 'the hand of the Master' in passages which to Dr *B* are trivial, absurd and quite unworthy of P. To carry on the game, I am in this case on the side of *A*: no one but P. could or would have written like this, and the passage gives us no less than his own attempt to compress into a few pages the essence of his later philosophy.

and disappointed, Plato is stung into the famous attack (quoted at the beginning of vol. IV) on any who claimed to put into writing 'the things he takes seriously'. It cannot be done, and if it could, he and no other should do it.

He now continues (342a): 'I should like to speak at greater length about this, for perhaps by so doing I can make my meaning clearer.' So begins the passage at which, as students of his philosophy, we must look more closely. Dion died in 354,[1] Plato in 347. In 353 he would be about seventy-five, so that, if genuine, it is his last philosophical testament, as well as being the only surviving statement of it in his own name. It is often referred to as 'the philosophical digression', but I have tried to show briefly how Plato introduces it as an integral part of a carefully composed whole. Regarded as the response to a request for immediate guidance in a political crisis, it may seem ludicrously out of proportion, but he has made it clear from the beginning that his intentions go far beyond that.[2] The letter is nothing less than a short apologia for his whole life and thought.

The question as introduced is epistemological. How is knowledge of objective realities possible, and what are its necessary preconditions? In another way one could call it a statement of the respective roles of intuition and discursive or methodical thought in Plato's philosophy. Their relations are sometimes misinterpreted according to the philosophical predilections of the expounder, and the best modern account of them which I know is that of Richard Robinson. Since I cannot improve on it, I hope I may be allowed to quote it (*PED* 65):

The alternative to orderly and systematic procedure might nowadays be said to be intuition. It is a familiar idea in our times to contrast the plodder who approaches the goal by careful planning with the genius who gets there in a stroke. This contrast seems to be entirely absent from Plato. He possesses the idea of intuition as well as that of method; but he does not contrast them in this way ... Intuition is not for him an easy way of shortcircuiting method;

---

[1] '[Harward's] date for the death of Dion (354) is an improvement on mine (353)' (L. A. Post in *CQ* 1930, 115).

[2] Cf. 324b: To learn the manner in which he reached (the τρόπος τῆς γενέσεως of) the beliefs that he shared with Dion will, he says, be instructive to young and old, 'and I shall try to explain it to you from the beginning, since present circumstances make it opportune'. Some have even thought that the letter from the friends of Dion was a fiction devised by P. as a peg on which to hang his manifesto (e.g. Harward, *Epp.* 190).

but the reward reserved precisely for the master of method. The contrast is between method crowned by intuition, on the one side, and random, fruitless effort, on the other.

Plato's reply to the question about knowledge is that it requires the presence of five [things]:[1] first a name, a definition and a sensible representation (*eidōlon*, image). These three are the *sine quibus non* of knowledge itself, which counts as the fourth. Fifth and finally there must be an existing object to be known.[2] Plato takes a circle as a single illustration to serve for all.

(1) *Name*, in this case the word 'circle'. This is purely conventional. If people decided to call the circular 'straight' and the straight 'circular', these would no less certainly be their respective names for those who had changed them round (343a–b).[3] Nevertheless some agreed label is necessary, for we can neither discuss nor think without words. (Thought is silent conversation of the mind with itself, *Soph.* 263e.) There is also a more strictly philosophical reason, arising out of the doctrine of Forms, why the name 'circle', when applied to the visible circles of our experience, has no natural correctness, namely that, in contrast to the Circle (i.e. the Form of circle, here 'the Fifth'), they are all imperfect and contain some straightness as well. 'Every circle actually drawn or turned is full of the contrary to the Fifth, for it everywhere touches a straight line,[4] but the Circle itself contains no part, great or small, of the opposite nature' (343a).

(2) *Definition* (*logos*), a compound of names with other parts of

---

[1] I have commented before on the enviable Greek privilege of omitting nouns, thus dispensing with tiresome makeweights like 'things' or 'factors', which, vague as they are, may not seem appropriate to all of a group which the Greek can call τρία or πέντε. For us it would be anomalous to include in a single list the objects of cognition as well as its modes and conditions. Not so for P. (which is an important clue to his particular brand of realism), and his native language conspired to make it easy for him.

[2] The trio ὄνομα–λόγοι–οὐσία at *Laws* 895d reads like a preliminary sketch for this more elaborate classification. It is not further explicated there, where P.'s immediate problem is to define the soul.

[3] Here P. sides with the Hermogenes of his *Cratylus*. (See ch. 1.) In that dialogue his Socrates was critical of both sides in the debate whether words were νόμῳ or φύσει, but his strongest objections were to any idea that names by themselves contained, and so could communicate, the essence of what they named, that as Cratylus put it, 'he who knows the names knows the things' (435d).

[4] Cf. p. 31 above. P. doubtless had in mind Protagoras's denial of the mathematical proposition that a circle only touches a straight rod at a point. (See vol. II, 486; III, 267.) In so far as he was speaking of sensibles ('a straight *rod*', κανών), the only realities that he recognized, he was right.

speech.[1] In Plato's example of a circle it is 'the figure whose extremities are everywhere equidistant from its centre' (342b). For Socrates, the ability to define was itself proof of knowledge, but in Plato's developed doctrine even this was not enough, let alone the mere names which satisfied Cratylus and his neo-Heraclitean friends.

(3) *Image*. Third come the imperfect and impermanent copies of Realities, exemplified by the circles or wheels which are drawn and erased, constructed and destroyed. This recalls the mathematicians of the *Republic* (510d, trans. Cornford):

> They make use of visible figures and discourse about them, though what they really have in mind is the originals of which these figures are images: they are not reasoning, for instance, about this particular square and diagonal which they have drawn, but about *the* Square and *the* Diagonal; and so in all cases. The diagrams they draw and the models they make are actual things, which may have their shadows and images in water; but now they serve in their turn as images, while the student is seeking to behold those realities which only thought can apprehend.

Plato uses circles and squares as his examples because it was the Pythagorean belief in the cosmic importance of mathematical truth that gave him most help in solving the Socratic problem of knowledge by postulating the existence of the Forms (see especially vol. IV, 35 f.); and for that reason his philosophy retained the geometrical character which we have often observed, most notably in the *Timaeus*. But as a follower of Socrates he extended his theory far beyond the mathematical, and especially into the ethical field. In the *Republic* he also says that if the state ensures that every man sticks to one job, that will be an *eidōlon* of Justice (443c), *eidōla* of true pleasure are mentioned at 586b, and *eidōla* of virtue at *Symp.* 212a. The third class, then, consists of what most people call realities, things and events in the world of sensible experience, though they have long been familiar to us as, in Plato's ontology, only imitations, reflections, images—in a word *eidōla*[1]—of the eternal Forms.

---

[1] Or possibly 'predicative phrases' (Taylor). At *Soph.* 262b ῥήματα are confined to verbs, but see pp. 155 n. 3 and 11 n. 4 above. According to von Fritz (*Essays* ed. Anton and Kustas, 443 n. 18), for P. ὀνόματα included nouns and adjectives and ῥήματα all other types of words.

[2] 342b2. On the meaning of *eidōlon* see further p. 135 n. 1 above. Though I have mentioned *Rep.* 6, one need not try to fit *Ep.* 7 precisely into its four-fold scheme. P. is thinking out the whole problem afresh, having written the later dialogues in between.

(4) *Knowledge* (of the first three).[1] Under this head Plato groups together knowledge or science (*epistēmē*), *nous*[2] and true belief. These, he says, must come under a single head, their unity lying in the fact that they are to be found neither in spoken words (φωναί) nor in bodily shapes, but in minds (cf. *Soph.* 263c, p. 404), which distinguishes them alike from the previous three and from 'the nature of the Circle itself'. One could not wish for a clearer proof that to the end of his life Plato thought of the Forms not as concepts or universals but as independently existing realities. It may be at first a surprise to find true belief brought so close to knowledge, considering the pains that he took to separate them in the *Meno* and *Republic* 5, but two points are relevant.

(*a*) Since then, in *Phaedrus*, *Sophist*, *Politicus* and *Laws*, he has polished and refined the method of scientifically dividing or classifying 'according to kinds', and we know that what is generically one may be specifically many, like virtue.[3] So here, the three that are united as members of the genus 'mental states' differ in their relations to the object, the truly real; *nous* is more nearly akin to it than the rest and resembles it most closely (342d1–2). This harks back to the *Phaedo* (in which the as yet undivided soul is equivalent to the *nous* of the letter): the reason why it can apprehend the Forms is that it is akin to and resembles them (*Pho.* 79d–e).

(*b*) One can detect elsewhere also a significant change at least in terminology since the day when knowledge and belief were necessarily directed to different objects, respectively the changeless Forms and the changing sensible world (*Rep.* 477b). By the time of the *Philebus*, *epistēmē* itself has been widened so that 'knowledge differs from knowledge, one kind regarding the things that come to be and perish, the other those that do neither, but remain for ever the same and unaltered'. Plato can no longer deny the name of knowledge to an acquaintance

---

[1] περὶ ταῦτα (342c5) cannot refer to anything else. The peculiar object of *nous*, as P. goes on to make clear, is real Being (the 'Fifth'), by virtue of its kinship with it. However, the higher knowledge includes the lower and, though transcending it, uses its data as springboard.

[2] It will be best to keep the Greek word. On its meaning cf. vol. IV, 253: '*Nous*, the highest intellectual faculty, is not the ability to reason things out to a conclusion; it is . . . what gives an immediate and intuitive grasp of reality, a direct contact between mind and truth'; also 421, 425 and 514.

[3] *Laws* 963d. The first steps had of course been taken in *Prot.* (vol. IV, 217f.), but as yet only in a tentative and unsure way, Socratic rather than Platonic. See pp. 191f., 371f. above.

with, and ability to use, the physical environment, without which human life would be impossible.[1] The ontological contrast between Being and Becoming, so emphatically repeated at *Timaeus* 27 d–28 a (p. 251 above), remains, but although in that dialogue (and even at *Laws* 632 c) he reiterates also the distinction of faculties (51 d–e), in others we find a blurring of the distinction which seems to represent a real change of emphasis and interest. It is not yet operative in the *Theaetetus*, which depicts the philosopher as almost comically aloof from practical matters and denies that true belief, even if accompanied by a *logos*, can be knowledge; but appears clearly in the *Sophist*[2] and *Philebus*, and especially in the more practical trend of the political theory of the *Politicus* and *Laws*. But this enlargement of the scope of knowledge had had the way prepared for it if the view put forward in vol. IV, 489–91, is correct, that the two accounts of the relation between knowledge and true belief in the *Meno* and *Republic* 5 can be reconciled. Belief arises from sense-perception, and its object is the sensible world, but since that is modelled on the eternal and unchanging, it also gives the philosophic spirit its first uncertain glimpse of the Forms, from which it can gradually recover by *anamnesis* its full ante-natal vision of them.[3] That the search for Forms must start from the evidence of the senses was already taught in the *Phaedo* (vol. IV, 345 f.).

(5) *Realities, the genuine objects of knowledge*. 'Fifth we must reckon that which is in itself knowable[4] and truly being' (342 a–b). A little later Plato enumerates the sorts of things concerning which we must in some measure[5] acquire items One to Four—name, definition, sensible image and knowledge—if we are ever to gain an insight into the Fifth. There must therefore be a Fifth—i.e. a transcendent Reality or Form— corresponding to them. This is his last word on the scope of the world of Forms, about which the dialogues left a certain doubt.[6] The list is

[1] *Phil.* 61 d–62 b. See pp. 104f., 229 above.
[2] The fact that δόξα appears in *Tht.* (189e–190a) as well as *Soph.* (263e–64a) as the outcome of διάνοια suggests perhaps that P., as so often, is using his terms loosely, for at *Rep.* 511 d διάνοια is equated with the exact sciences. It may nevertheless have some significance for his thought.
[3] I agree with Wilamowitz's warning (*Pl.* II, 296) against supposing that P. has given up the belief in knowledge as recollection.
[4] γνωστόν. For the equivalence of this to νοητόν cf. *Rep.* 517b.
[5] Or 'somehow or other' ((ἀμῶς γέ πως 342e1). Without the final vision none of these four can be an object or a vehicle of perfect knowledge.
[6] See index to vol. IV under 'Forms: scope of theory'.

remarkably comprehensive, including shapes, colours (cf. *Crat.* 423e), moral qualities, fire, water and the other elements (*Tim.* 49a–51c, especially 50c), all physical objects whether natural or artificial, living creatures, personal characters, actions and events ('everything done or suffered'). Forms of many of these are known from the dialogues, and the whole list is perhaps a natural extension of the account of the cosmos and its relation to the intelligible order on which the Demiurge modelled it, at *Tim.* 30c–31a. The model contained every kind of living thing, and therefore every kind must be reproduced in our world. Whether or not already in Plato's mind,[1] it was an easy step from 'every living thing' to 'every thing'. All these can be named, defined and experienced in the sensible world. Even the fourth prerequisite can be pursued in respect of this world, namely the methodical classification and evaluation of the continuous random flow of sense-impressions to create the natural, mathematical and moral sciences. Yet these cannot of themselves supply the actual contact with the real, intelligible and changeless essences for which the soul longs as itself belonging to their world, not to the world of bodies to which it is temporarily attached. It seeks, in Plato's terse phrase, the τί of an object, and they offer it only the ποῖόν τι: they enumerate its characteristics without conveying its essence.[2]

Their limitations are due to the inadequacy (lit. 'weakness', 343a1) of words, on which all alike rely. There is nothing stable or lasting (βέβαιον) about words. They can shift their meanings as we have seen, and different people give different names to the same things. Definitions are composed of words, and can be no more permanent than their constituents, and the same is true of the ordering and universalizing of experience into scientific theses.

[1] On this see pp. 257–59 above. Concerning Forms of artefacts, the remarks on the Form of shuttle in *Crat.* (pp. 19–22) above may be of some help. Cf. also vol. IV, 549 n. 2, and Bluck's long note on 342d, *Letters VII and VIII* 124f.

[2] 343b–c. This seems to me to show the earlier sentence at 342e2–43a1 to be an understatement quite in P.'s manner (οὐχ ἧττον = μᾶλλον). (Von Fritz thinks differently, *Essays*, ed. Anton and Kustas, 418.) *Tht.* 186b–c is important in this connexion. The distinction between ποῖόν τι and τί goes back to the *Meno* (71b), and it is interesting to notice P.'s change of front. There Socrates maintains (as he did in real life) that one must know what a thing is before one can say whether or not it has a particular property. For him definition was evidence of full knowledge. In this latest version of the theory of Forms knowledge (for reasons which P. gives) has been divided: the scientific knowledge expressed in a definition by genus and species is itself only of the ποῖόν τι, and preliminary to the complete revelation of a thing's essence or Form.

On the level of these images (343 c 7) of Reality we can converse with our fellow-men without appearing foolish, but when we try to lift them to the plane of the Fifth, we are at the mercy of any Sophist who likes to make us appear ignorant fools.[1] It is the plight of those in the *Republic* (517d) who after escaping from the Cave and seeing the divine sights in the full sunshine of the world above, appear awkward and ridiculous when they return and try to accustom their eyes again to the darkness and shadow-plays of the Cave. At the same time, continues Plato, it is through familiarity with the Four, by training the mind to move up and down between them, that the philosopher can with difficulty rise to knowledge of what is good and true. This knowledge is, as in the *Republic*, compared to visual clarity, and no one, says Plato, will be able to *see* unless he has a natural affinity with the object. Nor conversely, he adds, will those who have this kinship but whose minds are sluggish and forgetful ever discover as fully as possible the truth about virtue—or about its contrary either, for they must be learned together.[2] Plato's version of the old, especially Pythagorean and Empedoclean, belief that like knows like is familiar. In the *Phaedo* the mind can know the Forms because it is akin to them, and the idea is repeated several times in the *Republic*.[3] Interesting in its bearing on the relation between discursive reason and intuition is Plato's assertion not only that reasoning powers are useless without the flair imparted by affinity to the object but that this special aptitude will remain dormant in any who cannot submit themselves to the discipline of a long, hard training of mind and memory. (Cf. also 340d–e.) The affinity without

---

[1] I have ventured to interpret 343c5–d6 differently from others, who take P. to be referring solely to 'dialectical exercises' (Morrow) carried out within his own circle. I may be wrong—it is a loosely constructed piece—but had two reasons for the choice: (1) P. would not speak of himself and the Academy as people of πονηρὰ τροφή unaccustomed to seek the truth; (2) I did not want to translate ἀναγκάζωμεν as if it were passive ('are compelled' Morrow, 'il faut' Souilhé). That the philosopher is at the mercy of rhetoricians and their like is the theme of the description of him in *Tht.* As to 'Sophists' above, it seemed a suitable word for 'questioners who can tear to pieces and probe the Four . . . anyone who wishes of those skilled in refutation' (or 'in turning things upside-down').

[2] As Aristotle said more than once (and truly) τῶν ἐναντίων ἡ αὐτὴ ἐπιστήμη. Cf. also vol. IV, 508 n. 1.

[3] *Pho.* 79d, cf. p. 50 above. Morrow refers to *Rep.* 486d, 487a, 494d and 501d. 490b perhaps comes as close to the present passage as any of these. Of them, the Seventh Letter seems to echo especially the characteristics of the philosophic temperament as recapitulated at 494b–d. There is also my old favourite 500c–d, in which however the causal relationship is reversed. In all cases knowledge and resemblance go together.

the necessary powers of application might seem an impossibility, but Plato has a particular person in mind. It was young Dionysius who had shown him that it was possible to have a real bent for philosophy yet be incapable of the patient intellectual co-operation necessary to kindle the divine flame.[1]

'Co-operation' is the keyword. The goal is reached, if at all, through conversation (the basic and still operative meaning of 'dialectic'), in which ideas are put forward and tested by a group of like-minded people. In the well known sentence at 341 c–d, it is 'from much conversation and a life lived together' that the truth flashes on the soul like a flame, and after the philosophical exposition which we have just gone through, Plato reiterates that the truth and falsehood not only of virtue and vice but of the whole of Being must be learned in long and laborious study, and adds (344b):

At long last, when names, definitions, sights and other sense-impressions are rubbed together and tested amicably by men employing question and answer with no malicious rivalry,[2] suddenly there shines forth understanding about each one, and *nous* stretching human powers to their limit.

The figure of the sudden flash of illumination is not new. The *Republic* provides a good example of the process at work, in which name, definition and instances play their parts in leading, through their juxtaposition in dialectical discussion, to the intuition of the Form. Thus in bk 4, the discussion has led to the discovery of justice in the community. But, says Socrates, they cannot be sure that they have discovered the essence of Justice from this manifestation of it alone. They must investigate it in the individual too. If it turns out to be the same, well and good. If not, they must take the new definition back to the community to test it, and so, by comparing one with the other and rubbing them together like firesticks, they perchance may make the flame of Justice itself leap out.[3] It is to be hoped that comparisons like this may

---

[1] The application to Dionysius has been made explicit at 340b–41b.

[2] This contrast between competitive or eristic argument and friendly discussion or dialectic was brought out as early as the *Meno* (75 c–d).

[3] *Rep.* 435 a παρ' ἄλληλα... τρίβοντες, ὥσπερ ἐκ πυρείων ἐκλάμψαι ποιήσαιμεν τὴν δικαιοσύνην. Cf. *Ep.* 7, 344b τριβόμενα πρὸς ἄλληλα... ἐξέλαμψε φρόνησις. For a sensible explanation of this experience, in refreshing contrast to the mystical interpretation which has been a favourite in all ages, see von Fritz in *Essays*, ed. Anton and Kustas, 412 f.

further support the view[1] that we need not conclude, from Plato's condemnation of the written word here and in the *Phaedrus*, that he attached no serious philosophical weight to his own dialogues. The *Republic* is no ordinary written work (σύγγραμμα, *Ep.* 7, 341 c 5),[2] purporting to summarize his final conclusions about life and reality, but as I have called it, a *mimesis* of the living, spoken word as it passes to and fro between friends questioning and answering one another not in a competitive spirit, but with one common aim, the discovery of the truth.

'Whoever has followed this exploratory *mythos*',[3] concludes Plato (344 d), 'will know that if Dionysius or any lesser or greater man has written about the first and highest principles of reality (*physis*), he has not in my view heard or understood anything aright on the subject. Otherwise he would have reverenced these things as I do, and not exposed them to unfitting and unseemly treatment.' It is curious that we should owe to such an angry outburst Plato's only personal summing-up of his epistemological principles, yet so it appears to be. It is a *mythos* because the experience of intuiting the Fifth, the highest and most knowable Being, cannot be communicated literally, but only in metaphor—here the metaphor of spark and flame. Plato has never

---

[1] Expressed in vol. iv, 56ff.; cf. especially p. 63.

[2] For a contrary view see Krämer in *Idee u. Zahl*, 122 n. 54; *Mus. Helv.* 1964, 144f. I cannot believe that he and others are right in seeing a reference to P.'s own *Laws* at 344c. (See Krämer, *I. und Z.* n. 54, on p. 123.) P. is thinking of the actual laws drafted by practising lawgivers or politicians as at *Phdr.* 276d, where Hackforth translates: 'or in the role of a public man [δημοσίᾳ is expressly contrasted with ἰδίᾳ] who by proposing a law becomes the author of a political composition'. Thompson (following Stallbaum's 'indem er Gesetze gebend eine Staatschrift schreibt') commented *ad loc*: 'In his capacity as lawgiver, the statesman is in effect an author.' The point is clinched by 258a; see also 278c. Krämer's note on the meaning of σύγγραμμα (*l.c.* and *Mus. Helv.* 1964, 144 n. 17) should not be overlooked, but I do not think it would invalidate the point made in my text. The character of the dialogues as a compromise between the spoken and the written word has been well brought out by von Fritz in Anton and Kustas, *Essays* 428.

Another of Krämer's minor arguments may be disposed of here. In *Mus. Helv.* 1964, 145f., he says that P.'s pupils (the 'adepts') could not have owed their ideas to the dialogues because *Ep.* 7 speaks of them several times as having 'heard' them. He has temporarily forgotten that in fifth- and fourth-century Athens the usual way of becoming acquainted with a written work was to hear it read aloud. See vol. iv, 58, for ἀκούειν used by Thucydides of his history and by the Platonic Socrates of Anaxagoras's book (βιβλίον) on natural philosophy. (παρακούειν 340b6 and παρακούσματα 338d3 (not 341b2) do not of course refer to the 'adepts'.) This point is well brought out by Ryle in his *P.'s P.* See pp. 21ff.

[3] Treating μύθῳ τε καὶ πλάνῳ as a hendiadys. πλάνῳ is difficult. I cannot see it as 'digression', with Harward, Morrow and LSJ. (LSJ produce no other example of this sense.) For P. it is the centre and heart of his message. More likely is Howald's idea (*Briefe* 34) that it describes 'the uncertain, tentative progress of the investigator'.

hesitated to admit the existence of truths which outrun the resources of dialectical procedure. In the *Phaedo* and *Phaedrus* immortality can be demonstrated, but the details of life out of the body and of transmigration can only be reflected in mythical form.[1] The nature of the soul is a reality of this kind: one cannot say what it *is*, only what it resembles (*Phdr.* 246a). This leads through the chariot-simile to the whole *mythos* of the flight beyond the heavens to the realm of Forms. We face here the question of a mystical streak in Plato, on which opinion will doubtless continue to be divided according to the inclinations of individuals, who may read much or little into the same expressions of Plato. Howald claimed (*Briefe* 34) that by using the word *mythos* he puts his epistemology unexpectedly 'in a poetic-fantastic and even—let us dare to say— mystical setting'. Many would agree that this goes too far. That he compared its climax in his mind to the *epopteia* granted after ritual preparation in the Eleusinian or Orphic mysteries is likely enough: he has linked the philosopher with the initiate before.[2] It is also true that for Plato the Fifth is divine, and in so far as the mind can grasp it, it does so through its kinship with the divine. We do wrong if we belittle the theism of Plato and forget that the philosopher's aim is 'to become as like God as possible'.[3] But what we know of the mystery-religions suggests that even they offered little resembling the experience of those whom we now call mystics, whether Neoplatonic, Christian or other. Nor does Plato's philosophy seem very close to either, when we remember the character of the preliminary Four, all of which must be mastered before the goal can be attained. The term '*phantastisch*' seems especially inappropriate.

Knowledge and the Individual: Plato's problem. To understand a theory of knowledge, one must know the problem that its author intended it to solve. Can we see a still recognizable problem in Plato's case? In view of the exalted status of the Forms in his philosophy, the answer to be given here may seem paradoxical and improbable, but the risk must be run. It is that fundamentally he is concerned with individuals, the 'real things' of common sense and ordinary life, and his problem is whether

[1] Cf. vol. IV, 365 with n. 1, and this vol. p. 179.   [2] *Pho.* 69c–d, *Phdr.* 249c.
[3] ὁμοίωσις θεῷ κατὰ τὸ δυνατόν, *Tht.* 176b; πρὸς τῷ θείῳ γιγνόμενος, *Phdr.* 249d.

we can have knowledge of these; or rather, since he acknowledges various kinds or grades of knowledge, what kind or degree of knowledge we can have. The whole discussion in the *Theaetetus* seems to bear this out (cf. especially 208 d–209 d), and it is in fact a perennial problem. What kind of cognizance do we have of individuals, since there can be no science of them? One can write a scientific treatise on the behaviour of ants, but not of a particular ant. Higher up in the biological scale, a study of a single man may be a biography, a novel or a case-history. If the last, it will be filed by the psychologist, sociologist or anthropologist to serve with many others as the *material* for his study; but his *science* will be in the conclusions that he draws from them all, the theories which they enable him to support or test; in other (slightly Aristotelian) words, the common forms that he has extracted from a mass of cases inevitably differing slightly in their individual details or matter.

Plato, to be sure, says of the incorporeal Realities, 'the fairest and greatest of all, and revealed by reason alone', that 'all our present discussions are for their sakes'.[1] The Forms are the 'causes' (*aitia*) of the things and events of this world, that is, responsible for their natures and such properties—colours and sounds, moral and aesthetic values and so on—as in spite of their mutability they display. By their own presence, by 'sharing' or imparting their nature, by acting as standards or however it may be, the Forms save the sensible world from a state of incomprehensible Heraclitean flux.[2] But for Plato, as after him for Aristotle, a cause was ontologically as well as logically—and above all axiologically, or in worth—prior and superior to its effect. This is evident throughout his work, perhaps especially so in the 'intelligible Living Creature' after which the cosmos was modelled in the *Timaeus*. Once the existence of a Form is assumed (ὑποθέμενος, *Pho.* 100 b 5)— as a result, in the first place, of the evidence of the senses[3] (*ib.* 74 b)—it naturally takes precedence, but it is the precedence of *explicans* over *explicandum*. The starting-point of the enquiry is curiosity about

---

[1] *Pol.* 286 a. All Forms are of course incorporeal, but at the moment he is confining himself to those which have no perceptible likenesses, like Justice as opposed to Beauty (*Phdr.* 250 b–d). For translation and elucidation of the *Pol.* passage see pp. 177 ff. above.

[2] Stenzel rightly notes (*Kl. Schr.* 103) that a Form does not exist only on the Fifth plane; it has connexions with all the other stages too.

[3] See *Pho.* 74 b, and cf. p. 166 with n. 1 above, on *Pol.* 285 b 1.

individuals. Here are John and James, or two objects of different lengths. What makes one taller, or longer, than the other? (*Ib.* 96d–e.) Again, we look at an object and call it beautiful. Why? Because it has a beautiful colour? But it may lose that colour (like a Greek statue in a modern museum) and still be beautiful. Best to stick to the safe answer, 'simple, naive and foolish though it may be', that it is Beauty itself which makes it beautiful (*ib.* 100c–d). So too the wise are wise by wisdom and good things good by goodness (*H. Maj.* 287c). These well known examples are mentioned simply as a reminder that the Forms were first posited as a solution to puzzles about our perception of individual phenomena. The chief difficulties raised by their introduction are not concerned with their existence, even in the *Parmenides* (and cf. *Phil.* 15b), but with their relation to particulars.

The problem has been succinctly and lucidly stated by Aristotle, in a passage quoted at the head of ch. 11(2), p. 61, and *mutatis mutandis* a glance at his treatment of it may be instructive for our present purpose too. The *mutanda* arise from the fact that in his ontology Aristotle is a Platonist without the transcendent Forms. These he could not stomach, but he inherited from his Academic training a sense of the supreme importance of form which he never abandoned. He started from the commonsense premise that only particulars—*this* man, *this* horse—have full existence, or as he put it, are substances in the primary sense (*Cat.* 2a11–14). Universals have no independent existence. We say 'man begets man', but there is no such 'man'; we mean that Peleus begat Achilles, your father you and so on (*Metaph.* 1071a19–22). Yet the concept of universals, or forms, is necessary if we are to come to a better understanding of the primary substances. He even goes so far as to call them secondary substances,[1] and when he says that they do not exist he means only that they have no *separate* existence in fact, though since they are definable, they are separable in thought from the concrete objects of which they constitute the formal element.[2]

[1] Some think that in *Metaph.* Z they even usurped the position of primary substance in his mind, marking a change from the *Categories*. This may be doubted, but it must wait till we can turn our whole attention to Aristotle. His insouciant use of language is full of traps for the unwary. He can apply the term τόδε τι (individual) to specific nature or form (*Metaph.* 1070a11, 1042a29, 1049a35). At 1039a14–23 he sees the difficulty.

[2] They are χωριστὰ λόγῳ as opposed to ἁπλῶς, *Metaph.* 1042a26.

Consider next Aristotle's distinction between what is immediately recognizable to us (concrete, sensible individuals) and what is more fully knowable in its own nature (definable form or specific character, secondary substance, the substance or essence *of* the primaries). 'Logically speaking universals are prior, but in our perception the individuals come first';[1] and we must begin (as Plato did in the *Phaedo* because everyone must) from the things that immediately confront us (*EN* 1095b2–4). They are the data, the only starting-point that we have. Yet although these individuals are indefinable, the concepts which the philosopher draws from them are not mere logical structures, castles in the air with no foundations in reality, because even sensation implants an awareness of the first universal or specific form. 'We perceive the individual', he says (*An. post.* 100a17–b1), 'yet perception is of the universal, e.g. of man, not just of Callias *a* man'. It is an attempt to defend induction as a formally valid argument, which cannot of course be done on a purely empirical basis. Hence the conception of the common formal element in a set of particulars as the *substance* of that set, a reality which is *discovered* by the researcher. Aristotle therefore, in strong contrast to Plato, equates sensation with intuition (*nous* or *noēsis*), not as giving the final vision—for there is none—but as the faculty whereby we take the first step towards knowledge through definition by genus and species, the nearest that science can get to comprehension of the never wholly comprehensible chaos of appearances. Individual circles of bronze or wood (for a circle is Aristotle's example too) are not definable but recognized 'by sensation or *noēsis*'.[2] The only explanation offered is that the mind is so constituted as to be capable of this experience (*An. post.* 100a13). When not actually perceived their very existence is in doubt, but they are always spoken of and recognized by the general definition (*Metaph.* 1036a2–8).

For Plato too sensation yields immediate awareness of the individual, but *nous* or *noēsis* plays no part at this stage. The philosopher is on his

[1] *Metaph.* 1018b32. For this and a similar statement in *An. post.* see p. 117 above.

[2] *Metaph.* 1036a2–8. The two are more uncompromisingly identified at *EN* 1143b5 αἴσθησιν, αὕτη δ' ἐστι νοῦς. Plato himself said in *Tht.* (202b5–6), of what he there called elements or single letters, that they cannot be explained or known though they can be perceived. With the text here cf. pp. 119f. above.

own. First he, like his fellows, must adopt a name for it, not a proper name but one which relates it to others of its kind. ('Is this a *dagger* that I see?'; 'I recognized the *justice* of it'.) But how, unless one concedes to Aristotle that even in the act of perception the mind is given an inkling of what all members of a named class have in common? So Plato too believed that the gift of generalizing is bestowed on everyone, but for a different reason, namely that human souls have seen the Forms directly when out of the body, and through the human faculty of discursive reasoning (*logismos*), not *nous*, can begin the long, laborious journey towards their rediscovery.[1] Philosophic natures continue it until *noēsis* bestows the final reward for their pains. The second stage, which one might call the Socratic, serves to guard against the danger that two partners in dialectic may have 'only the name in common, but each have his own private idea of the reality to which he is applying it'.[2] Here dialectical skill relates its subject to the rest of the world by collection and division and so defines it. The aim of dialectic is often thought to be the discovery of the highest, most all-embracing Forms, or even higher principles if such there be. That is part of it, but the final aim is to reach, by successive correct divisions into genera and species, the smallest definable class—the atomic or indivisible species—and so come as near as possible to the individual.[3] Only then is it right to let the individual members 'slip away into the unlimited'.[4]

The lesson from the dialogues accords with the Seventh Letter (343e and 344b–c). The Four (sensible object or datum, its name, definition and scientific classification) can only tell the mind what *sort of* thing each individual (ἕκαστον) is: i.e. they classify but do not differentiate

[1] *Phdr.* 249b–c (vol. IV, 427). This faculty is closely related to the 'gift of the gods to men' of *Phil.* 16c, concerned with the one and the many, limit and the unlimited. It is of course possible to rationalize P. by discarding *anamnesis* and the rest as mythological or allegorical trappings; but this (as I hope has emerged from my study of *Phdr.*) would be to cut ourselves off from what is, whether or not it appeals to us, an integral part of his *Weltanschauung.*

[2] *Soph.* 218d. One might think of an official of the German Democratic Republic and a member of the American Democratic Party discussing the merits of democracy without a preliminary agreement on its definition.

[3] *Phdr.* 277b ὁρισάμενός τε πάλιν κατ' εἴδη μέχρι τοῦ ἀτμήτου τέμνειν (vol. IV, 427); *Soph.* 229d (after several divisions they must still consider) ἆρ' ἄτομον ἤδη ἐστὶ πᾶν ἢ τινα ἔχον διαίρεσιν. On *diairesis* see pp. 129–33, 166–8 above. Stenzel said its aim was actually 'to bring individual reality within the grasp of science' (vol. IV, 48 n. 1), and although that is unattainable, I welcome his confirmation that this was in fact P.'s problem.

[4] Or indefinite, undefined (*apeiron*), *Phil.* 16c–e. Cf. p. 209 n. 6 above.

between members of the same *infima species.*[1] In ordinary life we do that, as one might say, ostensively, through sensation:[2] we can point to one of a pair of canaries and say, 'I'll take that one.' But ostensive identification of a sensible 'copy' or 'image' is not Plato's idea of knowledge. For that, when one has agreed on the names, defined by collection and division, and organized one's findings into a science—natural, ethical or political—only then, and then only if one's mind is akin to the Fifth, the real, the godlike (*Phdr.* 249c6–d1), and if in addition one has had the opportunity for friction between one's own ideas and those of like-minded companions, will the flame burst forth. Then in a flash of insight the philosopher sees not only the divine Forms, and any higher principles there may be, but also, as far as human limitations allow,[3] the things of this world as each essentially is, and not only in relation to the concept of its class; for each and every one is stamped with the image of a Form, which, as Aristotle too would say of his wholly immanent forms, constitutes its Being or Substance,[4] and, humanly speaking, answers the question what it means to be that thing.

[1] Aristotle described the same quandary (ἀπορία, *Metaph.* 1039a14–16): εἰ γὰρ μήτε ἐκ τῶν καθόλου οἷόν τ' εἶναι μηδεμίαν οὐσίαν διὰ τὸ τοιόνδε ἀλλὰ μὴ τόδε τι σημαίνειν κτλ.

[2] Besides equating sensation with *nous*, Aristotle defined it as 'an innate power of discrimination' (*An. post.* 99b35).

[3] κατὰ δύναμιν, *Phdr.* 249c5; cf. *Tim.* 29d. For P.'s conception of knowledge as direct acquaintance see pp. 67–69, 107f. above.

[4] οὐσία, τί ἦν εἶναι; in P.'s terms the τί, not just the ποιόν τι.

VIII

PLATO'S 'UNWRITTEN' METAPHYSICS

Introduction: the modern thesis[1]

The reader who, either from these volumes or (it is to be hoped) from Plato's own dialogues, has learned to admire him as, with all his faults, a great philosopher, author and personality, might be well advised to skip this chapter. It deals solely with indirect evidence, which inevitably leads to controversy, and will only sow confusion and blur the vivid impression left by the dialogues. The historian however would rightly be blamed for ignoring a topic that is currently causing so great a stir among Platonic scholars.

It has always been known, and widely discussed,[2] that Aristotle mentions certain metaphysical tenets of Plato which at least in their expression and, as is generally thought, in content, differ from the lessons of the dialogues. Further information is to be gleaned from his Greek commentators from the third to the sixth century A.D. Since 1959 this subject has leaped to the forefront of Platonic debate through the efforts of a group of scholars, originating in Tübingen,[3] to make a much

---

[1] Professor E. N. Tigerstedt's book *Interpreting Plato* (1977) was sent to me by the author when this volume was already in the hands of the Press. Had it appeared earlier, I would certainly have made considerable use of a work so stimulating, refreshing and full of good sense. As it is, I can only add a note here to commend especially its sixth chapter, 'The Hidden System', a criticism of those whom the author calls 'Esoterists'. A single quotation cannot do it justice, but will indicate its point of view (p. 83): 'It seems an odd perversity to reject or to depreciate a philosopher's *ipsissima verba* in favour of obscure and contradictory second or third hand reports of what he possibly might have said.' The reader will also find in T.'s notes a fuller selection of references to scholarly literature than is given here.

[2] Of pre-1959 but still comparatively recent discussions may be mentioned Robin, *La théorie platonicienne des Idées et des Nombres d'après Aristote* (1908); Stenzel, *Zahl und Gestalt bei Platon und Aristoteles* (1924, 3rd ed. 1959); de Vogel, (1) 'La dernière phase de la philosophie de Platon et l'interprétation de Leon Robin' (orig. 1947), (2) 'Problems concerning Plato's Later Doctrine' (orig. 1949: both now in her *Philosophia* I, 1970); Wilpert, *Zwei aristotelische Frühschriften über die Ideenlehre* (1949); Leisegang in *RE*, 2520–2 (1950); Ross, *PTI* ch. IX, 'Plato's Unwritten Doctrines', and following chh. (1951). An excellent review of opinion from the late eighteenth cent. is in Cherniss's *ACPA* ix–xxii. For his own highly sceptical position see his *The Riddle of the Early Academy* (1945: German trans. 1966). Grote criticized the precursors of the Tübingen school, *Pl.* I, 273f.

[3] Hence already becoming known as 'the Tübingen school' ('die Tübinger Schule Schadewalts', Gadamer, *Idee u. Zahl* 9, and others).

Introduction

deeper and more systematic study of the 'unwritten doctrine' and its relation to the dialogues.[1] Since the general effect of this has been to weaken the claims of the dialogues to represent the Platonic philosophy, it has naturally met with opposition from scholars who cherish them and cannot believe that Plato produced such carefully composed and in some cases deeply philosophical works solely to encourage the study of philosophy and set out some of its problems, reserving the solution for private discussion with selected pupils.[2] Hence the suspicion in some minds that 'Krämer's procedure, despite its merits, has the unfortunate consequence of leading us to discount the central importance of the dialogues in favour of what must be regarded as fragmentary and conjectural secondary testimony'.[3]

The subject follows appropriately on a discussion of the Seventh Letter, which provides much of the circumstantial evidence for there being any 'unwritten doctrine' at all.[4] Something has been said of it already (vol. IV, 1–4, 64), as of the closely related question of Plato's attitude to the written word (ib. 56–64). All that can be done here is to

[1] The modern phase was inaugurated by H. J. Krämer's book *Arete bei Platon und Aristoteles: zum Wesen u. Gesch. der plat. Ontologie* (1959) and continued by him and K. Gaiser in a number of publications. Krämer has a powerful ally in Düring. See the latter's *Aristoteles* (1966), 183 f. (Note especially Gaiser's *P.'s ungeschriebene Lehre*, 1963, 2nd ed. 1968.) Since the bulk of the research is in German, English-speaking readers may welcome G. Watson's short but helpful book, *P.'s Unwritten Teaching* (1973 on title-page, actually published 1975). The author, who worked for a year at Tübingen, does full justice to the dialogues and makes a brave attempt to fit P.'s theology into the scheme. For orientation see J. Wippern's introduction to *Das Problem der ungeschriebenen Lehre P.'s*, pp. vii–xliii. Important collections of essays are *Idee u. Zahl* (ed. Gadamer 1968), the outcome of a symposium; *Das Platonbild* (ed. Gaiser 1969), which begins with Schleiermacher, and *Das Problem der ungeschr. Lehre P.'s* (ed. Wippern 1972), which goes back to 1918. An enthusiastic expounder of 'unwritten doctrines' is J. N. Findlay in *Plato: the Written and Unwritten Doctrines*. For bibliography see Gaiser, *PUL* 565–71, supplemented in 2nd ed. 575–7, and Wippern, *Das Problem* 449–64 (including many reviews).

[2] Since Krämer sees in the Plato of the dialogues only 'der Protreptiker, Elenktiker, Problematiker' (*Platonbild* 199), it is natural that he should look for something more positive elsewhere. But is not this a serious underestimate of their contribution to philosophy?

[3] S. Rosen, *P.'s Symp.* xvi. Krämer and Gaiser have stoutly maintained their position against powerful critics like Vlastos in *Gnomon* 1963 (repr. in his *Plat. Stud.* 379–98). No such detailed criticism will be attempted here. Best to read is probably von Fritz's in *Phron.* 1966 (English version in Anton and Kustas, *Essays* 1971) with K.'s riposte in *AGP* 1969, 22–9. More recent is A. Graeser's article in *AGP* 1974, a closely-reasoned rebuttal of K.'s view of the relation between the unwritten doctrine and some of the dialogues. G. J. de Vries has also written a criticism under the title 'Plato's Unwritten Doctrine: an attempt at deflation', which will appear in *Museum Philologicum Londiniense* vol. III, 1977.

[4] Hence titles like 'La VII epistola e Platone esoterico' (Isnardi Parente in *RCSF* 1969) and 'The Philosophical Passage in the Seventh Letter and the Problem of Plato's Esoteric Philosophy' (von Fritz in Anton and Kustas, *Essays*).

alert a reader to the existence of the question and offer a few general remarks and an indication of the kind of evidence available. In any case one of the Tübingen group has said himself that though its researches have already made possible a new insight into many aspects of Plato's philosophy, the major part of the work still lies ahead.[1] If that is so, any judgement at this stage must be provisional only.

At the heart of the new interpretation lies the thesis that the teaching on first principles ascribed to Plato by Aristotle and his commentators was not, as used to be believed, a late development in his philosophy, but lies behind the dialogues, as an unspoken presupposition, at least from the *Republic* onwards, and even in the *Meno* and *Lysis*.[2] This holding back was deliberate.[3] An example would be the refusal of Socrates to describe the Good itself in the *Republic*.[4]

The Tübingen school, as I have said, have had their share of detailed criticism, to which I do not propose to add; but in the spirit of Wip-

---

[1] 'Fast alles ist noch zu leisten', Wippern, *Das Problem der ungeschr. Lehre P.'s* xliii.

[2] See especially Krämer, Ἐπέκεινα τῆς οὐσίας, *AGP* 1969, and his essay on *Prinzipienlehre und Dialektik* in *Das Problem* (1972). In *Arete* he says (p. 502) that there never was a stage in P.'s written work which does not presuppose the *Prinzipienlehre* (that is, of the One as the first principle of Being). Gadamer (*I. u. Z.* 13) calls it 'the arithmos-structure of the logos', and finds hints of it in the dialogues from an early stage.

[3] Krämer, in *AGP* 1969, 22 and 23, nn. 67 and 68, opposes von Fritz's denial of 'eine absichtlich ungeschriebene Lehre'. On the question of a 'secret' doctrine, and its relation to the dialogues, it is difficult to be sure what is the view of the Tübingen scholars. K. certainly uses 'esoteric' and 'secret' ('*geheim*') in *Arete* and elsewhere (and has defined his use of the former in *Platonbild*, 204). It was not a matter of the impossibility of verbal formulation (as *Ep.* 7 might suggest) but of 'deliberate holding back' (*Mus. Helv.* 1964, 154; yet at *Platonbild* 198 he uses the word '*unsagbar*' of 'the essential'). In the same article he claimed that the inner-Academic teaching of Plato enjoyed priority over the dialogues both in method and in content. Two pages later he says that the content of the dialogues, though not false, is 'subordinate' to that of the oral teaching, which constituted 'a special esoteric doctrine' (*l.c.* 151, 153 n. 39, 154, 155). 'Plato did not consider the dialogue as in substance of equal value, but applied the devaluation ('*Abwertung*') of writing essentially to his own dialogues too.' 'Plato's devaluation of writing hits his own writings at the same time.' (*L.c.* 146, 147.) The reports of the oral teaching confirm 'that it is a matter of a special doctrine ('*Sonderlehre*') which deviates from the dialogues' (*Platonbild* 206). Yet in the same essay (221 n. 40) he can say 'that there can be no question of a "devaluation" of the dialogues in favour of the inner-Academic teaching', and in *Idee und Zahl* (p. 150) he repeats that from the unwritten doctrine properly understood there follows neither a secret doctrine nor a devaluation of the Platonic writings. Wippern too, in his indispensable introduction to the subject, denies that the doctrine taught in the Academy should be called either secret or esoteric, and describes the dialogues (Platonically but a little oracularly) as an εἴδωλον of the 'philosophy of the principles' (*Das Problem* xxxiv f. with n. 33). In opening the symposium that became *Idee und Zahl*, Gadamer suggested that the concepts ('*Begriffe*') of esoteric doctrine and secret doctrine should be completely banned from their discussion.

[4] 506d–e, cf. 535a. But see comment on p. 434 below.

pern's frank statement that 'only the first tentative steps have been taken', I offer a few general points on which caution seems advisable.[1]

1. The unwritten teaching, we are told, concerns primarily Plato's '*Prinzipienlehre*', his doctrine of the ultimate principles or sources (*archai*) of being. No doubt these must stand at the head of any ontology. The doubts arise when in Plato's case they are assimilated so closely to those of the Presocratics, as only a more advanced treatment of the same question. 'With his *Prinzipienlehre* Plato appears primarily as a continuator of Presocratic arche-philosophy.' 'The whole ontological approach of Plato, and his problem-formulation, is determined by the Presocratic arche-speculation.'[2] He certainly owed much to the Pythagoreans, but in linking him thus with the Presocratics in general one suspects that his interpreters have allowed themselves to be led astray by Aristotle.[3] Aristotle is an invaluable source of information on his predecessors provided that allowances are made for his known habits of mind. One of these is a tendency to regard earlier philosophers as forming a linear progression, trying one after the other to solve the same problems on much the same basic assumptions. A striking example is *Phys.* 189b8–16, where he equates a physical contrariety of the Presocratics like dense and rare with the later doctrine of the One and excess-and-defect as universal *archai*.[4] He himself inherited far more of the old Ionian spirit than did Plato.

2. This emphasis on Plato as successor of the Presocratic '*archē-philosophers*' has the unfortunate consequence that the influence of Socrates is practically ignored. Essay after essay on the unwritten doctrine does not mention him at all, and others give at most a perfunctory nod in his direction.[5]

---

[1] In stressing the provisional nature of their results, and therefore of any criticism, I wish to express my gratitude to Professors Krämer, Gaiser and Wippern, who have sent me offprints of some of their most important contributions, as have some of their critics.

[2] Wippern, *Das Problem* xlv; Krämer, *Platonbild* 224 (printed in italics for emphasis).

[3] See de Vogel, *Philos.* I, 272–4, and the passages there quoted.

[4] For the *archē* of the Presocratics, it might be helpful to consult the index to vol. I, *s.v.* F. P. Hager in *Studia Philosophica* 1964 has argued strongly that the *Prinzipienlehre* as described by Krämer and Gaiser is not P.'s own but his pupils'.

[5] Krämer has a remarkable note, *Platonbild* 227 n. 51. It has always been felt, he says, that the Socratic element by itself was insufficient to explain the doctrine of the two worlds and the Forms. (True enough that Pythagoreanism came to play an important part: see vol. IV, 35 f.) But, he goes on, 'in the *Prinzipienlehre* is revealed the element through which Platonism differed from

3. As already mentioned, the denial that the dialogues convey any positive ontological message, 'the repeated assertion that Plato's real philosophy does not lie in the dialogues, which . . . have only a protreptic character',[1] excludes a great deal that a perceptive reader will find in them.

4. To assert that for Plato all writings, and therefore his own dialogues, are 'only a game'[2] is unwarrantably crude, as I hope has been shown with reference to the *Phaedrus* and *Ep.* 7 (which are Krämer's witnesses) in vol. IV, 56–64.

5. The question of development. On pp. 222f. of *Platonbild* Krämer says 'We must at any rate free ourselves from the thought that Plato's dialogues reflect throughout an inner development of Plato . . . The sequence of the Platonic writings primarily follows other laws: didactic, protreptic, artistic . . . The *inner-academic* [K.'s italics] development of Plato, which in single details certainly took place, is difficult to establish because the dialogues offer no reliable criteria for it.'[3] If I understand this rightly, it amounts to a claim that the greater part of Platonic scholarship for nearly two centuries rests on false premises and should be jettisoned. When one compares the evidence and methods of argument which sustain it with the evidence and methods by which it is to be overthrown, one cannot feel that the case against real philosophical development in the dialogues is a strong one.

6. In describing what is now being called the esoteric or inner-Academic teaching of Plato, Aristotle often makes no mention of him by name, but may speak of 'we' (i.e. members of the Academy) or 'the believers in the Forms' or something similar. Krämer argues strongly for a 'common Academic system' upheld by Plato and his followers alike, claiming that it is unhistorical to try to separate them. This of

---

Socrates *from the beginning*, namely the Presocratic *arche*-speculation' (my italics). He does however make partial amends in 'Verhältnis von P. und A.', *Zeitschr. f. ph. Forsch.* 1972. See especially pp. 349f.

[1] Mittelstrass reviewing Gaiser's *Ungeschriebene Lehre* in *Phil. Rundschau* 1966, 38.

[2] 'die Schriften nur ein Spiel sind' (Krämer, *Platonbild* 198).

[3] To give an example, K. includes among the main achievements of his investigations in *Arete* the demonstration that because P. speaks of κόσμος and τάξις in *Gorg.* (503e–504d; vol. IV, 299f.), and of justice and σωφροσύνη as an orderly state of the soul, therefore 'in the κόσμος–τάξις doctrine of Being (*Seinslehre*) in the *Gorgias*', as well as in later dialogues, there is already present 'the general mode of being of all that exists (*die allgemeine Seinsweise alles Seienden*) which flows from the primary causes, the One and Many'. (See *Arete* 471 and *AGP* 1969, 24 n. 69.)

course considerably smooths the path to a reconstruction of Plato's thoughts from the Aristotelian evidence. On the other hand we know (from the same sources, Aristotle and his commentators) that Xenocrates, Speusippus and other early Academics (including of course Aristotle himself, though he still uses the 'we'-style) departed in important ways from their master's philosophy. Moreover Aristotle hints more than once at differences between different believers in the Forms. It would seem that the historian's preliminary task is not yet accomplished of either proving the existence of one single Platonic–Academic system or disentangling (if the evidence allows it) Plato from the rest.[1]

A glance at the evidence

This must necessarily be selective.[2] It is usual to start from two passages:

(1) *The 'unwritten doctrines'*.[3] In one of his less allusive moments (*Phys.* 209b14) Aristotle refers to 'Plato in what are called the unwritten doctrines' (ἄγραφα δόγματα). When therefore he attributes to Plato something not found in the dialogues, the natural assumption is that it belongs to this once mentioned oral legacy. It appears that what in the *Timaeus* is called space or the Matrix of becoming (which Aristotle rightly or wrongly identified with his own 'matter' or substratum) was referred to in the unwritten doctrines as 'the great and the small'.[4]

---

[1] Cf. Ross, *PTI* 151–3. For Krämer's view we may refer to *Platonbild* 210. A number of passages in Aristotle make it difficult to maintain, among them the οἱ μὲν at *Metaph.* 1091b13 and ὁ μὲν at line 32; the οἱ δὲ ... οἱ μὲν ... ὁ δὲ ... τῷ δὲ ... οἱ μὲν ... οἱ δὲ ... οἱ δὲ at 1087b4, 5, 6, 8, 13, 16, 17. All these appear to refer to differences among men who all alike believe in 'immutable substances' (1087a31). Cf. *Phys.* 189b15 τῶν ὑστέρων τινές, and οἱ μὲν ... οἱ δὲ who hold different views on the relation between Forms and numbers at *Metaph.* 1080b11–16. Again, at 1080b21–3 who is the 'other' who holds that 'the first number, that of the Forms, alone exists' (or 'is one', whatever either may mean), as opposed to the 'some' who identify it with the mathematical number? Cherniss has much to say on this subject in his *Riddle*.

[2] Easiest to consult is the collection of passages in de Vogel, *Gr. Phil.* I, 272–81. Gaiser has published a collection of *Testimonia Platonica* as an appendix to his *P.'s ungeschriebene Lehre*, 443–567, covering (A) organization, aims and mathematical studies of the Academy, and general information about P. as a teacher, (B) the content of the unwritten doctrine.

[3] For Cherniss's denial of any importance to unwritten doctrines of P., see his *Riddle*, especially pp. 15–17, 71 ff., criticized by Ross, *PTI* 142 ff.

[4] Comparing 209b13–16 with 209b35–210a2. The concept of the matrix, or space, in *Tim.* has been discussed on pp. 262–9 above.

Further references to the great-and-small (there is sometimes no article before 'small') suggest that this was a change of terminology rather than substance, the great-and-small being Plato's expression for the infinite or at least undetermined element, lacking the *kosmos* imposed by number and measure (pp. 428 ff. below).

(2) *Plato's 'On the Good'*. Aristoxenus, whose taste for piquant gossip and dislike of Plato are well attested, tells an amusing story which, he says, was a favourite of his master Aristotle. Its moral he intends, like Aristotle, to take to heart in his own work, namely that a prospective audience should always be warned of the general theme of a lecture.[1] Plato once gave a lecture on 'The Good'. Most of those who attended expected to hear a practical talk on the 'human goods' recognized by Greek society, like wealth, health, strength and happiness in general. When it turned out to be about mathematics—arithmetic, geometry and astronomy—and the thesis that Limit is the Good, a Unity,[2] it seemed to them utterly paradoxical, and some were contemptuous, others angry. This was because, says Aristoxenus, they were unprepared, and like eristics simply chased after the *name* 'Good' with mouths agape.

This story from a contemporary or near-contemporary[3] certainly leaves some questions unanswered. The lecture was evidently given, no doubt in the public gymnasium of the Academy (Düring, *o.c.* 359), to an uninstructed public audience of the sort that flocked to hear the *epideixeis* of the Sophists. Far from being fit to hear Plato's 'inner-Academic' doctrine, they could not even have known the dialogues or anything about Socrates, who taught that the good was knowledge and that the accepted 'goods' could lead to harm.[4] Why should Plato (especially in the light of what he said in the Seventh Letter) have taken it into his head to reveal to such an unworthy crowd the esoteric and

---

[1] Aristox. *Elem. Harm.* 2, p. 30 Meiborm, 122 Macran; also Gaiser *test.* 7, de Vogel 364c. Neither, however, quotes the passage in full. For that see either the text itself or Düring, *Ar. in Anc. Biog. Trad.* 357f. His comments are in any case worth reading.

[2] Following the sense given by de Vogel, *Gr. Ph.* 1, 274 n. 1. That the typically Platonic term πέρας has here only the adverbial force of 'finally' ('to crown all', Ross), as Cherniss (*Riddle* 87 n. 2), Ross, Krämer and others have thought (see Vlastos, *Plat. St.* 393 n. 21), seems, to me at least, most unlikely. There is nothing very strange in the grammar or word-order.

[3] Leaving Aristotle aside, Aristoxenus's own birth is put between 375 and 360 B.C.

[4] See e.g. Plato, *Meno* 87 e ff., *Rep.* 496b, Xen. *Mem.* 4.2.32.

highly technical mathematical basis of his philosophy of the Good as Limit and Unity? Later sources only deepen the mystery, for Simplicius says that 'Plato's lecture (or course)[1] on the Good' was attended by his own pupils, mentioning by name Aristotle, Speusippus, Xenocrates, Heraclides and Histiaeus. Afterwards they wrote down their own versions and so preserved its content.[2] Aristotle's version (also called 'On the Good'), from which we have a few attested quotations,[3] was still available to Alexander of Aphrodisias (third century A.D.) but probably not to later commentators.[4] For the Tübingen scholars 'On the Good' has become a *repeated* course. Krämer indeed supposes the name to have been applied to the oral teaching of Plato in general,[5] while still, apparently, identifying it with the 'On the Good' of Aristotle's reported cautionary tale.

Now the later commentators offer a considerable amount of information about the content of what they call the unwritten lectures (or instruction)[6] on the Good given by Plato and written down by Aristotle; so much in fact as to lend considerable support to the thesis that they embraced the main points of his Academic teaching, over a period of time, on the first principles of his ontology and axiology. *But can this be said about the unfortunate public lecture of Aristotle's story?* Everything goes to show (to adopt a phrase of our Tübingen colleagues) that the entertaining tale related by Aristoxenus, if more than *bien trouvé*, refers to an incident unconnected with the regular Academy seminars in

[1] The sing. ἀκρόασις, which appears in both Aristoxenus and Simpl., was used for both. Ross (*PTI* 148) favoured a course, but Allen (*Euthyphro* 143) reasonably objected that 'the reception described by Aristoxenus makes this difficult to believe'.

[2] Simpl. *Phys.* 151.8–11; 453.28–30 (Ross, frr. p. 117, Gaiser, *testt.* 8, 23B). What is said in this section slightly modifies the remarks in vol. IV, 21f.

[3] There is some evidence that Aristotle's Περὶ τἀγαθοῦ was not simply a reproduction of P.'s lecture. A late biographer of Aristotle uses a quotation from it as an illustration of Aristotle's own character. See the *Vita Marciana* on p. 103 of Düring's *Arist. in Biog. Trad.* or in the fragments ed. Ross p. 113.

[4] Zeller II.2, 64 n. 1; Cherniss, *ACPA* 119 n. 77. Περὶ τἀγαθοῦ appears in D.L.'s lists of the works of Aristotle, Xenocrates and Heraclides.

[5] Krämer, *Arete* 409, *Mus. Helv.* 1964, 143 and elsewhere.

[6] There are a number of references to unwritten συνουσίαι, in one place extended to 'unwritten συνουσίαι on the Good' (Simpl. *Phys.* 545.23, Ross frr. p. 112). Once only (*Phys.* 454.18, Ross p. 118) Simpl. uses the singular, but this has no significance because (*a*) the two are obviously interchangeable for him (as are ἀκρόασις and λόγοι; see *Phys.* 151.10, 453.28, both in Ross, p. 117), (*b*) the sing. συνουσία also meant instruction in general. See Plato, *Prot.* 318a, *Pol.* 285 c, Xen. *Mem.* 1.2.60 (Socrates never took fees for his συνουσία). Note also its force in the πολλὴ συνουσία of *Ep.* 7, 341 c6.

which Plato expounded, discussed and developed with his own pupils the mathematical and dialectical basis of his philosophy. Since Aristoxenus gives no hint of the motive for this venture into the light of publicity, which Aristotle considered a failure, we clearly cannot hope to recover it now. The little that is said of the content of the lecture is repeated as Plato's elsewhere, so we lose nothing if we dismiss the story as a red herring and turn to what in the first place Aristotle, but also his commentators, have to tell about Plato's oral teaching.

Content of the unwritten doctrine[1]

It may be remarked first that Aristotle's numerous explicit references to dialogues show that he did not consider them a less reliable source for Plato's philosophy than any oral doctrine. Next, the best starting-point will be the summary of Plato's philosophy in *Metaph*. A ch. 6,[2] a part of the general study of his predecessors which according to Aristotle's methodical rules was an essential preliminary to his own investigation. Plato he discusses immediately after the Pythagoreans, for he finds their philosophies in most respects alike. Where Plato differed, he attributes it to the combined effect of Socrates and Heracliteanism, a statement which our study of the dialogues has verified. The Heracliteans had represented the world as an unknowable flux, whereas Socrates's demands for universal definitions in the ethical sphere presupposed an unchangeable essence which could be the object of reason. Convinced by Socrates, Plato gave such realities the name 'Forms' (*ideai*) and said that sensible things were called after them because they owed their existence to 'sharing' in them.[3] After mentioning the mathematical objects between sensibles and Forms—unchangeable like the Forms but exhibiting many instances in each kind like sensibles[4]—Aristotle continues that since the Forms are causes of the rest, Plato held their elements to be the elements of all

---

[1] Since this section was written there has appeared the important work of Julia Annas, *Arist. Metaph.* M *and* N, which offers in the introduction a reconstruction, mainly based on Aristotle, of P.'s philosophy of mathematics.

[2] Supplemented from the parallel account in bk M, 1078b17–19, 23–4.

[3] What Aristotle thought of such language he makes plain a little later (991a20–2): it is 'empty talk and poetic metaphor'. On the modern objection that this argument for Forms rests on an error, see pp. 79–82 above, with notes.

[4] Cf. vol. IV, 342f., 523.

things.[1] These are the Great-and-the-Small and the One, for out of the Great-and-Small, by participation in the One, the Forms exist as numbers.[2] This theory is then carefully compared with the Pythagorean. The two agree in regarding the One as a substance, not just a predicate of something else, and in making numbers the cause of the existence of other things. But to posit a dyad instead of the Unlimited as a unity, making it consist of *great and small*, was Plato's own idea, as was also the separation of numbers from sensible objects and the introduction of the Forms. At this point Aristotle turns from description of the theories to criticism based on his own principles.[3]

In this exposition Aristotle makes no division, within the system of Plato himself, between an earlier and a later doctrine of Forms. The division is between two parts of the same theory, covering different subject-matter. The Forms are the causes, or explanation, of all that exists in the sensible world. Hence one part of the theory concerns the relations between the two. On this a critic may ask in what sense the Forms are causes, and whether they make good their claim to bring intelligibility into the world of sense. The nature and interrelations of the Forms themselves is another question. Plato thought of them as numbers, said Aristotle, and feels he must point out certain difficulties in this conception. Both parts of the criticism find their places successively in ch. 9 of the same book of the *Metaphysics*. Nevertheless a passage in a later book which partly repeats A6 more than hints that the association of the Forms with numbers was not a part of the original conception of them. The sentence runs: 'Regarding the Forms, we must first examine the actual conception of the Form, not connecting it in any way with the nature of numbers but *as it was originally understood by those who first asserted the existence of*

---

[1] Similarly the Pythagoreans had said that because things were numbers, the elements of numbers were ultimately the elements of things. (See vol. 1, 230 f.)

[2] τὰ εἴδη εἶναι τοὺς ἀριθμούς is the MS reading at 987 b 22, but it has often been disputed. Stenzel took τοὺς ἀριθμούς to be in apposition to εἴδη, but Zeller and Ross deleted τὰ εἴδη, while Jaeger followed Christ in deleting τοὺς ἀριθμούς. Asclepius added καὶ before τοὺς ἀριθμούς, 'inepte' said Jaeger, but Merlan has defended it. See Jaeger's Oxford text *ad loc.* and Merlan in *Phron.* 1964. Whatever the reading here, Aristotle several times identifies the Forms with numbers. (See pp. 435–37 below.)

[3] Though perhaps not everyone would agree, I believe that when Aristotle spoke of the resemblances and differences between Pythagorean and Platonic metaphysics he knew what he was talking about. Vol. 1, ch. iv, has I hope made plain the extent of Pythagorean influence on P., summarized in vol. iv, 35 f.

Forms.[1] In his irritating way Aristotle has omitted names, but 'the first to assert the existence of Forms' must refer primarily if not exclusively to Plato,[2] and the sentence accordingly means, as Ross said (*PTI* 154), 'without discussing Plato's later theory of Idea-Numbers'. The Socratic origin of the theory of Forms, which Aristotle immediately goes on to explain once again, makes it in any case highly unlikely that they had a numerical character from the start. That the impulse to this strange notion came from the Pythagoreans is certain, possibly as a result of Plato's visits to the Greek West. (Cf. vol. IV, 17, 284.) It is only natural that Aristotle, looking back after Plato's death, should in the general exposition of A6 have reported the theory in its latest form. When it took that form we cannot be sure, but may be confident that it was not a part of the original hypothesis of transcendent Forms which was Plato's solution to the Heraclitean–Socratic dilemma.

The archai *of the Forms: the Indefinite Dyad and the One-Good.* The question of the relation between one and many had haunted Greek philosophy and religion from its beginnings. For Plato as a post-Parmenidean it became the crucial question of his thought not only about the world but in his later years (as I would still suppose) about his cherished hypothesis of transcendent Forms. How, he asked in the *Parmenides* and *Philebus*, can each of these retain its unity and separateness yet be so connected with the members of natural kinds as to explain their existence as such? So far as this world is concerned, he feels he can now dismiss as childish and easy such questions as how one thing can possess several, even opposite, qualities, and how a person can still be called one though he be made up of many parts, a confidence born of

---

[1] *Metaph.* M, 1078b9. I have reproduced the singular after the plural (τῶν Ιδεῶν . . . κατὰ τὴν Ιδέαν), but Ross is doubtless right to see no difference. The passages from bks A and M are translated together in his *PTI*, 154f.

[2] A comparison with A6 makes this obvious. Nor is any difference discernible between the pl. here and the sing. τῷ τὰς Ιδέας τιθεμένῳ at 1090a4. Why Burnet should have found the identification 'impossible' he does not explain, while admitting that things are said here which are said of P. in A6. (See his *T. to P.* 313n.) He conjectures that Aristotle is thinking of the εἰδῶν φίλοι mentioned in P.'s *Soph.* Who these were, no one knows for certain, but on p. 141 above I have made out a case for supposing P. to be criticizing his own earlier views. As interpreted here, the sentence does not fit the Tübingen scholars' denial of an earlier and a later doctrine of P., and Krämer (*I. und Z.* 110) says that although Aristotle distinguishes a phase of the doctrine of Forms which was not numerical, one cannot 'in the face of modern research' (*sic*) invent ('*konstruieren*') a late date for the number-theory.

the hypothesis of Forms. (Cf. *Parm.* 129c–d.) The difficulties begin
when one thinks (as we should say) of universals, not oxen or men but
ox and man, not beautiful things or good deeds but goodness and
beauty, what they are in themselves and their relations to particulars.[1]
We are familiar with the idea that everything in this world is composed
of Limit and the Unlimited (*Peras* and *Apeiron*).[2] If Aristotle is to be
trusted, it is also true of the Forms. Can we make sense of this? I believe
we can, and what follows is a fresh attempt to do so, based on a colla-
tion of the indirect evidence (chiefly Aristotle's) with Plato's own later
dialogues. I may be wrong, but together these two sources, direct from
Plato and indirect, do seem to represent a coherent attempt to solve a
recognizable problem.

Aristotle says that the elements of Forms (and hence the ultimate
elements of all things of which Forms themselves are the *archai*) are the
Great-and-Small as matter and the One as substance or form.[3]
Aristotle's conception of 'matter' may be compared to the 'something
we know not what' of Locke, to that which Kant assumed to be left
when all experienced properties of a body were removed, or possibly
to the identity of Whewell's apple, now round, red and hard, when its
roundness, redness and hardness have all left it. It is the unqualified
substratum which never exists naked, but always clothed with a certain
form, or set of properties, to make the composite object which alone has
independent existence. Hence his justification for identifying it with the
mould or matrix of Becoming in the *Timaeus*.[4] Once we know that the
dyad Great-and-Small is only our old acquaintance the *Apeiron*, the
mists begin to clear; and that the Indefinite Dyad or Great-and-Small

---

[1] *Phil.* 14d–15b, *Parm.* 130e–31e.

[2] *Phil.* 16c: 'All things that are ever said to be consist of one and many, and combine in their
nature Limit and Unlimitedness'; also 23c: There are *Apeiron* and *Peras*, and thirdly a unity
compounded of the two. It will be convenient to use these terms here. The word *apeiron*, like the
word *archē*, had a long history in Greek philosophy, going back to Anaximander as well as the
Pythagoreans. It is discussed in vol. 1, 83–7. Its two main senses of 'indefinite in extent' and
'indeterminate in character' overlap in P.'s talk of *properties* as extending indefinitely in opposite
directions, i.e. of an as yet undetermined range of quantifiable properties like temperature, length
and weight.

[3] The substance of anything (οὐσία, cf. p. 414 above) is what Aristotle more commonly calls
its form. It must not therefore be confused with 'substance' as used by more recent European
philosophers for what Aristotle would call the sub*stratum* (ὑποκείμενον) or matter. Here he
avoids the word εἶδος for obvious reasons.

[4] *Phys.* 209b11. Cf. pp. 264f., 268f. above.

should have become Plato's technical term for the *Apeiron* finds support in his own writings. Thus in the *Philebus*: 'That the *Apeiron* is in a way a plurality I shall try to explain.'[1] The explanation is that so long as anything is *apeiron* it can range indefinitely between two opposite poles. Plato's examples include drier and wetter, quicker and slower, more and less, greater and smaller;[2] and it is natural enough that one of the more easily generalized of these contrasting pairs, great and small, should have come to stand for all, as Aristotle says it did. Whenever one can rightly apply not simply indefinite comparatives like 'bigger', 'smaller' and so on, but terms like 'equal', 'twice', 'three times' (the length, weight etc.), the *Apeiron* has been transformed by the imposition of quantity, measure, ratio or number—in short, some form of *Peras*. Everything in the world is such a mixture of *Apeiron* and *Peras*, but two further points should be noticed. First, Plato was a true Pythagorean in this, that in so far as *Peras* prevails in something, it is *good*. 'Evil belongs to the Unlimited, as the Pythagoreans surmised, and good to the limited', and *Peras* headed their column of goods.[3] So Plato himself: beauty and goodness reside in due measure and proportion (*Phil.* 64e); 'everything good is beautiful, and the beautiful is not disproportionate' (*Tim.* 87c). *Peras* has the double sense of any measurable quantity or ratio and the right one, just as the word *metrion* from *metron*, measure, normally meant within *due* measure (p. 169 above). Its imposition on an indefinite continuum puts an end to the conflict of opposites and makes them well proportioned and harmonious. So reconciled, their mixture produces health in the body,[4] music from the opposites high and low, fair weather from heat and cold, law and order

---

[1] What follows comes from *Phil.* 24a–26d, and involves in content a little repetition of pp. 212f. The passage is well explained by Hackforth, *PEP* 41–3. Cf. especially p. 42: 'In the *Philebus* the term δυάς is not used, but plainly the ἄπειρον is thus conceived.' Even in *Rep.*, though P. is still looking at the problem as one concerning the sensible world, we find more than the germ of the idea: reason perceives great and small as two separate entities, whereas the senses run them together.

[2] It might be thought that in one direction at least some of these must have a definite close, e.g. what gets slower and slower must finally come to a halt. P. did not see it that way It is *motion* which is *apeiron*, and motion excludes rest (*Soph.* 255e). Did P. have a Zenonian idea of indefinitely approaching a limit but never reaching it?

[3] Arist. *EN* 1106b29, 1096b5, *Metaph.* 986a23; vol. 1, 207, 245f., 248. In considering the relations between P. and the Pythagoreans, it may be worth while to re-read the full account of Pythagoreanism in vol. 1, ch. IV, especially § 2.

[4] Alcmaeon's theory again, for which see p. 212 n. 1 above, and vol. IV, 347 n. 3.

from the unruly and limitless passions of mankind and so on. Secondly, *Peras* is associated with *unity*, which is either identical with it or the first of its products when stamped on the *Apeiron*.

This too is a Pythagorean idea, but certainly adopted by Plato, who, says Aristotle (*Metaph.* 988a14), assigned the cause of good and bad to his two elements, the One and the Indefinite Dyad, respectively. In the dialogues it is mostly implicit, though at *Phil.* 16c we find that to be formed of one and many is the same thing as containing *Peras* and *Apeiron*.[1] The identification of unity and goodness naturally figures prominently in ethical and political contexts. Bad states have lost their unity, and the ideal city must be of a size consistent with its remaining one (*Rep.* 422e–23b). The laws must so far as possible secure the *unity* of the state (*Laws* 739d). The just man has brought the three parts of his soul into harmony and become *one* man instead of many (*Rep.* 443d–e). When these reflections on the importance of unity in human life were linked in Plato's mind with a universal metaphysical theory—whether before or after the *Republic*[2]—is perhaps not certain; but since one particular acquaintance of Plato, Euclides of Megara, is known to have identified the One with the Good, it is a fair guess that the discussions between them, when Plato stayed with Euclides after the execution of Socrates, helped him to formulate his own more complex theory.[3]

All this refers to the sensible world, not to the Forms,[4] but the *Philebus* does raise the question in relation to Forms.[5] Are they truly monadic, or is each in some way a one-and-many like their sensible copies (15b)? Cornford commented on *Parm.* 129c–30a (*P. and P.* 71):

[1] In the third hypothesis of the second part of the *Parm.* (158d), from the combination of the One with the Others there comes to be in the Others something else, which gives them a *peras* in relation to each other, whereas their own nature [plurality] gives them in themselves *apeiria*.

[2] Or the *Gorgias*, where although unity is not expressly mentioned, the introduction of organization, fitness and harmony into the soul (503e–504d) clearly has the same intent.

[3] For the philosophy of Euclides and his relations with Plato see vol. III, 499–505. (Possible examination question: Is Plato vulnerable to the following dictum of Ewing (*Fundamental Questions* 211): 'We cannot, from a general proposition about the unity of everything that is, conclude that unity ought to be realized in a particular way in human life, thus deducing our politics from our metaphysics'?)

[4] I suspect this is sometimes overlooked, as perhaps by Wippern, *Das Problem* p. x n. 40, where he cites (without quoting) *Tim.* 53d as evidence that the *Prinzipienlehre* can already be detected in the dialogues. It is the ἀρχαί of bodies that are there referred to.

[5] Of course if πάντα τὰ νῦν ὄντα ἐν τῷ παντί at 23c included the Forms, as many have believed, this would make the task easier; but I do not believe it. (See p. 213 with n. 1.)

'It would, as Socrates said, be a portent if . . . Unity were the same thing as Plurality. But it does not follow that the Form, Unity itself, cannot in any sense be many.' The *Parmenides* is a problem-setting dialogue, and as he adds, the full explanation is reserved for the *Sophist*. Now the *Sophist* is the first of a group of dialogues in which Plato develops the simple Socratic advice to define by 'dividing according to kinds' (p. 27 above) into his own highly systematized dialectical method. Socrates raised no ontological problem in his talk of generic or specific concepts (justice as a part of virtue and so on), but Plato with his divine and changeless Forms had given himself a harder nut to crack. (Cf. especially p. 161 above.) In the *Politicus* he links the twofold division of measure directly with the dialectical or 'diaeretic' (*Soph.* 229 c) art in general, and moreover claims that it will be necessary some time 'in the search for truth itself' (284 d ff., pp. 170 f.). Other lessons of the later dialogues are: (1) Just as particulars can 'share in' Forms, so Forms can share in, or combine with, each other (pp. 149 f.) (2) Forms are unities in the same sense in which a man is a unity, i.e. as wholes of parts, the parts being the more specific Forms in a single generic one. Thus in the *Timaeus* the Form *Zōon* (the 'intelligible Living Creature') is 'that of which the other intelligible *Zoa*, singly and in their families, are parts'. 'It embraces and holds them all in itself, just as our [living] cosmos contains us and the other visible animals',[1] while retaining its singleness (μόνωσις 31 b). So too in the *Sophist* knowledge is one, yet the several sciences and arts form parts of it, each marked off and given its own name.[2] (3) Forms are divisible. Only the narrowest Form, that of the *infima species*, is indivisible.[3] No definition of a smaller class, by addition of a differentia, is possible, and beyond it lie only the indefinable (*apeira*) particulars, of which there is an infinite, or at least indefinite (*apeiron* again) number.

Plato here presents a significant contrast to Aristotle and logicians generally. For them the *summum genus* is an empty box which gradually gets filled as successive differentiae are added. To the genus 'animal', to which little more than the property 'life' can be assigned, are added, in

---

[1] *Tim.* 30 c. Both μέρος and μόρια are used.
[2] *Soph.* 257 c–d, μέρος ἕκαστον. μόριον at d 7, 258 a 9 and 11.
[3] ἄτομον, *Soph.* 229 d, ἄτμητον, *Phdr.* 277 b.

man, the properties of being biped and rational, in fish those of being aquatic, cold-blooded and so on. For Plato the contrary is true. The more general Form includes, contains or embraces those of the subordinate genera and species. It is richer, not poorer, in content. (Cf. p. 258 n. 1.) This gives it a higher ontological status or degree of reality, and so down the scale until particulars are reached, which do not, strictly speaking, exist at all, but only 'become'. Such a hierarchical order depends on the Forms being pluralities (of parts) as well as unities (as wholes). But for Aristotle the presence of plurality implies the presence of matter.[1] Seen through his eyes, therefore, the Forms themselves contain both a formal element and what he would call an 'intelligible material' (ὕλη νοητή, *Metaph.* 1045 a 34). But whereas for him the material element of a definition was the genus, as being the less defined, and the formal the differentia which marked off the species, for Plato the reverse would be the case. Thus to continue with the *Timaeus* example, the Form *Zöon* has life as its own formal element but *contains* the Forms of all the animals there are. In traditional logical terms, the formal or unifying element of Forms is their connotation or intension, the material or indefinite element their extension or denotation. (Who can say how many species of living thing there are?) When we reach the lowest definable Form—the essence (οὐσία) of the St Bernard dog, say, or the corgi—may we say that it too comprised the elements of Unity and *Apeiron*, the latter represented by the unlimited number of particulars whose essence it is? To say that a Form 'is', or has as an element or part of it, the particulars that share its nature and name, may sound at first decidedly unplatonic; but in some way it is dispersed among them, and this could have been Plato's answer to the question he raised in the *Philebus* (15 b): 'Must we think of each of these unities [*sc.* Man, Ox, the Beautiful, the Good] as scattered among the unlimited number of things that come to be, and so becoming many, or else (what would appear to be utterly impossible) getting apart from

---

[1] *Metaph.* 1074 a 33. Aristotle's 'matter' (ὕλη) was very like the *apeiron*. See for instance 1029 a 20: 'By matter I mean that which by itself is neither a particular thing nor a quantity, nor is designated by any other of the categories by which being is determined.' There is no need to bring in the fifth-hand evidence that Simplicius got from Porphyry who got it from Dercyllides who got it from a book of Hermodorus the associate of Plato (Simpl., *Phys.* 247f. Diels; de Vogel, *Gr. Ph.* I, 277; Gaiser, *test.* no. 31).

itself as a whole and appearing in one and many at the same time without losing its unity?' The answer would be that the Forms themselves, the *archai* of things that become, have their own *archai*, the One and the *Apeiron*; and the One is Good. It is the completion of what was adumbrated in *Rep.* 6: the Forms which give intelligibility to the world of sense owe their own being and intelligibility to the Good. When Plato wrote the *Republic*, this was something of an act of faith. To give an account of the Good, says Socrates, is beyond his powers, and he protests against being made to express an opinion with no knowledge behind it. The best he can offer is a simile. It is more reasonable to believe that in these words Plato is speaking for himself and telling the truth than that the 'unwritten doctrine' known to Aristotle was already worked out, with all the dialectical science necessary to support it, but withheld as unsuitable for a written work.

The above is offered with due diffidence as a contribution to discussion. It may be thought to present too Aristotelian a view of Plato. In fact it is an attempt to see through the veil of Aristotle's concepts and terminology, such as form and matter, to the thoughts of the man with whom, in spite of their fundamental differences, he did associate for many years. As a final comment I would add that through Plato's work on dialectic Aristotle must have found the ground well prepared for his return to the doctrine of immanent form.[1] Not that Plato abandoned the Forms himself. How could the author of the *Phaedo*, *Symposium* and *Phaedrus* ever reject those divine essences whose place was beyond the heavens? The question sounds rhetorical, but (*a*) Aristotle's evidence that he maintained them to the end is incontrovertible, and not impugned by anything in the dialogues; (*b*) the religious and poetic colour persists in the later, dialectical writings, e.g. at *Soph.* 254d, where the philosopher, because his thoughts dwell continuously on the nature of reality, inhabits a bright region inaccessible to the eyes of ordinary men unaccustomed to gaze on the radiance of the divine. But as I tried to show in the chapter on that dialogue (pp. 160f.), the logic of the dialectical method and the 'noble doctrine of the Forms' made an un-

---

[1] In *Metaph.* Z ch. 14 he states the overwhelming objections which he sees against the idea that the Forms are separately existing substances but at the same time a Form consists of genus and differentiae.

easy partnership. No wonder that, as is plain from the pages of Aristotle, this was a central topic of discussion in the Academy, with Plato, Speusippus, Xenocrates and Aristotle each offering his own solution.

The Forms as numbers. 'Then came Pythagorizing, playing with numbers, superstititious demonology. To Aristotle with his healthy common sense, this was intolerable. Mathematics and astronomy did not interest him.' So Wilamowitz on Plato's old age (*Pl.* I, 728), simplifying and polarizing as he sometimes did. Yet there is something in it.[1] It does seem that as he got older, the influence of his Pythagorean friends, at least on his metaphysical and physical thought,[2] grew stronger. In the *Timaeus* he reduced all body to plane surfaces, seems to share the Pythagorean lack of discrimination between geometrical solids and physical bodies, and hints at prior principles which I ventured to supply from the Pythagorean background (pp. 285–8). Not having any word of Plato's own on the theory of Forms as numbers, so far removed in any case from our own habits of thought, we can hardly hope to reconstruct it fully.[3] Here are a few quotations to begin with.

Arist. *Metaph.* 988a10: 'As the Forms account for the essence of all other things, so the One accounts for the essence of the Forms.'

By itself, this accords with what Plato says of the Good in the *Republic*.

Idem, De an. 404b24: 'The numbers were said [by Plato] to be the actual Forms and principles, but are formed from the elements.'

That is, the Forms, now identified with numbers, are as they always were the *archai* of other things and events, but have their own *archai* or elements also, namely the One and the Indefinite Dyad.

Idem, Metaph. 991b9: 'If the Forms are numbers, how can they be causes?'

---

[1] As much and as little perhaps as in Shorey's comment on W.'s own book, that 'regarded as a historical novel it is deserving of all praise'.

[2] One must not forget that he was also writing the *Laws*. But even there, when he touches on such subjects, he speaks in Pythagorean fashion of three-dimensional as equivalent to sensible (894a, p. 288 above).

[3] For a vigorous denial that P. ever held any such theory, see Cherniss, *Riddle* 31–7. Annas also doubts it, *Metaph.* M *and* N 62–73. For further reff. in Aristotle, see *ib.* 64 n. 78 and 66f. Not all these passages mention Plato, and in some the subject is plural.

This is Aristotle's constant complaint against the Platonic hypothesis of the Forms, whether or not as identified with numbers, that it neglects what he calls the motive or efficient cause.

Alex. in Ar. *Metaph.* 987b33 (Ross, Arist. frr. p. 114; Gaiser, *test.* 22B): 'He [Plato] said the Forms were numbers.'

Alexander says more than once in this context that his source is Aristotle's *On the Good*, taken from Plato's teaching on the subject.

Many of Aristotle's criticisms of the Form–number doctrine mention no names, but speak vaguely of 'some' or 'those who speak of Forms'. A passage of Theophrastus is worth quoting in full, if only for its careful discrimination between individual exponents (*Metaph.* ed. Ross and Fobes from 6a23; fr. 12, p. 154 Wimmer).

But now most philosophers proceed to a certain point and then stop, as do those who posit the One and the Indefinite Dyad. When they have generated numbers and surfaces and solid bodies they practically leave out everything else, just touching on them and demonstrating no more than this, that some things proceed from the Indefinite Dyad, e.g. place, void and the *Apeiron*, and others from numbers and the One, like soul and a few more, time together with the universe and some others;[1] but about the universe and the rest they say no more. Nor do those who follow Speusippus, nor any of the others except Xenocrates. He does somehow distribute the other things about the universe, sensible, intelligible, mathematical and even divine. Hestiaeus, too, tries up to a point, and does not confine himself to the principles in the way I have described. Plato in referring things to the principles seems to touch on the other things [i.e. sensibles] when he attaches them to Forms, and the Forms to numbers, and from them goes to the [first] principles. Thence he follows the order of generation down to the things I have mentioned. But the others treat of the principles only.

Some specific questions arise.

Did Plato speak of Forms and numbers as the same, or of numbers as the archai *of Forms?* Theophrastus appears to contradict Aristotle on this, and Crombie (*EPD* II, 442) speaks of a 'clash' between them which makes it look as if Aristotle had been unfair to Plato on this point. Ross however attempts to reconcile them in his commentary on Theophrastus's metaphysical extract (pp. 58f.), and in his book on the Theory

---

[1] Adopting Wimmer's punctuation in preference to that of Ross–Fobes.

of Ideas (p. 218) he says (enigmatically?): 'It is probable, then, that Plato did not identify the ideas with numbers, but only assigned numbers to Ideas.' De Vogel has treated the matter at length in *La dernière phase* (*Philos.* I, 243 ff.), especially in connexion with the investigations of Robin, and affirms on p. 285 that 'Les Nombres–Idées forment donc une classe supérieure entre l'Un et les Idées proprement dits', thus siding with Theophrastus rather than Aristotle. There is, I imagine, no greater contradiction between saying that the Forms *are* numbers and that they are a product of numbers than there was in the original Pythagorean scheme between saying that things are numbers and that the elements of numbers are the elements of things,[1] or between saying that something is a window and saying that it is a glass rectangle.

Did Plato limit the numbers to ten?

Arist. *Phys.* 206b 32: 'Plato takes the numbers up to the decad.'

Idem, Metaph. 1084a 12: 'If number goes up to ten, as some say, in the first place the Forms will give out, e.g. if three is the Form of man, what number will be the form of horse?'

The implication is that there are far more than ten Forms of natural species alone.

Idem, Metaph. 1073a 18: 'Those who speak of Forms say they are numbers, but as to the numbers they sometimes speak of them as infinite, sometimes as limited to ten.'

At *Metaph.* 1090a 2 Aristotle asks what justification there can be for saying that numbers exist. Of course, he goes on, 'for him who assumes the Forms, numbers provide a cause for existing things, for each of them is a Form, and the Form is somehow or other the cause of the existence of other things' (and hence *a fortiori* exists itself). De Vogel, accepting the statement at *Phys.* 206b 32, concludes that this sentence cannot apply to Plato.[2] If Plato actually said 'Forms are numbers and numbers Forms,[3] but the numbers only go up to ten', what could he

---

[1] As to which see vol. I, 229f., 273. In any case, the ideal numbers which are either Forms or the ἀρχαί of Forms are distinct from mathematical numbers. Hence they can be incomparable with and inaddible to one another (ἀσύμβλητοι, Arist. *Metaph.* 1080a 19), as differing in kind, without affecting the addition etc. of numbers in mathematical operations.

[2] *Gr. Ph.* I, 275. Cf. *Philos.* I, 288.

[3] That the proposition is convertible appears from Arist. *Metaph.* 1084a 7–8, 1090a 5, *De an.* 404b 24.

have meant? Aristotle's vagueness, and his obvious lack of sympathy, are not reassuring. Certainly the idea would have its attractions for Plato through its association with the sacred Pythagorean tetractys and its musical and mystical overtones. Further, as Gadamer reminds us (*I. und Z.* 27): 'This is not only Pythagorean (the Tetractys). It is an undeniable fact about the decadic system that in all further numbering the first series is simply repeated.' Here perhaps lay Plato's escape from a merely captious criticism of Aristotle's. The one thing certainly incredible is that, numbers or not, there were only ten Forms. Nor need that be the consequence.[1] Whatever Plato thought about it, the belief that ten was both the complete number *and the foundation* (πυθμήν) *of all higher numbers* was held by Speusippus (fr. 4 Lang).

The generation of numbers. Plato, says Aristotle, posited the Dyad as the second principle because the numbers, 'except the first (or primary) among them, could be easily produced from it as from a plastic material'.[2] The generation of numbers[3] from prior elements, ultimately the Unlimited (which as we know was the same thing as Plato's Dyad) and Limit, was also taught by the Pythagoreans. (See vol. I, 240.) How the numbers were generated, and what Aristotle meant by 'except the primary' (ἔξω τῶν πρώτων), has been strenuously discussed. Opinions are collected by Ross in his edition of the *Metaphysics*, vol. I, 173–6,[4] who justly remarks that 'It is difficult to trace the lineaments of Plato's theory through the medium of Aristotle's external and unsympathetic account.' His own version of the generation of numbers is on pp. 187–205 of *PTI*. He gives qualified approval to van der Wielen's interpretation, which has been further explained and developed by Popper, *C. and R.* 91 n. 55. The details are complex, but Ross's summing-up of the

---

[1] Annas has now discussed this point in her *Metaph.* M *and* N 54f.

[2] *Metaph.* 987b33. Cf. other passages of Aristotle quoted with this one in de Vogel, *Gr. Ph.* I, no. 368, and those translated in Ross, *PTI* 190f. Annas (*Metaph.* M *and* N 45) follows Alex. in taking ἐκμαγεῖον in its other sense of stamp or die. (For the two senses see p. 263 n. 3 above.) But how could the *indefinite* imprint a form on anything? It must be the material (as at *Tim.* 50c2) on which the One or *Peras* can repeatedly stamp the definite characteristic of numerical quantity.

[3] That is, in Plato's case, the numbers which are Forms, excluding (as Ross points out, *PTI* 182) 'sensible numbers' or groups of things and 'mathematical numbers' of which mathematicians speak when they say 2 + 3 = 5. The Form–Numbers cannot be added to one another. Cf. Arist. *Metaph.* 1080a15 ff., 1083a32–5.

[4] Annas, *Metaph.* N *and* M 49f., may now be added.

general principle is refreshingly lucid (*o.c.* 204 f.): 'What I suggest, then, is that in Plato's generation of the ideal numbers the One answers exactly to the "limit" of the *Philebus*. The successive numbers were the result of successive applications of limit or definiteness to unlimited plurality.'

The general scheme or order of principles. So far as our inadequate and occasionally confused sources can take us, Plato's ontological hierarchy was ordered something like this. (1) First and highest stand the One and the Unlimited (*Apeiron*) or Indefinite Dyad. The One is the bearer of Limit and therefore of Good, for from it flow right measure, proportionate mixture, and all their beneficial products from health and strength to the harmonious strains of music. We can surely recognize here the unformed matrix of the cosmos in the *Timaeus* and the *kosmos* which, through the imposition of limit in the form of geometrical solids and their prior principles, is imprinted on it by the Divine Mind. (2) The One and the *Apeiron* combine to generate the number-series, beginning with 2.[1] (3) From numbers, identified with Forms (or perhaps their *archai*), spring points (or rather what Plato called indivisible lines or the *archai* of lines, believing points to be a geometrical fiction, Arist. *Metaph.* 992 a 21), from them lines, then surfaces, solids and the physical world. Prior to physical things, somewhere between them and the Form–Numbers, must have come the 'mathematicals', the intelligible pluralities with which the mathematician works when he speaks of equal triangles or multiplies seven by six, for Aristotle's repeated witness to these can scarcely be questioned.[2]

If this is anything like correct for Plato, there can be no doubt that Aristotle was right to say that his philosophy (that is, his metaphysics) in most respects followed the Pythagoreans,[3] including the thesis that numbers were the causes of other things. He differed from them, however, in introducing the Forms and the mathematical 'intermediates',

---

[1] For Greeks in general, the unit was outside the number-series. See vol. I, 240. Aristotle defined number as 'a plurality of units' or alternatively 'limited plurality' (*Metaph.* 1039 a 12, 1053 a 30, and cf. 1088 a 6; 1020 a 13). As to which definition he himself adopted, see Wilpert, *Zwei arist. Frühschriften* 177 n. 9.

[2] *Metaph.* 987 b 14–18, 997 b 1. See vol. IV, 342 f.

[3] For other (including religious) ways in which he followed them, and the questions in his mind to which Pythagoreanism seemed to hold the answers, see vol. IV, 35 f.

and in setting the numbers apart from other things, whereas the Pythagoreans had said that the things themselves *were* numbers.[1] Here at last was advance. Pythagoras and his followers, in the excitement of his great discovery of a numerical structure underlying the world of nature, and lacking any clearly expressed distinction between material and formal elements, announced the new truth by saying 'Things are numbers'.[2] In Plato's mind form and matter were already distinct, and there followed the distinction between the world of intelligible *archai*, the Forms, and the world of sensible, mutable nature, that only 'copied' or 'shared in' it. The next step was for Aristotle to return the Forms to the things to which they belonged, on the understanding that they were different conceptually, 'separable in thought though not in fact' as he put it.

Of the theory that Forms are, or are the product of, numbers, we simply do not know enough to make sense of it in conjunction with all we have learned about Forms from the dialogues. But one thing may be said. In Pythagoreanism the numbers were the basis not only of lines, surfaces, solids and physical bodies, but also of various abstractions, moral and other: justice, opinion, opportunity, marriage and so on, as well as soul and mind. So also in Plato. The fact that Aristotle's non-mathematical examples from him are all confined to cognitive faculties is doubtless explained by their occurrence in his work on the soul. At *De an.* 404b19–24 he says, speaking of Plato,[3] and after giving a geometrical explanation of the Form of living creature:

[1] *Metaph.* 987a20. Cf. 1090a20–3: 'But the Pythagoreans, because they saw many attributes of numbers inherent in sensible bodies, assumed real things to be numbers—not separate numbers: they actually thought existing things consisted of numbers.' The Pythagorean position has been fully discussed in vol. I, 229–38.

[2] This may of course, as I said in vol. I (p. 238), be the first expression of a great scientific truth, and Aristotle wrong when he asked contemptuously how qualities like hot or white could be numbers. If so, it was an inspired (and inspiring) guess, but no more. Science had to go through the stage of form and material substance and emerge on the other side before it could state with the authority of Professor Dingle (*BJPS* 1951, 94): 'The quantities occurring in our equations are the numbers we observe on the scales of our instruments when we perform certain operations with them. It is a gratuitous addition to suppose that they are the properties of some metaphysical stuff that we invent to adapt our thinking to the habits of childhood.'

[3] Whatever ἐν τοῖς περὶ φιλοσοφίας may refer to, there is no doubt in my mind that Aristotle is still speaking of P., whose *Tim.* he has just cited by name, and not Xenocrates whom he does not mention. For the controversy see Cherniss, *ACPA* 565 ff. and Gaiser, *I. und Z.* 54 ff. Cherniss argues that the reference is to Xenocrates. If Plato is meant, that is no reason why his pupils should have said the same (Krämer, *Plat. u. Hell. Ph.* 160 n. 233).

In another way too he says that *nous* is the one, knowledge two . . . the number of the plane [i.e. three] is belief and sensation is the number of the solid.

Which number should be assigned to which concept was a matter of dispute among the Pythagoreans (e.g. justice was sometimes four, the first square number, as representing reciprocity or requital, but sometimes nine, eight, five or three, marriage was three, five[1] or ten), and altogether the scheme had a strong element of fantasy to which one would like to think that Plato did not succumb. If he finally did, it is surely not wishful thinking to suppose that it could not have been in his mind when he wrote as he did about the Forms in the *Phaedo*, *Republic* and other dialogues.[2]

Were Plato's metaphysics monistic or dualistic? In vol. I (249) I ventured to state, against Cornford, that Pythagoreanism was ultimately dualistic, neither of its two first principles, the One and the *Apeiron*, being derived from the other or from anything else. I then, all too briefly (and possibly inaccurately; cf. the section on Speusippus's ontology, pp. 460 ff. below), attributed a form of monism to the Platonist Speusippus. Can we fathom Plato's own mind on this point? From what we have

---

[1] Ben Jonson did not mention his sources when he pythagorized in the *Masque of Hymen*:

> And lastly these five waxen lights
> Imply perfection in the rites;
> For five the special number is
> Whence hallowed union claims her bliss
> As being all the sum that grows
> From the united strength of those
> Which male and female numbers we
> Do style, and are first two and three.

He could have learned this from Plutarch, *Qu. Rom.* 288d or *De E.* 388c.

[2] Some may claim to see the Form–Numbers in the triad and pemptad of *Pho.* 104a. For myself I do not, though it may be that I can bring no conclusive argument against it. If they are Forms at all (which is doubtful; see vol. IV, 375 with n. 2), they are Forms *of* numbers, like the δυάς of 101c5, and de Vogel, to be sure, has argued that the Form–Numbers are not, on the ground that according to Aristotle 'those who introduced this theory [of Forms] did not allow Forms of things in which they saw priority and posteriority, for which reason they did not propose a Form of numbers' (Arist. *EN* 1096a17–19; de Vogel, *Philos.* I, 246f.). But her argument surely rests on a misunderstanding. What the Form-theorists meant was that no single Form can cover such a series *collectively*. There cannot be a Form of Number because numbers are to each other in the relationship prior–posterior (you can have five without seven but not seven without five), but this does not rule out a Form of Five or Seven. This (which occurred to me as obvious) appears to be a point made by J. Cook Wilson in 1904, but subsequently ignored by many scholars. See Cherniss, *ACPA* 513.

seen, it looks as if for him too the One and the *Apeiron* (or Indefinite Dyad) were both ultimate, but the *Timaeus* does not stop there. True, before time and the world began, they were there, and their intelligible product, the universe of Forms, was there also. For his act of creation the supreme God, the Demiurge, had to accept the *Apeiron*, in the guise of the Receptacle of Becoming, as a datum. But his creative Mind was there also, and it was he who made the world—and made it the best possible world—by combining the two, imposing the unifying power of Limit on the shapeless, heaving Receptacle, thereby articulating the primary bodies 'by figures and numbers' (53b). Clearly the divine Mind, with its power to act on these two *archai*, enjoys prior status and is itself the unique and primary cause. The Receptacle or matter (ἐκμαγεῖον) and Necessity are secondary (συναίτια). Forms (and prior to them their elements) are in the present scheme of things the causes or *archai* of the sensible world, but this they would never have been had not the divine Providence (30b8–9) decided to make a world in their image. Was the One too a datum, used by God as he used the material on which he stamped its imprint? Rather we may say that the One was in himself. Unity and its congeners—right measure, proportion, harmony and all their benefits—do not arise haphazard, but only where reason is at work. Plato saw plenty to criticize in Anaxagoras, and would never have called Mind *Apeiron*; but he took more than a hint from his predecessor's opening words: 'All things were confused, then Mind came and set them in order.' To Plato also could be applied Aristotle's splendid sentence about Xenophanes: 'Casting his eye on the whole heaven, he says the One exists, and it is God.'[1] Νοῦν μὲν τὸ Ἕν. The monism of Plato's latest metaphysics lies in his theism.

---

[1] *Metaph.* 986b24, and for Plato *De an.* 404b22 already quoted.

IX

POSTSCRIPT TO PLATO

The problems of the chapter just completed have their own interest, but are inappropriate as a final farewell to Plato. His fame as perhaps the greatest thinker of all times[1] rightly rests not on indirect evidence, but on the writings which we are fortunate enough to possess complete. To return our minds to the dialogues before we leave him, let us briefly recall the reasons for taking them one by one rather than ordering the study in separate subjects, at least if modern subject-headings were adopted. As I said at the beginning, no arrangement is ideal, and perhaps some further explanation is due to those who hoped that the chapters would pick out from the dialogues, synthesize and sum up in turn Plato's views on political, ethical and educational theory, his metaphysics, epistemology, psychology and so on,[2] instead of leaving the reader to do this for himself, with such help as the index could give.

I will not harp again on the loss that we should incur, not merely of literary enjoyment but also a philosophical loss, by wrenching the arguments from their setting in dramatically presented conversations and contrasts of character. (I have said something of this in vol. IV, 2f.) But suppose we take a few examples of Platonic teaching to see how amenable they are to arrangement in recognized philosophical kinds. Soul is immortal and akin to the divine, and, by the same token, to the changeless Forms, the eternal models of sensible things. In virtue of this it can have stable knowledge, for knowledge as distinct from shifting judgement is of Forms, not sensibles. Can one separate here psychology, metaphysics and epistemology? Virtue is knowledge. The

---

[1] Readers who have been offended by the anti-Platonic tone of Popper's *Open Society* vol. I may like to know that this verdict is from his article on P. in the *Internat. Ency. of Soc. Sciences.*

[2] My reviewer who found vol. IV more like a series of monographs than part of a history (see p. xiii) suggested that Zeller had solved the problem by providing a synthesis in his text and the analytical justification and documentation in the notes. On the other hand one of the vows made on starting this work was that, however inferior to Zeller's it might be in other respects, it must not run to footnotes of the inordinate length of his. (Another reviewer has expressed his appreciation of this feature.)

aim of conduct, both private and political, is the acquisition of virtue, which demands a knowledge of its true nature as the excellence peculiar to humanity, and more particularly in what way it is one and in what way many. What, demands Plato, is the relation of 'the virtues' to the one thing, virtue? Here as in all things one must learn to recognize one Form in many and many in one. Hence the primary importance of the science of dialectic, of classification by genus and species in such a way as to ensure that the logical divisions posited or discovered by the mind correspond to differences existing objectively in the nature of things. Thus ethical and political theory are entwined with metaphysics and the logical problems of classification and definition ('cutting at the natural joints', not inventing unreal class-divisions like those between men and other animals or Greeks and non-Greeks).

This world is the work of a God who is Reason, it is the nearest to perfection that can be realized in matter, constructed on a mathematical basis which accounts for the heavenly motions and the structure of physical bodies alike; and all this the human mind can learn to understand on the principle that like is known by like, by developing through the studies of mathematics, astronomy and dialectic that resemblance to the divine order and its Author of which its own possession of reason makes it capable, for by virtue of that capacity the human soul is akin to the divine . . . So a circle is completed by way of theology, cosmogony, cosmology and mathematical physics back to the nature of the soul or psychology. Moreover the world is good because it displays order, the product of limit, measure, harmony and number, and behind them all of Unity, which becomes for Plato the final *archē* and the source of all goodness, be it in the individual personality, in political communities, or in the *kosmos* at large. The reason for learning mathematics is that it 'furthers the search for beauty and goodness' (*Rep.* 531c). Again, how should we classify the doctrine of Eros, so central in Plato's philosophy, which embraces sexual relations, the nature of daemons, the possibility of immortality and the appreciation of beauty in all its forms, as it appears in bodies, souls, institutions, pure science, and so finally in the supreme beauty of the Form itself, revealed to the eye not of the body but of the mind?

Why then, it may be asked, should we not classify none the less, but in a Platonic framework, not our own? Let us have chapters, not on metaphysics or logic, but on Eros, the Forms, dialectic, and so forth? This would no doubt be a more practicable plan, but since the dialogues show plainly that they were not separated in Plato's mind, it would be wiser not to try. For him philosophy had a single aim, bequeathed to him by Socrates, though the search took him far beyond the master of his younger days: to discover the nature and conditions of goodness. Herein lay the difference between him and his great pupil Aristotle. For Aristotle, who based himself on the premise 'All men by nature desire knowledge', 'the eternal question' was not 'What is goodness?' but 'Where lies Reality?'[1] Yet just as Plato's quest for goodness led him to investigate the whole conception of existence, so Aristotle could not escape the consequence of his early training that the explanation of existence must be teleological.

[1] *Metaph. ad init.* and 1028b2–4.

X

PLATO'S ASSOCIATES

Something has already been said (vol. IV, 19–24) about the general nature, organization and interests of the Academy. It was a society of mathematicians and philosophers like that depicted in *Rep.* 7, the older among them privileged to enjoy long spells of peaceful theoretical study but all prepared to descend as necessary into the world and give the benefit of their intellectual attainments and (ideally at least) previous practical experience (539e–40a) to its statesmen and legislators. It was not only a college of teachers and taught, though its functions did include education in the preliminary disciplines of mathematics and the allied subjects, but also a community of fellow-seekers after truth, each one free to pursue it in his own way and defend the conclusions to which his own reasoning led him. Aristotle makes it plain that there was no single Academic doctrine, no orthodoxy, but a wide variety of theories within it, including of course his own. As for Plato himself, the impression given is of one who wished to provide no more than general guidance, to stimulate and assist that free intercourse of minds from which alone the flame of truth could be kindled. The present chapter offers a brief compendium of information on the best known of the other members and how each pursued his own researches and ideas, after which we should be ready to approach Aristotle, the only one from whom we have inherited a corpus of documentary remains, and the one who some thirteen years after Plato's death founded his own school to develop and promulgate his own different conceptions of philosophy and science. The chapter may tend to resemble a series of encyclopaedia articles and make correspondingly unattractive reading; but if it resembles them also in being informative, it will have achieved its purpose.[1]

---

[1] D.L. 3.46 names a selection of P.'s disciples, and an annotated list with sources will be found in Zeller, II.1, 982–4 (982 n. 1). If, as several sources state, two women, Axiothea of Phlius and Lasthenia of Mantinea, were of the number, this would accord with his affirmation in *Rep.* and *Laws* of their fitness for political office and military service. (The report is traceable to Aristotle's pupil Dicaearchus.)

Eudoxus

Eudoxus 'the mathematician' was better known for his mathematical and astronomical achievements, still respected today, than as a philosopher. Diogenes Laertius also mentions medicine, in which Philistion was his teacher, but nothing is known of his medical work. He also wrote a geography in at least seven books.[1]

Life. His home was Cnidus in south-west Asia Minor. It is difficult to reconstruct with certainty the order of events in his life.[2] His dates used to be thought of as roughly 408–356 (he died aged 52, D.L. 8.90), but recent re-examinations of the evidence favour (again approximately) 395–343 or even 337.[3] This means that he outlived Plato, a fact which has played its part in the controversy over the date of the *Timaeus*. At the age of twenty-three he came to Athens from his native Cnidus, attracted by the fame of 'the Socratics', but stayed only two months. After his return home he went to Egypt for sixteen months, thence to Cyzicus where he set up as a teacher,[4] and after visiting Mausolus the tyrant of Halicarnassus he at length returned to Athens, bringing many of his pupils with him. The Cnidians held him in high honour and had him write laws for them.

This meagre outline is mainly taken from Diogenes (8.86–8), from whom it also appears that he was in close touch with Plato. He is indeed commonly referred to as a friend or associate of Plato's, though Diogenes rightly omits him from the list of his pupils.[5] Like other brilliant mathematicians he evidently matured early, and talked with Plato on equal terms and as the leader of a school of his own. His teacher in geometry was Archytas and he himself was in later times called a Pythagorean.[6] It thus seems doubtful whether he was a member of the

---

[1] The fragments of Eudoxus have been collected by F. Lasserre (1966). Users of this serviceable aid should perhaps know of the highly critical review of Toomer in *Gnomon* 1968.

[2] For the evidence a reader may be referred to the careful study of Merlan in the appendix to his *Studies in Epic. and Arist.*, 98–104, 'The Life of Eudoxus'.

[3] Merlan, *o.c.* 100 with reff. in n. 23.   [4] σοφιστεύων, D.L. 8.87.

[5] D.L. 3.46. To Strabo (14.15, p. 915 Meineke) he is τῶν Πλάτωνος ἑταίρων, and Plut. (*adv. Col.* 1126d) brackets him with Aristotle as Πλάτωνος συνήθεις. For further reff. see Ross, *Arist. Metaph.* I, 198, and on P.'s relations with Eudoxus, Friedländer, *Pl.* I, 353 n. 15.

[6] D.L. 8.86, Iambl. *in Nicom. Arithm.* p. 10, 17 Pistelli. When he studied under Archytas we are not told. Even if Aelian's statement is true that he went to Sicily with Plato, i.e. on P.'s

447

Academy, though Merlan, like most scholars, states confidently that when Plato left for his first visit to Sicily he appointed Eudoxus as its temporary head. This is based on the statement in a late life of Aristotle that he joined the Academy 'in the time of Eudoxus'. The phrase is that used for dating events by naming the *archon* for the year, and the writer may have known no more than that Aristotle's entry coincided with Eudoxus's presence in Athens.[1]

Mathematics. It was here that Eudoxus won his greatest fame, and E. Frank may be right in saying that what we are accustomed to call Pythagorean mathematics is essentially the work of Archytas, Theaetetus and Eudoxus. The problem of irrationals, or incommensurable magnitudes, which had dealt such a blow at the arithmetical philosophy of the earlier Pythagoreans and seemed so crucial to Plato,[2] was solved by the theory of proportion due to, or at least perfected by, Eudoxus and incorporated in the fifth book of Euclid's *Elements*.[3] A second achievement concerned his theory of infinitesimals, or method of exhaustion, often claimed nowadays as a forerunner of the modern infinitesimal calculus. Historically it was developed from Anaxagoras's conception of the infinitely small (vol. II, 289f.) and a denial of the materialism of Democritus (*ib.* 484ff.) with its physically and mathe-

second visit (which Merlan was inclined to believe, *o.c.* 100 n. 16), that seems rather late for his pupillage. Theo Smyrn. brackets 'the followers of Eudoxus and Archytas' in connexion with the belief that there is a numerical ratio between concordant notes and that pitch depends on speed. See vol. I, 226.

[1] ἐπὶ Εὐδόξου, *Vita Marc.* p. 429 Rose, 99 Düring (largely restored from *tempore Eudoxi* in the *V. Latina*). See Merlan, *o.c.* 99 with n. 14; but also Jaeger, *Arist.* 16 n. 2, not mentioned by M., Düring, *Ar. in Anc. Biog. Trad.*, 159f. and Friedländer, *Pl.* I, 353 n. 15. M. himself says that Eudoxus was only 28 at the time, and had come to Athens in that very year. If that is so, P. would have regarded him as rather young to learn the science of dialectic, let alone to preside over a fraternity of dialectical philosophers.

[2] Cf. pp. 283 n. 2, 347.

[3] The evidence is a scholium to Eucl. v, Lasserre D 32, p. 22. On how much of Euclid was derived from Eudoxus see Hultsch in *RE* vi, 953. I borrow Frank's explanation of the theory (*P. u. sog. Pyth.* 226): ' $\sqrt{2}$ is the "mean proportional", the "geometric mean" between 1 and 2. By this so-called geometrical proportion the irrational quantity $\sqrt{2}$ can be brought into an exact mathematical relationship to the whole numbers (1 and 2) . . . It is called "geometrical" because the mean proportion in it ($\sqrt{2}$) can be precisely represented or discovered through geometrical construction, but neither *arithmetically*, through any rational number, nor *harmonically*, that is, by the string-length of a concordant note. Thus through the idea of proportion, the relationship between quantities becomes comprehensible irrespective of whether they are rational or irrational.' Cf. also Heath, *Aristarchus* 191, and for discussions of Eudoxus's contribution to the theory of proportion the references in Schofield, *Mus. Helv.* 1973, p. 5, n. 19.

matically indivisible atoms (*ib.* 484 ff. and appendix, 503 ff.), which 'confined pure mathematics to arithmetic and turned geometry into physics'.[1] Democritus in his own time was reacting against Eleatic monism, especially the dependence of Zeno's paradoxes on the notion of infinite divisibility. Eudoxus reintroduced this in a more advanced form as a geometrical conception and a solution to the problem of squaring the circle.[2] He is also credited by Archimedes with furnishing the proof of something discovered but not proved by Democritus, that a cone is one-third of the volume of a cylinder, and a pyramid of a prism, with the same base and equal height. (See vol. II, 488.)

Plutarch tells a story that Eudoxus and his pupil Menaechmus, and also Archytas, annoyed Plato by trying to solve stereometric problems like the doubling of the cube with mechanical aids, instead of working them out by reason alone.[3] They were, he said, undoing the good of geometry by turning it back to the sensible world instead of carrying it upward to the eternal and bodiless. This of course agrees precisely (perhaps suspiciously precisely) with Plato's theory of education for Guardians in the *Republic* (bk 7, 521 c ff.), especially 526 e: geometry will be useful only if it compels us to contemplate reality rather than the realm of change.[4] One can well understand that any method which involves only an asymptotic approach to the truth would seem to Plato to leave us stranded on the shores of empiricism and the sensible world. Diogenes on the other hand throws a rather different light on the matter

[1] Frank, *o.c.* 56, who saw in the rescue of mathematics from this threat a reason for the far-reaching importance attached by Plato to the idea of geometrical proportion or 'geometrical equality' (e.g. *Gorg.* 508 a 6).

[2] Described by Archimedes (2.294 Heiberg) as 'to find a rectilinear figure equal to a given circle and segment of a circle'. On Eudoxus's solution see Heath, *Maths. in Arist.* 96 f. Neither Eudoxus nor anyone else could *solve* the problem, but his 'great and fruitful' method cleared the way for further advances by showing that it was sufficient for the purpose to prove that the sum of the small segments left over between the sides of an inscribed polygon and the circumference of the circle can be made less than any assigned area.

[3] Plut. *Qu. conv.* 718 e–f and *Marcellus* ch. 14. The elegiac epigram quoted by Eutocius in his commentary on Archimedes (3.112 Heib., last four lines in DK I, 427), which ends with a warning to those who would double the cube to avoid 'the awkward cylinders of Archytas, the triads which Menaechmus produced by conic section and the curvilinear shapes of Eudoxus', seems only to be setting some empirical demonstrations against others.

[4] Purely in passing, I have just come across the following quotation from Einstein in Popper's *Logic of Scientific Discovery* (p. 314 n. 4): 'In so far as the statements of geometry speak about reality, they are not certain, and in so far as they are certain they do not speak about reality.' If we think of Plato as believing the exact reverse of this, we shall be near the heart of his metaphysics.

when he puts it the other way round and says that Archytas was the first to systematize mechanical methods by applying mathematical principles to them.[1]

Astronomy. Eudoxus's system of stellar motions, of which we have a summary from Aristotle himself,[2] is said to have been evolved in response to a problem set by Plato to the astronomers of his time. It was of course axiomatic for Plato that the stars and planets (the stellar 'gods') moved in perfect circles, on metaphysical and religious grounds as the *Timaeus* shows, grounds which still weighed with the young Kepler at the end of the sixteenth century A.D. The problem therefore was to demonstrate 'on what hypotheses the phenomena concerning the planets [including in that term, as was customary, sun and moon] could be accounted for by uniform and ordered circular motions'.[3] Eudoxus's solution was to suppose that the sun, the moon, and each of the planets was situated on the circumference of the innermost of a series of spheres whose common centre was the motionless earth. Each sphere, besides revolving on its own axis, was carried by the revolution of an outer sphere turning on a different axis at a different speed. The apparent departures of a visible planet from uniform circular motion could, he thought, be accounted for as the result of such composite movements if one assumed three spheres each for sun and moon and four each for the other five. The fixed stars, of course, since even their apparent motion was uniform, needed only one sphere, making a total of 27.[4]

Callippus, a younger contemporary of Eudoxus and close colleague of Aristotle, refined on this system by adding two spheres each for sun and moon and one for each of the planets except Jupiter and

---

[1] D.L. 8.83 τὰ μηχανικὰ ταῖς μαθηματικαῖς προσχρώμενος ἀρχαῖς μεθώδευσε. (For the verb cf. Diod. Sic. 1.81.2 on the derivation of Egyptian geometry from practical land-measurement: γεωμέτρου τὴν ἀλήθειαν ἐκ τῆς ἐμπειρίας μεθοδεύσαντος.) Diogenes does however add that Archytas 'introduced mechanical motion into a geometrical construction', when he sought by section of a half-cylinder to find two mean proportionals in order to double the cube. For the complete proof as given by Eutocius, and a modern explanation, see DK 1, 425–7.

[2] *Metaph.* Λ ch. 8. Our other source is Simpl. *Cael.* 492, 31 ff. Heiberg, going back to Eudoxus's own work Περὶ ταχῶν (*Simpl.* 294.12).

[3] Simpl. *Cael.* 492.31–493.4 and 488.21–24. On this passage see p. 296 n. 2 above.

[4] More detailed accounts are in Dreyer, *Planetary Systems* ch. IV and Heath, *Aristarchus* 194 ff. Both are written in acknowledged dependence on the pioneer work of Schiaparelli, and all three come in for some criticism by Dicks in his chapter on Eudoxus's astronomy, *Early Gk Astronomy* 176–88. See Dreyer 89 n. 3.

Eudoxus

Saturn,[1] but Aristotle himself modified it more fundamentally. He wrote that between each set of spheres governing the motions of a celestial body one must assume another set, fewer in number by one, to counteract the effect of one planet's motions on those of the next below it and so enable all but the outermost to perform their proper motions independently of those beyond them. The usual explanation of the difference[2] is that Eudoxus had treated the problem purely theoretically, in terms of geometry alone. 'The whole system was a purely geometrical hypothesis, or a set of theoretical constructions calculated to represent the apparent paths of the planets and enable them to be computed' (Heath, *Aristarchus* 196). He did not in any way connect the spheres moving one planet with those moving another. Aristotle on the other hand saw the problem in terms of the elemental substance, *aither*, of which he believed the heavenly bodies and their spheres to be composed. He 'transformed the purely abstract and geometrical theory into a mechanical system of spheres, i.e. spherical shells, in actual contact with one another' (*ib.* 217). Eudoxus would then provide a remarkable example of an astronomer faithfully following the precept of the *Republic* to treat the stars as a geometrician treats his figures, not simply as visible lines drawn with pencil on paper but as sensible aids to the discovery of intelligible, mathematical truth.[3] I have remarked (vol. IV, 524 n. 2(*b*)) that Plato did not by this intend to discourage the visual observation which provides an indispensable basis for the mathematical constructions no less than do the figures drawn by the geometer; and as we should expect from his methods in mathematics, Eudoxus did not neglect this aspect of astronomy. He made use of an observatory in Egypt and had one built at Cnidus,[4] and is recorded as using various

[1] Arist. *Metaph.* 1073b32–8. For Aristotle's relations with Callippus see Simpl. *Cael.* 493.5–8.

[2] It would be easy to add to the witnesses (Heath, Clagett, G. E. R. Lloyd) quoted in Wright's article mentioned in the next note, e.g. Karpp, *Eudoxus* 47 and 48, Popper, *Conj. and Ref.* 99 n. 6. Dreyer however was more cautious: 'Whether he merely adopted the spheres as mathematical means of representing the motions of the planets and subjecting them to calculation thereby, or whether he really believed in the physical existence of all these spheres, is uncertain' (*Plan. Systems*, 1906, 91).

[3] *Rep.* 530a–c, vol. IV, 524. This universally held opinion of the difference between the systems of Eudoxus and Aristotle (still upheld by Dicks in 1970, *Early Gk Astronomy* 257 n. 351) has recently been challenged by L. Wright, 'The Astronomy of Eudoxus: Mathematics or Physics?', in *Studies in Hist. and Phil. of Sci.* 1973.

[4] Strabo 2.14, p. 160 Meineke and 17.30, p. 1125.

instruments, even if their exact nature and stage of development in his time cannot now be determined. Cicero describes a celestial globe which he made, and Vitruvius credits him with something called the *arachnē* (lit. 'spider's web'), which he says was a kind of *horologia*.[1]

Ontology: Eudoxus and the Forms. In his *Metaphysics* Aristotle complains that owing to their transcendence the Forms can contribute nothing either to the being of sensible things or to our knowledge of them. He continues (991a14 = 1079b18) that if they were *in* the sensibles, they might possibly be thought to be causes as the white is the cause of something being white by being mixed with it.[2] But this explanation, used first by Anaxagoras and later by Eudoxus in his perplexity and a few others, is too vulnerable; it would be easy to collect against it many impossible consequences.

Aristotle does not say here what these objections are, but his commentator Alexander enumerates ten which he has taken from Aristotle's work *On Forms*, now lost.[3] Some of them resemble objections which Plato brought against his own Forms in the *Parmenides*, especially those at 131a–d.[4] We need not take Aristotle's comparison of Eudoxus with Anaxagoras too seriously, nor conclude with Hultsch (*RE* VI, 948) that 'to put it briefly, he replaced the Forms by Anaxagorean homoeomeries'. Aristotle's remark is no evidence for the unlikely idea that Eudoxus thought of the Forms as corporeal, and his general tendency towards

[1] Cic. *De rep.* 1.22 (cf. Dicks, *Early Gk Astronomy* 248 n. 252), Vitruvius, *De architect.* 9.9.1. On the *arachnē* (which he calls the spider; it could mean either) see Dicks, *o.c.* 257 n. 355. Hultsch (*RE* VI, 938) and others agree that he must have used an elementary form of dioptra (for which see *RE* V, 1073–9). Further information in *RE* VI, 744, II, 367. For his work on the calendar, see Dicks, *o.c.* 188 f.

[2] Cf. Alex. *im Met.* 97.18, which literally translated runs: 'Eudoxus said that individuals existed by the mixture of the Forms in the things which have their being with reference to them.' This is oddly phrased, for 'the things which have their being with reference to the Forms' are, one would suppose, the individuals themselves. Düring says (*Aristoteles* 253, n. 54) they are (or it is, for he conveniently translates τοῖς as singular, '*dasjenige*'), '*Stoffprinzip*', and presumably that is what Eudoxus intended.

[3] Alex. *in Met.* 79.3–83.30; Ross, *Arist. frr.* pp. 122–5. The list of objections in Alex. (thirteen according to Düring, *o.c.* 253 n. 55) is discussed by Cherniss, *ACPA* App. VII (525–39), much of which is taken up by a lengthy refutation of Karpp's arguments that some of the objections are Alex.'s own and not from the Π. Ἰδεῶν. See also K. von Fritz, 'Die Ideenlehre des Eudoxus etc.', *Philol.* 1926–7.

[4] Schofield ('Eudoxus in the *Parmenides*', *Mus. Helv.* 1973) sees an attack on Eudoxus's theory of the immanence of the Forms in the second part, *Parm.* 149d–150e.

anachronism in the assessment of his Ionian predecessors is particularly noticeable in his treatment of Anaxagoras.

All we know, then, of Eudoxus's views about the Forms is that being puzzled (διαπορῶν) about their relation to particulars he sought to remove the difficulty by making them wholly immanent, to which Aristotle (*ap.* Alex.) objected that along with their transcendence would have to be sacrificed their independence, imperishability and immobility —qualities, of course, which Plato prized in them above all else. At the same time the context in Aristotle's *Metaphysics* makes it clear that Eudoxus wished to retain their substantial existence. It is sometimes said that his doctrine of immanent Forms resembled Aristotle's own (e.g. by Ross, *Metaph.* vol. I, 198), which was therefore open to some of the same objections. However, the resemblance falls far short of identity, as may appear when the time comes to consider Aristotle for his own sake. Meanwhile a hint has been given on pp. 414f. above. In abandoning the famous *chorismos* ('separation') of the Forms, Eudoxus made a decisive break with Plato's theory. If the objections brought against his view went unnoticed by him, it looks as if his mathematical and astronomical gifts exceeded his aptitude for speculative philosophy, but our meagre information scarcely permits us to judge.

Ethics: pleasure as the Good. What Eudoxus taught on this subject is stated and commented on by his contemporary Aristotle (*EN* 1172b9–28 and 1101b27–34). He held that the Good, that perennial object of the Platonist's search, was *pleasure*, but according to Aristotle his arguments were accepted more on account of his personal virtue than for their own sake, for he was an exceptionally self-controlled and abstemious (*sōphrōn*) man. He gave five reasons for his belief.

1. Its universal desirability. All creatures, both rational and irrational, seek pleasure, and among all kinds what is chosen is suitable and what is chosen more than other things is the best. Thus the fact that all are drawn towards pleasure indicates that it is best for all. Everything discovers its proper good, no less than its proper nourishment, and what is good for all and desired by all is *the* Good.

2. Pleasure and pain are opposites. Pain *per se* is an object of universal

aversion, therefore its opposite must be *per se* universally choiceworthy.

3. Pleasure is chosen for its own sake, as an end in itself and not a means to something else. No one asks 'For what purpose is he enjoying himself?', and this implies that pleasure is chosen for itself.

4. Added to any other good thing, e.g. the practice of justice and self-control, it increases that thing's goodness. Nothing else therefore can be *the* Good, for that can only be increased by itself.

5. Pleasure, though an acknowledged good, is not praised. This is evidence that it is beyond praise, like God and the Good, which are the *standards* by which other things are judged.[1]

That pleasure could be the Good was of course fiercely denied by Plato in the *Republic* (505 c, 509 a), and combatted with more subtlety in the *Philebus*. Unfortunately we are not told what Eudoxus's conception of pleasure was, or what it included. Aristotle's tribute to his character, as well as the choice of examples in the fourth argument, suggests that he would have followed Plato, rather than Philebus or his own older contemporary Aristippus[2] and his Cyrenaic followers, in acknowledging pleasures of the soul apart from the body (Plato, *Philebus* 34c). Since he must have been aware of Plato's views,[3] it will be worth glancing back at the *Philebus* for a comparison. Plato too lays it down early in the dialogue (20d) as a necessary condition for the good that every creature (πᾶν, neuter) should desire it; but this consorts oddly with his challenging conclusion at 67b that pleasure cannot be, nor come near to being, the good,

No, not even if all the oxen and horses and every other animal should affirm it by their pursuit of enjoyment. Trusting to them, as diviners to birds, the common herd make up their minds that it is pleasures more than anything else that ensure a good life. They consider the desires of animals better testimony than that which results from the insight and reasoning of philosophers.

Reading this, we cannot absolve Plato from inconsistency on the

---

[1] The first four arguments are from the passage in the tenth book, the fifth from that in the first.

[2] For Aristippus see vol. III, 490–9.

[3] The unanswerable question of the exact relations between Eudoxus and the *Phil.*—whether it was deliberately directed against Eudoxus, or Eudoxus was replying to it, or Eudoxus's views had caused P. to modify his own in the *Phil.*—is discussed at length, with reff. to earlier opinions, y Karpp, *Eudoxus* 23–7.

grounds that universal desirability, though a necessary, is not a sufficient condition of being the Good. The Good, he has said, lies in the mixed life of reason and pleasure. On this hypothesis it would obviously be impossible for 'every creature' to desire the Good, nor do even the unphilosophical majority among human beings. It looks as if Eudoxus may have detected another flaw in this far from flawless dialogue.

The second argument is not mentioned in the *Philebus*, though at 31 b Socrates does say that they will find it impossible to examine pleasure apart from pain. The third is important as a direct contradiction of Plato, who claimed that pleasure was a process or coming-to-be (*genesis*) and a process is never good in itself but only as the means to an end beyond itself.[1] What Eudoxus said of pleasure Plato and Aristotle said of what they called happiness,[2] which they did hold to be the goal of human life. Eudoxus's language about pleasure is strikingly paralleled by Plato's on happiness in the *Symposium* (205 a): If someone is seeking happiness, 'there is no need for the further question why he wishes to be happy; the answer seems complete'. But for Plato the happy man, 'the possessor of good things', is the philosophic lover, not the hedonist. On the fourth argument Aristotle himself points out, recalling the *Philebus*,[3] that Plato used a similar one to prove the opposite, that the Good itself is not pleasure (*EN* 1172 b 26).

This argument [of Eudoxus] seems to show that pleasure is one of the good things, but no more so than another, for everything is more worth choosing when linked to another good than by itself. In fact it is by a similar argument that Plato *denies* that the Good is pleasure, because the pleasant life is more to be chosen when combined with wisdom than without it, and if the mixed life is better, pleasure is not the Good; for the Good cannot become more desirable by having anything added to it.

[1] *Phil.* 53 c–55 c. See pp. 228 f. above. Aristotle also disagreed with Plato on this point (*EN* 10 ch. 4).

[2] εὐδαιμονία. This is one of the many cases where no English word describes precisely the concept expressed by the Greek. 'Happiness' is the accepted translation, and probably nearer than any other, though 'good fortune' also comes near.

[3] Cf. in particular *Phil.* 60 d–61 a, where Socrates says that because the mixed life of pleasure and reason together is better than a life of either alone, therefore neither pleasure nor reason by itself can be the supreme Good.

Geography and ethnology.[1] Besides his mathematical, astronomical and philosophic interests, Eudoxus wrote a work not generally associated with the philosophical tradition but rather with men like Herodotus, Hecataeus and Ctesias. This was a Survey of the Earth or World-Survey[2] in at least seven books. From this we have a number of quotations or items of information, enough to suggest the flavour of the work, from which I take a few specimens. On Egypt Eudoxus could speak from the firm ground of personal experience. So he claims to have learned from Egyptian priests about the cause of the flooding of the Nile (fr. 287, and cf. 288),[3] explains the different rules of the priests at Heliopolis and elsewhere regarding the use of wine (fr. 300, from bk 2), tells of the burial place of Osiris (fr. 291) and gives the reason why the Egyptians do not sacrifice pigs. He also relates a strange Egyptian myth about Ammon (whom the Greeks called Zeus) and offers an allegorical explanation (fr. 299). In treating of Persia, too, he showed an interest in its religion, writing of Ormuzd and Ahriman, the spirits of good and evil, and the date of Zoroaster (fr. 341). He mentioned the Scythian custom of sacrificing to an upright sword as emblem of the war-god (fr. 303), already described in more detail by Herodotus (4.62), and on a different subject used the evidence of language in connexion with the Phrygian origin of the Armenians. Polybius compared him with Ephorus as an authority on the foundation of Greek cities, their relationships and their founding fathers (fr. 328).

The brief extracts are of course torn from their contexts. Some items, if Eudoxus simply recorded them as facts, would seem to show him up

[1] F. Gisinger devoted a treatise to this, 'Die Erdbeschreibung des E. von Knidos' (1921).

[2] Democritus, it is true, was coupled with Eudoxus as having done the same (fr. 15 DK). Such surveys formed a recognized class, and included information about manners and customs as well as geography. Thus Aristotle at *Pol.* 1262a18, speaking of peoples who have wives in common, says that relationships may nevertheless be detected from the resemblance of children to their mothers, 'which does actually happen according to some of those who compose world-surveys'. (Eudoxus himself spoke of this as a custom of the Massagetae in Asia (D.L. 9.8), but so had Herodotus before him, 1.216.1.) Again at *Rhet.* 1360a34, 'The world-surveys are useful for legislation, because from them can be learned the *nomoi* of foreign peoples.' In other contexts the phrase refers to maps, e.g. Hdt. 4.36.2, 5.49.5, Arist. *Meteor.* 362b12 and probably also at 350a16. For the map of Anaximander, called in our sources a πίναξ, see vol. I, 74. According to a scholium on Dionys. Periegetes (Gisinger, *Eudoxus* 14) Eudoxus himself made a πίναξ of the inhabited world, which is likely enough, though the scholiast's description of Democritus as a pupil of Thales does not inspire confidence.

[3] Fragments are referred to by the numbering of Lasserre's edition.

as considerably more credulous than Herodotus. He spoke for instance of a certain stone on a Phrygian mountain, such that whoever found it during the mysteries of Hecate went mad (fr. 338), and of two springs in Thessaly which turned sheep who drank of them respectively black or white—or piebald if they drank of both. According to Pliny he said that in southern India there were men with feet a cubit long, whereas the women's were so short that they were called 'sparrow-feet' (fr. 338).[1] In conclusion a few things may be mentioned to restore the balance of the great mathematician's reputation. First, I have omitted a number of pieces of straightforward geographical information quoted by the serious-minded geographer Strabo. Secondly, Dicks (*Astron.* 289) produces evidence tending to show that he was the first to apply mathematical principles to geography. Finally, he had a third-century namesake Eudoxus of Rhodes, who wrote 'Histories', and although attempts to make him out the author of the World-Survey have decisively failed,[2] some of the more fanciful items attributed simply to 'Eudoxus' may be owed to the Rhodian and not the Cnidian. In any case writers in this genre were expected by their public to retail items of folklore without always vouching for their truth. Some were repeated from author to author—commonplaces, one might say, of ethnological lore—and Eudoxus might well have said with Herodotus (7.152.3): 'My business is to record what people tell, but not necessarily to believe it. This may be taken to apply to my whole work.'

Speusippus

Speusippus, we are told, left a vast number of treatises and a good many dialogues: Diogenes (4.4–5) lists thirty as a selection. One wonders what we should make of him if we had even one of these works. As it is,

---

[1] It is an unfortunate oddity that the same Greek word, στροῦθος, means both sparrow and ostrich, but I assume that sparrows are meant here. Gisinger (*Eudoxus* 20) finds 'ostrich-footed' compatible with the smallness of the women's feet. He also finds the report '*durchaus glaubwürdig*'.

[2] It would suffice to cite the precise references to 'Eudoxus of Cnidus in the first book of his World-Survey' in Sextus Empiricus and Athenaeus and 'Eudoxus of Cnidus in the 7th book of his World-Survey' in Apollonius (fr. 278b, 284a, 323 in L.). These refer respectively to the marriage-customs of the Massagetae, the origin of the Phoenician custom of sacrificing quails to Heracles, and a Libyan people who make honey from flowers like the bees, where Eudoxus's authority appears to have been again Herodotus (4.194). Other references to 'Eudoxus in the World-Survey' may be regarded as similarly guaranteed. On the question of authenticity see Gisinger 2 ff. Lasserre 237–9.

we depend on scraps of information, spiced with criticism, thrown to us by others, largely (at least for his metaphysics) by Aristotle and his commentators. He was obviously a central figure in the great Academic controversy about the Platonic Forms, whether they were credible and what should replace them if they were not. Aristotle's own solution was very different from that of Speusippus, which he vigorously opposed. Where, as with Plato, we can check his interpretations, we know that if he disagrees he is not invariably understanding or fair, and with Speusippus we have not his own writings as a corrective. Moreover, attempts to reconstruct Speusippan metaphysics cannot confine themselves to passages in which he is named but must have recourse to many others in which Aristotle speaks of 'those who say' such-and-such, and which in the light of other evidence are with varying degrees of confidence assigned to him.[1] Nor is it always easy to reconcile apparently conflicting reports even on so crucial a question as the position of the One in his philosophy. All credit is due to those who have made the attempt at reconstruction,[2] but apart from any doubts about the accuracy of our sources, one gets the impression that the Academy in and after the last years of Plato's life was tending to lose itself in highly schematic and somewhat barren systems of 'reality' which were becoming more and more remote from reality as most men understand it. Perhaps the time was ripe for Aristotle with his sympathy for lay opinion, clarity of exposition and respect for the individual, to step in and rescue philosophy from aimless wandering in mathematico-metaphysical mazes of Pythagorean inspiration.

In their assessments of Speusippus modern interpreters differ widely. Merlan (see n. 2) on p. 117 says that on his own interpretation 'his system is a highly original, interesting, possibly unique system in the history of Western philosophy', and Cherniss too extols his originality (*Riddle* 43, 82). Tarrant on the other hand (p. 144) finds 'little cause for commending the originality of Speusippus' system . . . there is little which does not have its antecedent in Plato's *Parmenides*'.

[1] Ross, *PTI* 152f., lists passages in Aristotle where Sp. is either mentioned by name or referred to with certainty or high probability.

[2] I am thinking in particular of Merlan in ch. v of his *P. to N.* and H. A. S. Tarrant's article 'Speusippus' Ontological Classification' in *Phron.* 1974. See also the concise account of Cherniss in *Riddle*, 33–43. On the position of the One, contrast Krämer's and Merlan's views: 'Krämer places the One at the head of the list while Merlan excludes it altogether' (Tarrant, *l.c.* 131).

Speusippus

Life.[1] He was the son of Plato's sister Potone, and lived into old age. His dates have been estimated at approximately 410–339. He was probably a member of the Academy from its foundation, and he became its head on Plato's death in 347.[2] He died eight years later.

Ontology. Speusippus abandoned the Platonic Forms, replacing them with numbers. Aristotle more than once brackets him with the Pythagoreans, with whom he obviously had much in common. He differed from them however in that they identified numbers and things, whereas for Speusippus numbers were, like the Forms, independent substances separate from the sensible world, though at the same time 'mathematical numbers', not Plato's 'ideal numbers'. The axioms of mathematics are true, 'and gladden the soul', but do not apply to sensibles; so also with mathematical magnitudes. He and his followers, says Aristotle, did not believe in Forms, either in themselves or identified with numbers (as by Plato in his old age). Numbers and mathematical objects were the first of existing things, and the first principle or starting-point (*archē*) of numbers was the One. His additional (Pythagorean) dogma that ten was the complete, or perfect, number, and the foundation of all higher numbers, has already been noted on p. 438; and his substitution of numbers for the Platonic Forms is strikingly illustrated by his identification of the Creator's model (the 'perfect living creature' of *Tim.* 30c–31a) with the decad, to which he devoted half of his book on Pythagorean numbers.[3] Apart from sensibles, Speusippus posited only the

[1] Details and full reff. in Merlan's 'Zur Biogr. des Sp.', *Philol.* 1959. Only the barest outline is possible, and M.'s article gives the impression of one gallantly trying to make bricks with very little straw, eked out with frequent use of 'probably', 'possibly', 'it is natural to assume', and similar expressions. D.L. (4.1–5) relates several possibly legendary incidents. He has been thought to draw on two contrasting traditions, a favourable and a hostile. A letter of Speusippus to Philip of Macedon, giving evidence of his strong pro-Macedonian sympathies, is generally believed to have been fully authenticated by Bickermann and Sykutris in *Berichte Sächs. Akad.* 1928. For his friendship with Dion, whom he is said to have encouraged in his expedition against Dionysius II, see Plutarch's life of Dion and other sources mentioned by Stenzel, *RE* 1637.

[2] There is no point in speculating on the unknown reasons for this choice. It is not even known whether it was Plato's or made by the Academy after his death. Speusippus was already an established philosopher in his late maturity. Aristotle was some twenty-six years younger, and Xenocrates, evidently also younger, succeeded in due course, while Aristotle set up a school of his own. It has been suggested that the reason may have been purely practical, connected with the legal inheritance of the property (Jaeger, *Arist.* 110; Chroust in *REG* 1971).

[3] Fr. 4, p. 54 Lang. On the grounds for regarding ten as the perfect number see Heath, *Maths. in Aristotle* 258–60. This and the work on Pythagorean numbers found mention in vol. 1, 260.

mathematica, substituting mathematical number for ideal.[1] Aristotle objects that these people believe in two different 'ones', the *archē* itself and the One which is the first number (cf. vol. 1, 249), which, he thought, simply brought them back to Plato's distinction between ideal and mathematical numbers. As *archē* of 'the first of existing things', the One itself is 'not even existent' (Arist. *Metaph.* 1092a14). This must, one would think, mean that like the Form of the Good in the *Republic* (509b), it is not Being because 'beyond Being in dignity', a higher principle even than Being itself, and so it has been most frequently, but not universally, understood,[2] though this does not seem to suit the context in Aristotle very well. Iamblichus called it 'not yet a substance but the foundation-stone of substances, for the cause is not yet such as that of which it is the cause'.[3] Iamblichus also posits for Speusippus a *pair* of *archai* of numbers (and so of all substances), the One and its opposite the Many, or unity and plurality, as Aristotle had strongly hinted at 1091a31.[4] They apparently represented the formal and material principles respectively (Merlan pp. 88, 101).

Although by calling the One a supra-existential *archē* Speusippus would seem to have been seeking that ultimate unity of all reality in which Plato and Aristotle believed, Aristotle chides him for having made reality plural. 'Speusippus', he claims (*Metaph.* 1028b21), 'says there are several substances [kinds of substance] beginning with the One, and *archai* for each substance, one for number, another for magnitudes, then another for soul; and so he spins out the substances.'[5] Elsewhere he calls this 'making nature episodic' or disjointed, but, he complains, 'the phenomena do not suggest that nature is made of disconnected episodes, like a bad tragedy'. By calling this conception

[1] *Metaph.* 1083a20, 1086a2. The name of Speusippus is provided by ps.-Alex. See frr. 42a–g Lang. For σαίνει τὴν ψυχήν see *Metaph.* 1090a37.

[2] See Merlan, *P. to N.* 95 with n. 1. M. notes on p. 96 that the same expression (οὐδὲ ὄν τι Arist., οὐδὲ ὄν Plot.) was used by Plotinus of his own supernal One (*Enn.* VI. 9.3.38 Bréhier, p. 512.3 Volkmann).

[3] *Comm. math. sc.* p. 15, Tarrant, *l.c.* 132. The point about cause and effect occurs in Plato, *H. Maj.* 297a (if, as I believe, that dialogue is genuine). See vol. IV, 186. For the ascription of ch. 3 of Iamblichus to Speusippus, see Merlan's ch. in *P. to N.* already referred to.

[4] *Comm. math. sc.* p. 16, Tarrant 133. For comparison with Plato see p. 439 above.

[5] Merlan and Tarrant (see the latter, *l.c.* 131, 134, 141), relying on the passage from Iambl. *Comm. math. sc.*, suppose Speusippus to have posited five οὐσίαι in all, but differ over the lists which each draws up, as both do from Krämer.

'episodic' he means that 'no one substance contributes to another by its existence or non-existence'. Changing the metaphor (with a pun on the double meaning of *archē*, 'principle' and 'government') he says that nature cannot bear to be inefficiently governed, but as Homer says, 'The rule of many is not good: let one alone be king.' (See *Metaph.* 1090b 19, 1076a 1–4.) Pluralism did not suit Aristotle at all.[1] In the absence of Speusippus's own writings it is hard to assess the truth of this criticism, but the parallel criticism of Plato which immediately precedes it (1028b 19) is not reassuring. Plato, Aristotle says, posited three eternal beings, the Forms, the mathematicals, and sensible things; but it is hardly fair to say that the Forms made no contribution to the existence and nature of the sensibles.[2] If Plato believed in an ultimate plurality, it would be found rather in the Creator, the Model, and the Receptacle of the *Timaeus* (but on this see pp. 441 f. above).

Another essential respect in which Speusippus's system differed from both Plato's and Aristotle's is that he separated the One from the Good. The One was there in the beginning, but goodness was a late-comer. Aristotle was particularly severe on this, because it contradicted his own fundamental doctrine of potentiality and act, according to which actuality always preceded potentiality, the hen the egg, the perfect the imperfect. So he writes (*Metaph.* 1072b 30):

Those are wrong who suppose, like the Pythagoreans and Speusippus, that the finest and best is not in the beginning [or 'not in a first principle', ἐν ἀρχῇ] on the grounds that the beginnings of plants and animals are their causes but fineness and perfection are in the products. The fact is that the seed comes from previously existing complete creatures. One might call a man the cause of the sperm, not the one who is born from it but another from whom the sperm came.

At 1091b 32 he gives another reason, namely that Speusippus (the name is supplied by his commentator, fr. 35b Lang) avoided attaching the Good to the One, because since generation is from opposites, evil would

---

[1] 'The pluralist maintains that the cosmos is made up of a number of disconnected entities . . . [such] that they could quite well exist apart' (Ewing, *Fundamental Questions* 206f.). Ewing adds that 'Relatively few philosophers have adopted an at all radically pluralist view till very recent times.'

[2] It was nevertheless one of Aristotle's favourite criticisms of the Forms, e.g. at *Metaph.* 991a 8–14, 1033b 26–8.

be the same as plurality. His position is further described by Iamblichus thus:

But as for the One, it should not rightly be called beautiful or good owing to its being over and above the beautiful and the good. For as nature progresses further from the first stages, first the beautiful appears, and then, at a greater distance from the beautiful, the good.[1]

With one important qualification, then, Speusippus's metaphysics might be called evolutionary, as opposed to teleology of the Aristotelian type. That is, in so far as goodness and beauty are not among the first principles or causes but come later in the ontological series. The same is true of evil, if it is right to claim Speusippus as one of the 'others' who deny that goodness and evil are *archai* (Arist. *Metaph.* 1075 a 36, fr. 35 d Lang).[2] The qualification is that, so far as can be judged, Speusippus did not have in mind any temporal evolution, but only, like Aristotle, logical or causal priority and posteriority. Without the higher principles the lower ranks of being could not exist, but in fact all have existed from eternity. Numbers and geometrical figures are 'generated' from the One and plurality but their generation is to be understood as an intelligible or theoretical, not a creative or practical one. (So Proclus; see fr. 46 Lang.) This obviously applies to all real—that is, intelligible and incorporeal—beings. Did it apply also to the physical world? His interpretation of Plato's cosmology in that sense (p. 303 above) suggests sympathy with it. Note however the way in which Proclus in fr. 46 contrasts him with the mathematician Menaechmus.[3] Both are right, he says, the Speusippans because geometrical problems do differ from mechanical, the subjects of which are physical and undergo generation and all sorts of change. Presumably, like (one must suppose) Plato on the Speusippan view of him, Speusippus would regard the formation of the physical elements by the imposition of 'figures and numbers' on

---

[1] *Comm. math. sc.* p. 16.10 ff. in Tarrant's translation (*l.c.* 133).

[2] Yet if we trust Aristotle the primary *archai* are not totally divorced from values. The One, if not *the* Good, was *a* good, for here too, he says, Speusippus seems to have followed the Pythagoreans who placed the One in the column of goods (*Metaph.* 1096 b 5; for the Pythagorean columns see vol. I, 245). According to Iamblichus, as we have just seen, beauty and goodness only appear at a later stage. We can only *grope* our way back to Speusippus (if we think it worth while), as Merlan and Tarrant have done with ingenuity and acumen.

[3] For Menaechmus see p. 491 below.

sheer plurality as timeless, but the creatures put together from these elements as literally mortal and changeable. However, without his own writings there is little point in continuing to speculate along the shaky lines of tradition.[1]

Theology. Like Plato, Speusippus identified God with Mind and saw him as the Creator of the universe.[2] He also said that God was not the same as either the One or the Good, but of a nature peculiar to himself (ἰδιοφυῆ), presumably therefore another of the unconnected primary essences of which Aristotle complained.

Biology. In a work whose title (*Homoia*) may be rendered either 'Resemblances' or 'Homogeneous objects',[3] Speusippus developed the method of classification begun by Plato in his dialectical illustrations and vigorously pursued by Aristotle in the field of purely natural science. We possess a number of extracts, mostly from Athenaeus (frr. 5–26 Lang), which together name some fifty-five species and genera of animals, birds, fish and plants. Scholars have suggested that Speusippus

---

[1] A cosmological note in passing. Speusippus believed in five elements which he assigned respectively to the five Platonic figures. See fr. 4, p. 54 Lang, and cf. pp. 284f. above. Otherwise no details of his cosmology are recorded.

[2] Fr. 38 and fr. 4, p. 54 Lang, τῷ τοῦ παντὸς ποιητῇ θεῷ. Zeller (p. 1000 with n. 3) can hardly have been right in identifying the divine Νοῦς with the world-soul of *Timaeus*, and the passage about τὸ τίμιον in Theophr. (fr. 41 Lang), which he refers to the centre and extremities of the cosmic sphere, is corrupt and obscure. Tarrant (*l.c.* 139), in a passing mention, does not seem to give it a spatial reference. Frank (*P. u. sog. P.* 252) saw it as an instance of Sp.'s Pythagoreanism: the association of τὸ τίμιον with τὴν περὶ τὸ μέσον χώραν and τὰ ἄκρα shows, he thought, adherence to the Philolaic system in which fire occupied the centre of the universe because fire is τιμιώτερον than earth, the most honourable body should occupy the most honourable place, and limits are more honourable than what lies between them (Arist. *Cael.* 293a30; for the Philolaic system see vol. 1, 282ff.). Frank's view was accepted by Ross and Fobes (Theophr. *Metaph.* p. 74), but see Cherniss, *ACPA* 558ff., *Riddle* 64 with n. 23: 'there is some evidence that Speusippus held an astronomical theory different from all three [those of Plato, Eudemus and Heraclides], though not the so-called Philolaic system'. He refers to Arist. *De motu an.* 699a17–24, the relevance of which to the astronomy of Sp. is not very easy to see.

[3] Full information and discussion, including comparisons with Plato, in Stenzel, *RE* 2. Reihe, vi. Halbb. 1638ff. On the title Ὅμοια he points out that the Forms were for Plato τὰ ἀεὶ ὅμοια (e.g. *Rep.* 585c). Whether as transcendent Form or mental concept, ὅμοιον signifies that element in different things which can be summed up in the universal, τὸ ἐν πᾶσι ταὐτόν of the *Meno*. Of things themselves in the same genus it means homogeneous, e.g. pleasures, which, *qua* pleasures, are πάσας ὁμοίας (*Phil.* 13c). *Phdr.* 271a contrasts ὅμοιον with πολυειδές. Aristotle considered the study of ὅμοια to be a useful preparation for inductive and deductive arguments and definition (*Top.* 108b7). For his statement of the principles to be followed in zoological classification see *Part. an.* 1, chh. 2–4, and on his criticisms of the dichotomic methods of Speusippus, Cherniss, *ACPA* 56–62.

was not studying nature for its own sake, like Aristotle, but simply as a means to the perfection of dialectic,[1] though all agree that, whatever his ultimate aim, he made a significant contribution to natural science. The nearest parallel in Plato would be the zoological *diairesis* of *Pol.* 264b ff., the object of which is only to teach a more general lesson about the importance of correct *diairesis* in general. The only evidence for this judgement is that most of the extant biological fragments are quoted from the second book of the *Homoia*, and none from any other, from which it is conjectured that the other books contained similar divisions in non-biological fields. Lang suggested physics, ethics and metaphysics, but for this we have no evidence at all. Stenzel simply invoked the analogy with Plato's *Sophist* and *Politicus*, which begs the question.[2] It is no less likely that the new method inspired the more scientifically inclined among his companions, as it certainly did Aristotle, to use it as a tool for their own special interests. For Plato himself dialectic, though the highest of all branches of investigation, remained a method—an instrument to assist the mind in its progress as far towards the vision of truth as discursive reasoning can go;[3] and even for Plato the natural world was in his later dialogues assuming an ever-increasing importance. The often quoted passage from contemporary comedy depicts both him and Speusippus as instructors in botanical classification through empirical observations.[4]

Philosophical method and epistemology. We have already looked at the use made by Speusippus of the dialectical method in biology. In ch. 2 of *De part. an.* bk 1 Aristotle criticizes those who confine it strictly to dichotomy, and these are usually taken to include Speusippus.[5] As to

[1] So Lang 18f., Stenzel, *l.c.* 1640f. His researches 'did not spring from a genuine scientific interest'; 'the whole work was directed to the art of dialectic'; his biological studies 'were used as material for exercises in dialectic'. Lang's reluctance to take his biological achievement seriously seems to reveal itself in the double and triple negatives with which he admits the possibility: 'quamvis dissimulari nequeat fieri non potuisse quin studia illa . . . etiam scientiae rerum naturalium quadamtenus opitularentur . . .'

[2] See Lang p. 18, Stenzel *RE* 1648.

[3] Cf. Cherniss, *ACPA* 46f.

[4] Epicrates fr. 11 Kock, quoted by Lang on pp. 19f. For a translation see Field, *P. and Cs.* 38f. and cf. p. 132 above and vol. IV, 22 n. 2.

[5] Cherniss, *Riddle* 37f. and *ACPA* 56; Jaeger, *Arist.* 330 n. 2; Stenzel, *RE* 1651 and 1653. Unless I have overlooked something, there is no evidence for this either in the Ὅμοια or in the other fragments. The classification of words, to which we shall come shortly, includes a trichotomy.

definition, Aristotle mentions some who hold that it is impossible to define anything by *diairesis* without knowledge of all that exists, and his Greek commentators agree in ascribing the doctrine to Speusippus.[1] The argument is that the aim of definition is to distinguish its object from everything else; this necessitates being able to state in what respects it differs from all other things, which is impossible unless one knows the distinguishing characteristics of them also. The ancient commentators took this as a sceptical denial of the possibility of definition by division, but the moderns reject this as inconsistent with the rest of what we know about Speusippus, and claim (to quote Ross) that his point was rather 'an insistence on the unity of knowledge and the necessity of a wide knowledge of facts as a basis of theory'. This however would be very different from what Aristotle reports, namely that on this view 'one who would define must know *all* things' and that 'it is impossible to know how something differs from every other thing without knowing every other thing'.[2] If Speusippus had held the twin Platonic doctrines of the Forms and of knowledge as recollection, he might have had in mind the teaching of the *Meno* that all nature is related and the soul has learned everything in and between successive incarnations, but this would be even more unlike what we know about him.

Before leaving *diairesis*, we had better look at a much-discussed non-biological example of it, namely his classification of words[3] (fr. 32). It is as follows:

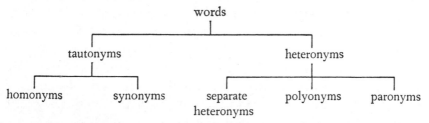

To explain: Where two or more things share the same name we have tautonymy. Homonymy gives the same name to different things (e.g.

[1] *An. post.* 97a6ff., to be found with the commentators in Lang, frr. 31a–e. The attribution goes back to Aristotle's pupil, Eudemus of Rhodes.

[2] For the views of Zeller, Cherniss and Ross see Ross's note on the passage in Aristotle, *An. post.* pp. 659f. For Stenzel the ancient view rested on 'an easily explained misunderstanding'.

[3] ὀνόματα, including at least nouns and adjectives.

bank where the wild thyme grows, bank where one keeps an account). Synonymy occurs when things share both name and nature, as 'animal' is synonymous when applied to man or ox. (The example is Aristotle's, *Catt.* 1 a 6. In this sense *synonyma* are obviously rather different from synonyms as commonly understood today.) Heteronymy connotes the giving of different names. 'Separate heteronyms' applies to things different in both name and nature (haddock, cow). Where several words are applied to one object, as for instance in poetic and prosaic diction, it is polyonymous, and the words are polyonyms. (The example given by Simplicius, our informant on all this, might be translated 'sword, brand, blade'.) Paronym applies to different inflections from the same root, its nominate being variously related to the same concept (just, justly, justice). The interest of all this for scholars has lain in its relationship to the somewhat similar scheme of Aristotle.[1]

Of more general interest is his theory of knowledge, and in particular the role of sensation in it. Sextus gives a clear account, which can be supplemented from Proclus.[2] Like Plato he divided the objects of cognition into intelligible and sensible, but whereas the intelligible were judged by 'epistemonic reason', the sensible were judged similarly by 'epistemonic sensation' ('epistemonic' meaning that both alike convey knowledge): 'Sensation can share in the truth of reason.' In this he is close to Aristotle, who actually identified sensation with *nous*, the faculty which has an intuitive grasp of the truth. Intuition, Aristotle believed, comes into play at both ends of the scale of knowledge. Through the senses it gives the mind its awareness of the lowest universal, and when the discursive reason (which can only deal with universals) has taken the dialectical process as far as it can, then *nous* makes the leap to the ultimate *archai*.[3] All this suggests that towards the end of Plato's life, his thoughts (as set down in the Seventh Letter, pp.

---

[1] Hambruch in 1904 argued that Aristotle treated homonymy, synonymy and the rest as properties of things to which words were applied, whereas Sp. treated them as properties of words, though the influence of Sp. led Aristotle on occasions to use the words in their Speusippan senses. Lang and Stenzel supported him, but his interpretation has been challenged by J. Barnes in *CQ* 1971.

[2] Sext. *Adv. math.* 7, 145; Procl. *Eucl.* p. 178 Friedlein, 148 of Morrow's translation (frr. 29 and 30 Lang).

[3] *EN* 1143a12–b14, where b5 αἴσθησιν, τοῦτο δ' ἐστι νοῦς and 10 καὶ ἀρχὴ καὶ τέλος νοῦς are especially to be noted. Also relevant is the last ch. of *An. post.* 2.

404–7 above) and those of Aristotle and Speusippus, though not coinciding, were at least converging, and from a comparison of the three colleagues one may get an impression of the stimulating discussions that must have gone on in the Academy.

The passage in Proclus quotes Speusippus's account of intuition and discursive reason, which may be rendered somewhat as follows: In general, says Speusippus, there are some things which the intellect in its researches simply puts forward without any elaborate process of thought, as preparation for the coming enquiry, and of these it has a clearer apprehension than has sight of what is visible. Others it cannot seize upon immediately, but progresses towards them by inference, and endeavours to track them down by way of their consequences.[1]

Psychology. Olympiodorus, writing some eight to nine hundred years after Speusippus, reports that he (and also Xenocrates) believed the irrational as well as the rational soul to be immortal. This, as Zeller says, would be a departure from Plato.[2] His only other recorded observation on the soul is one which I cannot claim to understand fully. Iamblichus, writing of those who give a mathematical explanation of the soul's nature, and more particularly an explanation in terms of figure and extension, i.e. geometrical, says that Speusippus located its essence 'in the form (shape or imprint, *idea*) of what is extended in all directions'. Lang (fr. 40) puts them under the heading 'soul of the world'. Diogenes (3.67) ascribes to Plato himself a notion of the soul as 'the form of the spirit (*pneuma*) which is extended in all directions'. The 'all-extended *pneuma*' shows the interpretation to be a Stoic one, and indeed Posidonius defined soul as 'the form of what is extended in all directions, itself constructed according to number that embraces concord' (Plut. *An. Procr.* 1023b, fr. 141a EK). From Speusippus onwards these post-Platonic writers evidently supposed themselves to be basing their definitions on Plato's conception of soul in the *Timaeus*, and indeed

---

[1] Stenzel (*RE* 1660) notes interesting coincidences of vocabulary with Plato. ἐπαφή recalls ἐφάπτεσθαι (with realities, truth and divinity as its objects; *Pho.* 79d, *Symp.* 212a, *Phdr.* 253a). διέξοδος is used of dialectical procedure at *Pol.* 277b. The metaphor of hunting (θήρα) in a similar philosophical context occurs at *Pho.* 66c.

[2] Fr. 55 Lang, Zeller II.1, 1008. Stenzel (*RE* 1657) on the contrary says 'like Plato in the *Phaedrus*'. For my own view on the *Phdr.* myth see vol. IV, 422–5.

Plato's expressions, whatever his intention, sometimes make it difficult to believe that he did not imagine the soul itself as extended. (Cf. pp. 314–17 above.) The inclusion of Speusippus among those who explained its being mathematically suggests that by 'the form or rational configuration (Cherniss)—of the extended' he meant something like the geometrical configuration which, in the *Timaeus*, the Demiurge imposed on the formless mass. So much at least is true, that for Plato number, regular figures, proportion, harmony—in a word Measure or Limit—constituted irrefutable evidence of the presence of soul.[1]

Ethics: Speusippus on pleasure. Speusippus wrote much on ethics. The list includes works on justice, friendship, wealth and pleasure, and an *Aristippus* which must also have been concerned with pleasure. Happiness for him lay[2] in the perfect functioning of one's natural powers. All men desired this, but the good man aimed at peace of mind (ἀοχλησία, freedom from disturbance). The virtues, he added, were instruments of happiness. This is not very different from Aristotle's 'activity in accordance with perfect virtue' (*EN* 1101a14). Aristotle in his practical way added the need for favourable external circumstances, as to which we read that Speusippus, while claiming that the wise man was always happy, did not deny that misfortunes like poverty, bereavement and physical pain were evils.[3]

Something is known of his view of pleasure, a central topic of discussion in the Academy, as Eudoxus, Speusippus, Aristotle and Plato's

[1] Any who wish to follow up this difficult and insufficiently documented matter may find assistance in the following: (1) Cherniss: (*a*) *Riddle* 73f., (*b*) *ACPA* 509–11, (*c*) notes on Plut. *De an. procr.* 1023b, Loeb ed., pp. 219–21. On the scanty evidence it seems daring to suggest (*Riddle* 73f.) that fr. 40 does not represent, indeed is incompatible with, Sp.'s own view. (2) Merlan: (*a*) *Philol.* 1959, 201f., (*b*) *P. to N.* 36–40. I still find it a difficulty that Aristotle, Sp.'s contemporary and colleague, accuses him of teaching that numbers, magnitudes and the soul had different ἀρχαί. (Cf. p. 460 above and Merlan, *P. to N.* 37.) (3) H. A. S. Tarrant in *Phron.* 1974, 141f. He refers to Theophrastus, *Metaph.* p. 12 R. and F. (Sp. fr. 51 Lang), but looking at this in its context I doubt whether Theophrastus intended to attribute anything more to Sp. than a refusal to pursue far enough the series of derivations from first principles.

[2] That is, according to the Christian writer Clement of Alexandria in the second century A.D. (fr. 57 Lang).

[3] The information comes from Cicero (fr. 58b Lang), whose source was Antiochus of Ascalon. (See Zeller II.1, 1009 n. 1, 995 n. 1.) Antiochus (second cent. B.C.) aimed at reconciling Academic, Peripatetic and Stoic doctrines, and this passage has a strongly Stoic flavour. It also unites Speusippus with a number of other philosophers by name, including Aristotle.

Philebus bear witness. He denied what Eudoxus and Aristotle maintained, that because pain is an evil and pleasure is the opposite of pain, therefore pleasure must be good. Using a mathematical analogy, he said that the greater and the less are opposed not only to each other but to the equal. This we have from Aristotle, who also reported the argument in the form: If pain is bad, it does not follow that pleasure is good, for evil may be opposed to evil, and both to what is neither.[1] Aristotle disagreed, but did not so much refute it directly as produce the counter-argument that all men seek pleasure, and what all seek must be the best (1153b25). This seems to have been the prevailing Academic view. It was one of the three criteria of the good in Plato's *Philebus* (p. 201 above), and repeated by Eudoxus (p. 453).[2] At the same time Speusippus's argument bears some resemblance to Aristotle's own idea that goodness lies in the mean: rashness and cowardice are opposites, but both are bad. The virtue of courage is opposed to both, and lies between. Similarly (say the scholia on Aristotle) Speusippus said that pain and pleasure were contrasting evils. Between them lay the intermediate state of painlessness, and this was good. Painlessness (ἀλυπία) corresponds to the undisturbed state (ἀοχλησία) mentioned by Clement, and brings him close to Epicurus in his ideals.[3]

Xenocrates

Life and character. Xenocrates was the last head of the Academy who could speak of Plato from personal acquaintance. He was also reported to have taught both Zeno and Epicurus, which is just possible and shows what a short bridge is needed between the early Academy and the Hellenistic philosophers.[4] The moderns like to speak of him in superior

---

[1] *EN* 1153b4, 1173a5. On the argument ἐκ τοῦ ἐναντίου see Cherniss, *ACPA* 36f.

[2] In view of this it is interesting that one scholiast (fr. 60d Lang) has taken the rather puzzling οὐ γὰρ ἂν φαίη ὅπερ κακόν τι εἶναι τὴν ἡδονήν of 1153b6 as if it were οὐ γὰρ ἂν φαίη τις: he writes οὐδεὶς γὰρ ἂν φαίη κτλ. It is in fact difficult to see how Sp. could have denied, on his own arguments, that pleasure was an evil.

[3] For the question whether Sp. is to be identified with the enemies of Philebus at Plato, *Phil.* 44b–d, as well as a fuller discussion of his views on pleasure, see M. Schofield in *Mus. Helv.* 1971. For the opinion, going back to Wilamowitz, that Sp.'s argument and Aristotle's rebuttal of it are alike unclear, see Schofield p. 17 and Stenzel, *RE* 1666. ἀλυπία is reminiscent of the τέχνη ἀλυπίας of Antiphon (vol. III, 290f.)—not that Sp. need have had him in mind.

[4] D.L. 7.2, 10.1 and 13; Cicero, *N.D.* 1.26.72; Numenius, *SVF* I p. 8 fr. 11. Hence information about X. is to be found in several recent books on the transition from Plato to later Greek thought. The Academy as a preparation for Stoicism is a theme of Krämer's *Platonismus und*

or condescending tones. T. H. Martin's judgement has already been quoted (p. 304 n. 2 above). 'This puritanical but rather insignificant man', says Lesky. Henry Jackson called him a kindly moralist who carried on Plato's philosophy out of piety but did not understand it, a verdict which Wilamowitz found '*treffend*'. More severe is Frank's 'boring scribbler' (we possess none of his writings), and Field found him an excellent character, but his contributions to philosophy less impressive.[1] In face of the scanty evidence one may well be more hesitant, but it does suggest that he was a highly moral, perhaps over-serious character, intellectually slow and solid rather than brilliant, but that he combined morality with wit may be suggested by the saying attributed to him that it is children rather than boxers who need ear-protectors.[2]

Unlike Speusippus, he was not an Athenian, but came from Chalcedon on the Bosporus. He lived to eighty-one, probably from about 395 to 314, became Plato's pupil 'in his youth' (D.L. 4.6), and was head of the Academy from the death of Speusippus in 338.[3] Apart from this, the *Academicorum Index* mentions only two events in his life: the invitation to himself and Aristotle to visit Hermeias, tyrant of Atarneus in north west Asia Minor, after Plato's death (of which more will be said in connexion with Aristotle), and his inclusion, though a metic, in the Athenian embassy to Antipater in 322. Diogenes speaks also of an

hellenistische Philosophie, who writes that the Academic '*Prinzipienlehre*' is the historical 'missing link' between Platonic and Stoic cosmology (1972, p. 129). Cf. also his earlier *Der Ursprung der Geistesmetaphysik, Unters. z. Gesch. des Platonismus zwischen Platon und Plotin* (1964, 2nd ed. 1967), and Merlan's *From Platonism to Neoplatonism* (1953). On the possible influence of the early Academy on Plotinus see also Dodds's article 'The *Parm.* and the Neoplatonic "One"' in *CQ* 1928, with its mention of Speusippus on p. 140.

[1] Lesky, *HGL* 543; Jackson quoted by Wilamowitz, *Pl.* I, 729; Frank, *P. u. sog. P.* 42; Field, *OCD s.v.* If we may with Dörrie (*RE* 1512) distinguish between 'the only [biographical] source to be taken seriously', i.e. the *Academicorum Index* from Herculaneum, and the 'later, purely anecdotal tradition', the evidence on which these writers rely comes wholly from the latter.

[2] Fr. 96 H. (p. 471 n. 2 below), from Plutarch. Plato is said to have remarked that he needed the spur, and advised him to sacrifice to the Graces (D.L. 4.6; cf. Plut. *De aud.* 47e). For reff. to his moral strength and integrity see Zeller, II.1, 988 n. 3.

[3] D.L. 4.14 is unusually precise about the date of his headship, 'for 25 years from the archonship of Lysimachus in the second year of Ol. 110'. According to the *Acad. Index* the head was elected by the members. Heraclides and Menedemus were a few votes behind Xenocrates, and Aristotle did not compete, being at the time at Philip's court in Macedonia. This account does not necessarily conflict with the story in Diogenes (4.3) that Speusippus in his last days asked Xenocrates to come and take charge of the school. See Merlan, 'The Successor of Speusippus', *TAPA* 1946.

earlier mission to Philip, of which Xenocrates was the only member proof against bribery.[1]

Writings. The list in Diogenes shows him to have been a prolific and versatile writer, and brings home once more how scanty and haphazard is our knowledge of these men. For example, he wrote a treatise on astronomy in six books, yet nothing is reported of his contributions to that subject, nor, in a different field, of the content of the four books on the elements of kingship which he addressed to Alexander.[2]

Being and knowledge. No more than Plato did Xenocrates keep these two apart. He posited three levels of being, which he put in a cosmological setting. There were the things beyond the heavens, the heavens themselves, and the things within the heavens. In terms of cognition, the first were objects of intelligence, the third of sensation, and the heavens themselves he called composite, as being both perceptible to sight and intelligible through astronomy, and objects of belief or opinion (*doxa*).[3] The combination of observation and intellect in the study of the heavenly bodies follows Plato closely,[4] but the tripartite division of cognition is new. The judgement of 'epistemonic reason' is firm and true, that of sensation is true, but less so than the first (*sic* in Sextus),[5] and *doxa*, the mixed, is partly true and partly false. Plato normally recognized only two main divisions of being, intelligible and sensible, equating sensation with *doxa* as at *Tim.* 27e–28a.[6] The intel-

---

[1] D.L. 4.8–9. On the embassy to Antipater cf. Dörrie, *RE* 1513; on that to Philip, Merlan, *Philol.* 1959, 205f.

[2] According to Plutarch (*Adv. Col.* 1126d) he had received a request for such advice from the great conqueror himself.

[3] Sextus, Xenocr. fr. 5 H. The fragments of Xenocrates were collected, with an essay on his philosophy, by R. Heinze in 1892, and reff. here will often be by name of source and fr. number only. Essential passages can be conveniently consulted in de Vogel, *Gr. Phil.* II, 274–82. None are fragments in the strict sense, and Dörrie's warning about their imperfect authority and trustworthiness (*RE* 1517f.) should be noted.　　　　[4] *Rep.* 7, 529d–30c; vol. IV, 524.

[5] Cf. *Plac.* IV.9.2 (Diels, *Dox.* p. 396): οἱ ἀπὸ τῆς Ἀκαδημίας [τὰς αἰσθήσεις] ὑγιεῖς μὲν ... οὐ μὴν ἀληθεῖς.

[6] The mathematical 'intermediates' form in some respects a third class (vol. IV, 343), but they still belong to the intelligible world (the upper half of the Line of *Rep.* 509d), and X.'s idea of the heavens as a separate object of *doxa* is his own. Asclepius in his commentary (fr. 34 H.) says that in second place after the Forms X. put the objects of διάνοια, that is of mathematics, namely lines and planes, then lastly physical objects. If both sources are correct, it remains obscure how this scheme is related to the one described by Sextus.

ligible essences beyond the heavens immediately recall *Phaedrus* 247 c ff., and cannot be other than the Platonic Forms, in whatever guise Xenocrates conceived them. 'Epistemonic *logos*' was also a phrase of Speusippus (p. 466 above), and one can imagine the arguments which must have taken place over the question whether sensation too could yield knowledge of truth, with Aristotle contributing his identification of it with *nous* (p. 415 above).

The chain of being. Theophrastus, in the passage from his *Metaphysics* already quoted,[1] exempts Xenocrates from his criticism of those who start from certain fixed principles, like the One and the Indefinite Dyad, but instead of completing the series of successive derivations from them, merely proceed to an arbitrary point and then stop.[2] 'But Xenocrates did somehow give everything its place in the cosmic order—sensibles, intelligibles, mathematicals, and divine things as well.' This may be taken with a passage in Aristotle (*Metaph.* 1028b24) where after mentioning Plato and Speusippus he passes to a third theory, of 'those who say that Forms and numbers have the same nature, and the rest depend on them, namely lines, surfaces, and so on until one comes to the heavens and sensible things'. This, says the commentator Asclepius, refers to Xenocrates.[3] The process starts from the One and unlimited Plurality, also called the Indefinite Dyad (as by Plato) and the everflowing. Later writers called it matter, though it does not look as if Xenocrates himself used this term.[4] Next come numbers, derived from the imposition of limit on undefined Plurality by the agency of the One, and so on.[5] The continuity of the scheme depends of course on the Pythagorean derivation of physical objects from mathematical numbers and figures: from the point (1) comes the line (2), from that the surface (3), from the surface the elementary solid (the tetrahedron, 4), and from that, in unbroken continuity, the physical, perceptible world. Such

[1] On p. 436. Part of it appears as fr. 26 in Heinze.
[2] Whom precisely he has in mind, it is difficult to say. Speusippus is separately mentioned as doing the same thing, and Plato is named and half-heartedly excused immediately afterwards.
[3] Fr. 34 H. The plural is common form, like οἱ περί for a philosopher himself.
[4] Fr. 28 H. Cf. especially ἀέναον τὴν ὕλην αἰνιττόμενος.
[5] Plut. *An. procr.* 1012d–e (fr. 68 H.). This is given as X.'s interpretation of the composition of the World-soul in *Timaeus*, but leaves no doubt that he adhered to it himself. The One and the Dyad he equated with the supreme gods. (See below.)

theories, as Aristotle frequently complained, treated units as if they were magnitudes, and derived things heavy or light from elements which were neither. They were pretty clearly followed by Plato himself, at least in his latest and most Pythagorean phase. (See pp. 285, 288 above.)

The Forms. Xenocrates defined the Platonic Form as 'a paradigmatic cause of naturally constituted things . . . a separate and divine cause'.[1] From its context this seems intended to apply to Plato's conception, but there is no reason to think that Xenocrates abandoned it himself.

The accepted view of the different Academic theories of the relation between Forms and numbers is as stated succinctly by Heath (*Maths. in Arist.* 220): Plato separated ideal from mathematical numbers, Speusippus recognized mathematical numbers only, and Xenocrates identified the two. We are still dogged by Aristotle's reluctance to mention names, but this deficiency is sometimes made up by his Greek commentators, and the distinctions seem pretty firmly established.[2] For Xenocrates we have just seen the statement that he identified Forms and numbers, and it seems safe to attribute to him the view mentioned at *Metaph.* 1083b2, that 'the number belonging to the Forms and mathematical number are the same'. Other passages suggest the same thing,[3] though our faith in the commentators, on whom we often have to rely for any explicit mention of the name Xenocrates, is somewhat shaken by their repeated association of him with Speusippus on this point.[4] Assuming the attribution to be correct, Xenocrates took from Plato the conception of ideal numbers as 'separately existing and the first causes of what is', and hence not mutually comparable or addible as mathematical numbers are,[5] and modified it by making no difference between the two kinds

---

[1] So Proclus (fr. 30 H.). On the limitation to τὰ κατὰ φύσιν ἀεὶ συνεστῶτα see Heinze pp. 52–6. Krämer (*P. und H. Phil.*, n. 40 on p. 116) takes it in its strict sense, as excluding Forms of artefacts, which contradicts *Ep.* 7, 342e (pp. 407f. above). Plato's own views on this are of course much debated, but here it could have been intended more loosely, as 'everything in the physical world'. As for ἀεί, on which Heinze has a note (p. 56), I take it to have its common meaning of 'from time to time': the things which are continually being produced in the natural world.

[2] On p. 152 of *PTI* Ross has collected references to the passages in Aristotle which may be assigned to X. either certainly or with high probability.

[3] See fr. 34 H.; also Ross's note on 1028b24 and his discussion in vol. 1 of the *Metaph.*, lxxiv–vi.

[4] See Ross on 1076a20–1 and Heinze, frr. 34 and 35 (ps.-Alex.) and fr. 36 (Syrianus).

[5] Arist. *Metaph.* 1080a12ff. Cf. p. 437 n. 1 above.

of number, or in the terms applied by Aristotle to Plato, between the Forms and the 'intermediates'. Of his development of this strange theme we know little, but it sounds like a further lapse into earlier Pythagorean ideas. Aristotle, no friend to number-metaphysics anyway, castigated it as 'the worst of the three modes'.

Theology: gods and daemons. Xenocrates tended to see everything in theological terms. For him indeed 'everything was full of gods', as Thales said. This starts with the first principles, and recalls the *Timaeus* (fr. 15 H.). The One for him was the supreme male deity, the Father, the Reason which rules in the heavens, Zeus. The Dyad was female, Mother of the Gods.[1] Her portion was the region beneath the heavens, which she animates as 'soul of the whole'. This has been called dualism, but as Dörrie has pointed out (*RE* 1520), the Dyad is clearly subordinate to the Monad. So in Plato the soul of the world was created by the supreme Reason. Being indefinite and unlimited, the Dyad seems to correspond rather to Plato's 'receptacle', or unformed matter, on which Mind imposed order 'by forms and numbers'. Xenocrates, it would seem, adapted this by making the matter alive, thereby settling on his own account a question which has bothered Plato's interpreters to this day, whether the aimless pre-cosmic motion was due to soul (pp. 271 f. above). As in Plato, the heavens and the fiery stars were also gods, eight in all: the sphere of the fixed stars (where the stars themselves are *dispersa membra* of a single god), the planets, sun and moon (Cicero, fr. 17 H.). Plutarch (fr. 18) speaks of a 'highest' Zeus, 'who dwells among the unchangeable and uniform realities' (which readers of Plato would instantly recognize as the Forms), and also a 'lowest', in the sublunary region. This must be Hades or Pluto, known also in Greek religion as 'another Zeus' or 'Zeus of the Underworld'.[2] The material elements also had divine powers, and were given the names of traditional gods.[3]

---

[1] Another Pythagorean echo? A so-called fragment of Philolaus (fr. 20a DK) runs: 'Philolaus says that the Dyad is the consort of Cronus.'   [2] Aesch. *Suppl.* 231, Hom. *Il.* 9.457.

[3] This goes back to Empedocles, about whose distribution of the divine names there is considerable doubt. X.'s identification of Hades with air (which may be taken as certain, in spite of a lacuna at this point in the text of fr. 15) may afford some slight support to those who suppose that E. did the same. It also fits with the assignment to Hades of the sublunary region (τὰ ὑπὸ σελήνην, fr. 18) rather than sub-terrestrial.

Xenocrates was a great believer in daemons, those denizens of the middle air of whom Plato speaks in the *Symposium*, and retailed much lore about them.[1] Though immortal and more powerful than men, they did not possess the divine pure and unmixed, but knew pleasure and suffering and were stirred by emotions.[2] To his pythagorizing mind the geometrical analogy intruded here as everywhere, and in a rather forced simile he compared the different forms of life to triangles, the gods to the equilateral, equal in every direction, daemons to the isosceles, equal in one way but not in another as possessing divine power but the feelings of mortals, and mortals to the scalene, in every way unequal. There were both good and bad daemons, and the unpleasant features of Greek cult, such as unlucky days, scourgings, fasting, abusive language and obscenity he explained as desirable not to the gods, but to the perverted taste of the bad daemons. He seems to have been perfectly serious, and it should be noted that Plutarch, our authority for all this demonology (frr. 23–5 H.), has his speaker attribute some features of it not only to Pythagoras earlier but to Plato and Speusippus as well. If he is to be trusted, the Academy must have been a strange place, where such superstitions could flourish alongside the serious philosophy, political theory and advanced mathematics of which we also know. As for Plato himself, in the light of the rest of his work it is more reasonable to take *Symp.* 202 d–203 a as symbolic or mythical, and the daemonic lore of Xenocrates as the mark of an inferior intellect. Its motive however seems to have been the worthy and Platonic one of denying to the gods any responsibility for the darker and less reputable side of Greek religion.

Cosmology and physics. A few scraps are recorded.[3] Xenocrates, like Aristotle, believed the cosmos to be ungenerated, and (unlike Aristotle) explained the *Timaeus* in that way. Doubtless he posited a fifth element (*aither*), which he also ascribed to his master (p. 284 n. 4). Plutarch's speaker in *De facie* credits him with an original scheme for the elemental

---

[1] They were of course objects of traditional belief, and Heinze outlines their previous history, from Hesiod onwards, on pp. 83 ff. For Plato see pp. 89–92.

[2] So of course were the gods themselves in Homer and popular belief, but a philosophic theologian would deny this. Cf. Plato, *Phil.* 33 b.

[3] Cf. also additional note on pp. 489 f. below.

composition of the heavenly bodies and the earth. I find it obscure, and since he has just given a wrong application to a passage from the *Timaeus*,[1] he is perhaps confused about Xenocrates too. Plutarch's statement is:

Xenocrates says that the stars and the sun are composed of fire and the first density, the moon from the second density and its own air, and the earth of water [and . . .?][2] and the third density, and that neither the dense nor the rare by itself is capable of acquiring soul.

The three densities (or dense substances; adjective without noun in the Greek) are neither explained nor mentioned elsewhere.[3] He is reported to have said that the stars all lie in one plane. This must refer to the planets, said Zeller; it must refer to the fixed stars, said Dörrie; and there we may leave it.[4]

Indivisible lines, atomic bodies, parts and wholes. Following Plato (if we may trust Aristotle; see p. 439 above), Xenocrates believed in minimum indivisible lines,[5] a conception vehemently opposed by Aristotle. His defenders said that this referred only to the Form of line or ideal line, which for him was, as we know, also the line as conceived by pure mathematicians. So for instance Proclus: 'To believe in an indivisible magnitude is absurd, but plainly Xenocrates thought it right to give this epithet to the *essential* line.'[6] The distinction between physical and mathematical divisibility of both lines and solids he employed against the Eleatic dilemma. Porphyry writes (fr. 45 H.):

[1] *De facie* 943f–44a, fr. 56 H. He applies 31b–c to the stars, whereas it describes the composition of the whole cosmos from all four elements. Of the stars Plato says simply that they were made 'mostly of fire' (40a). Though the reference to *Tim.* is unmistakable. Plutarch has confused it with *Epin.* 981e.

[2] One MS has 'water and fire', the other 'water and air'. Heinze prints πυρός. Cherniss in Loeb ed. excises the last two words.

[3] Zeller (II.1, 1024) and Cherniss (*ACPA* 143 and 485) offer explanations which, probably through my own fault, I find difficult to relate to the Greek. The differentiation of the elements by density and rarity goes back of course to Anaximenes (vol. I, 121), but three degrees of density, in some way separate from the elements (fire *and* the first density, etc.), seem an odd innovation. Nor is there any mention of three degrees of rarity, of which Cherniss speaks in *CP* 1951, 152.

[4] Fr. 57 H.; Zeller, II.1, 1025 n. 4; Dörrie, *RE* 1524.

[5] See on this Ross, *Metaph.* vol. I, 203–7; Furley, *Two Studies* (1) ch. 7. The evidence is in frr. 41–9 H.

[6] Fr. 46 H. Proclus is speaking as a Platonist, for whom the 'essential' (οὐσιώδης) line is the Form of line.

Xenocrates granted the first inference, that if what is is one it must be indivisible, but maintained that it is not indivisible and therefore not one. Nevertheless its division is not carried to infinity, but stops at certain indivisibles. These are indivisible in the sense of having no parts and being smallest in quantity, i.e. in matter; they are divisible and have parts, but in respect of their form they are indivisible and primary; for he posited certain primary, indivisible lines, and primary surfaces and solids formed from them. Xenocrates, then, thought that the problem of dichotomy, and in general of infinite divisibility, was solved when he introduced indivisible lines and indivisible magnitudes in general, thus escaping the dilemma that if what is is divisible it dissolves and disappears into what is not, since the indivisible lines out of which existing things have their being remain atomic and undivided.

Themistius was contemptuous of this argument, accusing Xenocrates of 'making the same thing a magnitude and not a magnitude'.[1] Several commentators link him with Democritus, and it does look as if he held a theory of physical atoms as smallest parts of the elemental masses (frr. 50 and 51 H.). If, as is generally agreed,[2] the Peripatetic treatise *On Indivisible Lines* is directed against Xenocrates, he argued that 'sensibles as well as intelligibles have their indivisible parts' (fr. 42, ll. 16–18 H.). The smooth Pythagorean transition from geometrical solid to physical body would facilitate this apparent confusion, but in any case our indirect sources scarcely give us the right to feel certain about how exactly his theories fitted together.[3]

This and the preceding argument in *On Indivisible Lines* make use of the dogma that parts are ontologically prior to wholes; that is, that a part can exist without the whole, but not a whole without the parts which compose it. A fragment of Xenocrates preserved in Arabic, and attested by name,[4] extends this to the relationship of species to genera: species are parts of genera, a part is prior to the whole, therefore species

---

[1] See second passage in fr. 44 H.

[2] See reff. in Krämer, *P. und H. Phil.* 336f., n. 355. This third argument for indivisibles is discussed in detail on his pp. 344–7.

[3] It is possible that more could still be deduced from a further study of the whole contemporary and earlier background. This might start from the first of Furley's *Two Studies*, that on 'Indivisible Magnitudes', noting in particular the evidence of Aristotle. If X. was not fully successful, this would not be surprising, for the problem of indivisibles has remained with philosophy for a long time. Cf. Furley's interesting chapter on Hume (*o.c.* ch. 10).

[4] First published in 1947, translation and commentary by S. Pines, *Trans. Amer. Philos. Soc.*, vol. LI pt 2 (1961), 3–34. See p. 6.

are prior to genera. This is reported by Alexander of Aphrodisias who proceeds to refute it. Here Xenocrates, who followed his master in so many things, went against him. For Plato too specific were parts of generic Forms and only the *infima species* was indivisible (*Soph.* 229 d); but the higher and more universal Form was ontologically prior to the specific.[1]

The existence of indivisible lines has an immediate bearing on the problem of irrational or incommensurable quantities,[2] and according to Pines (*l.c.* 15 ff., relying on Themistius, fr. 39 H.) this was ingeniously solved by Xenocrates through the assumption that ideal, or mathematical, quantities (and the problem is a geometrical one) *are* discontinuous (ultimately indivisible) and therefore rational: irrational quantity only exists on the corporeal plane. One cannot help thinking immediately of the statement already quoted from fr. 42 that sensibles as well as intelligibles have their indivisible parts, but Pines (p. 19) sees no necessary conflict here. The reader may judge for himself, but it looks as if on this question too our information is inadequate.

Method and logic. The list of his works shows Xenocrates to have written extensively on dialectic (14 books) as well as kindred subjects, but little has survived the inroads of time and chance. He is said by Sextus to have been responsible for the formal division of philosophy into three parts, physical, ethical and logical, which became standard in Hellenistic times, especially among the Stoics.[3] Mathematics he described as the 'handholds' whereby we get a grip on philosophy (fr. 1 H., Plut.), a truly Platonic sentiment. He drew a technical distinction between the

---

[1] I had not thought that this statement needed any defence, but have now read on p. 46 of Cherniss's *ACPA*, 'He [Plato] does not distinguish genus and species ontologically.' I still do not see how anyone can read the later dialogues and be left with that impression. The infinity of sensible particulars is of course ontologically inferior to any Form, and the successive divisions of a generic Form into ever more specific parts brings them nearer to the particulars. It is a progression from the one to the *apeiron* (*Phil.* 16 d–e; see pp. 209 f. above). *Tim.* 30 c brings out clearly the inferiority in the realm of Forms of τὰ ἐν μέρους εἴδει to the Form which embraces them all. Without using X.'s argument in so many words, Plato makes it perfectly clear that the Form of Animal could remain without the Form of Dog.

[2] The connexion is expressed in *De lin. insec.* 968 b 4 ff. (fr. 42 H.): 'From what the mathematicians themselves say, if lines measured by the same standard are commensurate. there must be indivisible lines' etc.

[3] Fr. 2 H. Cf. Krämer, *P. und H. Phil.* 114 n. 35. But who can say whether he preceded Aristotle (*Top.* 105 b 20)?

two words for wisdom, *sophia* and *phronēsis*, which in Plato had been interchangeable (vol. IV, 265), as follows (fr. 6 H., Clem. Alex.):

Xenocrates in his *On Phronēsis* defines *sophia* as knowledge of the first causes and of intelligible being. *Phronēsis* he divides into two, practical and theoretical, which indeed is *sophia* on the human plane. Hence *sophia* is *phronēsis* but not all *phronēsis* is *sophia*.

The dialectical division sounds Platonic, and the reference to a particular work (two books on *phronēsis* appear in D.L.'s catalogue) gives it an authentic air. It does not tally exactly with a brief note in Aristotle's *Topics*, which however may have been abbreviated for his immediate purpose, which was simply to illustrate the fault of using two words where one would do.[1]

Xenocrates and Andronicus [who lived much later] thought that everything was included under the headings of absolute and relative existence, so that there is no need for such a large number of categories. Fr. 12 H. (Simpl.)

This is evidently a criticism of Aristotle's ten categories, as Zeller said (II. I, 1013 f.), against which Xenocrates advocates the simple dichotomy of Plato. To Plato the distinction between absolute and relative being was fundamental, as marking off the world of Forms from the world of experience. Beautiful things were only beautiful relatively to others (and relatively to some could be actually ugly), but Beauty itself 'is not beautiful in one aspect but ugly in another, nor beautiful at one time but not at another, nor beautiful in relation to one thing but ugly in relation to another . . . It exists absolutely, by and with itself, uniform.'[2]

Psychology. Xenocrates defined the soul as a self-moving number, to which one's first reaction is to agree with Aristotle that this was 'much the most unreasonable thing said about it'.[3] More than once in the Greek commentators he is associated in this with Pythagoras, for whom of course anything whatever was a number. According to Plutarch his definition was based on an interpretation of the making of the world-soul in Plato's *Timaeus*, which is itself fantastic enough. From Aristotle's statement at 404b27 we may conclude that the soul's numerical charac-

---

[1] *Top.* 141a6. What kind of ὄντα are meant?

[2] *Symp.* 211a. Cf. *H. Maj.* 289a–b, *Phil.* 51c, 53d.

[3] *De an.* 408b32 (not in H.). For the evidence in general see frr. 60 and 68 H., and on Aristotle's detailed criticism Cherniss, *ACPA* 396 ff.

ter was connected with its mental, as distinct from motive, powers, and this would be derived from *Tim.* 37a–c, where its power of true discourse about both the intelligible and the sensible world is attributed to the numerical proportion and harmony in which its constituents are blended.[1] 'Number' for the Pythagoreans and their admirers is a compendium-word for proportion, measure, harmony—all the things which number was supposed to introduce. Nevertheless Plutarch's criticism is pertinent. Plato, he says, never called the soul a number, for to say that the soul is constructed on a numerical formula is not the same as saying that it is itself, in its own essence, a number.[2] Simplicius (fr. 64 H.) thought the definition was intended to demonstrate the intermediate status of the soul between the Forms and the things made in their likeness; for the Forms are numbers, but do not move.

The soul is incorporeal, and divided into reason and sense (frr. 66, 67, 70 H.). Xenocrates probably said that our *nous* came to us from outside, i.e. was divine.[3] Olympiodorus (fr. 75 H.) bracketed him with Speusippus as believing that the irrational as well as the rational soul was immortal, and Clement of Alexandria says that he 'did not give up hope that even the creatures without reason had some sense of the divine'. The expression ('did not despair')[4] shows him in the same attractive light as the anecdote of the sparrow which, pursued by a hawk, took refuge in his cloak. He hid it in the folds till the danger was past, then let it go, remarking that it would not do to betray a suppliant (fr. 101 H.). One can imagine such a man hoping that even a sparrow might have an immortal soul.[5]

So strong a believer in daemons can hardly have escaped the traditional belief that some at least were the souls of dead men, as they had

---

[1] See p. 297 above, and cf. further Krämer, *P. und H. Phil.* 348f.

[2] Plut. *De an. procr.* 1013c–d (not in H.). X.'s definition of soul, including Plutarch's account and criticism, has been discussed at length by Taylor, *Comm. on Tim.* 112–15.

[3] Fr. 69 H. This is simply a list of philosophers who said θύραθεν εἰσκρίνεσθαι τὸν νοῦν. The omission of Aristotle makes its accuracy suspect; cf. his expression at *Gen. an.* 736b28.

[4] οὐκ ἀπελπίʒει. The passage in Clem. Alex. is not in Heinze, but is quoted by Zeller, II.1, 1022 n. 4.

[5] At the same time, oddly enough, he is said to have written a book *On Animal Food* in which he said that meat was harmful to us because it might infect us with the unreasoning souls of the beasts. This too is from Clem. *Strom.* (fr. 100 H.) and is accepted by Heinze (p. 139) but Dörrie (*RE* 1517) is highly suspicious of its authenticity. The title is absent from D.L.'s list, nor does the argument figure among X.'s suggested reasons why Triptolemus should have enjoined abstinence from flesh (fr. 98 H.).

been for Hesiod and Empedocles, but there is no definite evidence.[1] He did however call the soul of a living man his daemon, taking the normal words for 'happiness' and 'misery', *eudaimonia* and *kakodaimonia*, in the literal sense of 'having a good—or bad—daemon'. This was right enough, but it means, he went on to say, having a worthy or unworthy soul, 'for each man's soul was his daemon'.[2] He was no doubt thinking of Heraclitus's aphorism (fr. 119 DK) that a man's character is his daemon, where however 'daemon' means rather fate, or a power controlling one's fate. Heraclitus was saying epigrammatically that what happens to a man is his own responsibility: 'You call it your daemon— your fate—but it's really up to you.' From Homer onwards a daemon is the external power that controls each individual's destiny. It could also mean a kind of guardian angel, a companion for the soul like the daemon which conducts each soul on its journey to the underworld, but not the soul itself.[3]

Ethics. Although like Speusippus Xenocrates wrote copiously on ethics, not much is now known about his opinions. What we have suggests that in many things he shared a common Academic viewpoint with Speusippus, Aristotle and no doubt others, much of which was absorbed by Zeno and the Stoics. For his philosophical investigation had an ulterior aim, peace of mind ('to put an end to the disturbance caused by the business of life', fr. 4). Only with Aristotle do we meet the scientific ideal of knowledge for its own sake as the natural goal for mankind (*Metaph. ad init.*). Sextus (fr. 76 H.) links Xenocrates with the rest of the old Academy, the Peripatetics, and the Stoics in classifying everything as either good or bad or neither. The classification, if it seems to pave the way for the Stoic doctrine of 'indifferents' (Krämer, *P. und H. Ph.* 229), was firmly rooted in Plato's own philosophy. We

[1] Hes. *Erga* 121–3, Emped. fr. 115; cf. Plato, *Crat.* 398c. Heinze saw it implied in a passage of Plutarch about daemons 'who have a kind of remnant of the sensuous and unreasoning part'. (See *Def. Orac.* 417b quoted in H. p. 83, where the words καὶ ἀλόγου have been accidentally omitted.) This however seems to have no connexion with X., whose name was mentioned back at 416c.

[2] The source is no late commentator but Aristotle himself (*Top.* 112a32–8, fr. 81 H.). He uses it to illustrate the eristic or rhetorical device of taking a term in its literal sense as if this were more proper than to conform to its established usage. I suspect it is doing the literal-minded philosopher too much credit to suppose him capable of such deliberate artifice.

[3] Plato, *Pho.* 107d, 113d. Burnet on 107d cites parallel passages from other classical authors.

remember the teaching of the *Meno* that health and wealth are in themselves neither good nor bad—it depends what use is made of them—and how ill health turned out to be a blessing for Theages.[1] Nevertheless it appears that for Xenocrates and Speusippus health had, in Stoic terminology, 'preferred' status (fr. 92 H.), but virtue remained supreme. Speakers in Cicero's dialogues seem sometimes to assimilate Xenocrates to the Stoics, in suspicious conjunction with Speusippus, Polemo and even Aristotle, as teaching that the virtuous man is happy in the most painful circumstances (frr. 84, 85 H.), but sometimes to distinguish him sharply from them. There may be some confusion here between Xenocrates and Polemo, his successor as head of the Academy.[2]

The basis of happiness was to live according to nature, in which Plutarch associates him with Polemo[3] (though it is equally true of Speusippus; p. 468 above), and says that Zeno followed them (fr. 78 H.). His recipe for securing it is in fr. 77 H. (Clem. *Strom.*):

Xenocrates of Chalcedon explains happiness as the possession of one's proper excellence and the powers ancillary thereto. In what does it occur? The soul. By whose agency? The virtues. What are the parts of which it is made up? Right actions, good states of mind, dispositions, motions and habits. What are its indispensable adjuncts? Bodily health and external resources.

So far as it goes, Aristotle's formal definition of happiness agrees exactly with this: it consists in 'activity in accordance with perfect virtue, combined with sufficient provision of external advantages and a life not cut short' (*EN* 1101a14).

The only other known ethical tenet of Xenocrates is that only philosophers are voluntarily virtuous. Plutarch speaks of 'the dictum of Xenocrates about true philosophers, that they alone do voluntarily what the rest of mankind do involuntarily under the compulsion of law, like dogs under the lash'. There is, says the same authority elsewhere, no fear that the removal of laws would reduce us to savagery, if we followed the 'laws' of philosophers like Parmenides, Socrates, Heraclitus

---

[1] *Meno* 87e–88e, *Rep.* 496c. Cf. also *Laws* 728d–e, the character of Eros at *Symp.* 201e, and the 'neither good nor bad' of *Lysis* 216e.

[2] See Cherniss's note in the Loeb Plutarch, xiii.2, p. 738, n. *a*.

[3] The germ of the idea is in Plato's view, expressed in *Lysis* and *Charm.*, that what is good is whatever properly belongs to one (τἀγαθὸν οἰκεῖον). See vol. IV, 149f., 159. In Heinze's opinion (*Xenokr.* 148) 'Polemo seems to have been the first to work out in detail the doctrine that following nature was the way to happiness, but it was already represented by Xenocrates.'

and Plato. 'Then, as Xenocrates says, we should do voluntarily what the law now makes us do against our will.' Humanity, it seems, is prone to sin, and can only be kept from it either by the law, as at present, or if all were converted to philosophy. This is not so different as it might seem at first sight from the Socratic paradox that no one voluntarily does wrong. According to Socrates we act wrongly through ignorance alone, whereas Xenocrates puts it that given the wisdom of the philosopher we should sin no more, but 'honour justice for its intrinsic worth'.[1]

Heraclides Ponticus[2]

Life. The dates of Heraclides of Heracleia on the Black Sea (hence 'Ponticus') may be taken as roughly 390 (or earlier)–310.[3] He was a member of the Academy who narrowly missed election to its leadership when Speusippus died (p. 470 n. 3 above); but the generally accepted story that Plato left him in charge on his last visit to Sicily in 361 (vol. IV, 27 n. 2) comes solely from the tenth-century Suda, and since he cannot well have been over thirty, and may have been only twelve, at the time, seems unlikely.[4] The same source[5] also tells the story of the tame snake which he employed to engineer his own apotheosis. Diogenes (fr. 3 W.), on the authority of Sotion, says that 'later he was a pupil of Aristotle'.[6]

Writings. We have the titles of forty-six dialogues, in which he seems to have paid at least as much attention to dramatic situation, character and mood as Plato did. Some, says Diogenes, were in the vein of comedy, others of tragedy, and others in a conversational style suited to the philosophers, politicians and military men whom he was portray-

---

[1] See Plutarch (and Cicero) in fr. 3 H.

[2] His fragments have been collected by F. Wehrli, Basel 1953 (2nd ed. 1969), and for general information see Wehrli's article in *RE Suppl.* XI (1968), 675–86, supplementing that of Daebritz in *RE* VIII, 472–85.

[3] *OCD* gives 390–10 approx., Sambursky (*PWG* 63) 388–15. Voss (*Heracl.* p. 8) says he was born between 388 and 373.

[4] It is strongly denied by Voss, *Heracl.* 11–13.   [5] See fr. 17 W.; also in D.L., fr. 16.

[6] Wehrli indeed includes him in his series 'Die Schule des Aristoteles', though he himself says that in view of A.'s departure from Athens on Plato's death and H.'s own return to Heracleia, any instruction by A. must have been in Plato's lifetime, when both were members of the Academy, not in the Lyceum. He adds that 'A.'s influence on H. was to say the least limited', but thinks that D.L.'s words imply membership of the Peripatos, and sees evidence of common interests with other Peripatetics like Clearchus and Aristoxenus. (See his *HP*, p. 60.)

ing. His scientific outlook is commonly spoken of today as marred by a weakness for fantasy and superstition, because he told tales like that of Empedocles's miraculous disappearance after reviving a woman who had been apparently dead for thirty days, and of a man fallen to earth from the moon.[1] But what would we think of Plato if the dialogues had vanished but we knew he had told a story about a man killed in battle who came to life on the funeral pyre twelve days later and described the marvels he had seen in the next world; and had spoken of the gods riding round the sky in chariots and afterwards stabling their horses and feeding them on ambrosia and nectar from a manger? If Heraclides had the Platonic art of blending *mythos* and *logos*, the man from the moon could have provided, as Hirzel suggested, the fictional framework for a serious cosmological discussion.[2] There is some evidence to suggest that his *Abaris*, called after the legendary Hyperborean wonder-worker, was identical with *On Justice*, just as the myth of Er occurs in a dialogue on the same subject.[3] He was certainly of a religious turn of mind, believed in the divine oversight of human affairs and was of those whom Diodorus called 'the piously inclined' who ascribed the terrible earthquake at Helike to divine wrath, as opposed to those (like Aristotle, *Meteor.* 366a24ff.) who looked for natural explanations of such disasters.[4]

Astronomy and cosmology. We may start with these, since in astronomy lies his greatest claim to fame, though the sources are so defective that after long controversy the most varied estimates of his achievements continue to be held. At a minimum he is known to have put forward, as a partial explanation of the celestial phenomena, the hypothesis that the earth was not motionless, but rotated once daily on its axis, while the heavenly bodies stood still.[5] In the view of many scholars he also taught that Venus and Mercury revolved around the sun as centre, a supposition that contains at least the germ of the theory of epicycles, generalized

[1] Frr. 83, 84 and 115 W. For Empedocles see vol. II, 134, and on Heraclides Περὶ τῆς ἄπνου, I. M. Lonie, 'Medical Theory in Heraclides of Pontus', *Mnemos.* 1965.

[2] Hirzel, *Dialog* I, 327. Some of the Pythagoreans, to whom Heraclides owed a great deal, believed the moon to be inhabited (vol. I, 285).

[3] The *Abaris* is not in D.L.'s list, which includes Περὶ δικαιοσύνης. See Hirzel, *Dialog* I, 328. But as Wehrli rightly warns (*HP* 76, 84), there is no proof.   [4] Fr. 46 W. Cf. fr. 75.

[5] For the possibility that two Pythagoreans, Ecphantus and Hicetas, should share the credit for this imaginative idea, see vol. I, 327f.

by Apollonius of Perge and brought to its final form by Ptolemy. Finally he has been claimed, and as forcefully rejected, as first begetter of the full heliocentric theory of Copernicus, usually credited to Aristarchus of Samos in the next century.[1]

For a pupil of Plato his most startling pronouncement, if he has been correctly reported, is that the cosmos is infinite (fr. 112 W., from Aëtius). Much of Plato's teleological edifice would have crumbled if he had not believed the cosmos to have been created unique, finite and spherical (*Tim.* 33b). For Heraclides however its infinity went with a still more extraordinary idea that each star is itself a whole cosmos, 'containing earth and air in the infinite *aither*' (fr. 113 W.). If this is true, each must have its own sphere of fixed stars, each of which will be a cosmos having its own sphere of fixed stars and so on *ad infinitum*. In our sources this theory is attributed jointly to Heraclides and the Pythagoreans, but even the (probably contemporary) Pythagorean Ecphantus said the universe was 'made spherical by divine power' (fr. 1 DK).

The moon was 'earth surrounded by mist' (fr. 114) and fr. 115 suggests that it was inhabited, as it was for his Pythagorean brethren (vol. 1, 285). Comets, he said, were high clouds brilliant with light from the upper region,[2] and he also offered an explanation of the tides as due to the action of winds (fr. 117 W.).

[1] For the texts see frr. 104–17 W. The full Copernican theory was credited to H. by Schiaparelli in 1898, denied by Dreyer in 1906 (*HPS* 134f.) and with more powerful arguments by Heath (*A. of S.* 1913, 275 ff., who gives the key passages in English), only to be revived equally emphatically by van der Waerden in his *Astron. d. Pyth.* (1951), § 9. (See also his 'Astron. des H. von P.', *Ber. d. Sächs. Ak.* 96 (Leipzig 1944), 47–56.) His authority is formidable, but opinion continues to go against him, e.g. A. Pannekoek, *The Astronomical System of Herakleides* (Amsterdam 1952), and Wehrli, *RE* 686. As to epicycles, Heath, while crediting H. with 'the great advance' of discovering that Venus and Mercury revolve round the sun, denied that this involved him in an epicyclic theory (*o.c.* 255–7). Recently, in *CQ* 1970, G. Evans has robbed him even of the theory that the two planets orbit the sun, though Sambursky in 1956 (*PWG*, with translation of passages) affirms it and adds that on this account he may be considered the founder of the theory of epicycles. Yet the suggestion of an epicyclic and heliocentric theory for the motion of Venus would appear to have been definitely refuted by Neugebauer's note on the meaning of 'superior' and 'inferior' in Chalcidius (*AJP* 1972, 600f.). The latest opinion of H.'s 'partial heliocentric theory' is that it 'ne paraît pas solidement fondée'. See J. Moreau in *Rev. d'hist. des sciences* 1976. I am scarcely competent to give a firm opinion but offer this selection of references to guide an interested reader in an investigation of the issues involved.

[2] Fr. 116 W. μετάρσιον ὑπὸ μεταρσίου φωτὸς καταυγαζόμενον. He may have had Xenophanes in mind, who called them 'ignited clouds' (vol. 1, 390, 392), but the expression in Aëtius suggests something different. Nor did H. follow X. in holding that this was also true of all the heavenly bodies. The two descriptions occur in the same short section of Aëtius recording the various views on these phenomena.

Physics. Heraclides adopted an atomic theory of matter, in which however he differed essentially from Democritus. His hostility appears in a work (possibly two)[1] *Against Democritus* and another *On Images* (*eidōla*, the Democritean word for the films of atoms which enter the eye in the act of sight), for Clement said that Heraclides trounced, or castigated, the *eidōla* of Democritus (fr. 123 W.). It is natural that a Platonic teleologist and believer in divine providence should want nothing to do with Democritus's purely mechanical and purposeless conception of causation.[2] Moreover he altered the theory at a vital point, making his ultimate particles, the *archai* of all things, subject to qualitative change.[3] For his model he appears rather to have looked to Empedocles, who went a long way towards the Democritean view, and where he differed from it did so in ways similar to those of Heraclides later. There were also, if the doxographers are to be trusted, coincidences of terminology, both having called their smallest particles not *atomoi* but *oncoi* (masses or lumps) and *thrausmata* (fragments).[4] Heraclides also, like his master (*Tim.* 67b), followed Empedocles in his explanation of sensation as due to the fitting of sensible materials into passages (*poroi*) of appropriate size in the body.

Heraclides applied to his *oncoi* a rare epithet (ἄναρμοι, lit. 'not joined') which unfortunately could mean either of two things: (1) not joined to each other, 'so that each is separate from the rest and moves on its own' (so Zeller, III, 1, 571 n. 4), or (2) not internally joined, i.e. loosely knit or loose-jointed. The second is adopted by Lonie in *Phronesis* 1964, and goes with his thesis that the *oncoi* are to be distinguished from the *thrausmata* as not indivisible but simply the smallest parts of the perceptible elements, which can be further broken up into the indivisible fragments. Thus the *oncoi*,

---

[1] Two appear in D.L.'s catalogue, but may be identical. (So Wehrli, *RE* 678.)

[2] Ecphantus too is said to have combined atomism with providential organization of the cosmos (vol. 1, 325, extract *d*).

[3] They were παθητά (fr. 120 W.). This would, I think, imply the possession of sensible qualities, like the physical bodies—earth, fire etc.—which they make up (perhaps in imitation of Empedocles, whom the doxographers associate with him; see vol. II, 150). Lonie argues (*Phron.* 1964, 157; see below) that παθητά here must mean divisible because ἀπαθῶν earlier in the same fr. is glossed as divisible, but with the article before ἀτόμων I am not quite convinced of the 'glossing'.

[4] For H. see frr. 118, 121 W.; for Empedocles, vol. II, 149, 150.

if they were conceived as particles of air, fire, etc. might be described as possessing quality . . . while the fragments, not being particles of any element in particular, were described as devoid of quality. Finally, both might be described as στοιχεῖα [elements], since both were in a sense ultimate.

This theory Lonie then connects with Plato's reduction of the four elements to geometrical solids and planes in the *Timaeus*. It is an attractive hypothesis, and I hope it is right, but our meagre sources say that Heraclides only changed the name of the atoms to *oncoi*, retaining their indivisibility, and regarded them as universal *archai*.[1]

Theology. In Cicero's dialogue on the nature of the gods, an arrogant Epicurean pours scorn on all theistic doctrines alike. Of Plato's he says that they 'are in themselves clearly false, and violently contradict each other'. This charge of self-contradiction is his favourite weapon. In the third book of Aristotle's *On Philosophy*, he claims, confusion reigns, and he elaborates the point in a passage which has greatly exercised the minds of those who would reconstruct that lost work. Then after dismissing Xenocrates as equally foolish he comes to Heraclides,[2] who, he says, 'stuffed his books with childish stories and at one time holds that the world, at another time that mind is divine. He also attributes divinity to the planets, deprives God of sensation and maintains that he is changeable in shape, and again in the same book puts earth and sky among the gods.' We can hardly hope to recover the real mind of Heraclides from such an attack. However, in spite of the deliberately misleading order, it sounds as if the original gave a fairly faithful reflection of the *Timaeus*. If he 'deprived God of sensation', that would be because he regarded him as pure mind, like the world-soul in Plato which had no need of sight or hearing (*Tim.* 33c) or the 'sacred mind' of Empedocles that penetrates the whole cosmos.[3]

Apart from this, nothing is known of his theology save that he up-

---

[1] (a) ἀμερῆ σώματα τοῦ παντὸς μέρη . . . [ταῦτα τὰ ἀμερῆ] ἐκάλεσεν ὄγκους. (b) ἀνάρμους ὄγκους τὰς ἀρχὰς . . . τῶν ὅλων (frr. 118 and 119a W.). The position is complicated by the fact that Asclepiades of Prusa (first cent. B.C.) in his corpuscular theory borrowed the phrase ἄναρμοι ὄγκοι from H.; and Asclepiades did believe that they were divisible. See Zeller III.1, 571 n. 4. Lonie's thesis of ὄγκοι divisible into θραύσματα has been accepted by Krämer, *P. und H. Phil.* 308.

[2] Cic. *N.D.* I, 13, 34. See fr. 111 W.

[3] Plato, *Tim.* 33c; Emped. fr. 134 (vol. II, 258–62).

held the doctrine of Plato in *Laws* 10, that gods both exist and concern themselves with human affairs (fr. 75).

The soul. Heraclides wrote a book on the soul, and was credited with another 'on the things in Hades', a title used by Democritus. The genuineness of the second was questioned in antiquity.[1] In any case, not much is known of the contents of either. Unlike Plato, he thought the soul material, though of the most tenuous sort of material substance, namely *aither*, and also said that it was, or resembled, light, which is in keeping with the shining quality of *aither* in common belief. Thus he kept closer to general and earlier philosophical beliefs in the fiery, aetherial or airy nature of the soul, which by no means excluded its divinity.[2] The story of 'The Woman without Breath' and her resuscitation bore the alternative title 'On Disease', and Galen treated it as a serious contribution to the literature of hysterical seizures (frr. 79, 80, 82 W.); but being colourfully told, with miraculous additions, as an exploit of Empedocles, it linked up with other legends of men rising from apparent death (Abaris, Aristeas, Hermotimus, Epimenides) and would inevitably lead to speculation concerning the whereabouts of the soul during such apparent absences from the body.[3] In similar mythical vein he told of a certain Empedotimus, who experienced a midday epiphany of Pluto and Persephone and a first-hand vision of 'the whole truth about our souls'.[4] Some Platonists, says Iamblichus, think of the soul as always embodied but alternating between a finer or more tenuous[5] and a solid body. Heraclides said that while awaiting their descent to earth souls were confined to the Milky Way, but others that they were distributed over all the spheres of the heavens (fr. 97 W.). Here again it would seem that the 'others' kept closer to Plato (*Tim.* 42 d), from whom Heraclides diverged in the direction of popular, and more specifically Pythagorean belief, for did not Pythagoras say that

[1] Fr. 72 W. For the Περὶ τῶν ἐν Ἅιδου of Democritus see vol. ΙΙ, 436–9.

[2] Cf. Euripides fr. 1014 on immortal soul and immortal *aither*. Vols. Ι and ΙΙ contain other reff. for the connexion in the earlier period.

[3] Cf. vol. ΙΙ, 436–8; vol. Ι, 318 f.

[4] Fr. 93 W. On Empedotimus see Rohde, *Psyche* (Eng. tr.) 330 n. 111. Rohde believed him an imaginary character in a dialogue by H. (An *alter Empedocles*? There is no great difference between κλέος and τιμή.)

[5] λεπτότερον. On λεπτόν see vol. ΙΙ, 276f.

the souls assemble on the Milky Way, which is so called from those who when they fall to birth are nurtured on milk?[1]

Pleasure. Heraclides wrote a dialogue *On Pleasure* described as being in the comic style, of which Athenaeus has preserved several extracts (frr. 55–9, 61 W.). One is a eulogy, outdoing Plato's Callicles in its extravagance, of pleasure, luxury, wealth and show. These develop the qualities of free men, work is for slaves and mean characters. It was an Athens revelling in fine clothes, jewellery and all sorts of luxury that humbled the might of Asia at Marathon. Those with the highest reputation for wisdom reckon pleasure the greatest good. This is presumably from the speech of the *advocatus diaboli*, and the other extracts all tell highly moral tales of cities demoralized and ruined by luxurious living (frr. 50 and 57), voluptuaries ending their lives in poverty and misery, and how the most intense pleasures are felt by the insane.[2] Unfortunately such stories monopolized the interest of later writers, so they are all that remains to us of his ethics, even of his dialogue *On Justice.* Of happiness he seems to have been content to repeat a Pythagorean dictum that it consisted in knowledge of the perfection of the numbers of the soul (fr. 44 W.). Altogether Pythagoreanism was probably the strongest influence on his thought, and his fragments are a useful source of information on the sect and its founder. (Cf. vol. I, 163–5.)

ADDITIONAL NOTE: THE NATURE OF SOUND

I have with some reluctance omitted from both this section and the one on Xenocrates an interesting passage from Porphyry's *in Ptol. Harm.*, which Zeller (II.1, 1036 n. 1) summarized as representing Heraclides's views on the subject of hearing and sight (in spite of having denied in vol. I. 1, 508 n. 1 that the Heraclides there mentioned was the Pontic). Wehrli has omitted it from the fragments of Heraclides and Heinze included it in those of Xenocrates. The epithet 'Ponticus' is not attached to Heraclides, and the quotation is said to be from his *Introduction to Music.* This exact title does not occur elsewhere, but an *On Music* is in D.L.'s catalogue. The arguments against an identification with our Heraclides are set forth by Heinze on p. 6 n. 2, and include the unlikelihood of his referring as he does to his contemporary

---

[1] Porphyry, *De antro nymph.* 28. For this and other quotations see Cook, *Zeus* II, 41 f.
[2] A point also made by Plato. See *Phil.* 45 e and p. 223 above.

Xenocrates as an authority. But in any case, is the identity of Heraclides relevant? The passage in Porphyry begins: 'Heraclides too writes on this subject in his *Introduction to Music* as follows: "Pythagoras, so Xenocrates says..."', and it continues with a detailed account of Pythagoras's discovery of the numerical basis of the musical intervals. It does not therefore in any way suggest that the theories which follow belong to Heraclides, but rather that they come from Xenocrates who ascribed them to Pythagoras, though they were probably at least partly Xenocrates's own as Heinze thought, who deals fully with the content of the extract on pp. 5–10 of his *Xenokrates*. Its most interesting feature is the discrete nature of sound. A sound is produced by a series of distinct blows (of air) falling on the ear.[1] Each blow 'occupies no time, but exists on the boundary between past and future', that is, on the instant between striking and being struck. Our hearing however is too feeble to distinguish the separate blows, which we perceive as one continuous sound. This temporal discontinuity of sound, as Heinze remarks, is analogous to the discontinuous magnitudes or indivisible lines of Xenocrates, but since he shared this atomic conception with his colleague Heraclides, that in itself would not help us to decide between them. All these contemporaries and colleagues in the Academy had many ideas in common, and many of these they shared also with the Pythagoreans, to whom Plato himself, as we know, was more than a little indebted.

Others

In view of our comparative ignorance of the other pupils of Plato, a few notes on some of them will suffice. They continue to come from a wide geographical area. *Philip* of Opus has already been mentioned in connexion with the *Laws* and *Epinomis* (pp. 321, 385 above). Like other members of the Academy, he wrote prolifically on a wide variety of subjects,[2] but what he said is unknown. *Hermodorus*, from Syracuse, is mentioned twice by Simplicius (*Phys.* 247, 31; 256, 32) as a pupil of Plato who wrote a book on him (perhaps the first) from which Simplicius quotes, though not directly. He is our authority for Plato's stay with Euclides at Megara after Socrates's death (D.L. 2.106 and 3.6). In a mathematical treatise he showed an interest in the astral religion of the Persian Magi, and offered an opinion on the date of Zoroaster and a

[1] Cf. Aristotle's definition of a letter as an indivisible unit of speech (*Poet.* 1456b 22).
[2] If we accept von Fritz's identifications in *RE* xxxviii Halbb., 2351f. For Philip see Tarán (p. 385 n. 1 above).

Greek etymology for his name.[1] *Histiaeus*, from Perinthos on the Sea
of Marmara, was a recorder of Plato on the Good (p. 425). Theophrastus
(*Metaph*. pp. 12–14 R. and F., cf. pp. 436, 472 above) commended him
as one who did not stop at the highest principles of being but attempted
'up to a point' to continue his investigations down to mathematical and
physical matters. He explained sight as a mingling of rays (from the eyes)
with images (from the objects), a purely Platonic (if not even Democritean) idea. His only originality lay in the invention of a technical
portmanteau-term for the result, namely *aktineidōla*, 'ray-images'
(Aët. in Diels, *Dox*. 403). Time he defined as 'the motion of the stars
relative to one another' (*Dox*. 318), which again is purely Platonic
(*Tim*. 38b–39e). *Menaechmus*, whom Proclus described as 'pupil of
Eudoxus and associate of Plato',[2] is mainly known for some notable
advances in geometry. He was credited with going some way towards
a practical, not merely theoretical, solution of the famous 'Delian problem' (of doubling the cube),[3] and with discovering the sections of a
cone. In astronomy Theon of Smyrna (pp. 201 f. Hiller) associates him
with Aristotle and (erroneously) Callippus in the introduction of
counteracting spheres into the motions of the planets and the idea that
the visible stars themselves are inanimate but moved by the spheres in
which they are fixed. *Theudius* of Magnesia is mentioned only by Proclus
as an outstanding mathematician and philosopher who (like Euclid a
little later) wrote a *Stoicheia*, or *Elements*, and generalized many
hitherto special, or partial, theorems.[4] *Euphraeus*, of Oreos in Euboea,
has been mentioned on p. 400. Demosthenes in his third Philippic
(59–62) tells how, after vainly opposing the pro-Macedonian party in
his city, he finally committed suicide, 'witnessing by his deed how

---

[1] D.L. 1.2 and 8. Aristotle and Eudoxus also gave opinions on the date of Zoroaster. For the
interest of the Academy in Persian religion (perhaps too much neglected here) see Koster, *Mythe
de P*., and the remarks of Jaeger, *Arist*. (Eng. tr.) 131–4. They were not however hypnotized by
it: Eudoxus found the idea of astrological prediction 'minime credendum' (Cic. *De div*. 11.42.87;
Koster, *o.c.* 16). For Plato himself, see p. 365 with n. 3 above.

[2] *In Eucl*. p. 67 Friedl., p. 55 in Morrow's translation.

[3] The 'credit' was given by Eutocius. See Kliem in *RE* xxix. Halbb. 700, but cf. p. 449 above.
To Kliem's references for M.'s mathematics may now be added Morrow's translation of Procl.
Eucl. p. 55 n. 43. See also J. Barnes, *CQ* 1976, 284–8.

[4] Procl. *Eucl*. p. 167 Friedl., 56 in Morrow's translation. For all these men anyone interested
should naturally consult the relevant articles in the *RE*. That on Theudius, by von Fritz, is in the
eleventh *Halbband* of the second series, 244–6.

justly and disinterestedly he had withstood Philip'. *Erastus* and *Coriscus* of Scepsis in the Troad, to whom Plato addressed the Sixth Letter (pp. 400 f. above), will be best reintroduced in the story of Aristotle's travel to Asia Minor after his death, which will find its place in the next volume.

BIBLIOGRAPHY

The following list contains particulars of books and articles referred to, usually in abbreviated form, in the text, together with a few additional items. For a plain text of all the dialogues there is Burnet's in the Oxford Classical Texts (prefaces dated 1899–1906). For a complete translation the one-volume Hamilton–Cairns collection (*q.v.*) is most convenient, and many dialogues are easily and inexpensively available in the Penguin Classics series. The Loeb Classical Library provides texts and translations for English readers, as does the Budé Association's series in French.

Many books on Plato contain select bibliographies, e.g. vols. II and III of Friedländer's *Plato* (1964 and 1969) provide separate lists for each dialogue at the beginning of the notes to the appropriate chapter, and general works may be traced in his list of abbreviations. Among other bibliographical aids may be mentioned Cherniss's well-known survey in *Lustrum*, Gigon's in the *Bibliographische Einführung*, Rosenmeyer's ten years of *Platonic Scholarship* and Schuhl's *Quinze années*. I am pleased to be able to welcome Skemp's useful survey of work on Plato which appeared just in time for inclusion in the bibliography. This year too Manasse has added a survey of Plato-literature in French to his previous two on works in German and English.

The lack of a complete word-index to Plato has long been felt. Hitherto scholars have had to rely on F. Ast's *Lexicon Platonicum* of 1835–8, for which reason it was recently reprinted. It is however incomplete, and special mention must therefore be made of L. Brandwood's computer-based *Word-Index to Plato* (1976).

I have retained a separate section for a selection of editions and translations of Plato's works, supplementing that in vol. IV and including commentaries without text, but have put it before the general section and ordered it under separate titles, not alphabetically by the modern scholars. (This list may be supplemented by those at the beginning of the notes to each chapter in Friedländer's *Plato*, vols. II and III.) This section covers Plato's works only. Editions of other authors, including collections of fragments, are entered under the editor's name in the general section. The Greek commentators on Aristotle are referred to in the text by page (and sometimes line) in the appropriate volume of the Berlin Academy's edition (*Commentaria in Aristotelem Graeca*, various dates). Items from the bibliography of vol. IV are not repeated here unless also relevant to this one. Thus editions of the earlier dialogues should be sought in vol. IV.

The flow of anthologies of previously published articles continues unabated, to the benefit of students and the embarrassment of bibliographers, and the last few years have also seen a considerable output of reprints, including books by outstanding scholars of the last century. Some of both kinds are sure to have escaped me.

Bibliography

1 A SELECTION OF EDITIONS, TRANSLATIONS AND COMMENTARIES

Collected dialogues

HAMILTON, E. and CAIRNS, H. *Plato, The Collected Dialogues including the Letters* (translations by various hands). New York, 1961; U.K. (Oxford), 1975.

JOWETT, B. *The Dialogues of Plato translated into English with analyses and introductions.* 4th ed. by D. J. Allan and H. E. Dale. 4 vols., Oxford, 1953.

Cratylus

MÉRIDIER, L. *Cratyle.* Introduction, text, translation and notes. Paris, 3rd ed., 1961 (Assoc. Budé).

Epinomis

NOVOTNÝ, F. *Platonis Epinomis commentariis illustrata.* Prague, 1960.

CASTORINA, E. Introduction, text, translation and commentary. Florence, 1967.

SPECCHIA, O. Introduction, text and commentary. Florence, 1967.

HARWARD, J. *The Epinomis of Plato.* Translation with introduction and notes. Oxford, 1928.

See also *Philebus.*

Gorgias

DODDS, E. R. *Plato, Gorgias.* Introduction, text and commentary. Oxford, 1959.

Laws

ENGLAND, E. B. *The Laws of Plato.* Introduction, text and notes. 2 vols., Manchester, 1921 (repr. Arno Press, New York, 1976).

TAYLOR, A. E. *The Laws of Plato.* Introduction and translation. London, 1934.

SAUNDERS, T. J. *Plato, The Laws.* Introduction and translation. Penguin Books, 1970, repr. (with minor corrections and expanded bibliographies) 1975. Further repr. in preparation.

Meno

BROWN, M. S. (ed.). *Plato's Meno.* Guthrie's translation with essays by various authors. Indianapolis and New York, 1971.

Parmenides

TAYLOR, A. E. *The Parmenides of Plato translated into English with Introduction and Appendixes.* Oxford, 1934.

CORNFORD, F. M. *Plato and Parmenides: Parmenides'* Way of Truth *and Plato's* Parmenides *translated with an introduction and a running commentary.* London, 1939.

Bibliography

Phaedo
HACKFORTH, R. *Plato's Phaedo*. Introduction, translation and running commentary. Cambridge, 1955.

Phaedrus
THOMPSON, W. H. *The Phaedrus of Plato*. Text, notes and essays. London, 1868.
VRIES, G. J. DE *A Commentary on the Phaedrus of Plato*. Amsterdam, 1969.
HACKFORTH, R. *Plato's Phaedrus*. Introduction, translation and running commentary. Cambridge, 1952. (Paperback repr. 1972.)

Philebus
BURY, R. G. *The Philebus of Plato*. Introduction, text, notes and appendices. Cambridge, 1897 (repr. Arno Press, New York, 1973).
HACKFORTH, R. *Plato's Examination of Pleasure. A Translation of the Philebus, with Introduction and Commentary*. Cambridge, 1945 (repr. 1958 etc.).
DIÈS, A. *Philèbe*. Introduction, text and French translation. Paris, 1949 (Assoc. Budé).
TAYLOR, A. E. Transl. (with *Epinomis*) posthumously edited by R. Klibansky and with an introduction by A. C. Lloyd. London, 1956.
GOSLING, J. C. B. *Plato: Philebus*. Translation with notes. Oxford, 1975.

Politicus
SKEMP, J. B. *Plato's Statesman*. Translation, essays and footnotes. London, 1952.
See also *Sophist*.

Protagoras
VLASTOS, G. *Plato's Protagoras*. Jowett's translation revised by M. Ostwald, ed. with introduction by G.V. New York, 1956.

Republic
ADAM, J. *The Republic of Plato*. Text, notes and appendices. 2 vols., Cambridge, 1926 and 1929; 2nd ed. revised by D. A. Rees, 1963.

Sophist and Politicus
CAMPBELL, L. *The Sophistes and Politicus of Plato, with a revised text and English notes*. Oxford, 1867.

Sophist
APELT, O. *Platonis Sophista*. Text, introduction and commentary. 2nd ed., Leipzig, 1897.
DIÈS, A. *Sophiste*. Introductions, text and French translation. Paris, 1925 (Assoc. Budé).
See also *Theaetetus* (Cornford).

Theaetetus

CAMPBELL, L. *The Theaetetus of Plato, with a revised text and English notes*. Oxford, 1883.

SCHMIDT, H. *Exegetischer Kommentar ʒu Platos Theätet*. Leipzig, 1880.

FOWLER, H. N. Text and translation, Loeb ed., Cambridge, Mass. and London, 1921 (repr. 1967).

CORNFORD, F. M. *Plato's Theory of Knowledge: the* Theaetetus *and* Sophist *of Plato translated with an Introduction and Running Commentary*. London, 1935.

APELT, O. Translation and commentary. 4th ed., Leipzig, 1944.

ZEPPI, S. and T. A. Introduction, commentary and translation. Florence, 1966.

RUSSI, A. and SANTANIELLO, M. Introduction, translation and notes. Messina, 1967.

MCDOWELL, J. H. *Plato, Theaetetus, translated with notes*. Oxford, 1973.

Timaeus

MARTIN, T. H. *Études sur le Timée de Platon*. 2 vols., Paris, 1841.

ARCHER-HIND, R. D. *The Timaeus of Plato*. Introduction, text and notes. London and New York, 1888.

TAYLOR, A. E. *A commentary on Plato's Timaeus*. Oxford, 1928.

CORNFORD, F. M. *Plato's Cosmology: the* Timaeus *of Plato translated with a running commentary*. London, 1937.

LEE, H. D. P. *Plato, Timaeus*. Introduction and translation. Penguin Books, 1965.

Timaeus and Critias

RIVAUD, A. *Timée, Critias*. Introduction, text and French translation. Paris, 1925 (Assoc. Budé).

Doubtful or spurious dialogues

CALOGERO, G. *Platone, 'L'Hipparco'*, with introduction and commentary. Florence, 1938.

CARLINI, A. *Platone, Alcibiade, Alcibiade Minore, Ipparco, Rivali*. Introduction, critical text, and translation. Turin, 1964.

SOUILHÉ, J. (1) *Dialogues suspects*, (2) *Dialogues apocryphes*. Introduction, text, translation and notes. Vol. XIII, parts 2 and 3, of the Budé series. Paris, 1930.

Letters

HOWALD, E. *Die Briefe Platons*. Introduction, text, German translation and notes. Zürich, 1923.

NOVOTNÝ, F. *Platonis epistulae commentariis illustratae*. Brno, 1930.

HARWARD, J. *The Platonic Epistles*. Introduction, translation and notes. Cambridge, 1932 (repr. 1976).

BLUCK, R. S. *Plato's Seventh and Eighth Letters*. Introduction, text and notes. Cambridge, 1947.

MORROW, G. R. *Plato's Epistles: a translation with critical essays and notes*. Indianapolis and New York, 1962.

Bibliography

PASQUALI, G. *Le lettere di Platone* (Essays). 2nd ed. Florence, 1967.
NEUMANN, W. and KERSCHENSTEINER, J. *Platon: Briefe, griechisch-deutsch.* Munich, 1967.

II GENERAL

ACKRILL, J. L. 'Symploke Eidon', *SPM* 199–206 (orig. 1955).
ACKRILL, J. L. 'Plato and the Copula', *SPM* 207–18 (orig. 1957).
ACKRILL, J. L. 'Plato on False Belief: *Tht.* 187–200', *Monist*, 1966, 383–402.
ACKRILL, J. L. 'In Defence of Plato's Division', *Ryle* 373–92.
ADAM, J. 'The Myth in Plato's Politicus', *CR*, 1891, 445 f.
AHLVERS, A. *Zahl und Klang bei Plato.* Bern, 1952.
ALLAN, D. J., 'The Problem of Cratylus', *AJP*, 1954, 271–87.
ALLAN, D. J. Review of Robinson's *Plato's Earlier Dialectic* in *PQ*, 1955, 173 f.
ALLEN, R. E. *Plato's 'Euthyphro' and the Earlier Theory of Forms.* London, 1970.
ANAGNOSTOPOULOS, G. 'Plato's, *Cratylus*: the two theories of the correctness of names', *Rev. of Metaphysics*, 1971–2, 691–736.
ANNAS, J. *Aristotle's* Metaphysics, *Books* M *and* N, *translated with introduction and notes.* Oxford, 1976.
ANTON, J. P. and KUSTAS, G. L. (eds.). *Essays in Ancient Greek Philosophy.* Albany, N.Y., 1971.
APELT, O. *Beiträge zur Geschichte der griechischen Philosophie*, Leipzig, 1891. (Contains 'Die Ideenlehre in Platons Sophistes', pp. 67–99.)
ARMSTRONG, D. M. 'Infinite Regress Arguments and the Problem of Universals', *Australasian J. of Philos.*, 1974, 198–201.
AUSTIN, J. L. *Sense and Sensibilia.* Oxford, 1962.
BACON, E. *See* GALANOPOULOS, A. G.
BACON, Francis. *Works*, ed. J. Spedding, R. L. Ellis and D. D. Heath. 14 vols., London, 1857–74.
BACON, Francis. *New Atlantis*, Ed. A. B. GOUGH, Oxford, 1915.
BAEUMKER, C. *Das Problem der Materie in der griechischen Philosophie.* Münster, 1890.
BALDRY, H. C. 'Who Invented the Golden Age?', *CQ*, 1952, 83–91.
BALTES, M. *Die Welterstehung des platonischen Timaios nach den antiken Interpreten.* Teil I, Leiden, 1976.
BAMBROUGH, J. R. (ed.). *New Essays on Plato and Aristotle.* London, 1965.
BAMBROUGH, J. R. *Reason, Truth and God.* London, 1969.
BARKER, E. *The Political Thought of Plato and Aristotle.* London, 1907. (Paperback, New York, 1959.)
BARNES, J. 'Homonymy in Aristotle and Speusippus', *CQ*, 1971, 65–80.
BARNES, J. 'Aristotle, Menaechmus and Circular Proof', *CQ*, 1976, 278–92.
BECKERMANN, E. and SYKUTRIS, J. 'Speusipps Brief an König Philipp', *Berichte über die Verhandlungen der Sächs. Akad. zu Leipzig, phil.-hist. Klasse*, 80 (1928).
BENFEY, T. 'Über die Aufgabe des platonischen Dialogs Kratylos', *Abhandlungen Göttingen, Phil.-hist. Klasse* 12, Göttingen, 1866, 189–330.

Bibliography

BIGNONE, E. *Studi sul pensiero antico*. Naples, 1938.

BLOCKER, H. G. 'The Truth about Fictional Entities', *PQ*, 1974, 27–36.

BLUCK, R. S. 'The *Parmenides* and the Third Man', *CQ*, 1956, 29–37.

BLUCK, R. S. 'False Statement in the Sophist', *JHS*, 1957 (Part 2), 181–6.

BLUCK, R. S. 'Forms as Standards', *Phronesis*, 1957, 115–27.

BLUCK, R. S. 'The Puzzles of Size and Number in Plato's "Theaetetus"', *PCPS*, 1961, 1–9.

BLUCK, R. S. 'Knowledge by Acquaintance in Plato's *Theaetetus*', *Mind*, 1963, 261–3.

BLUCK, R. S. *Plato's Sophist* (posthumously edited by G. C. Neal). Manchester, 1975.

BOCHENSKI, I. M. *Dogmatic Principles of Soviet Philosophy*, Eng. tr. by T. J. Blakeley. Dordrecht, 1963.

BONDESON, W. B. 'The "Dream" of Socrates and the Conclusion of the Theaetetus', *Apeiron* III.2 (1969), 1–13.

BONDESON, W. B. 'Perception, True Opinion and Knowledge in Plato's Theaetetus', *Phronesis*, 1969, 111–22.

BONITZ, H. *Index Aristotelicus. Aristotelis Opera*, vol. 5, Berlin, 1870.

BOUSSOULAS, N. J. *L'être et la composition des mixtes dans le Philèbe de Platon*. Paris, 1952.

BOUSSOULAS, N. J. 'Note sur la dernière doctrine platonicienne', *Bulletin de l'Assoc. Budé*, 1963, 404–36. (On the *Philebus*.)

BOUSSOULAS, N. J. 'Notes sur la pensée platonicienne', Πλάτων, 1963, 87–125. (All on the *Philebus*.)

BOYANCÉ, P. 'La "doctrine d'Euthyphron" dans le Cratyle', *REG*, 1941, 141–75.

BRAMWELL, J. *Lost Atlantis*. London, 1937.

BRANDWOOD, L. *A Word Index to Plato*. Leeds, 1976.

BRANDWOOD, L. See COX, D. R.

BRENTLINGER, J. A. 'Particulars in Plato's Middle Dialogues', *AGP*, 1972, 116–52.

BRINGMANN, K. 'Plato's Philebos und Heraklides' Pontikos' Dialog π. ἡδονῆς', *Hermes*, 1972, 523–30.

BROAD, C. D. *The Mind and its Place in Nature*. London, 1925.

BROCHARD, V. *Études de philosophie ancienne et de philosophie moderne*. Paris, 1926.

BROWN, M. S. (ed.). *Plato's Meno, transl. by W. K. C. Guthrie, with essays, edited by Malcolm Brown*. New York, 1971.

BROWN, M. S. 'Plato Disapproves of the Slave-Boy's Answer', *Plato's Meno*, 198–242 (orig. 1967).

BROWN, M. S. '*Theaetetus*: Knowledge as continued learning', *JHP*, 1969, 359–79.

BRUMBAUGH, R. S. *Plato's Mathematical Imagination*. Indiana, 1954.

BRUMBAUGH, R. S. *Plato on the One: the hypotheses in the Parmenides and their Interpretation*. Yale, 1961.

BURNET, J. *Greek Philosophy: Part I, Thales to Plato* (all published). London, 1924.

BURNYEAT, M. F. 'The Material and Sources of Plato's Dream', *Phronesis*, 1970, 101–22.

BURY, J. B. 'The Later Platonism', *J. of Philol.*, 1894, 161–86.

BURY, R. G. 'The Theory of Education in Plato's *Laws*', *REG*, 1937, 304–20.

CAIRNS, H. 'Plato as Jurist', ch. xvi of Friedländer, *Plato*, vol. I.

CAIZZI, F. D. *Antisthenis Fragmenta*. Milan, 1966.

CHARLTON, W. *Aristotle's* Physics *Books I and II*. Oxford, 1970.

CHERNISS, H. 'The Philosophical Economy of the Theory of Ideas', *SPM* 1–12 (orig. 1936).

CHERNISS, H. *Aristotle's Criticism of Plato and the Academy*. New York, 1944.

CHERNISS, H. *The Riddle of the Early Academy*. Berkeley and Los Angeles (Univ. of California Press), 1945.

CHERNISS, H. 'Notes on Plutarch's *De facie in orbe lunae*', *CP* 1951, 137–53.

CHERNISS, H. Review of G. Müller's *Studien zu den platonischen* Nomoi, *Gnomon*, 1953, 367–79.

CHERNISS, H. 'The Sources of Evil According to Plato', *Plato* II (ed. Vlastos), 1971, 244–58 (orig. 1954).

CHERNISS, H. '*Timaeus* 38A8–B5', *JHS*, 1957 (I), 18–23.

CHERNISS, H. 'The Relation of the "Timaeus" to Plato's Later Dialogues', *SPM* 339–78 (orig. 1957).

CHERNISS, H. 'Plato 1950–1957', *Lustrum*, 1959, 5–308, and 1960, 321–648.

CHERNISS, H. *Plutarch's Moralia*, Loeb ed., vol. XIII, ii. Text, transl. and notes. Cambridge, Mass. and London, 1976.

CHERRY, R. S. 'Timaeus 49 c 7–50 b 5', *Apeiron*, 1967, 1–11.

CHROUST, A. H. 'Speusippus succeeds Plato in the Scholarchate of the Academy', *REG*, 1971, 338–41.

CHUNG-HWAN CHENG. 'On the *Parmenides* of Plato', *CQ*, 1944, 101–14.

CLAGETT, M. *Greek Science in Antiquity*. New York, 1955.

CLAGHORN, G. S. *Aristotle's Criticism of Plato's 'Timaeus'*. The Hague, 1954.

CLEGG, J. S. 'Self-Predication and Linguistic Reference in Plato's Theory of the Forms', *Phronesis*, 1973, 26–43.

COOPER, J. M. 'Plato on Sense Perception and Knowledge: *Theaetetus* 184 to 186', *Phronesis*, 1970, 123–46.

COX, D. R. and BRANDWOOD, L. 'On a Discriminatory Problem connected with the Works of Plato', *J. of Roy. Statist. Soc.* B, 1959, 195–200.

CROMBIE, I. M. *An Examination of Plato's Doctrines*. 2 vols., London, 1962 and 1963.

CROMBIE, I. M. Review of *SPM* (*q.v.* in list of abbreviations), *CR*, 1966, 311f.

CROMBIE, I. M. 'Ryle's New Portrait of Plato', *PR*, 1969, 362–73.

DAEBRITZ, R. Article 'Herakleides (45)' in *RE* VIII, 472–85.

DEANE, P. 'Stylometrics do not Exclude the Seventh Letter', *Mind*, 1973, 113–17.

DERBOLAV, J. *Platons Sprachphilosophie im Kratylos und in den späteren Schriften*. Darmstadt, 1972.

DETEL, W. *Platons Beschreibung des falschen Satzes im Theätet und Sophistes*. Göttingen, 1972.

33-2

Bibliography

DICKS, D. R. *Early Greek Astronomy to Aristotle*. London, 1970.

DIELS, H. and KRANZ, W. *Die Fragmente der Vorsokratiker* (Greek and German). 6th ed., 3 vols., Berlin, 1951–2 (or later eds.; pagination remains the same).

DIELS, H. and SCHUBART, H. C. (eds.). *Anonymer Kommentar zu Platons Theätet*. Berlin, 1905.

DIÈS, A. *Autour de Platon*. 2 vols., Paris, 1927.

DILLER, H. 'Der vorphilosophische Gebrauch von κόσμος und κοσμεῖν', *Festschrift Snell*. Munich, 1956, 47–60.

DINGLE, H. 'The Scientific Outlook in 1851 and in 1951', *BJPS* II (1951–52), 85–104.

DODDS, E. R. 'The *Parmenides* and the Neoplatonic "One"', *CQ*, 1928, 129–42.

DODDS, E. R. 'Plato and the Irrational', *JHS*, 1945, 16–25. Repr. in *idem*, *The Ancient Concept of Progress and other Essays*, Oxford, 1973, 106–25.

DODDS, E. R. *The Greeks and the Irrational*. California U. P., 1951.

DÖRRIE, H. Article 'Xenokrates' in *RE*, 2. Reihe, XVIII. Halbb., 1512–28.

DREYER, J. L. E. *History of the Planetary Systems from Thales to Kepler*. Cambridge, 1906.

DÜMMLER, F. *Akademika: Beiträge zur Litteraturgeschichte der sokratischen Schulen*. Giessen, 1889.

DÜRING, I. *Aristotle in the Ancient Biographical Tradition*. Göteborg, 1957.

DÜRING, I. *Aristoteles*. Heidelberg, 1966.

DÜRING, I. and OWEN, G. E. L. (eds.). *Aristotle and Plato in the mid-fourth century*. Göteborg, 1960.

DYBIKOWSKI, J. C. 'Mixed and False Pleasures in the *Philebus*: a Reply', *PQ*, 1970, 244–7.

DYBIKOWSKI, J. C. 'False Pleasures and the *Philebus*', *Phronesis*, 1970, 147–65.

EDELSTEIN, L. *Plato's Seventh Letter*. Leiden, 1966.

EDELSTEIN, L. and KIDD, I. G. *Posidonius*, vol. I, *The Fragments*. Cambridge, 1972.

EDWARDS, P. and PAP, A. (eds.). *A Modern Introduction to Philosophy: Readings from Classical and Contemporary Sources*. New York and London, 1957 (3rd augmented ed. 1973).

ELIADE, M. *Le mythe de l'éternel retour*. Paris, 1949 (English trans., London, 1954).

Encyclopedia of Philosophy, The. 8 vols., New York and London, 1967. Paul Edwards, Editor in Chief.

EVANS, G. 'The Astronomy of Heracleides Ponticus', *CQ*, 1970, 102–11.

EWING, A. C. *The Fundamental Questions of Philosophy*. London, 1951.

Exegesis and Argument. Studies presented to G. Vlastos, edd. E. N. Lee, A. P. D. Mourelatos, R. M. Rorty. Assen, 1973.

FEHLING, D. 'Zwei Untersuchungen zur griechischen Sprachphilosophie: I. Protagoras und die ὀρθοέπεια, II. φύσις und θέσις', *Rheinisches Museum*, 1965, 212–30.

FIELD, G. C. *Plato and his Contemporaries*. London, 1930.

FIELD, G. C. *The Philosophy of Plato*. Oxford, 2nd ed., 1969.

Bibliography

FINDLAY, J. N. *Plato: the Written and Unwritten Doctrines*. London, 1974.

FINLEY, M. I. (ed.). *Slavery in Classical Antiquity*. Cambridge, 1960.

FINLEY, M. I. *Aspects of Antiquity: Discoveries and Controversies*. London, 1968. (Penguin Books, 1972.)

FLEW, A. *An Introduction to Western Philosophy*. London, 1971.

FONDATION HARDT. *Entretiens sur l'antiquité classique*, xviii; *Pseudepigrapha* I. Ed. K. von Fritz. Vandœuvres–Geneva, 1972.

FORRESTER, J. W. 'Arguments an Able Man Could Refute: Parm. 133b–134e', *Phronesis*, 1974, 233–7.

FRAENKEL, E. *Rome and Greek Culture* (Inaugural Lecture). Oxford, 1935.

FRANK, E. *Plato und die sogenannten Pythagoreer: ein Kapitel aus der Geschichte des griechischen Geistes*. Halle, 1923.

FREEMAN, K. *The Pre-Socratic Philosophers: a companion to Diels*, Fragmente der Vorsokratiker. Oxford, 1946.

FRIEDLÄNDER, P. *Plato*, transl. H. Meyerhoff. Vol. I, *An Introduction*, London, 1958 (2nd ed. 1969); vol. II, *The Dialogues, First Period*, 1964 [actually 1965]; vol. III, *The Dialogues, Second and Third Periods*, 1969.

FRITZ, K. VON. 'Die Ideenlehre des Eudoxos von Knidos und ihr Verhältnis zur platonischen Ideenlehre', *Philologus*, 1926–7, 1–26.

FRITZ, K. VON. Article 'Megariker' in *RE Suppl*. v, 707–24 (1931).

FRITZ, K. VON. Article 'Theaitetos' in *RE*, 2. Reihe, x. Halbb., 1934, 1351–72.

FRITZ, K. VON. Article 'Philippos von Opus', *RE*, XXXVIII. Halbb., 1938, 2351–66.

FRITZ, K. VON. *The Theory of the Mixed Constitution in Antiquity*. New York, 1954.

FRITZ, K. VON. 'The Philosophical Passage in the Second Platonic Letter, and the Problem of Plato's "Esoteric" Philosophy', Anton and Kustas, *Essays*, 408–47. (Translation of German article in *Phronesis*, 1966, 117–53.)

FRITZ, K. VON. *Plato in Sizilien und das Problem der Philosophenherrschaft*. Berlin, 1968.

FRITZ, K. VON. *See also* FONDATION HARDT.

FROST, K. T. 'The *Critias* and Minoan Crete', *JHS*, 1913, 189–206.

FRUTIGER, P. *Les Mythes de Platon*. Paris, 1930.

FUJISAWA, N. '῎Εχειν, Μετέχειν, and Idioms of "Paradeigmatism" in Plato's Theory of Forms', *Phronesis*, 1974, 30–58.

FURLEY, D. J. *Two Studies in the Greek Atomists*. Princeton, N.J., 1967.

GADAMER, H.-G. (ed.). *Idee und Zahl: Studien zur platonischen Philosophie*. Heidelberg, 1968. (Abh. Heidelb. Ak., ph.-hist. Kl., 1968, 2.)

GAISER, K. 'Quellenkritische Probleme der indirekten Platonüberlieferung', *Idee u. Zahl* (see GADAMER), 31–84.

GAISER, K. (ed.). *Das Platonbild*. Hildesheim, 1969.

GAISER, K. *Platons ungeschriebene Lehre* (including in appendix '*Testimonia Platonica*'). Stuttgart, 2nd ed. 1968.

GALANOPOULOS, A. G. and BACON, E. *Atlantis, The Truth behind the Legend*. London, 1969.

GALE, R. M. Article 'Propositions, Judgments, Sentences, and Statements' in *Ency. Phil.*, vol. VI, 494–505.

GALLIE, W. B. *Pierce and Pragmatism*. Harmondsworth (Penguin Books), 1952.

GALLOP, D. 'True and False Pleasures', *PQ*, 1960, 331–42.

GAUSS, H. *Philosophischer Handkommentar zu den Dialogen Platons*. 3 vols., 6 parts, Bern, 1952–61.

GIGON, O. *Platon: Bibliographische Einführungen in das Studium der Philosophie* 12. Bern, 1950.

GIGON, O. 'Das Einleitungsgespräch der Gesetze Platons', *Mus. Helv.*, 1954, 201–30.

GIORNINI, R. 'Osservazioni sul testo del *Timeo* ciceroniano', *Riv. di cult. class. e med.*, 1969, 251–4.

GISINGER, F. *Die Erdbeschreibung des Eudoxos von Knidos*. Leipzig, 1921.

GOLDSCHMIDT, V. *Essai sur le Cratyle*. Paris, 1940 (Bibl. des Hautes Études, fasc. 279).

GOMBRICH, E. H. *Art and Illusion*. London, 2nd ed., 1962.

GOMPERZ, T. *Greek Thinkers: A History of Ancient Philosophy*. 4 vols. London, 1901–12. (Vol. I transl. L. Magnus, vols. II–IV by C. G. Berry.) Paperback repr., London, 1964.

GOMPERZ, T. 'Die Composition der Gesetze', *S.-B. Wien, phil.-hist. Klasse*, 1902, no. 11.

GÖRGEMANS, H. *Beiträge zur Interpretation von Platons Nomoi*. Munich, 1960 (*Zetemata* 25).

GOSLING, J. C. B. 'False Pleasures: Philebus 35 c–41 b', *Phronesis*, 1959, 44–53.

GOSLING, J. C. B. *Plato*. London, 1973.

GOSLING, J. C. B. 'Father Kenny on False Pleasures', *Phronesis*, 1961, 41–5.

GOULD, JOHN. *The Development of Plato's Ethics*. Cambridge, 1955.

GRAESER, A. 'Kritische Retraktationen zur esoterischen Platon-Interpretation', *AGP*, 1974, 71–81.

GROTE, G. *Plato and the other Companions of Sokrates*. 3rd ed., 3 vols., London, 1875.

GRUBE, G. M. A. *Plato's Thought*. London, 1935 (and later reprints).

GULLEY, N. 'Plato's Theory of Recollection', *CQ*, 1954, 194–213.

GULLEY, N. *Plato's Theory of Knowledge*. London, 1962.

GUTHRIE, W. K. C. *The Greeks and their Gods*. London, 1950.

GUTHRIE, W. K. C. *Orpheus and Greek Religion*. London, 2nd ed., 1952.

GUTHRIE, W. K. C. 'Plato's Views on the Nature of the Soul', *Entretiens Hardt* III. Vandœuvres–Geneva, 1955, 3–22.

GUTHRIE, W. K. C. *In the Beginning: Some Greek views on the origins of life and the early state of man*. London, 1957.

GUTHRIE, W. K. C. Review of A. Wedberg, *Plato's Philosophy of Mathematics*, *Philosophy*, 1957, 369f.

HAAG, E. *Platons Kratylos: Versuch einer Interpretation*. Stuttgart, 1933.

Bibliography

HACKFORTH, R. 'Plato's Theism', *SPM* 439–47 (orig. 1936).

HACKFORTH, R. 'False Statement in Plato's Sophist', *CQ*, 1945, 56–8.

HACKFORTH, R. 'Platonic Forms in the Theaetetus', *CQ*, 1957, 53–8.

HACKFORTH, R. 'Notes on Plato's *Theaetetus*', *Mnemosyne*, 1957, 128–40.

HACKFORTH, R. 'Plato's Cosmogony', *CQ*, 1959, 17–22.

HAEBLER, C. 'Kosmos: eine etymologische-wortgeschichtliche Untersuchung', *Archiv für Begriffsgeschichte*, 1967, 101–18.

HAGER, F. P. 'Zur philosophischen Problematik der sogennanten ungeschriebenen Lehre', *Studia Philosophica*, 1964, 90–117.

HAGER, F. P. *Der Geist und das Eine*. Bern–Stuttgart, 1970.

HALL, J. 'Plato's Legal Philosophy', *Indiana Law Journal*, 1956, 171–206.

HAMBRUCH, E. *Logische Regeln der platonischen Schule in der aristotelischen Topik*. Berlin, 1904.

HAMLYN, D. W. 'The Communion of Forms and the Development of Plato's Logic', *PQ*, 1955, 289–302.

HAMMER-JENSEN, I. 'Demokritos und Platon', *AGP*, 1910, 92–105 and 211–29.

HARDIE, W. F. R. *A Study in Plato*. Oxford, 1936.

HARVEY, F. D. 'Two Kinds of Equality', *Classica et Mediaevalia*, 1965, 101–46.

HEATH, B. 'On Plato's Cratylus', *J. of Philol.*, 1888, 192–218.

HEATH, T. L. *Aristarchus of Samos, the Ancient Copernicus: a history of Greek astronomy to Aristarchus together with Aristarchus's treatise on the sizes and distances of the sun and moon*. Oxford, 1913.

HEATH, T. L. *Mathematics in Aristotle*. Oxford, 1949.

HEINIMANN, F. *Nomos und Physis: Herkunft und Bedeutung einer Antithese im griechischen Denken des 5. Jahrhunderts*. Basel, 1945 (repr. 1965).

HEINZE, R. *Xenocrates* (including fragments). Leipzig, 1892 (repr. 1965).

HEISENBERG, W. 'Platons Vorstellungen von den kleinsten Bausteinen der Materie und die Elementarteilchen der modernen Physik', *Im Umkreis der Kunst*, Wiesbaden, 1954, 137–40.

HEISENBERG, W. *The Physicist's Conception of Nature*. Eng. tr. London, 1958 (German original 1955).

HERMANN, A. *Untersuchungen zu Platons Auffassung von der Hedone*. Göttingen, 1972.

HERMANN, K. F. *Geschichte und System der platonischen Philosophie*. Heidelberg, 1839 (repr. 1976).

HERTER, H. 'Die Bewegung der Materie bei Platon'. *Rh. Mus.* 1957, 327–47.

HICKEN, W. F. 'Knowledge and Forms in Plato's "Theaetetus"', *SPM* 185–94 (orig. 1957).

HICKEN, W. F. 'The Character and Provenance of Socrates's "Dream" in the Theaetetus', *Phronesis*, 1958, 126–45.

HILPINEN, R. 'Knowing that one Knows and the Classical Definition of Knowledge', *Synthèse*, 1970, 109–32.

HIRST, R. J. Article 'Perception' in *Ency. Phil.* VI, 79–86.

HIRZEL, R. *Der Dialog.* 2 vols., Leipzig, 1895.

HOFFMANN, E. 'Der gegenwärtige Stand der Platonforschung', Appendix to Zeller, II. 1, pp. 1051–1105.

HORN, F. *Platonstudien.* Vienna, 1893.

HOSPERS, J. *An Introduction to Philosophical Analysis.* London, 1956.

HOWALD, E. 'Eikos Logos', *Hermes*, 1922, 63–79.

HUBER, G. 'Platons dialektische Ideenlehre nach dem zweiten Teil des Parmenides'. Basel diss., 1951.

HULTSCH, F. Article 'Eudoxos (8)' in *RE* VI (1909), 930–50.

JACKSON, H. 'Plato's Later Theory of Ideas', series of articles in *Journ. of Philol.* 1882–8.

JACKSON, H. 'Plato's Cratylus', *Praelections Delivered before the Senate of the University of Cambridge.* Cambridge, 1906, 3–26.

JAEGER, W. *Aristotle: Fundamentals of the History of his Development.* Eng. tr. 1934, 2nd ed. 1948 (paperback 1962).

JOHANSEN, K. F. 'The One and the Many: remarks concerning Plato's Parmenides and the Method of Collection and Division', *Class. et Med.*, 1957, 1–35.

JONES, R. M. 'The Ideas as the Thoughts of God', *CP*, 1926, 317–26.

JOSEPH, H. W. B. *Knowledge and the Good in Plato's Republic.* Oxford, 1948.

KAHN, C. H. 'Plato's Cretan City' (review article on Morrow's book), *JHI*, 1961, 418–24.

KAHN, C. H. 'The Greek Verb "To Be" and the Concept of Being', *Foundations of Language*, 1966, 245–65.

KAHN, C. H. 'Language and Ontology in the *Cratylus*', *Exegesis (q.v.)*, 152–76 (1973).

KAMLAH, W. *Platons Selbstkritik im Sophistes.* Munich, 1963.

KAMLAH, W. 'Zu Platons Selbstkritik im Sophistes', *Hermes*, 1966, 243–5.

KANT, I. *Critique of Pure Reason.* Eng. tr. by N. Kemp Smith, London, 1929.

KARPP, H. *Untersuchungen zur Philosophie des Eudoxos von Knidos.* Würzburg–Aumühle, 1933.

KENNY, A. 'False Pleasures in the Philebus: a Reply to Mr. Gosling', *Phronesis*, 1960, 45–52.

KERFERD, G. B. 'Plato's Noble Art of Sophistry', *CQ*, 1954, 84–90.

KERN, O. *Orphicorum Fragmenta.* Berlin, 1922.

KERSCHENSTEINER, J. *Kosmos: quellenkritische Untersuchungen zu den Vorsokratikern.* Munich, 1962.

KEYT, D. 'Aristotle on Plato's Receptacle', *AJP*, 1961, 290–300.

KEYT, D. 'Plato's Paradox that the Immutable is Unknowable', *PQ*, 1969, 1–14.

KING, H. R. 'Aristotle without Prime Matter', *JHI*, 1956, 370–90.

KING-FARLOW, J. and ROTHSTEIN, J. M. 'Paradigm Cases and the Injustice to Thrasymachus', *PQ*, 1964, 15–22.

KIRK, G. S. 'The Problem of Cratylus', *AJP*, 1951, 225–53.

KIRK, G. S. *Heraclitus, the Cosmic Fragments.* Cambridge, 1954.

Bibliography

KLIBANSKY, R. *The Continuity of the Platonic Tradition*. London, n.d. (Preface dated 1950.)

KLIEM. Article 'Menaichmos (3)' in *RE*, XXIX. Halbb., 1931, 700f.

KNEALE, W. and M. *The Development of Logic*. Oxford, 1962.

KOSTER, W. J. W. *Le Mythe de Platon, de Zarathoustra et des Chaldéens: étude critique sur les relations intellectuelles entre Platon et l'Orient*. Leiden, 1951.

KOUTSOUYANNOPOULOU, D. 'Τίς ὁ 'Αριστοτέλης τοῦ Πλατωνικοῦ "Παρμενίδου"; ', Πλάτων, 1966, 205–6.

KRÄMER, H. J. *Arete bei Platon und Aristoteles: zum Wesen und zur Geschichte der platonischen Ontologie*. Abh. Heidelberger Akad., ph.-hist. Kl., 1959.

KRÄMER, H. J. 'Retraktationen zum Problem des esoterischen Platon', *Mus. Helv.* 1964, 137–67.

KRÄMER, H. J. *Der Ursprung der Geistesmetaphysik: Untersuchungen zur Geschichte des Platonismus zwischen Platon und Plotin*. Amsterdam, 1964 (repr. 1967).

KRÄMER, H. J. 'Die grundsätzlichen Fragen der indirekten Platonüberlieferung', *Idee u. Zahl* (*see* GADAMER), 106–50.

KRÄMER, H. J. 'Επέκεινα τῆς οὐσίας, *AGP*, 1969, 1–30.

KRÄMER, H. J. *Platonismus und hellenistische Philosophie*. Berlin and New York, 1971.

KRANZ, W. 'Kosmos als philosophischer Begriff frühgriechischer Zeit', *Philologus*, 1938–9, 430–48.

KRANZ, W. 'Kosmos', *Archiv für Begriffsgeschichte*, 1958, 3–282.

KRETZMANN, N. 'Plato on the Correctness of Names', *APQ*, 1971, 126–38.

KRIEG, M. *Die Überarbeitung der platonischen 'Gesetze' durch Philippos von Opus*. Freiburg-im-Breisgau, 1896.

KUCHARSKI, P. 'La "théorie des Idées" selon le "Phédon" se maintient-elle dans les derniers dialogues?', *Rev. Philosophique*, 1969, 211–29.

KÜHN, H. Review of John Gould, *The Development of Plato's Ethics*, *Gnomon*, 1956, 336–40.

LACEY, A. R. 'The Mathematical Passage in the Epinomis', *Phronesis*, 1956, 81–104.

LANG, P. *De Speusippi Academici Scriptis*. Bonn, 1911 (repr. Hildesheim, 1965).

LASSERRE, F. *Die Fragmente des Eudoxos von Knidos* (ed. with translation and commentary). Berlin, 1966.

LEE, E. N. 'Hoist with His Own Petard: Ironic and Comic Elements in Plato's Critique of Protagoras', *Exegesis* (*q.v.*), 255–61.

LEISEGANG, H. Article 'Platon' in *RE*, 2. Reihe, XI. Halbb., 1941, 2342–537.

LESKY, A. *Kosmos*. Vienna, 1963 (inaugural lecture).

LESKY, A. *A History of Greek Literature*. Transl. from 2nd German ed. 1963 by Willis and de Heer, London, 1966.

LEVINSON, R. B. *In Defense of Plato*. Cambridge, Mass., 1953.

LEVINSON, R. B. 'Language and the Cratylus: four questions', *Rev. of Metaphysics*, 1957–8, 28–41.

LEVISON, M., MORTON, A. Q. and WINSPEAR, A. D. 'The Seventh Letter of Plato', *Mind*, 1968, 309–25.

LEWIS, F. A. 'Foul Play in Plato's Aviary: *Theaetetus* 195 B ff.', *Exegesis* (*q.v.*), 262–84.

LEYDEN, W. VON. 'Time, Number and Eternity in Plato and Aristotle', *PQ*, 1964, 35–52.

LLAÑOO, A. *Los Viejos Sofistas y el Humanismo Griego.* Buenos Aires, 1969.

LLOYD, G. E. R. *Polarity and Analogy: two types of argumentation in early Greek thought.* Cambridge, 1966.

LLOYD, G. E. R. 'Plato as a Natural Scientist', *JHS*, 1968, 78–92.

LLOYD, G. E. R. *Early Greek Science: Thales to Aristotle.* London, 1970

LONIE, I. M. 'The ἄναρμοι ὄγκοι of Heraclides of Pontus', *Phronesis*, 1964, 156–64.

LONIE, I. M. 'Medical Theory in Heraclides of Pontus', *Mnemosyne*, 1965, 126–43.

LORENZ, K. and MITTELSTRASS, J. 'Theaitetos fliegt: Zur Theorie wahrer und falscher Sätze bei Platon', *AGP*, 1966, 113–52.

LORENZ, K. and MITTELSTRASS, J. 'On Rational Philosophy of Language: the programme in Plato's *Cratylus* reconsidered', *Mind*, 1967, 1–20.

LOUZECKY, D. J. *See* TELOH, H.

LUCE, J. V. 'The Date of the Cratylus', *AJP*, 1964, 136–52.

LUCE, J. V. 'The Theory of Ideas in the Cratylus', *Phronesis*, 1965, 21–36.

LUCE, J. V. 'Plato on Truth and Falsity in Names', *CQ*, 1969, 223–32.

LUCE, J. V. *The End of Atlantis: New Light on an Old Legend.* London, 1969.

LURIA, S. 'Die Infinitesimaltheorie der antiken Atomisten', *Quellen und Studien zur Geschichte der Mathematik*, Abt. B, Band 2, Heft 2, 1932, 106–85.

McLAUGHLIN, A. 'A Note on False Pleasures in the *Philebus*', *PQ*, 1969, 57–61.

MAIER, H. *Die Syllogistik des Aristoteles.* I. und II. Teile, Tübingen, 1896 and 1900.

MALCOLM, J. 'Plato's Analysis of Τὸ ὄν and Τὸ μὴ ὄν in the Sophist', *Phronesis*, 1967, 130–46.

MANASSE, E. M. 'Platonliteratur', I, II and III, Philosophische Rundschau, Beihefte 1, 2, 7, Tübingen, 1957, 1961 and 1976. (Critical reviews of the literature in German, English and French respectively.)

MANASSE, E. M. *Platons Sophistes und Politikos: das Problem der Wahrheit.* Berlin, 937.

MANNEBACH, E. *Aristippi et Cyrenaicorum Fragmenta.* Leiden, 1961.

MEKLER, S. (ed.). *Academicorum philosophorum index Herculanensis.* Berlin, 1902.

MERLAN, P. *From Platonism to Neoplatonism.* The Hague, 1953.

MERLAN, P. 'Zur Biographie des Speusippos', *Philologus*, 1959, 198–214.

MERLAN, P. *Studies in Epicurus and Aristotle.* Wiesbaden, 1960.

MERLAN, P. 'Das Problem der Erasten'. *Horizons of a Philosopher: essays in honor of David Baumgardt*, Leiden, 1963, 297–314.

MERLAN, P. 'Aristotle, *Met.* A 6, 987b 20–25 and Plotinus, *Enn.* V 4, 2, 8–9', *Phronesis*, 1964, 45–7.

MILL, J. S. *A System of Logic* (orig. 1843). London, 1892.

MITTELSTRASS, J. Review of Gaiser's *Platons ungeschriebene Lehre*, *Philos. Rundschau*, 1966, 27–40.

Bibliography

Monumenta Asiae Minoris Antiqua, vol. IV, ed. Buckler, Calder and Guthrie. Manchester, 1933.

MOORE, G. E. 'The Nature of Judgment', *Mind*, 1899, 176–93.

MOORE, G. E. *Principia Ethica*. Cambridge, 1903.

MORAVCSIK, J. M. E. 'Συμπλοκὴ εἰδῶν and the Genesis of λόγος', *AGP*, 1960, 117–29.

MORAVCSIK, J. M. E. 'Being and Meaning in the *Sophist*', *Acta Philos. Fennica*, 1962, 23–78.

MOREAU, P. Article 'Quinta Essentia' in *RE*, XLVII. Halbb. 1171–1263 (1963).

MOREAU, J. 'The Platonic Idea and its Threefold Function: a Synthesis', *IPQ*, 1969, 477–517.

MOREAU, J. 'L'essor de l'astronomie scientifique chez les grecs', *Revue de l'histoire des sciences* 29 (1976), 193–312.

MORROW, G. R. *Plato's Law of Slavery in Relation to Greek Law*. Urbana, 1939.

MORROW, G. R. *Plato's Cretan City: a historical interpretation of the Laws*. Princeton, N.J., 1960.

MORROW, G. R. 'Aristotle's Comments on Plato's Laws', *A. and P. in Mid-Fourth Cent.* (see DÜRING), 145–62.

MORROW, G. R. *Proclus: a Commentary on the First Book of Euclid's Elements*. Princeton, 1970.

MORTLEY, R. J. 'Plato's Choice of the Sphere', *REG*, 1969, 342–5.

MORTLEY, R. J. 'The Bond of the Cosmos: a significant metaphor (*Tim.* 31cff.)', *Hermes*, 1969, 372f.

MORTLEY, R. J. 'Plato and the Sophistic Heritage of Protagoras', *Eranos*, 1969, 24–32.

MORTON, A. Q. and WINSPEAR, A. D. *It's Greek to the Computer*. Montreal, 1971.

MORTON, A. Q. *See* LEVISON, M.

NAKHNIKIAN, G. 'Plato's Theory of Sensation', *Rev. of Metaphysics*, 1955–6, 129–48 and 306–27.

NATORP, P. Article 'Hermogenes (21)' in *RE*, VIII, 1913, 865.

NELSON, E. J. 'The Category of Substance', in *Philosophy for the Future*, ed. Sellars, McGill and Farber. New York, 1949, 106–24.

NEUGEBAUER, O. 'On the Allegedly Heliocentric Theory of Venus by Heraclides Ponticus', *AJP*, 1972, 600f.

NEWELL, R. W. *The Concept of Philosophy*. London, 1967.

NEWIGER, H.-J. *Untersuchungen zu Gorgias' Schrift Über das Nichtseiende*. Berlin–New York, 1973.

NEWTON, Isaac. *Mathematic Principles of Natural Philosophy*, 2 vols., transl. A. Motte, ed. F. Cajori. Berkeley, 1946.

NICOL, A. T. 'Indivisible Lines', *CQ*, 1936, 120–6.

NILSSON, M. P. *Greek Popular Religion*. New York, 1940.

O'BRIEN, M. 'Plato and the "Good Conscience": *Laws* 863e5–64b7', *TAPA*, 1957, 81–7.

OSCANYAN, F. 'On Six Definitions of the Sophist: *Sophist* 221 C–231 E', *Philos. Forum*, 1972/3, 241–59.

OWEN, G. E. L. 'The Place of the *Timaeus* in Plato's Dialogues', *SPM* 313–38 (orig. 1953).

OWEN, G. E. L. 'Aristotle on the Snares of Ontology' in Bambrough, *New Essays* (*q.v.*), 69–96.

OWEN, G. E. L. 'Notes on Ryle's Plato', *Ryle*, 341–72.

OWEN, G. E. L. 'Plato and Parmenides on the Timeless Present', *Monist*, 1966, 317–40.

OWEN, G. E. L. 'Plato on Not-Being', *Plato* I (*see* VLASTOS), 223–67.

OWEN, G. E. L. 'Plato on the Undepictable', *Exegesis* (*q.v.*), 349–61.

OWEN, G. E. L. *See* DÜRING, I.

PANAGIOTOU, S. 'Vlastos on *Parm.* 132a1–b2: Some of his Text and Logic', *PQ*, 1971, 255–9.

PANNEKOEK, A. *The Astronomical System of Herakleides*. Amsterdam, 1952. (Circular no. 4 of the Astronomical Inst. of the Univ. of Amsterdam.)

PARENTE, M. ISNARDI. 'Per l'interpretazione dell'excursus filosofico della vii epistola platonica', *Parola del Passato*, 1964, 241–90.

PARENTE, M. ISNARDI. 'La vii epistola e Platone esoterico', *RCSF*, 1969, 416–31.

PAVLU, J. 'Der pseudoplatonische Dialog *Theages*', *Wiener Studien*, 1909, 13–37.

PECK, A. L. 'Plato and the μέγιστα γένη of the Sophist: a Reinterpretation', *CQ*, 1952, 32–56.

PECK, A. L. 'Plato's *Sophist*: the συμπλοκή τῶν εἰδῶν', *Phronesis*, 1962, 46–66.

PECK, A. L. 'Plato versus Parmenides', *PR*, 1962, 159–84.

PENNER, T. 'False Anticipatory Pleasures: Philebus 36a3–41a6', *Phronesis*, 1970, 166–78.

PETERSON, S. 'A Reasonable Self-Predication Premise for the Third Man Argument', *PR*, 1973, 441–50.

PFEIFFER, R. *A History of Classical Scholarship*, vol. I. Oxford, 1968.

PFISTER, F. 'Die Prooimia der platonischen Gesetze', *Annuaire de phil. et d'hist. orientales et slaves* 6 (Mélanges Émile Boisacq, II, 1938), 173–9.

PHILIP, J. A. *Pythagoras and Early Pythagoreanism*. Toronto, 1967.

Philosophy for the Future. See SELLARS, R. W.

PINES, S. 'A New Fragment of Xenocrates and its Implications', *Transactions of the American Philosophical Society*, vol. 51, Part 2 (1961), 3–34.

PINI, F. (ed.). *M. T. Ciceronis Timaeus*. Milan, 1965.

PLATON, N. *Zakros*. New York, 1971.

POHLE, W. 'The Mathematical Foundations of Plato's Atomic Physics', *Isis*, 1971, 36–46.

POPPER, K. R. *The Logic of Scientific Discovery*. Eng. transl. London, 1959, 8th impression 1975.

POPPER, K. R. *The Open Society and its Enemies*, vol. I, *The Spell of Plato*. 5th ed., London, 1966.

Bibliography

POPPER, K. R. Article 'Plato' in *International Encyclopedia of the Social Sciences*, London and New York, 1968.

POPPER, K. R. *Conjectures and Refutations.* 3rd ed., London, 1969.

POPPER, K. R. 'Scientific Reduction and the Essential Incompleteness of All Science', *Studies in the Philosophy of Biology*, ed. F. J. Ayala and T. Dobzhansky. London, 1974.

POPPER, K. R. and ECCLES, J. C. *The Self and its Brain.* Springer International, 1977.

POST, L. A. 'The Seventh and Eighth Platonic Epistles', *CQ*, 1930, 113–15.

PUHVEL, J. 'The Origins of Greek *Kosmos* and Latin *Mundus*', *AJP*, 1976, 154 ff.

RAEDER, H. *Platons philosophische Entwicklung.* Leipzig, 1905.

REES, D. A. (and STRANG, C.). 'Symposium: Plato and the "Third Man"', *Arist. Soc. Suppl. Vol.* 37 (1963), 165–76. (Strang's contribution repr. in *Plato* 1, ed. Vlastos, 1971.)

REICHE, H. A. T. *Empedocles' Mixture, Eudoxan Astronomy, and Aristotle's Connate Pneuma.* Amsterdam, 1960.

REITZENSTEIN, R. and SCHAEDER, H. H. *Studien zum antiken Synkretismus aus Iran und Griechenland.* Leipzig and Berlin, 1926.

REVERDIN, O. *La religion de la cité platonicienne.* Paris, 1945.

RICH, A. 'The Platonic Ideas as Thoughts of God', *Mnemosyne*, 1954, 123–33.

RICHARDSON, M. 'True and False Names in the "Cratylus"', *Phronesis*, 1976, 135–45.

RIDGEWAY, W. 'What led Pythagoras to the Doctrine that the world was built of numbers?', *CR*, 1896, 92–5.

RIST, J. M. 'Plotinus and the Daimonion of Socrates', *Phoenix*, 1963, 13–24.

RIST, J. M. 'The Immanence and Transcendence of the Platonic Form', *Philologus*, 1964, 219–32.

RIST, J. M. 'Knowledge and Value in Plato', *Phoenix*, 1967, 283–95.

RIST, J. M. 'Parmenides and Plato's *Parmenides*', *CQ*, 1970, 221–9.

RITTER, C. *Neue Untersuchungen über Platon.* Munich, 1910 (repr. 1976).

RITTER, C. *Platon, sein Leben, seine Schriften, seine Lehre.* 2 vols., Munich, 1910 and 1920 (repr. 1976).

RITTER, C. *The Essence of Plato's Philosophy* (transl. of 1931 German ed.). London, 1933.

ROBIN, L. *La théorie platonicienne des Idées et des Nombres d'après Aristote.* Paris, 1908.

ROBINSON, R. *Plato's Earlier Dialectic.* Oxford, 2nd ed. 1953.

ROBINSON, R. 'A Criticism of Plato's Cratylus', *Essays*, 118–38 (orig. 1956).

ROBINSON, R. 'The Theory of Names in Plato's *Cratylus*', *Essays*, 100–17 (orig. 1955).

ROBINSON, R. *Essays in Greek Philosophy.* Oxford, 1969.

ROBINSON, T. M. 'Demiurge and World Soul in Plato's *Politicus*', *AJP*, 1967, 57–66.

ROBINSON, T. M. 'The Argument for Immortality in Plato's *Phaedrus*', ANTON and KUSTAS, *Essays* (*q.v.*), 345–53.

RODIER, G. *Études de philosophie grecque*. Paris, 1926.

ROHDE, E. *Psyche: the cult of souls and belief in immortality among the Greeks*, transl. W. B. Hills, London, 1925. (Paperback, 2 vols., New York, 1966.)

RORTY, A. O. 'A Speculative Note on some Dramatic Elements in the *Theaetetus*', *Phronesis*, 1972, 227–38.

ROSE, H. J. *A Handbook of Greek Mythology*. London, 1928.

ROSEN, S. *The Symposium of Plato*. Yale U.P., 1968.

ROSENMEYER, T. G. 'Platonic Scholarship, 1945–55', *Classical Weekly*, 1957, 173–82, 185–96, 197–201 and 209–11.

ROSS, W. D. *Aristotle's Metaphysics*, a revised text with introd. and Commentary. 2 vols., Oxford, 1924.

ROSS, W. D. *Plato's Theory of Ideas*. Oxford, 1951.

ROSS, W. D. 'The Date of Plato's Cratylus', *Revue Internationale de Philosophie*, 1955, 187–96.

ROSS, W. D. *Aristotle De Anima*, ed. with introduction and commentary. Oxford, 1961.

ROTH, M. D. 'An Examination of Plato's Cratylus.' Unpublished doctoral dissertation submitted to the University of Illinois, 1969.

RUNCIMAN, W. G. 'Plato's *Parmenides*', *SPM*, 149–84 (orig. 1959).

RUNCIMAN, W. G. *Plato's Later Epistemology*. Cambridge, 1962.

RUSSELL, B. A. W. and WHITEHEAD, A. N. *Principia Mathematica*. 3 vols., Cambridge, 1910–13, 2nd ed. 1927 and later reprints.

RYLE, G. 'Plato's *Parmenides*', *SPM* 97–147 (orig. 1939).

RYLE, G. *The Concept of Mind*. London, 1949.

RYLE, G. *Dilemmas*. Cambridge, 1954.

RYLE, G. *Plato's Progress*. Cambridge, 1966.

Ryle. See WOOD, O. P.

SACHS, E. *De Theaeteto Atheniensi mathematico*. Berlin, 1914.

SAMBURSKY, S. *The Physical World of the Greeks*. London, 1956.

SAUNDERS, T. J. 'Two Passages in Plato's *Laws* (794a–c and 848a)', *CR*, 1961, 101f.

SAUNDERS, T. J. 'The Structure of the Soul and the State in Plato's Laws', *Eranos*, 1962, 37–55.

SAUNDERS, T. J. Review of Ryle's *Plato's Progress* in *Rev. Belge de Philol. et d'Hist.*, 1967, 494–7.

SAUNDERS, T. J. 'The Alleged Double Version in the Sixth Book of Plato's *Laws*', *CQ*, 1970, 232–6.

SAUNDERS, T. J. 'Penology and Eschatology in Plato's *Timaeus* and *Laws*', *CQ*, 1973, 232–44.

SAUNDERS, T. J. *Bibliography on Plato's Laws 1920–1970, with additional citations through May 1976*. New York, 1976. (U.K. agents Aris and Phillips.)

SAYRE, K. M. *Plato's Analytic Method*. Chicago, 1969.

SCHADEWALDT, W. 'Platon und Kratylos: ein Hinweis', *Philomathes* (essays in memory of Merlan), ed. Palmer and Hamerton-Kelly, The Hague, 1971, 3–11.

SCHIAPARELLI, G. *I precursori di Copernico nell'antichità*, in his *Scritti*, vol. I, 361–458. (Orig. 1873.)

SCHIAPARELLI, G. 'Le sfere omocentriche di Eudosso, di Callippo e di Aristotele', in his *Scritti*, vol. II, 3–112. (Orig. 1877.)

SCHIAPARELLI, G. 'Origine del sistema planetario eliocentrico presso i Greci', in his *Scritti*, vol. II, 113–77. (Orig. 1898.)

SCHIAPARELLI, G. *Scritti sulla storia della astronomia antica*, 3 vols., Bologna, 1925–7.

SCHIPPER, E. W. 'The Meaning of Existence in Plato's Sophist', *Phronesis*, 1964, 38–44.

SCHOFIELD, M. 'Who were the δυσχερεῖς in Plato, *Philebus* 44a ff.?', *Mus. Helv.*, 1971, 2–20.

SCHOFIELD, M. 'A Neglected Regress Argument in the *Parmenides*', *CQ*, 1973, 29–44.

SCHOFIELD, M. 'Eudoxus in the "Parmenides"', *Mus. Helv.*, 1973, 1–19.

SCHOFIELD, M. 'Plato on Unity and Sameness', *CQ*, 1974, 33–45.

SCHOFIELD, M. 'The Antinomies of Plato's *Parmenides*', *CQ*, 1977, 65–84.

SCHRÖDINGER, E. *Nature and the Greeks*. Cambridge, 1954.

SCHUHL, P. M. 'Platon: quinze années d'études platoniciennes', *Actes du Congrès Budé*, Paris, 1954.

SCIACCA, M. F. *Platone*. 2 vols., Milan, 1967.

SELLARS, R. W., ed. with V. J. McGill and M. Farber. *Philosophy for the Future: the quest for modern materialism*. New York, 1949.

SHINER, R. A. *Knowledge and Reality in Plato's 'Philebus'*. Assen, 1974.

SHOEMAKER, S. Article 'Memory' in *Ency. Phil.* v, 265–74.

SHOREY, P. *The Unity of Plato's Thought*. Chicago, 1903.

SHOREY, P. *What Plato Said*. Chicago, 1933.

SILVERTHORNE, M. J. 'Militarism in the *Laws*? (*Laws* 942a5–943a3)', *Symbolae Osloenses*, fasc. 49 (1973), 29–38.

SINGER, C. *A Short History of Scientific Ideas*. Oxford, 1959.

SKEMP, J. B. *The Theory of Motion in Plato's Later Dialogues*. Cambridge, 1942.

SKEMP, J. B. '῞Υλη and ὑποδοχή', *Arist. and Plato in Mid-Fourth Cent.* (*see under* DÜRING), 213–35.

SKEMP, J. B. *The Theory of Motion in Plato's Later Dialogues*. Cambridge, 2nd ed., 1967.

SKEMP, J. B. *Plato*. Oxford, 1976. (Greece and Rome: new surveys in the classics no. 10.)

SOLMSEN, F. *Plato's Theology*. Ithaca, N.Y., 1942.

SOLMSEN, F. *Aristotle's System of the Physical World*. Cornell U.P., Ithaca, N.Y., 1960.

SOLMSEN, F. Review of Edelstein, *Plato's Seventh Letter*, *Gnomon*, 1969, 29–34.

SOLMSEN, F. 'Beyond the Heavens', *Mus. Helv.*, 1976, 24–32.

SOUILHÉ, J. *Étude sur le terme* δύναμις *dans les dialogues de Platon*. Paris, 1919.

SPEISER, A. *Ein Parmenides-Kommentar: Studien zur platonischen Dialektik.* Leipzig, 1937.

SPOERRI, W. 'Encore Platon et l'Orient', *Rev. de Philol.*, 1957, 209–33.

SPRAGUE, R. K. *Plato's Philosopher-King: a study of the theoretical background.* Univ. of S. Carolina Press, 1976

SPRUTE, J. 'Über den Erkenntnisbegriff in Platons *Theaitet*', *Phronesis*, 1968, 47–67.

STEBBING, L. S. *A Modern Introduction to Logic.* 2nd ed., London, 1933.

STENZEL, J. *Zahl und Gestalt bei Platon und Aristoteles.* Leipzig–Berlin, 1924.

STENZEL, J. Article 'Sokrates (Philosoph)' in *RE*, 2. Reihe, v. Halbb., 1927, 811–90.

STENZEL, J. Article 'Speusippos' in *RE*, 2. Reihe, vi. Halbb., 1929, 1636–69.

STENZEL, J. *Plato's Method of Dialectic*, transl. and ed. D. J. Allan. Oxford, 1940.

STENZEL, J. *Kleine Schriften zur griechischen Philosophie.* Darmstadt, 1957.

STEWART, M. A. Review of T. M. Robinson's *Plato's Psychology*, *PQ*, 1971, 172f.

STOELZEL, E. *Die Behandlung des Erkenntnisproblems bei Platon.* Halle, 1908.

STRANG, C. 'Plato and the Third Man', *Plato* (ed. Vlastos, *q.v.*), 184–200. (Orig. 1963.) (*See* REES, D. A.)

STRAWSON, P. F. *Introduction to Logical Theory.* London, 1952.

STRIKER, G. *Peras und Apeiron: das Problem der Formen in Platons Philosophie.* Göttingen, 1970.

TARÁN, L. Review of Novotný's *Epinomis*, *AJP*, 1962, 315–17.

TARÁN, L. 'The Creation Myth in Plato's *Timaeus*', *Essays*, ed. ANTON and KUSTAS (*q.v.*), 372–407.

TARÁN, L. *Academica: Plato, Philip of Opus, and the pseudo-Platonic Epinomis.* Philadelphia, 1975.

TARRANT, D. 'Plato's Use of Extended *Oratio Obliqua*', *CQ*, 1955, 222–4.

TARRANT, H. A. S. 'Speusippus' Ontological Classification', *Phronesis*, 1974, 130–45.

TATE, J. 'On Plato: *Laws* x 899 cd', *CQ*, 1936, 48–54.

TATE, J. Review of Skemp's *Plato's 'Statesman'*, in *CR*, 1954, 115–17.

TAYLOR, A. E. *Plato, the Man and his Work.* London, 1926 (paperback reprint 1960).

TAYLOR, A. E. *A Commentary on Plato's Timaeus*, Oxford, 1928.

TAYLOR, A. E. 'Plato and the Authorship of the *Epinomis*', *Proc. Brit. Acad.*, 1929.

TELOH, H. and LOUZECKY, D. J. 'Plato's Third Man Argument', *Phronesis*, 1972, 80–94.

THOMPSON, W. H. 'Introductory Remarks on the Philebus', *J. of Philol.*, 1882, 1–22.

TIGERSTEDT, E. N. *The Legend of Sparta in Classical Antiquity.* 2 vols., Stockholm, 1965 and 1974.

TIGERSTEDT, E. N. *Interpreting Plato.* Stockholm, 1977.

TIGNER, S. 'The "Exquisite" Argument at *Tht.* 171A', *Mnemosyne*, 1971, 366–9.

TOEPLITZ, O. 'Die mathematische Epinomisstelle', *Quellen und Studien zur Geschichte der Mathematik*, ser. B (*Studien*), vol. II (1933), 336–46.

Bibliography

TOOMER, G. J. Review of Lasserre's *Die Fragmente des Eudoxos*, in *Gnomon*, 1968, 334–7.

TOULMIN, S. and GOODFIELD, J. *The Architecture of Matter*. London, 1962. (Also published in paperback by Penguin Books, Harmondsworth.)

TREVASKIS, J. R. 'The Sophistry of Noble Lineage (*Sophist* 230a5–232b9', *Phronesis* I (1955), 36–49.

TREVASKIS, J. R. 'Classification in the *Philebus*', *Phronesis*, 1960, 39–44.

UNTERSTEINER, M. *The Sophists*, transl. K. Freeman. London, 1957.

VERSENYI, L. 'The Cretan Plato', *Rev. of Metaph.* 15 (1961–2), 67–80.

VIDAL-NAQUET, P. 'Athènes et Atlantide: structure et signification d'un mythe platonicien', *REG*, 1964, 420–44.

VLASTOS, G. 'The Disorderly Motion in the *Timaeus*', *SPM* 379–400 (orig. 1939).

VLASTOS, G. 'The Third Man Argument in the *Parmenides*', *SPM* 231–64 (orig. 1954).

VLASTOS, G. 'Creation in the *Timaeus*: Is it a Fiction?', *SPM* 401–20 (orig. 1964).

VLASTOS, G. 'Parmenides' Third Man Argument (*Parm.* 132A1–B2): Text and Logic', *PQ*, 1969, 289–301.

VLASTOS, G. (ed.). *Plato: a Collection of Critical Essays*. 2 vols., New York, 1971.

VLASTOS, G. *Platonic Studies*. Princeton, 1973.

VLASTOS, G. 'Plato's Testimony concerning Zeno of Elea', *JHS*, 1975, 136–62.

VLASTOS, G. *Plato's Universe*. Oxford, 1975.

VOGEL, C. J. DE. Review of Philips' *Pythagoras and Early Pythagoreanism*, in *JHS*, 1969, 163–5.

VOGEL, C. J. DE. *Greek Philosophy: a Collection of Texts with Notes and Explanations*. Vol. I, *Thales to Plato*. Leiden, 3rd ed. 1963.

VOGEL, C. J. DE. *Philosophia, Part I: Studies in Greek Philosophy*. Assen, 1970.

VOSS, O. *De Heraclidis Pontici vita et scriptis*. Rostock, 1896.

WAERDEN, B. L. VAN DER. 'Die Astronomie des Heracleides von Pontos', *Berichte der Sächs. Ak.* 96, Leipzig, 1944, 47–56.

WAERDEN, B. L. VAN DER. *Die Astronomie der Pythagoreer*. Amsterdam, 1951.

WAHL, J. *Étude sur le Parménide de Platon*. Paris, 1926.

WAKE, W. C. 'Sentence-Length Distributions of Greek Authors', *Journal of R. Statistical Soc.* Series A, 1957, 331–46.

WALKER, M. G. 'The One and the Many in Plato's *Parmenides*', *PR*, 1938, 488–516.

WASZINK, J. H. *Timaeus a Calcidio translatus commentarioque instructus. In societatem operis coniuncto P. J.* JENSEN *edidit*. (*Plato Latinus*, ed. Klibansky, IV.) London, 1962, 2nd ed., 1975.

WATSON, G. *Plato's Unwritten Teaching*. Dublin, 1973 (actually 1975).

WEDBERG, A. *Plato's Philosophy of Mathematics*. Stockholm, 1955.

WEHRLI, F. Article 'Herakleides der Pontiker', in *RE Suppl.* XI, 1968.

WEHRLI, F. *Eudemos von Rhodos* (Die Schule des Aristoteles, Texte und Kommentar VIII). 2nd ed., Basel, 1969.

WEHRLI, F. *Herakleides Pontikos* (Die Schule des Aristoteles, Texte und Kommentar VII). 2nd ed., Basel, 1969.

WEIL, R. *L'Archéologie de Platon*. Paris, 1959.

WEINGARTNER, R. H. *The Unity of the Platonic Dialogue: Cratylus, Protagoras, Parmenides*. Indianapolis and New York, 1973.

WHEWELL, W. *The Philosophy of the Inductive Sciences*. London, 1840 (and later eds. and reprints).

WHITE, F. C. 'ὡς ἐπιστήμη οὖσα. A Passage of Some Elegance in the *Theaetetus*', *Phronesis*, 1972, 219–26.

WEIZSÄCKER, C. F. VON. *The World-View of Physics*, 1952 (tr. M. Grene from 4th German ed., 1949).

WHITEHEAD, A. N. *See* RUSSELL, B. A. W.

WHITTAKER, J. '*Timaeus* 27 d 5 ff.', *Phoenix*, 1969, 181–5.

WILAMOWITZ-MOELLENDORFF, U. VON. *Platon*. 2 vols., Berlin, 1920.

WILLIAMS, B. A. O. and BEDFORD, E. 'Pleasure and Belief', *PAS*, Suppl. vol. 33 (1959), 57–72 and 73–92.

WILPERT, P. *Zwei aristotelische Frühschriften über die Ideenlehre*. Regensburg, 1949.

WINSPEAR, A. D. *See* LEVISON, M., MORTON, A. Q.

WIPPERN, J. (ed. with introd.). *Das Problem der ungeschriebenen Lehre Platons*. Darmstadt, 1972.

WITTGENSTEIN, L. *Philosophical Investigations*, transl. by G. E. M. Anscombe, with German text. Oxford, 1953.

WOOD, O. P. and PITCHER, G. (eds.). *Ryle*. London, 1971.

WRIGHT, L. 'The Astronomy of Eudoxus: Mathematics or Physics?', *Studies in the Hist. and Phil. of Science* 4 (1973–4), 165–72.

WUNDT, M. *Platons Parmenides*. Stuttgart–Berlin, 1935.

WYLLER, E. A. *Platons Parmenides in seinem Zusammenhang mit Symposium und Politeia*. Oslo, 1959.

YOH, May. 'On the Third Attempted Definition of Knowledge, *Theaetetus* 201 c–210 b', *Dialogue*, 1975, 420–42.

ZEKL, H. G. *Der Parmenides: Untersuchungen über innere Einheit, Zielsetzung und begriffliches Verfahren eines platonischen Dialogs*. Marburg, 1971.

ZELLER, E. *Die Philosophie der Griechen, Zweiter Teil, erste Abteilung: Sokrates und die Sokratiker, Plato und die alte Akademie*. 5th ed., Leipzig, 1922 (repr. Hildesheim, 1963).

'ZELLER–MONDOLFO'. *La filosofia dei Greci*, Florence, various dates from 1932. (Zeller's work translated and enlarged by R. Mondolfo.)

'ZELLER–NESTLE'. E. Zeller, *Die Philosophie der Griechen*, I. Teil, 1. Hälfte (7th ed. 1923) and 2. Hälfte (6th ed. 1920), edited by W. Nestle (Leipzig).

ZEYL, D. J. 'Plato and Talk of a World in Flux: *Timaeus* 49 a6–50 b5', *HSCP*, 1975, 125–48.

INDEXES

I. INDEX OF PASSAGES QUOTED OR REFERRED TO

Indexes

Indexes

PLATO (*cont.*)

(206b), 116; (206c–210b), 117–20; (207c–209b), 67; (208c–10a), 70; (208d–209d), 413; (210c), 73 n. 2, 109

Theages (126d), 393; (128a), 393; (129e6), 393

Timaeus (17a), 123 n. 3; (18c), 307; (20a), 244; (20d–25d), 247–50; (21a), 248; (21c), 248 n. 2; (22b–23b), 249; (22c–e), 330 n. 2; (22c–d), 246 n. 1; (22c), 194 *bis*; (23dff.), 249; (23e), 248; (24a), 248 n. 3; (24c), 248 n. 4; (27a), 244; (27b), 254 n. 2; (27d–47e), 319 n.; (27d–28a), 232, 256 n. 2, 298, 381, 407; (27d), 246 n. 1, 251; (27e–28a), 471; (28a), 304 n. 3; (28a4–6), 302 n. 2; (28b), 145; (28b6ff.), 304 n. 3; (28c), 253 n. 2, 255, 279, 304 n. 5; (29a–30b), 261; (29a), 141 n. 2, 145 *bis*, 254 n. 2; 255 n. 1, 260, 261, 309 n. 5; (29a5), 302 n. 2; (29b–d), 252; (29b), 254 n. 3; (29c–d), 251; (29c), 367; (29d–30b), 215, 275; (29d–30a), 255; (29d), 417 n. 3; (29e), 216; (30a), 253 n. 2; (30a2), 269 n. 3; (30a3), 274 n. 1; (30b), 215 n. 3, 253 n. 2; (30b1), 275 n. 1; (30b8–9), 442; (30c–31a), 459; (30c), 257, 432 n. 1, 478 n. 1; (30c3), 259 n. 2; (30d), 253 n. 2, 259; (31a–b), 275–6, 292; (31a), 276; (31a6), 276 n. 2, 293 n. 3; (31b–34b), 276–80; (31b–32c), 281; (31b–c), 476 n. 1; (31b), 253 n. 2, 255 n. 1, 432; (31b3), 232; (32b), 253 n. 2, 278; (32c–33a), 275; (32c), 279; (32c2), 278 n. 1; (32d9–33a1), 278; (33a–c), 480; (33a1), 279; (33b), 290, 485; (33b3–4), 282 n. 3; (33b4–6), 280 n.; (33b7), 296 n. 2; (33c), 487, 487 n. 3; (33d), 255 n. 1; (34a), 253 n. 2; (34b–36d), 292–9; (34c4), 292 n. 2; (35a), 149 n. 5, 232; (35a1–b3), 293; (35a2–3), 293 n. 2; (35a6), 293 n. 4; (35b–36d), 294; (35b1), 293 n. 4; (36a2), 294 n. 2; (36b5–6), 295; (36c7), 296; (36e), 295; (37a–b), 149 n. 5; (37a), 293 n. 4; (37b–c), 293; (37b), 251; (37c–38c), 146; (37c–d), 255 n. 1; (37c), 253 n. 2; (37dff.), 281; (37d2), 274 n. 1; (38b–39e), 491; (38b8–c1), 277; (38c), 145 n. 1; (39a), 259; (39b), 194; (39d), 194; (39e–40a), 258; (39e), 254 n. 2, 255 n. 1; (39e1), 144 n.; (39e8), 259 n. 2; (40a), 284, 476 n. 1; (40a5), 305; (40b–c), 306 n. 1, 343 n. 1; (40b), 96 n. 3;

(40c–d), 295; (40d–e), 251; (40e), 251 n. 2, 306 n. 1; (41a–b), 146; (41a), 96 n. 3, 253 n. 2 *ter*, 302 n. 3; (41bff.), 182 n. 1; (41b), 279; (41c8), 312; (41d–42e), 307–10; (41d), 253; (41e4), 312; (42a), 306 n. 2, 307, 309; (42a3–4), 308; (42c4–d2), 308; (42d), 488; (42d2), 312; (42d3–4), 308 n. 2; (42e), 215 n. 3, 253 n. 2, 309 (43a–44d), 310–11; (43b–c), 309 n. 2; (43c), 23 n. 2; (44a), 297 n. 4; (44a7–9), 310; (44c), 318 n. 2; (45b–46c), 273, 314 n. 4; (45b), 23 n. 2, 276, 289 n. 1; (45c–d), 315; (46c), 164 n. 2, 273 n. 1; (46c8), 274 n. 1; (46d), 164 n. 2, 315; (46e–47c), 272; (46e), 273; (47a–c), 300; (47c), 251; (47e–69a), 319 n.; (47e–48a), 272, 273; (47e), 272, 273, 319; (48a), 255 n. 1, 291; (48a2), 286 n. 2; (48a7), 273; (48b–c), 266, 281; (48d–53c), 262–9; (48d–49a), 319; (49d), 251; (48e–49a), 262; (49a–51c), 408; (49a–b), 266; (49b–50b), 266 n. 1; (49b), 263; (49b8), 283 n. 3; (49c7), 283 n. 3; (49d), 81 n. 2; (50a–b), 263; (50a), 263; (50a3), 271 n. 2; (50b–c), 267; (50b), 267; (50c), 81 n. 2, 214 n., 236 n. 2, 263 *bis*, 269, 408; (50c1), 264 n. 4; (50c2), 263 n. 3, 438 n. 2; (50c5), 267 n. 2, 268 n. 3; (50d), 263 n. 3 *bis*, 266 n. 1; (50d7), 264 n. 4; (50e), 263, 265 n. 3; (50e5–8), 264; (51a–b), 263, 367; (51a), 255 n. 3, 264, 267; (51a2), 264 n. 4, 267 n. 2; (51a7), 264 n. 4, 269 n. 3; (51b–52a), 298; (51b), 269, 287; (51d–e), 407; (51d), 105; (51d3–52a7), 256 n. 2; (51d3ff.), 106; (51e–52a), 293 n. 3; (52a–b), 263, 264; (52a), 80 n. 2, 232, 268; (52a5), 267 n. 2; (52a8–b1), 264; (52a8), 214 n.; (52b2), 269 n. 3; (52c), 268; (52d–53a), 290; (52dff.), 301; (52d), 263 n. 2, 264, 319; (52d4), 304 n. 5; (52d5), 263; (52d6), 270 n.; (52e), 271, 272 n. 2; (52e1), 269, 269 n. 3; (52e3–5), 264; (53a–b), 270 n., 278, 290; (53a7), 304 n. 5; (53b), 255 n. 1, 442; (53b3–4), 269; (53b5), 274 n. 1; (53c–57d), 280–92; (53c–d), 283; (53c), 252 n., 277, 285 n. 1, 288, 319; (53c7), 283 n. 1; (53d), 251 n. 2, 285, 431 n. 4; (53e–54a), 288; (53e7), 282; (54b), 283 n. 3; (54d–55c), 288; (55a), 279 n. 3; (55a3), 282 n. 3; (55c), 253 n. 2, 292; (55c6), 284 n. 1; (56b–c), 282; (56b), 250 n. 2, 253 n. 2, 304 n. 5;

525

Indexes

II. GENERAL INDEX

General Index

atomism (*see also* Democritus), 138 n. 2, 266 n. 1, 299 n. 2, 486
Atreus, 181, 193, 195
Austin, J. L., 82 n. 1
Axiochus, 394–6
Axiothea of Phlius, 446 n. 2

Bacon, Francis, 242, 249
Baeumker, C., 263 n. 1, 264 n. 3, 265 nn., 268 n. 5
Baldry, H. C., 182 n. 2, 194
Bambrough, J. R., 69f., 171 n. 2
barbaroi, 168
Barker, E., 374
Barnes, J., 466 n. 1, 491 n. 3
'be', various senses of, 147f., 298
becoming, relation to being, 144, 169 n. 1, (in *Philebus*) 232, 233 n. 3, 237, (in *Timaeus*) 251, 256
Bedford, E., 218 n. 4
being (*see also* becoming, *alētheia*), 298; equated with truth, 154; as ingredient of soul of cosmos, 293, 297
belief, *see doxa; for relation to knowledge see* knowledge
Benfey, T., 31
Bergk, T., 321 n. 3
Berkeley, G., 78 n. 3, 267 n. 1
Bignone, E., 222 n. 4
biology, 132, 463f.
Bluck, R. S., 38 n. 1, 50 n. 1, 102 n. 2, 105, 122 n. 1, 130 n. 1, 161
Bochenski, I. M., 247
Bondeson, W., 107, 112 n. 4, 117 n. 1
Boyancé, P., 8 n. 2, 9 n. 2
Bramwell, J., 247 n. 2
Brandwood, L., 243 n. 2
Brémond, A., 218 n. 5
Brentlinger, J. A., 1
Bringmann, K., 222 n. 4
Broad, C. D., 83 n. 1, 327 n. 4
Brochard, V., 265 n. 5, 322, 378, 380f.
Brown, M. S., 63 n. 1, 76 n. 1
Brumbaugh, R. S., 53 n. 1, 55 n. 4
Burnet, J., 54 nn. 1 and 2, 128 n. 2, 141 n. 3, 266, 284 n. 1, 362 n. 4, 385 n. 2
Burnyeat, M. F., 114 nn. 1 and 3, 115 n. 3
Bury, J. B., 36 n. 1
Bury, R. G., 345 n. 5; on *Philebus*, 197, 213 n. 2, 218 n. 5, 222 n. 5, 232, 235 nn. 2 and 5

Cadmus, 181 n. 4
Cairns, H., 324 n. 3, 334 n. 4, 381
Callias, 4, 198, 395

Callippus, 450
Campbell, L., 33 n. 1, 66 n. 1; on *Theaetetus*, 61, (date) 62 n. 1, 78 n. 3, 111 n. 1; on *Sophist*, 125, 127, 129 n. 1, 136 n. 2, 140 n. 3, 141 n. 3, 147 n. 2; on *Politicus*, 176
catastrophes, natural, 194, 330
cause (*see also* Forms; mind): first cause in *Philebus*, 212, 214–16, 238; in *Timaeus*, 269
Chalcidius, 241
chance, 95, 273, 361, 362
Charlton, W., 265 n. 1
Charmides, 17, 65, 109, 390
Cherniss, H., 59 n. 2, 66 n. 1, 92 n. 2, 93 n. 1, 144, 149 n. 5, 253 n. 2, 259 n. 2, 440 n. 3; on Plato's conception of evil, 95f., on Forms of vices, 100 n. 3; on *Timaeus*, (date) 243 n. 2, 266 n. 1, 283 n. 3; on *Epinomis*, 385 n. 1, 386 n. 2; on 'unwritten doctrine', 423 nn. 1 and 3, 435 n. 3; on Eudoxus, 452 n. 3; on Speusippus, 458, 463 nn. 2 and 3
Cherry, R. S., 81 n. 2, 243 n. 2
children, 336 n. 5
chronos, 299f.
Chung-Hwan Chen, 60 n. 1
Cicero, 241
circular motion (*see also* heavenly bodies), associated with reason, 96 n. 3, 297, 300, 305f., 364
Claghorn, G. S., 265 n. 5
Clegg, J. S., 42 n. 2, 47 n. 3, 271 n. 4
Clinias (Cretan), 323f. and elsewhere in ch. V
Clitophon, 384, 387–9
Cnossus, 323, 333
Cohen, M., 58 n. 1
'collection', 27, 33, 61, 131, 166, 210 n. 1
concepts, formation of, 29, 308
conservatism, Plato's, 327, 368, 381f.
constitutions, classification of, 185
Cooper, J. M., 66 n. 1, 74 n. 3
Copernicus, 242, 485
Coriscus, 401
Cornford, F. M., 16 n. 1, 20, 26f., 28 n. 1, 38 n. 1, 42 n. 1, 50 n. 1, 52 n. 2, 97 n. 4, 101 n. 2, 108 n. 3, 110 n. 2, 121, 197 n. 1; on forms and particulars, 46; on immanent forms, 48 n. 1; on transcendent forms in *Parmenides*, 51 n. 1, 59 n. 2, 431 f.; on second part of *Parmenides*, 54 n. 1, 55, 56 n. 1, on the fluxdoctrine, 80 n. 1; on *Theaetetus*, *Sophist* and *Timaeus*, 61–163 *passim*, 241–320 *passim*
Corybantic ritual, 346 n. 1
cosmogony, *see table of contents*, pp. viii–ix; human orientation of, 300

General Index

III. INDEX OF GREEK WORDS

Greek words transliterated in the text will be found in the general index